RELIGIOUS RESOURCES
for
PERSONAL LIVING AND SOCIAL ACTION

Books by KIRBY PAGE

NATIONAL DEFENSE

LIVING CREATIVELY

LIVING TRIUMPHANTLY

LIVING COURAGEOUSLY

MUST WE GO TO WAR?

RELIGIOUS RESOURCES FOR PERSONAL LIVING
AND SOCIAL ACTION

RELIGIOUS RESOURCES

for

PERSONAL LIVING AND SOCIAL ACTION

by

KIRBY PAGE

In a Day of
Personal Insecurity and Frustration,
Social Conflict and Disintegration,
How Can I Experience
the Deeper Satisfactions of Life,
and Render Maximum Service to Society?

An Exploration
with an
Anthology of Verse and Prose

FARRAR & RINEHART

INCORPORATED

NEW YORK   TORONTO

CONTENTS

FOREWORD

PART I

PART II

Fourteen Weeks of Daily Readings
Four Pages Each
Covering These Seven Themes
An Anthology of Verse and Prose

Monday — The Ideal
Tuesday — The Actual
Wednesday — Concern
Thursday — Transformation
Friday — Proceed Resolutely
Saturday —- Comradeship
Sunday — Worship

PART III

Study Outlines for Fourteen Weeks
for Discussion Groups, Classes, and Forums

PART IV

Worship Services for Special Occasions

INDEX

Foreword

THIS volume is designed for use by individuals and by groups. Daily readings are provided for fourteen weeks, as well as an abundance of material for fourteen sessions of Epworth Leagues, Christian Endeavor Societies, Baptist Young Peoples' Unions, YMCA and YWCA classes and cabinet meetings, young peoples' and adult Bible classes, men's and women's clubs, teacher training institutes, and fellowship groups in homes. It is hoped that numerous individuals will take the initiative in assembling groups of friends in homes for weekly discussion and worship. In Part III will be found discussion outlines for fourteen weeks.

Classes and discussion groups will prove to be more rewarding if the various members will follow regularly the daily readings of four pages each. *A minimum of three copies of the book will make possible effective use of this material in classes:* one copy for the leader and two copies to be cut up and pasted on loose leaves for special assignment of different sections to various members. Twenty-five cents or fifty cents from the members of a class will obtain the three volumes needed.

Individuals who are called upon to lead services of public worship will find a great variety of material in this volume. A topical index makes it easy to find appropriate selections.

The reader will soon discover my heavy indebtedness to numerous sources. I am grateful to all the persons who have made possible this anthology as a tool for use by individuals and by groups. My special thanks go to our daughter Mary for help in the library, and to my secretary Myrtle Kahlmeyer for typing the manuscript.   KIRBY PAGE

PART I

Chapter I

Concentrate upon the Ideal for the Individual and for Society

PERSONAL religion and social reconstruction alike are imperatively required in this hour of crisis. It is not enough to convert individuals; it is not sufficient to change the structure of society; both are indispensable. In succession one may read two books which emphasize respectively these needs. The first volume concentrates upon the futility of attempting to build a new society out of old men, and calls for repentance and utter surrender to the will of God. With this emphasis I find myself in complete agreement. The other book analyzes the present social order and shows the urgent need for a new method of producing and distributing necessities and comforts if civilization is to avoid suicide on the industrial and international battlefields. This conclusion seems to me to be inescapable. But the first author pays little attention to the necessity of creating a new *structure* of industry, whereas the second one says nothing of the task of converting individuals. Thus we are confronted with the spectacle of personal evangelists and social reconstructionists running up and down parallel tracks without meeting.

Tragic indeed is the fallacy that changed environment would in itself produce the kind of men and women needed to operate the institutions of a prosperous and harmonious society. And equally tragic are the consequences which flow from the idea that genuinely converted individuals could make satisfactory use of any social system. The causes of the barbaric cruelty and appalling misery of the present hour cannot be removed or appreciably diminished until we act upon the recognition that converted individuals and a changed structure of society are both desperately needed. It is not adequate for one group to stress personal evangelism and another company to seek social transformation. Truly sensitive persons will become active participants in both endeavors.

1

"The world is wrong," writes Dr. J. S. Whale, "not because it has not yet discovered a new social technique, but because individual hearts are wrong. Sin would still be our stark intractable problem even if we all woke to find ourselves in Utopia tomorrow morning; 'You cannot build the Golden Age out of leaden men.' Problems innumerable wait for their solution at the hands of statesmen, scientists, economists and teachers; but there is not a social problem under heaven which can advance toward real solution unless the greater problem of which it is an aspect is first met and dealt with in the secret places of the individual heart. It is there that the solution must be found if it is to be found at all. Only redemption and conversion can meet our case. . . . The causes of the folly and woe of our time and of all times do not lie exclusively in vast intangibilities such as the Economic System or the National System, but in me and others everywhere like me who make the systems what they are. I find that my failure, my greed, my fear, match yours and that our lives interlock to form an organized system of evil."[1]

> All Social Schemes, all Planned Economies,
> All specious blue-prints of man's Ideal States,
> All vain attempts at just Democracies,
> Utopias, or Cities of High God
> Have failed—and must for long time fail—for lack
> Of only one essential thing: enough
> Just men and true to make Peace possible.[2]

Concerning the structure of society, the query arises: if all men were truly surrendered to the will of God, could they then live with equal satisfaction under fascism, communism, individualism, and socialism? If the answer is that one system is preferable to another, how does a genuinely religious person decide which one to favor? Is a competitive community preferable to a cooperative society? Is it desirable to have the chief means of production owned and controlled by a small proportion of the population, or is it better to have common ownership of essential industries together with private ownership of property which is personally used

[1] *What Is a Living Church?* Published by Harper and Brothers, New York.

[2] Edwards Davis, *Lovers of Life*. Published by Baker & Taylor Company, New York.

and consumed? Is love toward God and love toward man equally possible under various social systems? If the Lord's Prayer should be fully answered and God's will should be done on earth as it is in heaven, would the Kingdom of God resemble fascism or communism or individualism or socialism? If the answer is that it could not possibly be mistaken for any of these systems, then we need to ask: what changes in existing social systems are required before the divine society on earth can become a reality? In the meantime, should a true Christian be neutral in the conflict between totalitarianism and democracy, between individualism and socialism? In what soil does Christian fellowship flourish most luxuriantly: competitive or cooperative? If structure is important, how does a religious person decide where to cast his influence? If democracy is preferable, what steps must be taken to preserve and extend it?

In the effort to find correct answers to these questions, Christians must saturate themselves with the mind of Christ and must also become students of contemporary economics and politics. It is not possible to love neighbor as self unless we are familiar with the conditions under which he lives, and until we understand the consequences of respective courses of action which we may take. Underlying this volume is the conviction that in Jesus and his way of life are to be found in our day illimitable resources for personal living and social action. Illumination and power alike are available to men and women who resolutely commit themselves to this way. This book is an exploration of two profound questions: how may we more utterly love God, and how may we more sincerely love neighbor? To these ends, what changes in individuals and what changes in society are required?

II

At the beginning of our exploration, it is desirable to inquire into the nature of man. Giving due consideration to the organic structure of man, what kinds of changes are possible? If the evidence of radical conversion is convincing, what types of conduct are possible for a converted individual? Out of the combination of the raw stuff of human nature and redeemed personalities, what kind of society may be created? Experience and observation reveal a vast range of possibilities. Man is able to scale the steepest pinnacle and also to plunge into the deepest abyss. Courage and cowardice alike are possible responses. Compassion and cruelty, generosity and covetousness, love and hatred, self-sacrifice and murder, humility and arrogance, worship and blasphemy—these constitute only a few of the contrasting possibilities open to every person.

Human nature is potential. It is capable of becoming. Stimulus determines response. We are what we have been stimulated to become—by sensations, ideas, emotions, and ideals. Heredity and environment place boundaries beyond which we may not go, but within the vast territory thus enclosed we are driven about by countless external and internal stimuli. Stretched out before us are enormous ranges of possibilities.

Consider the extent to which heroism is latent. In an early year of this century Andrew Carnegie established the Carnegie Hero Fund Commission for the purpose of recognizing and rewarding acts of heroism. By the end of January, 1938, more than three thousand medals had been presented for conspicuous acts of bravery. Various annual reports of the Commission furnish impressive evidence of the heroic way in which ordinary men and women respond when confronted with emergencies:

Earl L. McJones, a colored laborer, aged twenty-two, died attempting to save James Fontana, Jr., aged thirteen, schoolboy, from drowning, Chicago, Illinois. James fell from a bridge pier into the Chicago Drainage Canal and drifted to a point seventy-five feet from the bank, where the water was twenty-two feet deep. The water was very cold and heavy with sewage. After a futile effort was made to reach James by means of a rope, and men, who were good swimmers, made no move to swim to James, McJones, who was heavily clothed, waded from the bank and swam a hundred feet to James. With one hand McJones took hold of James under his left armpit and swam thirty feet toward the bank. McJones then released his hold, raised himself slightly, and sank. James feebly swam ten feet nearer the bank. A rope was thrown to him, but he did not take hold of it and sank. Both were drowned.

Charles F. Lentino, aged twenty-two, plumber, saved Carrie J., and Mary A. Shallow, aged twenty-one and fourteen, respectively, Annie Carifi, aged thirty-one, and others, from burning, New York, N. Y. Lentino entered a burning tenement house and assisted Carrie Shallow through smoke from the second floor to the street, and then climbed up a water spout on the outside of the building, and helped Mary Shallow reach a place of safety from a narrow ledge upon which she stood. He then climbed the fire-escape to the third and fourth floors and assisted Mrs. Carifi and thirteen others to the ground, at one time entering a room on the third floor and bringing out five children, all of whom he carried down the fire-escape to safety. While on the fourth floor fire-escape helping an old man out of a window, Lentino, feeling a rush of smoke, looked down and saw flames and smoke issuing from the first floor door and the windows below him and was about to jump to the street, when firemen raised a ladder and he climbed down. The old man was safely taken to the ground.

Lucy E. Ernst, aged twenty, saved Harry E. Schoenhut, aged sixteen, from death from snake-bite, Porter's Lake, Pa. Miss Ernst, though having a fever blister on her lip, repeatedly sucked the venom from a rattlesnake bite on Schoenhut's arm near the shoulder.

Lyndon B. Phifer, aged thirteen, schoolboy, saved Paul I. Burrows, aged five, from being run over by a train, Rich Hill, Mo. Phifer ran out onto a trestle, released Burrows' foot from between two cross-ties, dropped him over the side into a small stream thirteen feet below, and then hung to the end of a cross-tie until the train passed.

Raymond I. Coldren, aged thirty-six, foreman of linemen, rescued Clark Trump, aged twenty-seven, lineman, from electric shock, Uniontown, Pa. Coldren ran to the assistance of Trump, who was unconscious and was held by his safety belt and spurs to a pole, near its base. A current of one hundred and sixty volts was passing through the pole. Coldren grasped Trump's clothes and tried to pull him away from the pole, but was rendered unconscious and hurled against a nearby fence. He made a second attempt, but was again rendered unconscious and thrown to the middle of the street. At the third attempt, he succeeded in pulling Trump away from the pole. Trump died from his burns three weeks later. Coldren escaped injury.

Herbert Aaron Friedlich, aged twenty-six, lawyer, saved Raymond Kraft, aged twenty-one, clerk, from an impending fatal fall, Glacier Park, Montana. Kraft alone ascended a mountain known as Pinnacle Wall for three hundred and fifty feet; and in attempting to cross a glacier thirty feet wide, he lost his footing and slid about seventy-five feet, injuring his ankle. He then attempted to descend the mountain on narrow ledges and finally reached a short ledge two feet wide. Kraft could go no farther and was greatly frightened. The face of the mountain below Kraft sloped down for one hundred and fifty feet at an angle of about twenty degrees from a perpendicular and was bare of vegetation. Friedlich with extreme caution and difficulty climbed toward Kraft from the base of the mountain. At two points in the ascent, where there were projections to surmount, he was forced to lean back for handholds, swing out with his feet unsupported, and pull himself up. He reached Kraft after climbing two hundred and fifty feet and with great difficulty helped him to descend. Two and a half hours were required to reach Kraft and descend with him.

George W. Weidinger, aged thirty-one, foreman welder, died saving one or more of about twenty-one men from an explosion, Buffalo, N. Y. One of a number of workmen in a building was handling a tank charged with acetylene gas. The tank began getting hot, and the man in charge of the workman told him to take the tank from the building, but the workman walked away from it. Weidinger hurried to it and dragged it through a door twelve feet away. Two feet outside the door the tank exploded, hurling Weidinger thirty-five feet. He was killed, and several men in the building were knocked down by the concussion.

John W. Smith, aged fifty-three, master, schooner "Elsie," with a volunteer crew of seven men, rescued eight passengers of the steamer "Larchmont," off Block Island, R. I. With the thermometer registering two degrees, the wind blowing thirty-five miles an hour, and the waves running twenty feet high, the "Elsie," a sixty-foot boat, was taken five miles to sea, to a raft on which were fifteen bodies. Seven of the castaways were found to have been frozen to death. The living were transferred to the schooner, by the crew, in twelve-foot dories.

These illustrative acts of sacrificial heroism remind us that it is slanderous to say that self-preservation is the first law of life. Under the impact of a powerful stimulus, average men and women jeopardize their own lives in the endeavor to rescue friends or even strangers from imminent danger. "We marvel at the utter disregard of self when the urge comes to help another who struggles for his life," says a report of the Carnegie Hero Fund Commission. "Without a moment's hesitation, one man will plunge into the very teeth of death—apparently willing to sacrifice his life that another may be saved. Not all men will do it, for countless numbers stand and watch the hero in his act. If there be something peculiar in the blood and fibre of an individual who does an heroic deed, it has not been discovered by the Commission in over thirty years of contacts. In appearance and behavior, the hero resembles the rest of mankind. He has the same strength, weaknesses, ills, and frailties that flesh is heir to. He comes from all the races into which the universe of mankind is divided. Riches, poverty, sex, youth, or age hold no distinguishing characteristics that set a hero apart from other men. . . . Although not germane to a discussion of the Carnegie Hero Fund, a word of mention is needed for all those who perform repeated acts of heroism as the monotonous, undramatic part of their daily duties. Surgeons, physicians, nurses, policemen, firemen, the ship's crew, and similar groups with social responsibility, constantly perform acts of bravery as a matter of course and with full premeditated knowledge of possible consequences. Their number is legion—so large that the Carnegie Hero Fund must ignore all of them."[1]

Truly their number is legion! And daily they confront us as living revelations of the latent heroism and sacrificial devotion of human nature!

III

Holding high rank among man's latent capacities is appreciation of beauty and harmony. So constituted is he that the glories of nature and of art and of music stir him profoundly and lift him to heights of ecstasy. Imagination takes wings and emotion surges exultantly when released by inspired words:

> If solitude hath ever led thy steps
> To the wild ocean's echoing shore,
> And thou hast linger'd there
> Until the sun's broad orb
> Seem'd resting on the burnish'd wave,

[1] Thomas S. Arbuthnot, *Heroes of Peace,* printed by The Carnegie Hero Fund Commission.

Thou must have mark'd the lines
Of purple gold, that motionless
Hung o'er the sinking sphere:
Thou must have mark'd the billowy clouds
Edged with intolerable radiancy,
Towering like rocks of jet
Crown'd with a diamond wreath.
And yet there is a moment
When the sun's highest point
Peeps like a star o'er ocean's western edge,
When those far clouds of feathery gold,
Shaded with deepest purple, gleam
Like islands on a dark-blue sea;
Then has thy fancy soar'd above the earth,
And furl'd its wearied wing
Within the Fairy's fane.

Yet not the golden islands,
Gleaming in yon flood of light,
Nor the feathery curtains
Stretching o'er the sun's bright couch,
Nor the burnish'd ocean-waves,
Paving that gorgeous dome,
So fair, so wonderful a sight
As Mab's ethereal palace could afford.
Yet likest evening's vault, that fairy Hall!
As Heaven, low resting on the wave, it spread
Its floors of flashing light,
Its vast and azure dome,
Its fertile golden islands
Floating on a silver sea;
Whilst suns their mingling beamings darted
Through clouds of circumambient darkness,
And pearly battlements around
Look'd o'er the immense of Heaven.[1]

Man's capacity to respond to the beauties of sunset at sea is illimitable. In many countries throughout long centuries countless human beings have experienced this rapture:

[1] Shelley, from *Queen Mab*.

Once, on a cliff, I saw perfection happen—
The full gold moon was balanced on the sea,
Just as the red sun rested on the moors.
The summer evening ripened and fell open;
And people walking through that fruit's rich core
Were suddenly what they were meant to be,
Quiet and happy, soft moving, lovely,
With still, translucent faces and clear eyes,
And all their heads and bodies brightly rimmed
With delicate gold; so radiantly, so gravely,
These people walked, so crowned, so golden-limbed.
The cliff seemed like an edge of Paradise.[1]

This insatiable thirst for beauty is an elemental characteristic of human nature, and under its dynamic man is driven forward into rich realms of experience:

Glory of sunrise and sunset,
Glory of night and the dawn,
Glorious flood of the moonlight
Washing with silver the lawn,
These have bound me and chained me,
Held my heart in the hills
These will envelop, surround me,
Hold my heart when it stills.

Wonder of birches at twilight,
Wonder of lights that enmesh,
Wondrous coolth of the waters
Caressing the swimmer's flesh,
These have conquered me, won me,
Held my heart all the years,
To these I will go on departure
Burying bodily fears.

Beauty of light on the waters,
Beauty of hills in their strength,
Beauty of wind on the corn-fields

[1] Winifred Welles, "The Heart of Light," in *This Delicate Love*. Published by The Viking Press, New York.

Rippling length on length,
These are the things I cleave to,
These will endure to the end;
Beauty, the quest of the ages,
Waits where the lost roads wend.[1]

Words are inadequate vehicles of human thought and emotion, yet lines of inspired verse bring vivid memories of enraptured solitude and of joyous fellowship by a forest stream:

There is always the sound of falling water here;
By day, blended with birdsong and windy leaves,
By night, the only sound, steady and clear
Through the darkness and half-heard through sleepers' dreams.
Here in the mottled shadow of glades, the deer,
Unstartled, waits until the walker is near,
Then with a silent bound, without effort is gone,
While the sound of falling water goes on and on.

Those are not stars reflected in the lake,
They are shadows of stars that were there aeons ago;
When you walk by these waters at night, you must forsake
All you have known of time; you are timeless, alone,
The mystery almost revealed, like the breath you take
In the summer dawn before the world is awake,
Or the last breath, when the spirit beyond recalling
Goes forth to the sound of water forever falling.

Swift as deer, half-thoughts in the summer mind
Flash with their hints of happiness and are gone;
In the dark waters of ourselves we find
No stars but shadows of stars which memory lost.
Dark are the waters under the bridge we crossed,
And the sound of their falling knows neither end nor start.
Frail are your stars, deep are your waters, mind;
And the sound of falling water troubles my heart.[2]

[1] Arthur S. Bourinot, "Enchantment," from *Selected Poems*. Published by Macmillan and Company, Ltd., Toronto. With the author's permission.

[2] Robert Hillyer, *Night Piece*. Published by Alfred A. Knopf, Inc., New York.

IV

And the sound of falling water troubles my heart! Beauty alone cannot quench man's burning thirst. Whence comes this loveliness? What is it in human nature that so easily becomes enthralled? How does it happen that man's spirit is so delicately attuned to the music of the spheres?

Lovely is daytime when the joyful sun goes singing,
Lovely is night with stars and round of sickled moon,
Lovely are trees, forever lovely, whether in winter
Or musical midsummer or when they bud and tassel
Or crown themselves with stormy splendors in the fall.
But lovelier than day or night or trees in blossom
Is there no secret infinite loveliness behind?

Beautiful is water, running on rocks in mountains,
Or bosoming sunsets where the valley rivers ponder;
Beautiful is ocean with its myriad colors,
In southern blues and purples, its arctic gray and silver,
Blown into green frost-fretted or wine-dark in the evening.
But still more beautiful than waters calm or cloven,
Than ocean thunder-maned or floored for delicate springtime,
Is there no beauty visible save to our eyes? . . .

Who lifteth in the eastern sky the dark, gold moon?
Who painteth green and purple on the blackbird's throat?
What hand of rapture scattereth sunshine through the rain
And flingeth round the barren boughs of spring returned
Dim fire? Who stenciled with caught breath the moth's wide wing
And lit the ruby in his eyes? Whose ecstasy
Set silver ripples on the racing thunder-cloud
And flared the walls of storm with terrible dead green?
What dreamer fretted dew upon the flat-leafed corn
And twined in innocence of useless perfect art
The morning-glory with its bubble blue, soon gone?
Was there no hand that braided autumn branches in
Their solemn brede and stained them with a sombre rust?
Was there no love conceived the one-starred rivered evening,
And dipped in crocus fire the gray horns of the moon?

They say there never was a god men loved but died—
Dead is Astarte, Astoreth is dead, and Baal;
Zeus and Jehovah share a single grave and deep;
Olympus hears no laughter, Sinai no voice;
Spring comes but Freia comes not nor Persephone;
On temple plinth and porch the random grasses run;
Of all their priests alone the white-stoled stars are faithful.
Dead are the gods, forever dead! And yet—and yet—
Who lifted in the eastern sky the dark, gold moon? . . .
There is a loveliness outlasts the temporal gods,
A beauty that, when all we know as beautiful
Is gone, will fashion in delight the forms it loves,
In that wide room where all our stars are but a drift
Of glimmering petals down an air from far away.[1]

The insistent "why?" coming from the heart of man leads him on to truer insights into the nature of life, and the end of the quest is worship of the living God. Beyond the questioning mood is an awareness of "a presence that disturbs me with the joy of elevated thoughts."

                              The sounding cataract
Haunted me like a passion; the tall rock,
The mountain, and the deep and gloomy wood,
Their colors and their forms, were then to me
An appetite; a feeling and a love,
That had no need of a remoter charm,
By thought supplied, nor any interest
Unborrowed from the eye.—That time is past,
And all its aching joys are now no more,
And all its dizzy raptures. Not for this
Faint I, nor mourn, nor murmur; other gifts
Have followed; for such loss, I would believe
Abundant recompense. For I have learned
To look on Nature, not as in the hour
Of thoughtless youth; but hearing oftentimes
The still, sad music of humanity,
Nor harsh nor grating, though of ample power

[1] William Alexander Percy, "A Canticle", in *Enzio's Kingdom*. Published by Yale University Press.

To chasten and subdue. And I have felt
A presence that disturbs me with the joy
Of elevated thoughts; a sense sublime,
Of something far more deeply interfused,
Whose dwelling is the light of setting suns,
And the round ocean and the living air,
And the blue sky, and in the mind of man;
A motion and a spirit, that impels
All thinking things, all objects of all thought,
And rolls through all things. Therefore am I still
A lover of the meadows and the woods,
And mountains; and of all that we behold
From this green earth; of all the mighty world
Of eye and ear,—both what they half create,
And what perceive; well pleased to recognize
In nature and the language of the sense,
The anchor of my purest thoughts, the nurse,
The guide, the guardian of my heart, and soul
Of all my moral being.[1]

Austere beauty is not enough. Man craves conviction that the universe is concerned about values and relationships. He desires assurance that at the heart of nature is intelligence and love and power. This is a perennial cry:

God of those splendid stars! I need
Thy presence, need to know
That thou art God, my God indeed.
   Cold and far off they shine, they glow,
In their strange brightness, like to spirit's eyes,
Awful, intensely on my naked soul;
Beautiful are they, but so strange, so cold,
I know them not: I shrink, I cling
Like a scared insect to this whirling ball,
Upon whose swelling lines I woke one morn,
Unknowing who I was or whence I came;
And still I know not: fastened to its verge
By a resistless power, with it I speed
On its eternal way, and those strange eyes,

---

[1] William Wordsworth, *Lines Composed a Few Miles Above Tintern Abbey.*

Those starry eyes, look over on me thus;
I wake, I sleep, but still they look on me,
Mild yet reproachful, beautiful but strange.
Visions are round me,—many moving things,
In clothing beautiful, soft and colored forms
With drooping heads caressing; eyes so meek
And loving and appealing, but they hold
A nature strange and different, each enwrapt
In its own mortal mystery: near they are,
And yet how distant,—familiar, fond,
Yet strangers all! I know not what they are.[1]

The satisfying answer which has come to an innumerable
throng throughout the ages is an experience of communion with
a loving Father: "God in His agony—a heart-beat; a lamentation;
an impassioned, low, insatiate cry."

It is impossible to be along here, even in this little cabin room,
After beholding the Glory of God through the somber splendor
    of twilight loom,
And the violet dusk of the mountains quiver, and the Holy of
    Holies glow through the gloom.

Dusk as a brooding spirit whispered over the face of the harrowed
    field;
Dusk as a dim-winged dragon darkened over the bay where the
    flame-points reeled;
As an angel, veiled and flaming-sworded; watched at the gates of
    the unrevealed.

Over the bay the lights of the city, a thousand blossoms of yellow
    flame,
Gleamed and twinkled out of the blue and ash-gray darkness; and
    there came
A slow wind thence: a murmurous rumor: human passion, sad-
    ness, shame.

And I beheld God in the mountains; God in the iris glow of the
    sky;

1 Eliza Thayer Clapp, *Hymn to the God of Stars* (1811-1888).

And I beheld in the throbbing lights of the city, God in His
    agony—
A heart-beat; a lamentation; an impassioned, low, insatiate cry.[1]

Long ago the Psalmist in imperishable words proclaimed the
message of unfaltering trust in the Eternal God:

> The LORD *is* my shepherd; I shall not want.
> He maketh me to lie down in green pastures: he leadeth
> me beside the still waters.
> He restoreth my soul: he leadeth me in the paths of right-
> eousness for his name's sake.
> Yea, though I walk through the valley of the shadow of
> death, I will fear no evil: for thou *art* with me; thy rod and
> thy staff they comfort me.
> Thou preparest a table before me in the presence of mine
> enemies: thou anointest my head with oil; my cup runneth
> over.
> Surely goodness and mercy shall follow me all the days
> of my life: and I will dwell in the house of the LORD for
> ever.[2]
> Bless the LORD, O my soul: and all that is within me,
> *bless* his holy name.
> Bless the LORD, O my soul, and forget not all his bene-
> fits:
> Who forgiveth all thine iniquities; who healeth all thy
> diseases;
> Who redeemeth thy life from destruction; who crowneth
> thee with loving kindness and tender mercies;
> Who satisfieth thy mouth with good *things; so that* thy
> youth is renewed like the eagle's.
> The LORD executeth righteousness and judgment for all
> that are oppressed. . . .
> He hath not dealt with us after our sins; nor rewarded
> us according to our iniquities.
> For as the heaven is high above the earth, *so* great is his
> mercy toward them that fear him.
> As as far as the east is from the west, *so* far hath he re-
> moved our transgressions from us.

[1] Kenneth Morris, *Dusk.*
[2] Psalms 23.

Like as a father pitieth *his* children, *so* the LORD pitieth them that fear him.

For he knoweth our frame; he remembereth that we *are* dust.[1]

O LORD our Lord, how excellent *is* thy name in all the earth! who hast set thy glory above the heavens.

Out of the mouth of babes and sucklings hast thou ordained strength because of thine enemies, that thou mightest still the enemy and the avenger.

When I consider thy heavens, the work of thy fingers, the moon and the stars, which thou hast ordained;

What is man, that thou are mindful of him? and the son of man, that thou visitest him?

For thou hast made him a little lower than the angels, and hast crowned him with glory and honor.

Thou madest him to have dominion over the works of thy hands; thou hast put all *things* under his feet:

All sheep and oxen, yea, and the beasts of the field;

The fowl of the air, and the fish of the sea, *and whatsoever* passeth through the paths of the seas.

O LORD our Lord, how excellent *is* thy name in all the earth![2]

O GOD, thou *art* my God; early will I seek thee: my soul thirsteth for thee, my flesh longeth for thee in a dry and thirsty land, where no water is.[3]

As the hart panteth after the water brooks, so panteth my soul after thee, O God.

My soul thirsteth for God, for the living God.[4]

In the parables of the lost sheep, the lost coin, and the lost son, Jesus interpreted the heart of the universe as a passionate concern about the fate of man. God is the Divine seeker who never falters in his pursuit.

So He told them the following story:

"What man among you, if he has a hundred sheep, and if he loses one of them, does not leave the ninety-nine in the desert and continue to look for the lost one until he finds it?

1 Psalms 103.
2 Psalms 8.
3 Psalms 63.
4 Psalms 42.

And when he finds it, with joy he puts it on his shoulders, and when he reaches home he calls in his friends and neighbors, and says to them, 'Rejoice with me, because I have found my lost sheep!' Just so, I tell you, there will be more joy in heaven over one sinful person who repents than over ninety-nine upright people who do not need any repentance.

"Or what woman, if she has ten silver coins and loses one of them, does not light a lamp and sweep the house, and look carefully until she finds it? And when she finds it, she calls in her friends and neighbors, and says, 'Rejoice with me, because I have found the coin which I lost!' Just so, I tell you, there is joy among the angels of God over one sinful person who repents!"

Then He said:

"There was a man who had two sons. The younger of them said to his father, 'Father, give me the share of the property that falls to me.' So he divided his property between them. Not many days after that, the younger son got together all he had and went away to a distant country, and there he squandered all his property by living in dissipation. After he had spend it all, a severe famine struck that country, and he began to suffer want. So he went and hired himself out to a citizen of that country, and he sent him to his fields to feed hogs. And often he craved to fill himself with the carob-pods which the hogs were eating, and nobody gave him a bite. Then he came to himself and said, 'How many of my father's hired men have more to eat than they need, and here I am dying of hunger! I will get up and go to my father, and say to him, "Father, I have sinned against heaven and in your opinion; I no longer deserve to be called your son; just treat me like one of your hired men."' So he got up and went to his father. But, while he was still a long way off, his father saw him, and his heart was moved with pity for him, and he ran and fell on his neck, and kissed him affectionately. His son said to him, 'Father, I have sinned against heaven and in your opinion; I no longer deserve to be called your son; just treat me like one of your hired men.' But his father said to his slaves, Bring out at once a robe, yes, the finest one, and put it on him, and put a ring on his hand and shoes on his feet; taken the fattening calf and kill it, and let us feast and celebrate, because this son of mine was dead and has come to life, was lost and has been found!' So they began to celebrate."[1]

V

High on the list of the potentialities of human nature must be placed the capacity for abstract thought. From the earliest times man has demanded explanations. An insatiable hunger for knowledge has driven him to keener and keener refinements of truth. He cannot be satisfied merely with enjoyment of the beauties of nature nor with reverent adoration of the Source of all being. He craves understanding and gives voice to interpretations. In the fullness of time this insistent quest has brought forth modern science with its miracles of thought and achievement.

Recent extensions of knowledge have not only revealed a universe of majesty and beauty and harmony of exquisite perfection, but have provided impressive witness to the greatness of the human mind. Kneel reverently before the revelations of astronomy! And bow down also before the mind of the astronomer!

The great nebula of Andromeda is so vast in dimensions that light, traveling at the rate of 186,000 miles per second (per second!), takes 50,000 years to cross it. So remote from the earth is this colossus that light from this source which reaches us today has been on its way for a million years.

"So far as the present astronomical instruments can sound the depths of space, to a distance of the order of 300 million light years, the universe is dotted with great star systems or nebulae. In that immense expanse there are millions upon millions of nebulae, great 'island universes' which each contain millions of stars."[2] The total number of stars in the entire universe is possibly 10,000 million-million-million—10,000,000,000,000,000,000,-000,000! "In other words, there are about as many stars in the grander universe as there are glasses of water in all of the oceans of the world."[3] The stuff out of which the Companion of Sirius is made weighs about a ton per cubic inch (inch!).

Unimaginably hot temperatures prevail on these stars. How

[1] Luke 15:3-24. *The New Testament: A Translation in the Language of the People*, by Charles B. Williams. Published by Bruce Humphries, Inc., Boston.
[2] Watson Davis, *The Advance of Science, pp.* 2, 3.
[3] W. F. G. Swann, *The Architecture of the Universe*, p. 232.

often do we complain when the thermometer registers 100 in the shade! Well, the surface temperature of the sun is 6000 degrees Centigrade, whereas the heat of its interior mounts to 40,-000,000 degrees. "Completely covering the sun's surface is a mass of intensely hot crimson gases. These gases are like a turbulent upper atmosphere with a depth of 5000 to 10,000 miles. Raging and seething in long tongues of flame, they swirl up for thousands of miles above the surface, or are thrown far above it in titanic explosions. . . . The colossal flames which rise above its surface are called prominences. Some of the prominences shoot up with a velocity ranging from 300 to 600 miles a second, sometimes to a height of 200,000 miles, and even higher. The largest so far recorded extended upward for 500,000 miles. Others extend horizontally for a distance of over 300,000 miles, racing forward at the rate of a thousand miles a minute."[1]

Revelations of modern physics remind us that the inconceivable vastness of stellar space is matched by the incomprehensible minuteness of electrons and protrons. "It would take about 2000 protons laid side by side to make up the diameter of an electron, about thirty thousand electrons side by side to stretch the diameter of a hydrogen atom, and about a hundred million hydrogen atoms side by side to stretch one third of an inch. . . . The mass of the electron is so small that if you should magnify all masses so that the electron attains a mass of one tenth of an ounce, that one tenth of an ounce would, on the same scale of magnification, become as heavy as the earth. Then we have the proton—the fundamental unit of positive charge—a thing 1800 times as heavy as the electron, but 1800 times smaller in size, so that if you should magnify it to the size of a pin's head, that pin's head would, on the same scale of magnification, attain a diameter equal to the diameter of the earth's orbit around the sun. . . . A cubic inch of air contains about five hundred million million million molecules."[2]

Sir James Jeans tells us that if the molecules contained in a pint of water "were placed end to end they would form a chain capable of encircling the earth over 200 million times. If they were scattered over the whole land surface of the earth, there would be nearly 100 million molecules to every square inch of

[1] Florence Armstrong Grondal, *The Romance of Astronomy*, pp. 212, 213.
[2] W. F. G. Swann, *The Architecture of the Universe*, pp. 46, 44, 45, 55.

land. If we think of the molecules as tiny seeds, the total amount
of seed needed to sow the whole earth at the rate of 100 million
molecules to the square inch could be put into a pint pot. These
molecules move with very high speeds; in the ordinary air of an
ordinary room, the average molecular speed is about 500 yards a
second. This is roughly the speed of a rifle-bullet, and is rather
more than the ordinary speed of sound. . . . It is the high speed
of molecular motion that is responsible for the great pressure
exerted by a gas; any surface in contact with the gas is exposed
to a hail of molecules each moving with the speed of a rifle-
bullet. For instance, the piston in a locomotive cylinder is bombarded by about 14×10^{28} molecules every second. This incessant
fusillade of innumerable tiny bullets urges the piston forward
in the cylinder, and so propels the train. With each breath we
take, swarms of millions of millions of millions of molecules enter our bodies, each moving at about 500 yards a second, and
nothing but their incessant hammering on the walls of our lungs
keeps our chests from collapsing. Perhaps the best general mental picture we can form of a gas is that of an incessant hail of
shot or rifle-bullets flying indiscriminately in all directions, and
running into one another at frequent intervals. In ordinary air
each molecule collides with some other molecule about 3000 million times every second, and travels an average distance of about
1/160,000 inch between successive collisions. . . . The reddest light
we can see, which is that of longest wave-length, has a wave-
length of only 3/100,000 inch (7.5×10^{-5} cms.); the most violet
light we can see has a wave-length of only half of this, or
0.000015 inch. Light of all colors travels with the same uniform
speed of 186,000 miles, or 3×10^{10} centimetres, a second. The
number of waves of red light which pass any fixed point in a
second is accordingly no fewer than four hundred million million.
This is called the 'frequency' of the light. Violet light has the
still higher frequency of eight hundred million million; when
we see violet light, eight hundred million million waves of light
enter our eyes each second."[1]

Do the revelations of modern science make it easier or more
difficult for an individual to believe in God? Dr. Hermann Weyl,
Professor of Mathematics at the University of Gottingen, opened
his series of Terry Lectures at Yale with these words: "A mathe-

[1] Sir James Jeans, *The Universe Around Us,* pp. 90, 91, 108.

matician steps before you, speaks about metaphysics, and does
not hesitate to use the name of God. . . . One common thought
holds together the following three lectures: Modern science, in-
sofar as I am familiar with it through my own scientific work,
mathematics and physics make the world appear more and more
as an open one, as a world not closed but pointing beyond itself. . . . Many people think that modern science is far removed
from God. I find, on the contrary, that it is much more difficult
today for the knowing person to approach God from history,
from the spiritual side of the world, and from morals; for there
we encounter the suffering and evil in the world which it is difficult to bring into harmony with an all-merciful and all-mighty
God. In this domain we have evidently not yet succeeded in raising the veil with which our human nature covers the essence of
things. But in our knowledge of physical nature we have penetrated so far that we can obtain a vision of the flawless harmony
which is in conformity with sublime reason. Here is neither suffering nor evil nor deficiency, but perfection only. Nothing prevents us as scientists from taking part in the cosmic worship that
found such powerful expression in the most glorious poem of the
German language, the song of the archangels at the beginning
of Goethe's *Faust*:

> The sun makes music as of old
> Amid the rival spheres of heaven
> On its predestined circle rolled
> With thunder speed; the angels even
> Draw strength from gazing at its glance,
> Though none its meaning fathom may:—
> The world's unwithered countenance
> Is bright as on the earliest day.

The world is not a chaos, but a cosmos harmoniously ordered by
inviolable mathematical laws. . . . Eddington recently spoke of
the fact that in Kepler's conception of the world, the music of
the spheres was not drowned by the roar of machinery and that
herein lies a deep relationship between his astronomical thinking
and the development of modern physics. The harmony of the
universe is neither mechanical nor psychical, it is mathematical and
divine. . . . Purely mathematical inquiry in itself, according to

the conviction of many great thinkers, by its special character, its certainty and stringency, lifts the human mind into closer proximity with the divine than is attainable through any other medium. Mathematics is the science of the infinite, its goal the symbolic comprehension of the infinite with human, that is finite, means."[1]

This attitude is maintained by many other outstanding scientists of the present day. Sir James Jeans, for example, writes: "Twentieth-century science, projecting the ideas of pure mathematics on to nature, finds that they fit as perfectly, and as uniquely, as Cinderella's slipper fitted to her foot."[2] "To my mind, the laws which nature obeys are less suggestive of those which a machine obeys in its motion than of those which a musician obeys in writing a fugue, or a poet in composing a sonnet. The motions of electrons and atoms do not resemble those of the parts of a locomotive so much as those of the dancers in a cotillion. . . . If all this is so, then the universe can be best pictured, although still very imperfectly and inadequately, as consisting of pure thought, the thought of what, for want of a wider word, we must describe as a mathematical thinker. . . . Thirty years ago, we thought, or assumed, that we were heading towards an ultimate reality of a mechanical kind. It seemed to consist of a fortuitous jumble of atoms, which was destined to perform meaningless dances for a time under the action of blind purposeless forces, and then fall back to form a dead world. Into this wholly mechanical world, through the play of the same blind forces, life had stumbled by accident. One tiny corner at least, and possibly several tiny corners, of this universe of atoms had chanced to become conscious for a time, but was destined in the end, still under the action of blind mechanical forces, to be frozen out and again leave a lifeless world. Today there is a wide measure of agreement, which on the physical side of science approaches almost to unanimity, that the stream of knowledge is heading towards a non-mechanical reality; the universe begins to look more like a great thought than like a great machine. Mind no longer appears as an accidental intruder into the realm of matter; we are beginning to suspect that we ought rather to hail it as the creator and governor of the realm of matter—not of course

[1] Dr. Herman Weyl, *The Open World*, pp. 1, v, 28, 29, 21, 25, 26, 7.
[2] Sir James Jeans, *The New Background of Science*, p. 294.

our individual minds, but the mind in which the atoms out of which our individual minds have grown exist as thoughts. . . . We discover that the universe shows evidence of a designing or controlling power that has something in common with our own individual minds—not, so far as we have discovered, emotion, morality, or aesthetic appreciation, but the tendency to think in the way which, for want of a better word, we describe as mathematical. And while much in it may be hostile to the material appendages of life; we are not so much strangers or intruders in the universe as we at first thought."[1]

Concerning the function of a mathematical physicist, Dr. W. F. G. Swann writes: "For himself he is one of the poets of science, or if you will, a harmonist of the universe; and, in welding into consistency the various parts of nature's structure, he is as a musician who takes a tune which before we knew only as a waltz, a melody which we knew only as a song, and a theme which we knew only as a military march, and welds them as part of a grander structure, the symphony of the universe. . . . In some respects, our mathematical physicist is like a Dr. Jekyll and Mr. Hyde. Or, let me perhaps liken him to two distinct animals. . . . No longer in physics are we satisfied with a picture of angels carrying the planets around the sun. No longer do we hope to push the explanation of things back to some fundamental causes which of themselves need no explanation. Rather does the man of science today seek satisfaction in the expression of nature's laws in a beautiful and harmonious form. . . . In a sense, science becomes an art; and, in so doing, it loses none of that power characteristic of the spirit of the scientific method, but rather does it gain in that power, since no longer is there left anything in the way of preconceived mechanisms to hinder its theories in seeking accord with the facts. And so, in a sense, the man of science and the artist become one. If we should consult some great potentate of wisdom concerning the question, 'What is art?', I can imagine his answering thus: 'There is one great work of art; it is the universe. Ye men of letters find the imprints of its majesty in your sense of the beauty of words. Ye men of song find it in the harmony of sweet sounds. Ye painters feel it in the design of beauteous forms, and in the blending of rich soft colors do your souls mount on high to bask in the brilliance

[1] Sir James Jeans, *The Mysterious Universe*, pp. 167, 168, 185-187.

of nature's sunshine. Ye lovers are conscience of its beauties in forms ye can but ill define. Ye men of science find it in the rich harmonies of nature's mathematical design. And so, dear mortals, if ye should pray for anything, pray that ye may find senses to which all nature's beauties bring response, for then shall ye be as angels, and heaven shall be your habitation.' "[1]

VI

Human nature being what it is, how does an individual act when he is normal and natural? He may climb or he may plunge. Man's capacity for sordidness and greed and cruelty should never be minimized. But it is equally possible for him to respond to the appeal of beauty and truth and goodness. Truly man does not live by bread alone, but by ecstatic beauty, rapturous harmony, sublime thought, noble deed, and fervent adoration of the Eternal God.

VII

What kind of society can be built out of the raw stuff of human nature? The entrancing possibility presented by high religion is that of the Kingdom of God on earth. "Thy Kingdom come, thy will be done on earth as it is in heaven," is the most exalted petition ever uttered. In the language of poetry, prophets and seers throughout the centuries have portrayed the good society.

The people that walked in darkness have seen a great light: they that dwelt in the land of the shadow of death, upon them hath the light shined. Thou hast multiplied the nation, thou hast increased their joy: they joy before thee according to the joy in harvest, as men rejoice when they divide the spoil. For the yoke of his burden, and the staff of his shoulder, the rod of his oppressor, thou hast broken as in the day of Midian. For all the armor of the armed man in the tumult, and the garments rolled in blood, shall be for burning, for fuel of fire. For unto us a child is born, unto us a son is given; and the government shall be upon his shoulder: and his name shall be called Wonderful, Counsellor, Mighty God, Everlasting Father, Prince of Peace. Of the increase of his govern-

[1] Dr. W. F. G. Swann, *The Architecture of the Universe*, pp. 17, 18, 423-424.

ment and of peace there shall be no end, upon the throne of David, and upon his kingdom, to establish it, and to uphold it with justice and with righteousness from henceforth even for ever.[1]

The wilderness and the dry land shall be glad; and the desert shall rejoice, and blossom as the rose. It shall blossom abundantly, and rejoice even with joy and singing; the glory of Lebanon shall be given unto it, the excellency of Carmel and Sharon: they shall see the glory of Jehovah, the excellency of our God.

Then the eyes of the blind shall be opened, and the ears of the deaf shall be unstopped. Then shall the lame man leap as a hart, and the tongue of the dumb shall sing; for in the wilderness shall waters break out, and streams in the desert. And the glowing sand shall become a pool, and the thirsty ground springs of water: in the habitation of jackals, where they lay, shall be grass with reeds and rushes. And a highway shall be there, and a way, and it shall be called The way of holiness; the unclean shall not pass over it; but it shall be for the redeemed: the wayfaring men, yea fools, shall not err therein. No lion shall be there, nor shall any ravenous beast go up thereon; they shall not be found there; but the redeemed shall walk there: and the ransomed of Jehovah shall return, and come with singing unto Zion; and everlasting joy shall be upon their heads: they shall obtain gladness and joy, and sorrow and sighing shall flee away.[2]

And I saw a new Heaven and a new earth; for the first Heaven and the first earth were gone, and the sea no longer exists. And I saw the holy City, the new Jerusalem, coming down out of Heaven from God and made ready like a bride attired to meet her husband. And I heard a loud voice, which came from the throne, say,

> "God's dwelling place is among men
> And He will dwell among them
> And they shall be His peoples.
> Yes, God Himself will be among them.
> He will wipe every tear from their eyes.

[1] Isaiah 9:2-7.
[2] Isaiah 35:1, 2, 5-10.

Death shall be no more;
Nor sorrow, nor wail of woe, nor pain;
For the first things have passed away." ...

So in the Spirit he carried me to the top of a vast, lofty mountain, and showed me the holy City, Jerusalem, coming down out of Heaven from God, and bringing with it the glory of God. It shone with a radiance like that of a very precious stone—such as a jasper, bright and transparent. ...

I saw no Sanctuary in the City, for the Lord God, the Ruler of all, is its Sanctuary, and so is the Lamb. Nor has the City any need of the sun or of the moon, to give it light; for the glory of God has shone upon it and its lamp is the Lamb. The nations will live their lives by its light; and the kings of the earth are to bring their glory into it. And in the daytime (for there will be no night there) the gates will never be closed; and the glory and honor of the nations shall be brought into it. And no unclean thing shall ever enter it, nor any one who is guilty of base conduct or tells lies, but only those whose names stand recorded in the Lamb's Book of Life. ...

And there will be no night there; and they have no need of lamplight or sunlight, for the Lord God will shine upon them, and they will be kings until the Ages of the Ages."[1]

VII

The visions of the prophets emerge from the great concepts and high experiences of religion:

1. God is creator and sustainer of the universe.
2. Personality is the most precious of all values.
3. Kinship with every other human being is the normal relationship.
4. Concern about values and relationships is the most dynamic motivation.
5. Justice is required in all relationships.
6. Fellowship travels far beyond justice.
7. Evil can be overcome only with goodness.

[1] Revelations 21:1-4, 10, 11, 22-27; 22:5. *New Testament in Modern Speech,* by R. F. Weymouth. Published by The Pilgrim Press, Boston.

8. Risks must be run and consequences endured.

9. God can be and must be trusted and obeyed.

The religious concept of the good society begins and ends with God. This earth is our Father's home. True enough it is only one room of many mansions, but the jurisdiction of His reign extends throughout the world. The cattle on a thousand hills belong to Him, and man can never be more than a trustee utterly dependent upon the Giver of every good and perfect gift.

Personality towers above all other values because man is created in the image of God, and therefore reverence for personality is an essential element of high religion. The inherent worth and dignity of a person demand that he ever be treated as an end and never merely as a means to an end. "Whoever shall occasion the fall of one of these little ones who believe in me, it would be better for him to have a millstone hung round his neck and to be drowned in the depths of the sea."[1]

Kinship with every other person is the normal relationship because all are children of God. Men of all races and nations and classes are members of our common family and all are dwelling together in the home of our Father. High barriers which arbitrarily divide mankind into antagonistic units based upon color or speech or status constitute disloyalty and treason to the one family.

Concern about values and relationships is the most dynamic motivation of human behavior. Love of God and love of neighbor lead to the most creative forms of activity. Human nature is so equipped that man's highest satisfactions may be derived from commitment to the task of creating a new society in which the value of personality will be exalted and the harmony of human relationships will be experienced.

Justice is the minimum requirement of reverence for personality and recognition of kinship. "Do unto others as you would have them do unto you," is an inherently reasonable admonition.

> He hath showed thee, O man, what is good; and what doth Jehovah require of thee, but to do justly, and to love kindness, and to walk humbly with thy God.[2]

Justice however is not enough and must be supplemented with fellowship. No family can long remain harmonious if a

[1] Matt. 18:6, Weymouth.
[2] Micah 6:8.

wife always gives her husband just what he deserves! Generous
portions of forgiveness and forbearance and sacrificial loyalty
are required.

> Love is so patient and so kind;
> Love never boils with jealousy;
> It never boasts, is never puffed with pride;
> It does not act with rudeness, or insist upon its rights;
> It never gets provoked, it never harbors evil thoughts;
> Is never glad when wrong is done,
> But always glad when truth prevails;
> It bears up under anything,
> It exercises faith in everything,
> It gives us hope in everything,
> It gives us power to endure in anything.
> Love never fails; . . .
> And so these three, faith, hope, and love, endure,
> But the greatest of them is love.[1]

Evil must not be resisted with evil but only with goodness:
this is the message of exalted religion. Retaliation compounds
and extends evil. Persevering goodwill alone can break the vicious
chain. "You have heard that it was said, 'Eye for eye, tooth for
tooth' (Exod. xxi. 24). But I tell you not to resist a wicked
man, but if any one strikes you on the right cheek, turn the
other to him as well. . . . You have heard that it was said, 'Thou
shalt love thy neighbor (Lev. xix. 18) and hate thine enemy.'
But I command you all, love your enemies, and pray for your
persecutors; that so you may become true sons of your Father
in Heaven; for He causes His sun to rise on the wicked as well
as the good, and sends rain upon those who do right and those
who do wrong. For if you love only those who love you, what
reward have you earned? Do not even the tax-gatherers do that?
And if you salute only your near relatives, what praise is due to
you? Do not even the Gentiles do the same? You, however, are
to be complete in goodness, as your Heavenly Father is complete."[2]

"Your love must be true. You must always turn in horror

---

[1] Cor. 13:4-8, 13. *The New Testament,* Williams.
[2] Matt. 5:38, 39, 43-48, Weymouth.

from what is wrong, but keep on holding to what is right. . . .
Keep on blessing your persecutors; keep on blessing and stop
cursing them. . . . Stop returning evil for evil to anyone. . . . If
your enemy is hungry, give him something to eat. If he is thirsty
give him something to drink. For if you act in this way, you
will heap burning coals upon his head! Stop being conquered by
evil, but keep on conquering evil with good."[1]

"Master, how often am I to forgive my Brother when he
wrongs me? As many as seven times?" But Jesus answered: "Not
seven times, but 'seventy times seven.' "[2]

Risks must be run and consequences endured if the way of
forgiving love is to be followed. Resistance to evildoers is dangerous irrespective of the method of resistance, whether by violence or by persuasive goodwill. Futile, however, is courageous
resort to violence; whereas, heroic loyalty to the way of love is
redemptive.

"Listen! I am sending you out as sheep surrounded by
wolves. So you must be sensible like serpents and guileless
like doves. Be on your guard against men, for they will turn
you over to the courts and will flog you in their synagogues,
and you will be brought before governors and kings for my
sake. . . . One brother will turn another over to death, and
a father his child, and children will take a stand against their
parents, and will have them put to death. And you will be
hated by all men, because you bear my name; but whoever
bears up to the end will be saved.[3]

"If any man wishes to walk in my steps, let him renounce
self, take up his cross, and follow me. For whoever wishes
to save his life will lose it, and whoever, for my sake and
for the sake of the Good News, will lose his life shall save
it.[4]

I am giving you these commands that you may love one
another. If the world hates you, you know that it has first
hated me. . . .

They will expel you from their Synagogues; indeed the

1 Rom. 12:9, 14, 17, 20, 21, Williams.
2 Matt. 18:21, 22, The Twentieth Century New Testament. Published by
Fleming H. Revell Company, New York.
3 Matt. 10:16, 17, 21, 22, Williams.
4 Mark 8:34, 35, Twentieth Century.

time is coming when any one who kills you will think that he is making an offering to God.[1]

Trust in God is required of persons who faithfully follow the way of the cross. The ultimate outcome of the struggle against evil is not in our feeble hands. While we are called upon to co-operate loyally with God, He alone is able to create the divine society. Not victory, but heroic faithfulness is demanded of us. "Love is the law of life and not merely some transcendent ideal of perfection," writes Reinhold Niebuhr. "It is important to recognize that the Kingdom of God, according to the biblical conception, is never purely an other-worldly perfection, not even when it is interpreted in a gospel which is directed primarily to the Greek world. The Christian is taught to pray constantly 'Thy Kingdom come.' The hope of this prayer, when vital, is a constant pressure upon the conscience of man in every action.[2]

Except the LORD build the house, they labor in vain that build it: except the LORD keep the city, the watchman waketh *but* in vain.[3]

God is our refuge and strength,
A very present help in trouble.
Therefore will we not fear, though the earth do change,
And though the mountains be shaken into the heart of the
    seas;
Though the waters thereof roar and be troubled,
Though the mountains tremble with the swelling thereof.
                                                    [Selah
There is a river, the streams whereof make glad the city of
    God,
The holy place of the tabernacles of the Most High.
God is in the midst of her; she shall not be moved:
God will help her, and that right early.[4]
Lord, thou hast been our dwelling-place
In all generations.
Before the mountains were brought forth,

[1] John 15:17, 18; 16:2, Twentieth Century.
[2] *Beyond Tragedy*, pp. 258, 277, 278.
[3] Psalms 127:1.
[4] Psalms 46:1-5.

Or ever thou hadst formed the earth and the world,
Even from everlasting to everlasting, thou art God.
Thou turnest man to destruction,
And sayest, Return, ye children of men.
For a thousand years in thy sight
Are but as yesterday when it is past,
And as a watch in the night.

The days of our years are three-score years and ten,
Or even by reason of strength fourscore years;
Yet is their pride but labor and sorrow;
For it is soon gone, and we fly away.
Make us glad according to the days wherein thou hast afflicted
    us,
And the years wherein we have seen evil.
Let thy work appear unto thy servants,
And thy glory upon their children.
And let the favor of the Lord our God be upon us;
And establish thou the work of our hands upon us;
Yea, the work of our hands establish thou it.[1]

Bless Jehovah, O my soul.
O Jehovah my God, thou art very great;
Thou art clothed with honor and majesty:
Who coverest thyself with light as with a garment;
Who stretchest out the heavens like a curtain;
Who layeth the beams of his chambers in the waters;
Who maketh the clouds his chariot;
Who walketh upon the wings of the wind;
Who maketh winds his messengers;
Flames of fire his ministers;
Who laid the foundations of the earth,
That it should not be moved for ever.
I will sing unto Jehovah as long as I live:
I will sing praise to my God while I have any being.[2]

"Do not sparrows sell for a cent apiece? And yet not one
of them can fall to the ground without your Father's notice.

1 Psalms 90:1-4, 9, 10, 16, 17.
2 Psalms 104:1-5, 33.

Even the very hairs on your head have all been counted by
God. So stop being afraid; you are worth more than many
sparrows . . . Keep on asking, and the gift will be given you;
keep on seeking, and you will find; keep on knocking, and the
door will open to you. For every one who keeps on asking,
receives, and everyone who keeps on seeking, finds, and to the
one who keeps on knocking, the door will open. What human
father among you, when his son asks him for bread, will give
him a stone? Or if he asks for a fish, will he give him a
snake? So if you, in spite of your being bad, know how to give
your children what is good, how much more surely will your
heavenly Father give what is good to those who keep on
asking Him?[1]

VIII

The pulling power of an ideal is revealed most clearly in the
character and teaching of Jesus Christ. In the Fourth Gospel,
these symbolic words are attributed to him: "And I, if I be lifted
up from the earth, will draw all men to me." The extravagance of
this utterance appears less extreme the longer one reflects upon
the magnetic influence of Jesus upon multitudes of individuals
of all races and classes throughout the centuries. More than sixty
thousand volumes have been written in the insistent endeavor to
account for him. "The name of Jesus is not so much written as
ploughed into the history of the world," wrote Emerson. And
Rabbi Enelow has testified: "Jesus has become the most popular,
the most studied, the most influential figure in the religious history of mankind. . . . Jesus has fascinated mankind."

The most exalted concepts of religion were in the person of
Jesus clothed with flesh and blood. From the realm of abstraction
down into daily conduct he brought reverence for personality and
recognition of kinship with every other person. With utter selflessness he carried upon his own shoulders the burdens and miseries
of the bereaved and distressed. To an unparalleled extent he
sought fellowship with individuals of different races and classes.
Loathing evil with refined sensitivities, he refused to do evil
in the endeavor to protect the helpless. He persisted in living every
day as a loyal member of God's home, and when confronted with

[1] Matt. 10:29-31; 7:7-11, Williams.

the necessity of abandoning his chosen way of life or being crucified as an enemy of the people, he stedfastly set his face toward the cross. From the abyss of agony he struggled upward with power derived from supreme trust in God.

So massive was the impact Jesus made upon his disciples that they could account for him only in terms of a unique relationship to God. "So high, so pure, so holy, of such unearthly grandeur and might, did Jesus appear to those who confessed Him as their Saviour," writes Dr. Warschauer, "that they had in some way to mark their sense of His elevation above the common plane of humanity. St. Paul does not state it in the same terms as the Fourth Evangelist, nor the latter in the same terms as Matthew and Luke; yet they one and all, each in his own dialect, put into words the same conviction, born of the same consciousness. In reading the accounts of the Lord's miraculous entry into the world, the true question we have to ask is this: *What must have been the quality of a Life to which such an origin was attributed?* As has been wisely and happily said concerning these narratives—which we would assuredly not miss from our Gospels—'they are trustworthy testimonies, not to the reality of certain incidents, but to the quality and magnitude of Jesus' character; not the history of His birth, but products of the quality of His ministry.' "[1]

Stricken humanity in this hour of world crisis needs nothing quite so desperately as the reproduction and extension of the spirit of Jesus in personal living and in social action. The more thoroughly we become saturated with His spirit the more exultantly do we sing:

> Fairest Lord Jesus
> Ruler of all nature
> O thou of God and man the Son!
> Thee will I cherish,
> Thee will I honor,
> Thou my soul's glory, joy and crown.
>
> Fair are the meadows,
> Fairer still the woodlands,
> Robed in the blooming garb of spring;

[1] J. Warschauer, *The Historical Life of Christ*. Published by the Macmillan Company.

Jesus is fairer,
Jesus is purer,
Who makes the woful heart to sing.

Fair is the sunshine,
Fairer still the moonlight,
And all the twinkling, starry host;
Jesus shines fairer,
Jesus shines purer,
Than all the angels heaven can boast.[1]

---

[1] Anonymous. From the German, Seventeenth Century.

Chapter II

Deepen Understanding of the Actual

HOW CAN a man believe in God when faced with an appalling mass of cruelty and hatred and misery? The deeper one probes into the present state of affairs, the more earnestly he inquires: could a man believe in God if we were now reaping a harvest of peace and prosperity from the seed sown during the past century? What kind of universe would yield violets from thistle seeds? Or giant sequoia from raspberries? Integrity of the law of the harvest is essential to confidence in an orderly universe ruled over by an intelligent Creator. We can believe in God because "whatsoever a man sows that shall he also reap."

Human nature is potential. It is capable of becoming; what it becomes is determined by the relative impact of various stimuli. Environmental influences are enormously important not only in determining the external forces which produce human sensations, but also in shaping the ideas and ideals which operate as internal impulses. Consider the contrasting stimuli bombarding the youth of Fascist Italy, Soviet Russia, Nazi Germany, Imperial Japan, primitive Liberia, socialized Sweden, and competitive United States. From within and from without human nature is constantly being driven.

The political and economic structure of society must be examined if we are to understand the forces and factors which shape human nature. In the course of this exploration we should, however, be on guard against the error of assuming that environmental influences completely dominate human responses. Certain individuals in Italy and Russia and the United States bear a much closer resemblance to each other than to their respective countrymen. Various persons react differently to the same stimulus. But surely the life of Hitler would not have been the same if he had grown to maturity in a comfortable and happy Norwegian home. How widely would Gandhi now be known if all his days had been spent in Greenland? What kind of person would Mussolini be if he were a native of Tanganyika?

Some of the most dynamic stimuli which influence the present generation are released by individualism, nationalism and secularism. Of the utmost importance therefore is an exploration of the meaning and significance of the present social order.

II

The people of the United States are now living under a system of qualified competitive-individualism. The prevailing economic ideas and practices are a heritage from the pioneer conditions which prevailed upon this continent until recently. Since deeper insight into contemporary situations may be gained from the perspective in history, let us remind ourselves of the fundamental economic beliefs dominant in this country at the close of last century:

1. Self-interest is and must continue to be the primary incentive to efficient economic activity. The individual who most successfully advances his own interests becomes the greatest servant of society. An ancestor of J. Pierpont Morgan, the Reverend Joseph Morgan, actually praised greed more highly than love: "Each man coveting to make himself rich, carries on the Publick Good: Thus God in His Wisdom and Mercy turns our Wickedness to Publick Benefit. . . . A rich Man is a great friend of the Publick, while he aims at nothing but serving himself. God will have us live by helping one another; and since Love will not do it, Covetousness shall."[1]

2. An individual is entitled to all the money and property that he can acquire honestly. It is legitimate and even desirable for the ablest and most thrifty members of the community to acquire great riches, even though the mass of people are unable to rise above the level of poverty and want. The Honorable Samuel J. Tilden in 1877 thus soothed his rich friends: "While you are scheming for your own selfish ends, there is an over-ruling and wise Providence directing that the most of all you do should inure to the benefit of the people. Men of colossal fortunes are in effect, if not in fact, trustees for the public."[2] Four decades ago in the

[1] Lewis Corey, *The House of Morgan*, p. 20.
[2] Corey, *op. cit.*, p. 80.

House of Representatives, Congressman Walker exclaimed: "The golden rule runs through all economic law, and no man can resist it, be his motive good or bad. No man can accumulate a fortune in manufacturing who does not serve his fellows a thousand-fold more than his personal interest in the operation, be his motive moral or immoral.[1]

3. Therefore competition is the most satisfactory method of carrying on production and distribution. The inefficient are thus weeded out as the chief rewards go to the skillful and the industrious. At the beginning of this century, Andrew Carnegie surveyed the scene with unalloyed satisfaction: "We accept and welcome, therefore, as conditions to which we must accommodate ourselves, great inequality of environment; the concentration of business, industrial and commercial, in the hands of the few; and the law of competition between these, as being not only beneficial, but essential to the future progress of the race."[2]

4. Government should keep out of business and confine its operations to safeguarding the public, compelling fair observance of the rules of the game, and serving its citizens in the realms of education and culture. In the middle of the nineteenth century Francis Bowen, Professor of Moral Philosophy in Harvard College, wrote: "Laissez-faire; 'these things regulate themselves,' in common phrase; which means, of course, that God regulates them by his general laws, which always, in the long run, work to good. In these modern days, the ruler or governor who is to be dreaded is, not the tyrant, but the busybody. Let the course of trade and the condition of society alone, is the best advice which can be given to the legislator, the projector, and the reformer. Busy yourselves, if you must be busy, with individual cases of wrong, hardship, or suffering; but do not meddle with the general laws of the universe."[3]

5. Nationalism became the instrument through which these ideas were extended to the world scene. The doctrine of national interest rested upon the same foundation as the dogma of self-interest, and the idea that a nation is entitled to the highest possible standard of living for its own citizens regardless of the welfare of the rest of humanity was rarely questioned. "The gist of

[1] *Congressional Record,* January 30, 1894, p. 1648
[2] Andrew Carnegie, *The Gospel of Wealth,* p. 4.
[3] Francis Bowen, *Principles of Political Economy,* pp. 22, 23.

the matter," says Harry Emerson Fosdick, "lies in the fact that the dogma of nationalism, as it has developed in the last two centuries, has become a competing religion. I think it the most dangerous rival of Christian principles on earth. The crucial conflict today is not primarily Christianity versus Buddhism or Christianity versus Mohammedanism, but Christianity versus nationalism, and until one has clearly envisaged that fact one does not understand the crux of our situation."[1]

6. The method of competition when extended on a world scale became militaristic imperialism under which the strong seized as much of the earth as their respective opportunities and powers made possible. "One cannot study this period," writes Professor Langer of Harvard in his monumental history of imperialism, "without marvelling at the exuberance and optimism which went hand in hand with recklessness and confidence in the conduct of foreign affairs. It was taken for granted that the world was marked out by Providence for exploitation by the European white man and that the principle of every man for himself and the devil take the hindmost was natural law. In the writings of the statesmen and in the writings of journalists there is very little trace of deeper understanding. The rise of Japan, the Adua disaster, the Boxer rising, none of these epoch-making events really opened the eyes of Europe. Even Lord Salisbury could see in the world nothing but a few virile nations and a large number of dying nations. The basic problem of international relations was who should cut up the victims."[2]

7. The idea of governmental non-interference took the form of international anarchy as sovereign nations sought to do as they pleased in the struggle for privilege. "Every one ought to know," writes W. Arnold-Forster, "as part of his historical equipment, how anarchic, how really lunatic, were the assumptions upon which responsible statesmen conducted international relations, at least so lately as twenty and thirty years ago. All the Foreign Offices were engaged in a deadly game of bluff and counter-bluff and genuine menace, with war as their ultimate instrument. The Kaiser described the game with refreshing candour when he wrote in 1899, apropos of The Hague discussions on arbitration, 'In practice I, at any rate, will henceforth rely and call upon God and

[1] *The Christian Century*, January 19, 1928, p. 74.
[2] William L. Langer, *The Diplomacy of Imperialism*, Vol. II, p. 797.

my bright sword alone; and damn their resolutions.' The Kaiser was not alone: that is what they were all doing in greater or lesser degree—relying upon their own bright swords and their exclusive alliances with God."[1]

Once the idea became firmly embedded in the popular mind that the individual serves society best by concentrating upon his own interests, and that the nation's first duty is to look after its own welfare, free reign was given to the spirit of covetousness. Human nature is equipped with enormous possibilities of greediness, and insatiable is the demand for privilege and power under the stimulus of admonition, approval and opportunity. Especially malignant is that form of covetousness which seeks privilege in the name of high ideals—love of family and devotion to country. So completely did individualism and nationalism capture the Western mind that education and organized religion were drafted into the service of self-interest and national interest. Selfishness was exalted into a national creed.

On the American continent the case for individualism appeared irrefutable because of the fortunate combination of circumstances under which it operated. A vast domain with apparently inexhaustible supplies of minerals and other natural resources, the development of modern science and technology, and successive generations of sturdy pioneers enabled competitive individualism to produce wealth on a fabulous scale. Nothing succeeds like success and the beneficiaries of a given system rarely take seriously criticisms of the source of their privileges. "We are much better off than people used to be, and we enjoy a far higher standard of living than that of any other nation at the present time." What could be more convincing?

Therefore the soil of American life was spread thickly with the seed of covetousness and fertilized with the enthusiastic approval of many wise and good men. The growth of greed became more luxuriant through the corruption of the religious doctrine of stewardship and consequent assumption that it is legitimate for an individual to acquire great riches if he will use the money wisely, especially if he will "give a tenth of his income to the Lord." It is not easy to imagine a social order in which the

1 W. Arnold-Forster, "Order and Self-Defence in the World Community," *Problems of Peace,* 5th Series, p. 231.

passion to make money would be more highly inflamed than under the system of American individualism.

III

It is doubtless an exaggeration to say that "the love of money is the root of all evil," but surely the terrible consequences of greed cannot be overlooked. This is harvest time and we are now reaping after the manner of the sowing. Four fruits of the harvest demand serious consideration: extreme concentration of power, gross inequality of privilege, devastating conflict, and enervating secularism.

In a complex and highly industrialized society, control of the primary means of production and distribution carries with it stupendous power over the lives of all the people. To the extent therefore that such control is concentrated in the hands of a tiny fraction of the population, the basic economic policies of the nation are dominated by rich financiers and industrialists. And under a profit system this enormous power is wielded in such a way as to increase the privileges and influence of the most highly favored section of society. Thus concentration of wealth and income becomes more and more extreme.

Consider certain relevant facts: President Roosevelt, in his message to Congress on April 29, 1938, thus summarized the trend toward monopoly: "Among us today a concentration of private power without equal in history is growing. This concentration is seriously impairing the economic effectiveness of private enterprise as a way of providing employment for labor and capital and as a way of assuring a more equitable distribution of income and earnings among the people of the nation as a whole. Statistics of the Bureau of Internal Revenue reveal the following amazing figures for 1935: Ownership of corporate assets: Of all corporations reporting from every part of the nation, one-tenth of 1 per cent of them owned 52 per cent of the assets of all of them . . . the Bureau of Internal Revenue reports that estate tax returns in 1936 show that: 33 per cent of the property which was passed by inheritance was found in only 4 per cent of all the reporting estates. (And the figures of concentration would be far more impressive if we included all the smaller estates which, under the law, do not have to report.)"

Under the auspices of the Social Science Research Council of America and under the direction of the Columbia University Council for Research in the Social Sciences, Professor Adolf A. Berle, Jr., and Professor Gardiner C. Means assembled a vast quantity of evidence revealing extreme concentration of control of corporate wealth in the United States in 1930. From their volume, *The Modern Corporation and Private Property*,[1] the following summary is taken:

"The great extent to which economic activity is today carried on by such large enterprises is clearly indicated by the accompanying list of the two hundred largest non-banking corporations, compiled as of January 1, 1930. Nearly all of these companies had assets of over one hundred million dollars, and fifteen had assets of over a billion dollars. . . . When we compare the combined assets of the two hundred largest non-banking corporations with the assets of all non-banking corporations, their dominant role is further emphasized. These companies, 42 railroads, 52 public utilities, and 106 industrials, each with assets over ninety million dollars, had combined assets at the beginning of 1930 of $81,074,000,000. According to an estimate based on Income Tax figures, the total assets of all non-banking corporations at the beginning of 1930 amounted to $165,000,000,000. Thus the two hundred big companies controlled 49.2 per cent of nearly half of all non-banking corporate wealth, while the remaining half was owned by the more than 300,000 smaller companies. . . . A very rough estimate, . . . indicates that at least 78 per cent and probably a larger proportion of American business wealth is corporate wealth. Since the two hundred largest corporations controlled approximately 49 per cent of all corporate wealth, the rough calculation would indicate that they controlled 38 per cent or more of all business wealth. . . . Since the total assets of the two hundred big companies in that year amounted to $81,077,000,000, they controlled roughly 22 per cent of the total wealth of the country. . . . It must further be remembered that the influence of one of these huge companies extends far beyond the assets under its direct control. Smaller companies which sell to or buy from the larger companies are likely to be influenced by them to a vastly greater extent than by other smaller companies with which they

1 Published by Commerce Clearing House, Inc., New York, pp. 19, 28, 31, 32, 33, 46.

might deal. In many cases the continued prosperity of the smaller company depends on the favor of the larger and almost inevitably the interests of the latter become the interests of the former. The influence of the larger company on prices is often greatly increased by its mere size, even though it does not begin to approach a monopoly. Its political influence may be tremendous. Therefore, if roughly half of corporate wealth is controlled by two hundred large corporations and half by smaller companies it is fair to assume that very much more than half of industry is dominated by these great units. This concentration is made even more significant when it is recalled that as a result of it, approximately 2,000 individuals out of a population of one hundred and twenty-five million are in a position to control and direct half of industry. . . . Approximately 2,000 men were directors of the 200 largest corporations in 1930. Since an important number of these are inactive, the ultimate control of nearly half of industry was actually in the hands of a few hundred men."

IV

Since privilege always flows toward power, concentration of control leads to excessive congestion of income. President Roosevelt, in his message on monopoly, thus summarized the trend: "The year 1929 was a banner year for distribution of stock ownership, but in that year three-tenths of 1 per cent of our population received 78 per cent of the dividends reported by individuals. This has roughly the same effect as if, out of every 300 persons in our population, one person received 78 cents out of every dollar of corporate dividends, while the other 299 persons divided up the other 22 cents between them. The effect of this concentration is reflected in the distribution of national income. A recent study by the National Resources Committee shows that in 1935-36: 47 per cent of all American families and single individuals living alone had incomes of less than $1,000 for the year; and at the other end of the ladder a little less than 1½ per cent of the nation's families received incomes which in dollars and cents reached the same total as the incomes of the 47 per cent at the bottom."[1]

Even at the height of prosperity in 1929 approximately 40 per cent of all American families received an income of less than

[1] April 29, 1938.

$1,500. The following table,[1] showing classifications of income for 1929, deserves careful consideration:

| Group | Income Range | | Number | | Per-centage of Total Popu-lation |
	Families	Un-attached In-dividuals	Families	Un-attached In-dividuals	
Wealthy.......	$25,000 and over	$15,000 and over	160,000	66,000	0.6
Well-to-do.....	10,000 to 25,000	5,000 to 15,000	471,000	241,000	1.8
Comfortable...	5,000 to 10,000	2,500 to 5,000	1,625,000	632.000	5.9
Moderate cir-cumstances..	3,000 to 5,000	1,500 to 2,500	3,672,000	1,900,000	13.7
Minimum comfort.....	1,500 to 3,000	750 to 1,500	9,893,000	3,649,000	35.7
Subsistence and poverty.	Under $1,500	Under $750	11,653,000	2,500,000	40.6

"The 11,653,000 families with incomes of less than $1,500 received a total of about 10 billion dollars. At the other extreme, the 36,000 families having incomes in excess of $75,000 possessed an aggregate income of 9.8 billion dollars. Thus it appears that 0.1 per cent of the families at the top received practically as much as 42 per cent of the families at the bottom of the scale. At 1929 prices, a family income of $2,000 may perhaps be regarded as sufficient to supply only basic necessities. However accurate this gen-

[1] Maurice Leven, Harold G. Moulton and Clark Warburton, *America's Capacity to Consume*, p. 87. Published by The Brookings Institution, Washington, D. C.

eralization may be, it is significant to note that more than 16 million families, or practically 60 per cent of the total number, were below this standard of expenditures." [1]

In the ninth year of the great depression which began with the crash in October, 1929, the tragic plight of millions of Americans was thus summarized: "Few people realize how desperate the relief problem in the United States has become. Few people, that is to say, beside the twenty million or more men, women and children who depend upon local, state or federal government assistance for the necessities of life. . . . The most conservative estimates put the total figure for unemployment at 12,000,000 and it is probably closer to 14,000,000 in reality. And while the rolls of relief applicants grow (often double, sometimes treble), the appropriations for relief are everywhere being curtailed. Everybody is sick of the problem. . . . In some respects the problem today is more difficult than it was in 1932. The prosperity that preceded the depression of 1929 had enabled a great many families to build up some sort of reserve to fall back on in case the income source should be cut off. Men who had held jobs all their lives, who had built up savings accounts and bought homes and automobiles, were able to carry on for several years, in many cases, after they were fired. They sold their possessions, borrowed money on their homes and insurance policies until every last resource had been tapped and they were forced to make application at the relief bureau. . . . The survey made by the American Association of Social Workers uncovered a picture of unbelievable destitution throughout the country. In Douglas County, Nebraska, for example, the average amount of relief per family is $6.90 a month, and only about 20 per cent of the families that need help are getting it. . . . In Arkansas the average monthly relief allowance for a family is $6. In Little Rock, during February, it was discovered that two thousand families without any income were receiving no aid whatsoever and were on the verge of starvation. . . . In St. Louis, the Board of Education reports that out of the 70,000 school children given physical examinations during the past year 6,000, or about eight per cent, are undernourished. This in spite of the fact that the schools give free milk and balanced free lunches to counteract the poor food the children get at home." [2]

[1] *Ibid.*, pp. 55, 56.
[2] Bruce Bliven, Jr., in *The New Republic,* April 13, 1938.

V

In a highly mechanized society where self-interest has been exalted for a sufficiently long time to bring about a high degree of concentration of economic power, industrial conflict tends to become more and more destructive. The units of combat become gigantic in size: huge corporations and chain stores frequently crowd to the wall small producers and distributors; labor is compelled to organize in larger and larger unions and to engage in strikes which dislocate entire industries and even threaten the operation of essential social functions. Class consciousness becomes increasing acute and the effort to preserve vested interests assumes a more ruthless form as the privileged section of the population becomes frightened. Swarms of industrial spies are employed in many plants to report on activities of union organizers, and sometimes thugs are hired as strike-breakers. In numerous communities sheriffs and policemen are under the control of powerful industrialists and financiers, with the result that government agencies are often used to break strikes. Sometimes pitched battles with machine guns and other weapons of war break out. With abundant justification does Professor Slichter of Harvard exclaim: "Had we deliberately planned an industrial system which would create intense conflict between capital and labor, we could scarcely have devised one which would have achieved this result more completely than does the existing economic order."

A graphic picture of recent industrial warfare in the steel industry is presented by Paul Y. Anderson, one of the most alert and reliable newspaper correspondents in Washington: "For several months an important section of American industry, led by the Republic Steel Corporation, has been in a state of open, armed rebellion against the authority of the United States government as expressed in the Wagner Act, and its mercenaries have inflicted heavy casualties in dead, wounded, and captured, without suffering any appreciable losses. . . . The object of this dispatch is to parade recent incidents of the rebellion in a connected sequence, and thereby attempt to explain why the commission of mass murder in certain localities of the United States has become bolder, safer, and more systematically organized during the last two months than at any other period since Al Capone, Dion O'Banion, the Genna brothers, and Bugs Moran made Chicago their private battleground. The two periods are alike in one respect, that the motive was profit. But whereas the police were merely corrupt and quiescent when the gangsters were killing one another, they are now doing the killing themselves; and whereas all sides in the gang wars were well armed, the police victims have all been unarmed workingmen or innocent bystanders. On the afternoon of Memorial Day Sunday a holiday crowd of some 2,500 men, women, and children attended a mass meeting several blocks distant from the South Chicago plant of the Republic Steel Corporation, where a strike was in progress. At its conclusion most of them proceeded to a point a few blocks removed from the plant, and there a group of about 400 detached themselves from the main body and walked along a dirt road across an open field in the general direction of the plant, with the intention of marching past the gates, displaying signs appealing to the non-striking workers to come out and join them. At the far corner of the field before the gates were in sight, the paraders were halted by a long line of uniformed Chicago policemen, numbering 200 or more. During a parley which lasted not more than four minutes individuals at the front of the procession asked the police for permission to proceed through the line and establish peaceful picketing, as had been promised by Mayor Kelly, and were told in reply to 'get the hell out of here.' Then, upon a signal which consisted either of the firing of a shot in the air or the tossing of a gas grenade into the midst of the crowd, police charged into the left flank of the crowd, clubbing its members ferociously. From back in the throng a shower of small stones and sticks was thrown toward the police. Instantly there was a terrific roar of pistol shots from all along the police line, and as the front rank of the marchers went down in a bloody tangle the bluecoats charged with smoking guns and flying nightsticks. Total dead: ten, of whom seven were shot in the back. Total suffering from gunshot wounds: approximately 50, of whom 62 per cent were shot in the back. Total injured from all causes: approximately 75, of whom at least two will be crippled for life. Three policemen were hospitalized. No policemen were shot. Cook County authorities took the position that the victims, including those shot in the back, were killed by policemen acting in self-defense. The coroner's jury sustained that position."[1]

[1] Paul Y. Anderson, "Armed Rebellion on the Right," *The Nation*, August 7, 1937.

An incident in the industrial warfare which rages across the continent is thus described by J. Warren Madden, chairman of the National Labor Relations Board: "I have seen a man as gentle and as deserving of the protection of the law as you and I, whose head was hammered to a bloody pulp with an iron hammer on the main street of a great American city in plain view of many witnesses . . . but because the man was a union organizer, no arrests were made." The background of this incident has been thus outlined: "The man whose 'head was hammered to a bloody pulp with an iron hammer' is Norman Smith, organizer for the United Automobile Workers of America. Unfortunately Chairman Madden did not give the facts behind the attack on Norman Smith. If he had, he would have laid bare a lamentable state of affairs in the city of Memphis—political bossism, police brutality, wholesale violations of civil liberties, and corporation domination of the city government. . . . The Ford Motor Company has tried to prevent the organization of its outlying assembly plants by the same methods that it has used at the giant Ford plant in Dearborn, Michigan, methods which were outlined in the decision against the Ford Company recently handed down by the NLRB. These include the establishment of company unions, the open flouting of the principle of collective bargaining, the use of thugs to coerce workers and to beat organizers, and the use of the machinery of the city government both to assure the immunity of the thugs and to harass union workers with false arrests and police intimidation."[1]

A vivid illustration of the mob violence against union officials and their sympathizers which breaks out periodically throughout the nation is furnished by the recent experiences of Norman Thomas in Jersey City and Newark. Here is the story as told on the front page of the *New York Times:* "Newark, N. J., June 4.—Chanting 'We Want Americanism—Not Reds,' and following a band playing patriotic music about fifty men, mostly war veterans, broke up a meeting in Military Park in the heart of the city tonight, at which Norman Thomas, former Socialist candidate for President, was to have spoken. They pelted Mr. Thomas with rotten eggs and ripe tomatoes, drowned out his efforts to

[1] George Lambert, in *The Nation*, January 22, 1938.

speak and his appeals for fair play with howls and band music, and finally forced him to abandon the attempt. Three persons were hurt, one being taken to a hospital, in rioting around the speakers' stand. . . . Before tonight's riot a committee representing war veterans' organizations and American Federation of Labor unions made an unsuccessful attempt to have Mr. Thomas's permit revoked. The permit was granted some time ago by the Commissioner of Parks and Public Property. . . . After the Thomas party left, the men who had broken up the meeting continued to march around the park behind their band. Their leader identified himself as Adam Cassell, adjutant of Good Fellowship Post 189 of the American Legion, one of the organizations which had tried to have Mr. Thomas's permit cancelled earlier in the day. He said his group had hired the band and organized deliberately to break up the meeting."

VI

Just as the dogma of self-interest blossoms into the doctrine of national interest, the justification of a competitive struggle for private profit leads to militaristic imperialism and war. Industrialism has made the nations interdependent and unable to live alone, with consequent need of raw materials, markets and fields of investment in other lands. The current doctrine of patriotism produces national egotism to an extravagant degree, with the result that patriots find it is easy to justify whatever foreign policy may seem to be necessary in serving national interests. Armed intervention in other countries is the habitual practice of imperialist powers. The government of the United States has without declaring war sent our armed forces into foreign lands a hundred times in a hundred years.[1] No informed person believes that the present size of the American navy is required in order to defend our shores. The enormous addition to the fleet just authorized is being made for the purpose of enabling this country "if necessary" to fight Japan in Far Eastern waters in defense of our interests in China and other areas in Asia.

The nations are now plunging ominously near the abyss of another cataclysmic war because the general practices of the nations have produced five crucial problems: the Treaty of Versailles,

[1] See details in M. Offutt, *The Protection of Citizens Abroad by the Armed Forces of the United States.*

the economic problem, the empire problem, the armaments problem, and the anarchy problem.

At the end of the World War the French were determined to prevent another invasion of their land by the double process of breaking Germany's power and of strengthening their own defenses. The military, naval, territorial and economic provisions of the Treaty of Versailles reduced Germany to the rank of an inferior power; whereas the impregnable border fortifications and a series of military alliances raised France to a degree of dominance on the continent not equalled by any nation in modern times. But all this did not make France safe, but on the contrary fanned to white heat German passions of hatred and insatiable desire for revenge. The effort of the Allies to crush Germany was a primary cause of the rise of Hitler to dictatorial power.

The economic problem is produced by the practice of the favored nations of using their superior economic advantages in such ways as to handicap, if not to strangle, the weaker countries. The essence of the problem is access to markets, because raw materials may easily be purchased if sufficient foreign exchange is available. Japan, for example, secures dollars with which to make purchases in this country by sales of her products in this country or by exchanging for dollars the pounds or francs obtained by sales in England or France. If the favored nations raise tariff walls high enough to shut out goods from the handicapped countries, the economic position of the latter group becomes desperate.

The empire problem is the result of the determination of latecomers to follow the example set by their predecessors in seizing foreign territory and controlling the economic resources of other peoples. The nations chiefly responsible for empire-building are clearly revealed on a map of the world. It is natural that the privileged countries should desire to end the process and maintain the status quo; whereas equally understandable is the determination of Germany, Italy and Japan to play at least one more inning before the game is called off. Before the United States, Great Britain and France can convince other powers that they have repented and reformed, they must bring forth fruits of penitence.

The armaments problem is created by the refusal of the Allies to reduce substantially their own armaments after Germany was paralyzed by the Treaty of Versailles. Tragic blindness made possible the illusion that sixty million Germans would accept permanently a status of military impotence. Which other great power would have for such a long time refrained from re-arming? The Allies are directly responsible for the terrific race of armaments now being run along the edge of the international chasm.

The anarchy problem grows out of the reluctance of peoples to widen the jurisdiction of government sufficiently to make possible pacific settlement of economic and political controversies. The assumption that that government is best which governs least is the foundation upon which rests the doctrine of national sovereignty. So long as the respective nations cling tenaciously to the sovereign right to do as they please in realms where the interests of other peoples are involved, war will hover as an imminent threat. The League of Nations has been rendered relatively impotent by the refusal of several great powers to become members or to retain membership, and by the effort of the favored nations to use it as an instrument for preserving their vested privileges.

Greed and egotism, armaments and anarchy, in a world of suspicion and hatred, are driving the nations furiously toward war. And war on the present scale with available weapons constitutes a terrifying threat to all high values. The prospect before us is thus described by an eminent Frenchman: "We open the newspaper. 'Canton was bombarded,' we read. 'There are about 1,500 victims.' We sigh, yawn, turn the page, read another report: 'The little town of Granollers in Spain—' These completely useless massacres shock us, but we feel powerless to stop them. We have lost not only our courage but our desire to act. The humane ideal, whose noble aims were generally respected before the World War, has declined during the last ten years to a condition of primitive violence and cruelty. We are again becoming accustomed to the ferocity of which several centuries of civilization had seemed to cure the human race; and this new barbarity is far more dangerous than that of the savages because it is armed by science. . . . At nearly every point the forces of civilization seem to be sounding a retreat. In 1913 physical security for Europeans was assured. The idea that a town could be half destroyed in a single night without declaration of war, that thousands of women and children could be killed by bombs, nuns massacred by rioters, non-belligerent ships torpedoed in the Mediterranean by pirates would have seemed mad. . . . A good part of the world is already at war. Menacing shadows loom threateningly over the rest of the planet. The destructive power of modern armaments and the ruthlessness of the new doctrine of warfare are such that, in case of conflict, almost total ruin for victor and vanquished alike is inevitable. Civil and religious liberty is denied to thousands of people, and the countries which still remain faithful to liberal institutions are wondering anxiously whether these very institutions will not lead them to disaster. . . . During the war of 1914 humanity once more served a gruesome apprenticeship to violence. The tiger which has tasted blood no longer hesitates to attack man; men who have learned to kill no longer have the same respect for human life. To bombard an open town would have been criminal lunacy in 1913. But to us, in 1938, who have become familiar with the idea through war itself and through photographs and films of warfare, it has become no more than an 'unavoidable necessity.' Violence engenders violence. The torrents of blood which were spilled in the cellars of Moscow, like those shed under the guillotine in Paris in 1793, have raised an almost insurmountable barrier between fellow-countrymen. The middle classes, menaced in many countries by revolutionary parties, have given their support to authoritarian governments. The movement which has been called fascism is a reaction of despair on the part of societies seeking order at any cost. . . . It is in these doctrines of violence, common to the extremists of right and left, that the most serious danger of our times lies. For if these opposing-systems came into violent conflict all over Europe in a war of religion, as is now the case in Spain, the physical means of destruction are today so great that our civilization might perish altogether. In any case, the happiness of a whole generation would be irreparably damaged. Is such a catastrophe inevitable?"[1]

VII

Secularism is the root evil which yields industrial conflict and international warfare. In economic activities and political affairs, God is almost completely ignored by a vast proportion of people. The processes of production and distribution of goods and services are carried on with practically no recognition that God is creator and sustainer of the earth and that all wealth belongs to Him. Even individuals who are deeply religious usually fail in

[1] Andre Maurois, in *New York Times Magazine,* June 19, 1938.

their economic and political behavior to act upon the realization that they are now living with their brethren in God's home. Reverence for personality does not habitually characterize dealings with competitors and employees. Literally true is the statement that in a vast proportion of business offices God is never taken into account when policies are determined. Industry and commerce and finance have become almost completely secularized.

Wide areas of education have likewise been secularized. That this is God's world and that we are all His children are ideas rarely brought into discussions of economics, sociology and political science. Even when reform and revolution are under consideration, man's utter dependence upon God is usually ignored altogether. Although the mechanistic theory of the universe is being undermined by recent developments in physics and astronomy, many outstanding scientists are agnostics and some are convinced atheists. To say that a spiritual interpretation of the universe is not usually presented in the classroom is putting the matter mildly.

In the high degree of secularization of modern civilization is found the chief reason for its decay. Human nature is potential and responds to stimulus. When the most powerful forces that play upon human beings are stimuli to be greedy and belligerent, society becomes a battleground. If man's capacities for sacrificial devotion to the common good are to be developed, he must be subjected to appropriate stimuli. And of these the most dynamic are released by worship of the Eternal God and commitment to the task of creating the divine society on earth. When God is ignored and a spiritual interpretation of life is rejected, human nature is played upon predominantly by stimuli which produce discord and chaos.

Therefore, modern society is characterized by brutality and triviality. "The plain truth is," says the *Literary Review,* "that as a civilization we are less sure of where we are going, where we want to go, how and for what we wish to live, than at any intelligent period of which we have full record."

I am riding on a limited express, one of the crack trains of the
    nation.
Hurtling across the prairie into blue haze and dark air go fifteen
    all-steel coaches holding a thousand people.

(All the coaches shall be scrap and rust and all the men and women
    laughing in the diners and sleepers shall pass to ashes.)
I ask a man in the smoker where he is going and he answers:
    "Omaha."[1]

This is a record of a radio conversation which encircled the
globe:

"I caught a fella last night in the South Pacific—
He was on a freighter way beyond New Zealand.
And what do you think he said to me, that guy?"
The young radio man was talking.

" 'How did the Cubs come out today?' he said.
"How did the Cubs come out?" Nothing he wanted
But that fool game! "They got it in the neck,"
I answered him—ten thousand miles across—
"The Pirates chewed 'em up." "The hell they did!"
"Say, where's the sun out your way?" I ticked off—[2]

The fate of man is thus portrayed by Theodore Dreiser:

Wandering endlessly
Through innumerable rooms,
All of them empty
And without windows:
No sky—
No hope—
And only one door for entrance
And another for exit.
Doors opening
Doors closing
Automatically behind one.
Yet
I will not let myself expect
More of these rooms
Than is here
Or think of them
As other
Than that which they are—
Empty—

[1] Carl Sandburg, "Limited." Published by Harcourt, Brace and Co., New
York.
[2] Harriet Monroe, "Radio," in *Poetry*.

Or myself
As other
Than an automaton
Shunted colorlessly
From one to another
By a power that will not let me rest—
Or stay—
Nor will I believe
That the darkness
Into which I pass
Is different to that from which I entered
But can not remember—
Nor will I look forward
Or back
With either hope or resentment
But endure—
Since I have not chosen so to wander—
In the emptiness
Of each and every room—
The sum total of astounding emptiness
That includes them all.[1]

Bertrand Russell in a frequently-quoted passage gives his creed: "That Man is the product of causes which have no prevision of the end they were achieving; that his origin, his growth, his hopes and fears, his loves and his beliefs, are but the outcome of accidental collocations of atoms; that no fire, no heroism, no intensity of thought and feeling, can preserve an individual life beyond the grave; that all the labours of the ages, all the devotion, all the inspiration, all the noonday brightness of human genius, are destined to extinction in the vast death of the solar system, and that the whole temple of Man's achievement must inevitably be buried beneath the debris of a universe in ruins—all these things, if not quite beyond dispute, are yet so nearly certain, that no philosophy which rejects them can hope to stand. Only within the scaffolding of these truths, only on the firm foundation of unyielding despair, can the soul's habitation henceforth be safely built."[2]

[1] Theodore Dreiser, "Empty Rooms," *Moods.* Published by Simon and Schuster, New York.

[2] Bertrand Russell, Philosophical Essays, II, *The Free Man's Worship*, pp. 60-61.

The utter futility of all living is a favorite theme of many contemporary poets:

> The stone falls, the bird flies, the arrow goes home,
> But we have no motion, we scatter like foam.
> O, give me a song to sing for your sorrow,
> A song that will lift, like a wave from the reef,
> You and myself, that will fling like an arrow
> My poor scattered words to the target of grief:
> I want to forget, to remember no morrow,
> To go with the petrel, to go with the leaf. . . .
>
> We would fly with all things to the goal of their flying,
> We would turn with all things to the magnetic star,
> But we never can live, because of our dying,
> And we never can be, for the things that we are.
>
> We alone of all creatures—the stones more than we—
> Have no end, no motion, no destiny.[1]

VIII

"And every one who hears these my teachings and does not act upon them will be found to resemble a fool who builds his house upon sand. The heavy rain descends, the swollen torrents come, and the winds blow and burst upon the house, and it falls; and disastrous is the fall."[2]

Therefore I will make the heavens to tremble, and the earth shall be shaken out of its place . . . Their infants also shall be dashed in pieces before their eyes; their houses shall be rifled, and their wives ravished.

Behold, I will stir up the Medes against them, who shall not regard silver, and as for gold, they shall not delight in it. And *their* bows shall dash the young men in pieces; and they shall have no pity on the fruit of the womb; their eye shall not spare children. And Babylon, the glory of kingdoms, the beauty of the Chaldeans' pride, shall be as when God overthrew Sodom and Gomorrah. It shall never be inhabited, neither shall it be dwelt in from generation to generation: neither shall the Arabian pitch tent there; neither shall shep-

[1] Genevieve Taggard, "The Futile." Published by Thomas Seltzer.
[2] Matt. 7:26-29, Weymouth.

herds make their flocks to lie down there. But wild beasts of
the desert shall lie there; and their houses shall be full of dole-
ful creatures; and ostriches shall dwell there, and wild goats
shall dance there. And wolves shall cry in their castles, and
jackals in the pleasant palaces: and her time is near to come,
and her days shall not be prolonged.[1]

It has happened before.
Strong men put up a city and got
      a nation together,
And paid singers to sing and women
      to warble: We are the greatest city,
            the greatest nation,
            nothing like us ever was.

And while the singers sang
and the strong men listened
and paid the singers well,
      there were rats and lizards who listened
      . . . and the only listeners left now
      . . . are . . . the rats . . . and the lizards.
      And there are black crows
      crying, "Caw, caw,"
      bringing mud and sticks
      building a nest
      over the words carved
      On the doors where the panels were cedar
      and the strips on the panels were gold
      and the golden girls came singing:
            We are the greatest city,
            the greatest nation:
            nothing like us ever was.

The only singers now are crows crying, "Caw, caw,"
And the sheets of rain whine in the wind and doorways.
And the only listeners now are . . . the rats . . . and the lizards.[2]

[1] Isaiah 13:14-22.
[2] Carl Sandburg, "The Past is a Bucket of Ashes." Published by Harcourt,
Brace and Co., New York.

Chapter III

Be Concerned Because of the Gulf Between the Actual and the Ideal

PENITENCE is a powerful dynamic in determining human conduct. If the ideal is vivid and if understanding of the actual is adequate, sensitive individuals are stricken with a sense of guilt because of the chasm which divides present achievement from the possible. When we test ourselves by the fullness of the measure of the stature of Christ, and when we contract our present social order with the divine society on earth, we realize how feebly we have drawn upon the vast reservoirs of potentialities in human nature, and are therefore filled with contrition. Deep sorrow over man's failure to claim his heritage is an essential condition of spiritual power.

Have mercy upon me, O God, according to thy loving kindness:
According to the multitude of thy tender mercies blot out my transgressions.
Wash me thoroughly from mine iniquity,
And cleanse me from my sin.
For I know my transgressions;
And my sin is ever before me.
Purify me with hyssop, and I shall be clean:
Wash me, and I shall be whiter than snow.
Make me to hear joy and gladness
That the bones which thou hast broken may rejoice.
Hide thy face from my sins,
And blot out all mine iniquities.
Create in me a clean heart, O God;
And renew a right spirit within me.
Cast me not away from thy presence;
And take not thy holy Spirit from me.[1]

I am made of flesh that is frail, sold into slavery to sin. Indeed, I do not understand what I do, for I do not practice

[1] Psalms 51:1-3, 7-11.

what I want to do, but I am always doing what I hate. . . .
For I know that nothing good has its home in me; that is, in
my lower self; I have the will but not the power to do what is
right. Indeed, I do not do the good things that I want to do,
but I do practice the evil things that I do not want to do. . . .
Wretched man that I am! Who can save me from this deadly
lower nature? Thank God! it has been done through Jesus
Christ our Lord! So in my higher nature I am a slave to the
law of God, but in my lower nature, to the law of sin.[1]

Another time, speaking to people who were satisfied that
they were religious, and who regarded every one else with
scorn, Jesus told this parable—

"Two men went up into the Temple Courts to pray. One
was a Pharisee and the other a tax-gatherer. The Pharisee stood
forward and began praying to himself in this way—

'O God, I thank thee that I am not like other men—thieves,
rogues, adulterers—or even like this tax-gatherer. I fast, twice
a week, and give a tenth of everything I get to God.' Meanwhile the tax-gatherer stood at a distance, not venturing even
'to raise his eyes to Heaven'; but he kept striking his breast and
saying 'O God, have mercy on me, a sinner.' This man, I tell
you, went home pardoned, rather than the other; for every one
who exalts himself will be humbled, while every one who
humbles himself shall be exalted."[2]

If we say that there is no sin in us, we are deceiving ourselves, and the Truth has no place in us. If we confess our sins,
God may be trusted, in his righteousness, to forgive us our sins
and purify us from all wickedness. If we say that we have not
sinned, we are making God a liar, and his Message has no place
in us.[3]

Complacency and cynicism alike are deadly enemies of the
human spirit. A low estimate of human nature is unwarranted
because of man's kinship with God; while vainglory is unjustifiable
because the individual so frequently trifles with rich potentialities.
Alertness to possibilities and awareness of actualities combine to
produce penitence and determination.

[1] Romans 7:14, 18, 19, 24, 25, Williams.
[2] Luke 18:9-14, Twentieth Century.
[3] 1 John 1:8-10, Twentieth Century.

II

"Perfectionism" is the charge sometimes hurled at persons who endeavor to use the standards of Christ as measuring rods in determining attitudes toward social practices. That feeble and stumbling human beings cannot climb to his level is indisputable; that immature individuals cannot build a perfect society is likewise obvious. Indeed, it is wholly improbable that any member of this generation will equal the nobility of Jesus' character; and it is entirely unlikely that the Kingdom of God in fullness and power will come upon the earth within any time that we are now able to foresee.

Nevertheless, the stature of Christ and the concept of the Kingdom of God on earth are the only ultimate standards of judgment for Christians. We must never be content with that which falls far short of the ideal; we must constantly struggle to approach more nearly to perfection; and daily we must be moved with contrition because of our sins.

The idea is sometimes advanced that Jesus adopted one standard for himself and a different standard for other individuals, that Christians cannot be expected to follow his example. This note, however, is completely missing from the teaching of Jesus himself. On the contrary, he made drastic demands upon his disciples and gave voice to superlative expectations:

> Then He called the people to Him along with His disciples, and said to them, "If anyone wants to be my disciple, he must say, 'No' to self, put the cross on his shoulders, and keep on following me. For whoever wants to save his higher life, will have to give up the lower life, and whoever gives up his lower life for me and for the good news, will save the higher life. For what benefit will it be to a man to gain the whole world and fail to gain the higher life? For what price can a man give to buy back life?"[1]

> Jesus looked at the man, and his heart went out to him, and he said: "There is still one thing wanting in you; go and sell all that you have, and give to the poor, and you shall have wealth in Heaven; then come and follow me." But the man's face clouded at these words, and he went away distressed, for he

[1] Mark 8:34-37, Williams.

had great possessions. Then Jesus looked round, and said to his disciples : "How hard it will be for men of wealth to enter the Kingdom of God."

The disciples were amazed at his words. But Jesus said again : "My children, how hard a thing it is to enter the Kingdom of God! It is easier for a camel to get through a needle's eye, than for a rich man to enter the Kingdom of God." "Then who can be saved?" they exclaimed in the greatest astonishment.

Jesus looked at them, and answered : "With men it is impossible, but not with God; for everything is possible with God."[1]

I am not saying these things on my own authority, but the Father who always remains in union with me is doing these things Himself. You must believe me, that I am in union with the Father and that the Father is in union with me, or else you must do so because of the very things that I am doing. I most solemnly say to you, whoever perseveres in believing in me can himself do the things that I am doing; yes, he can do even greater things than I am doing, because I am going to the Father. And anything you ask for us bearers of my name I will do for you, so that the Father may be glorified through the Son. Yes, I repeat it, anything you ask for as bearers of my name I will do it for you. If you really love me, you will keep my commands.[2]

Love toward God and love toward man constitute the essence of high religion and the chief purpose of life is to participate creatively in the task of building the divine society. "Thy Kingdom come, thy will be done on earth as it is in heaven," must ever be the petition of a religious person, and by this standard every social institution must be judged.

III

When we utter the words of the Lord's prayer, what are we praying for? What will be the economic and political characteristics of the Kingdom of God on earth? What social institutions will be required in order to bring about reverence for personality,

1 Mark 10:21-27, Twentieth Century.
2 John 14:10-15, Williams.

recognition of kinship among all people, rendering of justice, enjoyment of fellowship, and adoration of the Eternal?

If mutuality and sharing are to characterize human relationships, the structure of society must be so constituted as to produce cooperation and peace rather than grabbing and fighting. This means that the present social order stands condemned by the standards of Christ, because of its exaltation of self-interest and competition and because it so prolifically breeds greed and warfare. A society which stimulates a tiny fraction of the population to live luxuriously and complacently in the midst of a vast sea of human destitution and suffering, and whose primary processes drive men to slaughter their fellows on the battlefield, must be denounced in the name of God. Classification of human beings by races, with varying standards of treatment for different groups, including discrimination and segregation along racial lines, must be condemned if we are to show loyalty to the mind and spirit of Christ. Therefore, when we pray the Lord's prayer with sincerity, we are asking for fundamental and drastic changes in the present social order. In our day, as in previous periods of history, prophets of religion must sound a warning of impending doom upon a society which ignores God and violates his commandments. Contrition and the bringing forth of fruits of penitence are urgently demanded of this generation.

Woe unto them that call evil good, and good evil; that put darkness for light, and light for darkness; that put bitter for sweet, and sweet for bitter!...

Therefore as the tongue of fire devoureth the stubble, and as the dry grass sinketh down in the flame, so their root shall be as rottenness, and their blossom shall go up as dust; because they have rejected the law of Jehovah of hosts, and despised the word of the Holy One of Israel.[1]

For your hands are defiled with blood, and your fingers with iniquity; your lips have spoken lies, your tongue muttereth wickedness.... Therefore is justice far from us, neither doth righteousness overtake us: we look for light, but, behold, darkness; for brightness, but we walk in obscurity. We grope for the wall like the blind; yea, we grope as they that have no eyes: we stumble at noonday as in the twilight; among them that are lusty we are as dead men. We roar all like bears, and

1 Isaiah 5:20, 24.

moan sore like doves; we look for justice, but there is none; for salvation, but it is far off from us.[1]

Come, you rich men, weep aloud and howl for your sorrows which will soon be upon you. Your treasures have rotted and your piles of clothing are moth-eaten; your gold and your silver have become covered with rust, and the rust on them will give evidence against you, and will eat your flesh like fire. You have hoarded up wealth in these last days. I tell you that the pay of the labourers who have gathered in your crops—pay which you are keeping back—is calling out against you; and the outcries of those who have been your reapers have entered into the ears of the Lord of the armies of Heaven. Here on earth you have lived self-indulgent and profligate lives. You have stupefied yourselves with gross feeding; but a day of slaughter has come.[2]

"Alas for you, Scribes and Pharisees, hypocrites, for you pay the tithe on mint, dill, and cumin, while you have neglected the weightier requirements of the Law—just judgment, mercy, and faithful dealing. These things you ought to have done, and yet you ought not to have left the others undone. You blind guides, straining out the gnat while you gulp down the camel!

"Alas for you, Scribes and Pharisees, hypocrites, for you wash clean the outside of the cup or dish, while within they are full of greed and self-indulgence. Blind Pharisee, first wash clean the inside of the cup or dish, and then the outside will be clean also.

"Alas for you, Scribes and Pharisees, hypocrites, for you are just like whitewashed sepulchres, the outside of which pleases the eye, though inside they are full of dead men's bones and of all that is unclean. The same is true of you: outwardly you seem to the human eye to be good and honest men, but, within, you are full of insincerity and disregard of God's Law.

"Alas, for you, Scribes and Pharisees, hypocrites, for you repair the sepulchres of the Prophets and keep in order the tomb of the righteous, and your boast is, 'If we had lived in the time of our forefathers, we should not have been implicated with them in the murder of the Prophets.'

[1] Isaiah 59:3, 9-11.
[2] James 5:1-5, Weymouth.

"So that you bear witness against yourselves that you are descendants of those who murdered the Prophets. Fill up the measure of your forefathers' guilt. O serpents, O vipers' brood, how are you to escape condemnation to Gehenna?" [1]

IV

Denunciation of evil is not enough, but it is an essential part of the task of building the good society. If religious people in our day would withdraw their approval and support from armed preparedness and war as methods of seeking safety and justice, governments would be required to find other ways of settling international controversies. If racial segregation were recognized as sinful by Christians, and if they took seriously the teachings that all men are kinspeople, an enormous stride in the direction of social justice could quickly be taken. If the economic system of competitive individualism were branded as the source of terrible iniquities, a cooperative commonwealth would be much easier to create.

Even though we may not be able to draw a blueprint of a perfect alternative to the present social system, we are nevertheless obliged to condemn all attitudes and practices which constitute flagrant violations of the ideal. Frequently the difficulty which confronts us is not lack of understanding and inability to form a clear judgment: we *know* that war as a method is utterly irreconcilable with the teaching and example of Jesus; we *know* that the ruthless competition now prevalent throughout the economic order is thoroughly anti-Christian; we *know* that placing individuals in arbitrary categories and treating them as white men or yellow men or black men is contrary to the mind and spirit of Christ. There are areas in which we do not know precisely where to draw the line between right and wrong, but lack of insight at these points does not excuse us from vigorous action in zones of brilliant illumination. Hatred is always wrong and goodwill is always right, even when dealing with enemies. The massacre of populations by high explosive and fire and poison gas and starvation is always wrong and can never be transmuted into right, although atrocity may be committed in the name of high ideals. Burning a man at the stake is always wrong, even though the lynching may be perpetrated by church members in defense of womanhood.

[1] Matt. 23:23-33, Weymouth.

If religious people would resolutely turn away from behavior which they know to be flagrantly in contrast to their ideals, and would penitently seek forgiveness for their disloyalty to the will of God, rapid strides could be taken in the direction of a just society. A vital element in high religion is the readiness of God to forgive his penitent children. While the prodigal son is still a long way off, the Father runs to greet him. Consciousness of having been forgiven is in turn a powerful dynamic to right conduct. Sinful individuals in the midst of a wicked and perverse generation must be stricken with contrition, pray passionately for forgiveness, and resolutely determine to bring forth fruits of repentence.

"If we confess our sins, He is so faithful and just that He forgives us our sins and cleanses us from all unrighteousness." [1]

A voice is heard upon the bare heights, the weeping *and* the supplications of the children of Israel; because they have perverted their way, they have forgotten Jehovah their God. Return, ye backsliding children, I will heal your backslidings. . . . If thou wilt return, O Israel, saith Jehovah, if thou wilt return unto me, and if thou wilt put away thine abominations out of my sight; then shalt thou not be removed; and thou shalt swear, As Jehovah liveth, in truth, in justice, and in righteousness; and the nations shall bless themselves in him, and in him shall they glory. [2]

Yea, I have loved thee with an everlasting love; therefore with loving kindness have I drawn thee. [3]

[1] I John 1:9, Weymouth.
[2] Jeremiah 3:21, 22; 4:1, 2.
[3] Jeremiah 31:3.

Chapter IV

Endeavor to Transform the Actual into the Ideal

I T is easier to say that humanity has reached the end of another era and that we are now witnessing the emergence of a new period of history than it is to act as if we believe this statement to be true. In one of the volumes prepared for the ecumenical conference at Oxford, J. H. Oldham writes: "The relative stability of the world which existed before the war has gone. The foundations of human society are quivering. The fact itself none will dispute, but our minds become dulled by familiarity to its significance. We give it our indolent assent, and contentedly resume the tenor of our habitual attitudes. There can, however, be no true wrestling with the realities of the contemporary situation except in so far as we allow their meaning to break through the crust of our customary thinking into those deeper levels of our being in which our experience is absorbed and organized, so that there will take place progressively, and to a large extent subconsciously, a reconstruction of our whole outlook and a reorientation of our fundamental attitudes." [1]

We urgently need new men and a new structure of society, and we will betray the responsibility which rests upon us if we concentrate exclusively on one or the other of these requirements. Some of the evils of the society which is passing have been thus summarized by R. H. Tawney: "Its emphasis on the supreme importance of material riches; its worship of power; its idealization, not merely of particular property rights, but of property in general and as an absolute; its subordination of human beings to the exigencies, or supposed exigencies, of an economic system; its erection of divisions within the human family based, not on differences of personal quality or social function, but on differences of income and economic circumstance—these qualities are closely related to the ends which capitalist societies hold to be all-important. In such

[1] *The Church and Its Function in Society.* Published by Willett, Clark & Company, Chicago.

societies, as the practice of the latter clearly shows, they are commonly regarded, not as vices, but as virtues. To the Christian they are vices more ruinous to the soul than most of the conventional forms of immorality." [1]

From these and other vices many members of this generation need to be converted. Personal evangelism is indispensable to the creation of a just society. "What shall we do?" you ask. "What is the answer?" In commenting upon these questions, Samuel M. Shoemaker writes: "America should turn to God. Thousands and millions of Americans remembering the God of their fathers, and getting down on their knees again in repentence for the years of neglect and indifference—that is the answer. Thousands and millions of Americans being absolutely honest with their families, with their companies, with their creditors, with their neighbours, and making every wrong right. Thousands and millions of American homes where the day begins with the Bible and listening to God, and His Word as the decisive factor in every problem. Thousands and millions of American homes where father and mother bow before the same Authority as rules brother and sister, where sharing clears misunderstandings, where laughter comes back, and unselfishness, and homes are homes once again, and the children love them, and the neighbours come in to find what has brought this great change. Thousands and millions of Americans, not stalling off the minister with some money for his church, but going there, going with something to give, pushing right on through the weaknesses of organized religion, and helping to create a true church. Can it happen? Why not? The negative front has accomplished very much the same thing in another direction—made thousands and millions change their minds, their values, their aims, their procedure. This is a staggeringly big answer for a staggeringly big problem, but it is the one thing that is working wherever it is being tried. The alternative to it is not just staying as we are: it is chaos. I am tired of cures that don't cure, of movements that don't move, of answers that don't answer. God's control is the answer for America. It begins with us. Let us begin to take that 'high line!' The real church has got something that nobody else has got: it has got the secret of God. It gets people into touch with the living God. Light in every soul, in every home of this land—that is what we want. The guidance of God. There is noth-

[1] *Ibid.*, p. 194.

ing eerie or mysterious about that. We are all guided by something—by fear, by the glances of the neighbours, by cupidity, by the effect something will have on us, or by the wife's disposition. There *is* something new under the sun, after all: it is that the wisdom of life does not lie in everybody's doing what you want, or in everybody's doing what I want, but in everybody's doing what God wants. We can find out what that is by listening. A whole nation listening to God—that is the answer for America. Let us make listening to God a national institution, and obeying Him a national habit!" [1]

Every sensitive Christian recognizes the validity of the challenge for converted individuals and changed homes. Only on this foundation can the good society be built. But a further insistent question cries aloud for an answer: how shall redeemed individuals conduct themselves in their economic, political, racial and other social relations? If all men were truly surrendered to God, *could they live with equal satisfaction under fascism and communism; under individualism and socialism?* Mr. Shoemaker exclaims: "Don't swing further to the right, or further to the left. There is a third way to swing: swing up, to God!" That we are under obligation to swing up, to God, will not be questioned by any faithful follower of Christ. But the question persists: *when we swing up toward God, how do we act in economic and political affairs?* Do we support individualism? Do we favor fascism? Do we desire communism? Do we work for socialism? Are we neutral as between the conflicting claims of clashing systems? Do we say that the structure is irrelevant and that true Christians can satisfactorily operate the institutions of any given social order?

Could loyal followers of Christ dwell together in fellowship with equal ease under any given system of property ownership and control? Shall we favor unlimited acquisition of all types of property by the individual, with the assurance that a true Christian will prove himself to be a wise and faithful steward of possessions which he recognizes as belonging to God? Should we favor common ownership by all the people of certain types of property? Mr. Shoemaker says: "Of course there are situations in which it is right for the state to own and control property for the benefit of its citizens also. The great question always is: What will make men unselfish with what they have, whether it be little or much?

1 *The Church Can Save the World*, pp. 72-74.

The answer is: Bring them under God's control themselves. . . ."

In which situations will God-controlled individuals favor state ownership of property? How does a devoted Christian reach a decision concerning such questions? We must respond to the challenge of Jesus to love God with our minds and form judgments in the light of sound diagnosis and Spirit-illumined conscience. It is imperative, therefore, that we clearly understand the nature of the existing property system, and that we become vividly aware of its chief consequences.

II

Imperative is the necessity of distinguishing between property which is used or consumed by the owner, and property which is an instrument of power over other persons. To me the desirability of private ownership of a modest home, appropriately equipped, appears incontestable. It is this type of property that Mr. Shoemaker has in mind when he writes: "God-control is increasingly seen as the way to make people unselfish about private property. Since the day when the prophet saw, as an element in the fair world that was to be when men accepted the rule of God, every man sitting "under his vine and under his fig tree," most men with insight have believed that private property used unselfishly for others was the best solution to the whole question of ownership. It certainly makes a man a better steward of a set of tools if they belong to him, rather than if they belong to the company. It certainly follows that you will not hammer so many tacks in your own wall as into the wall of a landlord. Private ownership is a way of developing responsibility."

The case for private ownership of a modest home, furnishings, clothing, food and many other commodities required for use or consumption by individuals and families seems invincible. I am personally convinced that private ownership of a moderate amount of land by a farmer, suitably equipped, is highly desirable. It may be that human experience will demonstrate the continuing value of having certain types of small-scale production and distribution carried on by private enterprise, especially in the areas of highly skilled handicraft and artistic production.

Sharply divergent, however, is the social significance of another type of property, illustrated by electric-power generators, coal mines, railways, steel mills, and banks. The significance of this kind of property is not found in its use or consumption by private owners, but in the power bestowed upon owners to control economic instruments which are essential to the existence and comfort of all the people in a highly industrialized society and to extract for these owners a disproportionate share of the national income. Should devout Christians favor the system of private ownership of these giant instruments of production?

Privately owned instruments of production and distribution must be used competitively or monopolistically or by moving in the direction of the latter. Privately operated industries cannot continue indefinitely without profit for the owners, although severe losses may be sustained within time limits set by capital reserves. Profit is obtained by competing with rival companies or by combining with them. The executive officers of a great corporation are employed for the purpose of so operating the plants that profit will accrue to stockholders. The test of efficiency in a private corporation must be profit and by this criterion policies and practices must be judged if bankruptcy is to be avoided.

Cooperation within a corporation is possible and even indispensable, but it is cooperation for the purpose of more efficient competition or with the intention of moving toward monopoly. If the words "competitive" and "cooperative" are used to emphasize the contrast between two types of economic activity, the conclusion seems inescapable that *a genuinely cooperative society cannot be built upon the foundations of private ownership of the chief instruments of production.*

The stimuli released by a competitive society are so terrific that human nature except in rare instances is unable to resist the driving power of covetousness. The extent to which the gambling spirit now prevails in this country is pointed out in an editorial in the official journal of The United States Chamber of Commerce which deserves publication in full. Under the caption, "We must speculate!" the editor writes: "As this is written the afternoon papers, in front page, seven column head-lines, say: Stocks Jump in New Buying Stampede. America always has been a nation of speculators. We came by it naturally. We must speculate if we are to go forward. Nor could we stop speculation if we would. We may make it difficult here, we may penalize it there, only to see it break out elsewhere. We have placed barriers against speculation in industrial undertakings through market regulations, federal requirements as to stock issues, and penalty taxes. What has happened? No one who has eyes in his head can fail to see the tremendous increase in petty speculations, or call it gambling if you will. According to a habits study of the Northwestern National Life Insurance Company this shift of 'risk-bearing' mounts up to $3,500,000,000 yearly. Betting on horse races is now legal in 22 states. Horse or dog racing has become legal in 12 states within the past four years. Bookmakers operate in many other states. Far more widely distributed than the major forms of racetrack gambling are foreign sweepstakes tickets, available to the clerk and stenographer virtually everywhere. Mr. John Citizen pays his $2.50 for a sweepstakes ticket; drops a quarter or a dollar into an office baseball or football pool; gives a slot machine a few whirls on his lunch hour; shakes dice for his cigars or cigarettes. He goes home to find that his wife has put 15 cents on a number peddled by a door-to-door solicitor in the hope that the last three digits on her ticket will tally with those of the total bank clearings for the day. Mrs. Citizen has invited the Joneses over to play bridge at a tenth of a cent a point. Junior had two nickels which went into the pinball machine setup near the high school, and he holds a punchboard chance that may win him a miniature radio for his bedroom. Sister won't miss going to the neighborhood movie house this evening; it is bank night; the purse is up to $275, and she feels lucky. Then there is the drawing in the lodge raffle, to decide what fortunate family will win a new set of dinner silver, or maybe even a sedan. The profits will help furnish the new club rooms, or perhaps buy a piano for a settlement house that is the lodge's charitable activity. So it goes. Slot machines are illegal in nearly all states. But operation depends on strictness of local law enforcement. After a local crusade has forced the slot machines into hiding, pinball machines appear. . . . Church raffles and 'Bingo' parties have become popular means of raising money for expenses, although prominent churchmen have recently voiced vigorous objections. School alumni associations, lodges, and various charitable organizations have found in the desire of the human race to take a chance the quickest, simplest way of raising money for their purposes. Volume of money wagered in football pools increases each fall. Every business office of any size has its perennial 'jackpot' organizer. Reform drives against bookmakers, gambling houses and slot machines gather momentum; sweep new local officials into power; clamp down the 'lid'; usually peter out. 'What's the use to try to stop it when 95 per cent of the public wants to gamble in one form or another?' asks an eastern enforcement official." [1]

Again the question must be faced: *can individuals who are surrendered to God dwell in fellowship with equal ease in a competitive society and a cooperative society?* Does the stimulus to compete and the stimulus to cooperate produce the same behavior? If God's will were loyally followed on earth as it is in heaven, would His children compete for private gain to be administered as faithful stewards, or would they mutually cooperate for the common good?

The evils of competition are numerous and conspicuous, but the vices of private monopoly are even more disastrous. In an earlier section we presented evidence showing an unmistakable trend toward monopoly in this country.[2] Already a tiny fraction of the total population wields incalculable economic and political power over the lives of all the people. So long as concentrated control of our economic resources persists, the population will continue to be divided into privileged rich, relatively comfortable middle class, and impoverished masses. In such a society talk of Christian fellowship among all the people is sheer mockery.

III

The emergence of a new property system is essential to the growth of a genuinely cooperative society in which universal fellowship may flourish. The nature of the new system is revealed in this paradox: There is urgent need for much more private property and an equal demand for much less private property; at present there is not enough private property in consumers' and users' goods because there is too much private property in the chief means of production and distribution.

Starting from here, how do we reach the desired system of property ownership and control? The following steps are suggested:

1. Create public opinion favorable to the new system, through evangelism and education. Increase the number of citizens who

[1] *Nation's Business,* August, 1938.
[2] See pages 40 ff., 192 ff.

understand the significance of private ownership of essential economic resources and who are determined to move progressively in the direction of a truly cooperative society through the common ownership of the giant instruments of production and distribution. Reveal the superior advantages of an equalitarian cooperative society to those of a competitive community with its deep cleavages between rich and poor and its devastating social conflict. Emphasize the fact that the most satisfying satisfactions are derived from mutuality and sharing rather than from covetousness and grabbing.

2. Differentiate clearly one type of property from another and point out the various kinds of ownership. The possibilities open to us includes these:

(a) Private ownership of homes, furnishings, clothing, food, and numerous miscellaneous articles which are used or consumed personally.

(b) Private ownership of various small units of production and distribution, especially in the areas of skilled craftsmanship.

(c) Group ownership by members of churches, fraternal orders, labor unions, farmers' organizations, business associations, etc., for mutual advantages in the realms of education, recreation, health, etc.

(d) Cooperative ownership by groups of consumers of stores, dairies, bakeries, and numerous other units of production and distribution.

(e) Municipal ownership.

(f) County ownership.

(g) State ownership.

(h) Joint ownership by two or more states.

(i) Federal ownership.

3. Elect to public office candidates who favor extensions of common ownership and cooperative utilization of various types of property through action by local, state and national agencies of government.

4. Pass appropriate legislation authorizing the socialization of selected industries, under the right of eminent domain.

5. Make payment to private owners by exchanging government bonds for private stocks and bonds, these new government securities to be based not on public credit but upon the value of the new properties acquired, with a time limit providing for the

complete amortization of the entire indebtedness within say twenty years.

6. Operation of nationalized industries not by committees of Congress but by boards composed of technicians, workers and consumers, or by a board of experts as in the case of the Tennessee Valley Authority, or by a single expert administrator as in the case of some other Federal power projects. The operating personnel of socialized industries would, of course, remain substantially the same as under private ownership—that is to say, the railroads would be operated by the same engineers, firemen, conductors, etc., but with a different board of control and with a different objective: public service rather than private profit for investors.

7. Reliance upon other incentives than the "profit" motive, including dependence upon various types of "income" motive for individuals who have not yet developed sufficient public spirit to be impelled by concern for the common good. It may be well to remind ourselves of the types of incentive which will motivate individuals under socialized industries:

(a) Desire to receive an income in the form of salary or wages.

(b) Desire to rise above the minimum income. In a community where citizens truly reflect the spirit of Christ, distribution will be made according to relative needs. In the meantime, as a concession to an unfortunate heritage, it may be necessary to set the maximum income at a figure ten times as high as the minimum, that is to say, if the legal minimum income is placed at $1,500, the maximum legal income might be placed at $15,000.[1]

(c) Desire to receive to public approval and applause.

(d) Desire to avoid disapproval and penalties for failing to do good work.

[1] Among the more than one million employees of the Federal Government are many of the ablest individuals in the country: statesmen, administrators, scientists, inventors, judges, etc. Yet the number of high salaries constitutes an extremely small proportion of the total number. A list compiled in 1935 showed 989 salaries as high as $10,000, with 7,223 between $5,000 and $10,000. Only eleven employees of the Federal Government receive a salary above $15,000 per year— the President $75,000; the Chief Justice $20,500; eight Associate Justices of the Supreme Court $20,000; the Governor General of the Philippine Islands $18,000. (New York Times, May 5 and 6, 1935) The Governors of only 10 states receive a salary of $10,000 or more.

(e) Desire to wield authority and carry responsibility by climbing to the top.

(f) Creative satisfaction derived from engaging in congenial activities.

(g) Concern for human welfare prompted by patriotic duty and religious devotion.

8. Appropriate regulations by various units of government of industries remaining under private operation to safeguard the public against the extremes of monopoly and cut-throat competition.

9. Use of taxation as an instrument of social policy, as well as a source of public revenue.[1] By removing all tax-exempt sources of income and fixing sharply graduated rates of income tax and inheritance tax, it will be possible within a single generation to eliminate excessive congestion of income and wealth.

10. Social security and public privileges in the realms of health, education and recreation should progressively be extended in the light of experience.

IV

Among the instruments of economic change which must be utilized and strengthened are these:

1. Educational institutions of various kinds.

2. Churches and synagogues, with their various agencies of evangelism, education and nurture.

3. Labor unions.

4. Consumers' cooperative societies.[2]

5. Units of business men who are working for the new property system.

6. Organizations of engineers and other technicians who are seeking to establish a cooperative commonwealth.

7. A political party which is committed to the task of creating a socialized society.[3]

[1] See pages 417-419.

[2] For full information concerning consumers' cooperation, write to The Cooperative League, 167 West 12th Street, New York City.

[3] Most of us who are now members of the Socialist Party under the leadership of Norman Thomas favor the formation of a new political party with mass support of workers, farmers and middle class for the pacific socialization of the chief means of production and distribution.

Plenty for everybody is within reach of the American people. We have been blessed with the required physical basis: soil, climate, natural resources. Man-power in abundance is available. Machinery and mechanical energy are ready to use. Administrative genius is at our disposal. Assets of incalculable worth are to be found in our heritage of political democracy and religious liberty. Squalor and strife are unnecessary. Plenty and peace are within reach. But we must cease glorifying competitive struggle for private gain and exalt cooperative effort for the common good, and we must create a property system which will make possible mutuality and genuine cooperation.

V

The structure of nationalism as well as that of individualism must be changed. When reflected on a world scale, self-interest becomes national interest, competition becomes militaristic imperialism, and the theory that government should keep its hands off business becomes international anarchy. The unity of all God's children in a universal fellowship will remain a vain hope so long as many of the prevailing attitudes and practices and institutions of nationalism are perpetuated. Therefore, it is the duty of religious persons to recognize and proclaim the sharp contrast between their ideal and the actual doctrines of nationalism.

The following steps seem to me to lead in the direction of a sound foreign policy:[1]

1. Support the reciprocal trade agreements and other methods of opening channels of international trade. Especially desirable is the lessening of economic tensions in Germany, Italy and Japan by making it easier for them to sell commodities in the United States.

2. Urge the entrance of the United States into the World Court and the signing of the optional clause accepting the compulsory jurisdiction of this tribunal.

3. Advocate the entrance of the United States into the League

[1] See my book *Must We Go To War?* for an extended discussion of this subject, with chapters on What is War? Why Do Nations Fight? What Must Be Done If War Is To Be Averted? Is An International Police Force Needed? Can the United States Stay Out of Another Great War? What Should Church and Synagogue do About War? What Shall We Do About Civil War? 278 pages. Price $1.00. Published by Farrar and Rinehart, New York City.

of Nations on a basis of the Pope Resolution, that is, with the reservation that this country is not obligated to use armed force in support of the League's decisions.

4. Endeavor to strengthen the neutrality law, especially through the explicit provision that all trade and all travel by Americans in a war zone must be done at the risk of the trader or the traveler and that the United States assume no responsibility to use armed action in defense of its citizens abroad; by making mandatory an embargo on materials of war (oil, iron, steel, etc.) beyond a peacetime quota, with a cash-and-carry provision; and by adopting the Fish amendment making effective in peacetime as well as in wartime the embargo against the exportation of munitions and other implements of war.

5. Support the proposal of a nationwide referendum on this question: shall citizens of this country be drafted for war service outside continental United States.

6. Oppose all bills providing for conscription through the device of an industrial mobilization plan.

7. Support the Ludlow amendment providing that Congress shall not declare war unless such action is previously approved by a nationwide referendum of American citizens.

8. Urge the adoption of income tax rates which in wartime will absorb all war profits and thus reduce profiteering.

9. Support the plan of nationalizing the munitions industry and thus eliminate the provocative actions of merchants of death.

10. Oppose military training in civilian colleges and high schools, as well as Citizens' Military Training Camps, on the ground that they tend to militarize the minds of American citizens.

11. Hasten the complete independence of the Philippine Islands on terms that safeguard the economic interests of the Filipinos; and that relinquish all military and naval bases of American forces in that land.

12. Advocate the placing of Orientals on a quota basis in our immigration law on equality with peoples of other lands.

13. Urge the withdrawal of all American armed forces from China; and adopt officially the permanent policy of refraining from sending American troops beyond our own borders.

14. Support the establishment of a National Peace Department, with a Secretary of Peace and an adequate budget.[1]

15. Urge the Government of the United States to take seriously the obligation imposed by the Kellogg-Briand treaty "that the settlement or solution of all disputes or conflicts of whatever nature or of whatever origin they may be, which may arise among them, shall never be sought except by pacific means."

16. Advocate drastic reductions in armaments, as a step toward total disarmament and the abandonment of the practice of using armed force as an instrument of policy.

VI

It is necessary to influence governmental policy if war is to be averted. The United States is one of the countries in which it is possible for rank and file citizens to exert substantial influence on decisions of government. The voters of the nation have it within their power to decide which public officials are sent to Washington, and through various devices they can let their demands be known to their public servants. Literally dozens of ways of exerting direct and indirect influence are open to them. By personal contact or personal communication they can set forth their views on public questions; and in numerous ways they can help to create the public opinion which dominates governmental action.

Public opinion is made up of ideas, traditions, myths, illusions, frustrations, passions, interests, loyalties, and ideals. And every individual can have an effective part in shaping and directing these potent forces. The minds of other individuals can be changed, their motivations and loyalties can be shifted, their emotions can be directed into new channels. Judgments and feelings form public opinion; public opinion in the long run decides governmental action; governmental action determines whether we are to have war or peace. From the following list of suggested courses of action, every reader will find a dozen or more that are open to him.

1. Study of international problems is required of persons desiring to be effective participants in the peace movement. Through books, magazines, lectures, classes and radio programs one must

[1] A step in this direction has been taken by the recent establishment in the State Department of a Division of Cultural Relations.

keep informed. To the person who insists that he does not have the time needed for this study, the question should be put: is every hour of your daily program now being spent in ways that are more important than in helping to prevent the suicide of civilization in another world war? Are the lives and destinies of all those you love worth the time required to equip yourself for effective action against war?

2. Take membership in one or more peace societies and thus secure additional access to information and suggested courses of action; and, moreover, strengthen much needed cooperative agencies of persons determined to prevent war. Literature received from these societies will help one to evaluate the significance of news in the morning paper.[1]

3. Persuade other individuals to inform themselves more thoroughly concerning international problems through reading, attendance at lectures and classes, and through careful selection of radio programs.

4. Help to organize and strengthen peace committees in local organizations, including churches, synagogues, clubs, fraternal orders, commercial organizations, labor unions, educational socie-

[1] American Friends Service Committee, 20 South 12th Street, Philadelphia, Penn.

Carnegie Endowment for International Peace, 405 West 117th Street, New York City.

Catholic Association for International Peace, 1312 Massachusetts Avenue, Washington, D. C. (Consultative).

Central Conference of American Rabbis, 117 Gibbs Street, Rochester, N. Y.

Committee on Militarism in Education, 2929 Broadway, New York City.

Department of International Justice and Goodwill of the Federal Council of Churches, 105 E. 22nd Street, New York City.

Fellowship of Reconciliation, 2929 Broadway, New York City.

Foreign Policy Association, 8 West 40th Street, New York City.

Institute of International Education, 2 West 45th Street, New York City.

League of Nations Association, 8 West 40th Street, New York City.

National Committee on the Cause and Cure of War, 1641 Grand Central Terminal Bldg., New York City.

National Council for Prevention of War, 532 17th St., N.W., Washington, D. C.

National Peace Conference, 8 West 40th Street, New York City.

National Student Federation, 8 West 40th Street, New York City.

Women's International League for Peace and Freedom, 1734 F Street, N.W., Washington, D. C.

World Alliance for International Friendship Through the Churches, 70 Fifth Avenue, New York City.

World Peace Foundation, 40 Mt. Vernon Street, Boston.

World Peaceways, 103 Park Avenue, New York City.

ties, etc. Help to increase the effectiveness of these committees as agencies of peace education and peace action.

5. Send telegrams and letters to Senators and Representatives. Concerned citizens should file their names, addresses, and telephone numbers with some local peace agency, and indicate a willingness to communicate with Washington promptly upon notification that a timely moment has arrived for communications dealing with specific legislative measures. Similar communications should also be sent to the President of the United States and to the Secretary of State, since they exercise great influence on legislation. In such communications the asking of questions which call for a definite answer is desirable. Volume is what counts in sending communications to public officials. An individual should not feel that his telegram or letter is unnecessary or futile, any more than he regards his individual ballot on election day as negligible in significance. Frequency in communicating with governmental officials is desirable. Alert citizens may wisely write or telegraph Senators and Representatives several times during a session of Congress. An effective practice is to take time at a public meeting or session of a discussion group then and there to write letters to public officials. Foresight in making available stationery, postcards, and stamps is required.

6. Pass resolutions and circulate petitions. Copies of resolutions and petitions should be sent to local newspapers, as well as to United States Senators, Representatives, the President, and the Secretary of State. Care should be taken to indicate the nature and place of the meeting and the number of persons present. It is highly desirable that resolutions calling for specific legislative action be passed by a wide variety of local organizations and sent to Washington. Volume, variety and frequency are needed.

7. Visitation of public officials in behalf of peace legislation is helpful. Wherever practicable, delegations of representative citizens should call upon Senators and Representatives, either in Washington or when these officials are present in their home communities. More detailed suggestions concerning these various methods are contained in a leaflet entitled *Peace Pressure Primer,* which may be secured upon request from the Women's International League for Peace and Freedom, 1734 F Street, N.W., Washington, D. C.

8. Active participation in local party politics opens the way to effective pressure in behalf of peace legislation. In election years such activity is necessary to secure the nomination and election of suitable candidates.

9. Engage in systematic conversation daily with friends and acquaintances concerning problems of war and peace and seek to awaken their concern and enlist their activity.

10. Teachers, clergymen and other public speakers may wisely select subjects dealing with war and peace, emphasizing especially specific programs of action.

11. Write letters for publication in correspondence columns of newspapers and magazines emphasizing vital aspects of the peace message.

12. Contribute financially to one or more peace societies. The effectiveness of peace education and peace action obviously depends upon funds available. In determining the amount of one's gift, the relative importance of averting war and of other good causes should be kept in mind.

13. Cooperate in presenting anti-war plays and pageants, and in this way appeal to both intellect and emotion.[1]

14. Help to arrange peace parades and other public demonstrations for the purpose of arousing citizens and challenging them to action in behalf of peace.

15. Enlist the cooperation of leaders of orchestras and bands and other musicians in increasing the effectiveness of peace meetings and demonstrations.

16. Display anti-war window cards and billboard posters and in this way challenge the attention of numerous persons who never attend peace meetings.[2]

17. Make use of anti-war stickers on window shields of automobiles. Local groups may print their own stickers at small cost, or information may be secured from various national peace agencies.

18. Use illumined maps in schools, churches, libraries, and

[1] Information concerning plays and pageants may be secured from the National Council for the Prevention of War, 532 17th St., N.W., Washington, D. C.; or from the Women's International League for Peace and Freedom, 1734 F Street, N.W., Washington, D. C.

[2] Information may be secured from World Peaceways, 103 Park Avenue, New York City; and from The American Friends Service Committee, 20 South 12th Street, Philadelphia, Penn.

other institutions to call attention to current events that affect the peace of the world. At a modest cost a map of the world may be equipped with tiny sockets in the principal cities of the various countries. Various colored bulbs (or thumb-tacks) may be used to designate types of events, and ribbons stretched to the margin of the map will call attention to brief typed descriptions or to clippings.

19. Arrange peace exhibits in windows of temporarily vacant stores or in other accessible places. These exhibits may include posters, window cards, stickers, leaflets, pamphlets and books dealing with war and peace. The practice of arranging peace exhibits in connection with conferences and conventions of various organizations is effective.

20. Distribute peace literature, including leaflets and pamphlets. Call attention to significant articles in magazines and to important books on war and peace.

21. Take advantage of anniversaries and special occasions for peace education and peace action.

22. Cooperate in sending youth deputations from colleges and churches to speak on war prevention before various groups in surrounding communities.

23. Encourage student protests against war and cooperate in promoting student peace demonstrations, especially by helping to make effective the annual national student strike against war.

24. Cooperate with the American Friends Service Committee in enrolling students as peace volunteers during the summer. Under this plan carefully selected mature students are trained for two weeks in special institutes and then sent in teams of four to carry on peace education in strategic rural regions throughout the summer.[1]

25. Place on record your determination not to approve of or to participate in any future war, or your purpose not to support any war on foreign soil.

26. Cooperate in opening a register in a church, synagogue, college or other institution, which may be signed by persons desiring to record their determination not to approve of or to participate in any future war, or to declare their purpose not to support a war on foreign soil.

[1] Full information may be secured from Ray Newton, 20 South 12th Street, Philadelphia.

27. Churches, synagogues and other institutions may wisely conduct house-to-house visitations and every-member-canvasses in behalf of world peace. Through conversation and the distribution of literature new recruits for the peace movement may be won.

28. Seek by pacific means to transform competitive capitalism into a cooperative commonwealth; especially by helping to strengthen the labor movement and the consumers' cooperative movement; and by political activity in behalf of a new social order.

29. Be vigilant in safeguarding freedom of speech, assembly and press.

VII

Evangelism, education and organization are indispensable instruments of social change. Conversion and nurture must be supplemented by the creation of a new social structure. Through vocation and avocation concerned individuals are called upon to devote their lives to this triple task.[1] Youth especially is challenged to conquer new frontiers and to blaze new trails. Competitive individualism and militaristic nationalism must be transformed into cooperative commonwealths banded together in mutual endeavor to serve the common good.

Is there really any basis for hope that the required changes can be brought about without resort to civil war? Communists usually answer in the negative, while many of us who are socialist Christians hold the deep conviction that there is a sufficient possibility of success to justify maximum expenditure of energy to achieve pacific transformation of the existing economic order. The social consequences of prolonged civil war in a highly industrialized nation would be devastating beyond imagination. The degree of interdependence of the people in an urban civilization and the destructiveness of chemical and aerial warfare would transform congested areas into infernos. The demolition and dislocation of an infinitely complex productive and distributive sys-

1 See *Creative Pioneers,* by Sherwood Eddy and Kirby Page, Building a New Society Through Adventurous Vocations and Avocations on the Frontiers of the Labor Movement, the Cooperative Movement, Political Action, Racial Justice, and Socialized Religion. Published by Association Press, 347 Madison Avenue, New York City, in a 50-cent edition.

tem would quickly produce hunger and starvation on an appalling scale in metropolitan communities. Modern warfare is ghastly beyond exaggeration, and civil war among industrial populations is the most diabolical form of conflict.

The ethical and religious case against revolutionary violence is made even more conclusive when we recognize the part played by hatred in Communist tactics. Not class solidarity alone, but class hatred is deliberately engendered as necessary to effective hostility against the owning class. Communist literature abounds with direct incitations to hatred and every effort is made to infuriate the workers into armed rebellion against their oppressors when the situation is ripe. Class enmity is to take the form of suppressing all opposition. That virulent hatred and enmity are irreconcilable with high religion seems obvious beyond dispute.

My conclusion, then, is that the Socialist program of persuasion and social coercion through economic and political pressure is more consistent with religious idealism than any other method which offers hope of building a just social order; and that the Communist strategy of violent class war is pragmatically indefensible and morally unjustifiable.

I do not contend that a non-violent strategy is bound to succeed. On the contrary, I have pointed out to a hundred audiences the fact that the odds are overwhelmingly against us, and that, judged by visible and audible evidence, the probabilities are that this generation of Americans will not succeed in creating a just society. It may be that the processes of decay in Western civilization have advanced too far to be arrested and that we are destined to be buried in its ruins. But I am convinced utterly that the strategy of radical religious pacifism is far more likely to prevent such a catastrophe and to create an equable and harmonious community than is the alternative of civil war.

Moreover, it is my deep conviction that hatred and slaughter are never justifiable, no matter how impotent goodwill and non-violence may appear to be in a given crisis. Again and again in human history that which appeared to be victory turned out to be tragic defeat, and often that which seemed to be failure proved to be glorious triumph. I simply cannot believe that hatred will be driven out by hatred, or that war will be ended by war, whether the war be international or civil. "Do men gather grapes from thorns or figs from thistles?" Surely the evidence is incontrovertible that Jesus rendered an incomparably greater service to humanity by "defeat" on the cross than he would have been able to do if he had resorted to armed revolution.

This question of the relative effectiveness of a non-violent and a war-like strategy of revolution is so crucial that it may be desirable to explore it further. Most radicals are convinced that the present owners of heavy industry will not relinquish their privileges voluntarily, but they differ as to the most effective means of coercion. *In order to expropriate by violence those persons who now own and control, what steps would have to be taken?* First, enroll a sufficiently large minority of workers to enable insurrectionists to cope with the armed forces at the disposal of vested interests. Second, equip revolutionists with ample supplies of the weapons and munitions of modern war. Third, win the active support, or at least the sympathetic acquiescence, of a majority of the population, especially that of a considerable proportion of the workers in heavy industries and chief means of transportation. Fourth, wage civil war successfully in strategic centers throughout the nation. Fifth, after the initial victories, suppress armed counter-revolutionaries. Sixth, socialize industry with sufficient rapidity to provide for the basic requirements of the masses, in order to prevent desperation and despair from driving multitudes into the ranks of the counter-revolutionaries. These are minimum conditions of successful armed revolution.

Even if an adequate minority of active revolutionists could be enrolled, and even if a majority of the middle class would consent to the revolution, *large-scale and prolonged fighting would be required to consolidate victory*. And when the destructiveness of modern warfare is kept vividly in mind, and the complexity and delicacy of present-day industry are recalled, it becomes evident that civil war in the United States under present conditions, and much more so under the intensified industrialism of the 1940's and 1960's, would destroy and dislocate production and distribution to such a degree that standards of living would drop calamitously, even if wholesale starvation could be avoided. The prospect of being able to satisfy the basic needs of the people under such circumstances appear to be slight. For this reason, revulsion of these masses might result in the triumph of counter-revolutionaries.

What should be the attitude of truly religious persons toward the workers, if in desperation they resort to armed action in an endeavor to secure justice? My own answer is clear and unequivocal. I am on the side of the victims of exploitation and injustice, and make no pretense of being neutral in the class conflict. I have been endeavoring to make my position clear that under no circumstances will I participate in armed warfare, whether it be international or class warfare. Moreover, I will never sanction or approve any kind of armed hostilities. But even if the workers follow the fatal example of their oppressors and resort to retaliatory violence, I shall continue to believe in the justice of their cause, and to give them my non-warlike support. A Belgian pacifist who refused to take up arms against Germany did not thereby assume an attitude of neutrality, but chose to express his loyalty to Belgium in higher ways than by killing Germans. Such a man was not acting as a parasite, profiting by the suffering of his countrymen. Likewise, it is possible for a non-violent revolutionist to refrain from participating in or sanctioning armed hostilities, without abandoning his loyalty to the workers. Being convinced that all armed warfare is ineffective and unethical, a radical religious pacifist should refrain from hatred and murder, and should depend utterly upon persuasion and ethical forms of coercion.

One of the objections most often raised against pacifism in the class war is based on the assumption that fascism can in the last resort be resisted only by taking up the weapons of battle. This argument overlooks the fact that *nowhere has fascism been successfully resisted by violence,* certainly not in Italy, Germany, or Austria. Fascism is a product of economic collapse and intense suffering, accompanied by national frustration and bitterness. Its emergence is improbable except as a result of paralyzing defeat in war or terrible disappointment over the outcome of war. Three factors combined to produce Hitlerism: appalling misery; venomous hatred toward France and deep resentment against any German Government that accepted the Treaty of Versailles and continued reparation payments; and despair of the future under the existing régime. The significance of the time factor can scarcely be stressed too heavily. Hitler did not succeed in the fifth year of Germany's bondage, or in the tenth. Even after a decade of degradation and agony, the German people would have rejected

Hitler if the Allies had cancelled reparation payments, removed the sole guilt clause from the Treaty of Versailles, taken even moderate steps in the direction of disarmament, and revealed a disposition to restore Germany to a status of equality among the great powers. Year after year, the suffering masses of Germany endured and hoped, until they cracked under the strain in the fourteenth year, and turned to the most chauvinistic and reckless of the available alternatives.

To organize the workers, consumers, and voters, and to achieve power by economic pressure and the ballots of electors: this task is enormously difficult, but it is far easier than to convert a majority of the American people to the doctrine of proletarian dictatorship, and to train them for the violent seizure of power. It is imperative that emphasis be placed upon the incalculable significance of the middle class in this country. The course of events in Italy and Germany reveals clearly the dynamic power of this class when aroused. *The quickest and most certain way to guarantee the emergence of a Fascist dictatorship in the United States is by creating a Communist Party that is strong enough to convince members of the middle class that they are about to be subjected to a reign of terror under a proletarian dictatorship.* If socialism is to succeed in America, powerful sections of the middle class must join forces with a majority of the working class. It is imperative, therefore, that Socialists disavow with all possible emphasis any intention of seeking power through civil war. Appeals to violence will not lead to socialism, but to fascism.

Let the fact be emphasized with the utmost vividness that the tides of economic life are sweeping us on toward socialization. The competitive system is breaking down. Profits are diminishing to the disappearing point in several major industries, notably railroads and coal mines. The British Tories are now socializing the coal industry in an effort to save capital from the wreckage of competitive conflict. Is there any reasonable basis of doubt that most of the present owners of railroads and coal mines in the United States would sell their holdings at an equitable price, rather than to take up arms in opposition to a program of socialization? During recent weeks high officials of electric power companies have expressed themselves publicly as favorable to the sale of their properties to the government at a fair price.

The change in public opinion that is required in order to

*make advanced socialism possible in this country is not as pro-
found as that which has actually occurred within the past half
century*. Moreover, the incredibly rapid pace at which we are now
moving toward consolidation of economic power will by its very
velocity speed up the transformation of the public mind with regard to social ownership, as well as concerning social control.
Necessity is a stern but highly successful teacher, and the present
economic depression has produced a greater revolution in thought
than would have appeared possible ten years ago. A concluding
aspect of the American scene should be kept in mind, and that is
the rapidity with which public opinion changes. Sentiment concerning prohibition offers an impressive illustration. After decades of relatively ineffective agitation, prohibition swept the
country at an amazing speed, and after a decade of experience,
the nation went wet at an equally rapid pace. Shifts in attitude
toward economic questions are now occurring in the United States
at a speed which is too dazzling to be comprehended.

That we are confronted with titanic difficulties is obvious, but
the odds have usually been against persons who struggled to create the good society.

Chapter V

Proceed Resolutely When Confronted with the Consequent Opposition and Suffering

HIGHLY perilous is the endeavor to change habitual practices and social institutions. To an amazing degree men move along in ruts, and bitterly do they resent efforts to guide them into new pathways. The prevailing tendency is to accept whatever social system happens to be dominant and to conform to its customs. When the economic structure of society takes the form of chattel slavery, masters find it easy to produce convincing arguments that (1) slaves are better off than cannibals in the jungle, (2) slaves are more fortunate than dwellers in city slums, (3) slavery is necessary if masters are to have the leisure and facilities with which to produce civilization, (4) slavery is God's idea and is inherent in the nature of things. If the slaves are better off than people used to be and other people are at the present time, slavery must be a good system, especially so since it was ordained by God. The masters are easily convinced. And acquiescence is characteristic of slaves. Born into a world where they and their parents are bought and sold as property; treated as means to other persons' ends; compelled to obey orders and to exhaust themselves in labor from which they receive only bare subsistence; prevented from taking collective action to improve their lot or to obtain freedom; threatened with mutilation and death for even the mildest forms of subordination; victims of a corrupted religion which taught that their position was assigned to them by God and that their joys must be sought in heaven; it is inevitable that most slaves acquiesce and fatalistically live out their days with no hope of liberty.

The arguments used in defense of chattel slavery throw such floods of illumination upon contemporary problems that it will be well to cite vivid illustrations. It was considered axiomatic that Negroes are an inferior race and that without the leadership of white people they could never rise above barbarism. Professor

88

Thomas R. Dew, of William and Mary College, based a long argument on the proposition that "slaves are entirely unfit for a state of freedom among the whites." Chancellor William Harper once declared that "the Creator did not intend that every individual human being should be highly cultivated morally and intellectually. . . . It is better that a part should be fully and highly cultivated, and the rest utterly ignorant."[1] Governor J. H. Hammond once said: "I endorse without reserve the much abused sentiment of Governor McDuffie, that 'slavery is the corner-stone of our republican edifice'; while I repudiate, as ridiculously absurd, that much lauded but nowhere accredited dogma of Mr. Jefferson that 'all men are born equal.' "[2]

That slavery was the black man's best friend was often maintained. Chancellor William Harper quoted with enthusiasm from an article which said: "Slavery has done more to elevate a degraded race in the scale of humanity; to tame the savage; to civilize the barbarous; to soften the ferocious; to enlighten the ignorant, and to spread the blessings of Christianity among the heathen, than all the missionaries that philanthropy and religion have ever sent forth."[3]

The Reverend James Wilson called slavery "that gracious and benevolent system which elevates the heathen cannibal into the contented, civilized, intelligent, and happy domestics we see around us. Nay more, into humble, faithful, and most joyous worshippers of the true and everlasting God. Bless God for such a system. We don't apologize for slavery, we glory in it, and no society shall exist within our borders that disqualifies or stigmatizes the slave trade."[4]

That slavery was ordained by God was the unwavering belief of most Southern churchmen.[5] In 1852 appeared the fifth edition of a volume by the Reverend Josiah Priest entitled *Bible Defence of Slavery*. A total of 469 pages is devoted to proving the thesis that slavery came from God. "I firmly believe," said Governor J. H. Hammond, "that American slavery is not only not a sin, but especially commanded by God through Moses, and

[1] *The Pro-Slavery Argument*, p. 35. (1853, 490 pages.)

[2] Hammond's *Letters on Slavery*, pp. 109, 110.

[3] *The Pro-Slavery Argument*, p. 60.

[4] Report of the Anti-Slavery Society of New York, 1860, p. 281.

[5] See Henry Wilson (Vice President of the United States), *The Rise and Fall of the Slave Power in America*, 3 vols., 2164 pages, pp. 697-724, Vol. 3.

approved by Christ through his apostles."[1] In 1858, during the course of a debate with another minister, the Reverend W. G. Brownlow said: "Not only will I throughout this discussion openly and boldly take the ground that Slavery as it exists in America ought to be perpetuated, but that slavery is an established and inevitable condition to human society. I will maintain the ground that God always intended the relation of master and slave to exist . . . that slavery having existed ever since the first organization of society, it will exist to the end of time."[2] The Reverend J. C. Postell, of Orangeburgh, South Carolina, once declared: "So far from being a moral evil, slavery is a merciful visitation. . . . It is the Lord's doings, and it is marvellous in our eyes; and had it not been for the best God alone, who is able, long since would have overruled it. It is by divine appointment."[3]

The Nashville Christian Advocate, on June 14, 1861, defended slavery in this extravagant language: "Southern people feel profoundly assured that they are fighting for the only rights, the only comfortable life, and the only true social and political status the negro can ever have. They feel that they are fighting for the only true Christian civilization they can ever enjoy, either in this or any other country. Slavery is rapidly coming to be regarded as a providential system of African civilization. It has long since come to be regarded as a 'power' in general civilization; now, the idea of the present and eternal welfare of the Africans is involved in its defence. Southern men defend slavery now upon the same principle and with the same spirit as they do their religion, their homes, their wives and children, their personal honor and independence."

Upholders of slavery not only believed passionately in the righteousness of the institution, but were usually intolerant of any other opinion. As they became more fearful that the activities of abolitionists were undermining the sacred structure of slavery, they became increasingly bitter in their attacks upon their opponents. In dedicating a church building in Charleston in 1850 the Reverend J. H. Thornwell, a distinguished Presbyterian clergyman who was sometimes called the "Calhoun of the Church," said:

[1] *Governor Hammond's Letters to Thomas Clarkson,* p. 5.

[2] *Ought American Slavery to Be Perpetuated?* A Debate between Rev. W. G. Brownlow and Reverend A. Pryne, 305 pages.

[3] Quoted by Stephen S. Foster, *The Brotherhood of Thieves.*

"The Parties in this conflict are not merely abolitionists and slaveholders—they are atheists, socialists, communists, red republicans, jacobins, on the one side, and the friends of order and regulated freedom on the other. In one word, the world is the battle ground—Christianity and Atheism the combatants; and the progress of humanity the stake." This same procedure of labelling antislavery advocates with all the objectionable epithets then current was followed by the Honourable James Wilson, American Minister to Turkey. In one category he grouped "the advocates of 'free love,' the 'Socialists,' the Infidels, the 'Red Republicans,' and 'Abolitionists.' . . . But for the professed teacher of God's Holy Word; for the man who claims to be a disciple of Christ, and a follower of His holy counsels, but who prostitutes the pulpit to the purpose of inciting hatred instead of love . . . who teaches his congregation that all the other sins of the world are as nothing compared to the sin of slavery—who can regard him in any other aspect than as the enemy . . . of that meek and lowly Jesus whom he professes to serve?"[1] Red Republicans! The lowest estate to which a true Southerner could fall! And thus become an enemy of the lowly Jesus!

Defenders of the status quo do not stop with vituperation but go on to violent action as their fears rise and their passions boil. For many years prior to the Civil War it was highly dangerous to speak against slavery anywhere in the South. Ministers and teachers found their positions jeopardized and their lives threatened if it became known that they were sympathetic with the antislavery movement. Large rewards were offered for the capture dead or alive of certain noted abolitionists. Many post offices refused to deliver antislavery literature, this procedure being defended by at least two Postmaster Generals of the United States. Mob violence occurred frequently, both in the South and in the North. The classic assault upon Garrison by Bostonians of property and standing was not an isolated case. Vice President Henry Wilson in his monumental history has gathered together a mass of evidence on this point.[2] In Philadelphia, New York, Cincinnati, Utica, New Bedford, Nantucket, Portland, St. Louis, and other cities violence was used against the persons and property of abolitionists. Concerning the situation which prevailed

[1] *The South Vindicated*, pp. 70, 143, 144.
[2] *A Political History of Slavery*, Vol. 2, pp. 666-672; vol. 1, p. 662.

throughout the South, Wilson said: "The proscription, lawlessness and barbarism of slavery were the necessary conditions of its existence. . . . The mob was sovereign. . . . A merciless vindictiveness prevailed, and held its stern and pitiless control over the whole South. . . . Southern papers were filled with accounts of the atrocities perpetuated, and volumes alone would contain descriptions of all that transpired during this reign of terror. . . . The Texas 'Advocate,' the organ of the Methodist Church South, urged 'the thorough and immediate eradication of the Methodist Church North in Texas, with whatever force may be necessary.' If such were the teachings of their religious journals, little surprise need be felt that the mob reigned, and reigned ruthlessly."[1]

II

This tendency to accept the status quo and to defend it with violence may be illustrated by dipping into history at any point. Throughout the period when feudalism was dominant, men of privilege found it easy to believe that serfdom was good for the serfs, good for the lords of the manor, and divine in its nature. Vast estates were common wherever feudalism existed. At times small holdings disappeared almost entirely and an absolute monopoly prevailed. In an age when the church dominated so large a share of all life it was inevitable that it should accumulate much property. There came a time when "there was not a bishopric, an abbey, a chapter of canons or a collegiate church that had not become a great landholder." As early as the Ninth Century the richest clergy possessed from 75,000 to 140,000 acres of land and had an annual income of $85,000 to $225,000, while the income of the poorest bishops and abbots ranged from $5,000 to $14,000.[2] This was in the days before the church became really wealthy. During the next three centuries clerical wealth increased enormously. One abbot "had among his vassals 4 archdukes, 10 counts palatine and margraves, 27 counts and 28 barons and knights."[3] Princes, nobles, wealthy merchants, Jews, and monks alone could afford to live in great stone houses and be waited

[1] *Ibid.*, Vol. 2, pp. 666, 667.
[2] J. W. Thompson, *An Economic and Social History of the Middle Ages*, p. 650.
[3] G. G. Coulton, *Five Centuries of Religion*, Vol. 2, p. 35.

upon by many servants. It has been estimated that in the Thirteenth Century the church owned one third of the land of Germany, one fifth of France, the greater part of Italy, one third of England, vast areas in Spain, Scandinavia, and other parts of Europe.[1] The church was incomparably the greatest secular and economic power of the age. As late as the closing decades of the Eighteenth Century one fifth of the entire domain of France was owned by the church.

The serf differed from the slave in that he could not be sold. His obligations to his superior, however, were often so numerous and exacting as to make his condition one of actual slavery. He could not leave or establish himself elsewhere without his master's permission. The right of pursuit and capture was an unquestioned prerogative of the master. Among the recognized duties of serfs were the bearing of arms at the command of his master; the payment of taxes, either in money or goods; the filling of requisitions by the lord, including entertainment for the latter and his entourage when travelling; the obligation to perform physical labor for the master, such as ploughing, harvesting, and road making; the recognition of banalities, that is, certain obligations imposed by the master, including the requirement that the serfs patronize the master's mills and other monopolies. There were long periods when it was a rare occurrence for the owner to manage his estate personally. As a rule, supervision was delegated to an overseer, who managed the place, collected taxes, punished evil doers, and executed persons sentenced to death. Ordinarily the overseer received no salary or wages, earning his livelihood by retaining a portion of the taxes for himself. Under this arrangement nothing short of a miracle could prevent him from becoming a grafter and petty tyrant.

The helplessness of the vassals was further increased by the irresponsibility of the master. There was no state or outside agency to stand between the exploiter and his victims. The lord's wishes constituted the only justice received by serfs. "In almost all the documents of the middle ages," said Seignobos, "justice means the right of levying fines or the product of those fines. . . . Feudal society was not acquainted with justice that was the same for all. Justice, like peace, was not a common right; in the middle ages it was a privilege. There was a different justice and spe-

1 Clarence Flick, *The Rise of the Medieval Church*, p. 574.

cial courts for each class."[1] Tenants could not even gather together to discuss grievances without permission from the landlord. Illicit assemblage was a crime.

When it is recalled that for several centuries more than three-fourths of the population of great areas of Europe were serfs, the incalculable amount of misery caused by this economic and social system will be more clearly realized.[2] And all the while monasteries and churches were terribly entangled in the system.

The church accepted feudalism and made only the feeblest and most sporadic efforts to overthrow it. Regulations and reform was its motto. The long-established custom of patching up the existing order was adhered to and radical changes were frowned upon. Indeed, the church was a primary factor in prolonging the life of feudalism. Numerous synodical decrees prohibited the alienation of church property, including slaves and serfs. "The serf might often buy his freedom," says Professor Coulton, "but it was seldom given to him. It was on Church estates that bondage lasted longest."[3] Professor Thompson expressed the same opinion: "In the matter of serfdom itself the Church was conservative to the point of being reactionary. . . . In the matter of emancipation of serfs, the Church lagged behind secular Europe and even retarded emancipation."[4]

III

Throughout many generations the doctrine of the divine right of kings held sway. "It was essentially a popular theory," says J. N. Figgis, "proclaimed in the pulpit, published in the market-place, witnessed on the battle-field."[5] It is almost impossible for persons who have been reared in a democratic community to appreciate the extent to which men's minds were dominated for many centuries by this idea. The first two verses of the thirteenth chapter of Romans have been quoted an endless number of times as a justification of the perpetuation of infamous tyrannies: "Let every soul be subject unto the higher powers. For there is no

[1] Charles Seignobos, *The Feudal Régime*, pp. 18, 59.
[2] See W. S. Davis, *Life on a Mediaeval Barony*, pp. 253-274.
[3] Coulton, *op. cit.*, Vol. 2, p. 8.
[4] Thompson, *op. cit.*, p. 679.
[5] *The Divine Right of Kings*, p. 3.

power but of God; the powers that be are ordained of God. Whosoever therefore resisteth the power, resisteth the ordinance of God: and they shall receive to themselves damnation." To question the divine right of a king to rule his subjects was long regarded as both heresy and treason. Until recently orthodox ecclesiastics have usually sided with reactionaries and opposed efforts toward political democracy.

On July 30, 1682, John Whitfield preached a fifteen-thousand-word sermon before the Lord Mayor and aldermen of London on the subject, "The Dreadfulness of the Sin of Despising Dominion and Speaking Evil of Dignities," in which he said: "The Apostle makes it a main Master-piece of Christianity, when he joyns 'Fear God, and honour the King,' so indivisibly together. . . . He that is not a good Subject, cannot be a good Christian." On another occasion before the same distinguished company, Edmond Hickeringill said: "The King himself is accountable for his Errors to none but God, his Personal errors; but as King and in his Politick capacity, it is impossible he should have any Errors, for a King of England can do no wrong."[1]

In a volume the English edition of which was published in 1882 Bishop Martensen strongly indorsed the principle of a hereditary monarchy "because of its full manifestation of the fact that the king exists not by the will of the people, but by the will of God, that the king and his authority are given us, that subjective arguing is in this matter of as little use as it would be to complain that we have not other parents than those whom God has given us."[2] In his famous Konigsberg speech of 1910 the German Kaiser said: "Considering myself as the instrument of the Lord, without heeding the views and opinions of the day, I go my way." On another occasion, he said: "The king holds his power by the grace of God, to whom alone he is responsible."

IV

Further illustrations may be taken from the period beginning with the industrial revolution and continuing until the present day. During recent decades belief in competitive individualism has been as fervent as were former convictions about slavery and

[1] Edmond Hickeringill, *Curse Ye Meroz.*
[2] M. Martensen, *Christian Ethics,* Vol. 2, p. 187.

serfdom, while opposition to change has likewise found expression in multiple forms suppression. Holders of privilege and power have readily found arguments to entrench their position. It now seems incredible that wise and good men once regarded poverty not only as inevitable but as desirable. Yet it is possible for a present-day historian to devote an entire chapter to "The Doctrine of the Utility of Poverty." [1] Not a few writers of that period proved to their own satisfaction not merely that poverty is inevitable and desirable but that it is really a blessing. After all, the poor have less responsibility and fewer anxieties than the rich. One writer described the blessings of poverty in these words: "O ye children of poverty and toil, of misfortune and sorrow! God is better to you than ye know. Ye see but one side of the veil now, and that is fretted with troubles, and dark with adversity. But it has another side. On that side are angel faces and the smile of God. Your crowns are gathering lustre. Your harps are being attuned to sweeter notes and deeper melodies of joy." This same point of view was expressed by another theologian in these words: "Never mind: if you cannot have a piano on earth, you may have a harp in heaven." Edmund Burke once said: "The body of the common people . . . must respect that property which they cannot partake. They must labor to obtain what by labor can be obtained; and when they find, as they commonly do, the success disproportioned to the endeavor, they must be taught their consolation in the final proportions of eternal justice." [2]

Concerning the attitude of the churches toward social reform, Lord Shaftesbury, one of the foremost advocates of protective legislation for workers, said: "I find that Evangelical religionists are not those on whom I can rely. . . . To whom should I have naturally looked for the chief aid! Why, undoubtedly to the clergy, and especially those of the trading districts. Quite the reverse; from them I have received no support, or next to none. And this throughout my whole career. . . . I have had more aid from the medical than the divine profession." In describing the frame of mind which prevailed during this period Harold Begbie said: "Nearly every suggestion for bettering the condition of the poor was regarded as blasphemous republicanism and treated with a

[1] Professor Edgar S. Furniss, of Yale University, *The Position of the Labourer in a System of Nationalism,* chap. 6.

[2] *Reflections on the Revolution in France,* p. 359.

wrathful disdain. . . . Religion, politics, art, even literature, struck no blow for justice and advance."

V

Elsewhere I have gathered together some of the evidence showing opposition to almost every reform designed to curb the power of special privilege in the United States.[1] Here are illustrations from the record: The owning class long sought to perpetuate its reign by depriving the workers of the right to vote and to hold office. The early American Fathers utterly rejected democracy. Professor Parrington has pointed out that at one time among the two thousand members of Massachusetts Bay Colony, only a dozen freemen of the corporation exercised the right of franchise, this handful electing and constituting the officials of the community.[2] Universal white manhood suffrage was granted with extreme reluctance and only after a prolonged delay. Three years after the Constitutional Convention assembled only 1,303 male residents of voting age in New York out of 13,330 were permitted to vote, that is, one out of ten.[3] As late as 1821, nine of the 24 states retained property qualifications for voting.[4] In 1830 such eminent citizens of Virginia as John Marshall, James Madison and John Randolph supported a measure which excluded 50 thousand white men from the franchise.[5] Indeed, until 1850 landowners alone voted in Virginia, and another six years passed before North Carolina let down the bars.[6]

In conservative circles the protection of property was considered more important than safeguarding the rights of ordinary people. Consequently, the retention of political power in the hands of a small oligarchy was considered imperative. "Those who own the country ought to govern it," declared John Jay.[7] Long before Locke had advanced the idea that "the great and chief end, there-

1 See my *Individualism and Socialism*, pp. 31-64.

2 Vernon Louis Parrington, *Main Currents in American Thought*, Vol. 1, p. 19.

3 Claude C. Bowers, *Jefferson and Hamilton*, p. 142.

4 Arthur M. Schlesinger, *New Viewpoints in American History*, p. 87.

5 *Ibid.*, p. 87.

6 Charles A. and Mary Beard, *The Rise of American Civilization*, Vol. 1, p. 545.

7 Bowers, *op. cit.*, p. 178.

fore, of men uniting into commonwealths and putting themselves under government, is the preservation of their property."[1]

The Declaration of Independence solemnly declared that "all men are created equal," but in practice this sentiment was interpreted to mean "all white men who own property are created equal." The word *men* must be underscored, because the possibility simply did not dawn upon the Fathers that their mothers, wives, daughters and sisters should be accorded equal political rights. More than a century was to elapse before the Nineteenth Amendment to the Constitution became the law of the land and bestowed upon women the full franchise. The editor of a Seattle paper in 1871 paid his respects to Susan B. Anthony, saintly suffragist, in this language: "She is a revolutionist, aiming at nothing less than the breaking up of the very foundations of society, and the overthrow of every social institution organized for the protection of the sanctity of the altar, the family circle and the legitimacy of our offspring, recognizing no religion but self-worship, no God but human reason, no motive to action but lust. . . . The whole plan is coarse, sensual and agrarian, the worst phase of French infidelity and communism." And communism!

Desirous of perpetuating control by property, and holding a low estimate of the masses, members of the owning class, with certain conspicuous exceptions, long opposed universal education and threw the tremendous weight of their influence against free public schools. Fifty years after the Declaration of Independence was promulgated, with the exception of certain portions of New England, free public schools "were the distant hope of statesmen and reformers." A terrific and prolonged struggle was required before the principle of universal free education was accepted. Concerning the long struggle for free schools, Dean Cubberley has written: "Excepting the battle for the abolition of slavery, perhaps no question has ever been before the American people for settlement which has caused so much feeling or aroused such bitter antagonisms. . . . Often those in favor of taxation were fiercely assailed and even at times threatened with personal violence."[2]

The doctrine of laissez-faire had led to the ruthless exploitation of women and children. Intelligent and devout employers

[1] Parrington, *op. cit.* Vol. 1, p. 270.
[2] *Encyclopaedia Britannica,* 14th edition, vol. 7, p. 993.

have often lived in luxury from the proceeds of industries which devoured human flesh and blood. Callous indifference and pious protestations of inability to remedy these evils have frequently been the responses of industrialists to inhumanly long hours and starvation wages. One of the arguments used by Alexander Hamilton in urging an American protective tariff in 1791, was that the extension of machine industry would make possible the profitable employment of women and children of "tender age."[1] In 1833 it was estimated that two-fifths of all the factory workers in New England were children under sixteen years of age.[2] Not until 1842 did Massachusetts pass the first law limiting the hours of children in industry, prohibiting the employment of children under twelve for more than twelve hours per day. In 1856 Connecticut restricted the hours of children under fourteen to twelve per day. But even these inadequate laws were feebly enforced. Twice the United States Supreme Court has declared child labor laws unconstitutional. The National Association of Manufacturers conducted a vigorous campaign against the child labor amendment, rejecting "this revolutionary grant of power to the Congress as repugnant to our traditional conception of local responsibility and self-government. . . ."[3] Mr. James A. Emery, general counsel for the Association, declared: "The proposal is socialistic in its origin, philosophy and associations. . . . The word 'Socialistic' has been frequently and loosely applied to many proposals. This phrase is, however, related to the present proposal by unusual evidence of directing influence and sympathetic philosophy."[4] Senator King asserted: ". . . every Bolshevik, every extreme communist and socialist in the United States is back of the measure. . . . Of course, this is a communistic, Bolshevistic scheme, and a lot of good people, misled, are accepting it, not knowing the evil consequences which will result and the sinister purposes back of the measure."[5] And it was Senator Reed of Missouri who exclaimed: "I affirm that it is completely subversive of our form of government; that it is socialistic, bolshevistic, and I would almost say, anarchistic. It has all the vices of socialism

[1] Beard, *op, cit.,* Vol. 1, p. 348.
[2] Schlesinger, *op, cit.,* p. 204.
[3] Resolution adopted May 21, 1924.
[4] Pamphlet entitled *An Examination of the Proposed Twentieth Amendment to the Constitution of the United States,* pp. 4, 20.
[5] *Congressional Record,* May 31, 1924.

and none of its virtues. . . . It is a march from liberty toward despotism. It assassinates democracy, and upon its grave establishes a hybrid monstrosity. . . . It is as idiotic as it is destructive, and as wicked as it is imbecile."[1]

Ceaseless and bitter opposition to efforts on the part of the workers through organization and legislation to reduce the length of the working day has been put forth by employers as a class, with many exceptions. Huge volumes would be required to record the details of the sordid story of how industrialists in their mad scramble for profits have cruelly exploited their employees. As late as 1914, "fully 25 percent of the more than 7,000,000 workers in manufacturing industries were working from 60 to 72 hours weekly."[2] The 12-hour day, the 7-day week, and the 24-hour shift every two weeks were not abolished by the United States Steel Corporation until 1922, following a decade of nationwide public condemnation and an open appeal from the President of the United States. "The Eight-Hour bill, as it has been introduced in successive Congresses," declared the National Association of Manufacturers, "is the work of the agitator pure and simple."[3] To set limits to the working day in the navy yards would be "little less than treason."[4] President Parry of the Association declared: "The eight hour bill if enacted into law would mark a radical departure from the spirit of our free institutions and would work great harm to industrial interests. The bill belongs to the category of socialistic schemes which organized labor favors for the artificial regulation of industry. . . . Such paternalism and artificial regulation of industry as this bill contemplates is directly at variance with those inalienable rights of the individual to do as he pleases with his time, his labor, and his property, so long as he does not infringe upon the equal rights of another."[5]

In their frantic pursuit of profits, manufacturers have frequently been careless of or indifferent to the health and safety of their employees. Working conditions have often been insanitary and dangerous to a high degree. Yet employers have been slow to install adequate safeguards and to provide healthful shop

[1] *Ibid.,* June 2, 1924.

[2] Gordon S. Watkins, *An Introduction to the Study of Labor Problems,* p. 106.

[3] *Eight Hours By Act of Congress,* p. 39.

[4] *Ibid.,* p. 65.

[5] David N. Parry, *Disastrous Effects of a National Eight-Hour Law.*

conditions. Indeed, they have frequently resisted with vigor legislation designed for the protection of the workers. Decades of endeavor were required before industrial workers in general were provided with decent toilet facilities, separate dressing rooms for men and women, safeguards on dangerous machinery, protection against fire, satisfactory heating, lighting, and ventilation. During the 1932 Presidential campaign, Franklin D. Roosevelt reminded his audience that in the 1911 session of the New York Legislature, which passed the Workmen's Compensation Act, that "we youngsters who were in favor of it were called socialists and radicals."[1]

The desire for gain has expressed itself also in the form of shacks and tenement houses. Property owners have taken every possible advantage of the ignorance, inertia and poverty of the workers and have often herded them together in unspeakably vile quarters. For a full century the United States has been confronted with a tragic slum problem.

Throughout the realms of transportation, industry and banking, callous indifference to public welfare has frequently been manifested, while fraud and corruption have been widely practiced. Nevertheless, industrialists and financiers have usually resisted every extension of public control designed to curb the ruthless exploitation of the common people. The Interstate Commerce Commission, the Federal Trade Commission, the Federal Reserve System are now almost universally regarded as necessary and beneficial, yet when legislation of this character was first suggested, it was greeted with a storm of denunciation from vested interests whose autocratic and lawless reign was threatened. Three huge volumes are required to contain the testimony before the Senate Committee on Interstate Commerce in 1905. The following excerpts are typical of the hostile attitude toward governmental regulation: "in matters of railroad regulation, I am opposed to Federal interference in all or in part. . . . Competition is the law of business, with railroads which have transportation to sell, just as it is with merchants who have goods to sell. . . . There is no complaint except people who would be glad to see a condition amounting first to municipal socialism, and second to State socialism. . . . Rates of freight are the sales price for the service the railroad render, and it would be just as legitimate

1 Quoted by Abraham Epstein, *Insecurity: A Challenge to America,* p. 68.

for the Department of Commerce and Labor to take absolute control of the price schedules of all other corporations as to confer the power of making rates upon the Interstate Commerce Commission. The American public, I take it, is not prepared to submit to this method of confiscation of property rights."[1] In an address on railway regulation, Robert Mather said: "As a nation, we have no greater peril to fear than the constant interference of agents of Government in our daily affairs."[2] Every possible effort was made to prevent the creation of the *Federal Trade Commission*. Typical arguments of the spokesmen for business interests are those of Senator Townsend and Senator Sutherland. "It seems to me," said the former, "that the gun provided in the bill is out of all proportion to the real game sought. We would not think of hunting chipmunks with a cannon. The proposed effort to destroy illegal business is like firing grape and canister into a flock of sheep to kill a diseased one in their midst."[3] Senator Sutherland, who has since become a Justice of the Supreme Court of the United States, warned: "I believe it to be a dangerous measure, and in many respects an unjust measure, and a measure which we ought not to pass. . . . I am opposed to this bill from the beginning of it to the end of it, with its arbitrary powers, with its absurd requirements."[4]

An avalanche of pressure was brought to bear upon Congress to prevent the creation of the *Federal Reserve Banking System*, especially the inclusion of those features which enlarged governmental powers of control. Former Senator Aldrich of Rhode Island, one of the most faithful servants of big business ever elected to Congress, was extremely critical of many aspects of the bill, using such language as this: ". . . radical and revolutionary in their character and at variance with all the accepted canons of economic law. . . . If the attempt is successful it will be the first and most important step toward changing our form of government from a democracy to an autocracy. No imperial government in Europe would venture to suggest, much less enact, legislation of this kind. . . . The creation of this board, however, is clearly

[1] *Hearings before the Committee on Interstate Commerce,* U. S. Senate, May, 1905, vol. 3, pp. 2021, 2022, 2112.

[2] *Railway Regulation,* p. 25.

[3] *Congressional Record,* July 9, 1914, p. 11872.

[4] *Congressional Record,* July 27, 1914, pp. 12805, 12862.

a favorable response to socialistic demands."[1] Senator Sherman of Illinois, in the debate on the Federal Reserve bill, exclaimed: "For myself I would support a law to wind a watch with a crowbar as cheerfully as I will support any such bill. . . . Business is restrained by commercial laws superior to statutes. . . . Business is ruled by laws as inexorable as the tides. . . . The attempt to so control credit can end in nothing but disastrous failure."[2] While the Honorable Charles H. Fowler of New Jersey wailed: "I don't know what it will do to you central bankers, but it will put the country national banks out of business."[3]

The financial interests of the country were extremely hostile to the idea of establishing *postal savings banks*. In commenting upon the history of legislative efforts in this direction, Professor Kemmerer points out that success was not achieved until "after nearly forty years of discussion . . . after eight postmasters-general had recommended the establishment of postal savings banks and ten times as many bills had been introduced into Congress for this purpose."[4] From every direction the proposal was damned as paternalistic, socialistic and fraught with infinite peril to the Republic. The literature of the opposition abounds with such expressions as these: "Let us reason together before taking a fatal plunge into paternalism, the effects of which in the long run palsies human progress . . . the menace of this radical movement . . . the whole scheme may be said to be a radical innovation upon the powers, obligations and duties of the Government . . . communistically becoming their business competitor . . . may graft into the fabric of our government a principle destructive to liberty and therefore to the comfort and welfare of the toilers everywhere."[5]

The establishment of the *parcels post* was likewise opposed and long delayed by the relentless opposition of vested interests. In a widely circulated statement, John Wanamaker, Postmaster General, declared: "There are just four reasons against the establishment of a parcels post. They are the American, the Adams,

[1] *Proceedings of the Academy of Political Science,* vol. IV, Oct. 1913, pp. 37, 85, 87.
[2] *The Bankers Magazine,* November, 1913, pp. 522, 523.
[3] *Hearings before the Committee on Banking and Currency,* U. S. Senate, 63rd Congress 1913, p. 1899.
[4] *Political Science Quarterly,* 1911, vol. 26, p. 462.
[5] See *Outlook,* Jan. 16, 1909, p. 115; *Bankers Magazine,* vol. 78, p. 777; *American Banker,* Jan. 26, 1898; *Bankers Monthly,* Jan. 1909, p. 17; *Financial Chronicle,* Feb. 27, 1909, p. 1539.

the United States, and the Wells Fargo Express Companies."[1] That this was an incomplete statement of the case may be seen from the comment of an editor in 1911: "I have never heard of any association of retail dealers that is not on record against the extension of the domestic parcels post in any form . . . practically all the organizations of wholesalers and manufacturers are opposed to the parcels post, and like the retailers have been fighting it for years."[2]

Tons of ink were consumed in printing such statements as these: "Sugar coat the pill as you will, the parcel post agitation is a self-seeking commercializing sham, sought by the few, advocated by the few, and aimed at the many, who through ignorance or carelessness fail to grasp its scope or its perils. . . . If we do, we are going into socialism . . . paternalistic, socialistic legislation. . . . The country's commercial system will be revolutionized, the population of rural communities depleted, and their progress retarded. . . . It will cost the farmer in depreciation of farm values and removal of social advantages $10 to every $1 saving he can secure . . . the institution of parcels post would mean the destruction of thousands of hamlets, the lessening of activities in innumerable towns, and cessation of growth in many flourishing cities. . . . The tremendous losses entailed by revolutionizing the existing mode of distribution would spell disaster to hosts of wholesalers and manufacturers . . . an 11-pound limit will put two-thirds of the retail merchants in all lines out of business. . . . I believe that it is all bad. I hope to goodness we do not get it in this country. If we do, God help us."[3]

While the *income tax and inheritance tax* are now almost universally relied upon for substantial revenues by the various state governments as well as the Federal authorities, until the immediate past they were regarded with extreme hostility not only by the rich but by a large proportion of the American people. The first Federal income tax was inaugurated during the Civil War and was repealed in 1872. In 1894 this tax was revived but was declared unconstitutional by the Supreme Court. Not until 1913 was the income tax amendment to the Constitution ratified and a new

[1] E. M. Phelps, *Selected Articles on Parcels Post*, p. 93.

[2] *Independent*, June 12, 1911, p. 72.

[3] *Hearings before Subcommittee on Parcel Post of the Senate Committee on Post Office and Post Roads*, 1912, pp. 424, 549, 597, 730, 812.

income tax law passed. The income tax was denounced in unrestrained language by the wealthy. On the floor of the Senate, it was assailed as "an assault on Democratic institutions. Its adoption would be the most dangerous feature of the proceedings and operations of this Government since its establishment. . . . Sir, I oppose this bill, not in the interests of the rich, but in the interests of the poor. . . . I believe it will result in degrading men. . . . The men who offer this amendment as a sop to the discontented will be swept away by the rising tide of socialism. They will discover when too late, that in overturning the barriers which separate liberty from anarchy they have liberated ten thousand furies who will sweep over them and overwhelm them in a mad procession of anarchy and disorder."[1] In his argument before the Supreme Court, Joseph H. Choate made an unrestrained assault upon the principle of an income tax: "It is far more communistic in its purposes and tendencies. . . . It is defended here upon principles as communistic, socialistic—what shall I call them— populistic as ever have been addressed to any political assembly in the world."[2]

Opposition to the *inheritance tax* has been, if possible, even more severe than to the income tax. So unanimous was public opinion in the United States that little serious study was given to the question until the very end of the nineteenth century, and "if by chance the inheritance tax was mentioned in books or pamphlets upon taxation, it was only to be dismissed with Ricardo's comment that it bore upon capital and therefore was an evil thing. Few writers dared to defend it, and they were looked upon in those days with suspicion as being 'radical.' "[3]

Opposition to *unemployment insurance* is still so widespread that it is scarcely necessary to cite illustrations. As late as March, 1933, Merle Thorpe, editor of *Nation's Business,* the official organ of the United States Chamber of Commerce, in a signed editorial entitled "With Charity for All," said: "If we have really come to enjoy poor economic health, the surest way to prolong the malady is to talk about giving direct government aid to the man who says he cannot find a job. The idea is not quite that

1 *The Forum,* March 1894, pp. 7, 13.
2 *Income Tax Cases, Supreme Court of the United States, October Term, Closing Argument by Joseph H. Choate, March 12, 1895, and March 13th, pp. 4, 7.*
3 William J. Shultz, *The Taxation of Inheritance,* p. 102.

simple, of course, but the subsidy of idleness is its essence. The deadly atrophy of ambition creeps on men fast enough without accelerating it with a financial bonus. . . . There is neither logic nor salvation in seeking the rehabilitation of men by stultifying enterprise and enfeebling spirit. In vain shall we look for the 'beneficiaries' of a system which inherently outrages the instincts of ordinary manliness." "The government was set up to be primarily a rule-maker and an umpire," asserts John E. Edgerton, President of the National Association of Manufacturers. "Public unemployment insurance would be not only in conflict with, but subversive of these tested theories of government. . . . It (the capitalist system) has never yet been improved by the sewing into it of any patches of red bunting. To say that public unemployment insurance is socialistic, and thereby antagonistic to American institutions, is to say something that every real socialist will admit."[1]

It is not necessary to cite further evidence. Daily newspapers and current periodicals are filled with attacks upon innovators and "agitators." Those who wield power and enjoy privilege are more and more resolute in their opposition to drastic social change.

VI

Christians should not be surprised by the fact that defenders of the status quo make bitter attacks upon individuals who are endeavoring to transform existing institutions. Our Lord himself was nailed to a tree because men of authority and privilege looked upon him as a public menace. His teaching and conduct were interpreted as a threat to prevailing economic practices; his words sounded treasonable to embittered patriots writhing under the heel of the invader; his treatment of other races seemed treachery to his own people; his attitude toward religious institutions appeared blasphemous to members of the hierarchy. In the name of sound economics, love of country, loyalty to race, and devotion to religion, Jesus was "removed" or "liquidated."

The irreconcilable clash between the ideal and the actual made it necessary for Jesus to choose between the new way and the old way. Conformity to prevailing customs and existing institu-

[1] Quoted in *Compulsory Unemployment Insurance*, by E. C. Buehler, compiler, pp. 287, 288.

tions was the price demanded for survival. Only by descending
to the level of his contemporaries could he avoid crucifixion. To
meet this demand was impossible for one who enjoyed such intimacy of communion with the Eternal and whose every action
was impelled by a passionate determination to do the will of God.
In the valley of temptation, Jesus faced the alternatives and
"stedfastly set his face toward Jerusalem." He could not do less
than proclaim the good news of God's reign and summon men
to live now as good members of their Father's home. To the
extent that his challenge was accepted and his hearers followed
the way of love toward God and toward man, existing social institutions would be radically transformed. The division of the
community into privileged rich and impoverished masses would
be done away with if men recognized themselves as kinspeople
under a common roof. No longer would hatred of Romans be
manifested and no longer would members of other races be treated
with contempt. Salvation would not be sought in strict observance
of the ceremonial law, but accepted as a free gift by those who
yield themselves to the reign of God. Therefore, hostility toward
Jesus was inevitable on the part of those who sought to preserve
existing customs and institutions. Just because the changes which
would follow acceptance of his way would be so drastic, nothing
short of his death would remove the terrifying threat to vested
interests.

The tragedy becomes more poignant when we remember that
Jesus was crucified by officials of Roman law in response to the
insistent demand of representatives of Hebrew religion, and that
Roman law and Hebrew religion were man's noblest creations
up to that hour. Good men in the name of law and religion hanged
upon a tree the incarnation of perfect love. When insight and
understanding are lacking, zealous attachment to justice leads to
tragedy. Persecution of innovators in the name of family or tribe
or nation knows no bounds, and when "those who turn the world
upside down" are opposed in the name of God, ruthlessness has
no limit. As we see utter love crucified between two criminals, we
are witnessing the most profound spectacle of all time and one
that is a parable of all life.

Far more vivid appears the significance of Jesus' way of life
when we meditate upon the probable consequences if he had concluded that after all a man must live and had adjusted his ideals

to the actualities of the situation by joining the patriotic Zealots. Judas Maccabeas had succeeded in winning freedom for the Jews a hundred and fifty years earlier against terrific odds, and the oldest members of the community could still remember the days when their country enjoyed liberty, political independence having been preserved until about six decades before the birth of Jesus. To a unique degree Jesus was conscious of having access to the illimitable resources of God, and one of his most severe temptations was to seek divine support in the use of unholy means. If Jesus had taken up arms against Rome and had called upon his Father for "twelve legions of angels," what would have been the outcome? Even if he had succeeded in recovering political freedom for his people, he could not have become our Lord and Redeemer, not merely because he had a unique mission but also because of the irreconcilable contradiction between his way and that of patriotic war. He could adhere to his own ideals or he could follow the method of Barabbas, but he was compelled to make a choice. If he had placed reliance in the sword, his significance in history would probably be similar to that of Judas Maccabeas and other eminent military leaders.

VII

Are Christians supposed to seek the ends which Jesus sought and to rely upon the methods which he used? Did he adopt one standard for himself and proclaim a different standard for his followers? Is the Sermon on the Mount merely a picture of life as it will be lived in the divine society, or is it a practical method of conducting human relations on earth?

It is easy to demonstrate that the teaching of Jesus has no meaning whatever if the theory is accepted that he was merely describing ideal life in the Kingdom of God. Consider his admonition to love enemies. Will there be enemies in the millenium? If a man smite you on one cheek! Will blows be dealt in heaven? Forgive your brother seventy times seven! Will sinners need forgiveness in the perfect society? Beware of false prophets! Will there be deceivers in that glad day? Blessed are they which are persecuted for righteousness' sake! Will there be persecution when God's reign is acknowledged by all his children? The teaching of Jesus is rich with meaning only when it is regarded as guidance for daily life. His way of life is a method of starting here and moving toward the ideal community. The time to love enemies is when we are threatened by enemies; the time to forgive is when we are subjected to injustice; the time to endure persecution is when we are victimized. Jesus points the way, gives guidance, and presents means of reaching the end.

The idea that he believed in a double standard of conduct, one for himself and another for his disciples, is foreign to the record of his teaching. On the contrary, the evidence is consistent and cumulative that he challenged men to follow his way of life. Undivided allegiance to the task of creating God's Home is what he expects of his followers. The purpose of life is to participate in the endeavor to awaken men to a realization of their kinship to God and to each other, and to persuade them to live every day as if the ideal society has already been created. All other objectives must be subordinated to the supreme goal, and the consequent risks and penalties must joyously be accepted. An exquisite parable makes Jesus' meaning clear: "The Kingdom of the Heavens is like a jewel merchant who is in quest of choice pearls. He finds one most costly pearl; he goes away; and though it costs all he has, he buys it."[1] And again: "The Kingdom of the Heavens is like treasure buried in the open country, which a man finds, but buries again, and, in his joy about it, goes and sells all he has and buys that piece of ground."[2]

Illustrations of His teaching concerning the quality of devotion expected are easily assembled:

> But make His Kingdom and righteousness your chief aim, and then these things shall all be given you in addition.[3]

> Not every one who says to me "Master! Master!" will enter the Kingdom of Heaven, but only he who does the will of my Father who is in Heaven.[4]

> You are the salt of the earth; but if salt has become tasteless, in what way can it regain its saltness? It is no longer good for anything but to be thrown away and trodden on by the passers by. You are the light of the world; a town cannot be hid if built on a hill-top. Nor is a lamp lighted to be put

1 Matt. 13:45, 46, Weymouth.
2 Matt. 13:44, Weymouth.
3 Matt. 6:33, Weymouth.
4 Matt. 7:21, Twentieth Century.

under a bushel, but on a lampstand; and then it gives light to all in the house. Just so let your light shine before all men, in order that they may see your holy lives and may give glory to your Father who is in Heaven.[1]

Again and again Jesus emphasizes the fact that he is not calling men to conventional mode of life. From those who have been granted vision and privilege, much is expected. Sonship and brotherhood impose tremendous responsibilities.

For I assure you that unless your righteousness greatly surpasses that of the Scribes and Pharisees, you will certainly not find entrance into the Kingdom of Heaven. . . .

For if you love only those who love you, what reward have you earned? Do not even the tax-gatherers do that? And if you salute only your near relatives, what praise is due to you? Do not even the Gentiles do the same? You, however, are to be complete in goodness, as your Heavenly Father is complete in goodness, as your Heavenly Father is complete.[2]

So if your right eye causes you to do wrong, pluck it out of your way; for it is better to have one part of your body suffer loss than to have your whole body go down to the pit. And if your right hand causes you to do wrong, cut it off and put it out of your way, for it is better to have one part of your body suffer loss than to have your whole body go down to the pit.[3]

Then Jesus looked at him and loved him, and said to him, "You lack one thing. Go, sell everything you have, and give the money to the poor, and you will have riches in heaven; then come back and follow me." But his countenance fell at that command, and he went away in deep distress, for he owned a great deal of property.[4]

While they were going along the road, a man said to Him, "I will follow you wherever you go."

But Jesus said to him, "Foxes have holes, even wild birds have roosts, but the Son of Man has nowhere to lay His head." He said to another man, "Follow me."

[1] Matt. 5:13-16, Weymouth.
[2] Matt. 5:20, 46-48, Weymouth.
[3] Matt. 5:29, 30, Williams.
[4] Mark 10:21, 22, Williams.

But he said, "Let me first go back and bury my father."

Then He answered him, "Leave the dead to bury their own dead; but you go on and continue to spread the good news of the kingdom of God."[1]

He who loves father or mother more than me is not worthy of me; and he who loves son or daughter more than me is not worthy of me. And the man who does not take his cross and follow in my steps is not worthy of me.[2]

Jesus takes it for granted that his friends will suffer persecution and encounter numerous perils. Repeatedly he warns them not to be afraid, but boldly to live day by day as if the ideal society is a present reality.

Blessed are you when they have insulted and persecuted you, and have said every cruel thing about you falsely for my sake. Be joyful and triumphant, because your reward is great in the Heavens; for so were the Prophets before you persecuted.[3]

Now, go. Remember, I am sending you out as my Messengers like lambs among wolves.[4]

Jesus not only foresees his own doom, but also tells his disciples plainly that they too will be martyred. Many crosses will be required before the Family of God can be fully established. Suffering is inescapable for those who bear the burden of their kinsmen.

No pupil is better than his teacher, and no slave is better than his master. The pupil should be satisfied to become like his teacher, and the slave should be satisfied to become like his master. If men have called the Head of the house Beelzebul, how much worse names will they heap upon the members of His family! So you must never be afraid of them; for there is nothing covered that will not be uncovered, nor a secret that will not be known. What I speak to you in the dark, tell in the light, and what you hear whispered in your ears, you must proclaim from housetops. You must never be afraid of those who kill the body, but cannot kill the soul.[5]

If any man wishes to walk in my steps, let him renounce self, take up his cross, and follow me. For whoever wishes to

1 Luke, 9:57-60, Williams.
2 Matt. 10:37, 38, Twentieth Century.
3 Matt. 5:11, 12, Weymouth.
4 Luke 10:3, Twentieth Century.
5 Matt. 10:24-28, Williams.

save his life will lose it, and whoever, for my sake and for the sake of the Good News, will lose his life shall save it.[1]

VIII

Loyalty is indispensable to the effective functioning of any valid way of life. A true patriot does not say: "I rejoice in loving my country on Mondays, Wednesdays, and Fridays; but on other days I seek satisfaction in a different way." It is not enough for a patriot to be loyal to his nation in times of prosperity and safety; he is also called upon to demonstrate his devotion in periods of adversity and danger. Mussolini demands and receives unquestioning obedience from fascists. Followers of Stalin would be executed for treason if they alternated between support of communism and capitalism.

The way of love is terribly handicapped if an individual exhibits this attitude between demonstrations of hatred. Reverence for personality is nullified by atrocious assaults upon human beings, and the melting power of forgiveness is rendered impotent by exhibitions of venom. Goodness cannot overcome evil if this procedure is adhered to only intermittently between successive endeavors to obtain revenge. Complete consistency is impossible for immature beings, but at least a minimum of constancy is required if utter chaos of life is to be avoided. Imperfect Christians are unable to avoid some degree of oscillation between opposites, but the meaning of their religion is obscured when they indulge in practices which they recognize to be flagrant violations of the way of love. There would have been no consistency and no vitality in Jesus' way of life if he had alternated between urging love of enemies and hatred of Romans. Loyalty is indispensable.

The objection is sometimes raised that since mortal man in complex situations cannot clearly understand the meaning of the way of love, and since he is still less able to act at all times in accordance with its demands, he should not depend upon the law of love as a guide to human conduct. This point of view is illustrated by reference to a competitive economic order. An individual who is engaged in a highly competitive industry cannot meet the demands of perfect love. In spite of strong desire to live in fellowship with his employees and to show reverence for personality, a

[1] Mark 8:34, 35, Twentieth Century.

manufacturer may find himself unable to pay a living wage because ruthless competition makes it impossible for him to provide an income high enough to enable workers to live decently and comfortably. A citizen soon discovers that he cannot disentangle himself completely from the iniquities of his community and nation. How can he escape responsibility for exploitation if he patronizes a store where prices are low because its employees receive mere subsistence wages? The money he pays in taxes may be used to build armaments with which to enforce imperialistic exploitation of primitive peoples.

If we find that it is impossible to avoid some practices which violate the law of love, are we thereby absolved from following that way when it is possible to do so? The judgment is sometimes expressed that since a pacifist cannot possibly disentangle himself from all the social iniquities of capitalism, it is not reasonable for him to take the position that he will never approve of or engage in war. This observation prompts a query as to the nature and degrees of personal responsibility. Consider a wartime situation: one individual is enthusiastic about the war as a necessary means of resisting evil and enlists in a machine-gun corps; another individual is opposed to the war and exerted himself to the utmost to prevent a declaration of war, but now finds himself producing potatoes which may provide strength for soldiers as they wage war. If the premise is accepted that engaging in war is wrong for a Christian, are these men equally guilty? Is indirect and involuntary participation on the same level with direct and voluntary participation? Answer in terms of these additional illustrations: does inability to avoid purchasing some goods which are produced through exploitation of human labor bring the same quality of guilt that adheres to an individual who deliberately exploits the weak for his own enrichment? Are these two citizens equally guilty: an individual who is opposed to armed intervention in other lands but who pays taxes to a government which uses his money to carry out a policy of intimidation and exploitation, and a manufacturer of munitions who conspires to produce international friction in order that his profits may be increased? If no fundamental distinction may validly be drawn between remote and unwilling participation in evil, on the one hand, and direct and conscious participation, on the other, then moral conduct is impossible and it is an utter waste of time to discuss questions of right and wrong. In a wicked and complex society, no individual can remain entirely free from indirect entanglement in corporate evils. If conduct of this character is equally reprehensible with, say, hatred and murder, then moral choice is sheer illusion. If the payment of taxes to Caesar made Jesus equally responsible with Pilate for the cruel exploitation of the Jews, then distinctions between right and wrong are so blurred that no criterions of moral conduct are visible.

But the question of moral responsibility for a Christian cannot thus be evaded. Even though we cannot reflect untarnished loyalty to the way of love, we do possess at least minimum insight and minimum power to follow moral judgments. We know that some attitudes and some practices are wrong, and sometimes it is possible for us to refrain from what we know to be wrong. To the degree that we know and to the extent that we have power, we are obliged to refrain from participation in evil. Reference to a color scheme may be illuminating. If black is used to designate attitudes and practices which ought never to be maintained and committed, and if white be used to signify dispositions and deeds which are always appropriate, then every Christian has a list of blacks and whites. Many lists of black include these: a Christian should never hate another person; he should never seek revenge; he should never look upon another person merely as a means to his own advantage; he should never commit rape and certain other sexual offences; he should never join a lynching mob and help burn at the stake another human being; he should never place a higher value upon his own personal property than upon the life of another person; he should never be content to be a parasite without responsibility for the common good; he should never fail to acknowledge his own indebtedness to God and to his fellowmen; he should never manifest disrespect and defiance toward God.

On such a list uncounted numbers of Christians place approval of war and engaging as a belligerent in war. For them war is black. As far back as 1916 I was driven to the conclusion that the method of war is not a lesser evil but a combination of the worst of all evils: indiscriminate slaughter of men, women, and children, irrespective of the character of or the degree of their guilt, by explosive, fire, poison gas, and starvation-blockade; deliberate and massive use of false propaganda to engender hatred and to arouse brutal passions; corruption of religion by using it as a justification for venom and atrocity. If the method of war is not contrary to Jesus' way of life, then no method can be contrary to it; if we are not justified in reaching the judgment that the method of war is irreconcilable with his teaching and example, then we must conclude that Jesus has no distinctive message about the treatment of evildoers.

But many Christians find it impossible to reach this conclusion after examining the record. Cumulative testimony is available showing that Jesus was concerned not only with ends but also with means, and that his way of dealing with enemies stood in sharp contrast to that of Barabbas and other patriotic Zealots. The utter irreconcilability of the war method with Jesus' way of life has been proclaimed in numerous pronouncements by religious assemblies in recent years. When representatives of many Christian communions gathered in ecumenical conference at Oxford recently, they felt impelled to declare: "War involves compulsory enmity, diabolical outrage against human personality, and a wanton distortion of the truth. War is a particular demonstration of the power of sin in this world and a defiance of the righteousness of God as revealed in Jesus Christ and him crucified. No justification of war must be allowed to conceal or minimize this fact." And in the report of this conference these words were printed in italics for emphasis.

The General Conference of the Methodist Episcopal Church in 1936 said officially: "War as we now know it is utterly destructive. It is the greatest social sin of modern times; a denial of the ideals of Christ, a violation of human personality and a threat to civilization. Therefore, we declare that the Methodist Episcopal Church as an institution does not endorse, support or purpose to participate in war. . . . We therefore petition the government of the United States to grant to members of the Methodist Episcopal Church, who may be conscientious objectors to war, the same exemption from military service as has long been granted to members of the Society of Friends and similar religious organizations."

The college of Bishops of the Methodist Episcopal Church, South, in 1935 issued an official statement on war: "We shall hold in contempt this entire nefarious war business. War as a method of settling international disputes has not one single defensible argument in its behalf. We reiterate what we said a year ago to the General Conference: 'It is archaic, belongs to the jungle period of human development and should be branded as an iniquitous and inhuman procedure. . . . It is an unhallowed thing utterly contrary to the genius of Christianity.' . . . We shall teach our children and youth to despise the unclean thing and to swear eternal loyalty to the ways of peace and to the sacred honor of their brother man."

The General Convention of the Protestant Episcopal Church said: "As stated by the last Lambeth Conference: 'War, as a method of settling international disputes, is incompatible with the teaching and example of our Lord Jesus Christ. We believe that as the Christian conscience has condemned infanticide and slavery and torture, it is now called to condemn war as an outrage on the fatherhood of God and the brotherhood of all mankind.' "[1] In a Pastoral Letter issued by the House of Bishops of the Protestant Episcopal Church the statement is made that "war is murder on a colossal scale. . . . The Christian Church cannot and will not deny loyalty and fealty to its Lord by being partner in any scheme, national or international, that contemplates the wholesale destruction of human life."[2] The Northern Baptist Convention went on record: "War is the supreme social sin, and so long as the war system is maintained there can be no safety for our homes or for our civilization and no realization of the kingdom of heaven on earth."[3] The Synod of the Reformed Presbyterian Church declared: "War is essentially and inherently a supreme violation of the teachings and spirit of Jesus . . . as a method for securing national ends, however just and right, is antichristian."[4]

The International Convention of the Disciples of Christ said: "We believe that war is pagan, futile, and destructive of the spiritual values for which the churches of Christ stand . . . we therefore dissociate ourselves from war and the war system, and hereby serve notice to whom it may concern that we never again expect to bless or sanction war."[5] The Universalist Convention of California resolved: "That the Universalist principles of the Fatherhood of God and the Brotherhood of Man cannot be reconciled with the deliberate taking of life in war. That, since our country has renounced all war, we urge our people to adopt the historical position of the Friends, and take the attitude of conscientious

[1] Protestant Episcopal Church, General Convention, 1931.
[2] Quoted in the *Living Church*, Nov. 3, 1934.
[3] Northern Baptist Convention, 1928.
[4] Reformed Presbyterian Church, Synod, 1924.
[5] Quoted in *The Christian Century*, Oct. 31, 1934.

objection to all war. That the faith of the Universalist Church should be recognized by all governmental agencies in the same way as they accept the belief of the Society of Friends."

The General Council of Congregational and Christian Churches thus went on record: "The cleavage.between the way of Jesus and the system of war is clear. We of this council are convinced that we must now make this declaration, 'The church is through with war!' We of this council call upon the people of our churches to renounce war and all its works and ways and to refuse to support, sanction or bless it."[1] The 1934 General Assembly of the Presbyterian Church in the U. S. A. "declares anew its break with the entire war system. . . . Christians cannot give their support to war as a method of carrying on international conflict." The Southern Presbyterian Church asserts that "the church should never again bless a war, or be used as an instrument in the promotion of war."[2]

A *Manifesto Against War* was released on Armistice Day, 1934, under the auspices of the Church Peace Union. This forthright declaration was signed by more than 200 outstanding citizens of the United States, *including 60 bishops and 45 college presidents*. Here is a quotation from this pronouncement: "The time has come when organized religion must proclaim that never again shall war be waged under the sanction of the Church. . . . With the ruins of the last war piled high at its feet the Church should solemnly declare herself the implacable enemy of war. . . . We have had in our generation an appalling revelation of the true nature of war. War is not what it was. When science added the airplane, the submarine and poison gas, warfare entered on a new stage. With the advent of poison gas and bacteriological germs it laid aside the last vestige of decency. War has always been bloody and brutal. It is now an atrocity. . . . War is as futile as it is barbarous. . . . There is no victor. All are defeated. . . . Modern war is suicide. The sword is so sharp that a nation can cut not only the throats of its neighbors but its own throat also. Civilization itself is in jeopardy."

The Ohio State Pastors' Conference asserted: "We are convinced that war is un-Christian, futile, and suicidal, and we renounce complete the whole war system. We will never again sanction or participate in any war. We will not use our pulpits or

[1] General Council, 1934.
[2] General Assembly, 1929.

classrooms as recruiting stations. We set ourselves to educate and lead youth in the principles and practice of goodwill, justice, understanding, brotherhood, and peace. We will not give our financial or moral support to any war."[1] The National Study Conference on the Churches and World Peace declared: "War denies the fatherhood of God, scorns the brotherhood of man, mocks the sacredness of human life, is merciless to helpless women and children, uses falsehood, ignores justice, releases the passions, and cultivates hate. War means everything that Jesus did not mean, and means nothing that he did mean. We therefore hold that the Churches should condemn resort to the war-system as sin and should henceforth refuse, as institutions, to sanction it or to be used as agencies in its support."[2] While the Commission on International Justice and Goodwill of the Federal Council of the Churches of Christ in America said bluntly: "The war system of the nations is the outstanding evil of present-day civilization. It is the most ominous antichristian phase of modern life."[3]

Out of 20,870 clergymen who in 1934 replied to a questionnaire, 12,904 said "yes" to this question: "Are you personally prepared to state that it is your present purpose not to sanction any future war or participate as an armed combatant?" While 13,997 answered affirmatively: "Do you believe that the churches of America should now go on record as refusing to sanction or support any future war?"[4]

Thus many Christians are driven inescapably to the judgment that they should never approve of the method of war and should never go to war under any circumstances. Many of us are constrained to proclaim our resolute rejection of the method of war, even though we are unavoidably entangled in many of war's roots and even if we are unable to escape the coils of other forms of sin. We must take confident action with regard to blacks and whites even though we are confused about light grays and dark grays and are relatively impotent in dealing immediately with light browns and dark browns. Through constant saturation of self with the mind and spirit of Christ and through rigorous analysis of specific

[1] *The Nation, February* 10, 1932, p. 158.
[2] National Study Conference on the Churches and World Peace, 1929.
[3] *A Message to the Churches of Christ in America from the Federal Council's Commission on International Justice and Goodwill,* 1924.
[4] See *The World Tomorrow,* May 10, 1934, for an exhaustive analysis of the replies to 15 questions on international and economic questions.

situations, it is possible progressively to extend the zones of black and white and to be increasingly confident of the validity of our procedure over wider and wider ranges of life. And in the meantime we must move forward in a spirit of contrition, constantly manifesting anguish of soul because of inextricable entanglements in corporate iniquities and because of frequent exhibitions of treason to the highest good that we can perceive.

IX

Loyalty demands not only the negative attitude of refusal to engage in flagrant violations of the way of love but also positive endeavor to change the actual into the ideal, even when confronted with opposition and persecution. Cumulative evidence has already been presented showing the persistent hostility to basic changes in the structure of society. Individuals and groups which desire for various reasons to preserve the status quo are certain to view with alarm the actions of innovators, and in proportion to the intensity of their fears are likely to become ruthless in their efforts to remove threats to their own security.

This generation of radicals is especially subject to attack because in times of social convulsion fears are deeper and passions are hotter. Severe tremors are shaking the very foundations of the present economic order, with the result that even the most powerful beneficiaries of the existing system are overwhelmed with a feeling of insecurity and are terribly apprehensive about the future. International lawlessness and aggression are so widespread that peoples everywhere are afraid to reduce armaments, and certain types of patriots feel obliged to combat what they regard as the subversive and treasonable activities of pacifists.

Members of this generation who are endeavoring to bring about vital changes in the structure of society cannot hope to escape the charge that they are public enemies. An effective device used in every period is found in the calling of names, the pinning of labels, the hurling of epithets. The tendency is to pick out the most feared type and then lump together under this designation all individuals who refuse to acquiesce in the status quo. The word "communist" has been worked overtime as a bludgeon with which to beat down non-conformity to existing practices. During the past century this epithet has been hurled at almost every reformer.

The individuals who propose freedom for the slaves "are atheists, socialists, communists, red republicans, jacobins." They are "advocates of 'free love,' the 'Socialists,' the Infidels, the "Red Republicans.' An editor described the saintly Susan B. Anthony as "a revolutionist, aiming at nothing less than the breaking up of the very foundations of society. . . . The whole plan is coarse, sensual and agrarian, the worst phase of French infidelity and communism." The proposed child labor amendment to the Constitution of the United States was described by one Senator as "a communistic, Bolshevistic scheme," while another Senator described it as "socialistic, bolshevistic, and I would almost say, anarchistic. . . . It assassinates democracy, and upon its grave establishes a hybrid monstrosity."

At the present time there is a widespread tendency to lump together under the designation "communists" all opponents of the status quo. Many newspapers are engaged in a vigorous endeavor to convince their readers that it is un-American and subversive to advocate basic changes in the structure of society. Interpreting "communism" in highly distorted language, they seek to convince the public that "communists," that is, persons advocating radical social change, are depraved and vicious "agitators" or at best are deluded victims of unscrupulous conspirators. This trend has gone so far as to include President Roosevelt among the "communistic" enemies of the American way of life. So successful has this propaganda been that large numbers of citizens are sincerely convinced that the Executive Office in Washington is swarming with public enemies who are conspiring to destroy democracy and establish a "communist" dictatorship. How little foundation there is for this charge becomes evident when the New Deal is compared with the policies of the Tory Government of Great Britain. It is easy to demonstrate that the practices of the Chamberlain administration are in many respects more radical than the New Deal. President Roosevelt, for example, has not even remotely suggested the wisdom of immediate public ownership of coal mines; whereas the Tories of Great Britain are now engaged in socializing the coal industry of that country. The general policy of public ownership is much further advanced in the British Isles than in the United States; taxes for the average man are much heavier and the public debt is relatively higher than in America.

The obligation resting upon innovators to proceed resolutely in the face of bitter opposition is inescapable. The contrast between the ideal and the actual is flagrant; the status quo is always defended ruthlessly; the required changes can be brought about only by heroic and sacrificial loyalty. If they called the master "Beelzebub" they will call his disciples equivalent names. Several times Jesus warned his friends that loyalty to the new way would bring persecution and suffering. Listen to his farewell conversation with his intimate circle of disciples and observe the manner in which he stresses alternately suffering and joy: "I have told you all this so that my own joy may be yours, and that your joy may be complete. This is my command—Love one another, as I have loved you. No one can give greater proof of love than by laying down his life for his friends."[1]

"Thus I command you to love one another. If the world hates you, remember that it has first had me as the fixed object of its hatred. If you belonged to the world, the world would love its own property. But because you do not belong to the world, and I have chosen you out of the world—for that reason the world hates you. Bear in mind what I said to you, 'A servant is not superior to his master.' If they have persecuted me, they will also persecute you: if they have obeyed my teaching, they will obey yours also. But they will inflict all this suffering upon you on account of your bearing my name—because they do not know Him who sent me."[2]

"When the Advocate is come whom I will send to you from the Father's presence—the Spirit of Truth who comes forth from the Father's presence—He will be a witness concerning me. And you also are witnesses, because you have been with me from the first. These things I have spoken to you in order to clear stumbling-blocks out of your path. You will be excluded from the synagogues; nay more, the time is coming when any one who has murdered one of you will suppose he is offering service to God. And they will do these things because they have failed to recognize the Father and to discover who I am. But I have spoken these things to you in order that when the time for their accomplishment comes you may remember them, and may recollect that I told you."[3]

So much suffering is recorded in the New Testament that it might well be referred to as a book of martyrs. Yet, no volume in

[1] John 15:11-13, Twentieth Century.
[2] John 15:17-21, Weymouth.
[3] John 15:26-16:4, Weymouth.

all literature sounds more clearly and continuously the note of joyous triumph. This paradox possesses such immeasurable significance for our present discussion that it seems advisable to assemble a number of the most striking of these passages. Let the reader keep constantly in mind the fact that these words of exultation come from the lips of followers of the crucified Nazarene who themselves were subjected to all manner of persecution:

Now at last I can rejoice in my sufferings on your behalf, and in my own person I supplement the afflictions endured by the Christ.[1]

Yet all that was gain to me—for Christ's sake I have reckoned it loss. Nay, I even reckon all things as pure loss because of the priceless privilege of knowing Christ Jesus my Lord. And for His sake I have suffered the loss of everything, and reckon it all as mere refuse, in order that I may win Christ and be found in union with Him, not having a righteousness of my own, derived from the law, but that which arises from faith in Christ—the righteousness which comes from God through faith. I long to know Christ and the power which is in His resurrection, and to share in His sufferings and die even as He died; in the hope that I may attain to the resurrection among the dead.[2]

The Spirit Himself bears witness, along with our own spirits, to the fact that we are children of God; and if children, then heirs too—heirs of God and co-heirs with Christ; if indeed we are sharers in Christ's sufferings, in order that we may also be sharers in His Glory. Why, what we now suffer I count as nothing in comparison with the glory which is soon to be manifested in us. . . .

What then shall we say to this? If God is on our side, who is there to appear against us? He who did not withhold even His own Son, but gave Him up for all of us, will he not also with Him freely give us all things? Who shall impeach those whom God has chosen? God declares them free from guilt. Who is there to condemn them? Christ Jesus died, or rather has risen to life again. He is also at the right hand of God, and is interceding for us. Who shall separate us from Christ's love? Shall affliction or distress, persecution or hunger, naked-

[1] Colossians 1:24, Twentieth Century.
[2] Philippians 3-7-11, Weymouth.

ness or danger or the sword? As it stands written in the Scripture,

For Thy Sake They Are, All Day Long Trying To Kill Us. We Have Been Looked Upon As Sheep Destined For Slaughter (Ps. xliv. 22).

Yet amid all these things we are more than conquerors through Him who has loved us. For I am convinced that neither death nor life, neither the lower ranks of evil angels nor the higher, neither things present nor things future, nor the forces of nature, nor height nor depth, nor any other created thing, will be able to separate us from the love of God which rests upon us in Christ Jesus our Lord.[1]

Yes, even if I am pouring out my life as a libation on the sacrifice and service your faith is rendering, I am glad to do so and congratulate you all upon it; you too must do likewise, be glad of it and congratulate me.[2]

My Brothers, whatever may be the temptations that beset you from time to time, always regard them as a reason for rejoicing, knowing, as you do, that the testing of your faith develops endurance. And let endurance do its work perfectly, so that you may be altogether perfect, and in no respect deficient.

If one of you is deficient in wisdom, let him ask wisdom from the God who gives freely to every one without reproaches, and it will be given to him. But let him ask with confidence, never doubting; for the man who doubts is like a wave of the sea driven hither and thither at the mercy of the wind—such a man must not expect that he will receive anything from the Lord, vacillating as he is, irresolute at every turn.[3]

Therefore, surrounded as we are by such a vast cloud of witnesses, let us fling aside every encumbrance and the sin that so readily entangles our feet. And let us run with patient endurance the race that lies before us, simply fixing our gaze upon Jesus, our Prince Leader in the faith, who will also award us the prize. He, for the sake of the joy which lay before Him, patiently endured the cross, looking with contempt upon its

[1] Romans 8:16-18, 31-39, Weymouth.
[2] Philippians 2:17, 18, Williams.
[3] James 1:2-8. Twentieth Century.

shame, and afterwards seated Himself—where He still sits—at the right hand of the throne of God.

Therefore, if you would escape becoming weary and faint-hearted, compare your own sufferings with those of Him who endured such hostility directed against Him by sinners. In your struggle against sin you have not yet resisted so as to endanger your lives.[1]

But to God be the thanks who in Christ ever heads our triumphal procession, and by our hands waves in every place that sweet incense, the knowledge of Him. For we are a fragrance of Christ grateful to God in those whom He is saving and in those who are perishing.[2]

His commands are not burdensome, for every child of God continues to conquer the world. Our faith is the victory that has conquered the world. Now who is it that continues to conquer the world, if it is not the person who believes that Jesus is the Son of God?[3]

Now to Him who is able to keep you from stumbling and to make you stand in His glorious presence faultless and full of triumphant of joy—to the only God our Saviour, through Jesus Christ our Lord, be glory, majesty, might, and authority, as it was before all time, both now and forever and ever. Amen.[4]

[1] Hebrews 12:1-4, Weymouth.
[2] 2 Corinthians 2:14, 15, Weymouth.
[3] 1 John 5:3-6, Williams.
[4] Jude 24, Williams.

Chapter VI

Seek Comradeship in Thought and Prayer and Action

HUMAN nature being what it is, potentially this and potentially that, human conduct is determined by the relative impact of various outward and inward stimuli. And of all the forces which pull upward, fellowship is among the most magnetic. If the pressure to be covetous and belligerent is to be resisted, companionship with other persons who are endeavoring to be generous and cooperative is essential. Especially urgent is the need for comradeship if an individual refuses to conform to prevailing attitudes and practices and resolutely seeks to transform existing institutions. Loneliness and doubt and discouragement will overwhelm an innovator unless he is sustained by friendship.

That an individual may become a self-made and self-sustained man is a dangerous delusion. We are what we are stimulated to become by the impact of sensations and ideas and ideals which pour in upon us from a thousand sources. The power of selection which may be exercised over a wide territory enables us in considerable measure to shape our own destiny, but to a far greater degree than is generally realized we are products of society. One of the most significant choices we are able to make is that of selecting intimate friends, although the range of possibility is sharply limited by environmental factors. Almost impossible to exaggerate is the importance of moving into a circle of comrades who are devoted to a great cause and who are mutually stimulating one another to clearer thought and nobler living. "I suggest that the modern cultivated person is *over-estimating* his power of maintaining contact with the realm of spiritual in his present condition," writes Lawrence Hyde. "He imagines in his self-sufficiency that he can get along satisfactorily without rites and ceremonies, without private disciplines, without associating himself on a religious basis with a group of his fellowmen. But the plain fact is that he cannot —unless he is a very exceptional person indeed. The great mass of more highly educated men and women today—those anyway of a more spiritual type—are psychologically unstable, restless, unfulfilled, and morbidly self-conscious." [1]

The rich potentialities of corporate discussion and meditation are thus described by Miss Maude Royden: "For several years I have belonged to a little society which meets every week and spends a considerable time in silence. We have a subject in common, which is some difficulty that has arisen in our lives, or some 'hard saying' of Jesus Christ, or something that perplexes us. We decide to give our time to this particular difficulty, or saying, or problem. We sit in silence, waiting upon God, and if after a certain time any one of us has received any light, it is his or her duty to tell us. If anyone speaks, it is our duty to think over what they have said before we either agree with it or contradict it. That is a wonderful method. It was not my invention, of course, and we sometimes forget it, or fail to pursue it because it is difficult, but I commend it as a real psychological discovery. If you are really trying to find the truth, not trying to score off somebody else, not trying to push your own idea, but really trying to find the truth, sit and think about it together. When somebody speaks, your instinct almost at once is either to agree or to disagree. But if you wait a little, and think over what has been said, you will constantly find that there was some truth in it, and some truth that was new to you, though perhaps if you had commented on it at once, you would have disagreed with it or thought it a truism. If you take hold of it and give it the hospitality of your mind you will see that there is some truth in it. If you all work together on these lines, you get some light."

Dr. E. Stanley Jones, out of wide experience in many parts of the earth, writes: "Many Group Movements with varying emphases have sprung up throughout the world—the Oxford Groups, the Cambridge Groups, the Burma Gospel Team Groups, Kagawa's Fellowship of the Friends of Jesus Group, the Christian Ashram Group Movement in India, and various other types. I cannot help but feel that God's Spirit has been raising up these Groups to most particular needs. Not that I think that any one of them has the complete truth, but each does seem to have some particular phase of truth—partly neglected by others. The difficulty comes when

[1] Lawrence Hyde, *Prospects of Humanism.* Published by Charles Scribner's Sons, New York.

each becomes exclusive and self-righteous. Then the lilies that fester smell worse than common ordinary weeds. But God is speaking to this generation through groups. He spoke to the first generation through groups. The fact is that Jesus formed a Group Movement when He and His disciples fellowshiped and worked together. It was out of that fellowship that the New Testament came. The play of mind upon mind, of attitude upon attitude, of method upon method, of life upon life brought forth a body of common ideas and attitudes. These became the New Testament. Individual writers wrote them down, but the Christian groups produced them in their interaction with the Spirit of God and with each other. When the disciples said, 'It seemed good to the Holy Ghost and to us,' they could have said it not merely in reference to that particular decision, but in reference to the whole body of truth and attitude which was growing up. That Group had become not merely a collection of men, but an organism of the Holy Spirit. He was expressing His mind and redemptive purposes through that Group. Today God guides the individual through such closely knit fellowships as the groups. Each individual needs the correction and sustenance of some such group. For the group checks up and tends to keep the individual guidance from going astray. So God often guides through a group." [1]

As a member of a dynamic religious group, Dr. Hornell Hart shares his experiences in this summary: "For centuries, the Society of Friends (Quakers) have found the presence of God in silent worship, and have sought the guidance of the Inner Light through group meditation. By this communion with the unseen they became outstanding forces for peace, for liberation of slaves, for the freedom of womankind, for prison reform, and for economic goodwill. In their business sessions, Friends who still follow the early methods begin with a period of collective silent meditation. Then those who feel 'a concern' express it. Other Friends give their reactions, in the light of the Spirit. Renewed silence is employed, at times, when perplexities arise. The clerk waits until the sense of the meeting begins to take form in his mind. Then he writes out a tentative minute and reads it to the meeting. Friends express their approval or their wish for modification. No vote is taken. If substantial agreement develops, those who have been

[1] E. Stanley Jones, *Victorious Living*. Published by the Abingdon Press, New York.

unfavorable withdraw their opposition, and the minute is entered as a record of the action of the meeting. But if strong opposition continues, those favoring the minute ask to have it lie over until the meeting can be of one mind. The method is not perfect, but in so far as it embodies the attitude of seeking the unity of the Spirit, it succeeds. The Society of Friends has had power to the degree that it has been faithful to the leadings of the Spirit of Truth and of Love. In their meetings for worship, the Friends who have continued in the original Quaker methods sit in silence, waiting for the Spirit to move some one of their number with a message. Sometimes no one speaks during the entire hour; sometimes several utter what has come into their inner consciousness. Sometimes talkative people, with no deep spiritual experience, seize the opportunity for a harangue. Sometimes stereotyped phrases follow one another mechanically. But often the worshipers are led up to heights of inspiration and insight by some sincere and inspired utterance. Sometimes the silence is dead, because those who participate are drowsing, or letting their thoughts wander idly. At other times the spiritual power is almost tangible." [1]

The Fellowship of Reconciliation is made up of individuals in many countries who are attempting seriously to follow Jesus' way of life.[2] It began in England soon after the outbreak of the World War as a movement of protest against war and of faith in a better way than violence for the solution of all conflict. Although its members do not bind themselves to any exact form of words: "They refuse to participate in any war, or to sanction military preparations; they work to abolish war and to foster good will among nations, races and classes; they strive to build a social order which will suffer no individual or group to be exploited for the profit or pleasure of another, and which will assure to all the means for realizing the best possibilities of life; they advocate such ways of dealing with offenders against society as shall transform the wrong-doer rather than inflict retributive punishment; they endeavor to show reverence for personality—in the home, in the education of children, in association with those of other classes, nationalities and races; they seek to avoid bitterness and contention,

[1] Hornell Hart, *Living Religion*, pp. 50, 51. Published by The Abingdon Press, New York.

[2] The office of the Fellowship of Reconciliation in the United States is located at 2929 Broadway, New York City.

and to maintain the spirit of self-giving love while engaged in the struggle to achieve these purposes. It is intended that members shall work out these purposes in their own ways. There is no uniform program of social reconstruction to which all are committed. The movement depends not upon a large number of nominal adherents, but upon those who, accepting the principles fully for themselves, will give time individually and in groups to thinking out what is implied, and will set themselves seriously to apply their conclusions. Such an endeavor inevitably brings a consciousness of insufficiency; but strength and wisdom, far beyond the limits of our present experience, are available to all who open their lives to the leading of the Spirit of God." Members of the Fellowship are endeavoring to make real Jesus' way of unswerving goodwill in the areas of international problems, economic affairs, race relations, and the treatment of criminals.

Fellowship has ever been one of the most precious means of grace. The flow of God's love into our lives frequently comes through creative comradeship with His children. Exhilaration surges through us when we are submerged in the stream of loving companionship. Concerning the experiences of the early Christians, Dr. Johannes Weiss writes: "A tempestuous enthusiasm, an overwhelming intensity of feeling, an immediate awareness of the presence of God, an incomparable sense of power and an irresistible control over the will and inner spirit and even the physical condition of other men—these are ineradicable features of historic early Christianity. . . . The deep inner confidence in God as the Father, which radiated from Jesus' person and shone out from his unforgettable sayings, now took full possession of their souls; after the terrific trial by fire which it had undergone, this faith emerged once more like a phoenix, a joyous and unshakable trust. The moral earnestness, which owed its original impulse to this faith, now became a renewed strength for which love and self-discipline, sacrifice and even the facing of martyrdom were an easy task. In brief, Jesus' power over their souls was now at last fully realized. This is the personal and moral basis of the overpowering enthusiasm which welled up among them and overflowed like a flood into the spiritual life of mankind." [1]

[1] Johannes Weiss, *The History of Primitive Christianity.* Published by Wilson-Erickson, Inc., New York.

II

The realization that one's own life is a link in a long chain of builders of the good society stretching across the centuries and encircling the globe brings perspective and courage and joy. Biography often becomes a source of power. It is thrilling to be reminded that one is engaged in the same task which consumed the colossal energies of John Wesley. Here is his almost incredible record:

He traveled 250,000 miles, chiefly on horseback, averaging 20 miles per day for 40 years, in the days before Fords and streamliners hurled passengers furiously through space.

He preached more than 40,000 sermons.

He produced more than 400 books, as author, editor, and translator, while his own distinctive writings fill upwards of 25 massive volumes. And all this in his own handwriting!

He knew ten languages and made good use of them: Arabic, Hebrew, Greek, Latin, French, Italian, Spanish, German, Dutch, English.

He planted, watered and nourished innumerable religious groups, which ultimately became the mighty world-wide Methodist Church.

At the age of 83 he was annoyed by the discovery that he could not write for more than 15 hours a day without hurting his eyes, and at the age of 86 he was ashamed to admit that he could not easily preach more than twice a day! We notice in his diary an increasing tendency to lie in bed in the morning, sometimes as late as 5:30 A.M. In his 86th year he preached in almost every shire in England and Wales, and often rode from 30 to 50 miles per day.

This awareness that one is a member of an endless caravan of kindred spirits is vividly reflected in the inspiring autobiography of Miss Vida Scudder, professor in Wellesley College for nearly half a century, promoter of social settlement houses, biographer and devotee of St. Francis and St. Catherine, ardent socialist and Christian revolutionist.[1] The Preamble to this revealing pilgrimage opens with these words: "It is in this Florentine gallery that I begin to think of releasing into words, so far as possible, the story of my spirit. Around me spreads the vision of the past. Serenely,

[1] Vida Dutton Scudder, *On Journey*. Published by E. P. Dutton and Company, New York.

worshiping saints of every age venerate the Madonna, adore the Crucified. . . . All the human race is here; all the Mysteries; and much history happening at once. . . . Does my little modern self, with eyes too often sealed to heavenly things, belong in this room with all these Holy Ones? Yes, I claim my place. There are many people on these walls who are not holy. I don't mean the Roman soldiers at the Crucifixion; I refuse to be counted among them. Or even the attendants on the Nativity kings, who are too romantic for me. But crowds of little citizens in the background, onlookers merely; or, farther away, plain folk working in the fields, busy with tasks or pleasures, unaware often of marvels close at hand. Each life of supreme importance to itself; and supremely interesting, to anyone with eyes to see. I propose to press in among them, insignificant as I am, playing my own part in this World Redeemed. . . . The walls widen; they present the whole pageant of history, the procession of the human race. I am no onlooker; I am one of the actors, and I am going to tell my little story in the presence of all these Blessed Ones. May it be vouchsafed me to tell how my blind eyes have been opened to behold the spiritual drama, eternal behind this shifting scene of sense and time."

Miss Scudder then contrasts this sense of communion with saint and sinner with her distress of soul on another occasion: "Memory travels to a great room in an American institution of learning, where I was lecturing not many months ago. The startling murals on the walls are not likely, once seen, to be forgotten. They too, like these walls in Florence, present the pageant of human life. Or rather, as I said to the artist, the rout of the capitalistic order. Here, experience disintegrates in aimless conflicts and futile activities. We see the tape of the stock exchange; fat hands, making deposits at a bank window; hungry hands, quivering toward the soup of the bread-line. We see the Subway, with a big man absorbed in a pornographic Comic, and pallid girls hanging to straps; brutalized men, loading an ocean liner; a Salvation Army lassie, exhorting in vain. A night club, a speakeasy. A phantasmagoria of modern life, relentless, powerful. Here is not the semblance of a world redeemed."

To the task of helping to transform the actual into the ideal, Miss Scudder has devoted her long and creative life, and the reading of her story is a source of illumination and strength. Something of her spirit is reflected in these sentences: "I felt the social order

in which we moved to be poisoned at the roots, beneath its smooth
suave surface. . . . I became increasingly convinced that no revolution could bring ultimate salvation unless it proceeded from a
Christian conception of man. Before long, the word Humanism was
much on men's lips; but I was persuaded that humanity could
never pull itself up by its own bootstraps, and turned more and
more to seek my foundations in a full Christian philosophy. . . .
Realizing the dangerous, the revolutionary elements in the teaching
of Jesus, one hardly knows what to say to those who all down
the centuries try to find in the Gospels and in the Christian religion,
a defense of the status quo. . . . One morning at Adelynrood, at
the early Eucharist, not planning to receive, I knelt at the back of
the chapel. The voice of the celebrant was exceptionally clear to
my dull old ears. But suddenly came up a tumultous storm. Rain
thundered on the roof, winds howled, the world darkened. For
the moment, everything except consciousness of the storm was
blotted out. Then, after a few dazed instants, I heard again the
Voice at the altar. Much farther away it seemed, but steadily clear
and audible through the tumult of the elements. The sacred words
of the aspiration of the ages; the supreme words of Institution.
It was to me the Voice of the Church Eternal; persisting through
the passing storms of Time." [1]

Few individuals in any country in any century have explored
more thoroughly the depths of fellowship than has been done by
Charles F. Andrews, intimate comrade of Mahatma Gandhi and
Rabindranath Tagore. Perhaps no Anglo-Saxon of this generation
has caught so completely the spirit of St. Francis of Assisi and
has incarnated so fully the compassion of Christ as this saintly
friend of man who has ministered so creatively in India, South
Africa, Australia, Japan, China, the United States and his own
British Isles. A glowing tribute from Mr. Gandhi is reproduced
on an accompanying page.

Some years ago Mr. Andrews described in these vivid words his
early contacts with the Mahatma: "While the great movement of
Indian renaissance has been growing in depth and volume, year
after year, there has been one constant longing in my heart which
I have tried in different ways and at different times to put into
words. This intense longing has been that I might live to see this

[1] *Ibid.*, pp. 279, 306, 368, 370.

Segaon,

17·10·39   Wardha c. p.

India

Dear Friend ———

I am glad you are liberally
taking passages from C. F. A's pen in
your anthology of devotional literature.
For Charlie Andrews is a man of
prayer & deep faith. He is a Christian
to the marrow, but his Christ is
not the Jesus Christ of a narrow
sect. His Christ is the Anointed
of humanity. He sees Him in
Ramakrishna Chaitanya and many
other Teachers whom I can name
& who are of other faiths. We
in India, who know him, call
him Deenbandhu, Friend of the
Afflicted. Our friendship is of long
standing; we are like blood-brothers.
There are no secrets between
us. Charlie is simple as a
child, forgiving & generous to

a fault He is loving & lovable
like a woman who is purity
personified   In jest I call him
half woman & half man —
But I mean it

yours sincerely,

M. K. Gandhi

Kirby Page Esq.
La Habra
California

new movement in Indian life and thought tending more and more toward the 'things that are of God.' In other words, I have prayed not for India's sake alone but for the sake of humanity as a whole that the merely national and political spheres might not occupy the sole attention of the leaders, but that an open pathway might be found which should lead to a fresh realization of the vision of God. . . . With Mahatma Gandhi, from the very first, I felt that there had come into the world not only a new saintly personality but also a new religious message. I had found this to be true in the South African struggle itself. The scene out there reminded me of nothing so much as the early days of the Christian Church when the disciples of Jesus had everything in common. There was a sweetness and beauty that was inexpressible amid the sordid lust for gold and racial hatred of the Rand. Never can I forget the first evening which I spent in his religious retreat at Phoenix. Mahatma Gandhi was there with the little children round him whom he loved. One baby girl, an 'untouchable,' nestled in his arms and shared her place there with a weak little invalid Mohammedan boy. A young Zulu Christian woman had come over from the Zulu mission compound as a most welcome guest, and an elderly Kaffir woman was the friend and servant of us all. European comrades, Mr. Polak and Mr. Kallenbach, who had been with Mahatma Gandhi in gaol, were there also. Every word that was spoken about General Smuts and the Boers and the British in Natal was kindly and considerate. The only wealth in Phoenix Asram was the wealth of overflowing love."

This messenger of reconciliation has devoted much time to the effort to break down barriers erected by white men against colored peoples. In an article on "Christ and Race," he outlined some of his convictions and related some of his experiences:[1] "White racialism has infected the interior of the Christian Church. That is to me the crowning horror. When I was in South Africa, in 1913-1914, Mahatma Gandhi was refused admission to a Christian church though it was the Christmas season of peace and goodwill. An Indian Christian would have received exactly the same treatment at that particular church, and so would a Chinese Christian or an African Christian. We have a professing religion today which calls itself Christian but does not acknowledge the

[1] *The World Tomorrow*, April, 1929. See also the issue of March, 1929.

ultimate Christian principle of racial equality. It cannot truly say: 'We are all "one humanity" in Christ Jesus.' It cannot repeat this because it does not believe in it and does not practice it over large areas.

"Again and again when we go abroad—and even sometimes in England and America—the question is put to us by those who belong to other religions: 'Why do you Christians alone uphold racial inequality and judge men according to the color of their skin?' We are told again that the Christian religion is the religion of the White man and that it is a symbol of domination. If we protest and assert vehemently that Christ never taught such things, we face the fact that Christ's followers actually practice them on such a large scale that they fill the whole picture. They ask us the searching question: 'Did not Christ say "By their fruits shall ye know them? Can men gather grapes of thorns or figs of thistles?"' It is an African proverb which says: 'Your deeds speak so loud to me, that I cannot hear what your words say.' Surely in Africa our deeds have spoken so loud that our professions carry no weight at all. It is these loud-speakers all over the world—the imperial *deeds* of Christendom—which trumpet forth our sins. No wonder that the still small voice of the Holy Spirit cannot be heard. No wonder that the portrait of the meek and lowly Christ remains unknown and unloved.

"What is needed today is a revival of the spirit of martyrdom. That great word 'marytrdom' has a fine background and a noble meaning. It signifies witness in action. It is only those who have carried their faith to the test of action, those who have lived for their faith with the joyful consciousness that at any moment they might be called upon to die for it—it is only such men and women who are able to hold their own position without wavering when the crucial test comes. It is only these who can wrest victory out of defeat. There must be no compromise, no betrayal, no looking back. The test is crucial, for it is always, in some way or other, the test of the Cross. We can not, we must not, we dare not swerve one hair's breadth from the great charter of human solidarity and human redemption, which Christ himself has given us: In Him there can be neither Jew nor Greek, barbarian, Scythian, bond nor free, for all are one Man in Christ Jesus."

III

The cumulative testimony of biography and contemporary observation reveals clearly the illimitable power inherent in fellowship of devoted comrades in a great cause. Through fellowship in thought and prayer and action an individual finds himself flooded with illuminating and surcharged with power. But a sharp warning must be sounded: fellowship in thought and prayer must find expression in common endeavor to transform vicious social practices and unjust social institutions. The deepest comradeship can be entered into only by the payment of a heavy price. This truth is burned into our consciousness by vivid words of Archibald MacLeish in his "Speech to those who say Comrade:"

The brotherhood is not by the blood certainly:
But neither are men brothers by speech—by saying so:
Men are brothers by life lived and are hurt for it:

Hunger and hurt are the great begetters of brotherhood:
Humiliation has gotten much love:
Danger I say is the nobler father and mother: . . .

Who are the born brothers in truth? The puddlers
Scorched by the same flame in the same foundries:
Those who have spit on the same boards with the blood in it:

Ridden the same rivers with green logs:
Fought the police in the parks of the same cities:
Grinned for the same blows: the same flogging:

Veterans out of the same ships—factories—
Expeditions for fame: the founders of continents:
Those that hid in Geneva a time back:

Those that have hidden and hunted and all such—
Fought together: labored together: they carry the
Common look like a card and they pass touching.

Brotherhood! No word said can make you brothers!
Brotherhood only the brave earn and by danger or
Harm or by bearing hurt and by no other.

Brotherhood here in the strange world is the rich and
Rarest giving of life and the most valued:
Not to be had for a word or a week's wishing.[1]

IV

The price that must be paid for the most dynamic comradeship
has never been more vividly emphasized than in the words of
Jesus. Here is the startling summary of the challenge which he
held before his disciples, as assembled by Dr. Hornell Hart:[2]

1. The true disciple must give up his intellectual pride and self-
complacency, becoming repentant, humble, teachable, open-minded.
Read Matthew 18. 1-4; Luke 10. 21; 18. 9-14. (See also Matthew
5. 5; 7. 1-5; Mark 10. 15; Luke 6. 41-42; 15. 11-32; John 5. 14;
I Corinthians 1. 26-29.)

2. He must triumph, inwardly as well as outwardly, over the
lusts and greeds of his physical body. Read Matthew 5. 8; 15.
19-20; Galatians 5. 16-21. (See also Matthew 5. 27-28; 19. 11-12.)

3. He must stop worrying about his material needs; he must
trust himself to the Divine Love. Read Matthew 6. 25-34; Luke
11. 2-13.

4. In the conflict between his own financial advantage and the
advancement of the Kingdom, he must whole-heartedly choose
the Kingdom. Read Luke 12. 15-34; 16. 13. (See also Mark 6.
7-9; 10. 17-30; Luke 6. 20-21, 24-25; 9. 56-58; 14. 15-24, 33;
19. 8-9; 22. 35-36; James 5. 1-6.)

5. He must get beyond all resentment, anger, envy, antagonism
and intolerance; his attitude even toward his enemies must be one
of active love. Read Mark 11. 25; Luke 6. 35-37; 17. 3-5; Romans
12. 14; Ephesians 4. 26; 31-32. (See also Matthew 5. 7, 9, 21-24,
39-48; 18. 15-18, 21-35; Mark 9. 38-40; Luke 6. 27-34; 23. 34;
John 8. 1-11; Romans 12. 19-21; James 1. 19-20.)

6. He must give up all discrimination based on race, nationality,
economic status or sex. Read Acts 10. 28; Galatians 3. 28. (See also
Mark 16. 15; John 4. 4-42; 10. 16; Romans 10. 12; Colossians 3.
11; James 2. 2-10.)

7. He must even give up demanding justice for himself, because love for the other has taken the place of insistence upon his

---

[1] Archibald MacLeish, *Public Speech*. Published by Farrar and Rinehart.
[2] Hornell Hart, *op. cit.*, pp. 11-13.

own rights. (This teaching is not stated explicitly, but it becomes clearly evident if one reads as a single unit the following passages: Matthew 20. 1-16; Luke 10. 38-42; 12. 13-14; 15. 7, 25-32; 17. 7-10.)

8. He must cease to desire prestige, power or domination over his fellows; service must displace all that. Read Matthew 23. 8-12; I Corinthians 13. 4-7. (See also Matthew 6. 1-6, 16-18; Mark 10. 42-45; Luke 6. 22-23, 26; 14. 7-14; John 13. 12-16; 15. 18-20; Romans 12. 3, 10, 16.)

9. He must be ready to give up life itself joyfully, in following his Master. Read Matthew 10. 28; Luke 9. 23-25; John 12. 24-25; 16. 1-3.

All these self-seeking purposes, set forth in the nine points which have been listed above, must be displaced by whole-hearted, single-minded devotion to the Kingdom:

10. This devotion must dominate and transcend all other motives whatsoever. Read Matthew 13. 44-46; Romans 12. 1-2. (See also Luke 9. 49-62; 14. 15-27.)

11. The true disciple must love God with all his being. Read Matthew 22. 37-38.

12. He must love his neighbor as himself. We enter into this life of God as we take over the sufferings, aspirations, needs and creative purposes of our fellow men. Read Matthew 22. 39-40; Galatians 5. 22-23; I John 3. 14-17. (See also John 13. 34-35; 15. 12-17; Romans 12. 15.)

13. This love must take the form of service to those who are in need. Read Matthew 7. 12; 25. 34-40; Mark 10. 42-45; Romans 12. 4-13. (See also Matthew 11. 2-6; Luke 4. 17-21; 10. 25-37; 14. 12-14.)

14. He must live the teachings, not merely talk piously. Read Matthew 7. 21-27; 21. 28-31; I John 3. 18. (See also Luke 6. 43-49; John 7. 16-17; 14. 21-24; James 1. 22-27.)

15. He must be devoted to the truth. Read John 8.31-32; 16. 13; Ephesians 4. 25.

Verily! Verily! "The gate is narrow and the road is hard that leads to life, and there are few that find it." [1] To climb the steep ascent, we must hold together in close company.

---

[1] Matt. 7:14.

Chapter VII

Worship God in Silence and Beauty and Harmony

HUMAN nature is constituted with boundless potentialities: ability to plunge deep into the abyss of greed and lust and cruelty, and ability to climb to heights of beauty and truth and goodness. Latent within man is capacity to respond to the appeal of holiness. By nature he is equipped to worship. Long ago Clement of Alexandria exclaimed: "A beautiful, breathing instrument of music, the Lord made man, whereon the spirit of Life makes melody to God." "I have behind me a long line of evidence," writes Rufus Jones, "which convinces me that the infant cries of the seeking soul, the yearnings of the heart of man who was made in God's image, the resolve of the mind to leave the swine husks and go to the Father are human attitudes which bring an immediate response from Him to us. . . . There is something human in God and something divine in man and they belong together. If you bring a diamond into the light you occasion a double revelation. There is a revelation of the glorious beauty of the jewel. While it lay in the dark you never knew its possibilities. It was easily mistaken for a piece of glass. Now it flashes and burns and reveals itself because it has found the element for which it was meant. But there is also at the same time a revelation of the mystery of light. You discover now new wonders and new glories in light itself. Most objects absorb part of its rays and imperfectly transmit it to the eye. Here is an object which tells you its real nature. Now you see it as it is. So Christ shows us at once man and God. In a definite historic setting and in the limitations of a concrete personal life, Christ has unveiled the divine nature and taught us to say 'Father' and He has, in doing that, showed us the goal and type of human life. The Son of God and the Son of Man is one person." [1]

If man's inherent ability to scale steep ascents is to be released

[1] Rufus Jones, *The Double Search*. Published by John C. Winston Co., Philadelphia.

and developed, human nature must be subjected to appropriate stimuli. And of all the pulling powers which surround man, the most dynamic is vivid awareness of the holiness and power and love of God. Nothing, absolutely nothing, can so utterly revolutionize life as alert realization that every hour of existence is spent in the presence of, and subject to the yearning-power of the Good Shepherd who ever searches for the one who is lost. "God is bound to act," exclaimed Eckhart, "to pour Himself out into thee as soon as ever He shall find thee ready. Think not it is with God as with a human carpenter, who works or works not as he chooses, who can do or leave undone at his good pleasure. It is not so with God; but finding thee ready, He is obliged to act, to overflow into thee; just as the sun must needs burst forth when the air is bright and clear, and is unable to contain itself. . . . Thou needest not seek Him here or there, He is not farther off than at the door of thy heart; there He stands lingering, awaiting whoever is ready to open and let Him in. Thou needst not call to Him afar, He waits much more impatiently than thou for thee to open to Him. He longs for thee a thousandfold more urgently than thou for Him: one point the opening and the entering."

Concerning the objection that the God of illimitable celestial spaces cannot possibly be interested in a single individual, the late Canon Street wrote: "The imagination of many recoils before the facts of Astronomy. Against the background of the unthinkable distances and immensities of the physical universe the planet we inhabit is itself just a speck, indeed less than a speck. On this planet the individual is a speck upon a speck. Can we believe that the individual, his sufferings, and his doings, can matter in the slightest degree to the Power which produced and controls this vast immensity? But call in a microscope; through this we may contemplate a universe as infinitely minute as that which the telescope discloses to be correspondingly immense. The man of science does not regard the things shown by the microscope as less important than those which the telescope reveals. Indeed, for the theory of the nature of matter, as well as for the practical applications of science in regard to disease, manufacture, and the like, the important things are the microscopic. Why should the reverse be true of God?" [1]

[1] Burnett Hillman Streeter, *The God Who Speaks.* Published by The Macmillan Company, New York.

The longer I mediate the more certain I am that the most thrilling idea that ever entered the mind of man is this: we live continuously in the presence of a wise and powerful and affectionate God, holy and righteous altogether, who eagerly desires to enter into intimate comradeship with human beings created in His own image, and who challenges His children to become co-workers in the glorious adventure of creating a harmonious community of kinsmen.

II

Silence may become a gateway to God's presence and the alert individual will safeguard periods set apart for quietness with the same zeal with which he keeps appointments at the dining table. "What impresses me," writes Dr. L. P. Jacks, "is the deep *silence* of the universe, coupled with its unimaginable activity. I was recently hearing a distinguished man of science describing the wonders in the nebula of Andromeda—that faint mist of light in the depths of the firmament which the naked eye can sometimes detect—magnitude so vast, forces so stupendous, operations so immense, and yet so minute, that thought simply staggers in the presence of them. . . . The facts of astronomy are so overwhelming, so stupefying, that there are moments when human speech is stricken dumb, and one is almost tempted to cry like a child in the dark. . . . Verily, the highest cannot be spoken: the mere vastness of it completely baffles us. 'The stars above us, and the graves beneath us.' Great God, what a Universe!"

More or less frequently intimations of the Eternal come to most human beings. "At times in the lonely silence of the night," writes H. G. Wells, "and in rare lonely moments I come upon a sort of communion of myself with something great that is not myself. It is perhaps poverty of mind and language which obliges me to say that this universal scheme takes on the effect of a sympathetic person—and my communion a quality of fearless worship. These moments happen and they are the supreme fact of my religious life to me, they are the crown of my religious experiences." Thoreau once exclaimed: "It is always as if I met some grand, serene, immortal, infinitely encouraging, though invisible, Companion and walked with Him."

Discipline and perseverance are required if one is to appro-

priate the rich values of silence. Many beginners find it necessary
to fight against discouragement and a sense of futility as they discover themselves unable to make profitable use of prolonged
periods of solitude and quietness. "We deeply need to be reminded,"
writes Dr. Fosdick, "that every realm of spiritual excellence requires practical methods of nurture and discipline. Did not Paderewski say that if he stopped practising on the piano one day he
noticed the difference, if he stopped two days his family noticed
the difference, if he stopped three days his friends noticed the
difference, and if he stopped for a week the public noticed the
difference? That represents a universal law of life. . . . I know one
student of music who hopes sometime to be a concert pianist and
who in recent weeks has been practising five hours a day with his
right thumb alone. That is the test of his sincerity, his teacher says
to him. Does he want what he says he wants enough to master the
techniques? Yet how many of us spend five minutes a day on the
thoughtful nurture of our inner lives? 'Be not deceived; God is
not mocked: for whatsoever a man soweth, that shall he also
reap.' " [1]

In a rewarding little volume, *Christ and Prayer,* Charles F.
Andrews, out of profound and long-continued experience, answers
the question : "How do you begin to pray when you are all alone?"
"First of all," he says, "I spend some moments in complete and
utter stillness, remaining seated in such a manner that the body
becomes no clog or hindrance to the spirit, and a sense of outward
restfulness is attained. The inner stillness comes, however, not
through any mechanical means, but through that quiet and peace
of the soul when all is surrendered to God. My earlier mistake
was—I can see it now—to begin almost immediately with petition
and with thoughts of one's own needs, instead of resting in the
Lord and waiting patiently for Him in thankfulness and worship.
Now that I have begun to learn this lesson, I remain in stillness for
a much longer time until the spirit within is composed and I am
thus prepared to receive from God his own message for the day.
This listening attitude is needed, and it is clearly impossible to
hear God's voice so long as the outer world has its grip upon us
and continually obtrudes. It is essential to be the master and not
the slave of moods when we thus pray and worship. For if we

[1] Harry Emerson Fosdick, *Successful Christian Living.* Published by
Harper & Brothers, New York.

cease to pray whenever we do not feel in the mood for it, we shall soon cease altogether. In the active life of the world, we do not depend on our moods. We do things when we are least inclined to do them, and the right mood comes only when we make the effort. We must deal with our prayer life in a similar manner." [1]

III

Deliberate and frequent exposure of self to the appeal of beauty may be a source of spiritual power. Exultation in the glories of nature enables us to rise above the trivial and the temporary into an awareness of the majesty of the Eternal.

> Far up the dim twilight fluttered
> Moth wings of vapour and flame:
> The lights danced over the mountains,
> Star after star they came.
>
> The lights grew thicker unheeded,
> For silent and still were we;
> Our hearts were drunk with a beauty
> Our eyes could never see. [2]

With good reason does Studdert Kennedy say: "Nature seems to speak of God. Go, stand out on a summer night and look upwards to the sky where the million stars go sailing through that great wide sea of blue, like silent ships that pass in the night. Go, walk in the woods on a day in April and watch the beauty of nature repeating the eternal resurrection, and rising from the grave of winter to the splendour of spring. Go, stand and watch the daylight die, and all the west grow wonderful with a thousand colours past the power of human artists to express. Look at a mountain towering up to kiss the sun, pluck the tiniest flower that grows upon its side; and if you are a healthy man or a healthy woman there will be something that will call you—call you to the worship of the Maker and Creator of it all, and to the love of the great Artist in whose mind the ever-changing picture that the world presents was born."

---

[1] C. F. Andrews, *Christ and Prayer*. Published by Harper & Brothers, New York.

[2] George William Russell (A. E.), *The Unknown God*.

When in the affluent splendour of the day,
To heaven's cloudless blue I lift my eyes,
Thrilled with the beauty that around me lies,
My heart goes up on wings of ecstasy;
But when Orion and the Milky Way
Reveal the story of the midnight skies,
And all the starry hosts of space arise—
Mutely I bow in reverence to pray.

And so with life; the daylight of success
Rounds earth and pleasure to a perfect sphere,
But in the night of trial and distress
The quickened soul to vaster realms draws near,
And o'er the borders of our consciousness
Foretokens of the Infinite appear.[1]

The meaningfulness of beauty will be highly magnified if we constantly remind ourselves that God with infinite compassion is ever seeking to draw us nearer to Himself. Surely F. J. Gillman is justified in saying that "Beauty is a form of Divine speech: it reveals God to man. . . . Nor is God seen alone in the beauty of the natural world, in cloud and mountain, snow and vapour, green forest and spacious sea. Every artist in words or color or sound reveals something of His wisdom and power. The preacher and the theologian may reveal Him too, though sometimes they obscure and pervert His likeness; His ministers are not a close corporation of ordained clergy. Raphael is among them, and Millet, and Burne-Jones. Not David only, but Palestrina and Beethoven and Elgar sound His praises. Alike every builder of our stately cathedrals, and every humble workman who with heart and hand creates as best he can the meanest vessel that ministers to man's daily needs, are His artists and fellow-workmen."

I saw the new Jerusalem tonight.
The portals of the sky were opened wide;
The clouds were radiant with celestial light;
My lake gave back its answer, glorified.
Behold, there was a throne set high and clear;
An emerald rainbow circled it, all fair;

[1] Helena Coleman, "Day and Night", in *Canadian Poets,* edited by John W. Garvin. Published by McClelland and Stewart, Ltd., Toronto.

And four and twenty thrones, I think, were near,
For jasper, sardius, gold were everywhere.
Before the throne a sea of crystal glass,
And round about were creatures in the sky;
Across the sea a path of burnished brass,
And there, it seemed, angelic hosts drew nigh.
I thought I heard them singing as they trod,
Holy, holy, holy is Almighty God.[1]

The intimate relationship between beauty and holiness is vividly revealed in the life of St. Francis. "At the sight of beauty love always awakes;" writes Sabatier his biographer, "at the appeal of holiness the divine witness within us at once responds; and so we see, streaming from all points of the horizon to gather around those who preach in the name of the inward voice, long processions of souls athirst for the ideal. The human heart so naturally yearns to offer itself up, that we have only to meet along our pathway someone who, doubting neither himself nor us, demands it without reserve, and we yield it to him at once. Reason may understand a partial gift; . . . the heart knows only the entire sacrifice, and like the lover to his beloved, it says to its vanquisher, 'Thine alone and forever.' That which has caused the miserable failure of all efforts of natural religion is that its founders have not had the courage to lay hold upon the hearts of men, consenting to no partition. . . . Francis had given himself up too completely not to claim from others an absolute self-renunciation."

IV

Music also is a doorway to the presence of God. Time spent in exposing self to harmony will bring rich returns. Subjected as we are to all manner of discord, desperately do we need the unifying influence of the great masters. Through the eloquent speech of music, the Creator is eager to enter our lives. Well may the poet praise the orchestra conductor:

Strange magic he has worked with his baton:
That music comes upon us with a spell,
And when it leaves, discord and doubt have gone!

[1] Georgia Harkness, "Sunset," *Holy Flame*. Published by Bruce Humphries, Inc., Boston.

The potent sorcerer has fathomed well
A remedy for fevers of the heart
That burn to no availing; he can cure
The deep malignancies of strife that start
In subtlety; his wizardry is sure.
But more than medicine, the music throws
A charm upon the future and the past.
Who heeds the incantation truly knows
A healing efficacy that will last.
Not dark, but clear, the magic of this night,
Remembered for its radiance of light![1]

Now and then all of us enjoy experiences which enable us to
share in this poet's tribute to song:

Here shall remain all tears for lovely things
And here enshrined the longing of great hearts,
Caught on a lyre whence waking wonder starts,
To mount afar upon immortal wings;
Here shall be treasured tender wonderings,
The faintest whisper that the soul imparts,
All silent secrets and all gracious arts
Where nature murmurs of her hidden springs.

O magic of a song! here loveliness
May sleep unhindered of life's mortal toll,
And noble things stand towering o'er the tide;
Here mid the years, untouched by time or stress,
Shall sweep on every wind that stirs the soul
The music of a voice that never died![2]

Let no Christian revolutionist think that it is a waste of time
to nurture his sense of harmony. Even more than others he needs
to rise above discord and irritability, and to this end requires
the ennobling influence of music. The more resolutely we endeavor to change unjust social systems, the more urgently do
we need vivid awareness of the majesty and holiness and love
of God. So with frequency let us place ourselves under the spell
of symphony and solo.

1 Elinor Lennen, "Orchestra Conductor" in *The Christian Century*.
2 Thomas S. Jones, Jr., "To Song," from *Shadow of the Perfect Rose*.
Published by Farrar and Rinehart, New York.

We are the music makers,
  And we are the dreamers of dreams,
Wandering by lone sea-breakers,
  And sitting by desolate streams;—
World-losers and world-forsakers,
  On whom the pale moon gleams:
Yet we are the movers and shakers
  Of the world for ever, it seems.

With wonderful deathless ditties
We build up the world's great cities,
  And out of a fabulous story
  We fashion an empire's glory:
One man with a dream, at pleasure,
  Shall go forth and conquer a crown;
And three with a new song's measure
  Can trample a kingdom down.

We, in the ages lying
  In the buried past of the earth,
Built Nineveh with our sighing,
  And Babel itself in our mirth;
And o'erthrew them with prophesying
  To the old of the new world's worth;
For each age is a dream that is dying,
  Or one that is coming to birth.[1]

V

Under favorable circumstances corporate worship in a church provides silence, beauty, harmony, fellowship, sacrament, and preaching. Here is afforded dynamic stimulus to worship the Eternal, and here are available rich resources for personal living and for social action. Worship is essential not only to individual growth but also to the most effective action in behalf of the good society. "It is almost impossible to avoid a self-centered religion when one has no active share in the corporate worship of a larger religious fellowship," writes Douglas V. Steere, "This is

[1] Arthur O'Shaughnessy, "Ode," *Music and Moonlight* (1874). Reprinted by Yale University Press in *Poems of Arthur O'Shaughnessy*, selected and edited by William Alexander Percy.

particularly true of those who are not engaged in manual work. There is the subtle temptation to become one of those who mistake being 'agin' the group, being otherwise-minded, for following the dictates of conscience. Eccentricity, the sense of martyrdom, and an almost total absence of that precious element of 'creatureliness,' of humility in one's religious life as one of the great family of fellow creatures offering up their lives before the great Father—these frequently accompany this reluctance to share in corporate worship. Friedrich von Hugel used to tell of the sense of common need and of common love that came to him as he prayed through his rosary or listened to the mass while kneeling next to some Irish washerwoman. For this woman and millions of others, whatever their place in man's petty order of rank, would that very day perform the same act of love and devotion before a Father in whose loving regard each was of equal worth. It is this vivid sense of creatureliness and the felt attitude of the creature towards the creator that many have declared to be the central experience of worship or devotion and the very secret source of the religious refreshment at the base of their lives. For in this sense of creatureliness, the springs of the only enduring center of equality between men are forever being renewed. Here is the heart of a social gospel that is eternal. Here each is visited with a sense that he, in his need, is one and only one among other needy ones; that he is one among the many who have come to offer up their adoration and aspiration; that he is responsible for all and can never wrench loose from that responsibility. Howard Brinton has expressed the effect of this approach to the center in the fellowship of worship by the figure of the spokes of a wheel. The nearer the spokes of the wheel are to the center, the nearer they are to each other. If the worship is real this new sense of nearness to others will invade the rest of life and be brought to work on the barriers which retard it."[1]

Partaking of the sacrament of Holy Communion may be a holy experience. In a unified and beautifully conducted service where silence, beauty, harmony, fellowship, and admonition make their respective contributions, the spirits of the contrite and dedicated celebrants are ushered into the presence of the Living God. "We meet together at this Table that Christ may do for us here

[1] Douglas V. Steere, *Prayer and Worship*. Published by Association Press, New York.

what He has done for uncounted generations of Christian men,"
writes Dr. J. S. Whale. "What Christ does for us here is un-
searchably rich in meaning. Plainly enough, this central fact of
the Church's life has many aspects, yet three aspects have been
determinative from the beginning. There is, first, the historical
or memorial aspect; we remember here what was said and done
in time by Jesus; this feast is a memorial feast, commemorating
the mightiest of God's mighty acts of grace in the cross and the
resurrection. There is, second, the timeless or eternal aspect. Here
we are lifted out of time and have communion with the very
life of God. The feast mediates God's presence and His very Self
to us: here our fellowship with God and in God has all the actuality and wholeness of life. Thirdly, when by an act of faith we
partake together of Bread and Wine in this Sacrament, these two
aspects become one. At this Table there is a unique fusion or synthesis of what is historical and what is beyond history; of what
is in time and is remembered, and what is timeless and is experienced. . . . It is a vitally significant fact that not a single
Sunday morning has passed since the first Holy Week without
Christian men and women meeting at the Holy Table."[1]

VI

Truly may it be said that human nature is potential, potential greed and cruelty, and potential sacrifice and adoration. By
conscious selection of at least a portion of the stimuli to which
he is subjected, man may choose the direction of his course
through life, although, of course, he can never escape the powerful impacts of heritage and environment. The difference between
man and man is enormous, and the contrast between an individual at his best and at his worst is profound. We rarely use more
than a tiny fraction of our latent capacities. So constituted are
we that it is possible for us to live in fellowship with man and
in communion with God. Precious indeed is the privilege we
enjoy of being co-workers with the Father and His faithful children of every age and every land in building the divine society.
To the degree that we are loyal to our highest nature, we will
live today and every day as good members of God's Home.

[1] J. S. Whale, *What Is A Living Church?* Published by Harper and
Brothers, New York.

PART II

Human nature being what it is, stimulus determines response. We are what we are stimulated to be. Among the most powerful factors affecting behavior are ideas, ideals and emotions. The readings presented in this anthology are offered as stimuli. Because of the crushing weight of inertia and habit, serious endeavor is required if the individual is to rise above conformity and mediocrity. Long experience and wide observation convince me that the daily practice of devoting twenty to thirty minutes, as a minimum, to concentration upon a suitable theme brings rich returns. Through alert attention, calm reflection and fervent prayer, the higher side of human nature becomes dominant.

The cumulative effect of following this sequence may prove to be powerful if the daily readings are followed with regularity: ideal, actuality, penitence, action, suffering, comradeship and worship.

Many of these selections are suitable for use in devotional meetings and services of public worship.

151

Concentrate Upon the Ideal: First Monday

I. THE NEW TRINITY

Three things must a man possess if his soul would live,
    And know life's perfect good—
Three things would the all-supplying Father give—
    Bread, Beauty and Brotherhood.

> EDWIN MARKHAM, *New Poems*,
> Published by Doubleday, Doran & Company, Inc., New York.

THE IDEAL AS GUIDE

All mortals equally unequal are
To reach the goal the living Ideal sets
Before each as a star. Heed; follow it
Forever where it leads, searching all zones
Through Beauty's gracious Being to its Source.
Forever is that Ideal but a guide,
And never is it as pure passion quite
Possessed. As Heaven's guidance when despised
Ceases to lead, and leaves the follower,
Who once in faith had followed it, alone,
Each wanderer forlorn must, unled, fail
To find the way to God, except through Faith
In something more and nobler than himself.

> EDWARDS DAVIS, *Lovers of Life*.
> Published by Baker & Taylor Company, New York.

TE DEUM

If I could paint you the autumn color, the melting glow upon all
    things laid,
The violet haze of Indian summer, before its splendor begins to
    fade,
When scarlet has reached its breathless moment, and gold the hush
    of its glory now,
That were a mightier craft that Titian's, the heart to lift and the
    head to bow.

I should be lord of a world of rapture, master of magic and
    gladness, too, —
The touch of wonder transcending science, the solace escaping
    from line and hue;
I would reveal through tint and texture the very soul of this
    earth of ours,
Forever yearning through boundless beauty to exalt the spirit
    with all her powers,

See where it lies by the lake this morning, our autumn hillside of
    hardwood trees,
A masterpiece of the mighty painter who works in the primal
    mysteries.
A living tapestry, rich and glowing with blended marvels, ver-
    milion and dun,
Hung out for the pageant of time that passes along an avenue of
    the sun!

The crown of the ash is tinged with purple, the hickory leaves are
    Etruscan gold,
And the tulip-tree lifts yellow banners against the blue for a
    signal bold;
The oaks in crimson cohorts stand, a myriad sumach torches mass
In festal pomp and victorious pride, when the vision of spring is
    brought to pass.

Down the line of the shore's deep shadows another and softer
    picture lies,
As if the soul of the lake in slumber should harbor a dream of
    paradise,—
Passive and blurred and unsubstantial, lulling the sense and luring
    the mind
With the spell of an empty fairy world, where sinew and sap are
    left behind. . . .

So I will pass through the lovely world, and partake of beauty
    to feed my soul.
With earth my domain and growth my portion, how should I sue
    for a further dole?
In the lift I feel of immortal rapture, in the flying glimpse I gain
    of truth,

Released is the passion that sought perfection, assuaged the ardor
of dreamful youth.

The patience of time shall teach me courage, the strength of the
sun shall lend me poise.
I would give thanks for the autumn glory, for the teaching of
earth and all her joys.
Her fine fruition shall well suffice me; the air shall stir in my
veins like wine;
While the moment waits and the wonder deepens, my life shall
merge with the life divine.

BLISS CARMAN, Later Poems.
Published by Small, Maynard & Co., Boston.

A SINGING FIRE

A man saw the whole world as a grinning skull and cross-
bones. The rose flesh of life shriveled from all faces. Nothing
counts. Everything is a fake. Dust to dust and ashes to ashes
and then an old darkness and a useless silence. So he saw it all.
Then he went to a Mischa Elman concert. Two hours' waves of
sound beat on his eardrums. Music washed something or other
inside him. Music broke down and rebuilt something or other in
his head and heart. He joined in five encores for the young Russian Jew with the fiddle. When he got outside his heels hit the
sidewalk a new way. He was the same man in the same world as
before. Only there was a singing fire and a climb of roses ever-
lastingly over the world he looked on.

CARL SANDBURG, Chicago Poems.
Published by Henry Holt and Company, New York.

A TRUE SENSE OF DIRECTION

Canon Streeter of Oxford said recently, "The greatest need
of mankind today—socially and individually—is a true sense of
direction." . . . If we are lost in the woods, the one thing we must
seek first is altitude. We must find a hill, if we can, and on it a
high tree, but somehow we must get altitude so that around the
confusing close-up of the woods we can see horizons and perspectives. Recovering the sense of direction is always a matter of
elevation and vision.

Who does not need *that* today in his spiritual life? The canyons of these city streets sometimes become to us unbearable; the

pressure and tension of their noisy restlessness we cannot endure. We must away where there are distance and altitude, sky and horizon. So one lives with the terrific problems of our time—personal and social, economic and international—until the whole world seems mad and all its ways incoherently insane. But coming, it may be, into a service of great worship, see what may happen to a spirit so confused! "O God, who art, and wast, and art to come, before whose face the generations rise and pass away"— what a world of long distances and vast horizons this is! The world speaks no such language.

> Before the mountains were brought forth,
> Or ever thou hadst formed the earth and the world,
> Even from everlasting to everlasting, thou art God!

So the transient and temporal are not all; the insanities of man many a time have reared themselves against the Most High, and still the Most High he is. "While we look not at the things which are seen, but at the things which are not seen: for the things which are seen are temporal; but the things which are not seen are eternal." So one can know the east from the west and the north from the south and take up his way again. "Strengthened with power through his Spirit in the inward man"—so there are resources which can enable one to carry on.

HARRY EMERSON FOSDICK, *Successful Christian Living.*
Published by Harper & Brothers, New York.

A PRAYER

Enable us, Lord of sun and stars and the human soul, Who has made us in Thine own image a little lower than the divine, to be true to our Divine inheritance and grant us grace and power to reveal through our humanity the greatness of which Thou hast made us inheritors. Forgive us that we have so often made of our humanity an excuse for our faults and have so little used it for the ends for which Thou didst create us. In His name Whose life became the revelation of the Eternal. Amen.

GAIUS GLENN ATKINS.

Understand the Actual: First Tuesday

2. THE PEOPLE, YES

Who shall speak for the people?
Who knows the works from A to Z
    so he can say, "I know what the
    people want"? Who is this phenom?
    where did he come from? . . .

Who knows the people, the migratory harvest hands and berry
    pickers, the loan shark victims, the installment house wolves,
The jugglers in sand and wood who smooth their hands along the
    mold that casts the frame of your motor-car engine,
The metal polishers, solderers, and paint spray hands who put the
    final finish on the car,
The riveters and bolt-catchers, the cowboys of the air in the big
    city, the cowhands of the Great Plains, the ex-convicts, the
    bellhops, redcaps, lavatory men—
The union organizer with his list of those ready to join and those
    hesitating, the secret paid informers who report every move
    toward organizing,
The house-to-house canvassers, the doorbell ringers, the good-
    morning-have-you-heard boys, the strike pickets, the strike-
    breakers, the hired sluggers, the ambulance crew, the ambu-
    lance chasers, the picture chasers, the meter readers, the
    oysterboat crews, the harborlight tenders—
                    who knows the people?

Who knows this from pit to peak? The people, yes.
Have you seen men handed refusals
    till they began to laugh
    at the notion of ever landing a job again—
Muttering with the laugh,
"It's driving me nuts and the family too,"
Mumbling of hoodoos and jinx,
    fear of defeat creeping in their vitals—

Have you never seen this?
    or do you kid yourself
    with the fond soothing syrup of four words
    "Some folks won't work"?

Of course some folks won't work—
    they are sick or wornout or lazy
    or misled with the big idea
    the idle poor should imitate the idle rich.

Have you seen women and kids
    step out and hustle for the family
    some in night life on the streets
    some fighting other women and kids
    for the leavings of fruit and vegetable markets
    or searching alleys and garbage dumps for scraps?

Have you seen them with savings gone
    furniture and keepsakes pawned
    and the pawntickets blown away in cold winds?
    by one letdown and another ending
    in what you might call slums—
To be named perhaps in case reports
    and tabulated and classified
    among those who have crossed over
    from the employables into the *un*employables?

What is the saga of the employables?
    what are the breaks they get?
What are the dramas of personal fate
    spilled over from industrial transitions?
    what punishments handed bottom people
    who have wronged no man's house
    or things or person?

    Stocks are property, yes.
    Bonds are property, yes.
Machines, land, buildings, are property, yes.
    A job is property,
    no, nix, nah nah.

The rights of property are guarded
    by ten thousand laws and fortresses.
The right of a man to live by his work—
    what is this right?
    and why does it clamor?
    and who can hush it

so it will stay hushed?
and why does it speak
and though put down speak again
with strengths out of the earth?

CARL SANDBURG, *The People, Yes.*
Harcourt, Brace & Co., Publishers, New York. Reprinted by permission.

THAT'S NOT BUSINESS

John E. Edgerton, former president of the National Association of Manufacturers and now president of the Southern States Industrial Council, was the witness at hearings on the Black-Connery wages-hours bill.

Baldish and grim-faced, his sandy eyebrows knitted in a scowl, Edgerton had told the committee that he had "allowed" a number of grandmothers to work for $6 a week during the depression "as a humane thing."

Apparently shocked by his testimony, both Republicans and Democrats joined in close examination of the aggressive witness.

Representative Clyde Smith (Republican), of Maine, and Representative Reuben T. Wood (Democrat), of Missouri, asked him how a family could live on less than $16 a week. Edgerton, obviously irritated at the questioning and at the repeated laughter of spectators at his answers, snapped:

"I've never studied those social problems except in my church connections."

Q. Of course, some of your men might drink champagne on that fabulous wage you pay them. Answer the question, do you think $620 a year is enough? . . .

Edgerton burst out: "Why, I've never thought of paying men on a basis of what they need. I don't inquire into what they want. I pay men for efficiency.

"Personally I attend to all those other things, social welfare stuff, in my church work." (Here the crowd in the hearing room roared with laughter.)

Edgerton, glaring at the spectators, sneered:

"Of course, some people don't know about that sort of thing, church work and so . . . But that's the feeling side of life, church contributions and church work. That's not business."

Quoted in *Washington Post.*

THE SIN OF PRIDE

All power leads to pride and injustice; to the pride of "them that despise me," the pride of men who have forgotten that they are creatures and that no creaturely human strength is strong enough to make nature purely the servant of man rather than his nemesis; to the injustice of those who create their security at the expense of the security and freedom of others. The sin of pride, to which the prophets of Israel were so sensitive, is more obvious in our day than in theirs. Yet there are fewer prophets to recognize and challenge it. If this age is essentially irreligious, the basic cause of our irreligion is our sense of self-sufficiency. The achievements of science and technics have beguiled us into a false complacency. We have forgotten the frailty of man. We have overlooked the fact that no medicine for senility can be found by even the most advanced science. We have failed to consider that the mystery of death still challenges human pride; that man, for all of his enhanced physical strength, continues to be as grass which flourisheth in the morning and in the evening is cut down and withereth. He still "brings his years to an end like a tale that is told."

REINHOLD NIEBUHR, *Beyond Tragedy*.
Published by Charles Scribner's Sons, New York.

A PRAYER

O Thou Who are above all power and administration, hear, we beseech Thee, the complaint of the oppressed, the lament of the poor and all those who turn to Thy justice for their salvation. Thou hast long ago sent us the Long Expected but we have been so slow in making His laws the rule of our states and His spirit sovereign in our human ways. May we find in our perfect obedience to His will the fulfilment of all our hopes. Amen.

GAIUS GLENN ATKINS.

Be Concerned: First Wednesday

3. THE FALL OF MAN

I

O son of man, I give you earth and sea
And starry nights and lovely clouds that lie
At morn and eve fire-fretted in the sky.
I give you mind and summon you to be
A builder of the world along with me.
I give you power and courage to defy
The darkness and the tempest as you fly,
Exulting like an eagle, strong and free.
I give you dreams of beauty and the skill
Of artistry in marble, granite, gold.
With steadfast laws I serve your finite will
And lend you elemental forces old
As time, wherewith you have wrought marvels till
The angels pause in wonder to behold.

II

Apostate man! The holy angels weep
When they behold your slavery to lust,
Your love of lucre, leaving dry as dust
The streams of pity in your deadly sleep
Of conscience while you basely reap
What others sow. To me and man unjust,
Your violence is treason to my trust.
Your folly earns damnation long and deep.
You rain death and destruction from the sky;
With guileless blood your brutal hands are red.
In endless, ruthless war your bravest die,
While women wail and children cry for bread.
Your palaces and temples ruined lie,
Your capitals are shambles of the dead.

FRANK BROOKS COWGILL, *in The Christian Century.*

THE SPRING OF PENITENCE

To hear a man who believed in the moral being of God say
that he needed no forgiveness would affect us like the statement

of a friend, in a picture-gallery, that for him the works of the great masters had no beauty. At once we should recognize that we cannot make him see. But, if we ventured on advice, it would be the suggestion that he should contemplate some great picture, should look and look again, at intervals, with the confidence that something would happen. New perceptions would emerge. The beauty spread before him would by degrees become visible. Similarly, let the insensitive man take pains to see Jesus, let him not withdraw his attention from that Figure, and inevitably he will learn the truth about himself. True, it is not through the realization of Jesus only that God touches the spring of penitence in men: He may do it through many another deep experience; but the experience is always that of beholding a goodness that shames us. . . .

When we examine the past, or look around us, we discover that nothing in thought or experience is comparable to the cross for power to induce penitence in Christian or non-Christian, in old or young, in learned or simple. In the passion of Jesus there is that which breaks men down and melts them in contrition. Not in a remorse that goes out despairingly into darkness, but in a piercing and softening sorrow for all they are and have become; a sorrow which on its other side is an apprehension of the Father's mercy. To repent before Christ crucified and to trust because of Him—these are two aspects of one regenerating experience.

H. R. MACKINTOSH, *The Christian Experience of Forgiveness.*
Published by Harper & Brothers, New York.

CORPORATE CONTRITION REQUIRED

It is our belief that the problem of war illustrates in a manageable compass the central difficulties of the Christian's way of life; that by dealing with it we shall be facing the outstanding issue of our day; and that if we can see our way here we shall discover both the vision and the power for other and cognate tasks.

Why, then, do we claim that pacifism is the inevitable corollary of our theological and religious convictions? Because for us pacifism is involved in (*a*) our concept of God and of his mode of creative activity; (*b*) our understanding of Jesus and the method of his redemptive and atoning work; (*c*) our apprehension of the Holy Spirit and of the *koinonia* established by him. Put less technically these involve (*a*) a belief that in the nature of God and, therefore, in his dealings with man and in man's true way of life, love is always primary and justice derivative; (*b*) that in the teaching and atoning work of Jesus it is plain not only that those who take the sword perish by the sword, but that the sole redemptive activity is the power of the love that gives and suffers, that is of the cross; (*c*) that worship and fellowship, the love of God and the love of men, are inseparably united; that what is wrong for the individual cannot be right for the community; that the fruit of the Spirit is love, joy, peace—a way of living of which modern warfare is a flagrant denial; and that it is only as this way of life is realized that the ministry of the church can become creative, regenerative, and inspirational. . . .

Love, the love of God and the love of neighbor, is the end to be attained. The means of attainment must be consistent with that end. God cannot deny himself, and if God is love then love's way is universally applicable, and the use of any method that denies love will lead to damnation and ultimate disaster. We cannot do evil that good may come; for even though God can bring good out of evil, by choosing evil, we not only pass sentence upon ourselves but involve the innocent in unmerited suffering. It is to love's way that the Christian is committed when he accepts the cross as the token of his allegiance. . . .

It is strange that the church, accepting the cross as its banner and recognizing it as the means of our salvation, has been so slow to realize that to take up the cross is the essential condition of Christian fellowship, an obligation upon all its members, and that the way of the cross is the only road towards newness of life for it and them and the world. Can anyone who reflects upon the Crucified seriously argue that modern warfare, either in its course or in its effects, is or can ever be consistent with cross-bearing, though its victims, the men who struggle, the women who suffer, may find even there a veritable crucifixion? . . .

The valuation of human life which war accepts, the mass-hatreds which it fosters, the destruction which it achieves are manifestly incompatible with it. Nowadays, when the last rags of romance have been stripped from the trade of arms, when the shrinkage of the world has made all war civil war, and when terrorism and indiscriminate massacre have become the means to victory, the Christian ought no longer to shelter himself from the stark fact that "all war is contrary to the spirit and teaching of Jesus Christ."

CHARLES E. RAVEN, *The Universal Church And The World of Nations.*
An Oxford Conference Book.
Published by Willett, Clark & Company, Chicago.

A PRAYER

Heavenly Father, we speak to Thee out of the deep sense of need for ourselves and for our world. We see the suggestions of beauty and order upon the surface of life, the streams and the mountains, the magnificent buildings, the appearance of strength and character in men and women; and we know, too, the broken relationships in homes and in the community, the bitter struggles in the industrial world, the clash between races and the jealous rivalries of nations. We would know more of the power of love to restore and heal the wounds of life; we need a deeper knowledge of ourselves and the world about us; and a greater patience and courage to go on adventuring in the paths of sympathetic understanding, that we may be fellow workers with Thee in the creative work of building Thy Kingdom. When failure and disappointment have numbered our energies recall to us the noble lives of those who in every age have thought not of their own gain but have given themselves unsparingly to the life of the world. Save us from pride of opinion and cheap sophistication, that we may never lose our sense of awe and wonder in the presence of a growing world far greater than we can comprehend. Still more we feel the danger of viewing men cheaply and losing our faith in the capacity of each one of Thy children for noble and generous life. Save us from that blasphemy by revealing to us the riches of character that lie hidden under the unpromising exteriors of our associates; and grant us so to live that we may ever call forth the best in others, so that together we may rise to new levels of service. And when we think in large terms of the great problems of the world, may we never forget that no problem is so large but what its solution is made up of the sum of the efforts made by countless millions, that Thy Kingdom comes, not by some great cataclysm but as men and women enter into it day after day, living in terms of that way of life revealed most clearly in the words and life of Jesus Christ. In grateful recognition of His inspiration we commit our lives to Thee. AMEN.

BISHOP PAUL JONES.

Endeavor to Transform: First Thursday

4. PLENTY FOR EVERYBODY

Under modern conditions the earth has become so prolific that if mankind were to take the Sermon on the Mount seriously, the wants of every nation, and of all its citizens, could be abundantly secured.

CONRAD NOEL.

ETHICAL FOUNDATIONS OF PROSPERITY

Under our capitalistic system we have wrought one of the most amazing miracles in history, the creation of a productive system capable of supplying anything that mankind may need. But we need consumers who can buy what can be produced and there are not enough of them. So maldistribution rises up to confound us. We had supposed it was only an ethical question, but Jesus was right: ethical questions precede, underlie, dominate economic questions. Seek first righteousness, justice, humanity, or you never can be prosperous.

We used to say that we were punished for our sins, as though God were a judge on a bench who passed on the case and meted out penalty. The truth goes far deeper than that. We are not punished for our sins, but by them. It is our sins themselves that rise up to slay us. So we allowed maldistribution to continue and now maldistribution has plunged us into a major catastrophe. . . .

No private property can be considered merely private when it can have such enormous social consequences. We cannot call railroads and coal mines, forests and mineral resources, which God gave to all the people, private in the same sense in which a man's house or spade are private. Even if a man has an automobile society steps in to say, Such and such are the restrictions on your use of it. No private property can be merely private whose misuse can cause so much public damage.

We have gotten at least that far in our national thinking and no one socially intelligent supposes that these vast private properties based on natural resources, which belong to all the people, can be merely private any more. As to what the economic solution will be, whether it will be social ownership or social control, far be it from a preacher to prophesy! But a preacher has this advantage: he commonly stands outside the economic struggle and looks at it as a spectator. And this at least is what one preacher sees. At one end of our lives are areas which the government already by common consent has taken over. We rise in the morning and drink a glass of water from a government water system. We read our mail delivered by a government post office. We walk on streets that are owned, paved, cleaned, and lighted by the government. We see children going to governmentally owned schools and using governmentally owned text books. We enjoy governmentally owned libraries and public parks. If a crime is committed we hope the government will catch the criminal and if a fire occurs we trust the government to put it out. As long as four years ago it was reported that two thousand American communities already had their own electric light plants. Here at one end of the line is a great accumulation of functions once individual, now governmental. But at the other end of our lives are areas where, if any government tried to coerce and regiment us, as under communism or fascism, we probably would land in concentration camps, so angry would our protest be. For there are areas of life the essence of whose meaning is liberty and where the more liberty and the less government the better. In art certainly, in music, in religion, in scientific research we want no governmental intervention. Freedom to think and to say what we think; freedom of assembly and of protest even against the government; the right to own our homes if we can and to possess ourselves of property, for ourselves and for our children, which we personally use—such are the areas where we, along with all men and women brought up in the American tradition would say, Let the government keep out!

Now, between these two areas, one where the government is commonly accepted and one where it is commonly rejected, lies today the great American problem—a vast accumulation of private property which is no longer merely private, with the clash of antagonistic opinion sharp between the advocates of social ownership and the advocates of social control. . . .

For here, again, we confront Jesus. He knew nothing about our modern economic problems but he did know the laws of the moral world. And this is one of them: no nation can take the vast resources of a continent, which God gave to all the people, and use them in careless disregard of the welfare of millions of the people, without in the end being punished, not for its sins but by them. Still from that Galilean mountain the voice sounds which we may heed or neglect but which we cannot escape: first the kingdom of God and his righteousness or else not enough to eat or drink or wherewithal to be clothed.

HARRY EMERSON FOSDICK, A Sermon,
"The Ethical Foundations of Prosperity," January 13, 1935.

MOST COMPREHENSIVELY REVOLUTIONARY

Jesus' proposal was that man should surrender his life absolutely into the hands of God and should dedicate his life to the complete emancipation of his kind. In Jesus' thinking this proposal was revolutionary not merely in a spiritual sense but in a practical sense as applied to the actualities of the brutal injustices and cruelties of man to man. Jesus was against anything and everything that oppressed and exploited human life, divided men, races and nations into selfish competitive groups and made impossible the true brotherhood of man in a social order in which the Golden Rule would be taken seriously in a world order of human society in which the law of love would be supreme. . . .

There was dynamite in the original religion of Jesus. There is dynamite in it now! His original religion involved the most comprehensively revolutionary proposal for genuine human emancipation the world has ever heard. The word revolutionary is not used to imply that Jesus ever advocated the employment of physical violence. His challenge did not sanction the use of that kind of "dynamite." He was not that kind of revolutionist and attempts so to interpret His teachings are gross misinterpretations of His mind and message. We shall see this more clearly if we recall the historical actualities of the period in which He lived. . . .

The whole background of Jesus' day is filled with rebellion and blood. Jesus is impossible to understand if this is not clearly seen. When Jesus was a boy there was a terrible uprising of the Zealots. After they were beaten back and down and finally captured, hundreds of them were publicly crucified not far from Jesus' boyhood home. Whoever does not know these things does not know what dark, bloody and lurid forces played upon the mind of Jesus when He was growing into manhood. The whole background of His life and time is filled with the bloody business of the revolutionary hopes and uprisings of His people, always crushed out by the counter-strokes of the terrible might of imperial Rome.

JEAN S. MILNER, *The Sky is Red*.
Published by Bobbs-Merrill Co., Indianapolis.

A PRAYER

Teach us, good Lord, to serve thee as thou deservest; to give and not to count the cost; to fight and not to heed the wounds; to toil and not to seek for rest; to labor and not to ask reward, save that of knowing that we do thy will; through Jesus Christ our Lord. Amen.

A PRAYER

O God, Thou art Thyself the Master Workman, skilled Creator. Hast Thou not also revealed to us Thy very nature in Jesus the carpenter, whose roughened hands bear eternal testimony to the dignity of toil.

We sense Thy presence in the labor movement, in the upward surge of the masses, who with the awakened self-respect of children of God, have through the centuries cast off the shackles of slavery and serfdom, and stand now gazing toward the dawn of a greater freedom.

We praise Thee for those brave spirits who have led the way; who have dared to risk even their children's bread in organized endeavor to improve the lot of all; who for their unselfish devotion have been condemned as outcasts of society; suffered contumely; endured prison; sacrificed their lives as martyrs to the cause.

Help Thou the labor movement of our day to be worthy of its heritage. Unite in high purpose the workers in the factory and on the farm. Preserve them from temptation to selfish complacency in partial gains for any favored craft or race or nation. Guard their leaders from lust for personal power. Guide them in the service of the common good.

JAMES MYERS, *Prayers for Self and Society*.
Published by Association Press, New York.

Proceed Resolutely: First Friday

5. WHAT IF JESUS HAD BECOME ANOTHER MACCABEAN VICTOR?

The slumbering discontent of the Jews burst into a new flame of national zeal in the second quarter of the second century B.C., when the Syrian rulers had carried oppression to the point of endeavoring to wipe out the Jewish religion. That heroic struggle, known as the Maccabean revolution, continuing for approximately twenty-five years, finally issued in temporary political independence. Henceforth this was a period of history to be enshrined in memory along with the now idealized national triumph under David. It must have seemed to many Jews that they were now on the verge of realizing a happy theocracy, a veritable kingdom of God on earth. At no previous time since the Babylonian exile had the prospects for Jewish autonomy been so bright. Under the leadership of a John Hyrcanus (135–104 B.C.) the national fortunes of the Jews rapidly approached their zenith. . . .

The hope for permanent political autonomy under the Maccabean rulers was soon dispelled. Internal dissensions again rendered the Jews an easy prey for the conqueror, who this time was the Roman general Pompey. In 63 B.C. Palestine became a possession of the Romans.

SHIRLEY JACKSON CASE, *Jesus*.
Published by the University of Chicago Press, Chicago.

THROUGH THE EYES OF SIMON THE ZEALOT

The Prophet was a distant relative of mine. . . . As soon as I heard this news about the Messiah I pricked up my ears; for though all the young men of our village were keenly enthusiastic for the national cause, I was the keenest and most enthusiastic of them all. I was a Zealot of the Zealots—so much so that they had given me the nickname of Simon *the* Zealot. I was ready for anything: conspiracy, insurrection, assassination, if it offered the faintest chance of getting the Romans out of the country. But I knew, as we all knew, that we could do nothing without a leader. Suppose that Jesus should be the leader whom God had promised us! At any rate, it was worth investigating. . . .

We were high up in our glade on Hermon. For three days

now we had been resting, and Jesus had been teaching us. Some of us had been grumbling. In spite of the furious rush and hurry of those days down by the lake, I suppose we had secretly enjoyed being people of such importance. At any rate two or three of us (and I fear I was myself one of the most clamorous) had been reproaching the Prophet with his failure to take the splendid opportunity which had been offered him by those deputations of Zealots. Why did he not call a truce for the time being to all this talk about God and religion—all very well in its way, of course, but hardly practical in the present desperate state of our nation's fortunes? Why did he waste so many hours and days on healing the sick—for waste of time it surely was, so long as the Romans and the Roman-supported Herods were there to bleed the country white with their exactions; for most of this mass of disease was plainly due to poverty? As we grew more rested, we grew also more discontented. I myself, for instance, felt convinced that *now* was the time for the national uprising. I had forgotten my misgivings as to whether Jesus would ever make the kind of Messiah we needed. I thought only of his marvelous powers and of that unexampled popularity from which he had fled. . . .

We pressed him to return; we grew clamorous in our insistence that he should go back and take up the burden of leadership which God had so plainly laid upon him. In the name of the poor, of the oppressed, of those whose Rome-imposed poverty laid them open to disease (we knew by this time how to appeal to him), would he not return and declare himself? . . .

Suddenly he began to speak to us. I can hear his voice still.

"You are fortunate," he said, "in your poverty and hunger, even in the persecution which is to come. The people for whom you should be sorry are those in power, those with wealth, those who have all that heart can wish."

We listened incredulously. He went on to tell us that the truest happiness consists in humility and meekness, in purity of heart, and the desire to do God's will.

He spoke for long, and they were strange words. At the time I could make little or nothing of them. He spoke of truthfulness and love. He spoke of resisting not evil and of bearing oppression uncomplainingly. He spoke of true spiritual religion, of the kind of prayer which is really pleasing to God. He spoke of the folly of worrying about money and food-supplies if one really trusts

God, and of how God knows and meets the need of those who trust Him because He is their Father and they are His children. He spoke of the need of faithfulness and steadfastness and so forth. . . .

We disciples were impressed, I will not deny it; but in view of our Zealot cravings for direct and sudden action, you may imagine whether or no we welcomed such sayings as "Resist not evil; but whoever smiteth thee on thy right cheek, turn to him the other also." . . .

The spokesman of the crowd was a well-known Zealot from northern Galilee—a man with whom I had had a good deal to do in the old days. He said how wonder-struck they had all been at the healing of the man born blind. They did not believe a word of what the Pharisees said about Jesus—that he was insane, and that his marvelous powers were in truth the deeds of the devils of madness. Who had ever heard of a mad man opening the eyes of a man born blind? They were convinced that he could be none other than the Messiah, and to their great joy they had heard that on the previous day he had actually told the man whom he had healed that he was the Messiah. Let him keep them in suspense no longer. They were ready to follow him anywhere, and to do anything he might direct in the sacred cause of their country and their country's God. If he were the Messiah, let him declare himself openly, and the Kingdom was his in a few hours.

There were many thousands of them ready in the city—good hardy Galileans, men of their hands, mountain-bred, utterly reckless of their lives. With such men to back him, in addition to his divine power, he could not possibly fail. . . .

If ever I prayed it was then, while that Zealot was speaking. I besought Jehovah, with desperate urgency, that His Prophet might not fail; that he might be worthy of our great past and of our wonderful future: that he might be worthy of God's own high calling.

The others, I know, were feeling exactly as I did. I caught sight of John's face, an agony of expectant anxiety. Peter too: he was half across the line already, his hand clutching a sword which he had concealed under his long cloak, his lips parted to shout Hosanna—the battle-cry.

But no—ah, the bitterness of it! The opportunity passed once more.

The Prophet would not commit himself. He simply said: "You must judge of my Messiah-hood for yourselves, by the kind of things I do." We knew well enough what he meant—that he was not their kind of Messiah, but that he worked through pity and love. Think of taking refuge in pity and love at a moment like that! The chance of a lifetime, of a thousand lifetimes: and for our outraged country!

Then he went on to speak of his being the Good Shepherd, and about what it meant to be one of his sheep. Oh, it was too tragic!

He finished up with one of his mysterious sayings about his oneness with God; and with the fickleness of a crowd—they were terribly disappointed of course—they took up stones to kill him for blasphemy.

How we got him out I hardly know. For myself, the pain and shame of it were so bitter that I would have welcomed any death. In fact, I was so disgusted that I left the others to look after the Prophet, and came away at once, by myself. . . .

After that terrible disappointment, it was no longer possible for us to stay in Jerusalem. The tremendous loss in popularity which the incident immediately brought about meant also that the power and the malice of the priests and rulers were correspondingly increased. There was nothing for it, if Jesus wished to avoid arrest, but for him and the others of us to leave the city at once, and to retire to some remote district.

JOHN S. HOYLAND, *Simon the Zealot.*
Published by Williams and Norgate, Ltd., London.

A PRAYER

Almighty God, who dost prove us by the fires of tribulation, but who dost not try us beyond that we are able, strengthen us for the times of our passion, that we be not strangers to the sufferings of Christ. Give us at our latter end victory over the last enemies of our soul and confidence to commend our spirits into thy hand: through the same Jesus Christ our Lord. Amen.

WILLARD L. SPERRY.

Seek Comradeship: First Saturday

6. OUR CHRIST

In Christ I feel the heart of God
   Throbbing from heaven through earth;
Life stirs again within the clod,
   Renewed in beauteous birth;
The soul springs up, a flower of prayer,
Breathing His breath out on the air.

In Christ I touch the hand of God
   From His pure height reached down,
By blessed ways before untrod,
   To lift us to our crown;
Victory that only perfect is
Through loving sacrifice, like His.

Holding His hand, my steadied feet
   May walk the air, the seas;
On life and death His smile falls sweet,
   Lights up all mysteries;
Stranger nor exile can I be
In new worlds where He leadeth me.

            LUCY LARCOM (1826-1893).

WHAT POWER ON EARTH COULD RESIST IT?

Jesus and his friends tramping the roads of Galilee; Bernard of Clairvaux and his twenty-nine companions knocking at the door of the despairing reformed Benedictine congregation at Citeaux ready to enter and sustain it; Francis of Assisi and his devoted handful of daring confreres rebuilding San Damiano and discovering that security of fellowship that replaces security of possessions; the loyal lay-friends of Gerard Groote and Florentius Radewyn living together, supporting themselves by copying manuscripts, and offering hostel and religious instruction to the poor youth of Deventer in Holland; Ignatius Loyola, Francis Xavier, and their number conspiring together to found the Society of Jesus and to go to the end of the earth to open up new fields of conquest

for the church; George Fox and his early company in Lancashire
proclaiming the need not for words but for life here and now in
the new order; Newman, Pusey, Froude, and their friends at
Oxford restoring the organic sense of the Christian Society;
Kagawa and his New Life societies in Japan; Grenfell and his
socio-medical work in Labrador; Schweitzer and his medical-mis-
sion to Central Africa—these are all Christian associations that
a man who took the Christian way seriously could join. These are
authentic. They are evidences of men laid hold of by a devotion
that has made life, and a particular way of life, intensely important. If the Christian Church could multiply their kind, what power
on earth could resist it?

The power is there. How may it be laid hold upon? How can
Christians remain content with the apparently incurable mediocrity
of soul that fills the Christian ranks?

Prayer for them is a response to the prior love of God. Nearly
a thousand years ago Bernard of Clairvaux gave a matchless word
on this in a talk to his religious brotherhood: "Do you awake?
Well, He too is awake. If you rise in the night-time, if you anticipate to your utmost your earliest awaking, you will already
find Him waking—you will never anticipate His own awakeness.
In such an intercourse you will always be rash if you attribute any
priority and predominant share to yourself; for He loves both
more than you, and before you love at all."

Prayer then is simply a form of waking up out of the dull sleep
in which our life has been spent in half-intentions, half-resolu-
tions, half-creations, half-loyalties, and a becoming actively aware
of the real character of that which we are and of that which we
are over against. It is an opening of drowsy lids. It is a shaking
off of grave-clothes. It is a dip into acid. It is a daring to "read the
text of the universe in the original." "We should in ourselves learn
and perceive who we are, how and what our life is, what God is
and is doing in us, what he will have from us, and to what ends
he will or will not use us," says John Tauler, a disciple of Eckhart's.

DOUGLAS V. STEERE, *Prayer and Worship.*
Published by Association Press, New York City.

THE UNIVERSAL COMMUNITY

He conceived human society as based neither on the blood-
relationships of natural affinity, nor on the organized relationships

of political or ecclesiastical groupings, but simply on the practical sharing of life between any two individuals on a basis of their common humanity. At once there appears the possibility of a unification of all human beings in a single community, irrespective of race, nationality, sex or creed. The Kingdom of Heaven becomes the universal community of mankind based on the sense of unity between man and man, and expressing itself in the sharing of the means of life to meet human needs.

The conception of a universal community of mankind is in itself an enormous revolution in human thought. But for Jesus this is more than a bare possibility. It is the expression of the true nature of man himself and, therefore, it is grounded in the nature of reality. The creation of the universal family is the meaning of the religious impulse. Therefore it becomes at once the conscious end of all real human effort and at the same time the purpose of God for human life. It is this that brings God and man so closely together in the thought of Jesus, so that God becomes the universal father, and human life in its true expression the revelation of the Divine nature. The task of religion can now be seen in its full scope. The overcoming of fear and isolation is possible through the complete integration of mankind, through a conception which makes God their common father and the world their father's house. If this is the truth about the world, then faith triumphs completely over fear and re-establishes the continuity of all things without recourse to illusion. . . .

The tremendous idea of creating the community of all mankind as the fulfilment of the Divine purpose, does not lead him to an effort to secure the support of the cultured and ruling classes. The Roman Empire was already a political unification of a large part of the world. One might have expected that Jesus would have sought to use this approximation to a universal integration as a basis for the creation of the Kingdom of Heaven on earth. Yet this was precisely what he had already decided against in the temptation in the wilderness. He draws the conclusion that he must choose the band of disciples who are to help him create the Kingdom from the common folk, to which he himself belonged, and must resolutely turn his face away from the rich and the ruling classes. He saw from the beginning that the way to the Kingdom of Heaven lay through the destruction of the existing order. It is this discovery of the common people that is Jesus' great contribution to social history. It is the basis of democracy.

JOHN MACMURRAY, *Creative Society.*
Published by Association Press, New York City.

THE MIRACLE OF FELLOWSHIP

The recovery of Christendom will come, not by the formation of a new party, but by the miracle of fellowship. This we believe; and, believing it, we each desire to learn from others and to be helped by others; we each find that those who seem most to differ from us have often the most to teach us, and that often the very men whom we had been taught to oppose have the highest claim upon our admiration. Because we have been caught in the spirit of fellowship, we find ourselves less and less inclined to deny and ever more ready to respect and to affirm; in this we see the prospect of becoming ourselves more sane and reasonable, since men are apt to deny that which they do not understand, and to affirm those things in which they have found value. If the full presentment of Christ is not given by the Churches or the Church today, it is none the less to be found: it exists, scattered in the hearts of men, who when they come together in Christ's name find Him indeed in the midst of them, and seeing glimpses of His fullness, are made ashamed of their own fragmentariness—their obscurity and obscurantism—by the light which they discover.

PERCY DEARMER, in *A Picture of the Fellowship.*

A PRAYER

Lord of Life, King of Love, Father of our Lord Jesus, in whom all faithful souls have fellowship in the mystery of the Cross; joyously we praise Thee for the company of the shining ones who, rejecting the evil custom of the world, obeyed the heavenly vision in lives of heroic moral beauty, and by Thy grace ascended in triumph from the dark fields of time; humbly beseeching Thee to grant us some measure of their vision and victory who, in weakness were made strong, in sorrow found sanctity, and in death were not dismayed; that our faltering lives may be lifted out of dim shadows of fatality into the light and power and joy of the eternal communion; in Jesus Christ our Savior and Lord. Amen.

JOSEPH FORT NEWTON, *Altar Stairs.*
Published by the Macmillan Company, New York.

Worship God: First Sunday

7. OVERTONES

I heard a bird at break of day
　Sing from the autumn trees
A song so mystical and calm,
　So full of certainties,
No man, I think, could listen long
　Except upon his knees.
Yet this was but a simple bird
　Alone, among dead trees.
　　　　　WILLIAM ALEXANDER PERCY, *In April Once.*
　　　　　Published by Yale University Press.

A SENSE OF WHERE TO GO

On the shores of Lake Michigan
high on a wooden pole, in a box,
two purple martins had a home
and taken away down to Martinique
and let loose, they flew home,
thousands of miles to be home again.
　And this has lights of wonder
　echo and pace and echo again.
The birds let out began flying
north north-by-west north
till they were back home.
How their instruments told them
of ceiling, temperature, air presure,
how their control-boards gave them
reports of fuel, ignition, speeds,
is out of the record, out.
　Across spaces of sun and cloud,
in rain and fog, through air pockets,
wind with them, wind against them,
stopping for subsistence rations,
whirling in gust and spiral,
these people of the air,
these children of the wind,
had a sense of where to go and how,

how to go north north-by-west north,
till they came to one wooden pole,
till they were home again.
  And this has lights of wonder
  echo and pace and echo again
  for other children, other people, yes.
CARL SANDBURG, The People, Yes.

Harcourt, Brace & Co., Publishers, New York. Reprinted by permission.

ETERNITY

Utter no whisper of thy human speech,
But in celestial silence let us tell
Of the great waves of God that through us swell,
Revealing what no tongue could ever teach;
Break not the omnipotent calm, even by a prayer,
Filled with Infinite, seek nor lesser boon:
But with these pines, and with the all-loving moon,
Asking naught, yield thee to the Only Fair;
So shall these moments so divine and rare,
These passing moments of the soul's high noon,
Be of thy day the first pale blush of morn;
Clad in white raiment of God's newly born,
Thyself shalt see when the great world is made
That flows forever from a Love unstayed.
CHARLES ANDERSON DANA (1819-1897).

THE EYES OF GOD

I see them nightly in my sleep.
The eyes of God are very deep.
There is no cave, no sea that knows
So much of unplumbed depth as those,
Or guards with walls or spectres dumb
Such treasures for the venturesome.

I feel them burning on my back.
The eyes of God are very black.
There is no substance and no shade
So black as God His own eyes made;
In earth or heaven no night, no day
At once so black, so bright as they.

I see them wheresoe'er I turn.
The eyes of God are very stern.
The eyes of God are golden fires
That kindle beacons, kindle pyres;
And where like slow moon-rays they pass
They burn up dead things as dry grass.

They wait, and are not hard to find.
The eyes of God are very kind.
They have great pity for weak things
And joy in everything with wings;
And glow, beyond all telling bright,
Each time a brave soul dares a flight.

HERMANN HAGEDORN, in *The Outlook.*

SO BOUNDLESSLY PERSONAL

Personal as the Hebrew prophets had made God, none of them
dreamed of a God so intensely real, so boundlessly personal, so
amazingly akin to man. The boldness and the sweep of Jesus here
outrun description. The corollaries of his belief in God's personality are an entire transformation of the idea of righteousness
and a new emphasis on the significance of the human soul, that,
next to his belief in God, has been the most powerful thing in
history.

Plato had recognized the natural affinity of God and man, their
mutual intelligibility; man, he said, was made by nature to be
intimate with God; but Plato never came near such a sense as
Jesus had of God's kinship, interest, and nearness. Jesus pictures
a God who loves and who enjoys the world he has made down to
the last little sparrow in a nestful, who thinks in terms of color and
life and movement, and who above all else loves and enjoys the
nature of man, sees through man's limitations his worth and
grandeur, and cannot do without him. What teacher ever gave God
so thorough and so puissant a personality? He will have no God
remote if just, still less a God beyond being: he pictures a God involved in all the tragedy of all the world, who takes and keeps the
most resolute and self-sacrificing initiative, a God of energy and
hope. He pictures God as the good shepherd, who seeks the lost
sheep and who finds it and puts it on his shoulders with joy—God
as rejoicing with all his friends in heaven over one sinner that

repents—an emphasis beyond all others on man's personality. Other teachers more than half hinted failure in God, his world a mistake, to be made over again, the larger part of the men (for whom he was supposed to care) utter fiascos, mere fuel for the flames of hell and nothing more to be made of them. Not so Jesus; he saw better and read the triumph of God; the leaven leavens the meal; the seed brings forth a hundredfold; the lost sheep is found; the lost son comes home, drawn by his Father's invincible and irresistible love. God never made the wondrous human soul to be "cast as rubbish to the void." *Fecisti nos ad te,* said Augustine, "Thou hast made us for thyself"; and he learnt it from Jesus, who saw that God *will* have us, that he breaks down the obstacles between man and himself, and when man is angry with him or suspicious of him reconciles him to himself. Jesus "passed by the grand classical speech of religion, which was fast becoming a dead language to the living world . . . and took up the father and mother tongue, the dialect of the human heart, and at his summons and by the transfiguring power of his personality, the name of Father became pure and great enough to describe the inmost nature of the Eternal One."

T. R. GLOVER, *Jesus in the Experience of Men.*
Published by Association Press, New York.

A PRAYER

Save us, Our Father in Whose loving care even a sparrow takes its flight, from the peril of both of pride and discouragement, and help us increasingly so to live that without us some dear fellowship would be lonely, some worthy task less nobly accomplished and some hope of a happier order left unrealized. In His Name without Whom all our lives would be shadows. Amen.

GAIUS GLENN ATKINS.

Concentrate Upon the Ideal: Second Monday

8. DAWN IS FOREVER

I

I would be like the dynamo
That wakens in the city's night
The flowers of the million arcs—
A garden of exuberant light.

II

Let me be like the sun: his light
Shines though the tides of air are hurled
Across it; his unshaken might
Ignores the winds of all the world.

III

Love is wild like the sea—
It may drown us utterly:
But where is a better grave
Than the green light of a wave?

IV

The world—this cool green world we know—
More deeply seen is not the same:
Its heart a star, its life the sun,
This green world is a world of flame.

E. MERRILL ROOT, *Dawn Is Forever.*
Published by Packard and Company, Chicago.

FUGITIVE

What miracle of music lends a dream
Of hearts harmonious! Quick song rings clear
And beautiful, yet a hundred more supreme
We do not hear.

We glimpse a vista down the gloried west:
Twilight and river, sky and hill and lea—
But greater splendors lie beyond a crest
We can not see.

Beauty, what high compulsion do you give
to thought to make us noble! Even so,
What vaster wonder is that fugitive
We never know!

CARL JOHN BOSTELMANN, in *The World Tomorrow.*

BEAUTY'S SECRET

With all our busy seeking, we have not found the sorting house
where loveliness is extracted from the flux of things. We know
not why "great" poetry should move us to unspeakable emotion, or
a stream of notes, arranged in a peculiar sequence, catch us up to
heightened levels of vitality: nor can we guess how a passionate
admiration for that which we call "best" in art or letters can
possibly contribute to the physical evolution of the race. In spite
of many lengthy disquisitions on æsthetics, Beauty's secret is still
her own. A shadowy companion, half seen, half guessed at, she
keeps step with the upward march of life: and we receive her message and respond to it, not because we understand it but because we
must.

Here it is that we approach that attitude of the self, that point
of view, which is loosely and generally called *mystical.*

EVELYN UNDERHILL, *Mysticism.*
Published by E. P. Dutton & Company, New York.

BEAUTY OF LIFE

Why should this unending effort to interpret Jesus have begun at all? For it is not a simple thing that we should be concerned
today with a life lived nineteen hundred years ago. Men are
not ordinarily remembered after they are dead. It is estimated that
some sixty billion people have lived upon this earth since the dawn
of history. Of these the infinitely greater part have passed into a
silence beyond the dimmest recollection. . . .

This Man of Nazareth, hated, crucified, dishonored, has outlived all the mighty things that mocked him. With strange persistence, his influence endures. The thought of him haunts the minds of men with the unsolved problem of the secret of his power. His spirit comes alive and vibrant from those far centuries where that which once seemed the overwhelming significance of some of the greatest of his contemporaries is entombed with their forgotten dust. He challenges and disturbs us as others who were accounted conquerors and creators cannot do. . . .

How shall we explain this power of the man who died on Calvary? What was it that made him greater than the death he died there, and greater than many apparent burials of his influence in the course of history from which that influence has come again in recurrent resurrections?

WALTER RUSSELL BOWIE, *The Master.*
Published by Charles Scribner's Sons, New York.

POSSIBILITIES AND POWER

In Christ we have a revelation of both the human possibilities which are to be fulfilled and the divine power which will fulfill them. In Christ, too, we have the revelation of the significance of human history and of the ground of its meaning which transcends history. . . . We do not believe that the human enterprise will have a tragic conclusion; but the ground of our hope lies not in human capacity but in divine power and mercy, in the character of the ultimate reality, which carries the human enterprise.

REINHOLD NIEBUHR, *Beyond Tragedy.*
Published by Charles Scribner's Sons, New York.

THREE MEDICINES

By contrition we are made clean, by compassion we are made ready, and by true longing toward God we are made worthy. These are three means, as I understand, whereby that all souls come to heaven: that is to say, that have been sinners in earth and shall be saved: for by these three medicines it behoveth that every soul be healed.

JULIAN OF NORWICH.

A SILENT TE DEUM

We thank Thee, Lord,
For all Thy Golden Silences,—
For every Sabbath from the world's turmoil;
For every respite from the stress of life;—
Silence of moorlands rolling to the skies,
Heath-purpled, bracken-clad, aflame with gorse;
Silence of grey tors crouching in the mist;
Silence of deep woods' mystic cloistered calm;
Silence of wide seas basking in the sun;
Silence of white peaks soaring to the blue;
Silence of dawnings, when, their matins sung,
The little birds do fall asleep again;
For the deep silence of high golden noons;
Silence of gloamings and the setting sun;
Silence of moonlit nights and patterned glades;
Silence of stars, magnificently still,
Yet ever chanting their Creator's skill;
For that high silence of Thine Open House,
Dim-branching roof and lofty-pillared aisle,
Where burdened hearts find rest in Thee awhile;
Silence of friendship, telling more than words;
Silence of hearts, close-knitting heart to heart;
Silence of joys too wonderful for words;
Silence of sorrows, when Thou drawest near;
Silence of soul, wherein we come to Thee,
And find ourselves in Thine Immensity;
For that great silence where Thou dwell'st alone—
—Father, Spirit, Son, in One,
Keeping watch above Thine Own,—
Deep unto deep, within us sound sweet chords
Or praise beyond the reach of human words;
In our soul's silence, feeling only Thee,—
We thank Thee, Thank Thee,
Thank Thee, Lord!

Selected Poems of JOHN OXENHAM.
Published by Ernest Benn Ltd., London.

Understand the Actual: Second Tuesday

9. WATCHMAN, WHAT OF THE NIGHT?

Watchman, watchman, what of the night?
Lift high your lantern; show the light!
Is everything peace and quiet abroad;
The city guarded and free of fraud?
Do the stars shine down on a plenty to spare,
And is there laughter and love to share?
O, watchman, what of the night?

It's the zero hour, and this of the night:
Broken the lantern; gutted the light!
The city is guarded but not from fraud.
War and murder are rife abroad.
The cost of the killing mounts with a leap,
But human life is counted cheap.
The flares of riot are red on the sky,
And racial hatred takes long to die.
And there's never a star but a slithering fog
Where want and misery ride at a jog.
The children wail in the streets for bread,
And civilization is in the red.
The beggar still haunts the rich man's board,
But the crumbs are few from the rich man's hoard.
The worker stumbles his road alone—
And where's the finger to move a stone?
The multitudes mouth their numbing cry
Where king and bishop alike pass by;
And the churches bow to an empty form
While Christ the outcast trudges the storm.
And that is what of the night.

LESLIE B. WYNNE, in *Unity*.

THE IDOLATRY OF WEALTH

Few who consider dispassionately the facts of social history
will be disposed to deny that the exploitation of the weak by the
powerful, organized for purposes of economic gain, buttressed by
imposing systems of law, and screened by decorous draperies of
virtuous sentiment and resounding rhetoric, has been a permanent
feature in the life of most communities that the world has yet seen.

But the quality in modern societies which is most sharply opposed to the teaching ascribed to the Founder of the Christian Faith lies deeper than the exceptional failures and abnormal follies against which criticism is most commonly directed. It consists in the assumption, accepted by most reformers with hardly less naïveté than by the defenders of the established order, that the attainment of material riches is the supreme object of human endeavor and the final criterion of human success. Such a philosophy, plausible, militant, and not indisposed, when hard pressed, to silence criticism by persecution, may triumph or may decline. What is certain is that it is the negation of any system of thought or morals which can, except by a metaphor, be described as Christian. Compromise is as impossible between the Church of Christ and the idolatry of wealth, which is the practical religion of capitalist societies, as it was between the Church and the State idolatry of the Roman Empire.

"Modern capitalism," writes Mr. Keynes, "is absolutely irreligious, without internal union, without much public spirit, often though not always, a mere congeries of possessors and pursuers." It is that whole system of appetites and values, with its deification of the life of snatching to hoard, and hoarding to snatch, which now, in the hour of its triumph, while the plaudits of the crowd still ring in the ears of the gladiators and the laurels are still unfaded on their brows, seems sometimes to leave a taste as of ashes on the lips of a civilization which has brought to the conquest of its material environment resources unknown in earlier ages, but which has not yet learned to master itself. It was against that system, while still in its supple and insinuating youth, before success had caused it to throw aside the mask of innocence, and while its true nature was unknown even to itself, that the saints and sages of earlier ages launched their warnings and their denunciations. The language in which theologians and preachers expressed their horror of the sin of covetousness may appear to the modern reader too murkily sulphurous; their precepts on the contracts of business and the disposition of property may seem an impracticable pedantry. But rashness is a more agreeable failing than cowardice, and, when to speak is unpopular, it is less pardonable to be silent than to say too much.

R. H. Tawney, *Religion and the Rise of Capitalism*.
Published by Harcourt, Brace & Company, New York.

A SELFISH COMPETITIVE STRUGGLE

The fundamental evil of modern industrialism is that it encourages competition for private gain instead of co-operation for public service. This perversion of motive fosters : —

(a) An organization of industry which treats the workers as hands rather than as persons, and which deprives them of the control which they may reasonably claim to exercise over the conditions under which they earn their livelihood.

(b) The absence of responsibility on the part of those employed for the permanent results of their industry and of human interest in the work which they do : evils which are intensified by the mechanical and monotonous character of many of the processes and duties required.

(c) A disposition on the part of some of those engaged in industry to seek their own advantage at the expense of the community by unduly limiting the output, raising the prices, or deteriorating the quality of the work which they perform.

(d) Conditions of poverty which do not arise from individual defects or from natural scarcity, but which exist side by side with excessive riches.

(e) An organization of industry which creates a condition of insecurity among the workers and which makes their livelihood precarious and uncertain.

(f) An attitude of mutual antagonism and suspicion between the different parties engaged in industry.

The conception of industry as a selfish competitive struggle is unchristian. Industry ought to be regarded primarily as a social service, based on the effort of every individual to discharge his duty to his neighbor and to the community.

The Report of the Archbishops' Fifth Committee of Inquiry,
Christianity and Industrial Problems.
Published by the Society for Promoting Christian Knowledge, London.

CONCENTRATION OF WEALTH

There has been no great shift in the economic base since 1933. The party of wealth and talents as an economic order has not been decimated. Banks have not been nationalized, nor the railways taken over by the Government. Not a single instrumentality of economic power has been wrested from this party. The public debt has been increased, and its members hold bonds representing that debt. Even the financing of farmers has been assumed by the Federal Government on the basis of tax-exempt bonds. This operation has strengthened, not weakened, the party of wealth and talents; in the place of defaulted and decaying farm mortgages, it holds bonds guaranteed by the Federal Government. In the process of of liquidation now going on, all signs indicate a swift concentration of defaulted and distress paper in the hands of the shrewd and enterprising. There is no hint whatever of any change in the old practices of reorganizing bankrupt concerns. The "little fellow" is being frozen out as usual. At the end of the depression, if it ever ends, the concentration of wealth in the United States will doubtless mark a new high point in the evolution of American economy.

CHARLES A. BEARD, in *Scribner's Magazine.*

A PRAYER

God be merciful to us for we are sinners. We humbly confess that we are men and women of unclean lips, and that we dwell in the midst of a people of unclean lips. Lay a live coal upon our mouth, we implore Thee, and take our iniquity away, through Jesus Christ our Lord. Amen.

CHARLES E. JEFFERSON.

A PRAYER

Oh God, Thine enemies, Greed and Exploitation have come up against us! They have invaded Thy sanctuary, the Home, and defiled Thine altar. They have erected walls of unemployment against those who would worship at that shrine. They have built barriers of poverty between husband and wife. Children, who should be a blessing, they have made a calamity. The young have they dragged away to industrial slavery. But do thou, Oh, God, arise for our help! Bestow on us Thy strength in body, mind, and spirit, that we may assail and conquer the hosts of Mammon. Give us wisdom and courage for the building up of a free society, based on brotherly cooperation, in which marriage and the home may rightly flourish, undarkened by the shadows of ignorance, want, and fear, as institutions of enlightenment and happiness. We, thy Children, call upon thee to accomplish through us Thy holy will Amen.

KENNETH W. PORTER.

Be Concerned: Second Wednesday

10. THE ROOT CAUSE

The church is under obligation to proclaim the truth that the disintegration of society has one root cause. Human life is falling to pieces because it has tried to organize itself into unity on a secularistic and humanistic basis without any reference to the divine will and power above and beyond itself. It has sought to be self-sufficient, a law unto itself. Nor is there any hope in the ascription of sacred quality to nation or state or class. A false sacred, a false God, merely adds demonic power to the unredeemed passions of men. Though bringing about temporary and local unity it prepares for mankind an even worse and wider conflict. The recall to God in penitence must stand first.

Yet how shall men know who and what God is, and what it is of which they must repent, and in what new direction they must walk, and whence they may find strength to walk therein? The answer to these questions God himself has given in the revelation of his will and supremely in Jesus Christ. In God is the secret of true unity among men and in Christ is revealed the secret of God. The first task of the church, now as always, is to make known the gospel, and to assert the claim of Jesus Christ as the incarnate Word of God to the lordship of all human life. . . .

The life of the church is deeply infected with the very ills from which humanity suffers. The divisions and the conflicts of mankind have been reproduced and even justified within its own borders. Again and again Christian groups have persecuted and sought to destroy one another and with equal guilt have persecuted men of other faiths, and this is still happening today. The church's recall of the world to the feet of Christ must be preceded by the recall of itself. The church is under call to confess its sin and to seek anew from God forgiveness and the cleansing of its life.

But there is peril in these general propositions, true as they may be. The call to Christians to repent and submit their lives anew to God in Christ has to be obeyed in the midst of the concrete realities of the common life, where decisions have to be taken and acts with all their irrevocable consequences done. Perplexities and problems at once arise. They press the more heavily the more earnestly the Christian believer seeks to bring everything in his life into the obedience of Christ.

The difficulties arise in the main because the Christian finds himself called upon at every point to act in relation to systems or frameworks of life which partake of both good and evil; they are of God and yet also of human sin. The orders of family, community, people, nation, are part of the God-given basis and structure of human life without which the individual would have no existence at all; yet man's sin—his pride, greed, fear, idolatry—has infected them all. Hence the Christian who has seen the perfect will of God in Christ and would serve that will in the midst of his fellow men finds himself in perpetual tension and conflict. He accepts thankfully his community in order to live and to work in it and for it; yet if he would work in it and for it for Christ he must be in continuous protest against it.

The difficulty of deciding how far in particular instances the Christian should go in cooperation with ways of life which are in greater or less degree contrary to God's will is often great, and the danger of self-deception is always present. No general principle of guidance can be laid down. That the ways of the community or nation may reach such a pitch of evil that there is no option for the church but to repudiate them altogether, and even at times refuse cooperation with them, can hardly be questioned in view of contemporary events; but just where that point is must be left to the guidance of the Spirit. This, however, must be said: The church is under obligation never to lose sight of its one supreme calling to bear costing witness, in deed as well as in word, to the higher way of life in Christ. Where it must join in what it feels to be a partial approach to the perfect will of Christ, it must keep its spirit sensitive and humble by continual acknowledgment before God of the sin of mankind which is wresting the gifts of God to evil ends, and in which it is itself implicated. This is the tragic and continuous tension in which the church is always placed, the tension between the pure ideals of the kingdom and the unredeemed community of men in which it has to live and bear its witness. But so soon as it seeks peace by becoming unconscious of that tension then it is traitorous to its Master and Lord.

"Report of the Section on Church and Community."
The Oxford Conference: Official Report.
Published by Willett, Clark & Company, Chicago.

SQUALOR INSTEAD OF RADIANT GLORY

The clash of giant forces in the realms of international and industrial relations reverberates unceasingly around the globe, until there is scarcely a thinker of repute but is filled with combined fury and despair at the spectacle of man's life in the modern world. . . .

A Gospel which has no challenge, no revolution in it: a Gospel which constantly allows itself to be challenged and revolutionized by the suggestions of the secular crowd, is useless. Whatever men may think about it, they need to be told that they are sinners outraging a divine purpose: they need to believe in the Atonement wrought by God Incarnate: they need penitence and faith. . . .

The modern man can hardly believe himself a miserable sinner. He is either an employer, very angry about the sins of the workers; or he is a worker, very angry about the sins of the employers. He is not disposed to practice self-accusation. He is prepared to accuse only those forces and obstacles which obstruct him in the pursuit of what he regards as his own rights. And so the confusion grows. The mad oppositions continue. The world is sick and awaits deliverance; but the very nature of its sickness defines the shape which the Christian message must take today. . . .

The vital need of this day is that Christian men shall understand the world-constructive implications of their Faith, and shall see that their religion is not a mild sedative for frayed nerves, or a palliative of their mortal fears, and nothing more, but that it is a terrific energy and a shining star. The Gospel is in the world to renew and reform and control the world: to produce a society in which strength and skill shall become the instruments of love and not the servants of selfishness: to bind men with one indissoluble bond of loyalty: to produce beauty which shall banish ugliness and to awaken praise which shall silence the noises of war. The Gospel is here to evoke upon the chaos and squalor of this earth the radiant glory of that great city, the New Jerusalem . . . whereof the inhabitants do serve God day and night in His temple, and the sound of their joy is like the sound of many waters.

W. G. Peck, *The Divine Society.*
Published by the Student Christian Movement, London.

THIS MATTER OF OBEDIENCE

The nearer we are to perfect obedience, the less we sin, and the farther from it we are, the more we sin. In brief: whether a man be good, better, or best of all; bad, worse, or worst of all; sinful or saved before God; it all lieth in this matter of obedience. Therefore it hath been said: the more of Self and Me, the more of sin and wickedness. So likewise it hath been said: the more the Self, the I, the Me, the Mine, that is, self-seeking and selfishness, abate in a man, the more doth God's I, that is, God Himself, increase in him.

THEOLOGIA GERMANICA.

GOD SUFFERS

I cannot think that God could be content
To view unmoved the toiling and the strain,
The groaning of the ages, sick and spent,
The whole creation travailing in pain.
The suffering God is no vast cosmic force,
That by some blind, unthinking, loveless power
Keeps stars and atoms swinging in their course,
And reckons naught of men in this grim hour.
Nor is the suffering God a fair ideal
Engendered in the questioning hearts of men,
A figment of the mind to help me steel
My soul to rude realities I ken.
God suffers with a love that cleanses dross;
A God like that, I see upon a cross.

GEORGIA HARKNESS, *Holy Flame.*
Published by Bruce Humphries, Inc., Boston.

A PRAYER

O Thou, who are the Way, the Truth and the Life, grant that in Thee we may see the Way, may know the Truth and live the Life, that in the shadow of Thy cross we may catch the glory of that perfect love for all mankind which alone can heal the sorrows of a broken world. We ask it of Thee, our blessed Redeemer.

BISHOP PAUL JONES.

Endeavor to Transform: Second Thursday

II. PROPERTY

The freest government can not long endure when the tendency of the law is to create a rapid accumulation of property in the hands of a few and to render the masses poor and dependent.

DANIEL WEBSTER.

CONCENTRATION OF FINANCIAL POWER

The Bell System, with over five billion dollars of consolidated gross assets arrayed under the direct or indirect control of American Telephone & Telegraph Co., constitutes the largest aggregation of capital and resources that has ever been controlled by a single private company at any time in the history of business. The System consists of over 200 corporations directly and indirectly controlled by the American Telephone & Telegraph Co. This company controls, from its offices in New York City, between 80 and 90 per cent of local telephone service and 98 per cent of the long-distance telephone wires of the United States, including practically all wire facilities used in radio program transmission. It owns, leases, and operates about 15,000 teletypewriter machines (as compared with over 17,000 machines controlled by the telegraph companies) and gives the only teletypewriter exchange service (TWX) in the country. In addition, there are some 3,500 Morse telegraph machines used in the service of Bell Companies or leased for private line service. Transoceanic radio telephone service is a monopoly of the Bell System. A large part of press news and all of telephotograph service is dependent on Bell plant and service. . . .

The economic influence of the Bell System is pervasive in other directions as well. Its policies affect the interests of over 15,000,000 telephone users who obtain their service from one or another of the companies in the System. It is the largest private employer of labor. In 1929, it employed approximately 500,000 people; in 1937, about 300,000 people. The number of investors who have put their money in Bell System bonds and stocks is very large, approaching a million. Even though the average holdings are very small, still in the aggregate they represent a substantial public interest in the affairs of the System. As a purchaser of goods and services, the System has broad ramifications. Its annual purchases of raw materials reach into hundreds of millions of dollars, depending on the construction needs of the operating companies. As a bank depositor, using almost a third of the active banks of the United States, and as a purchaser of insurance, and in other commercial relations, the Bell System reaches out into the economic life of the country. . . . Naturally, there are social, political, and economic problems that arise from the sheer magnitude of such enormous wealth under single control. . . .

The dispersion as of the end of 1935 is indicated by the average holding per stockholder, which had declined to 28.1 shares. Entering into this 1935 figure of 28.1 shares were 244,566 stockholders with average holdings of but 2.87 shares each, and, at the other extreme, 43 stockholders with average holdings of 22,688 shares each. These 43 big stockholders owned over a quarter of a million shares more than the combined holdings of nearly a quarter of a million small stockholders.

So long as satisfactory dividends are received by the four-fifths of all stockholders who own slightly less than one-fourth of the total stock, the voting proxy constitutes a relatively simple expedient by which the management may obtain the voting power of a block of stock so large that its combination with the holdings of a few large holders, acting and voting in common, constitutes complete working control of the company. The chances of a successful challenge to this voting power control on the part of any independent or opposed financial group are nullified by the very size of the corporation itself. The total outstanding stock of the American Co. on December 31, 1907, was 1,315,514 shares with a par value of $131,551,400, not including the $150,000,000 issue of bonds convertible into stock, held by the banking syndicate. As of December 31, 1935, the total of outstanding voting stock was 18,662,275 shares of $1,866,227,500 par value. Obviously, management control of the American Co. never can be acquired by any rival financial interests through outright purchase of a majority or even a sizable minority of this voting stock. As related previously the Mackay group made that attempt, in 1907. Although their purchases reached a maximum of well over 70,000 shares, representing at one time an investment at market value of something over $10,000,000, the attempt did not succeed even to the extent of naming a single director to the company, and man-

agement control continued in the hands of those who constituted
the executive committee and the board of directors, all of whom
collectively held less stock than the Mackays. With the complete
failure of the company's largest single stockholder to gain any
voice in the management of the company, it is apparent that the
chances of a successful challenge to the voting power control of
the executive committee by any dissident stockholder or small
group of stockholders, regardless of the size of their individual
holdings, are negligible if not absolutely nonexistent. Furthermore, the probable heavy expense of any effective plan to circular-
ize the complete list of stockholders, running well over half a million in number, in order to compete with the incumbent management's control over the company-financed system of proxy solici-
tation, would further discourage any such effort. . . .

It follows that ultimate responsibility for Bell System policies,
and for their results, as set forth in the succeeding chapters of this
report, rests solely with the executive officers of the American Co.
These Bell System executives have continued in undisturbed possession of that responsibility, practically as a self-perpetuating
group, since the company's management control was changed in
1907, under the influence of those investment bankers who were
successful aspirants in the competition to attain dominance in the
field of communications.

Federal Communications Commission,
Proposed Report Telephone Investigation,
Pursuant to Public Resolution No. 8, 74th Congress.

ETERNAL VIGILANCE

Tolerance in any society very largely depends upon the degree
of security felt by those who govern it. They are willing to discuss when they have the sense that the basis of institutions is
not in dispute. Fear has always been the enemy of reason; and
men who feel that expectations they deem legitimate are in danger
have always been more ready to repress than to argue. . . .

Historically, in any society, men have rarely found it easy to
move from one way of life to another without conflict. We cling
to our habituations. We find it difficult to agree that the interests
we represent must give way before the claims of different interests. We fear novelty; we associate with our wonted ways ideas,
even ideals, of right behavior, challenge to which cuts at the

root of our adaptation to our environment. We want liberty; but we do not want the achievement of liberty to threaten a way of life in which we eagerly believe. . . . If there is any obvious lesson in the continental experience of these last two decades it is surely the lesson that representative government is, at best, a delicate and difficult adventure. To maintain it presupposes a people that is at unity upon all matters of fundamental importance. That is the essential condition of tolerance. Once that unity disappears, men begin to be afraid; and, as I have said, fear and tolerance are antithetic terms. . . .

There are no certainties in history; and I do not therefore share the views of those who believe that conflict is inevitable. But I do share the views of those who hold that there was never a time when vigilance was more urgent if our liberties are to be maintained. . . .

The true reading of the years since 1918 is that they are a warning whose significance no man can escape. All over the world, liberty is on the defensive; all over the world, also, those are at least its friends who most loudly proclaim their devotion to its service. To maintain its authority over the mind when differences are keen, and passions profound, is the most difficult exercise in the act of government. Few things are so easy as to reply to grievance by repression; few things are so hard as to surrender interests which have been made sacred to their possessors by time-honored prescription. After nearly three centuries of fortunate compromise, we have come once more to the parting of the ways.

HAROLD J. LASKI, *Dare We Look Ahead?*
By permission of The Macmillan Company, publishers, New York.

A PRAYER

O Thou, who art the true sun of the world, ever rising, and never going down; who, by thy most wholesome appearing and sight dost nourish and gladden all things in heaven and earth; we beseech thee mercifully to shine into our hearts, that the night and darkness of sin, and the mists of error on every side, being driven away by the brightness of thy shining within our hearts, we may all our life walk without stumbling, as in the day-time, and being pure and clean from the works of darkness, may abound in all good works which thou hast prepared for us to walk in. *Amen.*

ERASMUS (1467-1536).

Proceed Resolutely: Second Friday

12. THE MASSACRE

One day, when we were in Peraea, some grim and horrible news came down from Jerusalem. . . .

A great big mountaineer from the upper slopes of Hermon, far away to the north—rose to his feet, and in fierce, short sentences, which he hissed out in a tone of concentrated bitterness, told us a story which made us clamor furiously for vengeance— and yet it was, and is still, a story common enough in our oppressed and outraged country.

Three days before a party of them from a village in Upper Galilee had come to Jerusalem for some special sacrifices. Their leader had been a man named Barabbas, of whom I had heard. He was a well-known and determined Zealot.

On entering the city they had had trouble with the Roman guard at the gate over a question of whether they were going to be allowed to retain their arms in the city or not. Hot words had passed, and they had finally forced their way through (very unwisely no doubt), arms and all. I heard afterwards that there had been quite a little battle about it. The guard had been overpowered by weight of numbers, and some of them had been killed. They are fine fellows, our Galileans, fine dangerous men.

The party of them had gone straight to the Temple for their sacrifices; and there, right in the holy place, the vengeance of the Romans had overtaken them. . . . These fell upon the Galileans unexpectedly while they were sacrificing, killed a number of them, and captured Barabbas (his fate would be crucifixion). The rest had only escaped because they had managed to get lost in the panic-stricken Temple crowd. They had come straight down to Jesus in Peraea, for they knew, of course, that he was a Galilean, and they had heard all about his marvelous deeds. Now they appealed to him, as the destined Messiah of God, to arise in might and destroy these wicked pagans, these vile desecrators of our holy Jewish Temple, these heartless shedders of our sacred Jewish blood.

The man's speech was wonderful. There he stood, calling Jesus to vengeance. His right arm was roughly swathed in a blood-soaked bandage. His eyes flashed. He seemed to be the spirit of

our downtrodden country, summoning the greatest of her sons to
save her.

Again, as in the Temple a week or two before, I lifted up my
heart and prayed with feverish earnestness to Jehovah that His
Prophet at last might be worthy of Him.

But no—again nothing but disappointment and shame. Deliberately, heartlessly (I can use no other words), Jesus dragged in
the stale side-issue of religion. Think of talking religion at such
a time!

All he could say was: "Do you think that, because they suffered thus, these Galileans were worse sinners than the rest of
the Galileans? I tell you, no; unless you repent you will all perish
as they did."

You see? Not merely religion instead of patriotism, but a definite and deliberate threat to all patriotic Jews that unless we
adopted his views about God and repentence and so forth the
Romans would slaughter us too!

Oh, it was hard to be loyal to him sometimes: or hard, rather,
to know which loyalty to choose, our loyalty to him or our loyalty
to our glorious country and her God. . . .

I remember the third day of that Last Week chiefly on account of a series of conversations which took place in the Temple
between Jesus and various deputations from the Jewish leaders,
and for the teaching which arose from the questions asked by
these deputations. . . .

The question asked by this deputation was a very clever one.
Ought we to pay the Roman taxes or not? Quite apart from any
question of insurrection, were we or were we not justified in engaging in a campaign of passive resistance against the iniquitous
extortion and oppression of Rome?

You can see how cunning this question was. The Prophet's
enemies had staged their attempt to discredit him with great skill.
The occasion was as public as it possibly could be. There were
thousands of Passover pilgrims round him, many of them from
our own Galilee. Most of them, I believe, had arms concealed
under their outer garments. At the signal of revolt, had it been
given, they would have been transformed in a moment into an
armed mob, filled with a wild fanatical enthusiasm, thirsting to
shed their blood for their country. With the leadership which
Jesus could so well have given, they might have stormed the

Tower of Antonia, where the Roman garrison had its quarters, massacred every Roman in the city, freed our sacred soil from their presence, and (I at least have no doubt of this) established throughout the world the Divine Empire of the Jews. . . .

Again I found myself passionately praying to Jehovah that the committal might at last be made: that the opportunity might be seized and our country saved from her alien oppressors; that the Messiah might be worthy of his high calling.

But alas! another tragic disappointment was in store for us. When Jesus spoke, it was not to declare for non-payment of taxes —for resistance to oppression, in however mild a form—it was to lead his listeners off once more on what we could not but feel to be the false trail of religion: "Give to the Emperor what belongs to the Emperor, and to God what belongs to God."

It was too heart-rending for words! Another reckless squandering of God-given opportunity! Another wanton sacrificing of patriotism to religion! Another turning away from his country's need on the part of the greatest leader our country had ever known! . . . We could scarcely bring ourselves to remain his companions any longer. . . .

It was astounding how quickly the word was passed round amongst those pilgrims that Jesus was no good for our purpose. I was in close touch, of course, with the Galilean Zealots, of whom there were many thousands up at the Feast—hardy men, all prepared for instant action. There was not one of them who did not curse my Master to my face, after that decision about the Tribute Money, as a craven pietist, who would never do anything to help our country and to justify the hopes which he had aroused.

That occasion had been the decisive turning-point. Thenceforth Jesus' fate was sealed.

JOHN S. HOYLAND, *Simon the Zealot.*
Published by Williams & Norgate, Ltd., London.

WIND AND LYRE

Thou art the wind and I the lyre:
Strike, O Wind, on the sleeping strings—
Strike till the dead heart stirs and sings!
I am the altar and thou the fire:

Burn, O Fire, to a snowy flame—
Burn me clean of the mortal blame!

I am the night and thou the dream:
Touch me softly and thrill me deep,
When all is white on the hills of sleep.
Thou art the moon and I the stream:
Shine to the trembling heart of me,
Light my soul to the mother-sea.

EDWIN MARKHAM.
Published by Doubleday, Doran & Co., New York.

THERE'S A WIDENESS IN GOD'S MERCY

There's a wideness in God's mercy,
Like the wideness of the sea;
There's a kindness in his justice,
Which is more than liberty.

There is no place where earth's sorrows
Are more felt than up in heaven;
There is no place where earth's failings
Have such kindly judgment given.

For the love of God is broader,
Than the measure of man's mind;
And the heart of the Eternal
Is most wonderfully kind.

If our love were but more simple,
We should take him at his word;
And our lives would be all sunshine
In the sweetness of our Lord.

FREDERICK W. FABER, 1854.

A PRAYER

Almighty God, who in thy providence, dost not suffer us to evade life's sternest trials, give us an untroubled heart as we face our unknown future. Grant us day by day such measure of thy Hold Spirit that when the times of our proving come, the same Spirit shall speak for us right words and sustain us by its serenity. Amen.

WILLARD L. SPERRY.

Seek Comradeship: Second Saturday

13. LETTER TO AN ELDER GENERATION

We hold that life works haltingly through us,
Using for its dark ends our hands, our hearts,
That life is one vast movement and as men
We are its passing and eternal parts.

There is a force that drives us on and yet
We are that force and sometimes have controlled it,
There is an actual power that we are,
Our mind and actions, but we cannot hold it.

O splendid flame that madly makes us men,
Drives and defies, destroys but to create us,
Bring million-mannered life, brings single death,
We will accept what utter ends await us.

There is a long frontier in our own heart
That we will follow till the last shores bend
Blackly away down to the final land
With laughter and with courage to the end.

There is a forest where we walk our lives
Away beneath the spruces and the larch,
It is not that we die beneath those trees,
But always that we march, O that we march.

O South Pass where the ox and wagon broke
And men fought westward through the stone and snow.
O land beyond the great pass of the world,
Desert or Eldorado, still we go.

PAUL ENGLE, *American Song.*
Doubleday, Doran & Co., Inc., Garden City, N. Y.

UNITY IN DIVERSITY

Friendship is strong and valuable and durable in proportion
as it is centered in some good purpose, some noble ideal, some
service of the mind and soul. This is the groundwork of the most

lasting kind of friendship. This it is that makes friendship the source of noble character. And what is true of friendship is true also of all group fellowship, for friendship and fellowship are essentially the same.

The first principle of *Christian* fellowship is its belief that we have in common something in our nature that is unspeakably sacred, something which is capable of communion with God. In the Bible and the New Testament in particular this is generally called "the soul." When we talk about the sanctity of personality we are putting this belief in the language of today. Here then in personality is the sphere, the element, in which Christian fellowship is first and foremost rooted. The primary aim of Christian fellowship is the fulfillment of that higher and deeper possibility in human nature which we call personality, the perfection of that "character," which is the shape or form given to personality in the course of life. . . .

Now, according to Christianity, all souls have it in them to become like God; though few in fact show clear signs of this. In the mass of men the actual spirit or attitude of personality is mostly one not of divine power and love, but one of conventionality and self-seeking. Most men are, from the point of view of the ideal, still in a state of infantile immaturity. Until we realize the profound distinction just explained, the Christian principle of reverence for all mankind must appear "moonshine." But as Christians we believe that God looks at "the things that are not" as if they were, and bids His children value every man, woman, and child in virtue of the possibility that they can become like Jesus Christ.

Christian fellowship is friendship in the light of that idea, and that idea is a sure basis for fellowship. It gives supreme value to life, because it gives such infinite variety of interest. Personality is the most wonderfully varied and diverse achievement, and therefore the possibilities of friendship between persons are illimitable in their variety: there is so much hidden in the future, so much to be unfolded from the germ in which the ideal now lies hidden. And it is by fellowship with one another that we attain the fullness of life which God has in store for us.

The person who makes himself, his experience, his way of looking at things, the test and measure of all, says virtually, "I am a perfect man: all that is not according to my mind is abnormal." That, of course, is the blank negation of fellowship. The growth of personality depends upon the acquisition of the contrary attitude of mental co-operation, of magnanimity of heart, of instinctive looking beyond our circle, Christian or otherwise, for traces of the fellowship of the Kingdom of God. And here we can help each other by our very diversities. For surely most human beings are like organs, with only a very few of their many stops in use. It is by fellowship that we learn what stops are silent in our personalities, and how to pull out these stops and live with the whole of our capacity for receiving the life of God and transmitting it to others. For how far the Christian ideal reaches beyond the limits of the particular forms of it which we ourselves understand! "Unity in Diversity" is of the essence of human personality, as it is of the essence of the Christian fellowship which rests upon reverence for personality, in all its richness of possibility.

MALCOLM SPENCER and H. S. HEWISH,
Fellowship Principles and Practice.
Published by George Allen and Unwin, London.

BEYOND EDUCATION TO REDEMPTION

The urgency of the crisis in which we find ourselves and the necessity of much greater unity among Christians, if the church is to co-operate with the state and community in education, impel us in this ecumenical conference to make an attempt to sum up basic assumptions which underlie an education acceptable to Christians.

Christians share the conviction that there is one living and true God, Creator and Lord of earth and heaven, whose universe is planned and controlled by wisdom and love, and the chief of whose creatures is man, possessed of reason and conscience, and capable of becoming like him in character and sharing eternal life with him in an enduring society of the righteous. But Christians know themselves and all men as sinners and members of a race estranged from God in pride and at war within itself through selfishness. Man, both individually and collectively, needs redemption. God, the Creator and Lord, is also the Redeemer revealed in Christ, who died and rose again for us. God gives himself in his Spirit to re-create individuals and communities who turn to him in repentance and to guide them to discover for themselves the way of Christ and to grow into his stature in faith and hope and love.

The divine purpose to redeem, which is eternal in the will of God, was disclosed in the series of historic divine acts by which the purpose was realized in the life of man. The story of the revelation of this purpose and of its fulfillment, together with an inspiring record of the long history of the people of God—first as the Jewish church, inchoate, provisional, expectant, then divinely established as the body of Christ—is told in the Bible. To this we continually appeal. It is our charter, the main evidence for our belief that the heavens have been opened and that God is a God who lives and acts. The Bible has not always been wisely used, but the survival of Christianity will depend, as it has always depended, on its continual use. Because it comes from God the Bible has a universal quality, and by it man is judged. There is in the Bible a true revelation of the nature of God to men of every age, authenticated alike by the authority of the church and by the interior witness of the Spirit in the heart of man; there is an interpretation of human history; there is a view of life, which can be obtained from no other quarter. The Bible has that to say about God and about man which the present generation, perhaps more than any other, needs urgently to hear.

"Report of the Section on Church Community
and State in Relation to Education."
The Oxford Conference: Official Report.
Published by Willett, Clark & Company, Chicago.

A PRAYER

Eternal Father, from whom all love and friendship come, we thank Thee for our friends, and ask of Thee the spirit of true comradeship. Keep us faithful both in presence and absence; may the bond of loyalty hold us in our work and play; make us good and helpful in our common life, and let us not fail one another when difficulties or troubles come. In the name of Him who is the perfect Friend.

W. CHARTER PIGGOTT.

Worship God: Second Sunday

14. HEAVEN'S MAGNIFICENCE

Since o'er thy footstool here below
    Such radiant gems are strown,
Oh, what magnificence must glow,
    My God, about thy throne!
So brilliant here these drops of light,
There the full ocean rolls, how bright!

If night's blue curtain of the sky,
    With thousand stars inwrought,
Hung like a royal canopy
    With glittering diamonds fraught,
Be, Lord, thy temple's outer veil,
What splendor at the shrine must dwell!

The dazzling sun at noontide hour,
    Forth from his flaming vase
Flinging o'er earth the golden shower
    Till vale and mountain blaze,
But shows, O Lord, one beam of thine:
What, then, the day where thou dost shine!

Ah, how shall these dim eyes endure
    That noon of living rays!
Or how my spirit, so impure,
    Upon thy brightness gaze!
Anoint, O Lord, anoint my sight,
And robe me for that world of light.

           WILLIAM AUGUSTUS MUHLENBERG (1796-1877).

SUNSET ON THE BEARCAMP

A gold fringe on the purpling hem
    Of hills the river runs,
As down its long, green valley falls
    The last of summer's suns.
Along its tawny gravel-bed
    Broad-flowing, swift, and still,

As if its meadow levels felt
  The hurry of the hill,
Noiseless between its banks of green
  From curve to curve it slips;
The drowsy maple-shadows rest
  Like fingers on its lips. . . .

Touched by a light that hath no name,
  A glory never sung,
Aloft on sky and mountain wall
  Are God's great pictures hung.
How changed the summits vast and old!
  No longer granite-browed,
They melt in rosy mist; the rock
  Is softer than the cloud;
The valley holds its breath; no leaf
  Of all its elms is twirled:
The silence of eternity
  Seems falling on the world.

The pause before the breaking seals
  Of mystery is this;
Yon miracle-play of night and day
  Makes dumb its witnesses.
What unseen altar crowns the hills
  That reach up stair on stair?
What eyes look through, what white wings fan
  These purple veils of air?
What Presence from the heavenly heights
  To those of earth stoops down?
Not vainly Hellas dreamed of gods
  On Ida's snowy crown!

Slow fades the vision of the sky,
  The golden water pales,
And over all the valley-land
  A gray-winged vapor sails.
I go the common way of all;
  The sunset fires will burn,
The flowers will blow, the river flow,
  When I no more return.

No whisper from the mountain pine
　　Nor lapsing stream shall tell
The stranger, treading where I tread,
　　Of him she loved them well.

But beauty seen is never lost,
　　God's colors all are fast;
The glory of this sunset heaven
　　Into my soul has passed,
A sense of gladness unconfined
　　To mortal date or clime;
As the soul liveth, it shall live
　　Beyond the years of time.
Beside the mystic asphodels
　　Shall bloom the home-born flowers,
And new horizons flush and glow
　　With sunset hues of ours.

Farewell! these smiling hills must wear
　　Too soon their wintry frown,
And snow-cold winds from off them shake
　　The maple's red leaves down.
But I shall see a summer sun
　　Still settling broad and low;
The mountain slopes shall blush and bloom,
　　The golden water flow.
A lover's claim is mine on all
　　I see to have and hold,—
The rose-light of perpetual hills,
　　And sunsets never cold!

　　　　　The Complete Poetical Works of John Greenleaf Whittier.
　　　　　Published by Houghton, Mifflin and Co., New York.

VERTICAL SUPPORT

　　Faith in God is the only effective support to the individual life in a world which is the playground of vast aggregates and vast impersonal forces.

　　It is too often forgotten that the principle of the worth of the individual personality cannot stand by itself in our world, nor can it stand in the strength of a merely horizontal civilization. It needs a guarantee and support, vertical in nature. In other words, if the worth of the individual man is to be a compelling faith, it must be derived from the Fatherhood of God. For look what is happening to the inherent worth of the individual in our world. It is being flattened out by a parade of juggernaut cars. It is denied by many phases of our present capitalism. It is cynically despised by a steadily increasing militarism. It is trampled on by Fascism. It is smothered by Communism. It cannot hang in midair. It needs foundations. The only foundations robust enough for a support for the inviolable worth of the individual are indicated in the cry of the psalmist, "The eternal God is my refuge."

How easily this is forgotten is seen in a recent book by Joseph Wood Krutch, *Was Europe a Success?* Summing up some convictions of his own, he declares that he believes in "the sacredness of personality." And as those words march across the page one cries out, "Halt, who goes there?" For that word "sacredness" is a religious word. What does "the sacredness of personality" come from? With profound respect for Mr. Krutch we may still ask, What right has he to believe in the sacredness of personality, he who declares, in *The Modern Temper,* that "living is merely a physiological process with only a physiological meaning, and that it is most satisfactorily conducted by creatures who never feel the need to attempt to give it any other"? How firm a foundation for the "sacredness of personality" in that word, "merely physiological"! It is a striking instance of a very common process, pitching God out of the universe, and still using a vocabulary about man which is utterly meaningless without God.

HALLFORD E. LUBCOCK, *Christian Faith and Economic Change.*
Published by The Abingdon Press, New York.

A PRAYER

Breathe on me, Breath of God,
    Fill me with life anew,
That I may love what Thou dost love,
    And do what Thou would'st do.

Breathe on me, Breath of God,
    Until my heart is pure,
Until with The I will one will,
    To do and to endure.

E. HATCH (1835-1889).

Concentrate Upon the Ideal: Third Monday

15. THE SIGNATURE OF GOD

Our mansions shall be built on new-born dreams,
Buttressed more surely than those built on land
Like eagle-nests perched on these feudal steeps,
The world once battled for—and lost in flames.

Dawn breaks because it is too full of Heaven,
And spills its bliss upon a wakening world,
Where vernal lyric trees write down elate
Long shadows of the signature of God.

EDWARDS DAVIS, *Lovers of Life.*
Published by Baker & Taylor Company, New York.

ENTIRE SURRENDER

Science seems to me to teach in the highest and strongest manner the great truth which is embodied in the Christian conception of entire surrender to the will of God. Sit down before fact as a little child, be prepared to give up every preconceived notion, follow humbly wherever and do whatever abysses nature leads, or you shall learn nothing. I have only begun to learn content and peace of mind since I have resolved at all risks to do this.

HUXLEY.

AWAITING A NEW AGE

Jesus was born in one of the great moments of history. . . . The little strip of land, halfway across which Jesus lived, and over which for millennia armies had marched to defeat or victory, had become the channel through which the Far East poured its commerce and gold into the West.

To all this transformation Jesus was apparently indifferent. While a new world was in the making he was an unnoticed carpenter in a small town without history and without traditions. Yet his abiding significance was to be determined by these changes. As a Jew he shared in conditions set by the new epoch. For, without leading revolt, he was to live and teach in the atmosphere of revolution, use the language of revolution, make the revolutionary spirit the instrument of his message, and organize a movement composed of men who awaited a divinely given new age.

The approach to a true understanding of Jesus is through social psychology, and particularly through the messianic hope of his people. And the messianic hope is a phase of the psychology of revolution. To understand it one should be a student of revolutions. . . . Idealism, passionate and religious, was in this revolutionary psychology of messianism. . . . The sympathies of Jesus lay with men swayed by this revolutionary psychology. In time he joined them. He must have been aware of the serious nature of such a step. He must have known how insurrection had risen only to be crushed; how "robbers" had organized short-lived revolutions; how Judas of Gaulanitis and a Pharisee named Zaduk had headed a revolt, "professing an inviolable devotion to liberty, saying that God was their only ruler and lord." None the less he joined a mass movement under the leadership of John, a young man of his own age, who suddenly emerged from the wilderness of Judea as the prophet of the day. . . . Jesus was not dealing with abstract truth, but with young Jews on fire with revolutionary expectations which they had unified with their religious hopes.

SHAILER MATHEWS, Jesus on Social Institutions.
Published by The Macmillan Company, New York.

A NEW SPIRIT OF LIFE

The sermon on the Mount was never intended to be a code, either legal or moral. I suppose there is almost no one who thinks that the Sermon on the Mount was meant to be a *legal* code. . . . It does not lay down a standard up to which we ordinary people may reasonably be counted upon to live, and its standard cannot be modified to suit us and our circumstances, because the standard set up is a standard of perfection. "Be ye perfect, even as your Father which is in heaven is perfect."

If we do not love God as God is revealed to us in the life and teaching of Jesus, then we are not disciples of Christ, and the Sermon on the Mount lays no obligation upon us. For the Sermon on the Mount does not say, This is how people ought to be compelled or somehow induced to behave. It doesn't propose to offer any of us reasonable security that if we act in the way to prescribes we shall find plenty of other people keeping us company. It doesn't put us at all in a position where we are responsible only to other people as they are only responsible to us. It isn't based on a calculation of how people will probably behave under such and such circumstances. It puts us in direct relation to God, bids us consider, and then, for love, follow after the perfection of our Father in heaven. In so far as we accept it, it *commands* us, it is not mere advice. It is a command which follows upon dedication. Obedience is laid on those who love the truth as Jesus loved it. The Sermon on the Mount shows us a way of life we are to love for ourselves for its own sake. . . . Jesus was offering his disciples citizenship of a spiritual kingdom. . . . What matters in our acceptance of the invitation of the Sermon on the Mount is the spirit in which we are prepared to act and the standard of perfection which is held up to us in the love of God. . . .

"The unreasonable demands of Christ." That is not a reproach, but an acknowledgment of what the Gospel asks of us. If we ask to understand the relation of the Sermon on the Mount to life, and why it is that those who try to carry out its unreasonable demands are given grace, we must listen to what Jesus himself said: "If any man wills to do my will, he shall know of the doctrine whether it be of God or whether I speak of myself."

It has been the faith of Christians at all times that if they, however stumblingly, aim at carrying out this teaching of Jesus, then their faces will be set towards where the real forward fight is going on and that, whatever surprising things they may have to learn and whatever failures they may have to acknowledge, they will have God with them in the midst of the battle to direct and restore.

A. D. Lindsay, *The Moral Teaching of Jesus.*
Published by Harper & Brothers, New York.

THEY UPSET THE WORLD

They were hilarious, these early Christians. In their records we come constantly upon words that evince good spirits. Their delight in a new-found spiritual Friend triumphed over all their misfortunes. They upset the world with their joy and liveliness. They had the same sense of fellowship and enterprise as have the men of a regiment, and they went joyfully to meet persecution as men certain of victory go joyfully to battle. They felt themselves possessed by some external force of love and life which filled them with beautiful hopes and empowered them to carry out their desires. Lily Dougale.

STRONG SON OF GOD

Strong Son of God, immortal Love,
  Whom we, that have not seen thy face,
  By faith, and faith alone, embrace,
Believing where we cannot prove . . .

Thou seemest human and divine,
  The highest, holiest manhood thou;
  Our wills are ours, we know not how:
Our wills are ours, to make them thine.

Our little systems have their day;
  They have their day and cease to be:
  They are but broken lights of thee,
And thou, O Lord, art more than they.

We have but faith: we cannot know;
  For knowledge is of things we see;
  And yet we trust it comes from thee,
A beam in darkness: let it grow.

Let knowledge grow from more to more,
  But more of reverence in us dwell:
  That mind and soul, according well,
May make one music as before. . . .

          ALFRED TENNYSON, from *In Memoriam.*

A PRAYER

Oh God, light of all that is true, strength of all that is good, glory of all that is beautiful, we lift our eyes from the swiftly moving scenes about us by which we are often confused, that we may see again the wisdom and power and love sufficient for all our necessities. Enable us, we pray Thee, to walk in the Light, to share in the Wisdom, to rest upon the Love that we may be ready to play our part in the life of our times. Help us to think truly, to act kindly, to love wisely that we may leave the world better for our having lived. In Jesus' name. Amen.

          RAYMOND C. BROOKS.

Understand the Actual: Third Tuesday

16. THIS FAITH, THIS VIOLENCE

Is it not possible to believe without wanting to fight?

Can we have no faith without battles?

War is something for lions, for germs which must devour each other,

For bodies and anti-bodies, the corpuscles burning red and white in the blood,

For serums and toxins. But what of man? Is he only a germ or a lion?

There is room here for all of us; we do not eat each other with rich sauces,

Bones are worthless, we are not mice, we cannot build a house out of a skull.

Faith is something to share, to take joy in, pride in,

Showing it to others too, being generous, offering it around,

Because there is so much, more than enough, an inexhaustible treasure,

Faith in life, in ourselves and our destiny, in goodness and valor,

Call it God if you like, or call it whatever you please.

It is strong and positive, it is not hateful or spiteful.

It is a matter for joy, almost a matter of rapture

That here, on this earth, between the two freezing poles,

Not altogether burned by the sun or drowned by the wind,

In hunger and pain and sickness and fear of death,

Man lives, builds cities, grows wheat, and goes to church.

Do not be fooled, do not make any mistake—

We cannot afford to murder each other, even with flags and bugles.

For if those of us of one blood and mind were ever to destroy

Finally and irreparably, once and for all, forever,

Those others whose differing blood or ideas lash us to fury,

How bare would earth seem, how lonely her hills and water courses.

ROBERT NATHAN, in *Harpers' Magazine.*

SINCE THE ARMISTICE

In the nearly eighteen years since the war-to-end-war there have been seventeen wars, large and small. Two of these, the civil war in Spain and the undeclared war in the Far East, involve today one-fourth of the world's population. Over the entire world falls the shadow of conflict and nearly every nation wonders when its turn will come. . . .

Since 1930 the nations of the world have spent an estimated $48,000,000,000 on armaments, $12,000,000,000 of this amount having been spent in 1937. Before the present year is out it is believed that between $13,000,000,000 and $14,000,000,000 more will have gone for war machines.

New York Times.

"MAD ARMAMENTS RACE"

When other nations began a few years ago to crowd the air, the land and the sea with bombing planes, conscript armies, machine guns, tanks, cannons, battleships and submarines, President Roosevelt described this as a "mad armaments race" and a "grave menace to the peace of the world." Today, when the President urges this country to plunge into the same deadly whirlpool, we still believe that his earlier thought on the matter was right. For the proposed unprecedented peace-time expenditures for army and navy and air force are, in our opinion, unnecessary, wasteful and exceedingly dangeous.

This vast armament program is being sold to the country on the plea of defense. Defense against whom? Defense of what? The enemy is, of course, Japan and before long we will no doubt hear that there is a Japanese with a machine gun under every bed. Great arms programs are always put over by fear and war-scare propaganda.

What are the facts? Franklin D. Roosevelt told the country in the magazine "Asia" in 1923 that it was the consensus of opinion of military and naval men on both sides of the Pacific that Japan could not invade the U. S. and maintain an army here. No nation has ever been able to wage war when its source of supplies are more than 6,000 miles distant. This would require a battle fleet about five times greater than that of Japan and the entire present shipping tonnage of the world as transports and auxiliaries.

The effective range of a modern battleship is 1,500 miles; the maximum range of a bomber fully loaded is less than 500 miles. The minute battleship and bomber exceed these limits, the advantage goes definitely to the enemy. No wonder Lloyd's in London was ready to wager 500 to 1 that the United States would never be invaded. And Lloyd's generally bets on a sure thing.

Are we preparing to invade Japan? The project is just as futile. It cannot be done. Not only are there the 6,000 miles of ocean and the Japanese navy, but also a ring of island outposts through which no naval forces could make their way. Admiral Sir Roger Keyes once said: "As a naval man, Japan is untouchable. . . ."

Or does the Government propose to enter the wars of other nations "in order to save democracy"? Aside from the fact that the country is overwhelmingly opposed to such a course, there is no more certain way of destroying democracy than by going to war.

On the economic side, such arms expenditures are pure waste. They raise taxes, increase the cost of living, fatten the purses of the arms companies, and cause a general maladjustment of industry. The British experience of the last years is warning sufficient, while Germany has maneuvred herself into such a position today through armament making that it will be difficult for her to extricate herself without war or economic ruin. The Federation of British Industries, a group of powerful industrialists, warned that huge armament programs would be followed by "progressive reduction of labor and materials for civic requirements, as well as a further limitation of personal liberty and the impoverishment of living standards."

It is still time to prevent this "mad armaments race."

World Events.

THE POET IN THE DESERT

I have seen War.
I have heard it.
I have smelled it.
Even now I am waked from dreams
By the stink of bodies

Three days dead under the sun.
The life in the black mouths was maggots,
And flies crawled over the eyeballs,
Buzzing up angrily as we threw
Manhood as garbage into the pit of putrefaction.
Weeds will grow upon the lips of lovers
And grass will flourish out of the hearts of fathers,
But the father and the lover will return no more.
Nature will make excellent manure
Of the promise for the future.
Musicians, artists, artizans, artificers,
Mechanics, merry-makers, discoverers;
Poets, makers of soul.
I have hugged the grinning skeleton to my bosom
And have called him Honor, but his breath
Was the breath of the charnel-house.
I have, in my folly, endured
Burning summer and biting winter;
Thirst, hunger, fever; marching like marionettes
So that we lay down in the mud
And puked from exhaustion.
Incessant rain, Earth, becomes diluvian;
Man, mud-daubed, lizards, without sense or soul
Seeking their own destruction at a Masters' bidding,
Body and soul wallowing in primeval slime
At the bidding of Masters who stay at a table
And pulled the strings of their marionettes.
Was this for a great thing?
No it was for greed, and rivalry of power.
I have heard the screams of innocent, dumb horses,
Disemboweled;
And have stopped my ears
Against the cries of men,
Begging, for the pity of Christ, that they be shot.
Emperors, presidents, politicians, spinners of diplomacy
Have you ever heard the ravings of those
Who, through torture, begged that their agony be ended?
The agony which you had made?

CHARLES ERSKINE SCOTT WOOD, *The Poet in the Desert.*
Published by Vanguard Press, New York.

Be Concerned: Third Wednesday

17. BREAD-LINE

What's the meaning of this queue,
Tailing down the avenue,
Full of eyes that will not meet
The other eyes that throng the street,—
The questing eyes, the curious eyes,
Scornful, popping with surprise
To see a living line of men
As long as round the block, and then
As long again? The statisticians
Estimate that these conditions
Have not reached their apogee.
All lines end eventually;
Except of course in theory.
This one has an end somewhere.
End in what?—Pause, there.
What's the message in these faces
Modern industry displaces,
Emptying the factory
To set the men so tidily
Along the pavement in a row?
Now and then they take a slow
Shuffling step, straight ahead,
As if a dead march said:
"Beware! I'm not dead."
Now and then an unaverted
Eye bespells the disconcerted
Passer-by; a profile now
And then will lift a beaten brow,—
Waiting what?—The Comforter?
The pentecostal Visitor?—
If by fasting, visions come,
Why not to a hungry bum?
Idle, shamed, and underfed,
Waiting for his dole of bread,
What if he should find his head
A candle of the Holy Ghost?
A dim and starveling spark, at most,

But yet a spark? It needs but one.
A spark can creep, a spark can run;
Suddenly a spark can wink
And send us down destruction's brink.
It needs but one to make a star,
Or light a Russian samovar;
One to start a funeral pyre,
One to cleanse a world by fire.
What if our bread-line should be
The long slow-match of destiny?
What if even now the Holy
Ghost should be advancing slowly
Down the line, a kindling flame,
Kissing foreheads bowed with shame?
Creep, my ember; blaze, my brand!
The end of all things is at hand.
Idlers in the market-place,
Make an end to your disgrace!
Here's a fair day's work for you,—
To build a world all over, new.
What if our slow-match have caught
Fire from a burning thought?
What if we should be destroyed
By our patient unemployed?
Some of us with much to lose
By conflagration will refuse
To hallow arson in the name
Of Pentecost. We'd rather blame
The Devil, who can always find
For idle hand or empty mind
Work to do at Devil's hire.
The Devil loves to play with fire.
We'd rather blame him,—ah, but this
May be just our prejudice.

FLORENCE CONVERSE, Efficiency Expert.
Published by the John Day Company, New York.

MERE COGS

The modern industrial system is regarded with intense bitter-ness by masses of people, and I believe that their main quarrel with it is that they are considered only as means, cogs in the wheel, mere instruments. This widespread bitterness is a very noteworthy feature of the present situation, and it is our first duty to understand it. . . . It has produced in our time a stupendous revolution, and a new and militant religion. And yet, I repeat, we middle-class or professional people find it very hard to understand. Its watchwords are to us shibboleths, its philosophy a mass of fallacies, its apostle a cloudy preacher of hate. As one goes from the professional world to the world of class-conscious labor, one seems to move into a world of different assumptions where the meanings of language have changed.

A. D. LINDSAY, *Christianity and Economics.*
Published by Macmillan and Co., New York.

REPENTANCE MUST PRECEDE

The supreme duty of the churches in all countries as they face the present situation in the world of states and nations is to repent before God, not only by corporate acts of repentance, but by awakening the spirit of repentance in all their members : repentance for things done and things left undone. Judgment must begin at the house of God. If as Christians we are deeply disquieted by the political development of our age and our time, we have to acknowledge a large share of responsibility. We have not lived up to the word of our Lord: "Ye are the salt of the earth and the light of the world." We have not expressed our faith in the redeeming cross of Christ in terms of our social relations. We have accepted without clear protest existing social divisions. In like manner we recognize that churches have at times substituted for the true totalitarianism of Christ, which requires that every activity and every relation be subject to the will of God, a forced totalitarianism political in character. They have too often been far more concerned for their own security and prestige in this world than for fulfilling their Lord's commission and serving mankind in the spirit of self-sacrificing love. Today with deep humility we acknowledge our share in this guilt.

With repentance must go reconsecration. Penitence, if sincere, must bear fruit in action. We therefore resolve by God's grace to do our utmost to prevent the repetition of such sins in the future ; to discharge our duties as citizens in the spirit of Christian love ; and so far as in us lies, to create a spirit which will enable the state to fulfill its God-given task of maintaining justice and ministering to the welfare of the people.

"Report of the Section on Church and State."
The Oxford Conference: Official Report.
Published by Willett, Clark & Company, Chicago.

A PRAYER FOR PARDON

In all the wealth which Thou hast given
Who guidest every grace from heaven,
Forgive us for the blundering greed
Which keeps alive our brothers' need.

Forgive us for the dubious cant
Whereby we yet excuse their want;
The faults we deem beneath our own
Of which our hands the seed have sown.

Forgive our want of courage yet
To stay their robberies who get
The fruitage of the workers' toil,
Of which we fain would share the spoil.

O God, awaken us, before
The judgment breaks upon our shore,
And we, like Thebes and Rome of old,
Another people's wreck have told.

ROBERT WHITAKER, *in Unity.*

A PRAYER

Gracious Father, whose mercy is higher than the heavens, wider than our wanderings and deeper than all sin; receive back unto thyself thy bewildered and broken children. Forgive our folly and excess, our coldness to human sorrows, our envy of those who prosper and are at ease, our passion for the things of the moment that perish in the grasping, our indifference to those treasures of the spirit which are life and peace, our neglect of thy wise and gracious laws; and so change our hearts and turn all our desires unto thyself that we may love that which thou approvest, and do that which thou commandest, and with strength and resolution walk in uprightness and charity, to the serving of our brethren, and the glory of thy name. Amen.

Endeavor to Transform: Third Thursday

18. COOPERATIVE EFFORT AND MASS PURCHASING POWER!

Obviously there is nothing organically wrong. The country is full of people, the people are full of desire for a better standard of living, the fields are full of food, the mines are full of minerals, the factories are full of machinery, the railroads are full of rails, the roads are full of automobiles, the streets are full of labor, and the banks are full of safe-deposit boxes full of money. We have all the makin's of a mighty good time for everybody here in America, and it's hard to believe that we are just too dumb to do anything with them.

Editorial, Business Week.

CAUSE AND CONSEQUENCE

From 1920 through 1929, one-half the population was prosperous, the other half was sinking deeper into poverty. Inevitably, we arrived at 1933.

Business Week.

IDLE MONEY

Our banks are loaded with money ready to be invested in productive enterprise. Our plant capacity is near the peak of all time. Our worker efficiency was never higher, our power to consume is, for all practical purposes of calculations, limitless.

Yet, we are in the midst of a business recession which is keeping capital in idleness, turning plants out to weeds and obsolescence, adding workers to relief rolls every week and progressively restricting our enjoyment of the very things we are so able to produce.

JOHN W. HANES, in *New York Times.*

IDLE MACHINERY

Steel activity is practically unchanged this week. This makes the third week in which it has held between 30 and 31% of capacity and the twentieth week in which it has held between 26 and 36%. In other words, the rate of operations since the beginning of 1938 has been approximately 30% of capacity.

One can hardly overemphasize the trough into which business has fallen when operations in the most basic of manufacturing industries continue for four months at less than one-third of capacity.

Business Week, May 21, 1938.

PLANNED DEMOCRACY

The chief problem before the American people is how to evolve to a system of social planning which will be thoroughly democratic in all of its many ramifications.

To attain a democratically planned society, many things must be done. In the first place, the ownership of industry must be placed on a democratic basis. That means that industry as a whole must be owned by the community and by voluntary cooperative groups. Such ownership is a necessary preliminary to genuine social-economic planning and to the application of democracy to industry. Any comprehensive system of planning for the common good, a planning based on the full utilization of the human and mechanical equipment at the disposal of society and the equitable distribution of the products of industry among the masses of the people, is impossible without social ownership of the chief and essential industries of the nation.

This does not mean that all industry, under a socially planned society, must be publicly owned. A considerable section of industry might well be left to voluntary groups. At present consumers' cooperation in many lands is a powerful factor in the field of retail distribution. In the United States, agricultural cooperatives are growing in numbers and influence.

In a cooperative commonwealth, in a planned society, we are likely to see existing side by side with publicly owned industry many voluntary cooperative enterprises, particularly in the field of retail distribution, agriculture and intellectual production.

If social planning is to be truly democratic, furthermore, each socially owned industry should be administered democratically. That does not mean that the workers in each industry should completely control that industry, as syndicalists would urge. The final control of a publicly owned industry should be in the hands of society-as-a-whole. If the miners had complete administrative charge of the mining industry, they would be in a position to fix prices and the volume of production, boost wages out of line with the workers in other industries, and exploit the consumers. In any public industry, some plan should be worked out which would give each functional group adequate representation on administrative boards. The workers should be represented, since they are tremendously interested in the conditions under which they work. The consumer should have a say in the development of policies, since they are vitally interested in the quality, the volume and the prices of the goods produced. The administrative and technical staff should have a voice on the governing board because of their expert knowledge of the industry. All those groups should be represented on the directing body whose training and interest give them a significant stake in the enterprise. One of the major means of making social planning democratic is to adopt a system of democratic, of functional control of a publicly owned, as well as a cooperatively owned, industry.

Finally, if social planning is to be conducted in a democratic fashion, we must have, accompanying it, a democratic political structure. As it is difficult to build a genuine political democracy alongside of an industrial autocracy, so it is difficult, if not impossible, to develope an industrial democracy under a political autocracy or dictatorship. If the spirit of democracy is to permeate our planned economic structure, the spirit of democracy must also be shot through and through our political structure. If economic commissars are ever in fear of imprisonment or execution should they fail to follow the line laid down by the rulers of the political state, it is impossible to introduce true measures of democracy in the industrial structure over which they have control.

The maintenance and the extension of civil liberties—of the right of free speech, free assembly, free press, free association of political, economic and cultural groups—is essential to democracy within a planned economy, and everything possible should be done to make increasingly democratic our political institutions as we are democratizing and planning our economic life.

The old individualism is a thing of the past. Our planned semi-monopolized system is leading to increasing insecurity. Some form of social planning is essential to bring about a secure and abundant civilization. That planning should be democratic, if freedom and the finest development of personality and not merely economic security are to be our social goals. Democracy and social planning are thoroughly compatible. Let us do our part, in the development of planning in the United States, to see that everything possible is done to introduce democratic procedures in all phases of social planning and to bring about a cooperative fellowship of free men.

HARRY W. LAIDLER, in *The Socialist Review* July, Aug., 1938.

A PRAYER

O Divine Friend, who art our guide through life and also the goal toward which we are striving, we come before Thee with a deep sense of our own unworthiness. There are so many things that we have done badly, so many mistakes that we have made, so many times that we have let our evil and spiteful impulses direct us, so many things that we ought to have done that we have neglected, that we must ask Thy pardon. Thou didst make us for finer things and hast expected more of us. Help us in the future to make better use of our lives; that all who come in touch with us may be helped and blessed by that experience.

Our sympathy goes out to all who are in need, in sorrow, or distress, especially to those who have lost their faith in themselves, or their fellows, or in Thee.

We know that Thou carest, and we are strengthened by that thought; help us to commend that confidence to others.

We thank Thee for the blessings that have been showered upon us; for health and strength, for eyes to see the beauties of the autumn coloring, for ears to hear the voices of friends and the harmonies of song, for voices with which we can speak words of love and cheer to all. Grant that we may use these gifts as Thy children, sharing them in the building of Thy Kingdom of love and friendship here on earth.

All of which we ask in the name of our Master, Jesus Christ. AMEN.

BISHOP PAUL JONES.

Proceed Resolutely: Third Friday

19. AT A TIME OF SOCIAL CONVULSION

The atmosphere of Palestine was electric with revolutionary yearnings throughout the first century of the present era. The storm finally broke in full force in the year 66. When it had passed, the Jewish temple lay in ruins and even the semblance of national autonomy was completely shattered. The preaching activity of Jesus fell, roughly speaking, at a point halfway between the death of Herod the Great in 4 B.C. and the destruction of the temple at Jerusalem by the Roman army under Titus in 70 A.D. It was a favorable moment for the advocate of a new cause to get a hearing. The public ear was wide open to any message of hope for relief from society's mounting ills. But the moment was equally perilous. Emotions ran high and nerves were on edge. The crowd was fickle, not from lack of seriousness but from desperation and uncertainty. Enthusiasms were likely to be volatile; loyalties might evaporate overnight. Religious and political authorities were wont to act on impulse under high tension, while the loud voice of expediency often drowned out the whispering protests of more sober judgment.

These circumstances held out to Jesus no glowing prospects of phenomenal success in his efforts to reform his compatriots in preparation for the advent of God's kingdom. Rival panaceas were too distractingly numerous and conflicting interests were too powerful to yield right of way to the socially obscure Nazarene preacher. He might well have hesitated to enter upon so precarious a venture, or have proceeded with cautious step carefully anticipating difficulties or deliberately weighing chances and probabilities. But the ardent prophet is not much given to prudential considerations. He forges ahead to his envisaged goal in straightforward pursuit of duty regardless of probable success or failure. His cause is God's cause, and therefore it cannot fail, whatever may overtake the prophet himself. So it was with Jesus. He made friends, when friends were available, and he boldly withstood his most powerful enemies. He rendered supreme allegiance to God, whose will was to be obeyed whithersoever it might lead.

The foes of Jesus were sometimes members of his own spiritual household. He and they shared the same religious heritage from the revered past and served the same ancestral Deity. They were as confident as was Jesus that hope for the future depended upon the favor of God. But Jesus' ideals for the remaking of Jewish piety inevitably offended their sense of the proprieties. They deplored his seeming neglect of their sanctified institutions, and their well-trained leaders not unnaturally distrusted the unprofessional activities of a lay reformer. When he fell into disfavor also with the ever suspicious Roman police, who viewed all Jewish agitators as potential revolutionists, his activities were brought to a sudden and tragic close. The Romans crucified him, as they had crucified hundreds of other Jews during the previous period of their rule in Judea.

SHIRLEY JACKSON CASE, *Makers of Christianity.*
Published by Henry Holt & Co., New York.

TWO THOUSAND WERE CRUCIFIED

Next to Jerusalem the most important city of Palestine was Sepphoris, an easy hour's walk from Jesus' home in Nazareth. Sepphoris too was a thriving commercial center and was the capital of Galilee. . . .

The death of Herod the Great had been the signal for numerous uprisings in different parts of the country. In Jerusalem at Pentecost the revolt assumed threatening proportions, while agitators were active at many other points in Judea. In and about Jericho the revolutionists were led by one named "Simon," who had in his band of followers many persons from Perea. In Galilee a certain *Judas captured the military equipment stored at Sepphoris* and made it the center of a threatening revolt. . . . When the Romans finally restored order and punished only those who were believed to be the most guilty authors of the disturbance, they found two thousand persons to be crucified.

SHIRLEY JACKSON CASE, *Jesus.*
Published by the University of Chicago Press, Chicago.

THE HEART OF RELIGION

The Christian Church has instinctively turned to the cross to discover the essence of its message concerning Christ and God. The Father's love suffers in the blindness and wilfulness of his children; it bears and does everything which love can, with and for them. His Son reveals him by doing his all in word and life to redeem his brethren to the purpose of their God, and then by letting them do to him as they will, believing that in bearing what they inflict on him God will work an even greater deliverance for them. Those who are delivered follow Jesus in a service of like faith and courage and devotion.

This was the heart of the religion of Jesus to the most discerning Christians of the First Century to whom in the New Testament we owe the classic interpretation of Christianity. "God commendeth his own love toward us, in that, while we were yet sinners, Christ died for us." "Hereby know we love, because he laid down his life for us: and we ought to lay down our lives for the brethren." It is not that Jesus offers himself to alter God's attitude toward sinning men. His sacrifice of himself in life and death is a companion sacrifice to an already self-sacrificing Father who had patiently borne with man's selfishness and folly and given himself ungrudgingly to serve them. Father and Son are one in conscience, one in their toil for men, and one in their endurance of that which men cause them to suffer. Love only *is* power where the hearts of human beings are concerned. Love suffers where there is sin and by suffering love works redemption. . . .

Without closing our eyes to the grim facts of pain and wrong, we are obliged to grant that there is Something in the universe which made possible and sent forth Jesus. Is there a more adequate interpretation of that Something than Jesus' own—a God akin in purpose to him?

HENRY SLOANE COFFIN, *Ventures in Belief,*
edited by HENRY P. VAN DUSEN.
Published by Charles Scribner's Sons, New York.

THERE IS A MAN ON THE CROSS

Whenever there is silence around me
By day or by night—
I am startled by a cry.
It came down from the cross—
The first time I heard it.
I went out and searched—
And found a man in the throes of crucifixion,
And I said, "I will take you down,"
And I tried to take the nails out of his feet.

But he said, "let them be
For I cannot be taken down
Until every man, every woman, and every child
Come together to take me down."
And I said, "But I cannot bear your cry.
What can I do?"
And he said, "Go about the world—
Tell every one that you meet—
There is a man on the cross."

ELIZABETH CHENEY.

THE WAYS

To every man there openeth
A Way, and Ways, and a Way.
And the High Soul climbs the High Way,
And the Low Soul gropes the Low,
And in between, on the misty flats,
The rest drift to and fro.
But to every man there openeth
A High Way, and a Low,
And every man decideth
The Way his soul shall go.

Selected Poems of John Oxenham, Ernest Benn, Ltd., London, p. 23.

A PRAYER

Thou, O Christ, convince us by Thy Spirit; thrill us with Thy divine passion; drown our selfishness in Thy invading love; lay on us the burden of the world's suffering; drive us forth with the apostolic fervour of the early Church.

J. WILHELM ROWNTREE.

Seek Comradeship: Third Saturday

20. SOME FAR DESIGN

Beyond all talk of either mine, or thine;
Deeper than thought, than feeling more profound;
The human labors toward some far design
Wherein the stars companion with the ground.

Heartaches and aspirations, words and deeds,
Are of the woof wherewith we weave our part;
And to what timeless sea our moment leads,
Nothing shall fail that moves the human heart.

ROBERT WHITAKER, *The Call of the Human.*
Published by the Banner Press, Emory University, Atlanta, Ga.

REVERANCE FOR PERSONALITY

God is love. This is not the only thing that the Christian can say about God, but it is the only, or at least the most inclusive, thing that he can say about God's purpose in relation to persons, to men and women. . . .

In the revelation of the divine love in Christ is given the divine standard of human personal relationships, that which men were originally created to achieve and are still under divine command to seek to realize, that which, in so far as they fail to seek or to realize it, condemns them as sinful, needing forgiveness. Sin as manifesting itself in the world of persons is lovelessness, and lovelessness is sin.

It is the calling and privilege of the Christian disciple, in so far as he is truly a reconciled and forgiven person, to have increasingly in all his dealings with persons what it is not possible for the unreconciled man to have, namely, the mind of Christ. This is his vocation, and that which imparts at least something of distinctive quality to his life despite its abiding sinfulness and failure. He is called to be sanctified through the Spirit in the fellowship of the church. The fruits of the Spirit are the virtues of Christ; the virtues of Christ are relationships with persons. This having of the mind of Christ manifests itself in two directions. On the one hand it is manifested in the building up of the unity

of the Spirit within the Christian fellowship itself, which Christian
fellowship has no class or national limits or boundaries. On the
other hand it is manifested in the type of relationship the Christian,
or the fellowship, enters into with those outside the fellowship —
the world. Since in neither case the persons involved are free from
sin, the believer's personal relationships will derive such distinctive
quality as they may have from the constant reference of them to
the supreme revelation, in the cross of Christ, of God's way of
dealing with sinful persons. The believer's own sinful failures in
love will be seen for what they are, needing every day the patience
and pardon of God; the sinful failures of others will be seen in
their true light, needing also the patience and pardon of God and
calling for the believer's own costing endeavor that they, and he,
should be redeemed into the true life of fellowship with God.
Unless there is in the Christian disciple, in the sphere of human
relationships, an increasing sensitivity, practically implemented,
to the infinite demands of the love of God, to the shocking sin
and tragedy of lovelessness, to the costly way, revealed in Calvary,
which must be trod by God, and in some measure by those who
know God in Christ, if the thing is ever to be set right, it is difficult
to see what the specifically Christian vocation in human life really
amounts to in the end. What do ye more than others? was a question not infrequently on the lips of Jesus. . . . in proportion as a
person is treated, not as an individual having a value and significance in and for himself, but as a case for which any other could
be substituted—as a source of activity to be made subservient
wholly and instantly to one's own will; as an object in whom no
basis of confidence is sought, or believed possible, save as it is
played upon by powerful environmental stimuli—so in that proportion the relation is impersonal, even though it be to a person;
in that proportion it is loveless.

Suppose all human relationships arranged roughly in a scale
of increasing depersonalization; is there for the Christian at any
point in the scale a dividing line between the permissible and the
not permissible, so that he is bound to say at that point, out of
loyalty to his vocation, "Over that line I will not step, be the consequences what they may"? If there is such a dividing line, how is
the Christian to know where it is and when he is being invited to
step over it?

I presume that it will be generally agreed that there is such a dividing line somewhere. It is certainly possible to imagine depersonalized relationships which can be seen in advance of their ever happening to be so well over the line of the permissible that there can be no question that a final prohibition rests upon them for the Christian; thus a hard-pressed and conscienceless government might conceivably propose the torturing of prisoners in order to force the hand of a dangerous enemy at the gate . . . modern war when it is examined is seen to involve such a total depersonalization of human relationships that it cannot be yoked to the Christ style of life at all. It represents a cul-de-sac, a no-thoroughfare in the dimension of personal relations down which in the nature of the case a man cannot walk with Christ.

That war closely approximates to such a *ne plus ultra* of depersonalization, i.e., of evil, will hardly be questioned; whether it finally reaches that status can only be left to the individual conscience to judge as best it can. Certainly it is difficult to conceive of a use of force which (*a*) is more wholesale, undiscriminating, in the mass; (*b*) more completely excludes the possibility of any accommodation to, or from, the will of those to whom it is applied, for it aims with the help of every available mechanical invention at the maximum effect of blind force, namely, the complete smashing out of existence of the whole organic body-spirit unity of the person; (*c*) more unavoidably demands as indispensable to its prosecution, on the one hand, the repudiation of the basic requirements without which anything in the nature of truly personal relationship cannot even begin, such as truth and candor, and on the other hand, the manipulation of the psychological processes of the other man by any available trick of terrorism and propaganda; (*d*) more completely reduces the human agents involved from the level of self-directing persons to the mechanical level of the physical forces they are putting into operation, depriving them of rights of conscience against those in command. And all this it does necessarily. To imagine that it is possible to wage modern war and not be involved in this sort of thing is sentimental illusion.

HERBERT HENRY FARMER, *Christian Faith and the Common Life.*
An Oxford Conference Book.
Published by Willett, Clark & Company, Chicago.

A PRAYER

Lord, what a change within us one short hour
  Spent in Thy presence will avail to make!
  What heavy burdens from our bosoms take!
  What parched grounds refresh as with a shower!
We kneel, and all around us seems to lower;
  We rise, and all, the distant and the near,
  Stands forth in sunny outline, brave and clear;
We kneel, how weak! we rise, how full of power!
Why, therefore, should we do ourselves this wrong,
Or others—that we are not always strong—
  That we are sometimes overborne with care—
  That we should ever weak or heartless be,
Anxious or troubled—when with us is prayer,
  And joy and strength and courage are with Thee?

RICHARD C. TRENCH.

A PRAYER

Heavenly Father, who hast revealed Thy relationship to us in Thy Son Jesus Christ, who art near us the more deeply we enter into fellowship and understanding with our brethren, grant that we may never repudiate The by hardening our hearts against any of our fellows. Save us from that blasphemy by revealing to us the deep spiritual riches that await us on every side beneath the rough and imperfect exteriors of our associates; so that, day by day, seeking in people the true gold of love and honesty and the capacity for sacrifice that is so often covered by a veneer of pride, temper, greed, or lust, we may help to create that deeper fellowship in which Thou art Thyself revealed. So shall we all by one, even as Thou and Thy Son art one; through the same Jesus Christ Our Lord. AMEN.

BISHOP PAUL JONES.

Worship God: Third Sunday

21. SILENCE

Inaudible move day and night,
    And noiseless grows the flower;
Silent are pulsing wings of light,
    And voiceless fleets the hour.

The moon utters no word when she
    Walks through the heavens bare;
The stars forever silent flee,
    And songless gleam through air.

The deepest love is voiceless too;
    Heart sorrow makes no moan:
How still the zephyrs when they woo!
    How calm the rose full blown!

The bird winging the evening sky
    Flies onward without song;
The crowding years as they pass by
    Flow on in mutest throng.

The fishes glide through liquid deep
    And never speak a word;
The angels round about us sweep,
    And yet no voice is heard.

The highest thoughts no utterance find,
    The holiest hope is dumb,
In silence grows the immortal mind,
    And speechless deep joys come.

Rapt adoration has no tongue,
    No words has holiest prayer;
The loftiest mountain peaks among
    In stillness everywhere.

With sweetest music silence blends,
   And silent praise is best;
In silence life begins and ends:
   God cannot be expressed.

            JOHN LANCASTER SPALDING (1840-1916).

THE CHORISTERS

When earth was finished and fashioned well,
There was never a musical note to tell
How glad God was, save the voice of the rain
And the sea and the wind on the lonely plain
And the rivers among the hills.
And so God made the marvelous birds
For a choir of joy transcending words,
That the world might hear and comprehend
How rhythm and harmony can mend
The spirits' hurts and ills.

He filled their tiny bodies with fire,
He taught them love for their chief desire,
And gave them the magic of wings to be
His celebrants over land and sea,
Wherever man might dwell.
And to each he apportioned a fragment of song—
Those broken melodies that belong
To the seraphs' chorus, that we might learn
The healing of gladness and discern
In beauty how all is well.

So music dwells in the glorious throats
Forever, and the enchanted notes
Fall with rapture upon our ears,
Moving our hearts to joy and tears
For things we cannot say.
In the wilds the whitethroat sings in the rain
His pure, serene, half-wistful strain;
And when twilight falls the sleeping hills
Ring with the cry of the whippoorwills
In the blue dusk far away.

In the great white heart of the winter storm
The chickadee sings, for his heart is warm,
And his note is brave to rally the soul
From doubt and panic to self-control
And elation that knows no fear.
The bluebird comes with the winds of March,
Like a shred of sky on the naked larch;
The redwing follows the April rain
To whistle contentment back again
With his sturdy call of cheer.

The orioles revel through orchard boughs
In their coats of gold for spring's carouse;
In shadowy pastures the bobwhites call,
And the flute of the thrush has a melting fall
Under the evening star.
On the verge of June when peonies blow
And joy comes back to the world we know,
The bobolinks fill the fields of light
With a tangle of music silver-bright
To tell how glad they are.

The tiny warblers fill summer trees
With their exquisite lesser litanies;
The tanager in his scarlet coat
In the hemlock pours from a vibrant throat
His canticle of the sun.
The loon on the lake, the hawk in the sky,
And the sea-gull—each has a piercing cry,
Like outposts set in the lonely vast
To cry "all's well" as Time goes past
And another hour is gone.

But of all the music in God's plan
Of a mystical symphony for man,
I shall remember best of all—
Whatever hereafter may befall
Or pass and cease to be—
The hermit's hymn in the solitudes
Of twilight through the mountain woods,

And the field-larks crying about our doors
On the soft sweet wind across the moors
At morning by the sea.

BLISS CARMAN, *Later Poems.*
Published by Small, Maynard & Co., Boston.

AS THE BROOK FEELS FOR THE OCEAN

Prayer, whether it be the list of a little child, or the wrestling of some great soul in desperate contest with the coils of habit or the evil customs of his generation is a testimony to a divine-human fellowship. In hours of crisis the soul feels for its Companion, by a natural gravitation, as the brook feels for the ocean. In times of joy and strength, it reaches out to its source of Life, as the plant does to the sun. And when it has learned the language of spiritual communion and knows its Father, praying refreshes it as the greeting of a friend refreshes one in a foreign land. We ought not to expect that prayer, of the true and lofty sort, could be attained by easy steps. It involves appreciation of God and co-operation with Him. One comes not to it in a day. Even human friendship is a great attainment. It calls for sacrifice of private wishes and for adjustment to the purposes of another life. One cannot be an artist or a musician without patient labor to make oneself an organ of the reality which he fain would express. He must bring himself by slow stages to a height of appreciation. Prayer is the highest human function. It is the utterance of an infinite friendship, the expression of our appreciation of that complete and perfect Person whom our soul has found. "Lord, teach us how to pray."

RUFUS JONES, *The Double Search.*
Published by John C. Winston Co., Philadelphia.

A PRAYER

Our Father, teach us the joy of discovering the tokens of Thy presence always in the song of birds, the fragrance of flowers, the marvelous beauty of sunrise and sunset, in the ringing laughter and plaintive cry of little children, in the deep hunger in the hearts of our brothers and sisters and in our own souls so that we are never alone. Amen.

RAYMOND C. BROOKS.

Concentrate Upon the Ideal: Fourth Monday

22. INDIRECTION

Fair are the flowers and the children, but their subtle suggestion is
    fairer;
Rare is the roseburst of dawn, but the secret that clasps it is rarer;
Sweet the exultance of song, but the strain that precedes it is
    sweeter;
And never was poem yet writ, but the meaning outmastered the
    meter.

Never a daisy that grows, but a mystery guideth the growing;
Never a river that flows, but a majesty scepters the flowing;
Never a Shakespeare that soared, but a stronger than he did enfold
    him,
Nor ever a prophet foretells, but a mightier seer hath foretold him.

Back of the canvas that throbs the painter is hinted and hidden;
Into the statue that breathes the soul of the sculptor is bidden;
Under the joy that is felt lie the infinite issues of feeling;
Crowning the glory revealed is the glory that crowns the revealing.

Great are the symbols of being, but that which is symboled is
    greater;
Vast the create and beheld, but vaster the inward creator;
Back of the sound broods the silence, back of the gift stands the
    giving;
Back of the hand that receives thrill the sensitive nerves of
    receiving.

Space is as nothing to spirit, the deed is outdone by the doing;
The heart of the wooer is warm, but warmer the heart of the
    wooing;
And up from the pits where these shiver, and up from the heights
    where those shine,
Twin voices and shadows swim starward, and the essence of life
    is divine.

Poems by RICHARD REALF (1834-1878).
Published by Funk & Wagnalls Co., New York.

THE REALEST FORCES

In the grand days, alas, now gone, when Toscanini reigned like a king in Carnegie Hall, I have come from listening to symphonies there absolutely certain that the materialistic explanation of the universe would never do. Such beauty—the minds that created it and the souls that loved it—could not be the accidental consequence of colliding atoms. When an atheist like Krutch says, as in all good logic he must say, that life is "merely a physiological process with only a physiological meaning," that is nonsense, and as Professor Montague puts it, the chance of that's being true would have to be represented by a fraction with 1 for the numerator and with a denominator that would reach from here to one of the fixed stars. For in all our great moments the realest forces in the world are spiritual—goodness, beauty, love, and truth—and in the face of them it is desperately difficult to disbelieve in God.

HARRY EMERSON FOSDICK, *Successful Christian Living.*
Published by Harper & Brothers, New York.

THE ESSENCE OF CHRISTIANITY

It is the Christian faith that men in their search for the meaning of their lives cannot stop short of God. They need God as the intellectual explanation of their existence as well as for the sense of belonging to an order of things which gives coherence to their experience. . . .

It is the Christian faith that God is personal. That word is a stumbling block to many of our contemporaries. What it means can be put in this way. In the nature of the case God is unique. One cannot describe God by comparing him with anything else of the same kind. The most that we can do is to find suggestions or symbols in the world of our experience (the only world which is open to us at all) which seem fruitful in our thought about God. The possibilities among such suggestions are very limited. To say that God is personal is to say that God is more like a person than like a thing, more like a person than like a machine, more like a person than like a mathematical proposition, more like a person than like a tree. This last suggestion is pertinent, because the whole conception of God as blind life-urge is symbolized quite well by a tree. But, when we use the word "personal" as a description of God, we mean to include only a few of the characteristics of persons. Our human limitations which are inherent in our physical existence obviously do not apply to God. Those characteristics which do apply to God are : *awareness, intelligence, purposiveness, the capacity to appreciate, the capacity to respond to persons.* It is difficult to see how a God who lacks those qualities could be a fitting object of devotion or an adequate explanation of existence, or one to whom our conduct could make any difference.

It is the Christian faith that in Jesus Christ we have the surest clue to the nature of God. It is not enough to say that God is personal. That might leave it open to believe that God has the characteristics of a Napoleon or a Mussolini—the man of power. To say that it is in Christ-like personality that we have a true symbol of the nature of God becomes especially significant when we contrast Jesus with other types of persons. Moreover, God is revealed not only in the personality of Jesus but also in his teaching about God and in his religious response to God. His trust in God and his commitment to God form the clearest portrayal of man's right relationship with God.

It is the Christian faith that it is the purpose of God that the spirit of Jesus should be the norm for our lives, and that men should develop in the world a fellowship which knows no barriers of race or class or nation, and which is characterized by abundance of life, mutual loyalty, and a common devotion to God. So long as Christians take seriously the revelation of God and of his purpose which they find in Jesus they have a corrective for the most menacing perversions of our time, for racialism and nationalism, for economic injustice and war.

It is the Christian faith that there is a judgment of God which can be observed in personal life and in the events of history. God seeks to draw us, to persuade us, but we can resist him; and when we resist him too stubbornly we find ourselves up against punishment. This punishment is at work in the moral structure of things which makes evil in the long run self-defeating. . . .

It is the Christian faith that God can be trusted to deliver from frustration those who fulfill the conditions. The conditions are simple in the sense that they have nothing arbitrary or artificial about them, but they are not easy. They can be summed up in two words—commitment and trust. Men without the consciousness of God stumble on the fact that there is a healing power in life which goes beyond the obvious in delivering from frustration those who are not pre-occupied with self. Worship is both the act of commitment and the exposure of our spirits to those things which can lift us and make us capable of commitment. There is here no stereotyped solution of all our human problems. There are puzzles to which we cannot see the answer, especially the puzzle that so many persons are so controlled by fear and self-concern that they cannot know the experience of healing when they need it most. But it is a matter of record that countless persons who have fulfilled the conditions have in the face of all the tragedies of life found deliverance for their spirits. It is one of the meanings of the cross that Jesus found such deliverance, though he experienced almost every form of external evil.

The confidence of Christians in personal immortality has been a way of underscoring this trust in God. It is the trust that not even death (which has all the appearance of being the final frustration for persons) is beyond the range of God's deliverance.

JOHN BENNETT, Christianity and Our World.
Published by Association Press, New York.

A PRAYER

O Thou, unto whom all the hearts of men are dear and from whose love no man is shut out, quicken us that we may grow into the beauty of Thine own greatness. Save us from all our little and excluding ways that we may enter into all the fulness of understanding of the whole human family. Give us Thy seeing for our eyes that we may not shrink from beholding the ugliness and cruelty of life, and yet that we may never lose sight amid it all of the divinity and beauty that are in all men. Give us Thy strength for our hands that we may be able to build out of the fragments of men's failures a world of brotherhood fit for the glory of Thy Spirit. Give us Thy courage in our inward parts that we may keep holy the private places of our own integrity and always dare to stand firm for the dignity of human life. Give us Thy love for our hearts that we may not hate when we are hated or hurt those who seek to hurt us, but that we may learn the strategy of forgiveness and overcome evil with good. Inspire us with Thy compassion that in Thy gentleness we may be great enough to show Thy glory to the dull eyes of men. And unto Thy name we shall bring our songs. Amen.

FRANK KINGDON.

Understand the Actual: Fourth Tuesday

23. ENDS JUSTIFY MEANS?

We must be ready for sacrifice of every kind, and even if need be to practice everything possible; ruses and tricks, illegal methods; be ready to be silent and hide the truth; in short, it is from the interests of the class war that we deduce our morality.
LENIN, quoted in *Christianity and Communism*, edited by H. WILSON HARRIS.
Published by Marshall Jones Company, Boston.

PARALLELS

What Christianity says to the modern labor movement is something like this—that the startling thing about the labor movement, especially in its more thoroughly Marxist phases, is not its anti-capitalism, but precisely that, in spite of surface differences, its underlying assumptions are similar to those of our industrialist, capitalist civilization at its worst, and that unless the labor movement is purified, deepened and spiritualized, it too will contribute to the dissolution rather than the redemption of our civilization.

Among the devotees of Marx and Lenin, as among those to whom our industrial capitalist economy is god, one encounters:

The same pre-occupation with material abundance as the master-key to all human problems.

The same faith in the efficacy and sufficiency of external conditions or changes.

The same indifference to or contempt for the inner life of the soul—all that is sentimentalism, "escape from reality," to both systems.

The same subordination of cultural and spiritual life to economics.

The same reliance upon power, domination, violence, the same lapse into ruthlessness in critical times; the same contempt for gentleness, humility, love, fellowship.

The same degradation of morality into expediency and easy resort to the doctrine that the end justifies the means.

The same inability to break with war and presently the rationalization of war into the supreme and final means of the victory of the good.

The same confining of man's life exclusively to this world—
the secularization of all life.

A. J. Muste, in Federal Council Bulletin.

DICTATORSHIP IN SOVIET RUSSIA

There is an important fact about dictatorship which its
communist apologists too often forget. It is that there are psychological as well as purely economic laws which apply in the
affairs of men. Dictatorship, whatever its avowed object, concentrates power in the hands of the few, and "power corrupts,
and absolute power corrupts absolutely." . . .

Let us recite the inescapable facts which make the Russian
claims of democracy a fantastic misuse of words. Every Russian
citizen is kept track of by the most rigorous system of internal
passports in the world. He may belong to a church but it is
rigorously supervised and denied many rights which historically
churches have claimed. If he is a worker he must belong to his
union which in important ways serves his interests, but is nevertheless far more completely subordinated to the state apparatus
than the health of a socialist society requires. There is no right
to strike under any circumstances. Aside from his union, the excellent workers' club of his factory and some admirable scientific
societies, there is no club or association to which a Russian may
belong. No political party is legal except the communist. More
and more the Communist Party is bureaucratically controlled.
The Politburo, headed by Stalin, controls the party today, and
the party absolutely controls the army and the government. So
great is the fear of offending the dominant hierarchy or making
a wrong guess as to its decisions that wise men, even in the Communist Party, seek to evade political responsibility. When I was
in Moscow I was told of a communist unit in a very important
factory where out of three thousand worker-members not a single
one would stand as representative of that unit on a communist
central committee. They chose small bureaucrats to represent them
who had formerly worked in the factory. The old keenness of
political discussion in the party has almost died, at least in so
far as policy is concerned. (Criticism of administration is still
allowed.) A quotation from Stalin is a final answer to all argument. He receives the same sort of exaggerated veneration in

public appearances, in the display of his picture, and in written references to him that is accorded to a Mussolini or a Hitler.

Schools, the radio, the press are absolutely controlled by the government. The Communist Party, to be sure, has its own press distinct from the government press, and it is significant that *Pravda* is more powerful than *Izvestia,* the government organ. The newspapers are compelled to agree on every important issue.

Even those few Russians who might obtain foreign language publications and be able to read them are, with few exceptions, denied that right. When I was in Moscow a Russian woman had been held for three weeks incommunicado in some jail, the exact place unknown to her family, for no discoverable reason except that she had been the messenger of an American newspaper correspondent for delivering a package of English-language papers to another American who roomed with her at her home in Gorki. Episodes like this have produced an extraordinary fear among the politically articulate of any dealings whatsoever with foreign visitors.

It must be remembered, moreover, that while Russian justice in criminal cases is enlightened, in cases which we westerners would call political, the secret police and the secret tribunals are dominant. The great public works in Russia have been built in the main by convicts under armed guard, most of whom have never had what we should regard as a fair trial of any sort. . . .

The Trotskyist criticism of Stalin is weightier and better documented than that of the opponents of all social planning. It makes a good case that the communism of Stalin in the year 1937 is a far cry from the communism of Lenin. Nevertheless, neither Trotsky nor his supporters make a convincing case that his victory over Stalin would have altered the denials of liberty inherent in dictatorship. Trotsky now claims that in the days of his power he was opposed to a monolithic party, that is, a party in which differences of opinion were not tolerated. He certainly was not opposed in those days to the identification of the dictatorship of the proletariat with the dictatorship of the Communist Party. He was one of the chief apologists and practitioners of terrorism—not, however, by individual assassination—as a revolutionary weapon. First it was to be used against the enemies of the working class, but in practice that soon extended to its use against political opponents of the Communist Party within the working class. However much Trotsky today may deplore the attempt of communists in Spain to "liquidate" the anarchists he did not hesitate to do the same thing to Russian anarchists. Remember, moreover, his role in the ruthless suppression of the Kronstadt sailors. All the probabilities are that if Trotsky had won he would have been compelled by the logic of dictatorship to practice against his opponents what Stalin has practiced against him. Once more the end would have justified the means. Dictatorship is dictatorship, and he who accepts it is molded by it in its own image.

NORMAN THOMAS, *Democracy versus Dictatorship,*
a pamphlet published by The League for Industrial Democracy,
New York City.

A PRAYER

"Let justice roll down as waters, and righteousness as a mighty stream."

O God, together we confess our personal and social sin, beseeching Thee to forgive our blindness, our indifference, and our hardness of heart. Show us that we are members one of another, and that the hurt of one, even the humblest, is an injury to all and a sin against Thee. Deliver us from every form of the spirit of oppression, and the callous greed which seeks comfort, or ease, or gain at the cost of the misery of others. Create in us a passion for justice, that freedom may be a blessing and liberty bear the fruit of righteousness and good will.

Smite us, O Lord, with the conviction of Thy Holy Spirit; subdue us to true repentance. Evoke in us a new spirit of generosity, and unite us in one purpose to understand and to act, making our faith fruitful in the service of our fellow man in his struggle for a freer, fuller life. Endue us with the spirit of Jesus who saw Thy image in all who wear our human form; help us to toil with His patience and mercy, that we may do our part to heal the injustice of our time. Fill our minds with light, anoint our hearts with love.

JOSEPH FORT NEWTON, *Altar Stairs.*
Published by The Macmillan Company, New York.

Be Concerned: Fourth Wednesday

24. APOCALYPTIC

And down the vista'd boulevards of thought,
The Workingman came marching in battalions:
Scourged with the lash of Egypt, Babylon,
Persepolis, and lost Sumerian dynasts.
Makers of bricks without the requisite straw.
Makers of roads for Cæsar and Jay Gould,
Napoleon, Mussolini, and the baffled
Commissions for Relief of Unemployment.
Builders of Ziggurats and Pyramids,
Cathedrals, Boulder Dams, and Panama
Canals, and uninhabited Skyscrapers.
The sweated labor of the needle-trades;
The stunted generations of the children
From greedy cotton-mills; the grimy gnomes
From collieries; the old plantation darkeys;
The Kaffirs from the African diamond mines;
The coolies out of India and China;
Wat Tyler and his fourteenth century strikers,
And Sans-culottes, dancing the Carmagnole,
And Coxey's Army, and the Bonus Marchers;
And hungry farmers bearing burning sheaves
Of wheat for torches to give light to them
That legislate in darkness and the shadow
Of Revolution.—And beside him, Jones,
Respectfully silent, bent on keeping step
With an Expert's long, incalculable saunter.
All those past æons of exploited Helots
Epitomized in Jones, who would be scrapped
In a month or two.—Was this a sense of Sin,—
This raging anguish and this gallant shame,
This grief—at letting down the other fellow?
And if an individual could feel
So shaken,—what about Communal Sin,
That preface to the Mission worker's program?

What happened when a World turned penitent?—
By God, we're in for vomit and convulsion!

FLORENCE CONVERSE, *Efficiency Expert.*
Published by The John Day Company, New York

TESTING THE ECONOMIC ORDER

What guidance can those who must make these decisions concerning the economic order receive from their Christian faith? . . .

We suggest five such ends or standards, by way of example, as applicable to the testing of any economic situation.

(a) Right fellowship between man and man being a condition of man's fellowship with God, every economic arrangement which frustrates or restricts it must be modified—and in particular such ordering of economic life as tends to divide the community into classes based upon differences of wealth and to occasion a sense of injustice among the poorer members of society. To every member of the community there must be made open a worthy means of livelihood. The possibilities of amassing private accumulations of wealth should be so limited that the scale of social values is not perverted by the fear and the envy, the insolence and the servility, which tend to accompany extreme inequality.

(b) Regardless of race or class every child and youth must have opportunities of education suitable for the full development of his particular capacities, and must be free from those adventitious handicaps in the matter of health and environment which our society loads upon large numbers of the children of the less privileged classes. In this connection, the protection of the family as a social unit should be an urgent concern of the community.

(c) Persons disabled from economic activity, whether by sickness, infirmity or age, should not be economically penalized on account of their disability, but on the contrary should be the object of particular care. Here again the safeguarding of the family is involved.

(d) Labor has intrinsic worth and dignity, since it is designed by God for man's welfare. The duty and the right of men to work should therefore alike be emphasized. In the industrial process, labor should never be considered a mere commodity. In their daily work men should be able to recognize and fulfill a

Christian vocation. The workingman, whether in field or factory, is entitled to a living wage, wholesome surroundings and a recognized voice in the decisions which affect his welfare as a worker.

(e) The resources of the earth, such as the soil and mineral wealth, should be recognized as gifts of God to the whole human race and used with due and balanced consideration for the needs of the present and future generations.

The implications of even one of these standards, seriously taken, will involve drastic changes in economic life. Each one of them must be made more definite in terms of the problems which face particular communities.

Closely connected with the foregoing paragraphs is the whole question of property—so closely indeed that any action on the part of the community which affects property rights will also affect the application of the standards mentioned. This is a sphere in which Christian teaching on ends and principles in relation to economic life could have immediate results if it were translated into actual economic decisions. Christian thought has already supplied a background which is of great importance, but it has not been brought into effective relationship with the development of the institutions of property under modern economic conditions. This subject should be given close attention by any agencies for further study which may be established in the future. Meanwhile we suggest a few of the directions along which Christian thought should move.

(a) It should be reaffirmed without qualification that all human property rights are relative and contingent only, in virtue of the dependence of man upon God as the giver of all wealth and as the creator of man's capacities to develop the resources of nature. This fundamental Christian conviction must express itself both in the idea of stewardship or trusteeship and in the willingness of the Christian to examine accumulations of property in the light of their social consequences.

(b) The existing system of property rights and the existing distribution of property must be criticized in the light of the largely nonmoral processes by which they have been developed, and criticism must take account of the fact that every argument in defense of property rights which is valid for Christian thinking is also an argument for the widest possible distribution of these rights.

(c) It should further be affirmed that individual property rights must never be maintained or exercised without regard to their social consequences or without regard to the contribution which the community makes in the production of all wealth.

(d) It is very important to make clear distinction between various forms of property. The property which consists in personal possessions for use, such as the home, has behind it a clearer moral justification than property in the means of production and in land which gives the owners power over other persons. All property which represents social power stands in special need of moral scrutiny, since power to determine the lives of others is the crucial point in any scheme of justice.

"Report of the Section on Church, Community and State in Relation to The Economic Order."
The Oxford Conference: Official Report.
Published by Willett, Clark & Colby, Chicago.

GREATER GOOD AND LESS GOOD

He that will walk uprightly must not only distinguish between simple good and evil, but between a greater good and a less; for most sin in the world consisteth in preferring a lesser good before a greater. He must still keep the balance in his hand, and compare good with good.

RICHARD BAXTER.

A PRAYER

"Almighty God, unto whom all hearts be open, all desires known, and from whom no secrets are hid; cleanse the thoughts of our hearts by the inspiration of Thy Holy Spirit, that we may perfectly love Thee, and worthily magnify Thy holy Name, through Christ our Lord. Amen."

Old Sarum Collect.

Endeavor to Transform: Fourth Thursday

25. THE BUILDERS

Not in the dream of yesterday is found
  Substructure of the world that is to be;
  The pit was digged by no lone poet's plea,
Nor did the blood of martyrs break the ground.
Fear not! they shall be well-confessed and crowned
  Who played the prophets' part; yet shall men see
  The work was our humanity's, and we
Are all together in the building bound.
All life was in that quickening of the hand
  Which from the club wrought on to the machine;
  The airy uplift of the lumbering feet
To argosies which all the heavens command;
  The few as nothing, to the myriad mean
  In whom man's vast adventure is complete.
                    ROBERT WHITAKER, in *The World Tomorrow.*

IMPOSSIBLE TO FORESEE

If we looked backward over history, we can see how impossible
it is to stand in one age and predict the social philosophy of the
next. On what basis could anyone in the Roman Empire predict
the peculiar philosophy of feudalism? How could the wisest man
in the twilight of the Middle Ages have predicted the philosophy
which glorified the trader and made human greed the fountain
of justice and morals? How would it have been possible to have
foretold the development of the great modern corporate organization out of a philosophy of rugged individualism? Even Adam
Smith, who described his own time so accurately, stated with complete conviction that the development of the great corporation was
economically impossible because men would not work for corporations as they worked for themselves. Unless the profit motive
is to disappear, he argued, such organizations will be absolutely
impossible, because of the underlying factors which make up
"human nature."

So today, in the most highly organized and specialized society
the world has ever known, men are convinced that, except in

time of war (and we are going eventually to abolish war) centralized control by organizations which do not operate on the "profit motive" will lead to inefficiency, bureaucracy, tyranny, and worse.

And the curious thing is that so long as men think that way, the development of the new organizations always proves that they are right. Great corporations *were* actually inefficient in Adam Smith's day and the best work was done by individual craftsmen. Centralized governments today actually *are* tyrannical, bureaucratic, cruel, and so on. Germany, Russia, and Italy do not present attractive pictures of the world which is supposed to be created when a nation follows a consistent ideal.

However, one of the reasons that we are always able to prove our point, as Adam Smith did, is that our philosophy makes us judge the institutions which do not violate that philosophy by their successes and those which do violate it by their failures. Sweden is a much pleasanter country to live in today than Germany. Yet the non profit enterprises in Sweden, such as cooperatives and those subsidized by government, are the very things which we are sure would produce in this country conditions like those in Germany and Italy. . . . We escape from facts which contradict our theories by saying on the one hand, "One must not be fooled into condemning the good corporations by the bad," and on the other hand, "One must not be fooled into believing that a few instances of governmental efficiency are any excuse for its numerous failures." . . . In any combat situation each side will always look like villains to the other.

THURMAN ARNOLD, *The Folklore of Capitalism.*
Published by Yale University Press, New Haven.

CONSUMERS' COOPERATIVES

What is a cooperative? The idea was worked out and put into practice by twenty-eight hungry weavers (one of them a woman) in the town of Rochdale, England, in 1844. They set up a store, which they themselves owned, through an organization with the following principles: Each member has one vote; membership is open to everybody; the return on capital is to be limited (usually to the legal rate of interest); earnings are distributed to members in proportion to their patronage.

Consumer cooperation starts with retail trade, but it may extend, if successful, to wholesaling, to manufacturing, to credit. In short, it provides not only a way for helping the consumer to make savings or to get more for his money, but also a fairly complete scheme for the democratic reorganization of most of our economic processes. Local retail associations tend to federate into wholesales, and wholesales tend to take on manufacturing as they grow.

Consumer cooperatives engage in a great variety of business, for example: stores, restaurants, laundries, gas stations, credit unions, recreation, housing, the supply of electricity. Sales are made for cash at current market prices. Usually cooperatives assign some of their funds for education. Cooperatives are generally neutral as organizations in politics and religion, but the individual members express themselves as they wish on these issues. In the United States the farmers have led the way in the cooperative movement.

How do cooperatives get started? Let us suppose that a few individuals are aroused about high prices and resolve to do something by way of organization. They form a study club on consumer cooperation. As their information and interest grows, they form a buying club for a limited number of products. The training gained in this should equip them to expand into a cooperative grocery store dealing with the public. They must then form a consumer cooperative association under the laws of the state. Stock is sold to prospective members, often at five dollars a share. On this invested capital a fixed and limited return to be paid, say 5 per cent or less a year, after the store gets going. When enough funds are raised, a manager is employed, a store site is rented, goods are purchased at wholesale for resale to members and others.

At business meetings each member has one vote only and there is no voting by proxy. If at the end of the year—or a shorter period—the enterprise has been successful in accumulating a surplus, the usual action is to put part of it into a reserve fund, and to distribute the rest as a dividend to members on purchases or patronage. If the patronage dividend is 4 per cent of purchases and a family has bought a hundred dollars worth of products, then its dividend is four dollars. This is in addition to the interest paid on the capital. . . .

What is the hope in the people who give up their time and invest their money to make cooperatives a success? It does not seem to be confined solely to the lowering of prices. Those who participate actively in their cooperative say it is literally a school in economic democracy, where one learns by facing day by day the practical problems of supplying needs efficiently and justly. Many religious leaders have declared that there is a high ethical value in consumer cooperation in that individual competition for selfish gain is supplanted by working together for the common welfare. The growth of interest among the churches is one of the most notable developments in the cooperative movement during the past three years.

So far the volume of cooperative business is not very large in the United States. It is estimated at between 1 and 2 per cent of the retail business of the nation. But the cooperatives have been growing, especially during the depression. The farmers have about 8,500 marketing associations and 2,000 purchasing associations, making a total of 10,500. There are an estimated 5,000 consumer cooperatives of various types, including about 2,000 gas and oil stations and 100 grocery stores. In addition there are more than 6,000 credit unions, or small cooperative banks.

Can these cooperatives expect to affect the great volume of distribution in the United States? Can they expect, in time, to set up factories of their own, as they have done in England, and, without profit, manufacture goods for wide and cheap distribution through the local cooperatives? Certainly many of the devoted supporters of the idea hope to do exactly that. And in the course of doing that they expect to develop a democratically controlled economic system that will be more stable, and also more efficient than the present one.

Staff of the Council of Social Action.
Published in *Social Action,* April 15, 1938.

A PRAYER

Grant, O Lord, that we may be delivered from self-consciousness and self-love. Fill our minds with the sense of the needs of others, and of thy power to supply them, so that there may be no place for any thought of our own needs and powers; through Jesus our Lord. *Amen.*

Proceed Resolutely: Fourth Friday

26. THE FATE OF THE PROPHETS

Alas! how full of fear
Is the fate of the Prophet and Seer!
For evermore, for evermore,
It shall be as it hath been heretofore;
The age in which they live will not forgive
The splendor of the everlasting light,
That makes their foreheads bright,
Nor the sublime
Fore-running of their time!

HENRY WADSWORTH LONGFELLOW, From *The Divine Tragedy*.

THE AGONY OF GOD

I listen to the agony of God—
  I who am fed,
  Who never yet went hungry for a day.
I see the dead—
  The children starved for lack of bread—
  I see, and try to pray.

I listen to the agony of God—
  I who am warm,
  Who never yet have lacked a sheltering home.
In dull alarm
  The dispossessed of hut and farm
  Aimless and "transient" roam.

I listen to the agony of God—
  I who am strong,
  With health, and love, and laughter in my soul.
I see a throng
  Of stunted children reared in wrong,
  And wish to make them whole.

I listen to the agony of God—
  But know full well
  That not until I share their bitter cry—
  Earth's pain and hell—

Can God within my spirit dwell
To bring His kingdom nigh.

> GEORGIA HARKNESS, in *Radical Religion.*

THE GODLIKENESS OF JESUS

The Christian God is a God of sacrificial love, forever coming forth to communicate grace and truth to his creatures. The image of God, then, must be interpreted as man's capacity to respond gratefully to the divine love that patiently seeks him out, and to show his gratitude for God's patient mercy by exhibiting a similar magnanimity to his neighbors, even though they be his enemies.

This is that Godliness which Jesus held up before his disciples in the Sermon on the Mount, and which he himself exhibited when he went to the cross for mankind's sake, begging forgiveness for his enemies as they crucified him. No scientific anthropology could ever prove that man is capable of Godliness in this sense; though it might establish the fact that, like many of his humble mammalian ancestors, he knows "how to give good gifts to his children," and to some extent is accustomed to push the attitude of loving generosity beyond the limits of the natural family, to include members of other groups for which he has a strong "we-feeling." The confirmation of this Christian view of God and man is only to be found in the non-scientific observation, and that when the challenge to be Godlike is presented to him in the gospel, man does sometimes respond to it with a disinterested, reverent, self-forgetful devotion for which his devotion to wife and child, or country, or truth, or beauty, is only a partial analogy; so that even though he fails to live up to the challenge, his conscience remains uneasy and he bows down in penitence before the God of love whom he continues to crucify.

> WALTER MARSHALL HORTON, *The Christian Understanding of Man.*
> An Oxford Conference Book.
> Published by Willett, Clark & Company, Chicago.

STILL THE CROSS

Calvary is a continent
Today. America
Is but a vast and terrible
New Golgotha.

The Legion (not of Rome today)
Jests. The Beatitudes
Are called by our new Pharisees
Sweet platitudes.

We tear the seamless robe of love
With great guns' lightning-jets;
We set upon Christ's head a crown
Of bayonets.

"Give us Barabbas!" So they cried
Once in Jerusalem:
In Alcatraz and Leavenworth
We copy them.

With pageant and with soldiers still
We march to Golgotha
And crucify Him still upon
A cross of war.

O blasphemous and blind! shall we
Rejoice at Eastertide
When Christ is risen but to be
Recrucified?
E. MERRILL ROOT, in *The Christian Century.*

THE DISCIPLES

But if Himself He came to thee, and stand
Beside thee, gazing down on thee with eyes
That smile, and suffer; that will smite thy heart,
With their own pity, to a passionate peace;
And reach to thee Himself the Holy Cup. . . .
Pallid and royal, saying "drink with me";
Wilt thou refuse? Nay, not for Paradise!
The pale brow will compel thee, the pure hands
Will minister unto thee; thou shalt take
Of that communion through the solemn depths
Of the dark waters of thine agony,
Meets heart that praises Him, that yearns to Him
The closer through that hour. Hold fast His hand,
Though the nails pierce thine too! . . .

Therefore gird up thyself and come to stand
Unflinching prove the unfaltering hand,
That waits to prove thee for the uttermost.
It were not heard to suffer by His hand,
If thou couldst see His face;—but in the dark!
That is the one last trial:—be it so.
Christ was forsaken, so must thou be too:
How couldst thou suffer but in seeming, else?
Thou wilt not see the face nor feel the hand,
Only the cruel crushing of the feet,
When through the bitter night the Lord comes down
To tread the winepress.—Not by sight, but faith,
Endure, endure,—be faithful to the end!

HARRIET ELEANOR HAMILTON-KING (1840-1920).

A PRAYER

O thou whose patience we have too long tried, after so many ineffectual vows, we almost fear to repent, lest we only add one unfaithfulness more, and turn our last strength into weakness. Increase our faith that we may no longer lean on our broken will, but throw ourselves freely open unto thee, watch thy guiding light, and follow where thou mayst lead. Till we serve thy will with a surrendered heart, we know that thou canst not refresh our weary life. Accepting the meekness of Christ, may we find each holy truth grow clear, each sacred burden light, and the shadow of guilt dissolve away. Enlarge our souls with a divine charity that we may hope all things, believe all things, endure all things, and become messengers of thy healing mercy to the grievances and infirmities of men. In all things attune our hearts to the holiness and harmony of thy kingdom. And hasten the time when that kingdom shall come, and thy will be done on earth as it is in heaven. *Amen.*

JAMES MARTINEAU.

Seek Comradeship: Fourth Saturday

27. THE BALANCE

I ate the bread of beauty,
  I drank the wine of song,
And I was well fed
  And my body grew strong.

But what of my neighbor
  In a pit all day long,
Or the lad in the mill
  Who hears no glad song?

Have I any merit
  Which gives wine and bread
To me when my neighbor
  Is starving instead?
              MARGARET MILLER PETTENGILL, in *The Christian Century*.

THE LIVING PRESENCE

The religious movement headed by Jesus had apparently come to an end with his shameful execution upon the cross. The Sanhedrin, at any rate, apparently thought it unnecessary to pursue the matter further by the persecution of his followers. Whether this was because their numbers were too insignificant, or because they were so careful to remain inconspicuous that no one suspected them of forming a definite group or party—whatever the reason, we hear of no further measures taken either by the Jewish authorities or by the Roman Procurator. All the more surprising was it, therefore, when the movement presently raised its head again, not only unexhausted but with greater enthhusiasm than before. Jesus had been very reticent about his own person and in advancing his claims to Messiahship, so much so that it had been extremely difficult to formulate the charges upon which he was condemned. His followers, on the contrary, came forward not only with the message of the near approach of the Kingdom of God, but with the open proclamation: Jesus is in truth the Messiah. This was something unheard-of. None of the Messianic movements of the time had survived the fall of their leader (as Gamaliel's words imply, in Acts 5:35ff). Here, by contrast, the death of the Master provides the strongest incentive to a renewal of zeal. We must note also how bizarre this doctrine must have seemed. It was in fact nothing short of blasphemy— at the very best a wild delusion—which they maintained, viz. that the one "hanged on a tree" should be the King of Israel, foretold by the prophets. What had come over them, during the interval between Good Friday and the disciples' earliest Messianic preaching? . . .

. . . it appears as a fact that Jesus was not led to Jerusalem by any jubilant optimism, as hoping there to see the establishment of the Kingdom of God and to experience his own exaltation, but rather in the steadfast expectation that the way to glory led through a fearful crisis, through struggle, suffering, and death; that he tried to share this conviction, that the cross preceded the crown, with his disciples; and that they also, like himself, must face suffering—that is an idea of Jesus as assuredly as anything in the narrative of his life. It is quite conceivable that the final realization of the "passion-predictions" was overwhelming enough to prostrate the disciples; but it is equally conceivable that at once the recollection of Jesus' words and the memory of his majestic personality, ineradicable even in defeat and death, came into play—the "bent spring" began moving back into place. . . .

It is a real sign of an inherited capacity for hope, that the disciples of Jesus were not completely and permanently crushed by his death. And in dealing with the problem as a whole this undetermined yet perfectly real factor must be taken into account. Even so, one circumstance remains unexplained. We can understand how disappointed hope would soon revive, in some form or other; but how are we to account for the fact . . . that these hopes centered steadily in the person of Jesus, in spite of the apparent proof that he was not only not the Chosen One of God, but was only one more unmasked impostor? How came it that he was not deserted, as men had deserted the Baptist before him? Indeed, why was not the whole idea of a personal Messiah given up? The Reign of God, as Jesus had taught them to look forward to it, was entirely, and in fact even more satisfactorily, conceivable apart from the interposition of any human personality. Did not the deaths of both John the Baptist and Jesus show that men ought to look for the coming of God's Kingdom, but not in dependence upon any human persons? How then did it come to pass that the revived expectation clung nevertheless to Jesus?—and this not only in the sense that he was its prophet who in spite of everything to the contrary had nevertheless delivered a true message, but with the inspired proclamation: In spite of all he is Messiah! It is quite noticeable that Maurenbrecher, though he sets out to reduce as far as possible the personal factor of Jesus' influence upon the disciples, is again and again forced to admit this inextinguishable force of personality. "Naturally, of course, the historical Jesus must somehow have greatly stimulated and intensified the Messianic expectations of his disciples; otherwise we could not explain how, among thousands of his contemporaries, the dogma of the dying and rising Savior was to fasten itself upon him." Similarly, the brilliant passage: "Then came the new enthusiasm, which Jesus aroused in them: the more passionate message, the flaming Now, the audacity to live as if the New Age were already present . . . they were caught up by the same powerful movement that lay back of Jesus' own appearance. They dared to live as they had seen him live. . . . During the weeks while they companied with him, they had actually been lifted up above themselves." It was now an unforgettable memory, how during that flight amid the ravines of Lebanon he had talked with them about the Son of Man. They had known the teaching all along, but now it takes on new warmth. It becomes the symbol and clue to their own destiny. They look more deeply into the moral idea behind the myth, and resolve to stand fast in the face of whatever persecutions or dangers may arise, since the crown of life is not to be won apart from trial and suffering. This was the great achievement to which the ardor of Jesus' own inner life had led them—the dying and rising Son of Man was for them no longer a doctrine, a matter of speculation, a novel addition to the hope of the good time to come; it was an actual experience, a prototype and pledge of their own patient endurance and of its reward.

What Luke 24:32 relates of the disciples at Emmaus is "a tiny reflection of what these first disciples must have passed through, in fear and trembling: It was he himself! What he spoke to us about the Son of Man, it was himself he meant, and we simply did not understand. We were too dull, we were deaf and blind and stupid; we deserted, and took offense at him. . . . We were witnesses of the greatest drama that the world has ever seen in all its history, or will ever see, and we never suspected what was taking place before our very eyes."

Could one find more beautiful language in which to say that it was Jesus himself, his confident faith and his voluntary acceptance of death, which had preserved them in advance from sinking into despair, had rescued them from despondency and bound them more firmly to himself?

JOHANNES WEISS, *The History of Primitive Christianity.*
Published by Wilson-Erickson, Inc., New York.

SIGNIFICANCE OF THE CHURCH

What does a Church really do for the God-desiring individual; the soul that wants to live a full, complete and real life, which has "felt in its solitude" the presence and compulsion of Eternal Reality under one or other of the forms of religious experience?

I think we can say that the Church or institution gives to its loyal members:—

(1) Group-consciousness.

(2) Religious union, not only with its contemporaries but with the race, that is with history. This we may regard as an extension into the past—and so an enrichment—of that group-consciousness.

(3) Discipline; and with discipline a sort of spiritual grit, which carries our fluctuating souls past and over the inevitably recurring periods of slackness, and corrects subjectivism.

(4) It gives Culture, handing on the discoveries of the saints.

EVELYN UNDERHILL, *The Life of the Spirit and the Life of Today.*
Published by E. P. Dutton & Co., New York City.

A PRAYER

Oh God, we praise Thee for the dreams which have haunted the prophets of humanity for centuries, the dreams of peace which Christ inspires in human hearts. We pray that the knowledge and the power may be available to turn into reality the vision that has so long beckoned in vain. We rejoice in the heroic dead who have counted not their lives dear unto themselves, but have paid the price to obtain for us a freedom which they could not enjoy. We pray that we may be worthy of them, that we may be able to establish and complete their work, to build upon secure foundations the cooperative civilization for which they were willing to die. Amen.

RAYMOND C. BROOKS.

Worship God: Fourth Sunday

28. THE POET IN THE DESERT

Who can set a limit to the soul?
Who can explore the infinite?
Light, the swift messenger, which in the winking of
An eye can girdle the earth seven times,
Toils toward us half a million years bringing from
Some outer sentinel the message
Sent before man was "I am here."
And if we reach to the finest stardust of
The Milky-way—what's beyond?
Infinite is space—but not more infinite than the soul.
I cannot reach to the uttermost bounds
Of the soul of the one I love.
No, not even of the one I love.
Though we are comrades and eagerly try
To approach each other,
There are spaces not to be crossed,
And we wander alone; as much as the moon is alone,
Eager but inexorably forbidden—yearning but inarticulate.
I cannot probe even my own soul.
It eludes me; dissolves and flies like a rainbow
Or the mist in deep canyons, where none can follow.
I am a stranger even to myself.
Mixed, compounded and conditioned by unknown forces
Which have harnessed the stars.
A mystery to myself; to my dear one, a mystery.
He who shall look upon the last sunset
May boast he has known the soul of Man. . . .

As for me, I throw my arms out wide
To the green Earth, the air, the life-giving Sun,
Praying that the Unknown Miracle
Of which I am a part, make me as reverent
To the freedom of another as I
Insist on freedom for my own soul; as brave
For my struggle as those before me were brave.
Strengthen my heart for the path;

Put wings on my feet that I may walk
The higher way
Urging me desperately to know all things;
Humbly knowing I shall never know.
Guessing that Beauty is goodness, goodness beauty
And only Ugliness is sin.

O unseen, unknown, unapproachable, beautiful Mother,
Hushing, soothing, endlessly beneficent,
Continually rocking my cradle with soothing monotony;
Kiss me with your large tranquility,
And give me understanding.
Teach me the universal love
Which is the universal wisdom.
Make me in life reach toward death,
And in death toward the life
Which shall ceaselessly come after me;
Wherein lies my own immortality
And the eternal hope.
I know my ignorance.
I know my helplessness.
I know that I am compounded of you.
I began with you and shall end with you,
O Infinite Mother. . . .

Nature, lay on me your cool and benedictive hands;
Wrap me in your beautiful mantle.
Bathe me in your clear pools
And draw into your bosom all my fever.
Wash me clean of man's filthy turmoil.
Release me to embark upon the clouds
Or wander with the vagabond winds.
Lift me upon sunrise and unlock for me the sunset gates.
Into your quiet tent let me invite my soul.
Give into my hands the stars
And from your invisible fountains
Shed on me the dew of Peace. . . .

I, too, am part of the cosmos
And am entitled to sweep free in my orbit,
As the stars in theirs;

Though I take my place with this little lizard
As one of the motes of Creation.
Dimly, I begin to know that Nature
Has designed freedom for every one,
Without exception;
To each the possession of his own soul,
A mysterious cosmos.
These thoughts penetrate me,
Even as the insistent sap penetrates
To the very tips of the leaves,
Even as the sun of the Desert pieces my marrow.
And I know the order of the universe
And the salvation of the world is freedom. . . .

Behold how Nature in her elusive mantle,
More hushed that Night,
Soft-trailing as the clouds,
Goes, like a mother, to her perfect work.
Gentle as Sleep,
More comforting than Death,
She lifts the sea unto the mountain-top
Without a sound,
And pours continually the everlasting urns.
The rivers murmur as gods that dream,
And the benignant mountains guard their slumber.
Their heads are pillowed on Eternity;
Their never-sleeping voices are soothing.
Consider, also, the rain,
The very wine of days;
How noiselessly it seeks the slender roots,
As a bride creeps to her love;
And who has ever heard a cry or noise
From the frail and thready roots
Which uplift the trees,
Garnish the earth with grass
And spread abroad the blazonry of flowers?
The frail roots whose delicate fingers distill
Earth's miracle of nectared fruits,
And never make a sound.
Nature has laid her finger on her lips.

Night and day she teaches that Beauty is her state,
Silence her delight,
And Freedom her condition.

CHARLES ERSKINE SCOTT WOOD, *The Poet in the Desert.*
Published by Vanguard Press, New York.

A PRAYER

Eternal Spirit, high above us all yet deep within us all, we worship Thee. From the strife and confusion of the tongues of men we seek Thy sanctuary, not that we may find a selfish peace but that, with vision quickened for things unseen and eternal and with faith refreshed, we may tomorrow revisit the world and be more than conquerors.

We pray for height in our lives. We need altitude. Above the confusion and turmoil that baffle us, lift us today to some high outlook where we may catch large vistas and broad horizons.

We pray for breadth in our lives. We are shut in by the narrowness of our daily interests and even by the vindictiveness of our irritations. Lift us high that we may see broadly and, within the large comprehension of a more sympathetic care, take in all sorts and conditions of men.

We pray for length of outlook and of vison. The immediacies of these present days stare us out of countenance. O God, in Whose sight a thousand years are but as yesterday when it is past, give us long looks as the reward of our worship.

We pray for depth, that in these days of strain and storm we may have stout rootage and beneath our houses strong foundations. Give us depth that there may be inner adequacy, poise, and power. . . .

So blessed, may we lift up our hearts in thanksgiving in Thy sanctuary. Thanks to Thee for all that is excellent and beautiful in life, for all that cleanses the spirit, clarifies the mind, redeems the soul from destruction, and leads us in green pastures and beside the still waters. Put a song on the lips of Thy people—

"Bless the Lord, O my soul;
And all that is within me, bless his holy name."

HARRY EMERSON FOSDICK, in *The Church Monthly.*

Concentrate Upon the Ideal: Fifth Monday

29. HAIL, MAN!

This flesh is but the symbol and the shrine
Of an immense and unimagined beauty,
Not mortal, but divine;
Structure behind our structure,
Lightning within the brain,
Soul of the singing nerve and throbbing vein,
A giant blaze that scorches through our dust
Fanning our futile "might be" with its "Must";
Bearing upon its breast our eager span—
Beyond, above, and yet the self of man!

Look how the glow-worm with its feeble might,
Signals the presence of celestial fire;
How phosphorous upon the sea at night,
And the swift message o'er the radiant wire,
Proclaim the awesome thing existence covers;
Eternity emerging through our husk,
Sky through our vapor,
Glory through our dusk.

Behold the slender scarlet line that hovers
Between close fingers held against the sun,
Each like a swift and beaming taper
Afire from one.
And how each seems the token
Of a great mystery no man has spoken,
Wherein we walk and work and do our tasks,
Nor dream within what light the spirit basks. . . .

This creaking tent we call the universe,
One motion in a mighty caravan
Whose million, million orbits but rehearse
The miracle that swings the heart of man,
Is but the outward breathing from that Source—
Call it by whatsoever sounding name,
God or Jehovah, Life or Primal Force—

Which, like a vast, impalpable, pure flame,
Bears up the visible as 'twere a toy;
Shoulders our burdens like a singing boy;
Props with its permanence our mortal screen;
Hotter than hissing fires, than light more keen,
Solid as stone, simple and clean as glass,
Fluid as flashing waves that leap and pass. . . .

Yet doth obscuring flesh
Infinity enmesh,
While soul within its prison speaks to soul,
Hailing the habitation as the whole!
This flesh is but the visible outshowing
Of a portentous and a mighty thing,
Whereof, each mortal knowing,
Becomes a King!

ANGELA MORGAN, *Hail, Man!*
Published by John Lane Co., New York.

THE SUPREME MASTER

The supreme education of the soul comes through an intimate
acquaintance with Jesus Christ of history. One who wished to
feel the power of beauty would go to some supreme master of
color and form who could exhibit them on canvas and not merely
lecture about them. One who desired to feel the power of harmony would go, not to the boy with his harmonica, but to the
Beethovens or Mozarts of the race who have revealed what an
instrument and a human hand can do. So he who wishes to
realize and practice the presence of God must inform himself
at the source and fount, must come face to face with Him who
was the highest human revelation of God. No one of us can interpret his own longings or purposes until he reads them off in
the light of some loftier type of personality.

RUFUS JONES, *The Double Search.*
Published by John C. Winston Co., Philadelphia.

THE SUPREME VALUE

The most fundamental element in the Christian conception
of the social life is the intrinsic worth of every personality. For
Jesus each human individual has distinct and measureless value

as a child of God and a potential member of His Kingdom. The preciousness of a single life is suggested in parable after parable. The shepherd goes out to seek a single sheep, the woman sweeps the house to find one stray coin, the father yearns for a single wayward son. Nothing in the Gospel is clearer than this view of the sacred worth of all human life. . . .

The characteristic feature in His attitude was that He saw values where others did not, and refused to despair even of those for whom the Church in His day held out no hope. A lost son was still a son, and heir to all the father possessed. The "lost" man was so precious and of such potential value that "the Son of Man came to seek and to save that which was lost." He associated with the outcasts of His day. He saw in all men something of infinite worth. In Mary Magdalene he discerned the elements of true womanhood. In vacillating Peter there was something like a rock. In an unknown Syro-Phœnician woman there were elements of greatness. In a Roman soldier He found the greatest faith. In a thief on the cross there was something that could be welcomed in Paradise. The "common people heard him gladly," because in them he discovered and revealed rights and possibilities which others could not see. A new sense of human worth and dignity springs from the pages of the Gospel.

From the Christian estimate of personality it follows that each man has his own distinct place in God's plan, and is never to be regarded simply as a means for realizing the ends of others. Hence all slavery is wrong, because based upon a fundamental misconception of the value of personality. Ignoring the right of man as man to free self-development, it treats him not as a person but as a thing. It denies him his independent and inalienable place as a member of the family of God. And this Christian point of view is inconsistent not only with slavery in the crude form that now has vanished from the earth, but also with any social relationships that prevent full self-development by subordinating one human being to the uses of another and making one man little more than a means to another's convenience or gain. It runs counter to all valuing of people according to their utility to us rather than for their own intrinsic worth. Any civilization is, therefore, condemned by it so far as the well-being of the relatively few is built upon the continuing impoverishment of the many.

From the Christian conception of personality it follows also that material values are always to be secondary to human values. A man's life does not consist in the abundance of things that he possesses. They are to be regarded not as of primary concern but simply as a means to the worthiest living. "What doth it profit a man," asks Jesus, "to gain the whole world and forfeit his life?" And the principle applies not only to one's own life but to any impoverishment of the lives of others through one's pursuit of gain. According to the Christian scale of values, therefore, property rights are to be subordinate to human rights. The test of industrial efficiency is to be not the size of the profits but the effect on human lives. Men do not exist for the sake of industry; industry exists for their sakes, if personal values are the supreme thing in the world.

> The Committee on the War and the Religious Outlook,
> *The Church and Industrial Reconstruction.*
> Published by Association Press, New York.

BITTER OPPOSITION

From the very beginning . . . the course of Christianity was marked by persecutions and martyrdoms. No other of the faiths of mankind, religious or political, has quite so extensive a record of violent and bitter opposition to its growth. Jesus himself met it during most of his brief public career, and his cross is the prevailing symbol of the Christian religion.

> KENNETH SCOTT LATOURETTE.

A PRAYER

O God that dwellest in transcendental light
  Beyond our dreams, who grope in darkness here,
Beyond imagination's utmost flight,—
  I bless thee most that sometimes when a tear
  Of tender yearning rises unrepressed
Lo! for an instant thou art strangely near—
  Nearer to my own heart than I who rest
  In speechless adoration on thy breast.

> EDMOND GORE ALEXANDER HOLMES, *The God Within.*

Understand the Actual: Fifth Tuesday

30. THE WALL STREET PIT

I see a hell of faces surge and whirl,
Like maelstrom in the ocean—faces lean
And fleshless as the talons of a hawk—
Hot faces like the faces of the wolves
That track the traveler fleeing through the night—
Grim faces shrunken up and fallen in,
Deep-plowed like weather-beaten bark of oak—
Drawn faces like the faces of the dead,
Grown suddenly old upon the brink of earth.

Is this a whirl of madmen ravening,
And blowing bubbles in their merriment!
Is Babel come again with shrieking crew
To eat the dust and drink the roaring wind?
And all for what? A handful of bright sand
To buy a shroud with and a length of earth?

EDWIN MARKHAM.
Published by Doubleday, Doran & Co., New York.

ETHICS IN HIGH PLACES

Two of the nation's business leaders have been caught trying to cheat the government out of almost two millions in income taxes. The federal board of tax appeals has ruled that Pierre S. du Pont and John J. Raskob first tried to defraud the government with regard to their 1929 incomes, and then tried to cover up the fraudulent transaction by testifying under oath to a cock-and-bull story which the board refused to believe.

It would be hard to find two men who more nearly represent to the general public that type of great wealth which has been most jealous of its privileges and most bitterly opposed to every measure for public control.

When charges of income tax evasion were first leveled against the two millionaires, both made public statements holding the action of the government to be mere retaliation for their activities as Liberty Leaguers. "One could secure no better illustration," said Mr. Raskob, "of the tyranny which a government bureau can inflict on a citizen." And Mr. du Pont declared that the prosecution was "part of a scheme to injure me and to force a compromise of claims in a manner amounting to extortion." Those declarations make sorry but revealing reading when considered in the light of the facts brought out in the tax board's ruling.

The method which Mr. du Pont and Mr. Raskob used to cheat the government was a simple one. Shortly before the end of 1929 each man sold to the other more than $6,000,000 worth of stock at a price considerably lower than the purchase price. In January, 1930, the sales were reversed. Although, ostensibly, more than $29,766,000 had changed hands, the board of tax appeals found that the total actual difference in the sizes of the checks passed back and forth was only $46.86. On the basis of the "losses" the two men alleged they had suffered by these year-end sales and resales to each other, their income tax reports showed a capital shrinkage of $7,496,170 from their 1929 taxable incomes. But both men came out of the deal at the end of the month owning exactly the same stocks with which they started.

This slick little scheme for evading income tax will be seen to be simply an adaptation of the "wash sales" knavery now outlawed in Wall Street. It once was possible for brokers who were interested in manipulating the price of a certain stock to arrange for ostensible sales back and forth until the market price had been brought to the desired quotation. The practice was known as a "wash sale," and it was abolished even before the SEC began to pry into the workings of the stock exchange. Mr. du Pont and Mr. Raskob tried to work the old "wash sale" game on the government, but the tax board was not fooled.

Such is the verdict after more than two years of investigation into the tax returns of these two multimillionaires. It is a verdict rendered by a responsible tribunal of government on the ethics of men in high places. The language is restrained, as language in such documents must always be. Much of the testimony recapitulated is technical; the serried masses of figures may prove difficult for the common citizen to grasp. But what that common citizen does grasp, and will store away in his memory, is the fact that if the men who made this tax board ruling had been using the language of everyday life they would have employed such terms as trickery, cheating, crookedness, lying.

One astonishing feature of this affair has been the slight attention paid to it by most of the press. The newspapers could not entirely ignore so sensational a ruling, but it has been given prominence in few news columns and still fewer editorial pages have seen fit to call attention to its significance. One wonders whether there would have been a similar reticence had the person caught in an income tax evasion been someone like "Jimmy" Roosevelt or John L. Lewis or David Lilienthal! But when the men involved are outstanding champions of reactionary social and political views, and masters of far-reaching industrial enterprises, the press apparently is ready to say as little as possible about the matter, and to forget it as soon as possible.

There are those who assert that the American people are succumbing to an insidious process of moral decay. The sentiment is perhaps heard most frequently in the very circles which have expressed most admiration for men like Mr. du Pont and Mr. Raskob. If such a process is in truth at work, we do not believe that it has as yet widely undermined the national character. But this much we know: nothing can contribute more disastrously to the moral disintegration of a people than a belief that the rules of the game of life are whatever one can get away with. Yet that is precisely the lesson which, in rigging up their scheme to evade their just obligations to the government, Mr. du Pont and Mr. Raskob have been trying to teach.

The Christian Century.

TWENTY-FIVE BILLIONS

Despite the State "Blue Sky" laws the losses of investors have been appalling. Those who have considered the matter place such losses in this country at $1,700,000,000 annually even before the depression, and at more than $500,000,000 annually in the State of New York alone. Other statistics indicate that such losses have amounted to the colossal sum of $25,000,000,000 during the past ten years.

Senate Banking and Currency Committee, April 28, 1933.

BANK FAILURES

During the past twelve years, 10,484 banks, with deposit liabilities of $4,882,481,000, have failed in this country. Of this number, 1,571 were National banks, with deposits of $1,143,857,-

000, and 8,913 were banks other than National, with deposits of $3,738,624,000. Yet these figures do not reveal the whole of the damage done to our credit structure by bank failures since they do not include the millions of dollars withdrawn from deposit in going banks or the amounts which failed to find their way into banks for deposit through fear engendered in the minds of depositors by bank failures and fanned by rumors, which in many instances were malicious in character.

Annual Report of Comptroller of Currency, December 12, 1932.

A PRAYER

Oh God, who hast so curiously made us that from whatever heights we climb we see loftier heights before, and forever being thus dissatisfied behold what we ought to be outreaching what we are: *strengthen in us this divine discontent.*

From all manner of self-complacency, from pride in the actual and forgetfulness of the ideal, from the cowardice of time-serving and the contented living of mediocre lives on common levels: *save us, Oh God.*

We confess our temptation to measure our lives by the standards of the crowd and to excuse our disordered behavior by appeal to common practices. Oh Christ, who didst demand of thy disciples, "What do ye more than others?" grant us such clarity of vision, independence of mind, and courage of will that we may live according to our best conscience, without fear or favor of the multitude.

Disturb us with visions of a juster social order. From being contented while poverty and ignorance, lack of labor, and destitution of soul afflict our fellows: *save us, Oh God.*

From complacency with political corruption, racial prejudice, the hardships of unfair industry, the disunion of the Church, and the insanity of war: *good Lord, deliver us.*

Oh God, who without our asking it hast set us in this mysterious scheme of circumstance, give us light in order that we may know the path to walk in. Confirm in us the dreams of seers and the hopes of prophets; let not cynicism blight nor faithlessness uproot our confidence in thy coming kingdom of righteousness upon the earth, and at the fire of our faith let courage be kindled that we may live as we pray. Amen.

BISHOP WILLIAM SCARLETT.

Be Concerned: Fifth Wednesday

31. FAILURE

The world's tomorrow waits on us
   Who live the world's today,
And by our day's timidities
   Ages to come betray.

Who sells, for bread and butter now,
   The birthright of the whole,
Lays upon children yet unborn
   Intolerable toll.

They sleep on a volcano's crust
   Who only comfort seek;
And all their strength is less than dust
   Whose strength serves not the weak.

ROBERT WHITAKER, in *Social Song and Other Verse.*
Published by the Banner Press, Emory University, Atlanta, Ga.

THE CAUSES OF SOCIAL EVIL

In the social thinking of Christians there is vagueness and oversimplification in the diagnosis of the particular social evils which we face. The usual form which this tendency takes is to reduce all evil to one root—sin. Even if some account is given of the specific, proximate causes of such evils as war and economic injustice these causes are not taken seriously, and emphasis is placed too soon on the fact of sin, which, since it can be used to explain everything, really explains nothing in particular. Recently the concept of the "demonic" has come into Christian thinking and, while it is a useful concept in calling attention to the fact that many of the problems of life are created by social forces which have within them both constructive and destructive elements, it is rapidly becoming a new catch-all which throws very little light on any particular social fact. Another form of diagnosis which has become popular is to trace all moral and social evils to some quite general spiritual causes—secularism or human autonomy. Those words point to important aspects of our situation, but it is often not clear how far they explain the sources of specific social evils.

There are two reasons for the attempt in this paper to press for more precise thinking about the sources of the social evils of our time. The first is that these vague forms of diagnosis cover up the quite different ways in which various forms of evil must be cured. Most theological discussion of these matters obscures the necessity of a multiple attack upon our social problems—an attack along religious and moral, educational and technical, political and social lines at the same time.

The other reason for this attempt is that the social frustrations of our time have led Christian theologians to explore with new appreciation the pessimistic interpretations of human nature which have been an important strain in the Christian tradition, and in the light of those interpretations to make social judgments concernng what is possible in human history. We are thus being led from a dogmatic optimism which was founded on theories of progress and human perfectibility, for which there is insufficient empirical evidence, to a dogmatic pessimism which is founded on theological theories about man, for which there is also insufficient empirical evidence. It is my contention that one safeguard against this premature dogmatic pessimism is to remain longer than theological discussions usually remain within the area of specific social facts, and to seek to discover the roots of the particular social evils which have driven so many of us to this pessimism concerning the total human situation. . . .

It is the function of the church to call its people to repentance. The extension of the area over which Christian people feel a genuine sense of sin is an important part of the contribution of the church to the solution of the problems of society. But the church can do this most effectively if it does not assume that all men are equally sinful in relation to the whole mass of corporate evil, but rather if it shows up the evil which can be traced to the doors of each one of us in such a way that henceforth we become guilty in so far as we continue to consent to it. We may have been ignorant of the real consequences of our own ways of living, of the consequences of the social policies which we have instigated, by which we have profited, for which we have voted, to which we have consented, but when our ignorance is taken away we are without excuse. Moreover it must be realized that this ignorance is not merely a simple matter of the absence of knowledge of facts but it is far more the control of our minds by prejudices and patterns of thinking and feeling which cover up the real meaning of the facts.

In addition to the increase of actual moral responsibility through opening the eyes of men to evil which is connected with their lives, it is important to develop the inner attitude which fits the actual situation in connection with all social evil. Each of the types of experience, except the first—religious humility—described in the first part of this paper, has its own appropriate inner attitude corresponding to it.

This kind of analysis enables us to do justice to the stubbornness of evil in the human situation without blinding ourselves to the good in human nature. It becomes clearer how men can do evil on a vast scale in society and still in their personal lives, where issues are simpler and where imagination is active, show honesty, loyalty, and compassion. There can be fine strains in their motives even in relation to public policies which have evil consequences. Any sour view of human nature, any tendency to overlook the beauty and the nobility of countless persons, is terribly wrong. We must be able to understand why it is that human life contains so vast a contradiction as it does—devastating evil on the one side and on the other love and integrity and self-giving devotion in human hearts. Such a view as I have suggested indicates how it is possible that human nature caught in an evil situation, is still the fitting medium for the revelation of the divine.

JOHN COLEMAN BENNETT, *Christian Faith and the Common Life.*
An Oxford Conference Book.
Published by Willett, Clark & Company, Chicago.

A CALL TO THE CHURCH FOR PENITENCE

Impelled by the living presence of our Lord Jesus Christ and aware of our dependence on the Holy Spirit given to us by God for our guidance and enlightenment, we are moved to consider most earnestly how we may more fully give expression to our Christian faith in the affairs of our common life.

Before God, we confess our sins as individuals and as a Church. Too often have we yielded to the lust for wealth and power and compromised the teaching of the Gospel so that it would be acceptable to the powers of the social order. Too often have we set the welfare of the institution above the fellowship of saints. Too often have we given our blessing to the brutal and selfish struggle for profit without criticism of the impact of that struggle on the personalities of our fellowmen; to the whole structure of the social order that exalts wealth as the greatest good, establishes the profit-motive as normal, right, and necessary, and subordinates the rights of personality to the claims of property. Too frequently have we, while professing supreme loyalty to Jesus Christ, in reality given over our consciences to the keeping of the state and shared in the excesses of an unbridled, licentious, and imperialistic nationalism. We have blessed war and lent ourselves to the spreading of lies and incitement to bitter hatred against our brothers; too often have we identified the prejudices and conduct of our nation, of our race, of our class with the teaching of Jesus. For these our sins we do implore forgiveness —forgiveness of our fellowmen and of our God. We pray God for a truly penitent spirit and true repentance.

In the presence of God, we do put from us all loyalties that are not compatible with loyalty to our Lord which we confess anew.

The Joint Commission on Christian Social Action.
Submitted to the General Synod of the
Evangelical and Reformed Church.

APPROACHING GOD

When thou approachest to the One,
Self from thyself thou first must free,
Thy cloak duplicity cast clean aside,
And in Thy Being's being be.

AMOS BRONSON ALCOTT.

A PRAYER

O God, who knowest us to be set in the midst of so many and great dangers, that by reason of the frailty of our nature we cannot always stand upright, grant to us such strength and protection as may support us in all dangers, and carry us through all temptations, through Jesus Christ our Lord.

BOOK OF COMMON PRAYER.

Endeavor to Transform: Fifth Thursday

32. CONSUMERS' COOPERATIVES NOT ENOUGH

In Great Britain there are nearly eight million members of cooperative societies; that is, there is at least one cooperative member in about half the families of the country. These consumer members have provided the capital for and are ultimately in control of a loosely-knit but coherent trading system, employing over £360,000,000. About 10% of the retail trade of the country or 15-20% of the trade in foodstuffs is in the hands of the cooperative movement. One quarter of the liquid milk consumed in the country is supplied by cooperative societies. The trading undertakings of the movement are operating in all the main lines of industry and commerce. The cooperative method favors a large scale of operation. The Cooperative Wholesale Society Ltd. is among the largest trading concerns in the country, directly employing over 50,000 workers and with an annual trade of nearly £120,000,000. In very many towns the largest retailer is the local cooperative society. In several industries the largest units in the country are cooperative, in many more the average scale of cooperative organization is larger than that for capitalist undertakings. These facts indicate that cooperation is no "hot-house" experiment, but is a distinct form of industrial organization, well-established and operating on a sufficient scale to admit of valid comparisons between it and capitalism. . . .

Equally important at the present time are the limitations on cooperative expansion. There are, of course, certain industries—mainly transport, communications and power—which are unsuited for *voluntary* consumer control, but in which operation by the central or local government departments, or by public service corporations, is both practicable and increasingly common. Leaving these aside, there are fields of purely capitalist trade where immediate cooperative progress is unlikely. The movement has mainly developed in retailing and in the wholesaling and production of consumers goods; its progress in the extraction of raw materials, the earlier stages of manufacture and in the production of specialized machinery has been small. It must not be imagined that progress in these fields has been negligible, or that the cooperative form of organization is permanently inapplicable. But at the present stage of monopoly capitalism the gradual expansion of cooperative undertakings into many of these industries would be very difficult. The early home of the Cooperative Movement was laisser-faire capitalism and cooperative societies often occupy an anomalous position in the monopoly-capitalism of today. Perhaps one of their major problems is to develop constructive tactics in relation to marketing boards and all the new machinery of industrial control which is now growing up. These facts, however, make it clear that the dream of a "Cooperative Commonwealth" to be achieved by the steady and gradual expansion of the existing cooperative system until it covers the whole of industry is likely to be vain.

W. S. Symonds, in *Radical Religion.*

SOCIALIZED OWNERSHIP

Where is the money coming from? In the last analysis it can come only from tangible wealth, and wealth can only come from labor, materials, and technical skill. So long as there remains a margin above subsistence, new industries may be introduced—or refinements on old industries—to the benefit of the whole community. It makes no theoretical difference whether the new industry is public schools or television or airplanes. The money for each can be created.

What seems to bring business men up short is that they have great difficulty in visualizing a new industry launched on a cost of service basis rather than on a profit-risk basis. If the project is a gamble where investors either quadruple their money or lose their shirts, the business man has no attack of nerves. But if the project is a riskless one, specifically designed to fill a proven community need—like housing—he goes all to pieces. In his financial calculus, apparently, only uncertainties count. Even when avenues for risk-taking and profitable investment are blocked, as they have been for the last six or eight years, he grows dizzy at the thought of investing in certainties. If banked up savings are flung on the stock market to build a speculative bonfire which must end—and he knows it will end—in a lot of charred embers, he raises little objection. If the government borrows or taxes the savings to build new blocks of wealth, he writes hysterical letters to the *New York Times.*

New industries, whether public or private, have heretofore been monetized by borrowing. Savings have been borrowed, or new credit has been created by the banks and loaned. Today, as we have seen, private business is shy of incurring new debt for expansion. Public debt is growing rapidly, primarily as a result of financing emergency relief. If this drain continues indefinitely, it may end in a runaway inflation.

Are we then stalemated by these special circumstances?

The physical warrant for expansion in public business is drawn and ready. To secure the financial warrant the rules of the game will have to be changed. We cannot use the old rules, because interest-bearing debt has about reached its limit, as Bassett Jones has amply demonstrated. Getting more money at the future cost of a runaway inflation is a reasonably bad bargain. To my mind, three new rules are in order:

1. The use of income tax on the higher brackets as a prime method for financing public business. This does away with some of the borrowing, and also takes care of the excess savings for which the rich cannot now find productive investment.

2. The use of non-interest bearing revolving funds of publicly created credit for additional financing of public works. This knocks compound interest on the head. The government assumes the same powers which private banks now exercise, and proceeds to manufacture credit and lend it to cities, states, school districts, without interest, the principal to be amortized over a series of years. Many alternatives can be worked out.

3. The socialization of money and credit, to prevent sabotage by private bankers, and to keep compound interest in its place. An officer of the American Bankers' Association has proposed, as a protest against the New Deal, that the banks stop lending to the government. It is quite safe to say that until we know who is boss, the United States Government, or the private banks, no planned extension of new industries is possible.

In conclusion, Mr. Business Man, the money is coming as it has always come, but in order to keep the system stable, it is highly probable that credit must be socialized, and the government become the community's banker—as provided for, incidentally, by the Constitution.

STUART CHASE, in *Common Sense.*

THE LOVER OF LIFE

The lover of life holds life in his hand
  Like a ring for the bride.
The lover of life is free of dread:
The lover of life holds life in his hand
  As the hills hold the day.

But lust after life waves life like a brand
  For an ensign of pride.
The lust after life is life half dead.
Yea, lust after life hugs life like a brand,
  Dreading air and the ray.

  For the sake of life,
  For that life is dear,
  The lust after life
  Clings to it fast.

  For the sake of life,
  For that life is fair,
  The lover of life
  Flings it broadcast.

The lover of life knows his labor divine
  And therein is at peace;
The lust after life craves a touch and a sign
  That the life shall increase.
The lust after life in the chills of its lust
  Claims a passport of death;
The lover of life sees the flame in our dust
  And a gift in our breath.

                    GEORGE MEREDITH (1828-1909).

A PRAYER

Help us, we beseech Thee, so to live that we may partake
of the joy of our Lord. Keep our souls before Thee as a still
lake, that so there may be kindled in our hearts the glow of faith
and love; and may we, through such stillness and peace, find
strength for Thy service, O God, now and evermore.

                    JOACHIM EMBDEN (*Altered*).

Proceed Resolutely: Fifth Friday

33. AN EARLY TOTALITARIANISM

Early in the Empire, too, came the development of the worship of the Emperor. The longing for a saviour who would bring peace to the earth had seemed to have fulfilment in Augustus. In his lifetime, therefore, the belief arose that he was an incarnation of divinity. His image was erected and religious honors paid to his genius. . . .

For this religion temples were erected, not only in Rome itself, but in the many cities of the Empire. The shrines were among the public buildings, and their construction, adornment, and maintenance were matters of civic pride. In the provinces the upkeep of the temples and the celebration of the ceremonies of the cult of Rome were especially the charge of the aristocracy and of the official classes who prided themselves on their Roman citizenship and upon whom fell the burden of civic duties. The ruling classes looked upon them as an integral part of the established order, and regarded any attack upon them or any refusal to endorse them as a threat to the very existence of the state and of society. It was this conviction . . . which gave rise to the most severe persecutions which Christianity encountered.

KENNETH SCOTT LATOURETTE, *The First Five Centuries.*
Published by Harper Brothers, New York.

MARTYR TO MILITARISM

Dead in Germany is the civilian ideal and dead at last is its greatest defender. Carl von Ossietzky, the only pacifist ever to receive the full Nobel peace prize, won freedom after six years of imprisonment and unbelievable suffering by dying on May 4 in Berlin. Forty-eight years of age, he had for twenty years lived to champion civil as against military virtues, the civilian as opposed to the military state. When he died in the forced confinement which the nazi government ironically called a hospital, Carl von Ossietzky entered into immortality as one of the greatest modern martyrs in the struggle to maintain human liberty against the totalitarian state. Because growing militarization threatens all nations, including our own, with the same fascist pattern, we salute this great journalist in gratitude for having the insight to see the nature of the challenge militarism presents to civilization and the high courage to witness against it even unto death.

Before the Nobel award was granted a number of world famous English writers, including Bertrand Russell, Norman Angell, Aldous Huxley and H. G. Wells, issued a pamphlet supporting Jane Addams and Romain Rolland in urging that the prize go to von Ossietzky. Their words are truer today, now that he is dead, than when they were written. "If they decide to give him the peace prize," they said, "the committee will be crowning a true martyr. But we also suggest that they will be doing more than that. All of us have in some way or another tried to do something for the cause of peace. But we say that he has done more than any of us, and we believe that he has done most of all living men to deserve this acknowledgment from his fellow men.

"We believe that the strange and terrible fate which ruled his life made it possible for him to show the quality which, of all others, it is most difficult for a pacifist to demonstrate—fearlessness. We may possibly, each of us, possess his physical and moral courage, but (as yet) we dare lay no claim to be his equal here. We have not yet been tested as he has. Carl von Ossietzky has shown once for all, to the eager youth of the world, to all the natural hero worshippers, that heroism is not the prerogative of the soldier. He has marched up to the embattled enemy and taken from them the one emblem that really flamed there, the one token that truly adorned their ranks. He has taken for himself—for us —the red badge of courage." . . .

In November, 1931, he and Kreiser were brought to trial for treason. They were defended by some of the most prominent lawyers in Germany. The sessions of the court were held in secret, and each defendant was sentenced to eighteen months in prison. . . . An appeal was filed, while in the meantime, contrary to custom, the passports of the convicted men were not impounded by the police, and pointed hints were given that they flee. . . .

One morning in May 1932 after the appeal had been lost, a friend called for him in his automobile. In spite of the pleadings of the friend that he be permitted to turn his car toward the Czech border, von Ossietzky insisted that he drive to Tegel prison. There occurred one of the most dramatic struggles in modern history. The government still would gladly have permitted him to escape. Outside the prison a great crowd of his friends waited, to dissuade him from entering if possible; if not, to bid him farewell. Arnold Zweig, author of the famous war novel, *The Case of Sergeant Grischa,* was one of the group which walked to and fro among the scattered trees, arguing for an hour with von Ossietzky whether what he was doing was right. He was determined to let the full consequences of his unjust sentence fall on the government, and urged his friends to use the public concern that had been aroused to secure freedom for thousands of nameless political prisoners who had been forgotten. As for himself, he was prepared to pay to the full and had never considered political journalism as "health insurance." Finally he broke from them, strode to the prison gates. . . . Never again, except for a brief interval just before Hitler took power, was he to know freedom.

But the military were not yet satisfied. While he was in prison he was again brought to trial for publishing an article in which the author had said, "Soldiers are murderers." Ossietzky's defense was clear and courageous. "I have never stood before a court of law with greater pleasure. The article completely represents my opinion. I am not one of those who became a pacifist when Germany was defeated in 1918. I have fought war and been a member of pacifist organizations since 1912. And I repeat that what I saw of war only confirmed my earlier opinion of it—that war brings terror and despair to mankind, and that there is nothing heroic about it.

"It is our duty as pacifists to protest constantly and in plainest language against what we believe to be evil. All through literature, in the words of Laotze, in the Bible, in the works of Kant, you will find, couched in the same brief, lapidary style, denunciations of the profession of arms. All of them have stamped war as murder and those who wage it as murderers. There is an eternal divergence between the morality of the state and the morality of the individual. For two thousand years this divergence has been the subject of debate; the thing can be reduced to a formula. The retail murderer has his head cut off; the wholesale has his crowned with a wreath of laurel." . . .

He was acquitted, but returned to prison to serve out his sentence on the previous charge. Freed by the Christmas amnesty of 1932, he was again urged to flee when Hitler came into power a month later, but refused once more. The morning after the Reichstag fire he was swept into the police net as an "enemy of the state" and sent for "protective detention" to Spandau prison and thence to Sonnenberg, an old prison which had once been abandoned as too unhealthful, but was now a concentration camp. That he survived the horrors of three years in this hell to receive the Nobel peace prize is an amazing manifestation of the vitality of the human spirit when it is wholly committed to truth and brotherhood. . . .

The award of the Nobel prize to von Ossietzky almost paralyzed the German government with anger. An official communiqué sputtered, "The award of the Nobel prize to a notorious traitor is such a brazen challenge and insult to the new Germany that it will be followed by an appropriate and unequivocal answer." The Reich envoy at Oslo expressed both "astonishment and displeasure" to the Norwegian government. Chancellor Hitler, compelled to permit von Ossietzky to accept the award, issued a decree forbidding Germans to accept any Nobel prize in the future and establishing rival prizes for Germans.

Ossietzky was not returned to the concentration camp, but was imprisoned in a private sanitarium near Berlin from that time on.

Now the man who refused to flee from Germany because he said "a man speaks with a hollow voice across the border" is free to speak forever in ringing tones from across the border of death. In what land should his counsel be heard and his example be followed more assiduously than in the United States, which fought a war against militarism only to be baptized in a military spirit whose service today requires the chief energies of our government and in whose deceptive and deadly weakness our people are coming increasingly to trust? May von Ossietzky's voice raise up in this land which is yet free a million men and women who repudiate navalism and nationalism and turn America back from the military to the civilian way!

HAROLD E. FEY, in *The Christian Century.*

A PRAYER

O God, who hast made the earth so fair, and written Thy glory in the heavens, help us inwardly to respond to all that is outwardly true and beautiful, so that, as we pass through things temporal, we may have vision of the things eternal; through Jesus Christ our Lord.

Seek Comradeship: Fifth Saturday

34. FOREST MOODS

I hold that some melodious minstrel dwells
Close to the bosom of the streams and trees,
Haunting the dawnlit glades and twilight dells
With tremulous harmonies.

And not in bird-song only, or the roar
Of canyoned waters under spires of green,
One hears those charmed ethereal notes that pour
Out of the sweet unseen.

But when the night wears silence like a hood
And the hushed fields are robed in sunset grays;
Or in the bald ravine or windless wood,
That magic minstrel plays.

He sings the rapture of the crags and sky,
Of pine-groves chanting in the joy of birth;
And one who hears must go with glistening eye
Thankfully through the earth.

STANTON A. COBLENTZ, *Songs of the Redwoods.*
Published by Overland-Outwest Publications, Los Angeles.

AN EXPERIENCE OF KINSHIP

Religion is an experience of kinship with the Deepest Reality in the Universe and hence of membership in an infinitely meaningful world and of sharing in an ever unfolding life . . . in mankind God is creating creators and seeking to bring them into a community of love. . . . Without inner power, insight, and integrity no real participation in a meaningful world is possible, and without kinship and a vista of meaning stimulative of wonder the traits which make for individual participation will not be developed. . . .

The new theism will lay stress upon the insight that God works through "creating creators," and thus will deepen the ethical earnestness, as well as increase the interpretive power, of the theistic philosophy.

> Oh, brother men, if you have eyes at all,
> Look at a branch, a bird, a child, a rose,
> Or anything God ever made that grows,—
> Nor let the smallest vision of it slip,
> Till you may read, as on Belshazzar's wall,
> *The glory of eternal partnership.*[1]

The new theism will find in courageous attack upon our urgent human problems, in the applying of creative social intelligence to their solution, and in personal devotion to the building of the Beloved Community on earth, the living expression of the deepest reality of the cosmos. And it will find the fullest realization of God, the present experience of life eternal, in whatever increases the wisdom, good will, and joy of the world.

Eugene William Lyman, *The Meaning and Truth of Religion.*
Published by Charles Scribner's Sons, New York.

GLORY TO THEM

> Glory to them, the toilers of the earth
>   Who wrought with knotted hands in wood and stone
> Dreams their unlettered minds could not give birth
>   And symmetries their souls had never known.
> Glory to them, the artisans, who spread
>   Cathedrals like brown lace before the sun,
> Who could not build a rhyme, but reared instead
>   The Doric grandeur of the Parthenon!
>
> I never cross a marble portico,
>   Or lift my eyes where stained glass windows steal
> From virgin sunlight moods of deeper glow,
>   Or walk dream-peopled streets, except to feel
> A hush of reverence for that vast dead
> Who gave us beauty for a crust of bread.

Anderson M. Scruggs, printed in *The Golden Book Magazine.*

THE GRACE OF GOD

The doctrine of the Grace of God, expressed in the most general terms amounts to this—That man is ever within a natural order in which he is governed by his instinct for self-preservation;

[1] Edwin Arlington Robinson, "Sonnet," *Children of the Night.* Charles Scribner's Sons, publishers, New York. Printed by permission.

but that it is possible for him to rise out of that natural order into another order in which he is no longer governed by his instinct of self-preservation but by his relation with a power above humanity, yet personal; and that he attains to this relation, which is love, by the help of that power, a help which is called the Grace of God. . . .

But the full meaning of the doctrine is often unknown even to the devout, because they are not aware of all the ways in which the Grace of God comes to men. They suppose that a man who is possessed by it must himself be devout in an orthodox manner, must be full of the praises of that God whose Grace has possessed him. They do not know that the Grace of God comes to us in beauty and in truth, in beauty that they would call pagan, in truth that would seem to them merely scientific. Whenever a man forgets himself utterly in either of these, he has some experience of the Grace of God, though he may deny the existence of a God or of His Grace. Indeed, we cannot be aware of beauty until we are freed from the instinct of self-preservation; until we see things no longer in a merely economic relation to ourselves. Sheep, for instance, become beautiful to us only when they cease to be potential mutton. Nor can we be aware of the truth latent in a mass of facts until we cease to see those facts in a purely economic relation with ourselves. We must escape from that concern with our own individual survival, which is called selfishness, before we can be artists or men of science or philosophers, just as much as we must escape from it before we can be saints. . . .

According to the doctrine of the Grace of God we can attain to a positive freedom from the will to live, a freedom not by mere suppression but through another will, another passion. We can rise from the will to live to the will to love, because there is outside us that which calls for our love and which loves us, that which is of such a nature that it can be loved for itself. . . . Everywhere we see powers that remain futile and perverse, even when they win fame, because they lack the Grace of God That is a plain fact which no one can deny, even though he refuse to call that which is lacking the Grace of God. There is a sense of direction in all the higher human activities which seems to be independent of all other powers and which must be a sense of direction towards something. According to the doctrine of the Grace of God, it is a sense of direction towards God Himself. God is a fact, like the sun.

He exercises an attraction upon us all. But because He is a person and it is the attraction of His desire, and because we are persons with a freedom to desire or not desire, we are not utterly subject to His attraction, as other bodies are to the attraction of the sun. We can refuse it or yield to it. We can forget God in ourselves or we can forget ourselves in God. . . . Life is the power of choice; and the more fully it is life, the more it is the power of choice. We have more power of choice than the brutes, because we are more completely alive and less subject to the mechanical processes of the body. But this choice of ours, the choice between an alliance with God or a conflict, is not made once for all and in a moment. It is a choice that we have to be making always; it is never finally achieved either one way or the other. The man who seems utterly cut off from the Grace of God by his own choice may suddenly open himself to that grace; the man who seems to lie open to it always may suddenly shut himself against it. We are always growing and changing because we live; and the adventure of life is never determined for us one way or the other; because there is always the Grace of God pouring out for all men, and always in them the power to accept or refuse it.

A. CLUTTON-BROCK, *Studies in Christianity.*
Published by E. P. Dutton & Company.

A PRAYER

O Heavenly Father, who by loving us hast called forth our response in spite of all our weakness and sin, grant us faith always to approach our fellow men in that same spirit of love, that drawing upon those resources of fellowship present in every child of Thine we may continuously be building Thy Kingdom; through Jesus Christ Our Lord.   AMEN.

BISHOP PAUL JONES.

Worship God: Fifth Sunday

35. A FOREST HYMN

The groves were God's first temples. Ere man learned
To hew the shaft, and lay the architrave,
And spread the roof above them—ere he framed
The lofty vault, to gather and roll back
The sound of anthems; in the darkling wood,
Amid the cool and silence, he knelt down,
And offered to the Mightiest solemn thanks
And supplication. For his simple heart
Might not resist the sacred influence
Which, from the stilly twilight of the place,
And from the gray old trunks that high in heaven
Mingled their mossy boughs, and from the sound
Of the invisible breath that swayed at once
All their green tops, stole over him, and bowed
His spirit with the thought of boundless power
And inaccessible majesty. Ah, why
Should we, in the world's riper years, neglect
God's ancient sanctuaries, and adore
Only among the crowd, and under roofs
That our frail hands have raised? Let me, at least,
Here in the shadow of this aged wood,
Offer one hymn—thrice happy, if it find
Acceptance in IIis ear. . . .

But thou art here—thou fill'st
The solitude, Thou art in the soft winds
That run along the summit of these trees
In music; thou art in the cooler breath
That from the inmost darkness of the place
Comes, scarcely felt; the barky trunks, the ground,
The fresh moist ground, are all instinct with thee.
Here is continual worship; —Nature, here,
In the tranquillity that thou dost love,
Enjoys thy presence. Noiselessly, around,
From perch to perch, the solitary bird

Passes; and yon clear spring, that, midst its herbs,
Wells softly forth and wandering steeps the roots
Of half the mighty forest, tells no tale
Of all the good it does. Thou has not left
Thyself without a witness, in the shades,
Of thy perfections. Grandeur, strength, and grace
And here to speak of thee. This mighty oak—
By whose immovable stem I stand and seem
Almost annihilated—not a prince
In all that proud old world beyond the deep
E'er wore his crown as loftily as he
Wears the green coronal of leaves with which
Thy hand has graced him. Nestled at his root
Is beauty, such as blooms not in the glare
Of the broad sun, that delicate forest flower,
With scented breath and look so like a smile,
Seems, as it issues from the shapeless mould,
An emanation of the indwelling Life,
A visible token of the upholding Love,
That are the soul of his great universe.

My heart is awed within me when I think
Of the great miracle that still goes on,
In silence, round me—the perpetual work
Of thy creation, finished, yet renewed
Forever. Written on thy works I read
The lesson of thy own eternity. . . .

Be it ours to meditate,
In these calm shades, thy milder majesty,
And to the beautiful order of thy works
Learn to conform the order of our lives.

WILLIAM CULLEN BRYANT (1794-1878).
Works, Published by D. Appleton & Co., New York.

PURIFIES, ENLIGHTENS, TRANSFORMS

Worship, then, is an avenue which leads the creature out from his inveterate self-occupation to a knowledge of God, and ultimately to that union with God which is the beatitude of the soul; though we are never to enter on it for this, or any other reason which is tainted by self-regard. We see in its first beginnings man's emerging recognition of the Living Will which is the cause of all his living; and the gradual deepening and widening of this recognition, in diverse ways and manners, till at last all ways and manners are swallowed up in a self-giving love. By this door and this alone, humanity enters into that great life of the spiritual universe which consists in the ceaseless proclamation of the Glory of God. Thus worship purifies, enlightens, and at last transforms, every life submitted to its influence: and this not merely in the ethical or devotional sense. It does all this, because it wakes up and liberates that "seed" of supernatural life, in virtue of which we are spiritual beings, capable of responding to that God Who is Spirit; and which indeed gives to humanity a certain mysterious kinship with Him. *Worship is therefore in the deepest sense creative and redemptive.* Keeping us in constant remembrance of the Unchanging and the Holy, it cleanses us of subjectivism, releases us from "use and wont" and makes us realists. God's invitation to it and man's response, however limited, crude or mistaken this response may be, are the appointed means whereby we move towards our true destiny. Only in so far as this adoring acknowledgment of Reality more and more penetrates his life, does man himself become real; finding within himself the answer to the great Eucharistic prayer, "Make us living men!" and entering by way of unconditioned self-oblation upon the inheritance of Eternal Life. Each separate soul thus transfigured by the spirit of selfless adoration advances that transfiguration of the whole universe which is the Coming of the Kingdom of God.

EVELYN UNDERHILL, Worship.

Published by Harper & Brothers, New York City.

PERSONAL AND FAR MORE

We are right in thinking of God as personal; but we should never forget that he is very much more than personal and, in certain respects, very unlike a person. Our thought of God as Comrade, Guide, Helper, Father, One who may be known somewhat after the manner of our knowledge of a friend, needs ever to be supplemented by the reminder that, in another sense, we can never know him. The God of personal fellowship is also the God of the universe, of the immensities and the eternities. He who is "closer than breathing, nearer than hands and feet," is also the

Wholly Other, One whom no human concepts can portray and no human reach grasp. It is impossible to hold both ideas in one's mind at the same time, and that is not necessary; but both are true. In the fullest religious experience, one's thought moves constantly between these two poles by a process of alternation. Moreover, the recognition of the double character of our experience of reality as an experience of nature *and* of values aids our imaginations in keeping flexible and our thought balanced and rounded. No one who begins to comprehend the dimensions of his cosmic home will be too easily familiar with its Author and Sustainer. No one who lives deeply amid the richer of life's experiences and accepts their impress upon him will doubt that God is also in some grand sense akin to himself. The solution of the dilemma would seem to come just here—when thinking of God in relation to the cosmos, be careful to recall the mystery, the incomprehensibility, the impersonality of God; when thinking of God in his traffic with human life and those things which human life holds most dear, be bold to call him 'Father' and to fill the soul with all the meaning which that suggests.

To summarize our conclusion in this matter, God is to be thought of as personal, not because that is a wholly accurate or adequate characterization but because it is truer than any other which thought can provide and therefore better than any alternative designation which might be proposed. To paraphrase another, "If we err in speaking of God as personal, we err not that we say too much but that we say too little; and if we err in calling him 'Father,' we judge that we err less grievously than if we called him anything else."

HENRY P. VAN DUSEN, *The Plain Man Seeks for God.*
Published by Charles Scribner's Sons, New York.

A PRAYER

O Thou, who art the Light of the minds that know Thee, the Life of the souls that love Thee, and the Strength of the hearts that seek Thee; help us so to know Thee, that we may truly love Thee, so to love Thee that we may fully serve Thee, whose service is perfect freedom; through Jesus Christ our Lord.

GELASIAN PRAYER BOOK.

Concentrate Upon the Ideal: Sixth Monday

36. DREAM PICTURES

They do not die, the artists of my dreams,
 Nor do they serve for hire.
When the dawn-glory through my window streams,
 Or sunset glows expire,
I do not fear that these shall cease to be,
Or someone's gold will buy their gift from me.

Nor do I need to seek their gifts afar,
 In some appointed place;
Last night my closet door was swung ajar,
 And on its inner face,
At midnight, by the city lamps, I saw
Such pictures as no gallery might draw.

I crossed a ferry in a surging crowd,
 Their faces strange to me,
Yet was the throng so mystically endowed
 That I could seem to see
The human story since the world began,
And all that yet waits down the years for man.

There will be yet art-galleries for all,
 And none shall be too low
To understand them, and to heed their call.
 But wherefore wait to know
Such heritage of loveliness? Today
Behold what pictures crowd life's common way!

ROBERT WHITAKER, *Social Song and Other Verse.*
Published by the Banner Press, Emory University, Atlanta, Ga.

HEROES OF MEDICINE

There is something fine in the very quietness of brave deeds.
Perhaps the world can learn to pay homage to the silence of self-
sacrifice. One thinks of the individual who offers himself and perhaps his life to men, whose disease by its very nature casts them
apart on an island in the sea.

The suffering of man has long been the call that self-sacrifice
has heard with a listening ear. The call has never been too faint

or too far distant, when once it sounded in the heart, to stir the urge of man to render aid. Since sickness first touched the human race, there has been some individual to volunteer a comforting hand, even at the risk of life itself. History teems with the offers of men and women to go forth into areas of pestilence knowing full well that they might be cut down in their very acts of mercy. In the early days, when sickness was a mystery and feared with the fear of ignorance, there was something touching in the dumb, blind heroism that led men to the sick-bed, willing to accept consequences if they could relieve the sufferings of another.

The heroism of medical investigation is necessarily quiet. No predictions can be made, and there can be no promise of victory. The investigator goes forth merely to fight for an idea in which he may be proved wrong. He must endure in silence. Yet, in him, as in other heroes, there is the same willingness to risk life, whether his theory proves to be a life-saving success or a crushing failure. Within the memory of our day, what fine valor took that little group of men to Cuba to meet yellow fever in the face of such devastating odds! Here was a scourge, unknown in origin, loathesome in character, that took lives by the thousands with subtle, sudden cruelty. While men were fighting the Spanish-American war, death did not wait for bullets or for bayonets. It aligned itself with an ally just as deadly and far more treacherous—yellow fever.

The little commission under Walter Reed did not go with blinded eyes. They knew full well the lurking danger, and their valor grew in value with the thought that they knew no method of protection. The mosquito was suspected as a carrier. Was there not in those men a heroism, to which we bow our heads, when they deliberately permitted mosquitoes to bite them, mosquitoes collected from the bodies of those who had recently met death by the disease?

Some of these volunteers died; others, after sickness, recovered:—both groups were heroes in their search for knowledge and in their valiant effort to preserve life. We think of the young English doctor of such promise, who died within the past few years while studying yellow fever on the Gold Coast of Africa. When he was stricken he requested that a careful post-mortem be made of his body in case of death, and during his last few days he offered frequent specimens of blood for a study of the disease that was killing him.

Smallpox, too, has been cruel to those who have sought its mysteries—as have been typhus, scarlet fever, bubonic plague, influenza, and, of recent years, the X-Ray with its mutilations and its gnawing pains. Yet, the search for the unknown goes on, and scientists expose themselves to death or to lingering illness, aware of the peril but devoted to the ideals of their profession and to the pursuit of knowledge that may lessen the diseases of mankind. Disease-suffering humanity little knows the price paid by the intrepid investigators who offer all in an effort to give us cure and comfort.

The hero of medicine may never be received by the shouts of the multitude but in his self-renouncement, his sympathy, his sense of brotherhood, his courage, his willingness to die—he earns a life of veneration and a grave on which the gods themselves might sprinkle incense.

THOMAS S. ARBUTHNOT, *Heroes of Peace.*

DIMENSIONS OF SPLENDOR

The truth about man is that, so far, he has never lived more than a fraction of his possible life, and by far the greater part of human nature is unexplored and unrealized. Here and there along the centuries there have been great outgoings of light and fire from these hidden depths, evidence of energies and capacities of which the ordinary man is unaware. Yet the materials are buried in us which might raise the whole of life to dimensions of splendor and glory that would make the best of the past seem but the flicker of a rushlight. Some hints of what this life might be we can gather from the beauty of the Parthenon and the temple of the Wingless Victory, from the vision of prophets and poets who have descried afar off the grandeur of the human promise. You may see it all within the compass of a single life in Jesus of Nazareth. It is no idle dream that sees the whole level of life raised to the height of the high peaks of the past. For the materials of it are here, and God has not yet deserted his world. There is away "beyond the bound of the waste," a city of God awaiting its builders, a city whose dwellers shall be poets and prophets and seers, having the mind of Christ, a city of supermen and superwomen who spend their lives in works of love and beauty, and whose city reflects the light of their own loveliness. And that city shall not be left desolate,

nor shall time wear down its youth or despoil it of its fairness.
It is our task to build that city,—and what is more, we can.

RICHARD ROBERTS, *The Untried Door.*
Published by The Woman's Press, New York.

A PRAYER

With hearts responsive,
And enfranchised eyes,
We thank Thee, Lord—
For all things beautiful, and good, and true;
For things that seemed not good, yet turned to good;
For all the sweet compulsions of Thy will
That chased, and tried, and wrought us to Thy shape;
For things unnumbered that we take of right,
And value first when first they are withheld;
For light and air; sweet sense of sound and smell;
For ears to hear the heavenly harmonies;
For eyes to see the unseen in the seen;
For vision of The Worker in the work;
For hearts to apprehend Thee everywhere;
We thank Thee, Lord!

For all life's beauties, and their beauteous growth;
For Nature's laws and Thy rich providence;
For all Thy perfect processes of life;
For the minute perfection of Thy work,
Seen and unseen, in each remotest part;
For every wide-flung window of the soul;
For that Thou bearest all that Thou hast made;
We thank Thee, Lord!

J. OXENHAM.

Understand the Actual: Sixth Tuesday

37. ROBOTS IN THE OFFICE

Tillie the toiler, that independent pardon-my-gum stenog, is beginning to wonder. The changes in the old office during the past ten years have bewildered her and they are beginning to get on her nerves. . . .

The position of these office employees has been changing from that of clerk to machine-hand.

Today's mechanized offices constitute, in fact, a mass-production industry. Insurance premiums, light bills, checks, letters, reports pour out in thousands of units daily. The working conditions of office employees approximate those of industrial workers. Today their jobs are less secure than the jobs of auto workers in a Ford factory. Already thinned by the introduction of machinery, the ranks of office workers will be cut further as management increases the rate of productivity. . . .

Here are some illustrations of assembly lines in operation:

In the mailing department of a publishing company six girls around an addressograph must each produce 500 name stickers an hour so that the mailing-machine operator can keep pasting name stickers on magazines at the rate of 3,000 an hour.

The employee in the telephone filing department of an insurance company is called upon to consult his files eighty times an hour to keep the premium department going at top speed. . . .

In a mail-order house, workers in the Entry Department feed 24,700 orders an hour into the Pricing Department, where another group of workers check orders with catalogues at a rate that will satisfy the speed of the comptometers in the Checking Department which handle 125 invoices per hour. . . .

It is impossible to obtain any reliable estimate of the total number of workers already displaced by office machinery. Records show, however, that during the depression, from 1929 to 1935, American management invested about $500,000,000 in office machinery. During the same period there were produced about 754,700 adding, listing and bookkeeping-billing machines and 112,800 calculating machines.

To understand the full implication of these production totals it should be borne in mind that even under existing machine utilization:

The dictaphone displaces one out of every two stenographers;

The bookkeeping machine displaces about two out of every three bookkeepers;

The check-writing and billing machines displace three out of every four check-writers;

The statistical machine displaces four out of every five statistical workers;

And the tabulator, sorter and punch machines displace eleven out of every twelve tabulating clerks.

In the case of the tabulating machine alone, at least 300,536 hand calculators have lost their jobs within the past few years with the installation of 25,878 units of this mechanism.

MAL J. STUART, in *The New Republic*.

THE POET IN THE DESERT

But I have no gladness in the coming of day;
For I see an endless procession,
Flowing from life unto death;
Smileless, submissive, starvation-carved, soul-stunted,
Stolidly marching toward the hungry machines,
The clang of hammers and the clank of chains;
The clash and clamour of Industry
And the evil rattle of steel-cranes.
I hear the bellowing of monsters
Which feed on men, belching their black breath against the sky.
Naked men sweat in fires of the damned,
Slaves to the demons which they guide:
Grimy alchemists, with faces wan,
Who dully change dull iron to more sordid gold.
The patient sky above waiting;
The patient men below waiting.
The blue sky above forever listening;
Expectant.
The tired men below forever listening;
Expectant.
An iron world without a soul, forever devouring;
Devouring the men who are mates for mothers;
Fathers, steel-muscled, broad-chested, dominant;
The women, mothers of children, weary mothers;

Crypts of the ages; flexible, undulant;
Innocent children, with white bodies, fluent,
Seeds of the unknowable Future.
Devoured for a soulless profit which in the end
Is damnation. Glorious is creation.
But if justice and joy be lacking
Creation is death.

Let us watch miners creeping out of their hovels
As rats from their holes—the grime of yesterday
Unwashed from lustreless faces;
Battered tin buckets swing in their hands,
Their faces patient as a dog's before his master,
Blanched so pitiful that the smut upon them
Is dard, like the tally-mark of Death.
Into rayless galleries they bear feeble torches,
All the sun and moon their poor life knows;
And in their souls they bear feeble torches,
All the light their poor souls know.
The sun forsakes them as they go down into
The dripping corridors,
And sitting on the shoulder of each,
Crouching close at his ear, is—Death.
They rain gold into their owner's laps.
Their Masters bask in the sun
And breathe the bright air
Sifted by the leaves,
But to the toilers they toss only enough
Of the spoil of their own combat
To keep Life's thin, grey smoke ascending.
If the desperate souls rebel,
They are shot down by machine-guns worked
By professional assassins hired by the Master.
Yet this is not war—this is peace.
The peace of a great Republic, of wonderful "Patriots."
The peace that brings the death of a people.
The dull crowd applauds the slaughter.
Presently it will be their turn—for the wheel
Of God never ceases.

CHARLES ERSKINE SCOTT WOOD, The Poet in the Desert.
Published by Vanguard Press, New York.

SECURITY MUST BE SOCIAL

There are five major hazards of life which every family must face: sickness, accident, unemployment, old age, and the death of the breadwinner. The wealthy may be able to save against these contingencies. Families with only moderate income cannot save enough to make their permanent security certain. Wage-earning families must live in chronic fear of exhaustion of their meager resources from sickness, accident, or unemployment, and of spending their declining years in the almshouse to be followed by a pauper's grave. No wage-earner can save enough out of his small income to guarantee protection of his family from recourse to charity in the case of incurable illness or early death. Virtually all dependency, whether in periods of prosperity or depression, is traceable to these hazards.

JAMES FORD and KATHERINE MORROW FORD, *The Abolition of Poverty.*
Published by The Macmillan Company, New York.

A PRAYER

Lord, who art merciful as well as just,
Incline Thine ear, to me, a child of dust.
Not what I would, O Lord, I offer Thee,
    Alas! but what I can.
Father Almighty, who hast made me man,
And bade me look to heav'n, for Thou art there,
Accept my sacrifice and humble prayer:
    Four things, which are in Thy treasury,
I lay before Thee, Lord, with this petition:
My nothingness, my wants, my sin, and my contrition.
             R. SOUTHEY (*from the Persian*).

Be Concerned: Sixth Wednesday

38. THE INN THAT MISSED ITS CHANCE

"The Landlord Speaks: A.D. 28"

What could be done? The inn was full of folks!
His honour, Marcus Lucius, and his scribes
Who made the census: honourable men
From farthest Galilee, come hitherward
To be enrolled; high ladies and their lords;
The rich, the rabbis, such a noble throng
As Bethlehem had never seen before,
And may not see again. And there they were,
Close herded with their servants, till the inn
Was like a hive at swarming-time, and I
Was fairly crazed among them.

                    Could I know
That they were so important? Just the two,
No servants, just a workman sort of man,
Leading a donkey, and his wife thereon,
Drooping and pale—I saw them not myself,
My servants must have driven them away;
But had I seen them how was I to know?
Were inns to welcome stragglers, up and down
In all our towns from Beersheba to Dan,
Till he should come? And how were men to know?

There was a sign, they say, a heavenly light
Resplendent; but I had no time for stars.
And there were songs of angels in the air
Out on the hills; but how was I to hear
Amid the thousand clamours of an inn?

Of course, if I had known them, who they were,
And who he that should be born that night—
For now I learn that they will make him King,
A second David, who will ransom us
From these Philistine Romans—who but he

That feeds an army with a loaf of bread,
And if a soldier falls, he touches him
And up he leaps, uninjured? Had I known,
I would have turned the whole inn upside down,
His honour, Marcus Lucius, and the rest,
And sent them all to stables, had I known.

So you have seen him, stranger, and perhaps
Again will see him. Prithee say for me,
I did not know; and if he comes again,
As he will surely come, with retinue,
And banners, and an army, tell my Lord
That all my inn is his, to make amends.

Alas! Alas! To miss a chance like that!
This inn that might be chief among them all,
The birthplace of Messiah—had I known.

AMOS R. WELLS

Printed by permission of the author's widow.

CRITERION AND INDICTMENT

The relation of the commandment of love to the justice of political and economic systems is twofold. It is an ideal which reaches beyond any possible achievements in the field of political relations, but it is nevertheless also a standard by which various schemes of justice may be judged. . . .

The law of love which is the standard of the Christian life is properly to be regarded as being at the same time a present reality and an ultimate possibility. It is not only a criterion of judgment in all the fateful decisions which men must make in history, but also an indictment against all historical achievements.

As a criterion of judgment upon the relative merits of economic arrangements and social structures, the law of love gives positive guidance in terms of justice, even though it transcends the realities of all possible social structures. The obligation to love our neighbors as ourselves places clearly under condemnation all social and economic systems which give one man undue advantage over others. It must create an uneasy conscience (for example) in all Christians who are involved in a social system which denies children, of whatever race or class, the fullest opportunity to develop whatever gifts God has given them and makes their education depend upon the fortuitous circumstance of a father's possession or lack of means to provide the necessary funds. It must challenge any social system which provides social privileges without reference to the social functions performed by individuals, or which creates luxury and pride on the one hand and want and insecurity on the other. It makes the conscience of Christians particularly uneasy in regard to the deprivation of basic security for large masses of human beings.

"Report of the Section on Church Community and State in Relation
to the Economic Order."
The Oxford Conference: Official Report.
Published by Willett, Clark & Company, Chicago.

SELF-INTEREST PRODUCES FEAR

It was part of the realism of Jesus that side by side with His statement of the conditions of discipleship He set no less plainly His judgment as to the things which prevented such discipleship, or militated against it. We shall find that they are three in number, two internal and having their stronghold in the Christian himself, the other external. *Sin* could keep men out of the Kingdom and so could *fear;* these are the two internal causes of failure. The external cause which made it next to impossible for men to enter the Kingdom was *wealth.* Jesus shared with all the prophets a deep sense of the horror of sin, both individual and social. . . .

Yet, on exactly the same level with sin and equally potent to keep men out of the full free exercise of their citizenship in the Kingdom, and equally effective in cutting men off from God, was *fear.* Warnings against it occupy a definite place in the Sermon on the Mount and it is implied in His stress on the Fatherhood of God. He strove eagerly to combat it, and His chief instrument for the achievement of that end was to hold God up as utterly trustworthy and utterly loving. God sent His rain on the just and the unjust, He clothed the lilies of the field; not a sparrow fell to the ground without the Father. In the boat on the storm-driven lake He asks His disciples, "Why are ye so fearful?"—which means much more than, "What are you afraid of?"

How eagerly and how often He pleads for faith and utter trust in God. "Ask and it shall be given you, seek and ye shall find, knock and it shall be opened unto you." In dealing with fear He was dealing with a real situation. . . .

Fear is largely the product of self-centredness and self-interest. It is because we are so concerned with what is happening to ourselves that fear grips and dominates us; it swells with our self-regard, and just as an inflated toy balloon is more vulnerable than one not yet blown up, so the larger our self-esteem and self-regard, the larger the target we offer for "the slings and arrows of outrageous fortune." It is not until we find some interest so wide and large that it captures our attention and drains off attention from ourselves that fear ceases to grip us. . . . It is idle preoccupation with self which is the most fruitful source of fear; when we are actively engaged in a big issue, which "takes us out" of ourselves, life seems much less terrifying. Such a big issue Jesus offered to men in the conception of the Kingdom of God. Until men could get rid of self they could not be rid of fear; if, therefore, life was given wholly over to God in trust and obedience, fear would no longer have any dominion over men.

B. C. PLOWRIGHT, *Rebel Religion.*
Published by Round Table Press, New York.

TRUE OBEDIENCE

But what is true obedience? I answer, that a man should so stand free, being quit of himself, that is, of his I, and Me, and Self, and, Mine, and, the like, that in all things, he should no more seek or regard himself, than if he did not exist, and should take as little account of himself as if he were not, and another had done all his works. . . .

A PRAYER

Our Father Who art in Heaven, forgive us for our failure to honor Thee as we should, in the past. Help us to hallow Thy Name, and honor Thy Message, and trust Thy Word even as the dewdrop trusts itself to the sun, and the river gives itself to the sea. Amen.

GLENN CLARK, *I Will Lift Up Mine Eyes.*
Published by Harper and Brothers, New York.

Endeavor to Transform: Sixth Thursday

39. A PARTNERSHIP OF NATIONS

It may be well to summarise the conclusions which emerge from the line of thought we have been pursuing.

(1) That in the present state of international morality there is no infallible method of preventing war. The utmost we can hope for, or profitably aim at, is to render war progressively less attractive to war-makers.

(2) That all treaties, compacts, or covenants to suppress war by a general combination of armed force endure only so long as their application is not needed and are certain to collapse in the day of performance.

(3) That no future Covenant adopting the above method is likely to yield better results than its ill-starred predecessor, or to be anything else than the old medicine in a new bottle.

(4) That, therefore, the League of Nations, if it is to continue, must cease to be predominantly a League of *armed* nations and find for itself a new direction no longer dominated by war-making considerations, leaving these latter to be dealt with by whatever agencies exist for the purpose.

(5) That the new line of direction should aim at the creation of a common interest, at once co-operative in basis and business-like in pursuit.

(6) That in pursuing this new line of action efforts should be concentrated, at first, on establishing a nucleus for positive co-operation, a nucleus likely to grow and by its growth to act as an increasing deterrent on war.

(7) That such an enterprise, if wisely conceived, would, even in its inception, be one of considerable magnitude, and such as to challenge both then and afterwards the best talent of the covenanting nations.

(8) That in framing the requisite Covenant to embody these aims no higher demand should be made on the altruism of sovereign political states than is customary in business transactions or contracts intended for the mutual benefit of the contracting parties. . . .

L. P. JACKS, *Co-Operation or Coercion.*
Published by E. P. Dutton & Company, New York.
Reprinted by permission.

INTERNATIONAL ARMY NOT A POLICE FORCE

Let us consider some of the most obvious differences between a true police and a League army equipped and intended for war, "if necessary," as the saying goes; a foolish saying, for, if it were "necessary," we should not be arguing about it.

Police Force	*International Force*
1. Checks those who break a universally agreed law, and, if necessary, takes them into custody.	1. Could not appeal to universally agreed law and could not take a "criminal nation" into custody. It could only massacre its inhabitants.
2. Acts only when the offender is found *in flagrante delicto,* or on a warrant, which can be quickly obtained.	2. Could not act except after proof of aggression, which would cause dangerous delay.
3. Is a slenderly armed force, well-organized and loyal, dealing with individuals with no national backing and entirely unorganized.	3. Is a fully armed force, imperfectly organized, fighting another fully armed and organized force backed by patriotism.
4. Does not itself punish the alleged criminal.	4. Would itself carry out the punishment, and this would be indiscriminating, impossible to graduate, or adapt.
5. Is required to cultivate a mild and tolerant temper in itself and the public.	5. Would find much of its work impossible, unless it roused among the soldiers a ferocity unfamiliar to most of them as civilians; and among civilians a spirit of hatred and vengeance.

Police Force	*International Force*
6. Has no arms (in Britain) except a whistle and a truncheon and this latter it is required not to use except for necessity.	6. The nature of the arms would have to be the most modern and destructive yet known and they would have to be used with the utmost brutality for invasion of enemy territory as well as for the repelling of attack.
7. When it has arrested its man and handed him over to custody, even the small amount of force it has had to use ceases.	7. When it has started on its war, God knows when and after what holocaust of the innocent and the precious, what devastation of beauty and utility, of friendship and commerce and sanity that war would be concluded.
8. Operates in a country whose inhabitants are on its side.	8. Would be compelled to operate in a country whose inhabitants were bitterly hostile.
9. Does not depend upon extensive lying.	9. Would find in lies one of its chief weapons.
10. Is under the orders of a selected body of men (a municipality) chosen for their public character.	10. Is under the orders of men (governments) who, *ex-hypothesi,* are potential criminals, and in some cases have been declared criminals.
11. Operates in an environment favourable to law.	11. Would have to operate in an environment where "sacred egoism" is still the moral law of nations.

Police Force	*International Force*

Perhaps most important of all:

12. Is under the jurisdiction of one sovereign state acting for and responsible to its own nationals.	12. Would be under the jurisdiction of as many states as contributed to the force, and these states, though responsible to their own nationals, would be subject (more or less) to the decisions of an international authority.

H. M. SWANWICK, *Collective Insecurity.*
Published by Jonathan Cape, London.

A PRAYER FOR PEACE

Dear Lord, the world has known so many wars,
It bears such bitter, deep, and lasting scars,
Reach out Thy hand, O, Maker of us all;
Bend down Thy listening ear and hear our call
In this, and every other threatening hour.
Only Thy might, dear Lord, only Thy power
Can change the hearts of men—can bid them cease
Their avarice and greed—and bring us peace.
Lord of the nations, let no nation reign
To crush another. Free us from the stain
Of blood and slaughter—let us not forget
The loving kind example Thou hast set.
God help us lift the Golden Rule *so* high
That its bright words will flame against the sky:
"Do Unto Others As Ye Would That They
Do Unto You," and then will come the day—
The crushed will rise, the bound will find release,
And we shall know the blessedness of peace.

GRACE NOLL CROWELL.
Published by Harper and Brothers, New York.

Proceed Resolutely: Sixth Friday

40. THE GOOD SHEPHERD

O Shepherd with the bleeding Feet,
  Good Shepherd with the pleading Voice,
  What seekest Thou from hill to hill?
Sweet were the valley pastures, sweet
  The sound of flocks that bleat their joys,
  And eat and drink at will.
Is one worth seeking, when Thou hast of Thine
      Ninety and nine?
                    CHRISTINA ROSSETTI (1830-1894).

THE RANGE AND DEPTH OF LOVE

Why did Jesus lay down His life? For this means an attempt to understand in some measure the mind of Jesus Himself, when He went up to Jerusalem and to death; and the better we understand Him, the more do we find Him beyond us. . . . It is the range and depth of His mind which defeat our laboring apprehensions—that, and the unfamiliarity with the spiritual country in which He lived and moved and had His being. Hatred we know, and all its ways. Prejudice and fear, passion and caution, we know; but of love we know little, and our only chance of knowing the mind of Jesus is to understand what love is and what are its ways.

Love, as we know it, is often a give-and-take affair, where the mutual advantage is well in evidence, and it is part of the understanding that there are not to be any too unreasonable exactions on one side or the other. This is why the command of Jesus to love our enemies seems to many people absurd, and by many others is quietly deferred to some indefinite time to come, when possibly the absence of enemies may make obedience simpler. But occasionally we have seen instances of a rarer kind of love— a love which persists against contempt and indifference, which gives and receives nothing in return (save new demands), which survives the disillusionment of treachery and still refuses to despair. Whenever we see love of this quality, the wonder of it astonishes us as a thing incalculable, and hardly belonging to our world. . . .

I may be permitted to recall an instance which came within my own knowledge. A good many years ago I knew a workingman in the north of England whose wife, soon after her marriage, drifted into vicious ways, and went rapidly from bad to worse. He came home one Sunday evening to find, as he had found a dozen times before, that she had gone on a new debauch. He knew in what condition she would return, after two or three days of a nameless life. He sat down in the cheerless house to look the truth in the face and to find what he must do. The worst had happened too often to leave him much hope of amendment, and he saw in part what might be in store for him. He made his choice to hold by his wife to the end and to keep a home for her who would not make one for him. Now that a new and terrible meaning had passed into the words "for better, for worse," he reaffirmed his marriage vow. Later, when someone who knew them both intimately, ventured to commiserate him, he answered: "Not a word! She is my wife! I loved her when she was a girl in our village, and I shall love her as long as there is breath in my body." She did not mend, and died in his house after some years, in a shameful condition, with his hands spread over her in pity and in prayer to the last. . . .

They brought to Jesus a woman taken in adultery, quoted the law of Moses which enjoined the penalty of death, and asked His opinion, thinking to find occasion against Him. When at His challenge the accusers all melted away, Jesus dismissed the woman with the words: "Neither do I condemn thee. Go thy way," and added, "From henceforth sin no more." But is it to be supposed that when the woman was gone from His sight, she was dismissed from His mind, carrying away with her, as she did, not only some gift of peace, but also the problem of an infected mind and much besides? Or did He think no more of the still worse plight of her accusers who went away unforgiven? Did she, did they, have no place in His prayers at the day's end, and was the prayer just a "making mention"? Here surely were lost sheep, and He was the Good Shepherd. His character and His vocation supply the answer to our question. But the same question emerges continually in the daily contacts of our Lord's earthly life, and it demands the same answer. Jesus had no defense against human need. Necessity was laid upon Him. He "so loved that He gave." He so cared as to feel. Any man, any woman, who encountered Jesus any day, might leave with Him a fresh burden, a burden even to tears. . . .

Now, when we consider what it was to live after this fashion —never to hide Himself from any need or disclaim relationship with the meanest and the worst, to see His task daily increasing before His eyes and still retain the love that will not let us go—in a word, to bear the character of the Saviour of the world, it is no precarious inference to say that even the Son of man could not indefinitely carry in a human frame a burden so awful. His love, indeed, could not fail; His courage was not found wanting. But "the outward man," the bodily tabernacle, must break down under this ever-increasing strain.

Jesus knew this well, and felt it within Himself. He knew also that the manner of His dying must be a manifestation of His mission and of God's will. He knew, further, that death would not release Him from His vocation or end His work, but that it would free Him by the way of resurrection from human limitations, and put all authority and power into His hands. Therefore we see Him hastening to Jerusalem and to death, because He was also hastening to the resurrection and fullness of life and power. . . .

Seven words from the cross are reported, but there was another, which said, "I will never leave you nor forsake you." It was said by the only begotten Son of God with full purpose of heart, and it has never been unsaid. That pledge stands forever, and binds Him to our race in its deepest need. It binds Him: it confronts us. Every one of us must reckon with that word—or, rather, with the One who said the word. I may deny it; I may ignore it; I may never have heard of it; but it stands. If I sit in the courts of the House of the Lord, I may sing, "He loved me and gave Himself for me." But if I choose to sit at the table of harlots, and steep myself in sin's delirium, it is still true that He loved me and gave Himself for me, and His presence I cannot escape.

W. RUSSELL MALTBY, *Christ and His Cross.*
Used by permission of The Abingdon Press, New York.

O LOVE, THAT WILT NOT LET ME GO

O Love, that wilt not let me go,
  I rest my weary soul on Thee;
I give Thee back the life I owe,
That in Thine ocean depth its flow
    May richer, fuller be.

O Light, that followest all my way,
  I yield my flickering torch to Thee;
My heart restores its borrowed ray,
That in Thy sunshine's blaze its day
    May brighter, fairer be.

O Joy, that seekest me through pain,
  I cannot close my heart to Thee;
I trace the rainbow through the rain,
And feel the promise is not vain,
    That morn shall tearless be.

O Cross, that liftest up my head,
  I dare not ask to fly from Thee;
I lay in dust life's glory dead,
And from the ground there blossoms red
    Life that shall endless be.
                    GEORGE MATHESON, 1882.

A PRAYER

Grant to us, O Lord, the spirit of adventure. Give us initiative, and the strength to choose the pioneer's path. Give us to take life as Thou didst, as an adventure, gay and daring, full of high hope and lofty vision. And may we so live that we die in Thy service, having ventured all for an ideal that shall not fail, and a vision that brooks no tarrying.
                    J. B. GOODLIFFE.

Seek Comradeship: Sixth Saturday

41. PRAYER

At first I prayed for sight;
    Could I but see the way,
How gladly would I walk
    To everlasting day.
I asked the world's deep law
    Before my eyes to ope,
And let me see my prayers fulfilled,
    And realized, my hope;
But God was kinder than my prayer,
    And mystery veiled me everywhere.

And next I prayed for strength
    That I might tread the road,
With firm unfaltering pace,
    To heaven's serene abode.
That I might never know
    A faltering, failing heart;
But manfully go on
    And reach the highest part.
But God was kinder than my prayer,
    And weakness checked me everywhere.

And then I asked for faith;
    Could I but trust my God,
I'd live in heavenly peace
    Though foes were all abroad.
His light thus shining round,
    No faltering should I know;
And faith in heaven above
    Would make a heaven below;
But God was kinder than my prayer,
    And doubts beset me everywhere.

And now I pray for love,
    Deep love to God and man;
A love that will not fail,
    However dark his plan;

That sees all life in Him,
Rejoicing in his power;
And faithful, though the darkest clouds
Of gloom and doubt may lower.
And God was kinder than my prayer,
Love filled and blessed me everywhere.

EDNAH DOW CHENEY (1824-1904).

UNIQUE LOYALTIES

We should not overlook the influence of the group here. A company of individuals under the same religious stress introduces an element which is in itself a powerful means of heightening the suggestibility of the whole gathering. The mutual "continuing instant in prayer" of the believers in the Upper Room (Acts i. 14) acted and reacted on the individuals there. Each took fire from each; the whole group became religiously and psychologically infected by the experience of the individual members. After their renewed fellowship with Jesus risen from the dead, and overwhelmingly sure that He was soon to return with the Kingdom, they had returned to Jerusalem to await the promise of the Father in the coming of the power which should descend on them. The crisis was at hand. The days went by, and every disciple influenced the other in earnest desire, which increased the more they met and talked about it; they encouraged one another in joyfull hope, prayed continually, and every one was in a state of preparedness and likemindedness. The fulfilment came about. The big things happened. The clouds of heaven, as it were, burst upon them, mind and spirit received illumination, the limiting inhibitions which bound them to their religous antecedents were done away as in heart, mind, and will the believers were surrendered entirely to the new power that came upon them. The tides of emotion swept to and fro, and set up psychological abnormalities which have led some scholars to conclude that these were but mythical accretions, but which were rather the historical indices of a vital religious awakening which produced in its new loyalties results unique and life-changing.

P. G. S. HOPWOOD, *The Religious Experience of the Primitive Church.*
Charles Scribner's Sons, publishers, New York.
Printed by permission.

SIMPLE AND SUBLIME

The Christian religion is something simple and sublime; it means one thing and one thing only: eternal life in the midst of time, by the strength and under the eyes of God. . . .

Plato, it is true, had already sung the great hymn of the mind; he had distinguished it from the whole world of appearance and maintained its eternal origin. But the mind which he meant was the knowing mind; he contrasted it with blind, insensible matter; his message made its appeal to the wise. Jesus Christ calls to every poor soul; he calls to everyone who bears a human face: You are children of the living God, and not only better than many sparrows but of more value than the whole world. The value of a truly great man, as I saw it put lately, consists in increasing the value of all mankind. . . . But Jesus Christ was the first to bring the value of every human soul to light. . . .

In the combination of these ideas—God the Father, Providence, the position of men as God's children, the infinite value of the human soul—the whole Gospel is expressed.

ADOLF HARNACK, *What Is Christianity?*
Published by G. P. Putnam's Sons.

FOR GROUP WORSHIP

1—Each meeting begins with a reminder that during the discussion the aim is not to exert power "over" others but to gain power "with" others, not to beat somebody over the head with a dogma but share experience and find the truth.

2—Then a moment or two of silent meditation in which each person present thinks of every other person present with a special effort to understand and appreciate. That moment should also be one in which each person seeks to open himself as a channel for the best.

3—After social and personal issues are discussed and action planned, the lights are turned out. Each one in turn states in a sentence what comes to him as most significant at the time. He may even ask the group to pray every morning for a few days about this matter. Finally, with or without words, each one briefly prays. Either during these prayers or in the silence that follows, absent friends are remembered and contact is renewed with persons like Kagawa and with causes like the peace movement.

4—"Last thing before going to sleep, turn over all problems to God with some such prayer as this: 'Into Thy hands I commit my spirit.'

5—"Upon waking, turn your mind toward God instead of self, perhaps thinking of Him as 'Shining Beauty, Radiant Joy, Creative Power, All-Pervading Love, Perfect Understanding, Purity and Serenity.' As soon as possible commit the whole day to God."

6—Image members of the group, one after the other as living up to their best during the whole day, being surrounded by the light of God's presence.

7—Try such daily questions as these: Morning—"What shall I do today to help make war impossible?" Evening—"What, today, have I done?"

8—At various times this purpose is recalled: To embody in action the insight we discover together.

Before a Grate Fire.
Published by The Muriel Lester Group,
4611 Prospect Ave., Hollywood, California.

A PRAYER

God of the living, we praise Thee for the company of those gone before, who by their love and loyalty have left us a legacy of faith and hope. We give Thee thanks for the fellowship of those who gather here, our comrades and fellow workers, with whom we share Thy mercy and adore Thy name. Make us members one of another; unite us in one heart with all who seek Thee, in one communion with all who love Thee, in one steadfast purpose with all who serve Thy holy will in faithfulness and joy.

Bless the lonely of soul with Thy nearness, and the wounded of heart with Thy healing. Give to the hungry of spirit Thyself, his bread, even the hidden manna whereof if he eat he shall hunger no more. O Thou who hearest what our words cannot tell, lift our spirits to a loftier melody, that our song on earth may blend with the song of the redeemed. In the name of Jesus, Amen.

JOSEPH FORT NEWTON, *Altar Stairs.*
Published by The Macmillan Company, New York.

Worship God: Sixth Sunday

42. A SUN-DAY HYMN

Lord of all being, throned afar,
Thy glory flames from sun and star:
Center and soul of every sphere,
Yet to each loving heart how near!

Sun of our life, thy quickening ray
Sheds on our path the glow of day;
Star of our hope, thy softened light
Cheers the long watches of the night.

Our midnight is thy smile withdrawn;
Our noontide is thy gracious dawn;
Our rainbow arch thy mercy's sign;
All, save the clouds of sin, are thine.

Lord of all life, below, above
Whose light is truth, whose warmth is love,
Before thy ever-blazing throne
We ask no luster of our own.

Grant us thy truth to make us free,
And kindling hearts that burn for thee,
Till all thy living altars claim
One holy light, one heavenly flame.

OLIVER WENDELL HOLMES, 1860.

GOD IS PERSONAL AND ACCESSIBLE

Since the contemporary mind has most difficulty with the assertions that God is *personal,* that he is directly approachable or *accessible,* and that he is a *loving* Father, let us consider what these assertions mean, not in terms of recent popular liberalism, but in terms of classical Christian teaching.

(1) *That God is personal* does not mean that he is anthropomorphic,[1] nor that all his relations with us are personal; it does

---

[1] A convenient if somewhat formidable Greek term whose literal meaning is "man-shaped."

mean that he claims our loyal devotion as no sub-personal being could do, and that under the right conditions we can commune with him "as a man speaks with his friend."

No intelligent Christian seriously supposes that God is just like a human person. . . . Since, however, we are all children in relation to the ultimate mysteries of life, we have to think symbolically about God; and, as John Bennett remarks, the choice of symbols is "very limited." Either we think of God in terms of inanimate objects, or mechanical processes, or blind vital urges, or intelligent purposes. Unless we think of him in terms of our personal life, with its intelligent meanings and purposes, we are almost certain to think of him as an Ocean, or an Energy, or a Tree of Life, or an Organic Whole, or something else that is sub-human. It is far better to be a humanist, and worship the Family, or the Nation, or Humanity, than to bow down before such "stocks and stones" as these. Nothing sub-human can claim the full religious devotion of a human being.

If there is anything in the old maxim that "the stream cannot rise higher than its source," human personality is ultimately derived from a divine Source that is not less alive nor less intelligent than its highest known product, man. This Source must of course not be imagined in terms of our human intelligence and will, with their sharply limited focus of activity; traditional theology is full of warnings against pushing this analogy too far; yet Jesus, in his teaching about God, did not fear to pass from some high human quality to a similar but vastly expanded quality in God: "If ye then, being evil, know how to give good gifts unto your children, *how much more* shall your heavenly Father give the Holy Spirit to them that ask him." What their Master did, most Christians will not hesitate to do. . . .

For the Fathers of the Early Church, the universe was not an *embodiment* of God, but a *work* of God; and God's relationship to us through his works was an essentially *impersonal* relationship, like that which the modern scientific age expresses in the word *law*. In the natural and social orders, God touches us for the most part impersonally, through the constraints and the promises of the laws that prevail in these realms. But God also touches us more personally, through the subtle influences that play upon us and mold our characters in the little world of our intimate face-to-face communion with our friends and our ideals; and if, recognizing this personal touch in some transforming experience, we reach out appreciatively toward its Source as one might reach out toward a new-found Friend, Christian saints and mystics affirm with one voice that it is possible to establish a life-long, growing friendship with God in prayer, so intimate that it becomes inconceivable that death itself should break it.

(2) *That God is directly accessible* does not mean that we are ever alone with him without mediators; but it does mean that, through the medium of his works, his words, and our own thoughts and experiences, we are able to come into touch with him in such a way as to lay our needs before him, and receive his guidance and help.

From what has just been said about God's comparatively impersonal relationship to us in the natural and social orders, it is evident that Christian thought represents our access to him in these realms as indirectly mediated through the things that he has made. But in the sphere of personal religion, also, God never lacks for mediators: prophets, with their "Thus saith the Lord"; saints, with their luminous faces, translucent to the divine light; above all, Jesus, of whom it was said that he was the "express image" of God. Try if you will to brush aside all mediators, and deal with God directly, through what the Quakers call the "Inner Light," and you will still find that the veil of your own thoughts and feelings is between you and the Object of your quest. Mediation of some kind is inescapable in the religious life. Traditional piety has seen the perfect symbol of this fact in the vision of Jacob's Ladder, with "the angels of God ascending and descending on it." In a very real sense, we always come in contact with God through some "angel"; *i.e.,* some intermediary object, or person, or idea, which leads us toward God, or brings God near to us, without ever quite enabling us to see and grasp the divine Nature as it is.

Yet, if mediators are always present in the religious life, they fail to accomplish their function if they do not lead us toward *immediacy* in our relation with God. It is a perversion of the function of a mediator when—as has sometimes been the case in the popular practice of saint-worship—the impression is created that one gets better results by applying to a subordinate than by going to headquarters! If the Christian idea of God is sound, there is no saint, no Virgin Mother, no Christ, more compassionately sympathetic with our needs than God himself; and if God communicates with us through intermediaries, it is not in order to maintain himself in majestic apartness, but in order to get to us more effectively, by stepping himself down to our level. Mediators between God and man are like neurones in a nerve fiber or electronic particles in an electric circuit; their function is to bring needy human beings into sensitive, responsive touch with God. As experience grows, the intermediate process can be more and more ignored,[1] Jacob's Ladder can be kicked away, and the soul may enjoy foretastes of that "beatific vision" of which Dante writes in the last cantos of the *Paradiso*. Such at least is the prospect that the great saints and mystics hold out to their less experienced fellow-men, who stand below them on the ladder of the religious life and experience God largely through their mediation.

WALTER M. HORTON, *God*.
Published by Association Press, New York,
as one of the Hazen Books on Religion.

A PRAYER

O Heavenly Father, breathe into our souls the love of whatsoever is true and beautiful and good. May we fear to be unfaithful, and have no other fear. Help us to remember that we are Thy children, and belong to Thee. In Thy service may we live, and in Thy favor may we die; through Jesus Christ our Lord. Amen.

WILLIAM ANGUS KNIGHT.

A PRAYER

We beseech Thee, Who revealest Thyself in the true, the honest, the pure and the lovely, to help us make our minds Thy audience chambers. Forgive us our foolish and wandering thoughts. Feed our minds with Thy truth and guide our thoughts in Thy paths. We ask it all in His name in Whose mind Thy truth shone unshadowed. Amen.

GAIUS GLENN ATKINS.

---

[1] This might be smybolized by the progress of modern communications, from the telegraph and the Morse code, via the telephone, to radio and television. Radio and television still make use of a medium of communication, but they do not so clumsily get between us and the minds with which we are communing. In this respect, they furnish an analogy for God's universal simultaneous awareness of his whole creation.

Concentrate Upon the Ideal: Seventh Monday

43. HEROISM

So nigh is grandeur to our dust,
So near is God to man,
When Duty whispers low, *Thou must,*
The youth replies, *I can.*

RALPH WALDO EMERSON (1803-1882).

HEROES OF FAMINE

The trains from Moscow to Samara take now some forty hours as normal schedule. In the famine year of 1921, the special health train on which I traveled took ten days. . . . "How can you fight a famine this way?" I burst out impatiently. "The engines need repairing every few miles, the cars are inspected daily and some are always removed from the train, the fuel is damp wood that is cut while we wait, and there are only a few of these broken-down railway lines across tens of thousands of square miles of burned desert where harvest has failed! All the rest of Russia—workers, officials, everyone—is underfed and underclothed and inefficient from malnutrition. It is ghastly! It is utterly impossible!"

"There is nothing impossible," said Sonia in clear, firm tones. Sonia shared my cabin; she was the interpreter they had found for me in Moscow, a communist giving her month's vacation to famine work. She was born in England of Russian exiles and came to Russia with the revolution. England made her a textile worker; Russia made her a soldier on the Polish front and a commissar in a military hospital. Twice she had been wounded in battle; she had had typhus, smallpox and malaria. She had had a husband, and left him to fight at the front. She had always carried with her a tiny revolver "in case they capture me and find out that I am a woman."

"I also have thought in the past that there were impossible things," continued Sonia. "For eight months I ran a typhus hospital where a thousand men lay on wooden floors that could not be disinfected. The men had been in dirt so long that we had to cut the clothes from them; they were rotten with filth that crumbled in your hands. The lice were imbedded in their flesh; you had to scrub hard or use a razor to get them off. We had no beds, no mattresses, no sheets, no blankets, no soap. The doctors and nurses came down with typhus regularly in fourteen days; there was no possible way to protect them; when they took hold of those men you knew they would most of them be sick with typhus in two weeks.

"I thought it was impossible. But always something can be done. We commandeered a big school-building—the only building big enough for our sick. We took a great wooden tank that was used for washing clothes, and we scrubbed the men in it. . . . The best of my help came from the department in charge of deserters. We didn't shoot deserters; we got good use out of them. We detailed them to hospital work. It was really more dangerous than the front, but it didn't worry them so much. They were used to death in dirt and disease but not to death from guns. They would do any work quite fast and obediently to avoid being sent to the front. Every two weeks I would send for twenty deserters and in two weeks they would be down with typhus and I would send for twenty more. I never knew why I didn't get sick myself. They thought I was immune. I got my typhus later after my time at the front. I must have been weaker; I had been wounded twice. Also I was dirtier—covered with lice for weeks. Then I came down with everything, typhus, smallpox, malaria.

"But I learned that there is nothing impossible. There is always a way. . . ."

"Millions will die," I said to Sonia.

And Sonia answered: "Millions have already died."

ANNA LOUISE STRONG, *I Change Worlds.*
Published by Henry Holt and Company.

NOT BY BREAD ALONE

Jesus consecrated himself to one interest. In many ways he gives evidence of high talents any one of which might have made him distinguished; but they were all devoted to his vision of the Kingdom of God. . . .

He was the great seer of the real values of life. He knew what counts when man is estimated by eternity and not by time, by his infinite possibilities and not by his ephemeral whims, desires, vanities. He knew the heritage of man, his birthright in a kingdom not of this world, with this world's petty and factitious successes and honors. He knew that the body was more than raiment, and that, as it was written, man should not live by bread alone.

He saw through shams: the pretense of the complacent rich and sanctimonious—verily they have their reward, a miserable reward equal to their miserable fatuity. . . .

With courageous initiative and self-reliance he shifted the emphasis from action to motive, from the outer to the inner life: not that which entereth into the mouth defileth a man, but that which proceedeth out of the mouth, this defileth a man; everyone that looketh on a woman to lust after her hath already committed adultery with her in his heart; the Kingdom of God is within you. . . .

The life of Jesus was one long mediation, a conning over and over of all that he heard or observed, or read or felt or devised. Behold him, true kinsman of all the poets that he was, forever thinking and forever thinking. . . .

If the great poets are the answerers, as one of the greatest has told us they are, and as the response of our ears tells us they are, though the court musicians and singers come and go in their own right too, then is Jesus among the great poets—for his words are the bread of life. . . .

The truths of the spirit must be forever discovered and spoken anew; the soul too readily lapses with fatigue or disgust. It becomes blind: its eyes demand to be touched with the finger of a new prophet; hence the eternal need of new poets. But reiteration of spiritual truth is only a rediscovery and brings only an awakening when it comes from the mouth of a vitalizing personality. The originality of Jesus was not that he alone saw the heavenly vision, but that it gripped his whole being as it did. The originality of Jesus was that he spoke as one having authority and not as the Scribes and Pharisees. With this I do not mean that his originality was not also in his seeing more and farther, and in his speaking with more skill than any one other; but it is their emotional stress even more than their content and their form, the sincerity of conviction, the vital experience out of which they spring, that makes his words carry so far.

WILLIAM ELLERY LEONARD, *The Poet of Galilee.*
Published by the Viking Press, New York.

THE SOURCE OF ALL RAPTURE

This is my tribute to the poets with whom my spirit has held high adventure; they awakened and have nourished in me the most precious, the most terrible gift I possess, the Imagination—the source of all rapture and trembling; they have made me vividly aware of a glory that is in the world and a significance that is in common things; they have discovered to me shining ideals and disclosed a world of realities which are abiding and beautiful amid all the fluctuations of fortune; they have widened my sympathies and enriched my feelings, lifting me into the High Mood; they have put a philosophy in a sentence, or an unforgettable picture, and made duty seem a privilege; they have opened wide gateways into a realm of peace. . . .

The poets help us because they are mightily concerned with life. Poetry is a revelation or an interpretation of life in some of its aspects. Great poetry interprets life greatly: it reveals experience in amplest range, comprehensively and profoundly. The most gifted and permanent leaders of the world have all had the minds and usually the methods of poets.

CHARLES ALLEN DINSMORE, *The Great Poets and the Meaning of Life*.
Published by Houghton Mifflin Co., Boston.

THE HIGHER GOOD

Father, I will not ask for wealth or fame,
Though once they would have joyed my carnal sense:
I shudder not to bear a hated name,
Wanting all wealth, myself my sole defence.
But give me, Lord, eyes to behold the truth;
A seeing sense that knows the eternal right;
A heart with pity filled, and gentlest ruth;
A manly faith that makes all darkness light:
Give me the power to labor for mankind;
Make me the mouth of such as cannot speak;
Eyes let me be to groping men and blind;
A conscience to the base; and to the weak
Let me be hands and feet; and to the foolish, mind;
And lead still further on such as they kingdom seek.

THEODORE PARKER (1810-1860).

Understand the Actual: Seventh Tuesday

44. THREE CAR-SWEEPERS

Three women clatter down the train steps
Carrying pails and brooms and dirty mops . . . .
They should be knitting by a family fire;
They should be wearing caps of frilled white lace . . . .

O, Mothers of Men, is there no rest for you?
Must you go on forever sweeping trains? . . .
Scrubbing the filth of immaculate bankers and brokers?

Old Lady, I hear you calling to Timmy O'Leary,
Voicing your joy in the birth of beautiful twins . . . .
Clean forgetting that these twin girls may be
Two more sweepers fifty years from now.

High is our civilization! Great is its progress!
We have discovered adequate tasks for old women . . . .
Sweeping peanut shells . . . cleaning spit. . . .

HARRY ELMORE HURD, *Christ in the Breadline.*
Published by the Driftwind Press, North Montpelier, Vt.

IN THE GOLDEN NINETIES

At a dinner eaten on horseback, the favorite steed was fed flowers and champagne; to a small black and tan dog wearing a diamond collar worth $15,000 a lavish banquet was tendered; at one function, the cigarettes were wrapped in hundred-dollar bills; at another, fine black pearls were given to the diners in their oysters; at a third, an elaborate feast was served to boon companions in a mine from which came the fortune of the host. Then weary of such limited diversions, the plutocracy contrived more freakish occasions—with monkeys seated between the guests, human goldfish swimming about in pools, or chorus girls hopping out of pies.

In lavish expenditures as well as in exotic performance, pleasures were hungrily sought by the fretful rich delivered from the bondage of labor and responsibility. Diamonds were set in teeth;

a private carriage and personal valet were provided for a pet monkey; dogs were tied with ribbons to the back seats of Victorias and driven out in the park for airings; a necklace costing $600,000 was purchased for a daughter of Croesus; $65,000 was spent for a dressing table, $75,000 for a pair of opera glasses. An entire theatrical company was taken from New York to Chicago to entertain the friends of a magnate and a complete orchestra engaged to serenade a new-born child. In a burst of sentimental benevolence a family of destitute Negroes in the South was suddenly dowered with riches, garbed in luxury, and placed in a gorgeous house.

CHARLES A. AND MARY BEARD, *The Rise of American Civilization.*
Published by The Macmillan Company, New York.

LUXURY UNLIMITED

The plutocracy of the Mauve Decade was ascetic by comparison with the plutocracy of the present Black Decade. Point by point the most fantastic of the earlier extravagances, entailing the carefully studied waste of wealth produced by the people, are being duplicated or exceeded by the infinitely more monstrous extravagances of today.

In December, 1930, Mr. and Mrs. Henry L. Doherty arranged a coming-out party for Helen Lee Eames Doherty, daughter of Mrs. Doherty by a former marriage. This debut took place at the Mayflower Hotel, Washington, and guests were brought from New York in a special chartered train paid for by Doherty. Several floors of the hotel, in addition to the public entertaining rooms, were rented by the Dohertys for their entourage of guests, servants, and entertainers. The newspapers estimated the cost of the function at no less than $250,000.

At the close of 1936 Mrs. Evalyn Walsh McLean, the proud possessor of the $2,000,000 Hope diamond, heiress to a mining fortune, and married into a newspaper and Cincinnati public-utilities fortune, renewed her custom of staging a lavish New Year's Eve party in Washington.

Mrs. McLean, presiding in the turmoil, wore the Hope diamond, the Star of the East (another large stone), and six diamond bracelets. She was closely guarded, as befitted a walking fortune, by fifteen private detectives and a company of Washington police, who kept vigilant eyes as well on the scintillating jewelry of the guests.

We must disagree with Dixon Wecter when he writes in *The Saga of American Society:* "The greatest attempt ever made to achieve lordly splendor in America is William Randolph Hearst's 240,000 acre estate at San Simeon, California, with its estimated cost of $15,000,000 for furnishings and antiques alone. Its great dining-hall hung with Sienese banners and a magnificent Gothic chimney piece from the Château du Jour, its sixteenth-century refectory tables, Flemish tapestries, seventeenth-century Spanish candlesticks and old English silver, six Gobelin tapestries costing $575,000, a notable collection of armour, and Cardinal Richelieu's own bed are witnesses to the spoliation of Europe." Mr. Wecter is impressed by the fact that Hearst once transported a castle from Spain to New York in packing cases, that he purchased St. Donat's Castle in Wales, and that at San Simeon he owns a private railway spur and three cars and a diner to transport his guests to the main *palazzo.* Overlooking an entire Bavarian village that Hearst has constructed at Wyntoon, California, Mr. Wecter also overlooks the fact that all this is merely the minimum standard equipment of the contemporary multimillionaire. . . .

The Du Pont clan, because of its many members, probably owns more personal possessions than any other American family of the plutocracy, although the Vanderbilt group runs it a close second and the Rockefellers probably come third. A careful survey indicates that the Du Ponts own more yachts, more pipe organs, more swimming pools, more ducal estates, and more bathrooms than any other family in the world today. They employ more servants than the royal family of Great Britain, not excluding the King's Own Life Guards. . . .

Near the environs of Wilmington there are precisely two dozen Du Pont country estates, four of which are of the first magnitude. There is, for example, Winterthur, the ducal 150-room residence of the Henry F. du Ponts, boasting forty bedrooms, each with a radio installation, each replete with costly antiques; the cost of the building alone was $2,000,000, and including the grounds, trappings, furniture, and fixtures, the cost of the whole establishment easily touches $10,000,000.

Then there is Longwood, residence of Pierre du Pont, surrounded by 1,000 carefully tended acres which include six acres of glassed-over tropical gardens; in these are orangeries and separate orchard houses for the growing throughout the year of peaches, nectarines, and exotic fruits. The house has nearly two hundred rooms, and more than one hundred servants, including the gardeners who are employed there. A feature of the establishment is an organ of ten thousand pipes to transport which required fourteen railroad freight cars. According to *Fortune,* the volume of this regal instrument is sufficient to fill three cathedrals. The building was especially constructed to contain the apparatus, whose attendant is Firmin Swinnen, former organist at the Antwerp Cathedral. . . . All in all, the residential establishments of the Du Ponts, taking into consideration land, buildings, furnishings, and equipment, may be conservatively estimated as costing at least $150,000,000, or more than ten per cent of the total university and college endowment of the nation.

FERDINAND LUNDBERG, *America's Sixty Families.*
Published by The Vanguard Press, New York.

A PRAYER

O God of grace and truth whom the heavens cannot contain but who loveth to dwell with those who are of contrite heart, look mercifully upon us as we seek thy face. Thou art eternal and we are frail children of the dust; thou art holy and we are filled with pettiness; thy heart is love and we seek our own. Yet mean though we are, we are not wholly so. We are sick of our obsession with self. Help us to escape the tyranny of self by finding our brothers and living in them, by finding thee and losing ourselves.

Give us the grace to overcome the world's injustice, to hear the cries of the oppressed, to succor the fallen and to heal the victims of man's inhumanity to man.

Grant that as we worship thee we may come to a truer knowledge of ourselves. May we for knowing ourselves more honestly, seek thee more sincerely that thy grace may make us whole and thy strength may be made perfect in our weakness and thy will may make our wills thy tool, through Jesus Christ our Lord. Amen.

BISHOP WILLIAM SCARLETT.

Be Concerned: Seventh Wednesday

45. JUDGE ME, O LORD

"I press towards the goal unto the prize
of the high calling of God in Christ Jesus"

If I had been in Palestine
A poor disciple I had been.
I had not risked or purse or limb
All to forsake, and follow Him.
But with the vast and wondering throng
I too had stood and listened long;
I too had felt my spirits stirred
When the Beatitudes I heard.

With the glad crowd that sang the psalm,
I too had sung, and strewed the palm;
Then slunk away in dastard shame
When the High Priest denounced His name.
But when my late companions cried
"Away! let Him be crucified!"
I would have begged, with tremulous
Pale lips, "Release Him unto us!"

Beside the cross when Mary prayed,
A great way off I too had stayed;
Not even in that hour had dared,
And for my dying Lord declared;
But beat upon my craven breast,
And loathed my coward heart, at least,
To think my life I dared not stake
And beard the Romans for His sake.

SARAH N. CLEGHORN.

WE MUST CHOOSE

The fact is that, whether we like it or not, the real Jesus scandalizes us. We would be more aware of this, if we were not so hopelessly accustomed to him. One could sometimes wish that all of us could forget all we ever heard about him, and become sufficiently pagan to look on him with fresh eyes.

The scandal consists in his turning upside down all our values. . . . Before this Jesus, the Jesus presented in the Gospels, we can only conclude that he cannot be fitted in with our standards and conceptions, that we cannot really "understand" him, if understanding means to give him a place in the known world in which we really live. We must agree with Mr. H. G. Wells that "he is too big for our small hearts."

The situation is then that we must chose between Jesus and ourselves as we are. Since we cannot fit him in with our world, we stand before the alternative, either to forget him or to let ourselves be fitted in with his world. If he really goes his own royal way, we must decide between that way and ours.

The Christian is a man who has faced this choice, and who has come to the conclusion that Jesus is right and that he himself was and is wrong. To him it has become the simple truth of his life that Jesus speaks with authority and not as the scribes, not as the philosophers, the scientists, the theologians—and not as the little philosopher, scientist, or theologian within ourselves. He has discovered that if there is a contradiction between Jesus' world and our world, that means that our world is abnormal, out of joint, and that his is normal and true. He ceases therefore to "interpret" Jesus, and simply listens to him. He is willing to throw all "truths" away, to get hold of this truth. He sells all his pearls for the one pearl of great price.

W. A. VISSER T'HOOFT, "None Other Gods."
Published by Harper and Brothers, New York.

FROZEN RELIGION

No one knows better than the pastor of a church in an industrial community what a travesty on religion the faith and practice of allegedly godly men can be. Here we have church-school superintendents who are also mill superintendents, charged with the execution of harsh labor policies; elders and vestrymen, trustees and deacons, who drive hard competitive bargains; Mr. Barretts of Wimpole Street, whose religion has frozen in their veins; pious men who are exploiters of the labor of children; pillars of the sanctuary who are also pillars of a vicious political system;

"good" fathers who are cruel employers or defaulting bankers; women known as tender and faithful mothers and officers of the church guild who are hard mistresses to their servants and social climbers and spendthrifts. A recent writer accentuates the obvious when he says: "Christians are often blind to appalling injustices at their door. Sharp business practices, slander, envy, vulgarity, betrayal of confidence, evasion of contractual obligations, gaining one's ends through flattery of petty authorities obstructing the claims of justice, and being oblivious of the higher demands of the good life—such are not uncommon practices among Christians."

F. ERNEST JOHNSON, *The Church and Society.*
Published by the Abingdon Press, New York.

TURNING FEAR INTO HOPE

If fear were abolished from modern life, the work of the psychotherapist would be nearly gone. It was not without cause that the Master of the soul so often reiterated "Fear not," "Be not afraid," "Be not anxious."

Is this, then, an instinct we should suppress? That is both impossible and undesirable. The effects of fear are of two kinds: there is the fear that paralyses and the fear that inspires. Nothing paralyses our lives so much as fear, depriving them as it does of that abundance of power which is our birthright. But there is also the fear that nerves and inspires and expresses itself in the effective avoidance of imminent disaster. Now, we ask what constitutes the difference betwen the fear in these two cases? The answer is that fear paralyses when it offers no way of escape; it inspires when it is associated with hope. A hare, suddenly surprised, is either temporarily paralysed by fear, or stimulated to its topmost speed.

Fear which includes a large element of hope passes into confidence, and this, as we have seen, is the first essential of power. If we apply our principle to what we have said concerning morbid fear, we can see that our problem is to turn the fear that paralyses into the fear that inspires.

Those who have raised discussion as to whether we should "fear God" have, I think, failed to appreciate this difference between the fear that paralyses and the fear akin to hope that urges us to active service. To fear God may mean that we are afraid of God because He may punish us, and in this case the fear is paralysing and brings forth no good result—"I knew thee, that thou wert an austere man . . . and hid thy talent in the ground." But the fear of God may mean that, indifferent to ourselves, we are filled with reverent awe (in which emotion there is an element of fear), combined with a conviction of His willingness and power to help. This shifts the fear from ourselves, turns it into hope, and fills us with a confidence which stimulates us to great endeavours, and gives us that inspiration which only comes to those who humbly devote themselves to a noble cause.

J. Arthur Hadfield, in *The Spirit,* edited by B. H. Streeter.
Published by the Macmillan Company.

A PRAYER

O Thou, Whose ways and wisdom and love are the answers to all our needs, send us help, who need help so much from Thy sanctuary. Help us to seek forgiveness at Thine altars, to find strength in the fellowship of the aspiring and because we bow in prayer to be lifted up in strength. Make the place of Thy habitation glorious for us and through us. In His name Who sought Thy sanctuary and found it His Father's house. Amen.

Gaius Glenn Atkins.

A PRAYER

O Thou, whose commandment is life eternal, we confess that we have broken Thy Law, in that we have sought our own gain and good rather than Thy gracious Will, who willest good unto all men. We have sinned by class injustice, by indifference to the sufferings of the poor, by want of patriotism, by hypocrisy and secret self-seeking. But do Thou in Thy mercy hear us. Turn Thou our hearts that we may truly repent, and utterly abhor the great and manifold evils which our sins have brought upon the nation. Break down our idols of pride and wealth. Shatter our self-love. Open our eyes to know in daily life, in public work, that Thou alone art God. Thee only let us worship, Thee only let us serve, for His sake, who sought not His own will but Thine alone. Amen.

Endeavor to Transform: Seventh Thursday

46. THE MAGNIFICAT

One song, and but one song we have of her's,
    She, so revered and loved through ages long;
    Her's the Magnificat, that buoyant song
That every rebel of the centuries stirs.
Strange, is it not, her wonted worshippers
    Can be so patient with the prosperous wrong,
    While her high protest clamors like a gong,
Or horses thundering to the biting spurs?

"He hath put down the mighty from their seat,
    And hath exalted them of low degree;
Likewise He giveth to the hungry meat,
    And from the rich withholdeth good things, He."

No fawning ritual! no dead dogma, that!
Go! read again, Mary's Magnificat!

ROBERT WHITAKER, in Social Song and Other Verse.
Published by the Banner Press, Emory University, Atlanta, Ga.

THE MEANING OF STEWARDSHIP

It is the recurring emphasis on inwardness that continually discomfits him who would identify Jesus and the religion founded on his life with a social theory or program. "As he thinketh in his heart, so is he." "Not that which goeth into the mouth . . . , but that which cometh out of the mouth, this defileth a man." "God looketh on the heart." Nothing short of violence to Jesus' teaching can make it other than person-centered. The social gospel, if there is one, must take account of this, must embody it. And the explanation is to be found in the fact that what Jesus meant by the Kingdom was not what most of us mean by it. It was not an external project. It was the beloved community, existing, in fact, for everyone in whose heart the love of fellowship had been born. One can no more define the Kingdom in terms of externals than one can so define family, or home or native land. Family and home become meaningful to me as *my* family,

my home. Country, objectively, is nothing to be emotional about.
An alien looks upon it unmoved. But as *my* country, existing
within me as well as outside me, it becomes an emotional reality.
Hence "the kingdom of God is within you." And when one enters
the Kingdom the sense of kinship with one's fellows, of loyalty
to a spiritual society, is born. The test of citizenship in the Kingdom is therefore at once a personal and a social test. "We know
that we have passed from death unto life, because we love the
brethren." There is no more revealing word in Scripture.

It must be admitted that responsibility for the lack of sympathy, on the part of many church people, with the effort to
develop the social implications of the Christian message rests in
no small part on the exponents of the social gospel. Too generally
we have thundered the prophetic teachings of Christianity as mandatory without showing successfully how the social elements of
religious experience are, in fact, integrated with those of the
personal religious life. To reduce the gospel to a program of action
does as much violence to it as to confine it within definitions of
mystical experience. The message of Jesus is that man must be
born into a divine life and thus into membership in a divine
society. Since our world is filled with denials of this divine life,
the Christian affirmation can be upheld only as the individual
validates it in his own experience. That experience is but fragmentary and less than self-sustaining if it does not comprehend
in itself the entire social outreach of Jesus and his message. . . .

The limitation of self in the interest of other is a process to
which human nature offers stout resistance. It will always be so
until self and other are brought under a new synthesis. The heart
of my contention is that Christianity essentially offers that synthesis. It does not offer individual *and* social redemption—although the necessity for a convenient form of statement often
leads us to use such terms. In reality, it presents a spirit and a way
of life in which this conflict may be resolved.

The essence of sainthood is in the acceptance of this synthesis.
No matter how much or how little we may regard Christianity as
socially revolutionary, evangelical Christianity has always made
much of its revolutionary meaning as applied to the individual.
"For in Christ . . . a new creation!" The apostasy of modern
evangelism is in its denial of Jesus' own prescription for the
spiritual life. The prevalent effort to interpret regeneration as a

private and individual concern that may be effected as well in one social environment as in another is an irreverent blue-penciling of the New Testament. To say that Jesus' admonition to the rich young ruler is of limited application smacks of rationalization. Jesus found that young man spiritually barred from the Kingdom because his possessions stood between him and God. In other words, they barred him from that kinship with his fellows which is intrinsic in the Kingdom idea. But the fact devastatingly insisted on by Jesus is that it is the nature of wealth, standing over against poverty, to do that very thing. Cannot a rich man be saved, then? Yes, was Jesus' answer, but with very great difficulty. It is impossible unless he can in his own soul make those possession as if they were not! This is the meaning of stewardship, which the church has travestied by confusing it with tithing. As an admittedly arbitrary device for scaling one's giving tithing may have pragmatic value, but as a principle of measurement it is far less than Christian. It is nothing but ten-per-cent stewardship. The Christian doctrine here is essentially more radical than socialism, for it separates a man completely from his possessions in so far as using them for personal ends is concerned.

F. ERNEST JOHNSON, *The Church and Society*.
Used by permission of the Abingdon Press, New York.

A DECISION FOR GOD

That a man should find God and possess Him as *his* God,— should live in the fear of Him, trust Him, and lead a holy and blessed life in the strength of this feeling,—that is the substance and the aim of religion. . . . The Christian faith is not, as is so often maintained, a gentle exaltation of our earthly life, or a comfort and relief in its troubles and trials. No! it is a decision for God and against the world. It is an eternal life that is involved: the recognition that in and above Nature and her changes there is a realm of sanctity and love, a city not built with hands, whose citizens we are to be; and with this message there comes to us the demand that we should cleanse our hearts and deny ourselves. . . . When God and everything that is sacred threatens to disappear in darkness, or our doom is pronounced; when the mighty forces of inexorable nature seem to overwhelm us, and the bounds of good and evil to dissolve; when. weak and weary, we

despair of finding God at all in this dismal world—it is then that
the personality of Christ may save us. Here we have a life that
was lived wholly in the fear of God—resolute, unselfish, pure;
here there glows and flashes a grandeur, a love, which draws us to
itself. Although it was all a continual struggle with the world;
though bit by bit one earthly possession after another fell away,
and at last the life itself came to an ignominious end; yet no soul
can avoid the thought that whoso dies thus, dies well: he dies not,
but lives. For it was in this life and death that there first dawned
upon mankind the assurance of an eternal life, and a divine love
which overcomes all evil, nay, sin itself; and in the presence of a
glory which is beyond the reach of death, we have come to perceive the vanity of the world and of all earthy possessions. . . .
As surely as everything depends on the soul finding God and becoming one with Him, so surely is he the true Saviour, Guide and
Lord who leads the soul to God.

ADOLF HARNACK, Christianity and History.

A PRAYER

Almighty and most merciful God, we acknowledge and confess that we have sinned against thee in thought, and word and
deed; that we have not loved thee with all our heart and soul, with
all our mind and strength; and that we have not loved our neighbour as ourselves. We beseech thee, O God, to be forgiving to
what we have been, to help us to amend what we are, and of thy
mercy to direct what we shall be, so that the love of goodness may
ever be first in our hearts and we may follow unto our life's end
in the steps of Jesus Christ our Lord. Amen.

Devotional Services.

Proceed Resolutely: Seventh Friday

47. GETHSEMANE

His white hand rested on an olive tree.
He leaned a moment, wiping from His brow
The moisture from the climbing of the hill.
Sad unto death, He slowly raised His head.
The olive leaves were a strange dusky silver;
The groping starlight clung to them; all seemed
Dreamlike, unreal, yet too real for dreams.

The Son of Man looked down where Peter slept,
Peter and James and John, and gravely smiled
That even flesh so strong should be so weak.
He knew His hour was near. The sigh He breathed
Came back with some familiar redolence
Long past, that of a flower near Nazareth.
It summoned homely roofs, the loneliness
Of boyhood, the shrill whine of saws in beams,
Kind voices, human sounds that wove themselves
Into a childish human consciousness,
Dreaming the awful reveries of God.
Life seemed a jewel in the hand of death,
A brief dear boon, full of the beautiful
That dies in sunsets and in all farewells.
He knew what Never meant—that aching word
Heavy with loss, most musical with grief.
Grief for the stones His feet would press no more—
Never the pungent smell of olives crushed,
Never the clover where the grass was rich,
Never tall lilies, crimsoning at dawn,
Never the fresh ripe grapes at vintage time,
Never the fat figs rounding in the sun,
Never the mumbled blessings of the poor,
The timid touch of Mary's hand on His,
The clean night wind among the barren thorns,
The friendliness of near, white, dazzling stars,
The balm of work, the ecstasy of prayer—
No more, no more—the Son of Man must die.

He knelt. His strong hands met above His head
While long and long He prayed; not as men pray,
But lost in silence melting into God.
So still He lay, His body might have died
Pouring its spirit in the warm spring air
Like incense on the altar of the world. . . .
The whirling skies were mute; the night stood still.
Above a distant ocean throb he heard
In rhythm with the Pulse that sped the suns,
Slow time unraveling from eternity,
Time, like a thread unwound from the robes of God.
He saw His sheep dispersed. The pagan night
Descended on His tomb. The banqueters
Lay under falling roses, drunk with wine
And kisses, mad with impious despair,
And laughed His words away. Nero He saw,
And Elagabalus and Julian,
And old Rome's grandeur tottering down the years
To be the compost heap where presently
Should spring the perfect flower of Christian hope,
Sudden and strange, miraculously fair.
Swart cities, in the light crespuscular
That smoothed their ugliness, grew kind and gay,
Lifting on spires against the pearly skies
The rich dark promise of the Cross; and Christ
Could see it borne, stained red with martyres' blood,
To mountain wilds, dank rivers tropical,
Oceans of ice, and deserts cursed with heat,
Till all the globe was girt with charity,
And men who had been worse than beasts aspired
(Like spiders striving up from star to star,
Falling and bruised, to rise and climb again)
To stand before the very throne of God. . . .

Sin, sin that steals away the sleep of men,
Where will you lay your burden? How will God
Compound so great a guilt, unless He feel
Man's infinite remorse? And how shall God
Bear shame unless He stoop to share man's fall?
Here on this silent solitary back

Pile up your disillusioned agonies
Even to shroud the stars; no other back
Is innocent enough to bear them all. ...
All foulnesses that germinated deep
In the still womb of time—anger and pride;
Lust, the mother of fear; and envy, small
And Poisonous; dull, slothful ignorance,
Blind avarice, that wizens up the soul—
All frailties of men, Lord Jesus knew
And pitied, knowing hate was love turned sour,
And even greed perverted piety.
He was the purse-proud sybarite, the thief,
The slayer and the slain, the slanderer
And those he slandered; yes, the painted drab
Who slouched and shivered past some tavern door
Accursed and laughed at—He could love the good
Deep trodden in her heart, and knew its ache,
And how the lust and cruelty of men
Had twisted her poor soul. All human guilt,
All misery was His, all weariness,
When "Father," He cried, "Thy will, not Mine, be done!"
Then tortured, scourged, stretched through the void of night
Upon a cross that wracked the universe
From pit to unimagined heights of heaven,
He was the battlefield of life and death.
Time shriveled, and eternity was now;
Space crumbled, and the here was everywhere.
The whole creation groaned and parched with thirst,
And life moved swift and terrible to God,
And death gave up the ghost.

Now from His pain emerged a holy peace,
Serene, free, luminous and innocent,
The peace of God. Now kind hands bore Him up
To solitudes where nothing reigned but Love.
He was the light that kindled all the suns.
The little moons revolved beneath His feet.
The gemmed night veiled the glory of His face.
His thought was music, grave, majestical.
A flawless beauty was the air He breathed.

His heart was warmed with all-wise innocence,
And all things sang His praise.

With a great sigh that like an autumn wind
Passed shivering through the stars and saddened them,
The God bowed down again to mortal need,
Put off His glory and took up the cross
Of aching flesh, of hands that nails would pierce.
The cool night air brought to him hollowly
The sound of many voices. Torches glowed
Far down the slope. He walked with thoughtful steps
To meet the crowd, and when one came, He smiled,
And called poor Judas by the name of friend.

WILLIAM WALSH.

TRUTH ALONE IS STRONG

Though the cause of evil prosper,
  Yet 'tis truth alone is strong;
Though her portion be the scaffold,
  And upon the throne be wrong,
Yet that scaffold sways the future,
  And behind the dim unknown,
Standeth God within the shadow
  Keeping watch above His own.

J. R. Lowell.

A PRAYER

God, of Thy Goodness, give me Thyself; for Thou art enough
to me, and I may nothing ask that is less that may be full worship to Thee; and if I ask anything that is less, ever me wanteth,
—but only in Thee I have all.

JULIAN of Norwich.

Seek Comradeship: Seventh Saturday

48. SANCTUARY

How may one hold these days of wonderment
And bind them into stillness with a thong,
Ere as a fleeting dream they pass along
Into the waste of lovely things forspent;
How may one keep what the Great Powers have sent,
The prayers fulfilled more beautiful and strong
Than any thought could fashion into song
Of all the rarest harmonies inblent?

There is an Altar where they may be laid
And sealed in Faith within Its sacred care,—
Here they are safe into the very end;
For these are of the things that never fade,
Brought from the City that is built four-square,
The gifts of Him who is the Perfect Friend.

THOS. S. JONES, JR., in Shadow of the Perfect Rose.
Published by Farrar and Rinehart, New York.

MOST MARVELOUS AGE

That first century of the Christian faith was the most marvelous age of spiritual victory over material forces in all human history. The power of the Holy Spirit, working mightily within, was so great that it was able to crack the hard molds of convention in that ancient Roman world and to run deep beneath the surface of society, cutting everywhere new channels of its own.

In the joy of the glorious freedom of that new life of the Spirit of Jesus, men and women who were quite ordinary and commonplace people did extraordinary and uncommon things. The very weakest often proved the strongest. Slaves and freedmen and those of no account whatever in the world's estimation became valiant heroes of the new faith, ready to lay down their lives for Christ's sake. Their own bewildered and fearful hearts became suddenly filled to the brim with a strange new courage and amazing fortitude.

Throughout all these tremendous trials of their Christian faith they were noted for two qualities which shone out in their personal characters as individuals and made men take knowledge of them that they had been with Jesus. They had a joy in the midst of suffering that no earthly power could destroy; they also had the gift of peace in their inmost hearts that no suffering, however great, could take away.

One further vital fact needs to be emphasized relating to the Christian community. The Christ-life could never have been lived at such a high level if individual Christians had remained in isolation, separated from one another. But they were of "one heart and one soul" continuing "instantly in prayer." Their strength came from this unity and from the certain knowledge gained from inner experience that where two or three were gathered together in Christ's name he was in their midst. Thus the new commandment was fulfilled and in the power of the Holy Spirit the "greater works" were done.

What happened in the first century of Christian faith, with such results, can surely happen in our own day if we are ready to make a complete surrender of our hearts to the living Christ in the power of the Holy Spirit, for he, the Lord and the Master, has not left us comfortless. He is with us still through his strengthening and empowering Spirit. He is ready by the same Spirit to guide us into all the truth and to show us things to come.

C. F. ANDREWS, *Christ in the Silence.*
Used by permission of The Abingdon Press, New York.

A NEW HUMANITY

The new language on the lips of Christians was the language of love. But it was more than a language, it was a thing of power and action. The Christians really considered themselves brothers and sisters, and their actions corresponded to this belief. On this point we possess two unexceptional testimonies from pagan writers. Says Lucian of the Christians: "Their original lawgiver had taught them that they were all brethren, one of another. . . . They become incredibly alert when anything of this kind occurs, that affects their common interests. On such occasions no expense is grudged." And Tertullian (Apolog. xxxix.) observes: "It is our care for the helpless, our practice of lovingkindness, that brands us in the eyes of many of our opponents."

The gospel thus became a social message. The preaching which laid hold of the outer man, detaching him from the world, and uniting him to his God, was also a preaching of solidarity and brotherliness. The gospel, it has been truly said, is at bottom both individualistic and socialistic. Its tendency towards mutual association, so far from being an accidental phenomenon in its history, is inherent in its character. It spiritualizes the irresistible impulse which draws one man to another, and it raises the social connection of human beings from the sphere of a convention to that of a moral obligation. In this way it serves to heighten the worth of man, and essays to recast contemporary society, to transform the socialism which involves a conflict of interests into the socialism which rests upon the consciousness of a spiritual unity and a common goal. This was ever present to the mind of the great apostle to the Gentiles. In his little churches, where each person bore his neighbour's burden, Paul's spirit already saw the dawning of a new humanity, and in the epistle to the Ephesians he has voiced this feeling with a thrill of exultation. Far in the background of these churches, like some unsubstantial semblance, lay the division between Jew and Gentile, Greek and Barbarian, great and small, rich and poor. For a new humanity had now appeared, and the apostle viewed it as Christ's body, in which every member served the rest and each was indispensable in his own place.

ADOLF HARNACK, *The Expansion of Christianity in the First Three Centuries.*
Published by G. P. Putnam's, New York.

THE BIRTH OF A MIGHTY MOVEMENT

C. K. Ober, student secretary of the International Committee of Young Men's Christian Associations in North America, sent to Mott as a leader of the Cornell University Association an invitation to the first international, interdenominational student Christian conference ever held. Luther Wishard, Ober's colleague, had suggested to Moody, the famous evangelist, that he should hold a conference purely for students, on the lines of those that he had already for some years held for Christian workers in general at Northfield, in the Connecticut valley, where he lived. The idea pleased Moody, but he was reluctant to preside over students. When this hesitation was overcome invitations were sent over Moody's name by Wishard and Ober to colleges and universities throughout North America. The place of meeting of this Bible study summer school was to be Mount Hermon, which overlooks the Connecticut valley a few miles from Northfield, Moody's home. . . .

The students' summer school under Moody's leadership met for twenty-six days, from July 7 to August 1. It gathered 251 men from eighty-nine colleges and universities in different parts of the United States of America and Canada, with a small group from other lands. . . .

Robert Wilder's sister, Miss Grace Wilder, had it laid on her heart to pray that out of this conference to which her brother was going 100 students would volunteer for service in the foreign mission field. Her brother joined in these prayers and he shared his concern with a few others. He talked with Mott about it as they went down together to swim in the Connecticut River. A small group of these men who had decided to give their lives to service in the foreign field met every day at a given time for prayer. It began under a tree. As the meeting grew in volume the men went into a classroom in Recitation Hall. One after another, men came to the decision to volunteer for the field. Mott himself joined the group. He described the culmination thus in a speech: "The conference was drawing to a close when another meeting was held of which we do not talk much. It was too sacred. . . . We were meeting there in the dusk. Man after man arose and told the reason why he had decided to become a Volunteer. God spoke through reality. . . . It was not strange, therefore, that during the closing hours of that . . . conference the number of Volunteers greatly increased. At the beginning of the Mount Hermon conference less than half a dozen students were expecting to be missionaries. By the last day ninety-nine had decided and had signed a paper that read, 'We are willing and desirous, God permitting, to become foreign missionaries.' . . . Ninety-nine had signed that paper. . . . The conference closed, but the next morning those ninety-nine met for a farewell meeting of prayer. . . . It was in a room in Recitation Hall. There were not seats enough and some had to stand. We knelt, however, all of us, and while we were kneeling in that closing period of heart-burning prayer the hundredth man came in and knelt with us."

The author has before him a tiny olive-green pamphlet so small that it will go into a waistcoat pocket, in which the names of the 100 Volunteers were then printed. It is an historic document, for out of it two years later sprang the Student Volunteer Movement for Foreign Missions, over 13,000 of whose members have been thrust forth into all the mission fields of the world.

BASIL MATHEWS, *John R. Mott: World Citizen.*
Published by Harper and Brothers, New York.

Worship God: Seventh Sunday

49. WITH WHOM IS NO VARIABLENESS, NEITHER SHADOW OF
TURNING

It fortifies my soul to know
That though I perish, truth is so;
That, howsoe'er I stray and range,
Whate'er I do, Thou dost not change.
I steadier step when I recall
That, if I slip, Thou dost not fall.
ARTHUR HUGH CLOUGH (1816-1861).

TRUST IN GOD

Christianity believes in a God who created the world and will
redeem it; but it knows that the purposes of God may be mo-
mentarily and periodically frustrated by human wickedness. It
knows the heart of man to "be deceitful above all things and
desperately wicked." The basis of its trust and hope is, therefore,
not in some natural increase of human virture or some final
achievement of human intelligence. Christianity, at its best, is,
therefore, not involved in chaos and confusion when the imposing
structures of human contrivance fall, as they inevitably do and
must. The chaos of the destruction does not tempt it to a sense of
ultimate confusion. It knows that "the world passeth away and
the lusts thereof," and that the self-destruction in which the
world's empires become periodically involved is but a proof of the
immutability of God's laws and the power of his sovereignty,
which men defy at their peril. . . .

Ultimate confidence in the goodness of life can, in other words,
not rest upon confidence in the goodness of man. If that is where
it rests it is an optimism which will suffer ultimate disillusionment. Romanticism will be transmuted into cynicism, as it has always been in the world's history. The faith of a Christian is
something quite different from this optimism. It is trust in God,
in a good God who created a good world, though the world is not
now good; in a good God, powerful and good enough finally to
destroy the evil that men do and redeem them of their sins. This
kind of faith is not optimism. It does not, in fact, arise until

optimism breaks down and men cease to trust in themselves that they are righteous. Faced with the indubitable fact of human history that there is no human vitality which is not subject to decay and no human virtue which is not subject to corruption, hope in the meaningfulness of human existence must be nourished by roots which go deeper than the deserts of history, with their periodic droughts.

The Christian faith in the goodness of God is not to be equated with confidence in the virtue of man. But neither is it a supernaturalism and otherworldliness which places its hope in another world because it finds this world evil. Every distinction between an essentially good eternity and an essentially evil finiteness is foreign to the Christian faith. When Christians express their faith in such terms they have been corrupted by other types of religion. For the Christian who really understands his faith, life is worth living and this world is not merely a "vale of tears." He is able to discern the goodness of creation beneath the corruptions of human sin. Nor will he be driven to despair by the latter; for the God in whom he believes is the redeemer as well as creator. He has confidence, in other words, that evil cannot overwhelm the good.

Christianity is right in its general indictment, "Weep for yourselves." Sin is pitiful. The Saviour who utters these words dies upon the cross. He dies not because he has sinned but because he has not sinned. He proves thereby that sin is so much a part of existence that sinlessness cannot maintain itself in it. But he also proves that sin is not a necessary and inherent characteristic of life. Evil is not a part of God, nor yet a part of essential man. This Saviour is a revelation of the goodness of God and the essential goodness of man, *i.e.,* the second Adam. He is indeed defeated in history but in that very defeat proves that he cannot be ultimately defeated. That is, he reveals that it is God's nature to swallow up evil in Himself and destroy it. Life in its deepest essence is not only good but capable of destroying the evil which has been produced in it. Life is thus not at war with itself. Its energy is not in conflict with its order. Hence the Saviour truly says: "Weep not for me." Christianity stands beyond tragedy. If there are tears for this man on the cross they cannot be tears of "pity and terror." The cross does not reveal life at cross purposes with itself. On the contrary, it declares that what seems to be an inherent defect in life itself is really a contingent defect in the soul of each man, the defect of the sin which he commits in his freedom. . . .

The basic plan of life cannot be finally defeated. The will of God prevails even when the Son of God is crucified. In that very crufixion God has absorbed the contradictions of historic existence into Himself. Thus Christianity transmits the tragedy of history into something which is not tragedy. God is revealed as not only the ground but as the goal of human existence and man's rebellion against God is proved to be an abortive effort which cannot finally prevail. The suffering servant is the son of man.

This is the foolishness of God that is wiser than the wisdom of men.

REINHOLD NIEBUHR, *Beyond Tragedy*.
Published by Charles Scribner's Sons, New York.

FASCINATION OF THE GREAT PURSUIT

The central theme of the "Confessions" is religion. The most famous word Augustine ever wrote is: "For Thou hast made us for Thyself and our heart can find no rest until it rests in Thee." The words convey not only man's need of God but also the outgoing of the Divine Spirit towards human fellowship: *"Thou hast made us for Thyself."* The restlessness of his years of wandering had taught him this profound truth. He had gathered the riches of knowledge for his mind and it hungered for some deeper reality; he brought treasures from many lands and still was poor; he lived in the crowd and yet was lonely.

Many have written of the soul's search for God and have suggested that we pursue One Who ever eludes our quest. The most persistent search of the ages, they declare, is man's attempt to find One Whom he may worship. Augustine, who travelled far in the same quest, was made aware that he was not left alone. He came to realize that God is the Pursuer, the tireless Seeker, and man the object of His search. For this conviction he had the highest authority. Our Lord affirms that it is the Shepherd who seeks the sheep, and not the sheep that organize a search for the Shepherd. Constantly this sense of being pursued is made evident in the "Confessions."

The book reveals a mind satisfied and radiantly content.

Augustine lived in days of endless confusion. He saw the mighty civilization of Rome dissolving before his eyes and no man could tell what should take its place. Upon the Church also which he loved so dearly dark clouds were gathering. And yet he remained confident and undismayed because of that wonderful experience of God's presence and power that had come into his life. The God in whom he trusted was able to bring light out of darkness and order out of chaos. From the world within, so transformed and reorganized, he looked with serenity upon the world without which one day would yield itself to the same eternal and redeeming will. . . .

As we close the book there remains with us a profound sense of the central paradox of the Christian religion. Augustine was the merchant seeking pearls who found at last the pearl of great price and sold all he had to secure it. His "Confessions" are an account of the search, the discovery, the purchase, and the joy which was his in the great possession. But there was another Seeker Who also was searching for treasure and Who found it at last in Augustine. Some account of that other Seeker and of His tireless quest may also be found in the "Confessions" though none of the ransomed ever will know all the pain and peril of the divine pursuit. At last the seeker of treasure in human life found what He prized and sought. . . . The paradox of the doctrine of Grace stands revealed in imperishable glory in the Confessions of Augustine.

TREVOR H. DAVIES, *To Live Is Christ.*
Published by The Oxford University Press, New York.

A PRAYER

O God, by whom the meek are guided in judgment, and light riseth up in darkness for the godly; grant us, in all our doubts and uncertainties, the grace to ask what Thou wouldest have us to do; that the Spirit of wisdom may save us from all false choices, and that in Thy light we may see light, and in Thy straight path may not stumble, through Jesus Christ our Lord.

W. BRIGHT.

Concentrate Upon the Ideal: Eighth Monday

50. FANTASIA OF THE MIDDLE WEST

Here the vast corn fields lie
From east of sky to shimmering west of sky;
Here from world's end
To far world's end, each white and level road
Stretches (it almost seems) without a bend,
Bearing the traffic for its thunder-load.
Distant along each endless thoroughfare
Cities and little towns, strewn here and there,
Bulk huge or straggle. Here incredible
Space seems a miracle.

And on, and on, and very far away
Beneath the span of day
Extends and looms a monstrous bulk of loam—
Earth's mood grown monochrome.

Sluggish, amorphous, tawny, sprawling, slow,
Strange folds of moving earth, the rivers go
With a vast sullen patience in their flow.

Over the earth's supine monotony
The cyclone wanders free;
Or the wide gentler breezes whirl and run
Tossing the corn fronds softly in the sun.
Islands of shadowy trees
Loom dream-soft in the hot immensities;
And far white houses,—sudden, blinding,—glow
Like chalk cliffs in the corn's lush emerald flow.
Red silos bulge. Above, a windmill's wheel
Glitters—a giant sunflower of steel.
And, over all, the sky
Burns vast with thunder-cradling cumuli:
There the huge daylight ghosts of mountains go
Bearing the lightnings subtly to and fro—
Fierce golden pumas; and, immense, the air

Arches—the travelling sun's one thoroughfare.
Sky's vastitude, earth's vastitude,
Induce one mood:
Earth's monotone of rich immensity
Engulfs and shadows me.

And yet this land has beauty! Twilights fall
Lilac and lavender across the earth
Whence corn has birth,
Rich as the far blue of a mountain wall.
The silver and bark-pleated sycamores
Gleam over limestone floors
Where slow creeks drawl and drowse through shadow-spun
Dapple of sun;
Or red-buds toss their blossoms toward the skies—
Spring's fountains made of coral butterflies;
And cool sky-fallen clouds, the dogwood looms
With ivory blooms.
And here a free and friendly people go
Comradely to and fro,
Drawing their sure life from the deep black loam
Where they, even as the corn, find rooted home.
Generous, drawling, lavish, thrifty, they
Move as the winds move on their careless way . . .
Or as the clouds that cross their spacious skies
(Wherein the lightning lies).

And in this land my destiny and soul
Must (like the corn or red-bud) live and grow
Out of the deep earth, integral and whole,
From the seed's embryo.
My years must be a harvest for that bread
Whence more than flesh is fed . . .
Here must I reach, through earth, the strength and grace
Earth cannot wholly give, but may transmit;
Until I touch, within the finite place,
The placeless infinite.

E. Merrill Root, Dawn Is Forever.
Published by Packard and Company, Chicago.

A DEFENCE OF POETRY

Man is an instrument over which a series of external and internal impressions are driven, like the alternations of an ever-changing wind over an Aeolian lyre, which move it by their motion to ever-changing melody. But there is a principle within the human being, and perhaps within all sentient beings, which acts otherwise than in a lyre, and produces not melody alone, but harmony, by an internal adjustment of the sounds and motions thus excited to the impressions which excite them. It is as if the lyre could accommodate its chords to the motions of that which strikes them, in a determined proportion of sound; even as the musician can accommodate his voice to the sound of the lyre. . . .

Poetry awakens and enlarges the mind itself by rendering it the receptacle of a thousand unapprehended combinations of thought. Poetry lifts the veil from the hidden beauty of the world, and makes familiar objects be as if they were not familiar; it reproduces all that it represents, and the impersonations clothed in its Elysian light stand thenceforward in the minds of those who have once contemplated them, as memorials of that gentle and exalted content which extends itself over all thoughts and actions with which it coexists. The great secret of morals is love; or a going out of our own nature, and an identification of ourselves with the beautiful which exists in thought, action, or person, not our own. A man to be greatly good, must imagine intensely and comprehensively; he must put himself in the place of another and of many others; the pains and pleasures of his species must become his own. The great instrument of moral good is the imagination; and poetry administers to the effect by acting upon the cause. Poetry enlarges the circumference of the imagination by replenishing it with thoughts of ever new delight, which have the power of attracting and assimilating to their own nature all other thoughts, and which form new intervals and interstices whose void for ever craves fresh food. . . .

Poetry is the record of the best and happiest moments of the happiest and best minds. We are aware of evanescent visitations of thought and feeling, sometimes regarding our own mind alone, and always arising unforseen and departing unbidden, but elevating and delightful beyond all expression: so that even in the desire and the regret they leave, there cannot but be pleasure, participating as it does in the nature of its object. It is as it were the interpenetration of a diviner nature through our own: but its footsteps are like those of a wind over the sea, which the coming calm erases, and whose traces remain only, as on the wrinkled sand which paves it. . . .

Poetry thus makes immortal all that is best and most beautiful in the world; it arrests the vanishing apparitions which haunt the interlunations of life, and veiling them, or in language or in form, sends them forth among mankind, bearing sweet news of kindred joy to those with whom their sisters abide—abide, because there is no portal of expression from the caverns of the spirit which they inhabit into the universe of things. Poetry redeems from decay the visitations of the divinity in man.

Poetry turns all things to loveliness; it exalts the beauty of that which is most beautiful, and it adds beauty to that which is most deformed; it marries exultation and horror, grief and pleasure, eternity and change; it subdues to union, under its light yoke, all irreconsilable things. It transmutes all that it touches, and every form moving within the radiance of its presence is changed by wondrous sympathy to an incarnation of the spirit which it breathes: its secret alchemy turns to potable gold the poisonous waters which flow from death through life; it strips the veil of familiarity from the world, and lays bare the naked and sleeping beauty, which is the spirit of its forms.

SHELLEY's *Defence of Poetry.*

A PRAYER

As in the night beside the sea the moon sends its light to each man's feet, so send Thy radiance to every soul and deal with us one by one in the secret places of our hearts.

HARRY EMERSON FOSDICK.

Understand the Actual: Eighth Tuesday

51. CITY FERRY

(Chant of the Weary Workers)

A-drift. . . . Let us drift this night, let us drift on the river,
Herded and huddled. Our boat drifts on and on.
The dim far lights of the city shiver.
Dim in our hearts the lost lights quiver.
We are leaden and weary and wan.

Let us drift . . . let us drift, let us drift, let us drift forever.
A fog's in the air. . . . The river is white and still.
They are gleams, they are dreams, the ships that are faintly pass-
    ing;
They are gleams, they are dreams, that the river is softly glass-
    ing. . . .
O city, have pity this night! All day we have bent to your will!

Is it thy breath, O Death, that has touched the city?
That has made that hard face soft, and those hard eyes kind?
Is it Death that has brought and taught to our master pity?
Is it thy white breath, O Death, in the heart of the city,
And is it a corpse and a phantom we leave behind?

Is it Death? . . . Let us drift. We are weary, too weary for weep-
    ing;
Too weary to labor, to love, too weary to roam.
The waters, the air and the sky, they are sleeping, sleeping.
Let us drift. . . . On the air a silence like sorrow is creeping.
We are weary of going to work. O God! We are weary of going
    home!

                                EDWARD H. PFEIFFER, in *The Survey*.

DAILY LABOR OF THE PEOPLE

In the daily labor of the people
by and through which life goes on
the people must laugh or go down.

The slippery roads, icy tools, stalled engines, snowdrifts, hot boxes, cold motors, wet matches, mixed signals, time schedules, washouts,

The punch-clock, the changes from decent foremen to snarling straw-bosses, the sweltering July sun, the endless pounding of a blizzard, the sore muscles, the sudden backache and the holding on for all the backache,

The quick thinking in wrecks and breakdowns, the fingers and thumbs clipped off by machines, the machines that behave no better no worse no matter what you call them, the coaxing of a machine and fooling with it till all of a sudden she starts and you're not sure why,

A ladder rung breaking and a legbone or armbone with it, layoffs and no paycheck coming, the red diphtheria card on the front door, the price for a child's burial casket, hearse and cemetery lot,

The downrun from butter to oleo to lard to sorghum, the gas meter on the blink, the phone taken out, the bills and again bills, for each ten dollars due ten cents to pay with or nothing to pay with only debts and debts,

The human sardines of the rush hour car and bus, the gnawing fear of defeat till a workman never before licked says now-I'm-licked, the boy who says to-hell-with-work-you-never-got-anywhere-working-and-I'm-going-to-be-a-bum-good-by, the girl who doesn't know which way to go and has a wild look about it,

The pleasant surprises of changing weather when the saying passes it's-a-nice-day-isn't-it and they-can't-take-this-away-from-us, the shine of spring sunlight on a new planted onion patch after bright rain, the slow learning of what makes a good workman and the comfort of handling good tools, the joy of working with the right kind of a crew and a foreman who is "one of us," a foreman who understands,

The lurking treachery of machinery, good printers cursing "the innate cussedness of inanimate things," the pouring of molten ore at the right nick and the timing of the clutch of a crane or a lifting derrick or the dump of a steam shovel or the toss of a hawser from boatdeck to dockpost or the slowing to a stop for a red light or the eye on the clock for the deadline of a job marked rush,

The grades and lines of workmen, how one takes care and puts
the job through with the least number of motions and an-
another is careless and never sure what he is doing and
another is careful and means well but the gang knows he
belongs somewhere else and another is a slouch for work but
they are glad to have him for his jokes and clowning.

The people laugh, yes, the people laugh.
They have to in order to live and survive under lying politicians,
lying labor skates, lying racketeers of business, lying newspapers, lying ads.
The people laugh even at lies that cost them toil and bloody exactions.
For a long time the people may laugh, until a day when the laughter changes key and tone and has something it didn't have.
Then there is a scurrying and a noise of discussion and an asking
of the question what is it the people want.
Then there is the pretense of giving the people what they want,
with jokers, trick clauses, delays and continuances, with lawyers and fixers, playboys and ventriloquists, bigtime promises.
Time goes by and the gains are small for the years go slow, the
people go slow, yet the gains can be counted and the laughter of the people foretokening revolt carries fear to those
who wonder how far it will go and where to block it.

CARL SANDBURG, *The People, Yes.*
Published by Harcourt, Brace & Co., New York. Reprinted by permission.

FARE MORE REPULSIVE

Back in 1932 social workers in Chicago reported that many
people were poking around in the city's garbage dumps, seeking
means to stay their hunger. Each time a truck arrived and emptied
its refuse on the heap there was a scramble for first chance at
the new delicacies. The report shocked the public. But the social
workers were not surprised. The situation was and is commonly
observable in this richest nation in the world. The ups and downs
of prosperity decrease and increase the numbers of those who sub-
sist on fare more repulsive than the food for swine to which the
Prodigal Son turned during the famine in the far country. Some

people are always visiting the garbage dumps; in 1932 the number was unusually high.

But 1932 was no year of famine. American elevators never before held so much wheat as they held that year. It was no year of famine prices. Wheat was selling at the lowest price recorded since Queen Elizabeth's reign. Other agricultural markets were also glutted. Farm prices in general had fallen to about 44 per cent of 1929 figure. Perishable foods rotted in the fields, because prices would not pay costs of transportation.

With prices on the farm so low the farm families were pinched. Little clothing or furniture or machinery was purchased, which added to the distress in the cities. Even with the most rigorous thrift farm taxes and the interest on the mortgage could not be met. Tax sales and mortgage foreclosures kept sheriffs busy. These conditions do not merely illustrate the now familiar paradox of "poverty in the midst of plenty"; they illustrate the further fact that abundant cheap food does not guarantee an abundance to eat.

FERRY L. PLATT, in *Social Action*.

A PRAYER

God of all wisdom, source of light, and meaning behind our world, keep us from an ignorance which makes us think we know all things. May we have the humble heart and quiet mind of truly wise men, who sense the unknowable in the midst of card-catalogued knowledge, and sense the unseen beyond the bounds of sight. May we be as courageous as true science and as honest as true religion. May we dare to live what we know and find in it the joy of living, that the sons of men shall be free and become Thy sons O God, through Christ.

ALLAN KNIGHT CHALMERS, *The Commonplace Prodigal*.
Published by Henry Holt and Company, New York.

Be Concerned: Eighth Wednesday

52. CAVES OF ILLUSION

By false desires and false thoughts man has built up for himself a false universe: as a mollusc, by the deliberate and persistent absorption of lime and rejection of all else, can build up for itself a hard shell which shuts it from the external world, and only represents in a distorted and unrecognisable form the ocean from which it was obtained. This hard and wholly unnutritious shell, this one-sided secretion of the surface-consciousness, makes as it were a little cave of illusion for each separate soul. ... We see a sham world because we live a sham life. We do not know ourselves; hence do not know the true character of our senses and instincts; hence attribute wrong values to their suggestions and declarations concerning our relation to the external world.

EVELYN UNDERHILL, *Mysticism.*
Published by E. P. Dutton & Company, New York.

PRACTICAL ATHEISM

If we search for the root of the modern trouble we shall find it in that attitude of practical atheism which would confine human activity to the scope of the visible world, and finds the purpose of life in the gratification of the instinct for accumulating material goods. ... The ideal of material wealth has probably become more generally accepted in this age than at any other period of the Christian era. In company with individualism and the dogma or "self-realization" as we have described it, the pursuit of "success" has erected a kind of moral code and almost a religion of Mammon. There is no longer much hyprocrisy about the pursuit of money and the advantages which wealth can secure. We scarcely think it necessary to pretend to be doing anything else. The getting of gain is set forth as one of the supreme duties which a man owes to himself; and he who has not succeeded in this is quietly but surely estimated as a failure indeed. One conspicuous effect of this is that the masses of the poor, possibly quite as ready as the rich to burn incense in the temple of Mammon, are being taught to turn the political discussion into a purely economic discussion; and if the ideals of human life remain what they are today, and the poor do not get the better of the argument, the resort to other and more disastrous methods may yet be made in places far away from Russia. . . .

For the Christian, the question has arisen, To what ends, for what purposes, have I utilized my powers? When the soul thus begins with clear eyes to gaze upon itself, it discovers a spectacle not unlike the famous painting of Mona Lisa—that inscrutable face from which, as one beholds, the calm smile of purity sometimes seems to pass, revealing depths of treacherous insincerity. When Cardinal Manning was elevated to the Archiepiscopate of Westminster, he went into retreat, and recorded in his diaries the course of his self-examination. He therein declared that when he came to analyze *any one acton* of his past life, he was self-condemned, and desired to hide himself from himself. The soul enters into Christian experience only in one way. Reviewing itself and its whole activity, it must cry, "God be merciful to me a sinner." Nor does this self-conviction disappear with spiritual progress. The greatest Christian saints are most surely convinced of the enormity of their own sin; and thus man is in the paradoxical position that in his greatest spiritual advances he becomes only the more aware of his utter dependence upon the mercy of God. For the supreme answer of the spirit of man to the question of man's worthiness, according to the Evangelical testimony, is the admission that he is such a creature as has involved God Himself in the Sacrifice of Calvary. . . .

In the most fundamental relation of his existence, every man is a beggar; and his utter helplessness has been relieved only by an amazing adventure of generous love, undertaken by God. This is the explanation why not even the purest saint can ever achieve a standing of absolute moral credit. This is the explanation of Christian humility, which is numinous awe deeply charged with ethical penitence. No matter how great a thing a man may do, though he learn to speak with tongues of angels, or give his body to be burned, there is always an infinitely greater thing that has been done for him. He knows that he has cost God Bethlehem and Calvary, and his every prayer, as long as he live, must contain some strain of confession.

The heaviest batteries of the a-moralists have been turned upon the Christian ethic of meekness and humility. It has been described as "slave-morality," unfit for strong men. Yet it is a little curious that an age which has listened to such attacks seems extraordinarily lacking in strong men. The would-be supermen have assumed an appearance of paltriness. The glorification of "strength" has apparently produced a world incapable of managing its own affairs, a world which none but a lunatic can survey with much satisfaction. The superman in industry and *real-politik* has created a situation which is now sending cold shivers down his own spine. . . .

The acceptance of Evangelical experience logically involves collision with the whole social and economic structure which requires that our contribution to the world's well-being shall be based upon reward. Any man who believes that he is fundamentally in debt to start with, must know that the motive of his activity *in any sphere* ought to be nothing other than grateful self-offering. He must know that a system which requires him to advertise and proclaim his own merits, and expects him to sell his services to his fellow-men as dearly as possible: a system which requires him to push himself before his neighbour, and offers the greatest prizes to those who can push hardest, is utterly at variance with the Evangelical principle and a denial of its first assumptions. He must know that the whole category of private gain as the motive of work is the very antithesis of the spiritual attitude demanded by the Gospel. He must see that only by a subtle hypocrisy are men able to recognize themselves as beggars in the sight of God, while straining every nerve to appear as millionaires in the sight of men. They divorce the affairs of this world from the control of religion, and split themselves into unrelated compartments. The result is that the secular world is in complete confusion, and religion seems unreal. If the Gospel is to be determinative of a man's whole outlook, there is not the slightest doubt that it will cause him to feel the modern economic system as an irksome restraint upon his soul. . . .

The full impact of the Gospel upon modern life will never be felt, so long as official religion shrinks from proclaiming the social implications of conversion. It is strange, indeed, if man, so gravely a sinner that God must suffer shame and death for his redemption, and remaining in the mass still impenitent, has yet contrived a system of human relations which is sacrosanct. Is it not much more likely that the modern age, which has notoriously neglected religion, has produced a system which is damnable? Is it probable that while the world of individuals is heedless of God, the structure of society will have respect to God? Precisely how the transition from the present order is to be made may be a matter of debate; but that the Gospel demands some transition of a revolutionary character should be easily apparent to all who believe that God once walked as a poor man upon our earthly roads.

W. G. PECK, *The Divine Society.*
Published by the Student Christian Movement, London.

A PRAYER

God be in my head, and in my understanding;
God be in mine eyes, and in my looking;
God be in my mouth, and in my speaking;
God be in my heart, and in my thinking;
God be at mine end, and at my departing.

SARUM PRIMER.

A PRAYER

O Thou Great spirit of Truth and Freedom and Righteousness, we thank Thee that we dwell in a land of religious freedom, in which no creed or faith is given legal preference; in a land where every man may worship in whatever manner best pleases him, or not at all, according to the dictates of his own conscience.

We thank Thee that the rights of free speech, a free press, and free assemblage are guaranteed by the organic law of the nation. But, O God, save us from the sin of pride and overconfidence! On every hand we see countries in which religious and political freedom have been ruthlessly suppressed.

May we not, then, forget, as we enjoy these inestimable privileges, that they were won only by centuries of bitter struggle and suffering and can be maintained only by jealous watchfulness for and vigorous resistance to every threatened infringement.

We would especially petition, O God, to be kept from the arrogance and presumption which would deny to others, when we are strong, the rights we craved, when weak, for thou art a just God and will reward us according to our deeds.

Grant us then, O God, strength of body, mind, and spirit, that we may strive for the establishment of peace, justice, and freedom upon the earth, and that right speedily. Amen.

KENNETH W. PORTER.

Endeavor to Transform: Eighth Thursday

53. ABOVE EACH CALDRON

Above each caldron of disaster hangs
A star: and after Armageddon, light,
Unknown before, shall fall upon the world;
See, how beyond the blackness there, the deep
Of it turns blue. Wait patiently awhile.
The saffron edge of a supernal world
Appears to him who greets its grace as come.

EDWARDS DAVIS, *Lovers of Life.*
Published by Baker & Taylor Company, New York.

WITHOUT VIOLENCE

To those acquainted with the bloody history of labor struggles in Butte, Montana, it may be a surprise to know that this city has just ended a four and a half months' strike against the Anaconda copper mining company successfully. When the strike began the city was flooded with correspondents and writers of every description looking for blood and thunder copy. Hearing that a strike was in progress in "Bloody Butte" they all rushed to the kill. But this strike, even though one of the longest in recent history, failed to provide the sort of copy the news hounds were after, and few journals even saw fit to mention it. San Francisco and Minneapolis stole the front pages. "Bloody Butte" failed to live up to its reputation. Those hunting sensational news were forced to seek more fertile fields.

Butte labor may not have made good copy but it made history for it secured peaceably everything the workers in California and Minnesota fought and died for and failed to get. It secured a guaranteed minimum wage higher than the existing wage, for a period of six months to a year, with a sliding scale better than had ever been guaranteed this camp; a closed shop agreement that is not surpassed anywhere in the country; and an ideal set-up for the operations of the grievance board. It secured these concessions from a corporation which has maintained a stranglehold on the city, county and state for years; from a company which owns most of the banks, newspapers, radio stations, water systems, and controls most of the utilities in the state; secured all these things, I repeat, without loss of life, bloodshed, or violence in a long, drawn-out struggle. How was this accomplished?

It was accomplished because the peace officers and the governor refused to call out troops or deputize thugs and gunmen for the company to use against striking workers. When the strike began the company presented the sheriff with a list of names and asked that he deputize these men. This the sheriff refused to do, stating that he could very well pick men who would protect property when the occasion arose. This was the first time in the history of the county when a sheriff refused to do the bidding of the company in time of labor trouble. As a result, there were no legalized deputies to beat and gas men engaged in peaceful picketing. The sheriff also gave assurance that the strikers would be guaranteed the right to picket so long as no violence occurred.

Both the governor and the sheriff asked the company to keep its thugs off the streets so that serious trouble might be avoided. They told the company that if one of these gunmen was again found on the streets fully armed he would be arrested and jailed. This ultimatum was delivered because previous trouble had been started by gunmen armed with sawed-off shotguns, plenty of ammunition, tear-gas bombs, and automatic pistols. It was evident that trouble had not occurred until these hired gunmen came into town and forced it upon the striking men. . . . The strikers not only worked to prevent violence on the part of their own members, but also picketed with the object of preventing the company from instigating further violence intended to force the governor to call in the militia. As a result there were no more street fights, no more fires, and no more dynamiting.

After four and a half months the company officials sat around the conference table with the strike committee and settled their differences fairly and peaceably. The striking men did not win everything they asked for but they won the most vital points, and the cost to the company will be less than they paid to gunmen and scabs in trying to break the strike. The strike was settled without loss of life or property. It cost the city and county nothing for special police; it cost the state nothing for armed troops; the feeling is the best this city has known in the past decade; and settlement will be more permanent than any made in the past through the use of armed forces. It all came about because Montana has a governor who would not be swayed by the hysterics of a company-dominated daily press; because Montana has a governor who is not too far above the workers to talk with them and secure their cooperation in keeping peace; because Butte has peace officers, well trained, able to keep their heads, not easily frightened with threats of political annihilation if they failed to do the bidding of the company.

CHARLES E. SEBOLD, in *The Christian Century*.

AN EARLY CHRISTIAN DOCUMENT

You know that you servants of God dwell in a foreign land, for your city is far from this city. If, then, you know the city where you are to dwell, why provide yourselves here with fields and expensive luxuries and buildings and chambers to no purpose? He who makes such provision for this city has no mind to return to his own city. Foolish, double-minded, wretched man! seest thou not that all these things are foreign to thee and controlled by another? . . . So beware. Dwelling in a foreign land, provide thyself with nothing more than a suitable competency; and whenever the master of this city expels thee for opposing his law, be ready to leave his city and seek thine own, keeping thine own law cheerfully and unmolested. So beware, you that serve God and have him in your heart; perform his works, mindful of his commandments and of the promises he has made, in the faith that he will perform the latter if the former be observed. Instead of fields, then, buy souls in trouble, as each of you is able; visit widows and orphans, and neglect them not; expend on such fields and houses, which God has given to you (i.e., on the poor), your wealth and all your pains. The Master endowed you with riches that you might perform such ministries for him. Far better is it to buy fields, possessions, houses of this kind; thou wilt find them in thine own city when thou dost visit it. Such expenditure is noble and cheerful; it brings joy, not fear and sorrow. Practice not the expenditure of pagans, then; that ill becomes you, as God's servants. Practice your proper expenditure, in which you may rejoice. Do not stamp things falsely; never touch other people's property, nor lust after it, for it is evil to lust after what belongs to other people. Do thine own task and thou shalt be saved.

"The Parable of Hermas," quoted by Adolf Harnack, *The Expansion of Christianity in the First Three Centuries*. Published by G. P. Putnam's Sons, New York.

PEACE

Fed by the countless bodies of the slain,
    Out of the bones that crumbled into dust,
Catered to by the centuries of pain,
    At last will climb the hardy flower of trust. . . .
At last in every land forever freed,
    Over all vanished battle-lines, will rise,
Cemented by a stronger force than greed,
    Temples of peace to eavesdrop on the skies.
Nations, no longer by their own selves trapped,
    Will learn how boundaries of all countries start
And end in love-degrees—how lands are mapped
    Only by boundaries of the human heart;
How happy blood, that through each body sings,
    Arises from the same, immortal springs.
                    LOUIS GINSBERG, in *The World Tomorrow*.

A PRAYER

O God, who hast made of one blood all the nations of mankind, so that all are children and members one of another, how is
it that we are so slow to trace the family likeness, so reluctant
to claim our common kinship? We pray thee, O our God, to make
the peoples one.

We pray that since man's need is one, we all may find the
one way to thee, the one God. Forbid that in our highest things
we should find fellowship impossible. May the spirit of Christ
break down all barriers and answer the desire of all nations.
                    W. E. ORCHARD.

Proceed Resolutely: Eighth Friday

54. IF THERE BE FLAME IN YOU

We have had enough of hearth-ease, enough
Of the comfort-sodden soul, the slippered sloth:
If there be flame in you, if there be stuff
Of the swift blood laughing every rebuff
Down, unwrap your heart of its heavy cloth,
Shake out the dust, stamp out the stealthy moth
That feeds on disillusion and fat ease!
There, at your window, gloom the deep-chester seas!
The slaty peevish gulls, the plunging ships
Go down the wind together; and together
The wind and tide go in the sun-washed weather;
And the sun is clinging with sullen fingertips
To the horizon . . . inch by inch light slips. . . .

Go then, strip off your sick and woolen sloth!
Look, the young moon horned like a Visigoth!
Night is a blue leopard spotted with silver stars!
Adventure crouches where the sunset chars
To a last vivid puff! Go, leave behind
The nervous walls, the satisfied books, the kind
Cruelty of too much companionship, the blind
Routine! Go, empty of hands, cleaned out once more,
For the incalculable To-Morrow! Shut the door!

JOSEPH AUSLANDER, in *The World Tomorrow*.

EUGENE VICTOR DEBS

Susan B. Anthony was coming to town! The "female fire-brand" from the East was to speak in Terre Haute. Even the Occidental Literary Club, which had brought Wendell Phillips to the city, was afraid to sponsor the suffragette. One young member challenged, "All right, if you're afraid. I'll handle the matter myself!"

It was more of an undertaking than Eugene Debs had anticipated. He hired the hall and met her at the station. He escorted her through the main street. Her hat was on one side of her head; she chattered as they walked. A street loafer guffawed loudly. Gene stopped abruptly and faced the scoffer. There was fire in his wide blue eyes. The laughing stopped. But that evening there was no audience. The young idealist was fortunate to get the despised radical safely out of Terre Haute. Even his friends were disgusted with him.

At eighteen, this blue-eyed, muscular giant was firing a freight engine on the seventy-mile run from his home town to Indianapolis. He had a love for the railroad and became a pioneer in the Brotherhood of Locomotive Engineers and Firemen. The early years of his life were given to the organization of the railroad workers of America. . . .

The organizer of railway brotherhoods became the leader of the Socialist party in the United States. He was a sturdy campaigner for the rights of the laboring man. He was a socialist but not a communist. . . . Debs was a revolutionist, but he thought of a bloodless revolution that was to come about through peaceful and democratic methods, not by guns and executions.

With the beginning of the World War, Eugene Debs was outspoken in his opposition to the war. It was a violation of his faith in international brotherhood. He was arrested in June, 1917, after a speech in Cleveland, and tried by a jury of farmers. . . .

"I have been accused of having obstructed the war. I admit it. Gentlemen, I abhor war. I would oppose the war if I stood alone. When I think of a cold, glittering steel bayonet being plunged in the white, quivering flesh of a human being I recoil with horror. I have often wondered if I could take the life of a fellow man, even to save myself. . . . I do not believe that the shedding of blood bears any actual testimony to patriotism, to lead a country to civilization."

The American people were at war. The jury of farmers deliberated for five hours and gave the verdict, "Guilty as charged in the indictment." Debs received the sentence of ten years in the penitentiary with these words, "I can see the dawn of a better day of humanity. The people are awakening. In due course of time they will come into their own."

In Atlanta penitentiary he determined to dedicate the balance of his life to prison reform. He drew up his prison creed:

"While there is a lower class I am in it;
While there is a criminal element I am of it;
While there's a soul in prison I am not free."

Robert M. Bartlett, They Dared To Live.
Published by Association Press, New York.

LATENT ENERGY

Four years ago, at midnight, I witnessed an explosion at a great munition factory, and afterwards heard that a woman, after her day's work, had risen from bed and, in anxiety for the safety of her husband and son, had run practically the whole distance of seven miles to the scene of the explosion in an incredibly short time.

William McDougall quotes the case of a boy who, being chased by a furious animal, leaped a fence which he could never afterwards scale even as a grown man, and after continuous athletic training. The emotion of fear liberated powers which his strength of will could never equal.

I asked three men to submit themselves to test the effect of mental suggestion on their strength, which was measured by gripping a dynamometer. I tested them (1) in their normal waking condition; (2) after suggesting to them under hypnosis that they were "weak"; (3) after suggesting under hypnosis that they were "very strong." In each case the men were told to grip the dynamometer as tightly as they could—that is to say, to exert the will to the utmost. Under hypnosis the mind is very suggestible, and the response to the suggestions of weakness and strength gave very remarkable results. In the normal waking condition the men gave an average grip of 101 pounds. When, under hypnosis, I had given the men the idea that they were very weak, the average grip was only 29 pounds, one of them, a prize-fighter, remarking that his arm felt "tiny, just like a baby's." My suggestions of strength produced an average grip of 142 pounds as against the 101 pounds which was the best they could do in their normal waking conditions. A second test, measured by the time occupied in holding out a weight, gave similar results. In brief, when I suggested "weakness," the full flood of energy was checked and the men were capable of only one-third of their normal strength, whereas by suggestion of "strength" latent powers were liberated and their normal strength increased by half as much again.

Such an experiment shows us that, *when our minds our depressed with the idea of weakness, our strength may be diminished by two-thirds;* whereas if we have the stimulus of a great inspiration our strength may thereby be increased by one-half.

J. Arthur Hadfield, in *The Spirit,* edited by B. H. Streeter. By permission of the Macmillan Company, Publishers, New York.

MAN'S CRUELTY TO MAN

A cross is two pieces of wood, nailed together to make an instrument of torture, and death by torture. It carried originally no associations but those which a decent mind would shun. The lingering end of a crucified criminal was a sight to break the heart and sear the mind of any beholder. There was no sanctity which was not dishonored when they crucified a man. Stripped of its specifically Christian associations, a cross might fitly have symbolized the incredible cruelty of man to man. . . .

Such a death for such a Man! That *they,* being what they were, should crucify *Him,* being what He was—this might well have been remembered as the crowning infamy of human history. The cross might have remained as the symbol of man's incurable depravity, proof against the divinest appeal, and the Word of the cross only a verdict of infinite contempt for humanity.

But the New Testament knows no such word as this. Its message is far otherwise—"God forbid that I should glory, save in the cross of our Lord Jesus Christ." To Jews a stumbling-block, to Greeks a piece of foolishness, but to believers the manifestation of the power and wisdom of God. For this psychological reversal I see no other name than miracle.

W. Russell Maltby, *Christ and His Cross.*
Published by the Abingdon Press, New York.

A PRAYER

We thank Thee, O God, that Thou hast given us powers of mind to search into the laws of Thy universe; and we pray that our reverence may increase with our knowledge. With each advance in the researches and discoveries of scientists and economists, engineers and psychologists, may we be led to worship Thee in deepening humility. And seeing our own littleness in the light of Thy creative wisdom, may we devote ourselves to the fulfilment of Thy great purposes for mankind.

A. Margaret Worsdell,

Seek Comradeship: Eighth Saturday

55. BLIND

I am blind:
I cannot see.
Color is no bar to me.
I do not know
Nor black nor white—
I walk in night.
And yet it seems I see mankind
More tortured than the blind!
Can it be that those who know
Sight are thus condemned to woe?
Or is it that seeing
They never see
With the infinite eyes
Of one blind
Like me?

LANGSTON HUGHES, in *Christendom.*

"SCUM OF THE RACE"

"Scum of the race!" Know, out of scum
The world's enduring heroes come.
An amaranthine hero needs
Kinship with plebeian weeds
As well as with patrician flowers
Above them soaring like church towers.

"Scum of the race!" The stone you hurl
Would light on Nancy Hanks, would curl
Diogenes' large lips in scorn;
Nor would it miss a hero born
In Galilee of humble folk
As ever bore the patient yoke
Of poverty, a hero still
Who bends the Occidental will
Toward love and brotherhood, and lifts
Man's hope beyond the cosmic drifts. . . .

WILBERT SNOW, in *The World Tomorrow.*

CURRICULUM OF COMPANIONSHIP

Think of that first Christian theological seminary which was conducted by Jesus on the hills of Galilee. The first lessons were a long, long way from what many of us would have put first. In that curriculum there was an orientation course for new students; but it was not exactly of the kind which are designed in theological schools today, when the curriculum is revised every second year. I must confess that had I been Dean of that seminary I would have put in a course in "The Social and Political Problems of the Mediterranean Basin." Was that not the world which the disciples would have to face? I would have put in a course on "The Strategy of Propaganda Amid the Greco-Roman Culture." Jesus put first, in that curriculum of companionship, quite another lesson—Our Father. He saw clearly the issues involved in bringing the good news of the Kingdom into that world. He knew the clashes that would come. He told his disciples, "Ye shall stand before governors and kings." But he knew that if they did not face God it was not much use to face anything. That is elementary, but it is not irrelevant to our whole church life. Our first task is not to get people to *do* something, but rather to *receive* something, ourselves to share something. Jesus' first word to his disciples was not "go," but "come." We frequently reverse the order. We start with alarms and excursions, and the expeditions are often futile and short-lived, because we have not first freely received; we have not shared Jesus' calm faith in God and fellowship with God. . . .

Man needs God to bring the meaning of life into sharp focus. That meaning has blurred for millions. Somerset Maugham has recorded the spiritual odyssey of multitudes of his twentieth century in his symbolism of the figure in the Persian carpet as told in *Of Human Bondage*. The mysterious pattern wove into the carpet was supposed to hold the secret of the meaning of life. For a long time the hero of the story was baffled to find any clue to it. He finally discovered that the meaning of life was that there was no meaning. That novelist Ossorgin in *Quiet Street* paints a similar picture when he says that "life is entering by a narrow gate, stumbling like a lunatic as we go, and then making our exit at another narrow gate, where the turnstile clicks and the keeper lets us out with a ghastly grin as if to mock us." The same idea and almost the same words appear in an American prophet of blankness, Theodore Dreiser, who says that we enter the world, live through several decades, and as we make our exit, "catch no meaning from all we have seen and pass quite as we come confused and dismayed." Those passages may be dismissed as the speculations of intellectuals, or even as a literary post. But they represent a feeling which many have. A college paper a few years ago offered a prize for "the best definition of life" and many campus cynics had a wonderful time. Here are a few definitions which won "honorable mention": "Life is a bad joke which isn't even funny." "Life is a disease for which the only cure is death." "Life is a jail sentence which we get for the crime of being born." We can dismiss these as merely lively adolescent prancing. Yet they may stand as an indication of a lack of sense of high meaning to existence. They indicate a fact which has a bearing on both theology and psychology, that it is hard to keep unframed meaning. It is hard to keep clear a sense of deep meaning in life unless it is put in a cosmic frame. That is just what Jesus did—set life in the frame of a conviction of God. Such a conviction heightens and deepens the meaning of every experience of life. The absence of such a framework, the lack of an outlook and perspective which might throw a shaft of light on the picture of life and our place in it, is a major cause of the breaking down, the "tearing apart" of personality. . . .

Faith in man, if it is to stand the daily assaults which contemporary history makes upon it, depends on faith in God. A stout faith in man is desperately needed today, and desperately hard to maintain. We need a special grace these days before reading the daily paper, a grace to enable us to believe in the possibilities of man, in the face of the evidence of the daily spread of imbecilities recorded there. We can understand the mood of Thomas Carlyle when he said that the population of England was "thirty millions—mostly fools"; or of Bernard Shaw when he said that the other planets must use the Earth as an insane asylum. We can even understand the black bitter mood of Mark Twain when he wrote, back in 1887: "Special providence! That phrase nauseates me—with its implied importance of mankind and triviality of God. In my opinion these myriads of globes are merely the blood corpuscles ebbing and flowing through the arteries of God and we but animalculae that infest them, disease them, pollute them; and God does not know we are there and would not care if He did."

Our very sensitiveness to ethical wrong may betray us into a chronic neurotic contempt. If faith in the potentialities of man and of society is to survive under the ferocious pounding to which it is daily exposed, it will do so in the strength of other sources than confidence in our contemporary civilization. If we are to avoid cynicism, we must look at man with faith, faith in man's Creator, faith in the Divine Will acting through men.

HALFORD E. LUCCOCK, *Christianity and the Individual in a World of Crowds.*
Published by Cokesbury Press, Nashville.

OUTWITTED

He drew a circle that shut me out—
Heretic, rebel, a thing to flout.
But Love and I had the wit to win:
We drew a circle that took him in!

EDWIN MARKHAM.
Published by Doubleday, Doran & Co., New York.

A PRAYER

Grant unto us, O Lord, the royalty of inward happiness and the serenity which comes from living close to Thee. Daily renew in us the sense of joy, and let Thy eternal spirit dwell in our souls and bodies, filling every corner of our hearts with light and gladness: so that, bearing about with us the infection of a good courage, we may be diffusers of life, and meet all that comes, of good or ill, even death itself, with gallant and high-hearted happiness: giving Thee thanks always for all things.

The Splendour of God.

Worship God: Eighth Sunday

56. HIGH TIDE

Flood thou my soul with thy great quietness,
    O let thy wave
Of silence from the deep
Roll in on me, the shores of sense to lave:
So doth thy living water softly creep
    Into each cave
And rocky pool, where ocean creatures hide
Far from their home, yet nourished of thy tide.
    Deep-sunk they wait
    The coming of thy great
Inpouring stream that shall new life communicate;
Then, starting from beneath some shadowy ledge
    Of the heart's edge,
Flash sudden colored memories of the sea
    Whence they were born of thee
Across the mirrored surface of the mind.
    Swift rays of wondrousness
        They seem;
    And rippling thoughts arise
        Fan-wise
From the quick-darting passage of the dream,
    To spread and find
    Each creviced narrowness
Where the dark waters dwell,
    Mortally still,
        Until
    The Moon of Prayer,
That by the invincible sorcery of love
    God's very self can move,
    Draws thy life-giving flood
        E'en there.
    Then the great swell
    And urge of grace
Refresh the weary mood;
Cleansing anew each sad and stagnant place

That seems shut off from thee,
And hardly hears the murmur of the sea.

EVELYN UNDERHILL, *Theophanies.*
Published by E. P. Dutton & Co., New York City.
Reprinted by permission.

GOD SPEAKS

"God speaks." Aye, and with what voice? Ordinarily we men communicate, one with another, by perceptible signals—gestures, sounds, written symbols, and the like—which need to be interpreted by the observer, if the intent of the sender is to be revealed. . . . Through "the starry heavens above and the moral law within" comes general revelation; through illuminating crises, apparently slashing across but in fact carrying forward eruptively the stream of events, come special revelations. . . .

Jesus' life and death has brought into focus, for many, what otherwise would be a blurred and disheartening turmoil. Among "special revelations" it has a central place. But the meaning of it, too, needs to be discovered and apprehended through patient, penetrating study. It is not self-explanatory. For many besides the Jews and the Greeks of St. Paul's day, the cross has been a stumbling-block and an absurdity. Only to those who by faith, insight, devotion, have penetrated beyond the obvious, brutal denial of human decency and human hope in such a tragedy can it serve to reveal "the power of God and the wisdom of God."

Besides this more usual mode of communication through detailed, intentional signals, there is a rarer sort of communication between human persons, especially between those who know each other well through long life together. It is by no means confined to such long associations, and it need not be thought to involve other media than those ordinarily employed; but whatever the means, the outcome is of uncommon worth for living. There are clairvoyant moments when, without a word spoken or a conscious gesture made, the presence of another self comes home to one with vivid reality. One's friend, one's child, one's mate emerges from the fragmentary and often perfunctory contacts of routine association into galvanic aliveness and "immediacy." With such experiences, I venture to think, the visions of the mystics are to be compared. . . . And it is my strong persuasion now, mistaken or not, that in the true height of communion or confrontation, what is likely to be communicated is not some specific instruction for details of conduct, but such an unspoken word as "Fear not, I am with thee," or "Give in, and know that I am God!" Not one's stock of information, but stability of morale, joy of living, or basic direction of will, is primarily affected by the vividly felt presence of one's friend or of one's Maker. . . .

"The God of heaven, He will prosper us; therefore we His servants will arise and build." Here is no suggestion of rigid determinism nor of human futility. Here rather is the word of a vigorous human will, in the grip of firm conviction that God is a very present help in time of stress, and that *therefore* it is needful that men shall do with their might what their hands find to do. Divine support is no ground for human slacking. But neither does it leave room for human pride and self-satisfaction. "Except the Lord build the house, they labor in vain that build it"; and no thoughtful worker who is aware of God needs to be reminded that this is so.

ROBERT LOWRY CALHOUN, *God and the Common Life.*
Charles Scribner's Sons, publishers, New York. Printed by permission.

THE UNFATHOMABLE DEPTHS OF PRAYER

The passionate yearning which is poured forth in prayer does not spring from man's narrow heart but from God's eternal love to allure and to draw man upwards towards itself. . . . The longer a devout man continues in sincere supplication, and the more deeply he penetrates into the mysterious world of prayer, the more distinctly is the Invisible and the Eternal revealed to him. In prayer the vital feeling of the awful nearness of God is intensified until it issues in a spiritual vision of the Infinite, in an inner hearing of His word which summons, awakes, warns, and consoles. . . .

Since it is to him who prays in solitude that God reveals His nature and will, every new creation in the sphere of religion has its origin in solitary prayer. The great truths of revelation are ripened in the quiet of prayer and meditation; and here also great religious resolutions are taken. The solitude of prayer and of absorption is that which makes possible mysterious visions, ecstasies, and states of bliss, nay, it is the birthplace of world-religions and the source from which have sprung great religious reformations. In the lonely mountain of Sinai Jahve revealed Himself to Moses as the God of Israel; in secret fellowship with God the

Spirit of Jahve seized the awe-struck prophets and made them His messengers to proclaim His holy will to the people of Israel; in the stillness of prayer, at the baptism by the Jordan, this same Spirit came also upon Jesus of Nazareth and revealed to Him the profound secret of His divine sonship and Messianic task; in the lonely sojourn in the desert the Paul who had been laid hold of by Christ at Damascus won the power to become an Apostle to the Gentiles; on a solitary mount near Mecca Mohammed was called to be the messenger of Allah; in the remote crags of the highlands of Alverno, Francis of Assisi, as he prayed and meditated, was made one with his crucified Saviour and received the marks of His wounds; in private struggles in prayer Luther won at Worms that unshakable strength, assurance, and confidence with which he was able to defy a world of enemies, and as a man of prayer he became the great Reformer, the inaugurator of a new era in the history of Christianity. . . . Everything that is great, new, and creative in the history of religion rises up out of the unfathomable depths of prayer.

FRIEDRICH HEILER, *Prayer*.
Published by Oxford University Press, New York.

A SORROW AND A SHAME

But it is a sorrow and shame to think that the Eternal Goodness is ever most graciously guiding and drawing us, and we will not yield to it.

THEOLOGIA GERMANICA.

A PRAYER

O Heavenly Father, the Author and Fountain of all truth, the bottomless Sea of all understanding, send, we beseech Thee, Thy Holy Spirit into our hearts, and lighten our understandings with the beams of Thy heavenly grace. We ask this, O merciful Father, for Thy dear Son our Saviour, Jesus Christ's sake.

NICHOLAS RIDLEY.

Concentrate Upon the Ideal: Ninth Monday

57. THE STARRY HOST

The countless stars, which to our human eye
Are fixed and steadfast, each in proper place,
Forever bound to changeless points in space,
Rush with our sun and planets through the sky,
And like a flock of birds still onward fly;
Returning never whence began their race,
They speed their ceaseless way with gleaming face
As though God bade them win Infinity.
Ah whither, whither is their forward flight
Through endless time and limitless expanse?
What power with unimaginable might
First hurled them forth to spin in tireless dance?
What beauty lures them on through primal night,
So that for them to be is to advance?

JOHN LANCASTER SPALDING (1840-1916).

ASPECTS OF THE PINES

Tall, sombre, grim, against the morning sky
They rise, scarce touched by melancholy airs,
Which stir the fadeless foliage dreamfully,
As if from realms of mystical despairs.

Tall, sombre, grim, they stand with dusky gleams
Brightening to gold within the woodland's core,
Beneath the gracious noontide's tranquil beams,—
But the weird winds of morning sigh no more.

A stillness, strange, divine, ineffable,
Broods round and o'er them in the wind's surcease,
And on each tinted copse and shimmering dell
Rests the mute rapture of deep hearted peace.

Last, sunset comes—the solemn joy and might
Borne from the west when cloudless day declines—
Low, flute-like breezes sweep the waves of light,
And, lifting dark green tresses of the pines.

Till every lock is luminous, gently float,
Fraught with hale odors up the heavens afar,
To faint when twilight on her virginal throat
Wears for a gem the tremulous vesper star.

PAUL HAMILTON HAYNE (1830-1886).

THE MIRACLE OF DOING

I owe more to Christ for my unswerving conviction of the reality of God than to anything else in the universe. Whenever I find my way back to Him and really *see* Him living his marvelous life of love and trust and confidence and fellowship with God, I rise up in the strength of it and catch from Him a contagion of faith which is more than an anchor to the soul in the storm; it becomes a driving power that sends one forth to help build the Kingdom of God here and now. A prophet who wrote at the end of the apostolic period told of the coming of "new heavens and a new earth in which righteousness dwells." I am convinced that he put the two expectations in the right order. We shall not get, we shall not build, a new earth, ordered in peace and truth and righteousness, until we recover the reality of a living God and with it the reality of immortal life in Him and with Him. It is genuine faith in eternal values that makes a person struggle and suffer for great tasks and great issues. When once more that gripping power of faith in God returns to us we shall again accept crosses, prisons and scourgings. We shall rejoice to undertake the impossible and we shall see the miracle of actually *doing it*.

RUFUS JONES, *The Eternal Gospel*.
Published by The Macmillan Company, New York.

THE IDEAL WAY

Four great principles stand out clearly from His teaching. God is our Father and all men are our brethren. The Kingdom of God is at hand. Life is the measure of true value. All disciples are stewards. . . . God's Kingdom implies God's reign over the whole of human conduct, and carries with it a fellowship among His subjects. There is to be a Christian Society, a People of God, a Church, which shall be the light, the salt, the leaven of human life. But this Society is rather the means of realising the Kingdom than the Kingdom itself. Life, at its highest, is the knowledge of

God, but all human life comes within our Lord's purpose. Life itself is carefully distinguished from the material means of living; the service of Mammon is typical of the spirit of the "Kingdom of this age." Wealth is dangerous; and detachment from preoccupation with wealth is the first mark of the subjects of God's Kingdom. Men are responsible for their fellows, and for the use of the gifts which they themselves possess. "He that is faithful in that which is least is faithful also in much." In every station and position in life there must be fidelity. The Incarnation is a revelation of human duties. As the Son of God took man's whole nature upon Him nothing can be alien to Him. Man in the fulness of his nature is capable of fellowship with God, and the dominion of the spiritual must be extended over the whole of man's life in the world. The solidarity of the human race is implied in the universal manhood of our Lord. All the distinctions which cause division— nationality, class, sex—are merged in the Incarnate Son of God. "Ye are all one in Christ Jesus." Thus the Incarnation is the inexhaustible spring of brotherhood, and the Cross points to self-sacrifice as belonging to the very nature and character of God himself. Not self-development, but unselfish service, is the law of human life. The union of God and man, once accomplished, is continually effective. Men strive in dependence on a living God. "God has taken Humanity to Himself, and man redeemed in Christ is called to work out his destiny in reliance on the Holy Spirit." These central ideas found expression in the teaching of the New Testament writers and in the practice of the Early Church.

The Report of the Archbishops' Fifth Committee of Inquiry,
Christianity and Industrial Problems.
Published by the Society for Promoting Christian Knowledge, London.

WHY NOT GIVE CHRISTIANITY A TRIAL?

The question seems a hopeless one after 2000 years of resolute adherence to the old cry of "Not this man, but Barabbas." Yet it is beginning to look as if Barabbas was a failure, in spite of his strong right hand, his victories, his empires, his millions of money, and his moralities and churches and political constitutions. "This man" has not been a failure yet; for nobody has ever been sane enough to try his way. But he has had one quaint triumph. Barabbas has stolen his name and taken his cross as a standard. There is a sort of compliment in that. There is even a sort of loyalty in it, like that of the brigand who breaks every law and yet claims to be a patriotic subject of the king who makes them. We have always had a curious feeling that though we crucified Christ on a stick, he somehow managed to get hold of the right end of it, and that if we were better men we might try his plan. . . . The moneyed, respectable, capable world has been steadily anti-Christian and Barabbasque since the crucifixion; and the specific doctrine of Jesus has not in all that time been put into political or general social practice. I am no more a Christian than Pilate was, or you, gentle reader; and yet, like Pilate, I greatly prefer Jesus to Annas and Caiaphas; and I am ready to admit that after contemplating the world and human nature for nearly sixty years, I see no way out of the world's misery but the way which would have been found by Christ's will if he had undertaken the work of a modern practical statesman.

BERNARD SHAW, *Androcles and the Lion.*
Published by Dodd, Mead and Company, New York.

A PRAYER

Grant us, O God Who art our shield and sure defense, the grace of courage. Open our eyes to the power which attends Thy children if only they go quietly and confidently about their appointed tasks. Forgive us the distrust of ourselves, of life and Thee which find foes where there are none to make us afraid and besieges us by shadows, when the heights about us are full of the horses and chariots of God. In His name in Whose discipleship there is no place for fear. Amen.

GAIUS GLENN ATKINS.

A PRAYER

Grant unto us, Almighty God, that we, communing with one another and with thee, may feel our hearts burn within us; until all pure and just and holy things are lovely to us, and we find nothing to fear but that which is hateful in thine eyes. Let thy peace possess our souls, while we look to thy loving kindness and tender mercy to lift us above that which is low and mean; and, at last, give to the spirit within us a perfect victory, and bring us safe through death into life everlasting. Amen.

Services for Congregational Worship.

Understand the Actual: Ninth Tuesday

58. COMMISSIONED

You'll die for your country, you say;
    But dying is ill.
Your country wants more of you, boy;
    It wants you to kill.

Men, women, and children, to gas,
    Or to bomb into bits.
Not dying, but killing, my boy,
    Is the glory that hits.

It isn't for coffins and flowers
    You're taking the drill.
No! no! your commission, my boy,
    Is—TO KILL.

ROBERT WHITAKER, in *Social Song and Other Verse.*
Published by the Banner Press, Emory University, Atlanta, Ga.

THE MEN I KILLED

Strictly from the military point of view I have no regrets for having killed a subaltern of British infantry on that same morning I ordered our machine guns and rifles to be turned on the fleeing Portuguese. It happened on the Strazeel Road. It was a desperate emergency. I had to shoot him myself, along with a German who was running after him. My action *did* stem the tide; and that is what we were there for.

Vividly I still remember that scene. It might have been only yesterday. Never can I forget the agonized expression on that British youngster's face as he ran in terror, escaping from the ferocious Hun whose passions were a madness and who saw only red.

As I stood on the road, almost alone, after the incident, a car drove up. In it were a G.S.O.2 and C.R.E. One of them shouted out to me. Was all well? And he looked at the smoking revolver in my right hand.

Yes—all was well! And I *laughed.* . . .

It is very doubtful if the most highly trained, long-service troops in the world would stand up to modern war for long—let alone for four years—if the shadow of the death penalty did not always loom in the distance and the fear of the consequences of misbehaviour in face of the enemy was not constantly held in mind. . . .

Shooting out of hand is no pleasant task. But there are times when it is so terribly necessary, when, if it is not done, the public at home might read: ANOTHER BRITISH REVERSE. Of course it cannot be expected that this shooting business should be discussed in public—because battles are supposed to be won by valour and not by murder.

BRIGADIER GENERAL FRANK PERCY CROZIER, C.B., C.M.G., D.S.O.,
The Men I Killed.
Published by Doubleday, Doran and Company, Garden City, N. Y.

THE WAR NOBODY KNOWS

A few weeks ago the *New York Times* published a brief notice about armed conflict on the Northwest Frontier of India in which the casualties amounted to three dead and several wounded. That is about all the American public has been permitted to learn about a war that has been in progress now for more than a year, in which 37,000 British troops are engaged, in which the casualties for six months are officially given as 883 killed and 1,100 wounded, and which up to September has cost the Indian taxpayers about $5,000,000.

This war is in Waziristan on the Northwest Frontier of India. A British "White Paper" and a pamphlet written by Carl Heath and published by the Friends' Peace Literature Committee of England ("The Northwest Frontier of India") tell what has happened.

For ninety years this frontier has been the scene of bitter conflict and between 1849 and 1890 no fewer than 42 military expeditions have tried to "restore law and order" in this region. Ever since the World War the airplane has also been used in these wars by the British and bombings have been frequent and disastrous to the tribesmen. In 1925, for instance, a report was made on these bombings by the Air Vice-Marshal Sir Edward Ellington which contains a detailed account of the kind of bombs used (including some with delay action fuses) and the tactics employed on 42 consecutive days of bombing. In 1935, the Royal Air Force dropped 2,500 bombs in a single month on these helpless tribesmen. . . .

The reason for the constant disturbances on the Northwest Frontier have long been evident. The tribesmen of Waziristan suffer from ever-recurring winter starvation. Lacking food they make raids into Hindu and British controlled territory in order to live. By simple and constructive measures of economic cooperation this frontier could have been pacified long ago.

World Events.

CAVES

"Royal Air Force bombers are not employed on the N.W. Frontier or elsewhere for the purpose of attacking the civil population. . . . I do not think there can be any difficulty in the inhabitants of these places finding refuge . . . there are numerous caves in the vicinity."—Prime Minister, June 16th.

When British bombers go out to bomb,
Some frenzied fakir's redoubt to bomb,
They warn the tribes they're about to bomb
To take to the caves at hand,
And not till tribesmen have found the caves
They blast and batter and pound the caves
And wreck the landscape around the caves
By way of a reprimand.

There are caves throughout the North West Frontier,
A hitherto unsuppressed frontier,
And South Arabia's test frontier
Has caves for every beast and man.
There are excellent caves in the Hadramaut,
(Which Arabs appear so mad about
And Britain would feel so sad without)
And plenty in Waziristan.

No raid humane need destroy goodwill,
If bombed and bombers employ goodwill,
And every Power will enjoy goodwill
When our method is used by all.

There are refuge-caverns Arabian
Commodious caves in Waziristan
And through the Air Raid Precautions Plan
There are numerous caves in Whitehall.

SAGITTARIUS, in *The New Statesman and Nation.*

A PRAYER

Almighty and Everlasting God, who hast made of one blood all nations of men for to dwell on all the face of the earth, and who hast taught us by the mouths of holy prophets, which have been since the world began, that Thou art our Father and all men our brethren: Speak, we beseech Thee, amid the fear and sorrow of this hour, Thy rebuke of lust and hatred, violence and force, lest we forget that all Thy laws are loving kindness and all Thy paths are peace. Dispel the ignorance and blast the superstition which see in the drawn sword the security of nations, that we may learn to trust, in quietness and confidence, the work of right-eousness and love. Reveal to us our sins of prejudice and pride and passion, that we may see the sowing of the tares of misery now reaped in blood and tears, and know Thy judgments still are true and righteous altogether. Comfort with Thy pity and shelter with Thy grace the victims of violence who flee in unfamiliar places the waste of fire and sword. Strengthen those who minister to the wounded and forsaken. Bless the peacemakers of every land who live in hope and work in faith. Stay the tides of slaughter ravaging the world. And speed, O speed the happy day, fore-seen of old, when all nations and races and peoples shall be one, and wars and rumors of wars be at last no more. Amen!

JOHN HAYNES HOLMES.

Be Concerned: Ninth Wednesday

59. MAN TRIUMPHANT

Man triumphant—rides through the mountains—
Over the desert.
Man triumphant—builds a new heaven
Fifty stories high.
Man triumphant—laughs at the Gods
Who hid the ore, the coal, and the intricate processes that make
the steel.
Man triumphant—stands silent—alone,
His hands idle, beside the stopped machine.

*"At the gate"—we are all alike—"Spicks," "Dagoes," "Polacks,"
"Wops."*
Ours is the same answer—the same waiting.

I am Youth! Number 1533—Unemployed.
I walk the pavements, counting the cement blocks to the Yard
Office.
No Work Today! This must I do—that Number 1533 may live.

I know the ways of Man—the toil of idleness!
I know the pain of time—the quietness of the shutdown machine.
I have travelled the streets from shop to shop—
Stood outside the gates—walked along the red fence,
Barbed wire at the top. No Work Today! Yet the months toil on.
The stacks stand in silent rows. Not a cloud of smoke.
I can see the rust. The fires are out.
There are men everywhere. Strange—different.
Their faces are clean, pale, lost.
We sit on the street curb and talk—
But Hell! we can't—it's the same old "line."
The tomorrows are like the todays and yesterdays. "No Work To-
day."
Even with the gang I am lost, alone.
Only I can face my tomorrow.
I can see the rust. The fires are out.
I can see no further. The gates are closed.

NELS FRANCIS NORDSTROM, in *The Survey Graphic.*

THE DEBACLE

It is as though some invisible earthquake in the realm of mind and spirit had shattered our habitations, revealing fissures in what seemed to be solid and unshakable foundations, obliterating the old paths and levelling in ruinous chaos all temples made with human hands. Where once was a plain road, well-trodden and apparently an enduring highway, at the end of which was the Kingdom of God—a world of righteousness, peace and plenty—there is now an ill-defined track through a jungle, leading one hardly knows whence or whither. . . .

Suddenly the bomb fell, and the easy comedy was transformed in a flash into grim and stark tragedy. For four years, blood, lust, lying, disease, torture, and undiscerning death was let loose on Western Civilization. . . . More, man's experience in the War was confirmed by his post-war experience. To more than anything else he had trusted for prosperity and happiness to the industrial machine, and quite unexpectedly that industrial machine, of which he had been so proud, caught him in its toils and crushed him.

The very process of technological improvement in industry made man less indispensable for the working of those machines, and fewer and fewer people were able to buy the goods which the machines produced. Precisely because the cupboards were full, men were starved. Human unemployment and an unparalleled capacity for production were both parts of one and the same picture, aspects of one process. Industry was the supreme example of self-stultification: it was not merely a robot, but a Frankenstein robot which crushed the very men who made it.

Man's disillusionment was complete. He was the sport, the plaything of the deviltry in things, a half-crushed fly on the huge, relentless and irresistible fly-wheel of existence. With the best intention in the world, and precisely because he had made the completest use of one of the highest faculties within him—reason—he had made a sorry mess of things. So the fatalism of the War period was reinforced by the futilism of the post-war years. The Rake's Progress was complete. Man had begun by denying the reality of the otherwordly, then he had gone on to deny God, and last of all he had been compelled to deny himself. . . .

Such is the picture of our modern world—its economic life

patched, but disorganized and in the last state of repair, its political organization in the melting-pot, its spiritual foundations sapped and undermined. Never, in all probability, has any generation experienced such drastic disturbances in its life, or been compelled to adjust itself to them so swiftly as has ours; never was the ruin so complete. Yet in the very completeness of that ruin lies our hope. We are no longer bound to follow the old lines: as few generations have had it, we have the opportunity to build as we will. We are living in one of the greatest creative epochs of history, and what is certain is that for many generations to come civilization will keep the main outline and bear the stamp we set upon it. For good or for evil, life has become plastic and fluid once more, and we are making the mould into which it is being run.

B. C. PLOWRIGHT, *Rebel Religion.*
Round Table Press, New York.

THE DEEPER CAUSES

The causes of war lie much deeper than the will to war or absence of the will to peace. They lie today in the conflicts within nations that press them into rivalry in spite of the will to peace. . . . Modern wars are economic wars, not in the sense that they begin with conscious economic objectives, but in that peoples are driven by economic pressure to certain courses which are partly an internal relief and partly a provocation to other peoples.

The key to the tragic situation of a period marked by great peace activities and glaring preparation for war must lie in the aggressive nature of a human activity which is mistakenly regarded as pacific. It is not difficult to see that the insistent competition to sell without a corresponding competition to buy is at the root of an economic rivalry in which not only do some overreach others, but succeed only by making others fail. It is not merely increased prosperity but survival that is at issue. It is a grim struggle for one of the conditions of livelihood. It is not for goods, except to a minor extent. It is for employment as a condition of income. The roots of this rivalry are within each nation and it manages to dodge the worst effects by working for the foreigner. But an outside world ready to take goods to a greater extent than it sells, eventually develops the same need to export its unemployment problem. The world today is the field of a scramble to export as much and to import as little as possible. In preindustrial days men fought to get something it was easier to take than to make; now they fight because it is easier to make than to take. For society gives them income for the amount of their employment or trouble. Each seeks to give goods and to take work from the others. Milk poured down the drain at home, machinery exported on credit or on investment that is lost, shells bursting on a foreign soil, are all processes of an economic insanity that seeks maximum employment with minimum return. . . .

It is the absence of an economic mechanism for reciprocal trade in goods and services that prevents satisfaction of the claims of dissatisfied nations. Reciprocal trade implies that each nation can buy its own consumable production, and therefore distribute to its own people that part it keeps plus the equivalent from abroad of that part it exports. What makes this impossible is the same cause that impels organized destruction of foodstuffs and goods, governments not only encouraging such measures but penalizing those who produce too much. It is insufficient home income; income is insufficient because it is tied to employment. Under such conditions people will fight for more of the work that gives them paper claims on goods, while goods are being poured down the sink. . . .

There is no solution of the war problem; there is only a solution of the problem of social living. The modern world is trembling on the brink of peace and security. Collective productive skill has brought forth more than enough for all—and for most to be generous. . . .

Mankind today needs deliverance from the fear of peace. That deliverance requires such a re-ordering of social living within the national community that will earn the material security modern science has put into its hand.

V. A. Demant, The Universal Church and The World of Nations.
An Oxford Conference Book.
Published by Willett, Clark & Company, Chicago.

A PRAYER

O Lord, whose way is perfect, help us, we pray Thee, always to trust in Thy goodness; that, walking with Thee and following Thee in all simplicity, we may possess quiet and contented minds, and may cast all our care on Thee, for Thou carest for us: for the sake of Jesus Christ our Lord.

Christina G. Rossetti.

Endeavor to Transform: Ninth Thursday

60. BEYOND FASCISM

When fell Jerusalem of old
And Babylon prevailed,
With what dismay their hearts grew cold
Who feared that God had failed.

And when upon Golgotha's cross
The Christ was crucified,
How utterly were they at loss
Who thought that God had died.

Again and yet again the same,
While the slow ages run,
The rack, the scaffold, and the flame,
And always God undone.

Yet forth from ill success,
From all defeat of truth,
There dawns a larger righteousness,
There lives a wiser youth.

Thus do men's partial failures drive
Toward unities at last
Wherein their later counsels hive
The wisdoms of the past.

ROBERT WHITAKER, in *Unity*.

TWICE BEFORE

The Church should know how to proclaim the Good News of divine revelation in such a time as this, for at least twice before she has led the Western world through similar periods, triumphantly; once in the early days of her history, when Graeco-Roman civilization had experienced a "failure of nerve" and was slowly disintegrating, and once again at the time of the Reformation, when mediaeval feudal society was being rent asunder by new and explosive forces, carrying down in its collapse the ecclesiastical system which had been so closely united with it. In both of these periods, the Church's claim to possess light from above revealed by God Himself, was like an enheartening bugle call amid the confusion of the times, which stayed the rout and allayed the fears of those who rallied to her standard. It did not humiliate human reason; it saved panic-stricken men from fanaticism and superstition, and it eventually saved all that was best in the decadent secular culture of the time as a part—subordinate but valuable —of the body of Christian teaching.

WALTER M. HORTON, in *Revelation,*
edited by John Baillie and Hugh Martin.
Published by The Macmillan Company, New York.

THE CHRISTIAN'S DYNAMIC

This is a plea for a Protestant scholasticism. It may not be invented by a brilliant mind, nor hammered out by a committee in a few sessions. It must come by grant of God as men make themselves ready to receive it.

But, come it must, if we are to experience the "recovery of worship," need for which has so long been felt. For it was Liberalism's anti-theological temper that marked the decline and fall of worship in Protestantism.

The main marks of that culture called "modernity" were: monistic naturalism, excluding whatever reality had theretofore been sensed under the term "supernatural"; materialism with its corollary distrust of primary spiritual reality; optimistic belief in the self-containment of human nature, with its homocentric emphasis; and an arrogant secularity which could witness with glee the procession of "lost provinces" formerly claimed as sanctities. The self-sufficiency of man was the corollary proposition. . . .

We can no more than indicate the main lines of that scholasticism, and in that indication it will be seen how far afield the modern spirit has wandered from the essentials of fruitful faith.

God: Creator of all things, and as God of love, judge and grace-giver. He is transcendent and objective as Sovereign Lord. "The power not ourselves that makes for righteousness"; He is immanent as Indwelling Spirit.

Christ: The entrance of God into history in redemptive action.

Man: Creature of God and subject to his authority.

Redemption: Man is saved, not by his own righteousness but the free gift of God's grace accepted by faith, after penitence and evidenced by good works.

Church: Ordained of God, it is holy and catholic; essential to man's spiritual welfare and he may not be redeemed beyond its pales; pattern of the redeemed society through cooperative love; it is in the world but not of it, confronting the world as lost, but meeting it in compassion, and in love showing forth the judgment of God on all anti-social elements of society and the grace of God which is the social hope of redemption.

World: The world is evil and lost.

Final Things: The life eternal; the transiency of the seen world and its institutions; the permanency and ultimate victory of the unseen world; the consequent dualism and the cataclysmic contrast. This is the Christian's dynamic for good works and his inspiration to high fortitude in the face of visible hostile power.

GEORGE M. GIBSON, in *The Seminar Quarterly.*

THE DEEPER REVOLUTION

It cannot be too clearly understood in these days when so much talk about revolution is abroad, and Jesus is sometimes claimed as a proletarian leader, that there is nothing in his story—whether word or deed—that can be quoted in support of what is popularly called revolution. He saw that even if the Romans could be driven out, it would only leave the petty princes, the courtiers and the ecclesiastics a freer hand. And it almost seems as though Jesus disliked the Romans less than he disliked the native grandees. Certainly we have no record of his having spoken a harsh word concerning the Romans, while his language about the Pharisees never lacks vigour; and that profligate princeling, the Herod of his day, he called a fox. A successful revolution against the Romans would not remove the leprosy that was eating up society; it would only redistribute it. Nevertheless Jesus saw that nothing short of a revolution was called for by the state of the case. But the revolution that he saw necessary would move on a deeper level and would deal with the disease itself and not with its symptoms. And it was such a revolution that he preached.

RICHARD ROBERTS, *The Untried Door.*
Published by The Woman's Press, New York.

MOST PRECIOUS POSSESSION

Time is the inexplicable raw material of everything. With it, all is possible; without it, nothing. The supply of time is truly a daily miracle, an affair genuinely astonishing when one examines it. You wake up in the morning, and lo! your purse is magically filled with twenty-four hours of the unmanufactured tissue of the universe of your life! It is yours. It is the most precious of your possessions. . . . You have to live on this twenty-four hours of daily time. Out of it you have to spin health, pleasure, money, content, respect, and the evolution of your immortal soul. Its right use, its most effective use, is a matter of the highest urgency and of the most thrilling actuality. All depends on that.

ARNOLD BENNETT.

A PRAYER

O God, our Heavenly Father, thou who art the sum and source of all good, who givest and in thyself art every good gift, we thank thee for the ancient elemental things of life, for food and drink, for raiment and shelter, for family and friends. And at this moment we would particularly thank thee for the food now set before us for our nourishment as we gather here in social fellowship. May this meal be made a sacrament by thy presence. And may we realize that this food and drink, produced as it is by the sacrifice, be it sudden or slow, of the lives of men, our brethren, thy children, is in a true sense the body and blood of the Lord. We pray, then, in the name of Jesus of Nazareth, symbol both of the martyred workers of the world and of the necessities which they produce and which are unrighteously wrested from them, that we shall not forget those who go hungry as we eat, naked as we are clothed, shelterless as we sit beneath secure roofs, and that thou wilt bless this food to our use and us to thy service that our minds and our bodies, our souls and our wills, may be strengthened to the work of hastening the coming of thy kingdom, the reign of righteousness on earth, the co-operative commonwealth of Christ. We ask all this in the name of our friend and comrade, thy son, Jesus Christ. Amen.

KENNETH PORTER.

Proceed Resolutely: Ninth Friday

61. THIS IS ALONE LIFE

To suffer woes which hope thinks infinite;
To forgive wrongs darker than death or night;
    To defy power which seems omnipotent;
To love and bear; to hope till hope creates
From its own wreck the thing it contemplates;
    Neither to change, nor falter, nor repent;
This, like thy glory, Titan, is to be
Good, great, and joyous, beautiful and free;
This is alone Life, Joy, Empire, and Victory!

SHELLEY.

SUBLIMEST MEMORIES

Jesus had now continually to defend Himself against His friends. The very persons who adored Him would in their unwise enthusiasm divert His work into false paths. He was also compelled to turn against the leaders of the people because their hostility threatened to annul His aims and His plans. The struggle Jesus waged here against His opponents in order to preserve His aims reveals, when it is considered in its entirety, a dominating and persuasive force that is unique in the history of religious convictions. He, a solitary individual, confronts them in their collective power. A lone combatant, He proceeds to challenge their combined authority. . . .

The last days of Jesus in Jerusalem belong to the sublimest memories of the human race. His thought is fragrant with a freshness like unto the fragrance and freshness of the dawn, and all the powers of His highest person are completely mobilized. . . . A sudden and complete change now took place in the mood of the populace. A Messiah whom God would allow to be taken captive and bound as a criminal was utterly unthinkable to a Jewish populace, and a perfect fury of disappointment spent itself upon the head of Jesus. . . . He had to look on at what seemed to be the complete collapse of all His work, and to experience the full brunt of the ingratitude and ill will of this populace for whose salvation He had yearned more ardently and agonized more deeply than had any other man. There can be no question that He had to endure the betrayal and cowardly flight of His "faithful ones," and to bow to the total and brilliant victory which His enemies felt that they had achieved. Never did a man appear to suffer a more open, unconditional defeat. . . .

Let us picture to ourselves the ghastliness of His death complete—the suspension of the dead weight of His person from its pierced arms and legs, the inflamed wounds, the long, drawn-out torment induced by the distorted and swollen limbs, the violent stoppage of the circulation with all its attendant feelings of nameless terror; the parching thirst under the burning, pitiless sun, the hundreds of insect stings. The witnessing of this acme of humiliation on the one hand and the contrasting spectacle of the silent and speechless resignation of Jesus would have prostrated us. As long as our sensing of these hours of horror shall remain acute, all crucifixes somehow become paltry and superficial and all the hymns of the Church effeminate and weak.

Agony, it is true, wrests one more cry from the depths of His soul, but in it there is not one trace of hatred, disillusion, or revolt.

And now a stillness heavily charged with significance enfolds the cross, in which the greatest duel of our humanity is being fought out in His person. Utter distress is struggling to win the day over purest selflessness. Agony and torment are doing their worst to shake a will ready to carry trust to the point of abnegation. Triumphing malice is taking the offensive against tenderness that is divine. They conquer not. The silence that envelops the cross now suddenly becomes thicker still and of added solemnity. In the angry sea of human sin the most sublime of lives has gone down—but only as a prelude to a glorious and triumphant victory on Easter morn, imperishable forevermore.

FRIEDRICH RITTELMEYER, Behold the Man.

By permission of The Macmillan Company, publishers, New York.

TOO GREAT TO SUCCEED THAT WAY

We have seen that the prevailing temper of Judaism at the opening of our era was one of ardent longing for the Kingdom of God, which was the more surely expected in view of the very hopelessness of the outlook apart from such a supernatural intervention; the darkness of the hour was eagerly interpreted as predicting the dawn. The popular mind presented a mass of highly inflammable material; into this mass, ready to take fire from any spark, there fell like lightning the proclamation of the Baptist, "The Kingdom of God is at hand, at the very doors; repent, and be baptized in token of repentance!" Straightway men's hearts kindled in response throughout that tormented, restless country, and not least in Galilee. It would have been strange if a profoundly religious spirit like that of Jesus had not been deeply influenced by the eschatological hopes of His time—hopes which pointed to the end of the present evil age, and the inauguration of the Divine reign, when sorrow and sighing should flee away. . . .

It is all the more impressive to find how our Lord transcended these formal limitations of His thought concerning the Kingdom of God. Thus while, formally, He looked forward to the establishment by Divine intervention of an idealized Jewish theocracy, He has not one word to say on that favourite theme of his co-religionists, the Divine vengeance to be inflicted on the heathen. The vindictiveness which runs through so much of the apocalyptic thought of the age was as foreign to Him as the fevered dreams of world-dominion in which His countrymen indulged. If Judaism looked forward to a Messiah who should smite the earth with the rod of his mouth, and slay the wicked with the breath of his lips (Isa. xi. 4), what interested Jesus was solely the Reign of God, a reign of righteousness and grace; the political side of the Kingdom He left untouched, as of no importance to Him. Now it was just that political and secular side which loomed largest in the turbid imagination of His co-religionists, and it is at least a legitimate surmise that the non-political character of His preaching had not a little to do with the rapid waning of His popularity. To proclaim the glorious consummation as imminent—"nigh, even at the doors"—was to set every heart beating with anticipation; but when it was found that His programme lacked the very items by which the people set most store, they turned from Him in disappointment. . . .

He was too great to succeed in the only way in which He could have won temporal success.

J. WARSCHAUER, *The Historical Life of Christ.*
By permission of The Macmillan Company, publishers, New York.

BY THE STEPS I HAVE CUT

Where I lie down worn out, other men will stand young and fresh. By the steps that I have cut they will climb; by the stairs that I have built they will mount. They will never know the name of the man who made them. At the clumsy work they will laugh; when the stones roll they will curse me. But they will mount, and on my work; they will climb, and by my stair! . . . And no man liveth to himself, and no man dieth to himself.

OLIVE SCHREINER.

FOLLOW ME

Who answers Christ's insistent call
Must give himself, his life, his all,
Without one backward look.
Who sets his hand unto the plow,
And glances back with anxious brow,
His calling hath mistook.
Christ claims him wholly for His own;
He must be Christ's and Christ's alone.

JOHN OXENHAM.

A PRAYER

Almighty God, our heavenly Father, in whom we live and move and have our being, who hast created us for Thyself so that we can find rest only in Thee, grant unto us purity of heart and strength of purpose, so that no selfish passion may hinder us from knowing Thy will and no weakness from doing it, that in Thy light we may see light clearly and in Thy service find perfect freedom, through the Spirit of Him who taught us thus to pray, Our Father, which art in heaven, etc. AMEN.

EDWARD CAIRD.

A PRAYER

O God, who hast set before us the great hope that thy kingdom shall be established upon earth, so rule our lives by thy Spirit that all our thoughts, desires, and acts being made obedient unto thee, thy power, thy glory, and the mightiness of thy kingdom may be made known unto men; grant this, O merciful Father, for Jesus Christ's sake, thy Son our Lord. Amen.

Seek Comradeship: Ninth Saturday

62. PLEA FOR STILLNESS

O, may no sound corrupt this silence!
Let no small word
Alter for us this splendid stillness.
Dreamers have heard

Earth turning on her ancient axis,
Planets in space
Moving in solemn, lovely rhythm.
Here in this place,

Silence will make us heirs of wisdom.
Stars are our friends.
Dawn will behold us still enchanted,
When this night ends.

Then let our eager lips be quiet.
Only our eyes
Speak what the tongue can never utter.
Let us be wise.

RALPH FRIEDRICH, *The Lyric.*

A QUAKER MEETING FOR WORSHIP

"For when I came into the silent assemblies of God's people I felt a secret power among them which touched my heart; and as I gave way unto it, I found the evil weakening in me and the good raised up."

Robert Barclay.

The little meeting-house where I worship lies well out in the country, about four miles from Haverford. I get there just before eleven, enter in silence and sit down. There is no altar before me, no chancel, no choir loft, no organ. Only three rows of "facing benches," each of the back two being slightly elevated above the one in front of it. In former days and in many meetings still, certain older Friends and some "weighty" Friends who have often had insights to share with the group sat in these benches facing the meeting.

Our meetings are made up of a group of people gathered together in silent prayer. The first thing that I do is to close my eyes and then to still my body in order to get it as far out of the way as I can. Then I still my mind and let it open to God in silent prayer, for the meeting, as we understand it is the meeting place of the worshiper with God. I thank God inwardly for this occasion, for the week's happenings, for what I have learned at His hand, for my family, for the work there is to do, for Himself. And I often pause to enjoy Him. Under His gaze I search the week and feel the piercing twinge of remorse that comes at this, and this, and this, and at the absence of this, and this, and this. Under His eyes I see again—for I have often been aware of it at the time—the right way. I ask His forgiveness for my faithlessness and ask for strength to meet this matter when it arises again. There have been times when I had to reweave a part of my life under this auspice.

I hold up persons before God in intercession, loving them under His eyes—seeing them with Him, longing for His healing and redeeming power to course through their lives. I hold up certain social situations, certain projects. At such a time I often see things that I may do in company with or that are related to this person or to this situation. I hold up the persons in the meeting and their needs, as I know them, to God. . . .

When I have finished these inward prayers I quietly resign myself to complete listening—letting go in the intimacy of this friendly company and in the intimacy of the Great Friend who is always near. At this point, one could use Robert Barclay's words in describing our silent sitting together, "As our worship consisted not in words so neither in silences as silence, but in a holy dependence of the mind upon God; from which dependence silence necessarily follows in the first place until words can be brought forth which are from God's spirit." I do not know what takes place here. Often I am sure it is nothing at all. But there are times when a certain slowing-down takes place, a certain healing seems to go on, a certain centering, a certain tendering, a certain "dependence of the mind upon God." . . .

When I feel drawn to share something in the quiet meeting for worship, I simply rise and say it as briefly as I know how, seeking ever to "keep close to the root" and to avoid all vain and distracting ornamentation. The other worshipers often do not raise their heads or open their eyes. If they feel in unity with what I have shared and if it speaks to the condition of the meeting, out of which, if it be genuine, it originally sprang, then it becomes a seed for their meditation and something to search themselves in regard to. If it does not, they pay little attention to it and continue in their own worship. If this or something given by one of the other members of the meeting interprets the common need and exercise of the meeting, it is often added to by others and a common theme is developed that grips the mind of every participating worshiper who is present. I say "participating" worshiper, for it is possible to come to a Friends' Meeting and just "sit" or perhaps wait and often wait in vain for someone to "say something." Perhaps in no service of worship is so much left to the worshiper as in a Friends' Meeting. . . .

After about an hour whoever happens to be the "head" of the meeting on that day shakes hands with the person next to him or her and the "rise" of the meeting has come. Most of us linger and talk with one another for fifteen or twenty minutes before we leave. One of our members leaves directly and it is not her Sunday dinner that is responsible. She says that her cup is often so filled at meeting that she is not quite fit to talk about things in general at this point but feels that she must hold it full and get home as soon as possible to see what this means for her to do. "Was thee faithful?" and "Did thee yield?" are not archaic echoes of personal queries Friends used to ask themselves centuries ago in the first flush of their discovery. More than one member has hurried off to do something on which the divine accent has settled in the meeting. Concerns for certain social situations have sprung out of the meeting. Few leave without some refreshment, some sensitizing, and without at least a tiny nosegay of those mountain flowers that Frances de Sales declared to be there on the heights waiting to be plucked by every true worshiper.

DOUGLAS V. STEERE, in *The Woman's Press.*

DEEP CALLS TO DEEP

As they sang—
Of what I know not, but the music touched
Each chord of being—I felt my secret life
Stand open to it as the parched earth yawns

To drink the summer rain; and at the call
Of those refreshing waters, all my thoughts
Stir from their dark and secret depths, and burst
Into sweet, odorous flowers, and from their wells
Deep calls to deep and all the mystery
Of all that is, is laid open.

ANONYMOUS.

GRACIOUS SPIRIT

Gracious Spirit, dwell with me:
I myself would gracious be;
And, with words that help and heal,
Would Thy life in mine reveal;
And, with actions bold and meek,
Would for Christ my Saviour speak...

THOMAS T. LYNCH.

A PRAYER

Hush our hearts, O God, that we may hear within us Thine eternal song, and rise above the confusion and contradictions of life. Grant us release, if only for one dross-drained hour, from the woe that haunts us, that we may know the gospel of music and the truth it has to tell. Something within us sings, something deeper than our sin, deeper than our sorrow. We hear it when we are still; Thou hearest it all the time.

For the masters of melody, who have been the interpreters and deliverers of our spirits and the teachers of Thy truth, we praise Thee and give thanks. Thine they were, and Thou gavest them to us—winged spirits who listened to Thy voice, and told in song what they had learned in sorrow. Attune our faith to the truth that above all tumult, below it, through it, there is an eternal harmony yet to be revealed—when we have ears to hear it.

JOSEPH FORT NEWTON, Altar Stairs.

Published by The Macmillan Company, New York.

Worship God: Ninth Sunday

63. SILVER POPLARS

God wrote His loveliest poem on the day
He made the first tall silver poplar tree,
And set it high upon a pale-gold hill,
For all the new enchanted earth to see.

I think its beauty must have made Him glad,
And that He smiled at it—and loved it so—
Then turned in sudden sheer delight, and made
A dozen silver poplars in a row.

Mist green and white against a turquoise sky,
A-shimmer and a-shine it stood at noon;
A misty silver loveliness at night,
Breathless beneath the first small wistful moon.

And then God took the music of the winds,
And set each leaf a-flutter and a-thrill—
Today I read His poem word by word
Among the silver poplars on the hill.

GRACE NOLL CROWELL, printed in *Scribner's Magazine.*

THE UNSEEN WORLD

The words of Sénancour, "Let us keep our silent sanctuaries: for in them the eternal perspectives are preserved," might be taken as the main theme of this book. For it attempts to speak, from personal experience, concerning that inner life in Christ which has been for me the fountain head of outward speech and action. It seeks to bring the mind away from the tumult of the outer world to the "silent sanctuaries" of the Spirit, where Christ's voice alone is heard. . . .

There is a familiar refrain in Indian village folksongs which I have often heard on the lips of peasant singers. It tells how the diver must dive down to the depths of the sea of God's love if he would bring up the pearl of great price. Saint John's Gospel contains these precious truths about Christ's own deep love for us. Only quiet prayer and silent communion with him can bring their fullness to light. But when they are at last fully and consciously realized by man's inmost heart, they abide and bear fruit. They become an intimate part of life itself. They teach us slowly and almost imperceptibly that most difficult of all lessons, which each one of us has to learn—*not what to do, but how to be.* . . .

Yet this stillness of the inner spirit was, with Christ, no passive quality, unsuited for the active life of man; for, just before he had gone forth to the last agony of Gethsemane and the awful desolation of the cross, he had taken his wavering disciples apart into the quiet of the upper room where the doors were shut. He had pledged them his own inward gift of the Holy Spirit, the Comforter, who should lead them into all the truth and enable them to overcome the world. "Peace I leave with you," he had said to them in that parting hour, "my peace I give unto you: not as the world giveth, give I unto you. Let not your heart be troubled, neither let it be afraid."

All this I had often read about in books of meditation, and I had constantly thought of Christ's restfulness of soul as an infinitely precious treasure. But the deep inner need of it in my own life, as a necessary complement to action itself, had not come home to me in such a way as to carry final conviction. . . .

Thus very gradually the practice of the presence of God, with its deep and silent communion, became an abiding joy to me as my heart was more at leisure from itself. Instead of the former restlessness, a new peace came flowing in. Far beyond all human words to express it, my one supreme joy was this, that the consciousness of Christ's own living presence was brought intimately near to me with a fullness of love that I had never known before.

Just as I had felt a close companionship with Christ in the midst of human needs—among the poor and the needy, by the bedside of the sick and suffering, in the loneliness of the stranger, among the outcast and despised—so now I felt his presence in a new and living way through this deep peace which had flooded my whole being. What had been almost fugitive before became now more constant, and I longed to enter into its glorious completeness. There was a dual realization of his gracious presence, ever waiting to be fulfilled in my own life and ever ready to be made welcome. There were the sacrament of loving service in the outer world and the sacrament of silent communion in the inner chamber of the heart.

Surely the rhythm of such a twofold movement of the spirit, while the throbbing pulse of the universe beats to and fro, goes deep down into the mystery of life itself. There is the pure joy of alternate action and repose, like an unbroken strain of music, which integrates the outer and inner life of man. It is akin to the primal harmony of God's creation, when "the morning stars sang together and the sons of God shouted for joy.". . .

One further experience was mercifully vouchsafed to me which taught me most of all. For I was suddenly called upon to pass through the valley of the shadow of death. In a moment, the dread disease of Asiatic cholera attacked me just before night came on. It was like the "pestilence that walketh in darkness." No human aid was near at the time and it was long before a doctor could arrive. Yet Christ was intimately near me in that most desolate hour of all when I entered the dark valley, and he bade me fear no evil. . . .

Out of that intermediate state of death in life and life in death, through which I had passed for many days, I awoke at last into a new world. Old things had passed away and much of my former restlessness had gone. For when mortal weakness had reached its utmost limit, God's immortal strength had been revealed.

Very slowly indeed, during the long time of silent waiting till vital energy returned, my nature became transformed from within and I knew a deeper quietness and peace. The touch of the unseen and the eternal was upon me, and those who met me were conscious of a change, though they might not be fully aware of what had taken place. For the perspective of outward things had altered, and the unseen world was nearer to me than it had been before.

C. F. ANDREWS, *Christ in the Silence.*
Used by permission of The Abingdon Press, New York.

DAWN

The immortal spirit hath no bars
  To circumscribe its dwelling place;
My soul hath pastured with the stars
  Upon the meadow-lands of space.

My mind and ear at times have caught,
  From realms beyond our mortal reach,
The utterance of Eternal Thought
  Of which all nature is the speech.

And high above the seas and lands,
  On peaks just tipped with morning light,
My dauntless spirit mutely stands
  With eagle wings outspread for flight.

FREDERICK GEORGE SCOTT, in *Canadian Poets,* edited by John W. Garvin,
Published by McClelland & Stewart, Ltd., Toronto.

NOT BY THE MOUNTAIN'S MIGHT

It is not by the mountain's might of snow
Nor by the foaming turbulence of the sea,
The desert's fire, the night's immensity,
That nature moves me to a mystic glow
And leaves me spellbound; for I dimly know
That earth's expanse, the curve of heaven must be
Only a veil, beyond which lies the key
To the fixed Oneness whence the myriads flow.

Bewildering as the landscape of a dream
Are lake and forest, peak and star-clad height
When the vexed wanderer tries to read their face.
But he who stares unquestioning, finds they gleam
With the calm radiance of one changeless light,
Far-hung beyond the clouds of time and space.

STANTON A. COBLENTZ, *Songs of the Redwoods.*
Published by Overland-Outwest Publications, Los Angeles.

A PRAYER

O Thou Who hast called us to be Thy guests and touched our
temporal lives with the intimation of the Eternal, may the sense of
the enduring brighten all the swift passing of time. Hallow our
spirits and dignify all our enterprises by the revelation that we
sojourn here upon Thine invitation and may we so conduct ourselves as to be•worthy of Thy Divine hospitality. In His name
Who came to prepare for us a place in heavenly mansions. Amen.

GAIUS GLENN ATKINS.

Concentrate Upon the Ideal: Tenth Monday

64. SONG OF THE LOTUS-EATERS

There is sweet music here that softer falls
Than petals from blown roses on the grass,
Or night-dews on still waters between walls
Of shadowy granite, in a gleaming pass;
Music that gentlier on the spirit lies,
Than tired eyelids upon tired eyes;
Music that brings sweep seep down from the blissful skies.
Here are cool mosses deep,
And thro' the moss the ivies creep,
And in the stream the long-leaved flowers weep,
And from the craggy ledge the poppy hangs in sleep.

Why are we weigh'd upon with heaviness,
And utterly consumed with sharp distress,
While all things else have rest from weariness?
All things have rest: why should we toil alone,
We only toil, who are the first of things,
And make perpetual moan,
Still from one sorrow to another thrown:
Nor ever fold our wings,
And cease from wanderings,
Nor steep our brows in slumber's holy balm;
Nor harken what the inner spirit sings,
"There is no joy but calm!"—
Why should we only toil, the roof and crown of things?

TENNYSON (1809-1892).

THE VISION OF SIR LAUNFAL

For a cap and bells our lives we pay,
Bubbles we buy with a whole soul's tasking;
'Tis heaven alone that is given away,
'Tis only God may be had for the asking;
No price is set on the lavish summer;
June may be had by the poorest comer.

And what is so rare as a day in June?
  Then, if ever, come perfect days;
Then Heaven tries earth if it be in tune,
  And over it softly her warm ear lays;
Whether we look or whether we listen,
We hear life murmur or see it glisten;
Every clod feels a stir of might,
  And instinct within it that reaches and towers,
And, groping blindly above it for light,
  Climbs to a soul in grass and flowers;
The flush of life may well be seen
  Thrilling back over hills and valleys;
The cowslip startles in meadows green,
  The buttercup catches the sun in its chalice,
And there's never a leaf nor a blade too mean
  To be some happy creature's palace;
The little bird sits at his door in the sun,
  Atilt like a blossom among the leaves,
And lets his illumined being o'errun
  With the deluge of summer it receives;
His mate feels the eggs beneath her wings,
And the heart in her dumb breast flutters and sings;
He sings to the wide world and she to her nest,—
In the nice ear of Nature which song is the best?

Now is the high-tide of the year,
  And whatever of life hath ebbed away
Comes flooding back with a ripply cheer,
  Into every bare inlet and creek and bay;
Now the heart is so full that a drop overfills it,
We are happy now because God wills it;
No matter how barren the past may have been,
'Tis enough for us now that the leaves are green;
We sit in the warm shade and feel right well
How the sap creeps up and the blossoms swell;
We may shut our eyes, but we cannot help knowing
That skies are clear and grass is growing;
The breeze comes whispering in our ear,
That dandelions are blossoming near,
  That maize has sprouted, that streams are flowing,

That the river is bluer than the sky,
That the robin is plastering his house hard by;
And if the breeze kept the good news back,
For other couriers we should not lack;
    We could guess it all by yon heifer's lowing,—
And hark! how clear bold chanticleer,
Warmed with the new wine of the year,
    Tells all in his lusty crowing!

JAMES RUSSELL LOWELL (1819-1891).

AS A BEETHOVEN SONATA

A carpenter's baby. Thirty years of obscure village life. A young man, of whose secret growth nothing is revealed to us, coming with the crowd to be baptized by a religious revivalist. A refusal of all self-regarding or spectacular use of that immense spiritual power and effortless authority which the records so plainly reveal. Unlimited compassion especially extended to the most sinful, blundering, sickly, and unattractive among men. A self-oblivion so perfect that we do not even notice it. A balanced life of fellowship and lonely prayer. A genial love of, and yet a perfect detachment from, all human and natural things. Unflinching acceptance of a path that pointed to suffering, humiliation, failure and death. At last, a condemned fanatic agonizing between two thieves. These were the chief external incidents which marked the full expression of the Supernatural in terms of human personality. Yet within this sequence of transitory acts all sensitive spirits felt and still feel the eternal *state,* the interior life of Christ hidden in God, of which these "mysteries" are the sacramental expressions in space and time. Each scene in its own manner makes a sudden rift, and discloses a new tract of the supernatural world; and this with an even greater and more humbling splendour, with each advance of the seeing soul. . . .

The consummate personality of Jesus, in all the rich fullness of His sense of reality, His inclusive hold on the rugged and the tender, His energy and His peace, stands over against our jangled human character, as a Beethoven sonata stands over against the jangled world of sound. See how every now and then, in this apparently human history, the Transcendent, the utterly unearthly, is glimpsed through Him; and the "creature" recoils in awe. "They were amazed", say the Evangelists again and again. "No man durst ask him anything." "Verily, this man was the son of God!" says the Roman officer, watching that strange criminal die. Our blundering credal formulae, with their instinctive clinging hold upon the human—yet their sense that the human category at its highest here somehow becomes inadequate to the facts—manage little more than the constant reassertion of the paradox which has baffled, and yet enslaved, the Christian world. "Perfect God"; the Divine Word breaking through into Its creation, the utterance in human language of Reality. "Perfect Man"; the pattern of humanity, King of Saints. These completing opposites are here fused in one figure; perfectly historic, yet transcending the time-stream within which it emerged.

EVELYN UNDERHILL, *Man and the Supernatural.*
Published by E. P. Dutton & Co., New York City.
Reprinted by permission.

A VISIBLE PRESENCE ENFOLDED HIM

When John Wilhelm Rowntree was threatened with serious eye-trouble one of the best physicians was consulted. He could hold out no hope of improvement, or even of the arrestment of the evil, and John went out from the consultation into the street under the doom of coming and irreparable blindness. He stood by some railings for a few moments to collect himself, and suddenly felt the love of God wrap him about as though a visible presence enfolded him, and a joy filled him such as he had never known before. Instead of retreating before this insidious foe and leaving human wrongs to right themselves, as men would readily have excused him for doing, he only sought the more continually to fit himself for efficient service for God and his fellows, during every day which might yet be given him.

JOSHUA ROWNTREE.

A PRAYER

Oh God, source of the light that never fails and of the life that never ends, we bless Thee that some spark of the eternal flame has found its way into our spirits so that no one can ever be wholly satisfied with the possession of things however abundant they may be, but must find himself upon an endless pathway searching for ideals that are never wholly fulfilled. In Jesus' name. Amen.

RAYMOND C. BROOKS.

Understand the Actual: Tenth Tuesday

65. AN AUGUST NIGHT IN THE CITY

I know a sad park where, on breathless nights,
Throng those whom through the day the hot sun smites—
The pallid poor, unlettered and alone,
Whose hearts are hotter than the aching stone.

This is their dormitory; here they fare
After the Summer noon's relentless glare.
See! here they crowd like sheep without a fold,
While all around them rings the city's gold.

But there are coasts beside a lonely sea,
And hills and glens and many a wind-swept lea
Where man has never broken the silence deep. . . .
Yet here tonight an army falls asleep!

CHARLES HANSON TOWNE.
Published by Mitchell Kennerley.

PREFACE TO PEASANTRY

In the heart of the South there are approximately two hundred counties in which over half the population is Negro. These counties lie in a cresent from Virginia to Texas and constitute the "Black Belt." They contain the big plantation area of today and coincide with the location of the slave plantations of a few decades ago. The Black Belt includes the most fertile soil of the South, and contains a disproportionate number of its poorest people. The ownership of the best land is in the hands of a comparatively small group of white families; landlessness and chronic dependence is the lot of over half the white families and nearly nine-tenths of the colored. The Black Belt is the home of a few planters and many tenants. Thousands of families have no cow, no hog, not even chickens, and own no workstock or farm equipment, not even a hoe. Rickets and pellagra are common among those who till the most productive soils of the South. . . .

The collapse of the plantation system, rendered inevitable by its exploitation of land and labor, leaves in its wake depleted soil, shoddy livestock, inadequate farm equipment, crude agricultural practices, crippled institutions, a defeated and improverished people. Such is already the picture in a considerable part of the older Black Belt.

The Black Belt plantation economy, whether regnant or declining, prepares the land and the man for the emergence of a peasant rather than for the appearance of the traditional independent American farmer. Before the plantation structure crumbles, the owners dominate the economic and cultural life of the entire community, and a few of them may be relatively wealthy; but even then the majority of the plantation folk are subpeasants— no property, no self-direction, no hope of either. As the plantation crumbles, most of the erstwhile owners and some of the more alert tenants abandon the scene, leaving in the decadent area plantation families schooled in dependency, unaccustomed to responsibility, without experience in community leadership. These remaining families tend to become independent renters or small owners, and are characterized by very low but relatively secure planes of living. Such are the beginnings of peasantry in the New World—the collapse of the Black Belt plantation system is a preface to American peasantry. . . .

This most Democratic part of the nation is perhaps the least democratic part of the nation: from six to sixty times as much public money is spent for the education of the white as for the Negro school child; Negro officeholders are unknown; scarcely any Negroes register and vote in national presidential elections, almost none participate in local politics.

More than elsewhere in the South one finds in the Black Belt "unreconstructed rebels." Sherman's march to the sea is referred to daily; openly justified are the terroristic methods used to disfranchise the Negro, and revered is the white primary which legalizes this disfranchisement. With the financial, educational, and religious institutions maintaining the status quo and keeping the Negro "in his place," the threat of violence always hangs over his head and violence itself frequently is used upon slight provocation. . . .

The cash income of the families, varying by race and tenure class, averages less than a dollar a day per family, less than twenty cents a day per person.

It will be observed from the following table that in 1934 in

Greene the average cash income was $301.26 per rural white family and $150.74 per rural Negro family; in Macon, $872.21 for the white and $299.56 for the Negro. . . .

The public schools of Greene and Macon counties had less money spent upon them in 1934 than in 1928, and in each county the shrinkage of expenditures was greater for Negro than for white schools.

In 1928, the white child of school age in Greene had $36.53 of public money spent upon his education, the Negro child, $3.11—a ratio of twelve to one. In Macon, the white received $58.38 and the Negro $2.85—a ratio of eighteen to one. . . .

Between 1928 and 1934, the amount spent in Greene upon the white child had decreased by 16 per cent, upon the Negro child by 40 per cent; in Macon, the white child's decrease was 12 per cent, the Negro's 36 per cent. Thus the racial differentials were even greater than in 1928, seventeen to one in Greene, and twenty-five to one in Macon. . . .

The methods now employed in the production of crops in Greene and Macon counties utilize the labor of all the members of the farm family from sun to sun for a few months of each year. The rest of the time they have little opportunity for remunerative employment, and tire of idleness. By continuous labor and enforced idleness, by low incomes and restricted outlook, everybody gets fagged out and seems to stay that way. Earning a living under a system which keeps the workers dependent and the owners ridden by debt leaves both planters and tenants without security or hope. Where the majority of the population chronically receive small incomes and maintain low planes of living, they come to expect nothing better. In truth, the fatalism which accompanies their low plane of living does to their minds what inadequate food, malaria, and hookworm do to their bodies.

ARTHUR F. RAPER, *Preface to Peasantry.*
Published by University of North Carolina Press, Chapel Hill, N. C.

IS THERE NO HOPE?

In 1919, the total farm property of the nation had been valued at $78,000,000,000; by 1932, this value was $44,000,000,000. In 1919, the total farm income was $15,000,000,000; by 1932, $5,200,000,000. In June 1932, farm commodity prices were at 52

per cent of the prewar level while the prices of the things the
farmer bought were at 110 per cent of the prewar level. Thus, the
exchange value of farm products for the goods purchased by
farmers was 47 per cent of the prewar average. Mortgage indebtedness had increased from $3,300,000,000 in 1910 and $7,900,-
000,000 in 1920 to $9,500,000,000 in 1931; in the last year inter-
est and other costs on mortgage debts ate up fully eight per cent
of gross farm income, as compared with three per cent in the
prewar years. In 1931, taxes absorbed 11 per cent of gross farm
income as compared with four per cent in the prewar years. So
onerous were these fixed charges that during the five years ended
March 1, 1932, 9.5 per cent of the farms of the country changed
hands through forced sales (foreclosure of mortgages, bankruptcy, default of contract, sales to avoid foreclosure, etc.) while
3.5 per cent of the farms were sold for tax delinquencies. More
significant than any of these examples of agriculture's debased
position was the condition of agricultural real estate, that single
factor which heretofore had always succeeded in redressing the
balance. On the basis of the estimated value per acre of 100 for
1912-14, farm land in the whole country had been worth 170 in
1920, 116 in 1929 and but 73 on March 1, 1933! . . .

For the time being President Roosevelt is trying to carry
water on both shoulders: he is seeking to save American agriculture through subsidy and at the same time to recapture foreign
markets for the wares of our industrialists and bankers. But if
agriculture is to be saved, its monopoly of the home market and
a high price level for farm goods must be assured; and if industry
and banking are to be saved, low foodstuff and raw material costs,
cheap domestic labor and an open home market for the agricultural
products of the peoples buying our finished goods and borrowing
our money must be maintained. "You pays your money and you
takes your choice"; but choose you must. And because there can
be no question of the inevitable nature of the choice, American
commercial agriculture is doomed. No gifts of clairvoyance are
required to foretell that the future of the American farmer is the
characteristic one of all peasants for whom, in our present system
of society, there is no hope.

Louis M. Hacker, The Farmer is Doomed.
Published by the John Day Company, New York.

Be Concerned: Tenth Wednesday

66. LAPSE

Across the Oregon Trail
The paved road glares with grease
And the cars spring by like ghouls—
Raucous honks and laughter.

A place for the sky to bow,
A grave with rocks upon it;
Cobble stones from the stream
Placed one by one among tears.
A simple wooden cross
Saying only, "Pioneer Woman"
And the year and day of her passing.

Along the Oregon Trail—
And the motor cars spin and roar,
Reverence flung in a picnic basket,
Powdered faces leering.

"Pass that next car, honey!"
"There now, what'd I tell you?
The ox team's got a puncture;
Hind foot blew out an inner tube.
Get the thermos? Your flask's okay.
The wooden pail to the spring?"
"Cigarettes, kid! Whatcha think this is,
An Indian massacre?
You got your nerve taking
One of those rocks for a souvenir.
That jane that's dead under there
'Sapt to hafta take asperin,
Catch cold.
Funny to see this cross.
What a tombstone for—
Say, get going!
When do we eat?"

HELEN MARING, in *The World Tomorrow*

THE CRISIS OF RELIGION

It is likely that at all times in human history many men and women have spent their lives unaware of the deeper meaning of existence. But surely there have been few historical periods in which men were so disillusioned about the meaningfulness of life as they are in our own era. A majority of our contemporaries seem to lead the existence of drifters. . . . A spirit of uncertainty has shaken, it seems, all positive convictions. The most urgent human concern appears to be "security." All political movements, economic and cultural discussions, and religious longings are directed toward the overcoming of the feeling of "insecurity" which is abroad in all lands. The world-wide depression is not primarily economic but psychological in character. The morale of present-day mankind is not that of builders of civilization. There are comparatively few who can say *how* a civilization should be built and there are many who ask *why* it should be built anyway. . . .

The history of the modern Western mind may be said to be the history of a gradual secularization of man. Its outcome is apparent in the total structure of contemporary life, which as a whole moves along without a profound challenge from the spirit of religion, especially in so far as belief in God is implied. If that typical product of the modern age, the newspaper, can be considered an adequate mirror of the life of modern society, the world of religion has now been relegated to an insignificant corner in the existence of man, which is otherwise determined by the events and decisions in the fields of politics, business, sport and art. . . .

We cannot doubt the fact that Western civilization is today in a state of transition. More particularly, we should say that the doctrine of the autonomy of man which theoretically and practically has upheld the last phase of this civilization is now found wanting. What the ultimate effect of this breakup will be, no one can yet suggest with certainty. But it is evident that the realization of the inadequacy of a life dominated by the spirit of human self-determination is of great religious importance. This realization has already entered all fields of human endeavor. In this respect, our age is a religious period. The time is again fulfilled. It is our duty to know this and to be patient. Only by a comprehension of the changes which are befalling us can we be sufficiently prepared for a new religious certainty. . . .

The spirit of secularism has brought about the crisis of the old and of contemporary religion. A new religious sense, built upon a new certainty of God, must bring the spirit of secularism into a crisis. When this event occurs, we shall be saved. Perhaps the time is not far distant when a prophet will arise among us who, fully imbued with the mood and spirit of our era, will speak to us in the name of the living God with such power and authority that all who long for salvation will be compelled to listen. In the meantime, we must learn to be humble in the awareness that it is God, the Lord of all life, who has laid his hand upon us in this crisis. And we must learn to pray: We believe, O Lord, help thou our unbelief. He who will have authority to declare that this prayer has been heard will be the leader of the movement by which the crisis will be overcome.

WILHELM PAUCK, in *The Church against the World*.
Published by Willett, Clark and Company, Chicago.

HIS DISTINCTIVE STATUS

Man the animal is unable, as plain matter of fact, to live simply in the present. Perhaps a cow does; we have no way of knowing. But a man does not. He is aware of time, past and future as well as present. He is haunted by norms to which, often in contradiction of present desire, he tries to measure up. His animality is shot through with felt responsibility, and his life is continually in unstable equilibrium, as though its center of gravity were outside every present moment. To regard such a being as completely describable in terms of phenomena is to miss the most distinctive thing about him: his being haunted by what seems a perpetual summons from beyond every present appearance. To show how one phenomenal segment of his life is connected with other like segments is, we have said, necessary to any extensive understanding of his existence; but such descriptive explanation can never be sufficient.

There is needed further an explanation which pierces through the stream of appearances, in act rather than by observation; which seeks to *enact* with insight and in that sense to understand the more ultimate truth about man. Such enacted understanding is the Christian belief that man, this animal, is a responsible creature dependent for his being and his worth upon God. In response to God's creative word he has emerged from the stream of organic evolution, with ears partly though imperfectly attuned to God's continuing summons, which will not let him rest. That summons is partly conveyed, though by no means automatically interpreted, through the processes that go on within man, and in nature around him; which have their ultimate meaning not simply as being themselves, but as being vehicles for the divine word to which man is not merely subjected but *responsible,* having therein his distinctive status as man.

Robert L. Calhoun, *The Christian Understanding of Man.*
An Oxford Conference Book.
Published by Willett, Clark & Company, Chicago.

HALF-HEARTED AFFIRMATIONS

The real ground for anxiety on the part of the whole church is not our divergence over the things wherein we differ, but our half-heartedness in the religious affirmations that we share. At the foundation of our fellowship and at the heart of the creeds lies the confession of Jesus Christ as Lord, the recognition in Him of very God. Are we prepared to accept in our lives the implications of that confession, to permit Christ to be the Lord of our appetites, the Lord of our relations with our neighbors, the Lord of our family life, of our industrial and business relations? Every man who enters into the religious meaning of the ancient creeds stands upon his feet and joins hands with the great body of Christians throughout the centuries, and says that he believes in God; that he believes in a Righteous Will working in creation; he believes in Christ, the Son of God, the very life and love of God in terms of our human life; he believes in the Spirit, God working within us to draw us to Himself; he believes in the church, the fellowship of those who draw their strength from Christ; he believes in forgiveness, the undiscouraged love of God for us which demands an undiscouraged love for one another; he believes in our victory over death and the life of ever-deepening fellowship.

Letter from the Faculty of the Episcopal Theological School at Cambridge.

Endeavor to Transform: Tenth Thursday

67. AMERICA

From the National Ode, July 4, 1876

Foreseen in the vision of sages,
   Foretold when martyrs bled,
She was born of the longing of ages,
   By the truth of the noble dead
And the faith of the living fed!
No blood in her lightest veins
Frets at remembered chains,
Nor shame of bondage has bowed her head.
   In her form and features still
   The unblenching Puritan will,
Cavalier honor, Huguenot grace,
   The Quaker truth and sweetness,
And the strength of the danger-girdled race
Of Holland, blend in a proud completeness.
From the homes of all, where her being began,
   She took what she gave to Man;
   Justice, that knew no station,
      Belief, as soul decreed,
   Free air for aspiration,
   Free force for independent deed!
She takes, but to give again,
As the sea returns the rivers in rain;
And gathers the chosen of her seed
From the hunted of every crown and creed.
Her Germany dwells by a gentler Rhine;
Her Ireland sees the old sunburst shine;
Her France pursues some dream divine;
Her Norway keeps his mountain pine;
Her Italy waits by the western brine;
   And, broad-based under all,
Is planted England's oaken-hearted mood,
   As rich in fortitude
As e'er went worldward from the island-wall!
   Fused in her candid light,

To one strong race all races here unite;
Tongues melt in hers, hereditary foemen
Forget their sword and slogan, kith and clan.
    'Twas glory, once, to be a Roman:
She makes it glory, now, to be a man!
                  BAYARD TAYLOR (1825-1878).

TAXATION AS AN INSTRUMENT OF POLICY

Taxes are a privilege, not a burden, said Justice Oliver Wendell Holmes. How could so wise a man have had such an idea?

On the evening when you find the yearly bad news in the mailbox, sit down and figure out what it would cost you to buy separately the services covered by your local tax bill. Inside your house is running water. You paid for the plumbing; leave that out. But put down the cost of a well and a pump. Also a cesspool. You might put down the cost of one case of typhoid.

Then there is the morning's milk. Put down the cost of hiring a doctor to keep an eye on the milkman, his family, and his herd of cows. Look up your fine insurance policy, and figure the extra premium you would pay if there were no fire department.

Now go outdoors and look around. Oh yes, the paving out in front is a sore point. You paid plenty for that. But suppose that were the only strip of paving in town. Put down your guess at what it would cost you to get around through the mud. See the street light on the corner? Put down the cost of one lantern for each member of the family, and something for the smell of kerosene and the trouble of taking care of the lanterns. In the next block is the public school. Write down the cost of private schooling up to college age for your children.

There are plenty of other items, but these will do. Add them up and admit that Justice Holmes was right. Taxes are a privilege because through taxes you are able to buy dozens of services and conveniences at low rates—wholesale instead of retail.

It is true, of course, that some of these public services were foisted upon you, not because you wanted them, but because a politician wanted more jobs for his friends. Many of the services, however, in spite of their illegitimate origin, have turned out to be useful. With all the waste and graft counted in, your tax bill as a whole is an economy, not an extravagance.

Here are some of the things you buy with your taxes, local, state, and federal.

About 5 per cent goes into protection against fire, crime, and social disorder.

About 9 per cent is used up in overhead cost of legislatures, administration, and courts.

About 10 to 15 per cent goes into public business enterprises: the Post Office, banks, forests, docks, water supplies, and the like.

About 20 per cent goes for help to business, such as highways, conservation, agricultural research, and so on.

About 25 per cent goes into war costs and pensions, like it or not.

About 25 to 30 per cent of your tax bill goes for such services as schools, public health, recreation, and social welfare. . . .

Taxation as an instrument of public policy is the greatest tool of democratic self-government. Dictators can plan their economic systems and force the people to obey their orders. Democracies can plan their own development, and by a well-designed system of taxes, can carry out their plans with the least possible regimentation of the people.

We pay taxes, therefore, for two main reasons. One is that we can buy certain kinds of services more economically through the government than through individual purchase. The other is that we are obliged to adopt great national policies to protect ourselves against depressions, poverty, insecurity and loss of our liberties. By suitable taxation we can solve great national problems and yet preserve our democratic form of government. . . .

The graduated personal income tax includes two quite different measures. One is the tax on middle-class incomes, a tax designed to raise money for public purposes as fairly, and with as little disturbance to business, as possible. The other is the tax on the mammoth incomes, that swell like a great tidal wave, washing away the little men who stand in their path and threatening the safety of the nation. The taxes on mammoth incomes are not so much for revenue as for police purposes—to control these floods of money, and to direct them into harmless paths. We can avoid being confused in regard to income tax policy if we keep these two different purposes clear in our minds.

The best interests of the community are no longer served by letting the Horatio Alger heroes pile up uncounted millions. The unnecessary skyscrapers and multiplied oilwells are an illustration of the effect of wasteful investment, but in reality they are only symbols of something much larger and far more dangerous. Most of the big fortunes are used not for building, however wasteful, but for buying control over American business. . . .

If America is not to be ruled by unseen powers, responsible to no voters, caring for no interest but the increase of their own power, pushing their control farther and farther into the business of our country, the tax rates cannot stop at the point of diminishing return. America will not start to recover its lost freedom until it can enact and enforce upper bracket tax rates that will stop the growth of great fortunes and make them start to shrink away.

The place to get tax revenue, with the least possible damage and sacrifice, is from the "middle brackets." The top brackets are not cows to be milked and protected, but wolves to be controlled and reduced in number.

DAVID CUSHMAN COYLE, *Why Pay Taxes?*
Published by National Home Library Foundation, Washington, D. C.

NOTHING BUT A FRIGHTFUL MUDDLE

I have the profound conviction that the economic problem, the problem of want and poverty and the economic struggle between nations and classes, is nothing but a frightful muddle, a transitory and unnecessary muddle. For the Western world already has the resources and techniques, if we would create the organization to use them, capable of reducing the economic problem, which now absorbs our moral and spiritual energies, to a position of secondary importance. I still believe that the day is not far off when the economic problem will take the back seat where it belongs, and that the arena of the heart and mind will be occupied, or reoccupied, by our real problems, the problems of life and human relations, of creation and behavior and religion.

JOHN MAYNARD KEYNES, *Essays in Persuasion.*
Published by Harcourt, Brace & Co., New York.

PRAYER

O God, who art strength and power and harmony and love, so draw us to Thyself that we too may share in that peace which is the fruit of perfectly adjusted life; in order that we may be at one with ourselves, one with our fellows, one with Thee and one with Eternity. Amen.

BISHOP PAUL JONES.

Proceed Resolutely: Tenth Friday

68. THE PIONEER

You will observe my blood on the stones
And my blood in the hollow,
And you will come after; there will be bones
For you to follow.

I found my father's bones on the trail,
Bleached white with the weather:
Though he had failed, I could not fail
Him altogether.

As he found his father's before him I found
His blood on the bush:
And I felt that I stood on Holy Ground
In a grim hush.

You must come after and give a name
To the nameless one
Who perished here that the bush might flame
Some day for his son.

JOSEPH AUSLANDER, *More Than Bread.*
By permission of The Macmillan Co., publishers, New York.

Fellowship of Socialist Christians

I. PRINCIPLES

The Fellowship of Socialist Christians accepts the Christian faith as the only adequate interpretation and rule of life. Within terms of this faith its members have arrived at socialist political and economic convictions. They see in the processes of decay and destruction in contemporary capitalist society the judgment of God upon a society which violates the law of God and of life by its injustices. They believe that modern society is involved in progressive tendencies of self-destruction because the very technical achievements of an industrial age, from which a more optimistic generation expected salvation, accentuate the anarchy of our common life.

The Fellowship is committed to the belief that the social ownership and administration of natural resources and of basic means of production is a primary requisite of justice in our technological age. It affirms and supports the efforts of those who seek a cooperative society along socialist lines and it opposes those who seek to maintain the dominant contemporary system known as capitalism, which is characterized by private ownership of natural resources and the instruments of production. Capitalism, in its inevitable contracting phase, subordinates the needs of the masses to the preservation and enhancement of the privileges of a steadily narrowing class of owners. It destroys the opportunity of increasing numbers of people to earn a livelihood adequate for physical health, mental and moral development, and personal freedom. It thereby corrupts both culture and religion.

The Fellowship believes that the workers of the world, who suffer most from the injustices of the present society, have a peculiar mission to be the instruments and heralds of this new society. It therefore seeks to associate those who are not engaged in manual toil with the interests of those who are, striving to create political forces in which human need and moral decision will be united to bring in a new economic order.

The Fellowship differs from doctrinaire collectivist philosophies not only in its adherence to the Christian faith but also on empirical grounds. It is aware of the danger of unnecessarily mutilating organic forms of social life by coercing them into mechanical moulds. It seeks a socialist society because of its intent to enrich human life in both its social and individual aspects. Whether collectivism best serves this purpose in certain types of agrarian production and retail distribution is a question which it leaves open advisedly, believing that more experimentation is required to determine this issue.

The Fellowship believes that the process of change may involve conflict and destruction. It does not believe that good-will alone is a guarantee against the possibility of violent conflict. It does believe that the most certain way of mitigating conflict and violence is to enlist the largest number of the total community in the struggle for a new social order. The Fellowship does not share the optimism of those Marxists who imagine that a new mechanism of social ownership will eliminate all conflict in the world and solve all the problems of the human spirit. On the basis of its

Christian convictions it recognizes the inevitability of the conflict of interests in society as one of the forms in which human sin will always express itself.

II. OBJECTIVES

1. To strengthen the forces within the Christian Church which believe that socialism is a necessary next step in society by providing a fellowship in which such persons can find comradeship in thought and action and mutual assistance in vocational problems.

2. To present the challenge of radical Christianity to the people within Christian organizations, deepening our own awareness of our involvement in the interests and ideas of the present order.

3. To provide opportunities for developing and clarifying ideas in the field of the relation of the Christian ethic to the realities of the political struggle.

4. To encourage our members to a self-discipline involving: the careful stewardship of time and resources in the interest of radical social change; a responsible relationship to the cause of the workers, in terms of membership in or support of trade unions and political parties devoted to our objectivies; the exercising of responsibility, by protest, example and other means, toward all forms of racial and religious discriminations, unjust labor conditions and other forms of social injustice; and activities in the interest of international peace.

III. PROGRAM

1. Publication of the quarterly *Radical Religion* for the discussion of problems relating to Christianity and polico-economic radicalism, and the dissemination of news about significant activities in the field of radical religion.

2. Arrangement of conferences, national and local, for the discussion of common problems.

3. Financial support of religious work which is definitely related to the social struggle, such as labor churches, the training of religious workers in the radical cause, etc.

IV. MEMBERSHIP

1. Anyone who accepts the principles of the Fellowship may become a member by application to the Executive Committee.

2. Membership dues are voluntary. They should be measured

in terms of the financial resource of the member. They vary at present from $1.00 to $100 per year, each member being left free to determine the amount of his contribution. Student dues are 50 cents. It is expected that every member will subscribe to *Radical Religion,* the official organ of the Fellowship.

> Further information may be secured from
> The Secretary of The Fellowship of Socialist Christians,
> 3041 Broadway, New York City.

YOUNG WORDS

Old words can never drive a dream
Deep into frozen earth
And grow it to a fruited scheme
When young hope warms it to birth.
Old words can never quicken feet
Fastened by fear,
Or split the dark for the discreet
And bring a brave dawn near.

But young words! words that quiver and sing
And laugh as they storm the towers
Of ancient wrong; young words that ring
Like high bells heralding unknown hours
Golden and gay to come;
Words that are never silent of sorrow
Yet wing their burdens up to the sky;—
Oh, young words trill like a throbbing drum
As over the toiling world they cry:
Tomorrow! Tomorrow!

> DEVERE ALLEN, in *The World Tomorrow.*

A PRAYER

O God of unspeakable beauty, may such visions of Thy way come down upon us that we become touched with stillness in our hearts and in inner quietness and poised peace may there come Thy power through Jesus, the Christ, our brother. Amen.

> ALLAN KNIGHT CHALMERS.

Seek Comradeship: Tenth Saturday

69. CITY COMRADESHIP

Face on face in the city, and when will the faces end?
Face on face in the city, but never the face of a friend,
Till my heart grows sick with longing and dazed with the din of
    the street,
As I rush with the thronging thousands, in a loneliness complete.

Shall I not know my brothers? Their toil is one with mine.
We offer the fruits of our labor on the same great city's shrine.
They are weary as I am weary; they are happy and sad with me;
And all of us laugh together when evening sets us free.

Face on face in the city, and where shall our fortunes fall?
Face on face in the city,—my heart goes out to you all.
See, we labor together; is not the bond divine?
Lo, the strength of the city is built of your life and mine.

ANNA LOUISE STRONG.

GOD-CENTERED

Society has become disintegrated because it is made up of self-centered individuals. Should those individuals become wholly unselfish by self-surrender to that which transcends the human, a new society would inevitably be born. . . . The new society will come, not by a mechanical organization of chaotic elements, but by God breathing into this chaotic body of dust His breath of life.

Such a process will take time. Mechanisms are made quickly. Organisms develop slowly. We find ourselves in a desperate hurry. Yet unless human collectives devote themselves to a long, slow process of growth, there will be no salvation for society.

The possibility of unity on a high level is based on the doctrine of the Inner Light, that spark of divine fire which glows in every human heart. Man may or may not follow its guidance, but it is always there and always pleading to be followed. This fact gives the members of the group a confidence in each other and a respect for each other without which united action would be difficult. One member can always appeal to that in the other which will lead to the same divine Truth that he himself believes he sees. But in doing so he may find his own sense of leading corrected by the sense of leading of the other. The Light cannot be thought of in purely individual terms, for the individual is often incapable of discerning its leading correctly. It illuminates the group as well as the individual. . . .

The primary need today is for a society which will be God-centered and not group-centered nor self-centered. A God-centered group is both inclusive and exclusive. Here we do not halt half way between these two attitudes, but find a higher synthesis of both. Loyalty to a group, whether it be a race, a nation, a family, or some other unit is a virtue of a high order, but it need not be accompanied by a spirit of exclusiveness nor of antagonism to other individuals or groups. Only in a society created by the Father of all can man retain, not only those values inherent in a small closely united group, but those values which alone become possible of realization in a universal brotherhood.

HOWARD H. BRINTON, *Divine-Human Society.*
Published by The Book Committee of The Religious Society of Friends,
302 Arch Street, Philadelphia.

INNER CIRCLES

The church should be the place where barriers of race, nationality, class, sex and education are done away with, where the unprivileged, the downtrodden, the outcast and the despised, find a welcome and feel themselves at home; a meeting ground where those who are divided in questions of politics and economics can realize afresh their unity in loyalty to a common Lord, can discuss their differences in the reality of this fellowship and learn to understand one another. In the modern disintegration of social life the church ought to provide centers in which men can find protection, shelter and security in the care and love of their fellow men, and rediscover the meaning of community in the support and comradeship of a society the members of which bear one another's burdens and seek the good of all. The church ought also to be the place not only where support and encouragement are given those who need them, but where the more robust and vigorous may find their individualism and self-will disciplined and tempered and their purposes purified and strengthened in a common endeavor to learn and to fulfill the will of Christ.

When we speak of the fulfilling of this function by the church, however, we have again to make distinctions. If we look for something which from the nature of things cannot come about, we are doomed to disappointment and may lose courage. The church as an organized society includes a multitude of persons in very different stages of growth in the Christian life, if indeed in many instances they have entered on the Christian life at all. Many of them, like the disciples of whom we read in the Acts of the Apostles, "have not so much as heard whether there be any Holy Ghost." It cannot be expected, therefore, that they should manifest in full measure the gifts of the Spirit, the chief of which is love. What we must look for and work for is the growth of smaller groups who will seek to realize among themselves the relations of mutual trust and support and responsibility which are characteristic of the Christian society. Such groups, while they may, to begin with, be small, must not become esoteric and exclusive. They must continually be seeking to extend their borders. The purpose of the leaven is to leaven the whole lump, but it is necessary first of all that there should be the leaven. It is futile to waste our breath in demanding that the "church" be this or that. We have to begin with ourselves and those whom we can influence. Life becomes real when we face our own responsibilities. It has been "the few in every age who have been the soul of every reform and started every revival upon its daring course." The church has to be continually reborn as the living church within the church as an organized society. If within the larger body there are groups of persons actively engaged in discovering and realizing the meaning of Christian community as a fellowship of persons living together in relations of mutual trust, love, obligation and service, those outside who are brought by circumstances into touch with this life will feel its power and attraction and find Christ in and through his church.

Wherever there has been an enduring revival of Christianity it has generally found expression in the spontaneous activity of small groups meeting for mutual encouragement, fellowship and common effort. The conception of "cells" is wholly congruous with the genius of Christianity. May not the formation of such cells of Christian witness and service be the distinctive Christian contribution to the social and political struggles of our time? To be effectively changed a social system must be changed from within and in all its parts. This leaves entirely open the question at what stage a radical change of the whole system is required in order to allow the new, constructive forces the opportunity of further expansion. But to make an outward change of system while the mind remains unconverted and the old habits persist can result only in disillusionment; the existing evils will merely assume another form.

J. H. OLDHAM, *The Church and Its Function in Society.*
An Oxford Conference Book.
Published by Willett, Clark & Company, Chicago.

SACRED GIFT OF GOD

Christians have never known the Church as a society of man's contriving, an expression of human idealism like a mutual improvement society or a club for recreation, fellowship and good-will, with the minister of the Word and the Sacraments as its competent and salaried secretary. Christians know the Church evangelical and catholic as the sacred gift of God, which no merely naturalistic or revolutionary categories can explain; it is a wonderful and sacred mystery, the great company of the elect of God stretching beyond the sight of any man across the centuries and the continents: the host of the living God sharing His very life in all places and in all ages, on earth and in heaven; the Church which God loved, Christ purchased, and the Holy Ghost sanctified, and which Christ will present to Himself a glorious Church. All is of God; indeed we Christians cannot open our mouths to speak of any aspect of our religion without speaking of Him with whom we have to do.   J. S. WHALE.

A PRAYER

Oh God, my Creator and Preserver, teach me to obey the all-embracing law of universal love as exemplified in the life of Jesus Christ. Help me through daily meditation and prayer to search my heart, face my problems with courage, sublimate my earthly desires, and be lifted from consciousness of self to consciousness of Thee. At all times make me aware, in the silence of my soul, of Thy absolute presence, which, speaking the word of deepest wisdom, will sustain and guide me, and, if I be worthy, pass through me as an energizing and ennobling influence to my fellow men.   ALICE HEGAN RICE, *My Pillow Book.*
Published by D. Appleton-Century Co., New York.

Worship God: Tenth Sunday

70. THE LAKESIDE

The shadows round the inland sea
  Are deepening into night;
Slow up the slopes of Ossipee
  They chase the lessening light.
Tired of the long day's blinding heat,
  I rest my languid eye,
Lake of the Hills! where, cool and sweet,
  Thy sunset waters lie!

Along the sky, in wavy lones,
  O'er isle and reach and bay,
Green-belted with eternal pines,
  The mountains stretch away.
Below, the maple masses sleep
  Where shore with water blends,
While midway on the tranquil deep
  The evening light descends.

So seemed it when yon hill's red crown,
  Of old, the Indian trod,
And, through the sunset air, looked down
  Upon the Smile of God.
To him of light and shade the laws
  No forest skeptic taught;
Their living and eternal Cause
  His truer instinct sought.

He saw these mountains in the light
  Which now across them shines;
This lake, in summer sunset bright,
  Walled round with sombering pines.
God near him seemed; from earth and skies
  His loving voice he heard,
As, face to face, in Paradise,
  Man stood before the Lord.

Thanks, O our Father! that, like him,
    Thy tender love I see,
In radiant hill and woodland dim,
    And tinted sunset sea.
For not in mockery dost Thou fill
    Our earth with light and grace;
Thou hid'st no dark and cruel will
    Behind Thy smiling face!

The Complete Poetical Works of John Greenleaf Whittier.
Published by Houghton, Mifflin and Co., New York.

MYSTICISM

Mystical experience is marked by the emergence of a type of consciousness which is not sharply focalized, or clearly differentiated into a subject-object state. The "subject" and "object" are fused into an undivided *one*. Whatever is seen, heard, or felt in these moments is flooded with an inrush from the abysses of the inner life. Deep-lying powers, not ordinarily put into play, seem suddenly liberated. The usual insulations, which sunder our inner life into something like compartments, seem shot through. The whole being—in an integral and undivided experience—*finds* itself. Not only so, but transcendent energies from beyond the margin appear to "invade" the individual self, a larger environing consciousness, an enfolding presence, makes itself felt. These undifferentiated experiences—J. A. Stewart, in his *Myths of Plato* (London, 1905), calls them "transcendental consciousness"—occur in a great variety of fields, in numerous ways, and with all degrees of depth and inclusiveness. Lofty appreciation of beauty or sublimity, absorbed enjoyment of music, serene companionship with nature, sudden insight into the meaning of a truth, the awakening of love, moral exaltation of life in the pursuit of duty, illustrate some types of experience which immensely transcend "knowledge"—experiences in which "subject" and "object" are fused into an undifferentiated *one,* and in which self is identified with object.

Religious mystical experience is an intense, and strikingly dynamic, variety of this fused, undifferentiated consciousness. The individual soul feels invaded, vitalized with new energy, merged with an enfolding presence, liberated and exalted with a sense of

having found what it has always sought, and flooded with joy.
. . . The mystical experience, especially in the loftiest spiritual
geniuses of the race, may very well be the emergence of a new
type-level of life, a higher manner of correspondence with ultimate
sources of reality, an *élan vital* of the soul, a surge of the entire
self towards ineffable fullness of life. . . .

Christ's own personal experience, as it comes to light in the
Gospels, is the supreme model of true mystical experience. All His
words and acts are penetrated with an infinite depth of experience
and are fused with a warmth and intimacy of direct fellowship
with God. He reveals an interior *sense of life* which explores and
possesses new depths of reality and which releases for Himself
and others new energies by which to live. The active forces of His
will appear always to spring from a life-conjunction with the
Beyond. His ethical ideals—in the Sermon on the Mount, e.g.—
are inherently bound up with His prayer-experience. The kingdom
that is to come is the growing sway of the will of the Father to
whom He prays, and it is possibly only through expanding correspondence with a world of higher forces and of perfect conditions. The "altered fashion of countenance", the transfigured form
and face, which marked His prayer-experience before the journey
to Jerusalem, is such an experience as might well attach to a supreme crisis of personal decision. Prayer of illumination, altered
face, changed form, glorified figure, the radiation of light, have
marked many mystics, and these features seem to have characterized the Master as He adjusted His soul to the unseen realm, as
He formed His momentous decision to be faithful unto death in
His manifestation of Love. The agony of sweat as He rose, in
the shadow of the Cross, to the experience of communion and
fellowship of suffering with His Father, and was enabled to cry
"Abba," is psychologically true to nature and bears the genuine
mark of mystical experience.

The most important fact of this personal life, which ever since
has poured streams of power into the life of the world, is its complete adjustment to a realm of unseen reality, and its consciousness of correspondence with a personal heart and will, constituting
the essence of that unseen realm. Through all the story and behind all the teaching is the inner fact of personal experience of
God. In great moments of intercourse there is a flooding of con-

sciousness of sonship rising even to the audition, "This is my beloved son," and in times of strain and tragedy the onward course is possible because the Abba-experience is absolutely real.

Rufus M. Jones: Hastings "Encyclopaedia of Religion and Ethics.

THIS IS MY FATHER'S WORLD

This is my Father's world,
    And to my listening ears,
All nature sings, and round me rings
    The music of the spheres.
This is my Father's world,
    I rest me in the thought
Of rocks and trees, of skies and seas—
    His hand the wonders wrought.

This is my Father's world,
    The birds their carols raise,
The morning light, the lily white,
    Declare their Maker's praise.
This is my Father's world,
    He shines in all that's fair;
In the rustling grass I hear Him pass,
    He speaks to me everywhere.

This is my Father's world,
    O let me ne'er forget
That though the wrong seems oft so strong,
    God is the Ruler yet.
This is my Father's world,
    The battle is not done;
Jesus who died shall be satisfied,
    And earth and heaven be one.

Maltbie D. Babcock, *Thoughts For Everyday Living*.
Charles Scribner's Sons, publishers, New York. Printed by permission.

Concentrate Upon the Ideal: Eleventh Monday

71. REVELATION

One well might say the town was very dull
On such a winter's day as this has been,—
Till suddenly the stars were beautiful
Above stilled streets so fair for wandering in
That lonely walkers came, not knowing why,
Save to be lonely with such things as these,
When the last light is going from the sky,
And pale, starred dusks are in the thinning trees.

So had it been with me throughout the day;
No breath of beauty trembled anywhere,
No light upon the world that was not gray;—
And suddenly the stars were burning there,
And such grave mystery was in the street
That I walked home on hushed and timid feet.

DAVID MORTON, in *The World Tomorrow*.

FAR INTO QUIET DEPTHS

Our true life lies at a great depth within us. Our restlessness
and weaknesses are in reality merely stirrings of the surface. That
is why we must daily retire in silence far into the quiet depths of
our spirits, and experience the real life within us. If we do this, our
words and actions will come to be real also.

TAGORE.

MEANING AND DIRECTION

So many Christians are like deaf people at a concert. They
study the program carefully, believe every statement made in it,
speak respectfully of the quality of the music, but only really hear
a phrase now and then. So they have no notion at all of the mighty
symphony which fills the universe, to which our lives are destined
to make their tiny contribution, and which is the self-expression
of the Eternal God.

The people of our time are helpless, distracted and rebellious, unable to interpret that which is happening, and full of apprehension about that which is to come, largely because they have lost this sure hold on the eternal; which gives to each life meaning and direction, and with meaning and direction gives steadiness.

EVELYN UNDERHILL, *The Spiritual Life.*
Published by Harper & Brothers, New York City.

MUSIC

Music's the measure of the planet's motion,
    Heart-beat and rhythm of the glorious whole;
Fugue-like the streams roll, and the choral ocean
    Heaves in obedience to its high control.
Thrills through all hearts the uniform vibration,
    Starting from God, and felt from sun to sun;
God gives the key-note, Love to all creation;
    Join, O my soul, and let all souls be one!

JOHN SULLIVAN DWIGHT (1813-1893).

ELEMENTAL STUFF

It is stranger than fiction that even in the mere story of his life, Jesus still casts this spell over men. Here is H. W. Massingham, great soul and one of the bravest journalists of our time, toward the end of his life, making a fresh study of Jesus. And here is his report of it: "Going back to the Bible, and with the aid of modern criticism, simplifying the story of His life, as the imaginative reader loves to simplify it, I saw that it was elemental stuff and that out of it was made all the goodness I have ever come in contact with." *Elemental stuff,* please observe. . . . When you come to the cross you find yourself in the presence of something like an absolute ethical antithesis. In our human conflicts and crises we are never confronted by issues of simple right and wrong: there are endless cross currents and confusions of motive. Our choices have to be made not between black and white, but between shades of grey. But on the cross—and nowhere else— we find the contrast stark and absolute, black against white, midnight against midday, with no twilight zone. On the one side is the essential rightness of Jesus; on the other the forces that were bent on destroying him. . . .

There are personalities in the scene who are symbolical of "this world's unspiritual gods"—Barabbas, the preacher and practitioner of political violence; Pilate, the guardian of civil peace at any price; Herod, the idol of the fast set; Annas and Caiaphas, the crafty protagonists of vested interests; and the same old crowd that we know so well—ignorant, gullible, easily led by the nose, and fooled into shouting the catchword of the moment. Just the same violent, shrewd, vicious, selfish, stupid world that we have with us still. And over against all this, the antithesis of it at every point—Jesus.

RICHARD ROBERTS, in *Ventures in Belief,* edited by Henry P. Van Dusen.
Published by Charles Scribner's Sons, New York.

THE SUBSTANCE OF RELIGION

That a man should find God and possess Him as *his* God,—should live in the fear of Him, trust Him, and lead a holy and blessed life in the strength of this feeling,—that is the substance and the aim of religion. . . . The Christian faith is not, as is so often maintained, a gentle exaltation of our earthly life, or a comfort and relief in its troubles and trials. No! it is a decision for God and against the world. It is an eternal life that is involved: the recognition that in and above Nature and her changes there is a realm of sanctity and love, a city not built with hands, whose citizens we are to be; and with this message there comes to us the demand that we should cleanse our hearts and deny ourselves. . . . When God and everything that is sacred threatens to disappear in darkness, or our doom is pronounced; when the mighty forces of inexorable nature seem to overwhelm us, and the bounds of good and evil to dissolve; when, weak and weary, we despair of finding God at all in this dismal world—it is then that the personality of Christ may save us. Here we have a life that was lived wholly in the fear of God—resolute, unselfish, pure; here there glows and flashes a grandeur, a love, which draws us to itself. Although it was all a continual struggle with the world, though bit by bit one earthly possession after another fell away, and at last the life itself came to an ignominious end; yet no soul can avoid the thought that whoso dies thus, dies well: he dies not, but lives. For it was in this life and death that there first dawned upon mankind the assurance of an eternal life, and a divine love which overcomes all evil, nay, sin itself; and in the presence of a glory which is beyond the reach of death, we have come to perceive the vanity of the world and of all earthly possessions. . . . As surely as everything depends on the soul finding God and becoming one with Him, so surely is he the true Saviour, Guide, and Lord who leads the soul to God. . . .

ADOLF HARNACK, *Christianity and History,* 1896 edition.

CREATIVE OMNIPOTENCE

The childlikeness of an adequate religion lies not on this but on the other side of sophistication. It is not the childlikeness of primitive ignorance but the childlikeness of a wisdom which has learned the limits of human knowledge. It therefore approaches life with awe, hope and fear. With awe, because it knows that the mystery of life is something more than an unknown region not yet explored by an advancing science; with hope because "it doth not yet appear what we shall be" and no record of past history gives us an adequate clue of what creative omnipotence may bring forth out of the infinite possibilities of existence; with fear, because it knows the possibilities of evil, which appear at each new turn in history, are never adequately anticipated by any analysis of the past. The wisdom of such childlikeness will prefer its hopes to its fears, knowing that good is more primary than evil, that the world could not exist at all if it were not good, creation being a triumph over chaos. It will therefore approach life fearful and yet unafraid. Its serenity will be more lasting than that of a culture which based its confidence upon the illusion that human intelligence had overcome the chaos of the nature about us and the nature in us.

REINHOLD NIEBUHR, *Beyond Tragedy.*
Published by Charles Scribner's Sons, New York.

A PRAYER

Teach us, good Lord, to serve Thee as Thou deservest; to give and not to count the cost; to fight and not to heed the wounds; to toil and not to seek for rest; to labor and not to ask for any reward, save that of knowing that we do Thy will; through Jesus Christ our Lord.

IGNATIUS LOYOLA.

Understand the Actual: Eleventh Tuesday

72. LINES

Up and down the city there are clothes lines,
Full of clothes,
Washed and blowing in the sun.

All around the world there are class lines.
Full of horrors,
Hidden from the light.

Some women wash and iron clothes, day in and day out.
These women never have clean clothes.
They do not have time to wash their own clothes.

MARGARET LORING THOMAS, in *The Crisis*.

PREFACE TO PEASANTRY

The Negro mother or grandmother bears the brunt of the family's reverses. When her sister or daughter dies she takes the small children and rears them; when the family moves to another tenant house she puts up new clothes lines and clears the path to the spring or well and chops the weeds from the back door. When the busy season comes she prepares breakfast for the entire family, and, often leaving a small baby at the house with a young child, works until the middle of the day when she returns to the kitchen and prepares a hasty meal for her family. She goes back into the field in early afternoon and works until almost dark, returning to prepare supper and put tired children to bed. When the crop is poor she takes in additional washing or finds some neighbor who will give her a day's work now and then; when there is no work which she must do in the field or away from home, she gets out the family wash and attends to her housework, which usually includes the cultivating of whatever garden the family has and often the chopping of the wood for the stove. When "hard times" force the family to leave the home county, the father goes ahead to find work while the mother waits for word to come; then with bundles and belongings she gets her children on the train for a place where she hopes for an easier life but does not always find it.

The mother in the white tenant household, and even in that

of the small owner, is usually the chief burden carrier, frequently working in the fields in addition to doing her housework. In the planter family, the mother nearly always has heavy responsibilities. Scarcely any farm mother leads an idle or a sheltered life. The Negro mother bears all the load that the white mother bears, plus the additional burdens which her race imposes—a less stable family life, a circumscribed economic base, and inferior services from private and public agencies.

ARTHUR RAPER, *Preface to Peasantry.*
Published by University of North Carolina Press, Chapel Hill.

PEONAGE IN GEORGIA

When newspaper reports broke in September, 1937, on forced Negro labor in the cotton fields of Warren County, Ga., the situation revealed seemed to justify a first-hand investigation. The Southern Committee for People's Rights, the National Association for the Advancement of Colored People, the Workers Defense League, and the American Civil Liberties Union together sent an investigator into the field. He was a Southerner by birth who has lived all his life in the South devoting his time exclusively to economic and racial problems. . . .

On the 16th of September, 1937, the papers of the nation carried what was to many the shocking and revolting news that in Warren County, Georgia, Negroes were being forced into the fields to pick cotton at the miserably low figure of 40 cents per hundred pounds. Furthermore, the papers stated that an unruly and savage mob had invaded Warrenton, the county seat, and had terrorized the community by seeking out Negroes employed in various services and domestic servants, who sought protection in the homes of their employers, and by driving the larger part of the Negro community into the cotton fields.

While the practice is illegal and is shocking to the average American citizen, it is so universally practiced in the cotton-planting South as to cause little or no comment. By the planting interests it is looked upon as a very practical way of getting the cotton crop picked. The merchants and business men generally, in most southern cities and small towns, look upon the practice as an expedient and practical manner of relieving the city of "vagrants, loafers and relief hounds."

It is stated quite openly that the horse-whipping of tenants, particularly Negro tenants (I heard no reference to white men being whipped) is a common and accepted practice throughout the county on the large plantations. . . .

It is common practice for Warren County planters—and Warren County planters are not the only ones—to pay a tenant, always a Negro, out of debt, or as they say "to buy the debt" and place him on the buyer's plantation to work out the debt, which the unfortunate tenant rarely ever succeeds in doing. The action is tantamount to "buying the nigger," as I heard one farmer remark. If the tenant tires of his enforced bondage and tries to run away, the law steps in and returns the "run-away" to his master. While slavery has been legally abolished in these United States, there are areas in which for all practical purposes, it is still in existence. . . .

In an effort to secure sufficient pickers, farmers in Glascock went into the adjoining Warren County. Offering prices double what the planters in Warren were offering, they stood a good chance of securing the necessary labor. Trucks were sent to Warrenton and other nearby towns to secure the necessary pickers.

With thirty-cent prices being generally offered in Warren County few pickers had felt it worth while to respond. Thirty cents per hundred pounds meant that the average cotton picker could make around fifty cents a day. The average for Warren County, in my estimation, would be around 125-150 pounds per day. Some could pick 200-300 pounds per day but they would represent the exceptionally fast picker. At the outside, then, the best a good picker could expect was less than $1.00.

Warren County planters thought (1) that 30c. per hundred pounds was sufficient, although some paid 40c. but told their helpers to keep quiet about the extra ten cents; (2) that "the niggers ought to be loyal and pick Warren County's first"; (3) that to allow the pickers to get 60 and 75c. would "spoil our niggers"; and (4) that if the "niggers didn't come willingly, to force them to go to the fields and pick."

After some pickers from Warrenton had shown their reluctance to pick cotton in Warren County for 30c. and shown a marked preference for the 75c. being offered in Glascock, the planters decided that it was time to call a halt to the matter and "teach our niggers a little respect and loyalty."

So on the morning of September 13th, 1937, the citizens

were aroused by the angry shouting of violent men and the roaring of pistols and shotguns. A truck driver from Glascock who had come to get a load of pickers was pulled from his seat, roughly handled, threatened menacingly with an ax-handle and told to "git the hell out of town" and to stay out. It is evident from what transpired that the plans of the vigilantes had been carefully worked out and that it was not just a "popping off," as some sought to suggest. Following the assault upon the truck driver, the mob set upon the Negroes in the public square and began their lessons in patriotism to Warren County Negroes. . . .

The members of the mob made a systematic visit to each and every store. Wherever they found a Negro they told him to go to the fields and pick cotton. The bootblack in a barber shop showed some hesitancy about following the command and was given a clout over the head. . . . They forced open the doors of private homes and delivered their ultimatum—"We want you to pick cotton" and departed. Shots were fired into the air and into some of the homes—at least one received several shots—completely terrorizing the people. . . .

The vigilante placed armed patrols on the road to prevent any further molestation of their "niggers" by outside influences. It is alleged but obviously without getting proof that while the Negroes picked in the fields armed guards stood over them to see that they were not idle and did not leave the field. The actual presence or absence of guns is not relevant at all. The important and indisputable fact is that the Negroes of Warren County were so subdued by the terrorism and brutality of the mob that they were forced into the fields to pick cotton. The indisputable fact is that American citizens were forced against their wills to do labor for another through intimidation, through coercion, through bodily violence, and very probably, through the use of arms.

American Civil Liberties Union.

A PRAYER

Cleanse our hearts, we beseech Thee, of the dark sin of race prejudice; forgive us for our belief in the sacredness of human personality which Thou hast made in Thine own image; take away from us the uncontrolled passion of our hearts, and that violence of spirit which would make beasts of us all.

JAMES MYERS.

Be Concerned: Eleventh Wednesday

73. WISE AND GOOD MEN

Had the governing classes in France during the last century paid as much heed to their proper business as to their pleasures or manners, the guillotine need never have severed that spinal marrow of orderly and secular tradition through which in a normally constituted state the brain sympathizes with the extremities and sends will and impulsion thither. It is only when the reasonable and practicable are denied that men demand the unreasonable and impracticable; only when the possible is much different that they fancy the impossible to be easy. Fairy tales are made out of the dreams of the poor. . . .

There is no good in arguing with the inevitable. The only argument available with an east wind is to put on your overcoat. And in this case, also, the prudent will prepare themselves to encounter what they cannot prevent. Some people advise us to put on the brakes, as if the movement of which we are conscious were that of a railway train running down an incline. . . .

Not a change for the better in our human housekeeping has ever taken place that wise and good men have not opposed it—have not prophesied with the alderman that the world would wake up to find its throat cut in consequence of it.

JAMES RUSSELL LOWELL, *Democracy and Other Addresses*.

THE SAME INTENSE BELIEF

"Religion is the opium of the people." But the phrase was invented not by Karl Marx but by an anglican parson, Charles Kingsley. And too often it has been obviously true. No Christian can handle this subject with any sincerity who does not start by frankly confessing that some Churches claiming the name of Christ have allied themselves with reaction and obscurantism, and thus been used as the instruments of slavery.

The appalling events in the world of our time confirm the conviction of Christianity that Man *cannot* live by bread alone. The world to-day is hungry for God, for a life that is real, personal and satisfying; and man, if he cannot find God in heaven, must surrender himself to a god on earth. The collectives of contemporary politics offer that need a half-way satisfaction. But they leave what is deepest and most characteristic in the constitution of Man unfulfilled; and so long as that hunger remains unsatisfied the subterranean forces burst through, too often in blind, destructive fury. There is only one constructive rejoinder which can liberate all that is best and strongest in us in the venture of cooperative enterprise; and that is the Christian Revolution, which enthrones persons at the heart of politics because it enthrones God in the universe.

Christianity is a Gospel about God, the Father of our Lord Jesus Christ and the God to whom persons are dear. It is thus the religion of personality in a sense which can be claimed by no other. It stands for the fulfilment of persons in organic, ethical community. . . . It stands for the salvation of persons at all the levels of human experience—biological, psychological and spiritual—into right relationship with God and with one another in God. This it calls the Kingdom of God on earth and this it believes is the goal of history. And since for it all human institutions, political, economic or cultural, have their justification and reward in so far as they are instruments of His Kingdom, it can never accept the claim of the State as absolute.

Thus this faith is in essence revolutionary. If the God whom Christians believe in is the sovereign ruler of the universe and the overruling Providence of history, then Christians every time they repeat their creed are pledging their loyalty to a revolution— so to live that the order of this world may be conformed to that divine purpose which has been made manifest in Christ. . . .

In an iron age such as ours, a conventional and defensive Christianity is almost bound to be beaten off the field. It must show its faith by its works. It needs to revive its crusading ardour. The moral initiative is still ours, but it may not be so very much longer. The Christian religion can only win if it shows the same consecrated loyalty, the same power of sacrificial devotion, the same passion for emancipation, the same intense belief in its own cause, as the Komsomol and the Hitler-Jugend. Unless it appears as an exacting claim and demonstrates its effectiveness in action how are the hard-boiled young to believe in it?

F. R. BARRY, in *Christianity and Communism,* edited by H. Wilson Harris.
Published by Marshall Jones Company, Boston.

THE ARCHBISHOPS' COMMITTEE SPEAKS

Our "charity" has meant far too exclusively what may be
called ambulance work for mankind—the picking up of the
wounded and the curing of their wounds. We have neglected to
attack the forces of wrong. We have been content with the ambulance work when we ought to have been assaulting the strong-
holds of evil. We have allowed avarice and selfishness and grind-
ing competition to work havoc over the broad spaces of human
life. We want a strenuous reaffirmation of the principles of justice,
mercy and brotherhood as sovereign over every department of
human life. . . .

Founded upon the life and example of a unique Person, the
Christian Church claims to offer a spiritual ideal sufficiently definite and comprehensive to supply a criterion of human conduct
and institutions. It is a society which stands not only for a body
of doctrine but for a way of life. . . . We think it our duty to
point out that Christianity claims to offer mankind a body of
moral teaching which not only is binding upon individuals in
their personal and domestic conduct but also supplies a criterion
by which to judge their economic activity, their industrial organisation, and their social institutions. . . .

It is for the Church to humanise industry by upholding the
spiritual ends to which it ought to be directed, and the spiritual
criteria by which it ought to be judged. Industry is, in short, a
social function, which ought to be carried on, in the words of
Bacon, for "the glory of the Creator and the relief of man's
estate." Its character, organisation and methods ought to be such
as to make it unmistakable to observers that it is a main practical
activity of a Christian community. We think, therefore, that it is
the duty of the Church, while avoiding dogmatism as to the
precise methods of applying Christian principles to industry, to
insist that Christian ethics are as binding upon economic conduct
and industrial organisation as upon personal conduct and domestic life. . . . When Christian ethics and economic practice are
at variance, the latter must be adapted to the former, not the
former to the latter; and it is too often forgotten that avarice, in
the sense of the immoderate desire for gain, is a sin which Christian tradition regards as not less grave than some others which
to-day are more generally condemned. It can hardly be doubted,

indeed, that the common assumption that the attainment of riches is one of the main ends of man, and that the criterion of social organisation is its power to facilitate the pursuit of them, is not so much unchristian as anti-Christian; for it leads, when accepted, to the subordination of the religion of the spirit to a religion of gain. . . .

If it is true—and who can doubt it?—that the sanctity of personality is a fundamental idea of Christian teaching, it is evident that Christians are bound to judge their industrial organisation by that principle and to ask whether in modern industry human being are regarded always as ends and never as means.

The Report of the Archbishops' Fifth Committee of Inquiry,
Christianity and Industrial Problems.
Published by the Society for Promoting Christian Knowledge, London.

THE RICH YOUNG MAN

It seemed so mad a way to do—
To grieve so deep—to perish, too
For men He never even knew!
A life so lonely, meek, and bare!
I wonder why He made a prayer
For them that mocked and nailed Him there!
Vast wealth is mine; why do I see
My golden hoard without avail?
Why turns no man with love to me?
Why did He triumph, and I fail?
Poor and despised! how strange a thing
That mighty hosts, with worshipping,
Their homage to His name should bring!

Oh, 'tis a grievous mystery—
That mankind never looks to me
As to that spent and broken Christ
That drooped on Calvary!

LAURA SIMMONS.

A PRAYER

Forgive us who bear Thy name that, like the priest, we have many times passed by on the other side, leaving wounded humanity to be ministered unto by the good Samaritans of secular or political groups, whose courage and sacrifice have often put us to shame. JAMES MYERS.

Endeavor to Transform: Eleventh Thursday

74. THE INITIATED

Not from ourselves the subtle dreams we draw
    For our long intercourse of mind and mind.
We search in God for beauty and for law;
    We think, and share, ecstatic, what we find.

We are like children picking flowers in spring,
    In some sweet meadow rich with clover-yield;
And endless is the joy of gathering,
    And boundless is the field.

        EDITH LOVEJOY PIERCE, in *The Christian Century.*

A COMMUNITY OF EQUALS

The ideal aimed at in educational policy ought to be the deliberate formation of a community of equals, each of whom enjoys all the luxuries of knowledge, skill and culture, besides such training as will fit each to play a part in the common life. And for this purpose, in defiance of mediaeval authoritarianism under dictators, it is necessary that discussion of all possible opinions should be promoted in education, that all teachers and "leaders" should be freely criticized, that no fixed order of precedence should be granted to any class or group, and that all foreign contacts should be welcomed. A nobler and more living community can thus be formed than by an established orthodoxy.

The purpose of this policy is not merely to give to the poor or the ignorant what is now enjoyed by the rich and the learned. The purpose is far more radical. It is to remove the incompetence in the art of living in society, which is now prevalent in all circles; and to eliminate the evil characteristics of existing riches and traditional learning. Riches are too eagerly sought for private enjoyment; and learning is still affected by the obsolete slave-owner's idea that railwaymen and postmen are inferior persons who are instruments of the contemplative life of a select few. The chief purpose of educational policy is not the sharing of a tradition which already exists, but the creation of life in a community that does not exist. The purpose is the formation of a new way of living in common with others.

In that new community all personal activity will have its place in the life of the whole. Each occupation will be an honorable function, a service of a common purpose—the maintenance and progress of civilized life. One man's job will not be more respectable or noble than another's. But all will be levelled up; none will be levelled down. The docker is as clearly a servant of the community as the surgeon or the Prime Minister; and because the school is to make this new community out of the children of today, all schools should be in one system for all the new generation without distinction of the incomes or the functions of parents. The schools of today should be chiefly concerned with the formation of a new generation which will have the ability to make that life in common for themselves.

C. DELISLE BURNS, *Challenge To Democracy.*
Published by W. W. Norton Company, New York.

DEMOCRACY REQUIRES ECONOMIC EQUALITY

Social equality means . . . that, unequal as men are in every possible respect—and all the more because they are unequal—human Societies ought to be organised on a basis that will both avoid as far as possible adding artificial to natural inequalities and recognise the right of each man to have his happiness and well-being considered equally with those of any other in the framing of social policy, subject only to the right of Society to restrict the rights and claims of the individual for the purpose of promoting the greatest happiness and well-being of the greatest number.

This principle has been invoked repeatedly by democrats of many different schools of thought. Most of all it has been proclaimed as the justification for treating all men as "equal before the law," and for the adoption of forms of government resting on the foundation of "one man, one vote." But in no Society as yet have the democrats, even in these respects, ever had matters all their own way. . . .

The real roots of social inequality are mainly economic. It is simply not possible for men to be socially or politically equal as long as there exist among them differences of wealth and income so great as to divide them into distinct economic classes, with widely differing opportunities in childhood to become healthy, educated, travelled, and used to regard the world as a place made to suit their convenience. The slum child is not so healthy as the child whose parents can afford to give it the privileges of good food and sunlight. In the schools, the children of the poorest classes lag behind those who come from better equipped homes. . .

If we want a Society of social equals, we can hope to build it only on a foundation of economic equality. This is not to say that it is indispensable for all men and women, or all families, to have absolutely equal incomes, or incomes varying only with the size of the family. This may be desirable, in the long run, as the easiest way of solving the problem of distributing the national wealth; but it is not indispensable as the basis of democracy. It will suffice if there are no differences in wealth or income so large as to divide men into separate economic classes, with sharply contrasting standards of existence and habits of social life. For small differences of income among persons whose broad standards of living are the same will not confer on one great power over another, or interfere with their sufficient social equality in other respects— as voters, or before the law, or in their everyday intercourse one with another. But as soon as economic equality exceeds this limit, good-bye to the chance of real fraternity or of truly democratic institutions. Good-bye in fact to the chance of a Society that will take for its essential aim the greatest happiness and well-being of the greatest number.

Even among the relatively poor, objection is often taken to economic equality, even in this modified form, on the ground that it is inconsistent with the principle of rewarding men according to the quality of their service. It is argued that, if this principle is abandoned or limited, there will be no adequate incentive left to make men give of their best. We are not now raising the question whether or not Society will be able some day to dispense altogether with monetary incentives, by finding alternative incentives powerful enough to get the world's work done. But, quite apart from this, there is no evidence that, even if monetary incentives are required, they need be anything like so large as they are in most of the Societies of today. For the more equal incomes are, the smaller are the incentives needed to call out special effort. In an equalitarian Society, an extra penny may be as effective as a pound is now. Economic inequality bids up the price of effort, especially among the well-to-do, precisely because the more pounds a man has already the less an additional pound is worth to him.

Economic equality, in advanced industrial Societies, can come about only as an outcome of the social ownership of the resources of production. Private ownership of these resources means inequality; it is the foundation on which the major inequalities rest. Therefore, if we want equality, we must socialise.

We must do this, not only in order to get economic equality, but also in order to get social or political equality in any real sense. The pursuit of the greatest happiness and well-being of the greatest number is quite inconsistent with the treatment of the resources of production as the private property of a limited group of citizens. It implies their use as means of promoting the welfare of all. Political democracy cannot be real democracy unless it carries with it real control of the common means of life. For even if all men have votes, they cannot have an equal chance of using their votes aright unless they are tolerably on a level in standards of living, education and culture. When there are rich men and poor men, no merely political devices can prevent the rich from having more influence, man for man, than the poor. Nor can anything stop the rich, or most of them, from cohering together into a class for the preservation of their exclusive claims—from dominating the professions, the schools, the theatres, the newspapers, and from creating a socially stratified type of Society. Only collective control of the resources of production and of the distribution of incomes can prevent these things, which are the inevitable manifestations of a Society based on the recognition of unequal rights.   G. D. H. COLE and MARGARET COLE, *A Guide to Modern Politics.*
Published by Alfred A. Knopf, New York.

A PRAYER

O perfect Love and Beauty, Light of all minds that seek Thee, Joy of all souls that love Thee; before the wonder of Thy Being our souls bow down in adoration and awe, invoking the loftiest thoughts of Thy truth and the purest visions of Thy love; that our prayer may hallow Thy name in our hearts, and lead our spirits, if only for a moment, out of the shadows of time into Thy clearer presence, where truth and beauty blend in a fellowship ineffable and a praise unutterable; through Jesus Christ our Lord. Amen.   JOSEPH FORT NEWTON, *Altar Stairs.*
Published by The Macmillan Company, New York.

Proceed Resolutely: Eleventh Friday

75. FOR US THE JOY OF JOYS

We shall not travel by the road we make;
    Ere day by day the sound of many feet
Is heard upon the stones that now we break
    We shall be come to where the cross-roads meet

For us the heat by day, the cold by night,
    The inch-slow progress and the heavy load,
And death at last to close the long grim fight
    With man and beast and stone: for them the road

For them the shade of trees that now we plant,
    The safe, smooth journey and the certain goal—
Yea, birthright in the land of covenant:
    For us day-labour, travail of the soul

And yet the road is ours as never theirs;
    Is not one gift on us alone bestowed?
For us the joy of joys, O pioneers:
    We shall not travel, but we make the road!

HELEN FRIEDLAENDER.

MORE THAN CORRECT DIAGNOSIS

There is a mighty lot of good-will in the world and a large percentage is to be found among the members of Christian churches. The trouble is not so much that it is not "good" enough as that it does not "will" enough. What is lacking is not so much desire as drive.

To put through changes of the magnitude of those which many agree to be necessary today needs more than a correct diagnosis and a suitable prescription. It needs what may perhaps best be called moral dynamite. Where then are the factories from which it may be fetched? The obstacles are stupendous and therefore the supply must be unfailing until the task is accomplished. But it cannot be supplied wholesale: each person must procure his own supply, for it is through dynamic personalities that things happen in this world of persons.

It has been my lot to meet a number of truly dynamic people. Let me instance three: Hudson Taylor, Sun Yat Sen, Toyohiko Kagawa. The first was the creator of one of the largest missionary societies in the world. He was continually summoning people to new and apparently impossible tasks, and probably influenced more people to dedicate their lives to China than any other half-dozen people you could name. His life was one of tireless devotion to the vision he had of bringing the Gospel of Christ to the 400,000,000 of that country. The second risked his life and staked everything for the ideal he held before him in the rebirth of his nation. His dream took a political form, but it was inspired by a passionate love for his fellowmen, a sympathy with their pains and a belief in their personalities. Through evil report and through good report he remained true to his principles. China has honored his devotion and recognized his intrinsic greatness of soul and will continue to do so even if she does not in every detail adopt his program. The third, happily still with us, is a living example of how a frail body can be galvanized by a dauntless spirit. Utterly careless of the things men usually value—fame, wealth, ease, health, even life itself—he has lived among the poorest of the poor and made their cause his very own. The fire of his great love has well-nigh consumed him. Pouring out the wealth of his own talents for the sake of his weaker brethren, he has won a place in their hearts which no one can take away.

To contemplate the power which a life such as one of these has had over innumerable other lives almost takes one's breath away. In none of these cases was power due to prestige or social status or money; it was the direct outcome of something in the man himself, or something which came through his personality into the lives of others. In no case was it exercised through domination or violence or threat. Before such persons men have not fallen to be crushed as by a Juggernaut; rather have they risen upon their feet, stronger men and women, and have taken their own line and become in measure, themselves creative personalities.

Looking at these three men, can we put our finger on any of the secrets of their power? I suppose one may at once say that whole-hearted and selfless devotion to a cause is to be found in nearly every such person. A tremendous drive needs the entire concentration of personality, which is all too rare in these days of many interests, when we tend too long to balance the pros and cons and too seldom to make the life commitment. Nor can we fail to see the strength which comes from having not only an all-embracing ideal which tends to enlarge and recede as we approach it, but also a well-defined objective, difficult but achievable, to which the immediate energies can be fully directed. Another factor which it may be even more important to stress is direct contact with bitter need. . . . We do not find that rare gifts are needed, or great scholarship, or unusual background. What gave them their power is not beyond the reach of what we may call very ordinary people.

HENRY T. HODGKIN, in *The World Tomorrow.*

RELIGION IS REVOLUTIONARY

What has religion to do with radical social change? Consider the social laws of the Pentateuch, the safeguarding of life over property, the almost communistic legislation of the Jubilee Year, the social teachings of the prophets of Israel and of Jesus. Each one of these thoughts, in its age, advocated radical social change. The historical spirit of prophetic religion is radicalism. No intelligent person would dare to state that we must judge religion simply by the specific words of its prophetic souls in their own day. We have a right to ask what an Amos or a Jesus would say today. We have every right to infer that as they were radicals, socially, in their day, so they would be radicals, socially, today. . . .

Radical religion upholds a principle of social idealism. The tendency of all existing orders or social philosophies is to become static and dogmatic. Radical religion is the eternal ferment which prevents any social or economic order from becoming satisfied with itself. It is the one force that can prevent the revolutionary of today from becoming the reactionary of tomorrow. It has a social theory and idealism rather than a concrete economic panacea. It trades in specific economic and social projects simply because it is by means of these tangible projects that the constantly expanding goals of religious idealism are successively realized.

The truly dynamic revolutionary must be religious. It is the only thing that can give harmony and sequence to his philosophy of life. It is the only thing that can keep him eternally a revolutionary. It is the only thing that can give meaning to his striving for humanity. Faith in a cosmic unity is the only safeguard against dictatorial arrogance on the one hand and cynical despair on the other.

Today we advocate pacifism, the abolition of the profit system and the more practical realization of democracy. We advocate these salient points because humanity is cursed specifically by war, by economic exploitation and by a throttling of the freedom of the individual in political and civil expression. Tomorrow it may be an entirely different set of social evils which will distort humankind. Radical religion will change its set of concrete goals. Its guiding principle of a striving for full human expression will remain. The static revolutionary might be satisfied with the realization of a pacifist, socialistic society. His end has been achieved. Radical religion is never satisfied. It puts eternal unrest into the hearts of men. It holds up before mankind not a thing but a vision. At each moment it supports that thing which seems nearest the vision, but when the momentary thing is realized, it turns toward the next things that has been disclosed—a social idealism that our previous shortsightedness never could envision.

RABBI EDWARD L. ISRAEL, in *The World Tomorrow.*

A PRAYER

O Lord Jesus Christ, Son of the Living God, who didst say to Thine apostles, Come ye apart into a desert place and rest awhile, for there were many coming and going: grant, we beseech Thee, to us Thy disciples, that we may rest awhile with Thee. May we so seek Thee, whom our souls desire to love, that we may both find Thee and be found in Thee, and finally by Thy mercy attain to that eternal rest, where nevertheless they rest not, day and night, from Thy perfect service, who with the Father and the Holy Spirit livest and reignest ever one God, world without end. Amen.

C. F. ANDREWS, *Christ and Prayer.*
Published by Harper & Brothers, New York.

Seek Comradeship: Eleventh Saturday

76. OUR MASTER

Immortal Love, forever full,
  Forever flowing free,
Forever shared, forever whole,
  A never-ebbing sea! . . .

The letter fails, and systems fall,
  And every symbol wanes;
The Spirit over-brooding all
  Eternal Love remains. . . .

Our Lord and Master of us all!
  Whate'er our name or sign,
We own Thy sway, we hear Thy call,
  We test our lives by Thine.

Thou judgest us; Thy purity
  Doth all our lusts condemn;
The love that draws us nearer Thee
  Is hot with wrath to them.

Our thoughts lie open to Thy sight;
  And, naked to Thy glance,
Our secret sins are in the light
  Of Thy pure countenance. . . .

To Thee our full humanity,
  Its joys and pains, belong;
The wrong of man to man on Thee
  Inflicts a deeper wrong.

Who hates, hates Thee, who loves becomes
  Therein to Thee allied;
All sweet accords of hearts and homes
  In Thee are multiplied.

Deep strikes Thy roots, O heavenly Vine,
   Within our earthly sod,
Most human and yet most divine,
   The flower of man and God!

O Love! O Life! Our faith and sight
   Thy presence maketh one,
As through transfigured clouds of white
   We trace the noon-day sun.

So, to our mortal eyes subdued,
   Flesh-veiled, but not concealed,
We know in Thee the fatherhood
   And heart of God revealed.

We faintly hear, we dimly see,
   In differing phrase we pray;
But, dim or clear, we own in Thee
   The Light, the Truth, the Way! . . .

Apart from Thee all gain is loss,
   All labor vainly done;
The solemn shadow of Thy Cross
   Is better than the sun.

Alone, O Love ineffable!
   Thy saving name is given;
To turn aside from Thee is hell,
   To walk with Thee is heaven!
     The Complete Poetical Works of John Greenleaf Whittier,
     Published by Houghton, Mifflin and Co., New York.

MOUNTAIN RANGES

Here stand the mountain ranges, dark on flame,
   Stark in the light after the sun has gone,
Unchanged since man upon this planet came;
   Not farmed nor landscaped, quarried, built upon,
But still impregnable, reserved and sure,
   Whose rugged line the long horizon fills:
Across the earth God's mighty signature,
   Against the sky indelible blue hills.
        EDITH LOVEJOY PIERCE, in *The Christian Century.*

RADIANT JOY

For it was an experienced gospel with which the primitive Church was concerned as it was set on its agelong course in the world of human life. Combined with the traditional faith and apocalyptic vision of the Jewish religious environment was the experiential recognition and awareness that the Jesus they had known on earth was the risen and exalted Christ at God's right hand. . . . His personality, animated with His own force of His experience and knowledge of God, passed directly into the primitive Church experience as it took its rise from personal conviction about Jesus as He had been discovered to be in His earthly life and in what He had come to be for faith in His exaltation. Such is the unique content of the religious experience of the primitive Church. Little wonder, then, the joyous religious experience, for the first years at least, was for the believers one long feast of Pentecost, a prolonged day of power with the manifold manifestation of the Spirit's presence in signs and wonders, when joy was irrepressible, when unquenchable faith went hand in hand with a tremendous enthusiasm in witness and well-doing, accompanied by a communism of love expressed in self-denying devotion and benevolence, as the dynamic experience of an undimmed faith in Jesus their exalted friend and Messiah carried the believers onward through "the radiant spring morning of the Church." And if the literal apocalyptic hopes did begin to fade, the religious horizons were enlarged in more specifically moral and spiritual directions, for the real dynamic of the Spirit-possessed life had revealed in itself "that the new life had been given to men in Christ Himself and that fellowship with Him was the true fulfilment of the Kingdom of God." . . .

The Spirit was again attested by the overwhelming joy which possessed the primitive Church. The believers knew "gladness of heart" (Acts ii. 46), and their radiance found expression in "praising God," as the ground of their sure confidence. People took notice of such joy and love, and looked on the believers with favour, so that many were caught by the joyous contagion and added to the new community (Acts ii. 47). The apostles rejoice that they are accounted worthy to suffer dishonour for Christ's name (Acts v. 41). In so far as believers endured reproach for Christ they experienced all the greater joy in being permitted so to witness (1 Pet. iv. 13 f., 16). Joy inspires Stephen on his way to martyrdom (Acts vii. 55 f.). There was rejoicing in Samaria over Philip's visit, but the joy was motivated by gratitude for healings wrought, and lacks the pure spiritual quality of the characteristic radiance of the Church (Acts viii. 8). The Ethiopian goes on his way with joy after his conversation with Philip (ver. 39). The Church at Jerusalem rejoices over Peter's testimony concerning the Gentiles (Acts xi. 18) while Gentiles themselves share in the new-born, conquering joy of the gospel experience (Acts xiii. 46, 48, 52). Barnabas is radiant over the evidence of the Spirit's power in Antioch (Acts xi. 23). The primitive Church cannot be understood unless full justice is done to this radiance that possessed the believers.

P. G. S. Hopwood, *The Religious Experience of The Primitive Church.*
Charles Scribner's Sons, publishers, New York. Printed by permission.

THE CELESTIAL PASSION

O white and midnight sky! O starry bath!
Wash me in thy pure, heavenly, crystal flood;
Cleanse me, ye stars, from earthly soil and scath;
Let not one raint remain in spirit or blood!
Receive my soul, ye burning, awful deeps;
Touch and baptize me with the mighty power
That in ye thrills, while the dark planet sleeps;
Make me all yours for one blest, secret hour!
O glittering host! O high angelic choir!
Silence each tone that with thy music jars;
Fill me even as an urn with thy white fire
Till all I am is kindred to the stars!
Make me thy child, thou infinite, holy night—
So shall my days be full of heavenly light!

RICHARD WATSON GILDER (1844-1909).

Worship God: Eleventh Sunday

77. PROOF

If radio's slim fingers
　　Can pluck a melody
From night, and toss it over
　　A continent or sea;

If the petaled white notes
　　Of a violin
Are blown across a mountain
　　Or a city's din;

If songs, like crimson roses,
　　Are culled from the thin blue air,
Why should mortals wonder
　　If God hears prayer?

ETHEL ROMIG FULLER, *Kitchen Sonnets.*
Published by Metropolitan Press, Portland, Oregon.

DIVINE HARMONY

Paderewski's vibrating fingers speeding along the keyboard like electric waves through quiescent space arouse my emotions, and I wonder at the harmonious response of the billions and billions of organic cells to the coordinating physical processes which animate Paderewski's ethereal touch. But my wonder is amplified a thousandfold when I listen to the tuneful message which this performance of perfect physical coordination conveys to me from the internal world of Paderewski's consciousness, where it was recorded by the creative soul of some heaven-born genius. . . . To me Kreisler's violin is a bell. The smooth and silent movement of his bow communicates to the strings a rapid succession of tiny pulses identical in action to the strokes of a clapper upon the church bell. They are tiny but numerous clappers which impart to the strings the energy of their life. This life manifests itself in their melodious vibrations, carrying a wonderful tale to our listening soul. The tale is identical with . . . the language of the church bell. But one essential difference must be mentioned.

The violin-maker, just like the maker of the church bell, imparts to the bell, called the violin, its fundamental character. The virtues of a Stradivarius are among the glories of human ingenuity. But the temperament and skill of a Kreisler superpose upon this fundamental character of the violin an almost infinite variety of modulations. Kreisler makes the vibrating strings speak a language which is indeed a message from heaven. When Kreisler plays a Beethoven sonata he is the apostle of the great composer and delivers his master's message. The message is the embodiment of an inspiration the cradle of which is the soul of the heaven-born genius. . . . Each tiny flower of the field is a little bell responsive to some solar clappers, and so is the brilliant cloud figure which bids good-by to the setting sun or announces the approach of the early dawn. The whole terrestrial globe is a cosmic bell which, responding to the strokes of the solar clappers, glorifies the beauties of our mother earth. But that is one part only of the message which the sun and the luminous stars are sending to us. Each signalling atom in the sun and in the luminous stars sends us the history of its life and of the life of the star to which it belongs. Listen to a message which the spectroscope reports from a young star somewhere near the very boundary of our stellar system. The message says: "I am a million light years away from you. I am an astral baby now, and will be a baby still when a million years hence you receive this message. Many billions of years will pass before the ardor of my youth has cooled down to the moderation of your central star, the sun. Heaven only knows when I shall be as old as your old mother earth. But when I reach that age I shall be a beautiful cosmic bell just like your earth and responding to the clappers of the luminous stars, I shall add my voice to the celestial choir which is declaring the glory of God."

This is my answer to the question, What is light? The answer was prepared in the world of the human soul where a divine creative power resides, and it recalls to memory the faint strokes of the vesper-bell of my native village of sixty years ago and my mother's voice saying: "Michael, do you not hear the divine message which calls you to the altar of the Almighty God?"

MICHAEL PUPIN, *The New Reformation.*
Charles Scribner's Sons, publishers, New York. Printed by permission.

THE PROFOUNDEST OF ALL APPRECIATION

Music has a power of objective expression that is not to be found in any of the silent arts. Sound is more suggestive in its imagery than either sight or reflection. Music has a way of dipping deeply into the subconscious where it finds numerous hidden memories; takes them out of their subjective setting and thrusts them in objective relief. Music has an aggressive way of gripping our very being, of clutching at our roots, compelling us to respond totally to its mood. Few people have remained unstirred by the haunting and rousing strains of the masters. There is something fundamental in music. The music which has affected mankind profoundly has been that which has lifted man out of his simple setting and identified him with the vaster life, has lured him beyond his limitations and blended his being with illimitable existence. Great music has been objective music. Beethoven's "Fifth Symphony" and Brahm's "First" are superb demonstrations of the capacity of human genius to soar to heights of objective experience.

The objective mood is felt also in the great silent arts: Raphael's "Transfiguration," Ruben's "Fall of the Damned, "Michelangelo's "Last Judgment," and his frescoes in the ceiling of the Sistine Chapel in Rome are outstanding examples. . . .

For mysticism, more than being a creed, is an attitude toward life. It is simply an openness toward life, a sense of wonder that impels one toward inquiry, awe, and profound reverence. It flings open the doors of our minds and bids us look at life in all its vastness, its greatness, and its goodness. It releases the tension of our bodies and sends the tendrils of feeling deep into the environing mystery, and impels us toward communion with realities that sustain us. Mysticism illumines the mind by increasing its sensitivity. It warms the spirit by evoking awareness of our intimate kindship with the life of earth. Mysticism is the deep fountain of all life, the inmost spring of religion. For, as Havelock Ellis has said, in its quintessential core, mysticism is the art of finding our emotional relationship with the world conceived as a whole. In this sense, the mystical attitude is the æsthetic attitude extended to cosmic proportions. . . .

The appreciative level of life does not stop at man's creations; it reaches beyond into the cosmic mystery. It does not end with enjoyment of concrete beauty, but extends into awareness and contemplation of the unportrayable reaches of cosmic order. The highest level of appreciative living is achieved in the mystical response—a wide awareness of this total wealth of planetary life, with all its relevant activities, sustaining and bearing our being. Thus the greatest of all arts is the art of worship, and the profoundest of all appreciation, communion with God.

BERNARD EUGENE MELAND, *Modern Man's Worship.*
Published by Harper and Brothers, New York.

EPILOGUE

This wind upon my mouth, these stars I see,
The breathing of the night above the trees,
Not these nor anything my senses touch
Are real to me or worth the boon of breath.
But all the never-heard, the never-seen,
The just-beyond my hands can never reach,
These have a substance that is stout and sure,
These brace the unsubstantial sliding world,
And lend the evanescent actual
An air of life, a tint of worth and meaning.
Shall dust, fortuitously blow into
A curve of moon or leaf or throat or petal
And seeding back to vacancy and dust,
Content my soul with its illiterate
And lapsing loveliness? Or tired knowledge
Make credible the hard decree of living?
Oh, I have heard a golden trumpet blowing
Under the night. Another warmth than blood
Has coursed, though briefly through my intricate veins.
Some sky is in my breast where swings a hawk
Intemperate for immortalities
And unpersuaded by the show of death.
I am content with what I cannot prove.

WILLIAM ALEXANDER PERCY, *Enzio's Kingdom.*
Published by Yale University Press.

Concentrate Upon the Ideal: Twelfth Monday

78. PROPER CLAY

Their little room grew light with cries;
He woke and heard them thread the dark,
He woke and felt them like the rays
Of some unlawful dawn at work—

Some random sunrise, lost and small,
That found the room's heart, vein by vein.
But she was whispering to the wall,
And he must see what she had seen.

He asked her gently, and she wept.
"Oh, I have dreamed the ancient dream.
My time was on me, and I slept;
And I grew greater than I am;

"And lay like dead; but when I lived,
Three wingèd midwives wrapped the child.
It was a god that I had loved,
It was a hero I had held.

"Stretch out your mortal hands, I beg.
Say common sentences to me.
Lie cold and still, that I may brag
How close I am to proper clay.

"Let this within me hear the truth
Speak loud to it"—he stopped her lips.
He smoothed the covers over both.
It was a dream perhaps, perhaps.

Yet why this radiance round the room,
And why this trembling at her waist?
And then he smiled. It was the same
Undoubted flesh that he had kissed—

She lay unchanged from what she was,
She cried as ever woman cried.
Yet why this light along his brows?
And whence the music no one made?

Mark Van Doren, in *The Virginia Quarterly*.

AFIRE WITH GOD

Earth's crammed with heaven.
And every common bush afire with God:
But only he who sees takes off his shoes.

Elizabeth B. Browning.

HEROES WITH MINE AND QUARRY

Under the midnight sun in summer and the northern lights in autumn, under the winter shadow of Arctic night lies Karelia, a wilderness of primeval forests set with a hundred thousand tangled lakes and jeweled with mountains of marble and mica and iron and copper. It runs for almost a thousand miles north from Leningrad to the polar waters, a long thin strip of country between Finland and the White Sea. . . .

I went to Karelia. I learned in the following days why the people of Karelia love President Gühling; he is still their president, as I write this book in 1934. He is a man of wide culture; once an aristocrat in Finland, professor of statistics in Helsingfors University and a director of the Bank of Finland. Yet he was a leader in the revolution; and when counter-revolution came in Finland, it was he who stood quietly at his post in Viborg to organize the flight of the other people's commissars to Sweden. Six weeks thereafter he hid in a sewer pipe from which he briefly emerged at night into a cellar; every morning he heard above him the rattle of machine guns which killed his comrades by hundreds in the prison yards. From this past he had come to his work in Karelia, where he lived with his family in two rooms in the government building, with offices below. Like Suchanova and her friends, his family slept on mattresses laid on boards or even on the floors. He was a quiet, hard-working man accessible day and night to the needs of the simplest folk.

In other rooms of the state house or in the log cabins around it lived a government of men who never intended to be personally rich. Individually poor, they held in their hands the forests, mines and quarries of a vast, unpillaged empire; they talked in terms of millions. . . . They said: "Last year we got a million dollars' profit from our timber even in the midst of famine." But this million was profit for the state budget of Karelia, not for themselves. They personally had just begun to draw money wages and to hope that the local stores or their ration cards would soon give them clothes as well as food. They were too busy exploring, developing and building to think of personal comfort. They were pioneers—but of a new type. . . .

He was a Finnish-American quarryman who had returned to work for the revolution; he was developing mica mines and feldspar quarries north of the Artic Circle. Most of the state budget of Karelia came not from taxes but from its state-owned industries; Rimpalle's mines and quarries were among them.

In a little barn behind the state house I saw Veltheim receive the mica—one hundred thousand dollars' worth—on behalf of the Commissariat of Foreign Trade. Two men arrived in miners' shirts with the bronze of the far north on their faces. They had gone north the preceding spring with ten tons of flour and a few blunt axes as working capital. They had had not even a saw with which to build a dock, not even a change of clothes. Worst of all, in Rimpalle's eyes, they had neither pneumatic drills nor gunpowder for blasting; they had to blow mica out by dynamite which broke it wastefully.

They had waded waist-deep in swamps; they had poled their boats over streams and lakes and portaged over hills. They had trained unlettered peasants to work in quarries and mines. They had wrung wealth from the wastes. At summer's end they came south with their haul not to blow it in on one grand spree and not to bank it for some future stake, as had the Alaskan pioneers who came south to Seattle, but to hand it over to the state. Veltheim examined the samples, checked the weight, gave them a receipt and went back to his office in a building of unpainted boards. None of them thought that anything unusual had happened. Yet they had done something which, if repeated often enough, would wreck all the systems of industry in the capitalist world. They had done something which could check that orgy of speculation in Moscow streets—the only thing that could check it.

"What did you get for your summer's work?" I asked Rim-palle.

"I got rations of potatoes and good fat gravy and one resoling of my boots!" He laughed and patted the shabby but firm leather uppers. "I've swell boots! Brought them from America. They were on me when I ran the Finnish border through lakes and swamps. Everything on me I kept, but nothing else. Some of the men got boots for their work this summer. I didn't need them; my boots only had to be resoled.

"They tell me we're going on money wages now," he added. "But last year—say, who'd have thought a year ago that we'd have good fat gravy so soon!"

ANNA LOUISE STRONG, *I Change Worlds.*
Published by Henry Holt and Company.

PROPHECY

Somewhere Beauty dwells, all undefiled;
For I have seen a rose unfold
At dawn,
And wonder grow
In the eyes of a child.

Somewhere Love shall live, all unafraid;
For I have seen a woman clasp Death's hand
At child-birth,
And pass into the shadows
Undismayed.

Somewhere Life shall live, beyond the blue;
For I have seen the veil wear thin
And fall apart—
And the face of God
Shine through.

NELLIE B. MILLER.

A PRAYER

O Thou who art heroic love, keep alive in our hearts that adventurous spirit, which makes men scorn the way of safety, so that Thy will be done. For so only, O Lord, shall we be worthy of those courageous souls who in every age have ventured all in obedience to Thy call, and for whom the trumpets have sounded on the other side; through Jesus Christ our Lord.

A NEW PRAYER BOOK.

Understand the Actual: Twelfth Tuesday

79. SPIES IN INDUSTRY

The story of *Spy Overhead* is the story of the American industrial worker caught in a trap of commercialized espionage and violence. An odd assortment of evidence in the files of the Sub-Committee on Education and Labor tells this story; secretly mailed requests to the President or the Department of Justice for bodily protection; income tax reports; testimony of industrialists; of labor organizers, detectives, union men turned traitors, or union men who have refused to turn traitor; the testimony of labor pimps, munition makers, sluggers, and ex-convicts. Together they make a decipherable and appallingly true story more like fiction than fiction is itself. . . .

Pinkerton's agency was founded by Allen Pinkerton in 1854. Only twelve years later they had moved into a strike in Braidwood, Illinois. By 1870 so great was the increase in demand for industrial service, they already had a competitor. By 1892 when the Carnegie Steel Company's contract with the Amalgamated Association of Iron, Steel, and Tin Workers expired, Henry Frick sent for Pinkerton's to break a strike in Homestead. Pinkerton sent three hundred armed men, recruited from New York and Chicago, up the river in a boat. A battle followed in which many men were killed. Testifying in the Congressional investigation that followed, a member of the United States Secret Service said of the forty Pinkerton men whom he had interviewed: "There is not one out of ten that would not commit murder; that you could not hire to commit murder or any other crime."

This was strikebreaking by violence, and not espionage, and of strikebreaking we shall hear more later. But the groundwork of those gory decades, the last two of the old century and the first of the new, was always laid by spies. Continuously forward into the 1930's, when Congress legalized the union, labor history is richly documented by illustrations of the agencies' working principle that where there is spying to do and money to pay for it, detectives will stick at nothing. . . .

Out of such a market, detective agencies wheedled from General Motors $819,000 in the two years and seven months following January, 1933. Pinkerton alone got $419,000 of it. Chrysler

paid $211,000 to Corporations Auxiliary whose business in this period was $1,292,193. The combined known volume of business done by the four of the five big professional companies under subpoena in these thirty-one months amounted to $3,465,918, although these estimates are made from data known to be inconclusive. CLINCH CALKINS, *Spy Overhead.*
Published by Harcourt, Brace and Company, New York.

HOW TO BREAK A STRIKE

When the C. I. O. showed every sign of becoming a real mass movement, during the great automobile strikes and in the beginning of the steel-organization campaign, big industry gradually moved to meet it. . . . The financial interests which are behind both Big and Little Steel are by no means split. They merely function on two fronts—peace with the union in one sector, war on the union in the other. Nor did Little Steel go into the fight strategically unprepared. It had thought its tactics through. In the Little Steel strike, as indeed in every recent major strike, industry followed the so-called Mohawk Valley Formula.

This formula appeared in the form of an article in the Labor Relations Bulletin of the National Association of Manufacturers soon after the Remington Rand strike at Ilion, New York. It indicated in detail the steps to be taken in a campaign of national strikebreaking. . . . And here it is epitomized but with its essential outline unchanged:

First: When a strike is threatened label all union leaders as "agitators." In the plant conduct a forced balloting under the direction of foremen to ascertain the strength of the union and to make possible misrepresentation of the strikers as a small minority imposing their will upon the majority. At the same time disseminate propaganda, by means of press releases, advertisements, and the activities of "missionaries," such propaganda falsely stating the issues involved in the strike so that the strikers appear to be making arbitrary demands, and the real issues, such as the employer's refusal to bargain collectively, are obscured.

Second: Concurrently with these moves, by exerting economic pressure and threatening to move the plants, if that is feasible, align the influential members of the community into a cohesive group opposed to the strike. In this group, usually designated as a *"citizens' committee,"* include representatives of the bankers, real-estate owners, business men, ministers, etc.

Third: When the strike is called raise high the banner of law and order, thereby causing the community to mass legal and police weapons against their wholly imagined violence, thereby suppressing all the civil liberties of the strikers.

Fourth: Call a "mass meeting" of the citizens to coordinate public sentiment against the strike and to strengthen the power of the citizens' committee, which organization, thus supported, will both aid the employer in exerting pressure upon the local authorities and itself sponsor vigilante activities.

Fifth: Bring about the formation of a large armed police force to be built up by utilizing local police, state police if the governor cooperates, vigilantes, and special deputies, the deputies being chosen if possible from other neighborhoods. Coach the deputies and vigilantes on the law of unlawful assembly, inciting to riot, disorderly conduct, etc., and make them anxious and ready to use their newly acquired authority to the limit.

Sixth: Perhaps most important, heighten the demoralizing effect of the above measures by a "back-to-work" movement, operated by a puppet association of so-called loyal employees secretly organized by the employer. (In a superb psychological analysis Mr. Rand discusses the effect of this back-to-work movement upon the strikers, the community, and the authorities, showing that it is the best way to kill all collective-bargaining sentiments.)

Seventh: When a sufficient number of applications to go "back to work" are on hand, fix a date for the opening of the plant, which opening is of course requested by the "back-to-work" association. Together with the citizens' committee, prepare for such opening by making provisions for a peak army of police by roping off the area surrounding the plant, by securing arms and ammunition, etc. . . . Even if the maneuver fails to induce a sufficient number of persons to return, persuade the public through pictures and news releases that the opening was nevertheless successful.

Eighth: Stage the "opening" as theatrically as possible.

Ninth: Capitalize on the demoralization of the strikers by continuing the show of police force and the pressure of the citizens' committee, both to insure that those employees who have returned will continue to work and to force the remaining strikers to capitulate. If necessary, turn the locality into a warlike camp through the declaration of a state of emergency tantamount to martial law and barricade it from the outside world so that nothing may interfere with the successful conclusion of the "Formula," thereby driving home to the union leaders the futility of efforts to hold their ranks intact.

Tenth: Close the publicity barrage on the theme that the plant is in full operation and that the strikers were merely a minority attempting to interfere with the "right to work" . . . the campaign is over—the strike broken.

These ten scab commandments were followed religiously in the Little Steel strike. That's how the strike was broken.

BENJAMIN STOLBERG, in The Nation.

SLAVE MARKETS

A protest against the exploitation of young Negro women engaged for wages of $1 a day or 15 cents an hour for domestic work at "slave markets" on Bronx and Brooklyn thoroughfares was made yesterday by Miss Dorothy Height, Negro representative of the Harlem branch of the Y. W. C. A. She spoke before the youth welfare committee of the City Council.

The girls, desperate for work, wait at the curbs on the Grand Concourse at Highbridge Road, the Bronx, and on Prospect Avenue near Prospect Park, Brooklyn, and bargain for work with housewives who drive there in automobiles when they need help, according to Miss Height. Miss Height said these two locations were known in Harlem as "slave markets." . . .

New York Times.

A PRAYER

Eternal Love, enter into our being and possess us; manifest Thyself to us as our Father and Redeemer. Show us that Thou hast need of our little lives to fulfill Thy purpose of righteousnes, even as we need Thee to realize the fullness of life. Make our fairest vision of mercy and truth, of love and justice, so real, so commanding, that all that is within us shall rise up and follow it. Endue us with power, with the insight to read Thy word in the facts and events of our day, and the courage to obey it, following even where we cannot see the way.

JOSEPH FORT NEWTON, Altar Stairs.
Published by The Macmillan Company, New York.

Be Concerned: Twelfth Wednesday

80. PROLOGUE

                        Now I hear in the night
Rise from every corner of the world
The life-tormented yell of starving men,
From doorway beds or subway benches, wrapped
In newspapers—*Beauty Engaged, The Hardware Jones'
Leave For Europe, Agitator Jailed.*
The toes of children rip through old shoes and scrape
On the hot streets or in the deep snow. Women
Lift up their eyes, no longer filmed with patience,
In the question that is their birthright and their curse:
Here are my children, thin, the bones begging for food,
There are no more quarters for the gas meter, no
Credit at the butcher's, the heat turned off.
Here is a man glad for a chance to work
Hard, long hours, overtime, and yet
Must walk the streets or sit in a cold room.
I am a woman. I do not understand.
But has a man no more the right to work,
A child to eat? A woman at evening
To rest in her family without the fear
Morning will find them turned into the street
With a handful of clothes and an old chair?
                                         This is not
Your way, America.
                   Yet now I see
In Alabama cotton burned, in Iowa
Hogs slaughtered and buried, in Montana
Wheat plowed under. While ten million men
Shiver and hunger. This is not your way
America. Remember—if one man eats
While another starves, his very food is cursed.
The bread line is a rope will strangle you.

You've kidded yourself too long, America.
It's time you looked the straight fact in the eye.
The world's gone bust, gone haywire, and you with it,
You, the infallible, spoiled child. Fate's got

Your number, buddy, he's got the dope on you,
Either you act now or he'll slip up and say
You're through, fella, you're done, washed up, cold,
Out on your feet and you don't know it, you're
Dead from the ears up. Scraaam.
                          Remember
That living men do not forever crawl
Down in the gutter and die in sight of fire
Which burns the bread stuff that could nourish them,
That there is an ancient power in the world,
Blind and cruel and terrible in act,
And it is not in the stars or in your eyes
That you alone of all the world's lands will
Escape the unimaginable fury
Of the lean-bellied, too long patient poor. . . .
                  You will wake one morning
To hear the relentles hounds of hungry men
Crying destruction over your doomed hills.

O desert nation, jackaled with your dreams. . . .

We live darkly in the world's great darkness
Ringed round on the leaning hills with a fanged fire
That in the gray, bird-crying hour of dawn
Can run through the dry grass to leap and tear us,
Rip the lodge poles down, consume the permmican
Dried for winter, all the old and sick
Left screaming on the black ground, and a few
Escaped to the mountains with a medicine bag
And a knife, to live on roots and bark, and die
In the first blizzard, bones piled in the Spring
For the friendly buzzards. Or we can ourselves
Crawl up in the night to steal it from the gods
And carry it in a pouch to our own valley,
Fuel it with the dead and broken wood
Of a society we have proved rotten
And found the courage to destroy. O then
Having built up that man-exalting land,
The clear expression of the human thing
In the social multitude and in the lone
Individual with his single way

That is our self-created destiny,
I will become the true American flame
That will be deep fire in the nation's eyes,
That will burn steel but will not burn our hearts.

PAUL ENGLE, *Break The Heart's Anger.*
Published by Doubleday, Doran & Co., Inc., Garden City, N. Y.

THE CHURCH AND WAR

We approach this part of our subject with a profound sense of its urgency and of the inadequacy of the best that we can say. We know that multitudes are oppressed by the actual menace of war. While we may seek to influence actions which may avert the immediate danger, our main task is to probe the underlying sources of the evil and point to the ultimate remedy.

Here again our starting point is the universal fellowship of Christians, the *una sancta.* All Christians acknowledge one Lord, whose claim upon them is such as to transcend all other loyalties. Here is the first obligation of the church, to be in living fact the church, a society with a unity so deep as to be indestructible by earthly divisions of race or nation or class.

Wars, the occasions of war, and all situations which conceal the fact of conflict under the guise of outward peace, are marks of a world to which the church is charged to proclaim the gospel of redemption. War involves compulsory enmity, diabolical outrage against human personality, and a wanton distortion of the truth. War is a particular demonstration of the power of sin in this world and a defiance of the righteousness of God as revealed in Jesus Christ and him crucified. No justification of war must be allowed to conceal or minimize this fact. . . . (Italics in the original text.)

The church should remind its members that the principle of the unconditional supremacy of the state or nation, advanced either in time of peace or of war, is incompatible with the church's faith in Jesus Christ as its only Lord and is therefore unacceptable as the final norm of judgment or action. It is the church's duty to serve the nation in which it is placed, but the greatest service which it can render is to remain steadfast and loyal to its Lord and to test rigorously all claims of national interest by his gospel.

"Report of the Section on The Universal Church and the World of Nations."
The Oxford Conference: Official Report.
Published by Willett, Clark & Company, Chicago.

THE CREATIVE URGE

Ours is the most self-conscious, the most self-critical age the heavens have ever looked down upon. For centuries past civilized societies have been contracting certain habits, economic, political and moral, for the most part unconsciously. What we call our economic system, for example, would be more truly described if we called it our economic *habit*—a point to be remembered by those who desire to reform it. But now awareness has begun to dawn upon us of what these habits are and whither they are leading us. The consequence is that our age is becoming profoundly dissatisfied with itself and somewhat alarmed into the bargain. The critics of it are legion; indeed, one might almost say that criticizing civilization has become a recognized profession for civilized men. When I read the many books in which this self-criticism finds utterance, mostly in a pessimistic vein, it seems to me as though our civilization were repeating the gesture of the Publican in the parable, smiting upon its breast, so to speak, and crying out "God be merciful to me, a sinner." All this is a relatively new thing in the history of civilization. Unquestionably it is a portentous one. . . . Deeper than all knowledge, more powerful than any philosophy, there is in man a creative urge inherited from the universe whose offspring he is.

L. P. JACKS, *The Revolt Against Mechanism.*
Published by The Macmillan Company, New York.

A PRAYER

O Thou Who hast shown us Thyself in poet and prophet and artisan and teacher, we call Thee this day by Thy name of Advocate. In our need and our weakness we have none to plead our cause save Thyself. We are clients of The Eternal One and without hope apart from Thee. Now teach us, we beseech Thee, the secrets of Thine own pleading. As Thou dost plead for us, so would we plead for such as need our help. We would be advocates of all who have no other advocate, we would be friends to all who have no other friend, we would remember all whom everyone else forgets. Teach us Thy secret that in our measure we too may be a refuge and a strength to all in need. And this we ask that Thy name may be known in us. Amen.

—FRANK KINGDON.

Endeavor to Transform: Twelfth Thursday

81. LOST! 150 BILLIONS!

Why does Mr. Eastman hesitate to recommend immediate government ownership? Among major reasons is the fact that too many railroad workers will be displaced by consolidating terminals, eliminating duplicate lines, cutting down competitive sales forces. The pit of a depression is no time in which to displace more men.

These threats are real. Doubtless some sturdy individualists will presently use them as added reasons why the government should cease its meddling. What do the threats connote? They mean that equal output can be produced with less over-all manpower, which is the only abiding definition of efficiency. For its very competence, then, public administration is feared, and justly. The answer, however, is not to proscribe efficiency in the interest of incompetent private employment, but to develop new areas where the displaced manpower may perform useful service. The recent report of the National Resources Board can supply much information on this score. We could use in worthwhile public works, contributing to the budget of essentials, millions of workers for many years. Administration is one question, unemployment another.

Finally, private administration, admirable as it often is in detail, never considers the economy as a whole. As a result of the depression to date, 100,000,000,000 man-hours of work have been lost through unemployment (an average of 10,000,000 persons for five years at 2,000 hours a year), and goods and services worth from $150,000,000,000 to $200,000,000,000 have not been produced, although the equipment was in place to produce them. It would require, one suspects, quite an effort on the part of a public administration, charged with the performance of the economy as a whole, however green and inexperienced, to better this record of gross inefficiency. STUART CHASE, in *Current History*.

FOR A SOCIALIST AMERICA

1936 National Platform of the Socialist Party

On the basis of the present capacity to produce, a socialized society will make it possible to:

1. More than double the present annual production of wealth which properly distributed would provide every family with a minimum income of $2,500 to $4,000 per year.
2. Guarantee jobs to all persons willing to work and at the same time reduce the hours of labor to 30 or less per week.
3. Guarantee security for all persons against old age, sickness, and accident.
4. Provide a fine, modern home for every family in the city or on the farm.

Such a society cannot be obtained without a mighty struggle. The struggle must be waged by both workers and farmers—organized into labor and farmer unions, cooperatives, and their own political party.

WE PROPOSE . . .

To improve the conditions of life and labor and thereby to weld together the strength and solidarity of the masses, the Socialist Party pledges itself to fight for the following immediate steps:

1. THE CONSTITUTION

We propose to amend the Constitution to fit our needs through the Farmers' and Workers' Rights Amendment, ending the usurped power of the Supreme Court to declare social legislation unconstitutional and reaffirming the right of Congress to acquire and operate industries. We also propose to change the Constitution to make future amendments less difficult. We pledge continued support of the Child Labor Amendment.

2. SOCIAL OWNERSHIP

We propose the social ownership and democratic control of the banks, mines, railroads, the power industry, and all key industries.

3. RELIEF AND SOCIAL SECURITY

We propose an immediate appropriation by Congress of funds to insure adequate Federal relief to the unemployed, and a comprehensive program of useful public works at union wages, especially the immediate launching of a public housing program for the complete elimination of the nation's slums, and a Federal system of unemployment insurance and adequate old age pensions as provided in the Frazier-Lundeen bill, and disability and maternity insurance. We also propose adequate medical care of the sick and injured as a public function, duty and right, and not as charity.

4. YOUTH

We propose the passage of the American Youth Act to meet the immediate educational and economic needs of young people; adequate Federal appropriations for public schools and free city colleges with a view to making possible a full education for all young people. We oppose the C.C.C., the National Youth Administration and other government agencies dealing with the youth problem which threaten the wage and living standards of organized labor.

5. LABOR LEGISLATION

We propose the establishment of the thirty-hour week; the guarantee of the right of collective bargaining for all workers in industries and occupations—public and private; the abolition of injunctions in labor disputes; the prohibition of company unions, company spying and private guards and gunmen; the prohibition of the use of the police, deputy sheriffs and militia and federal troops against labor.

6. TAXATION

We propose a drastic increase in income and inheritance taxes and the introduction of the capital levy, together with a land values tax looking toward elimination of the unearned increment of land values.

7. AGRICULTURE

We propose:

A. That immediate relief be provided for debt-laden working farmers by advancing government credit on such terms as do not threaten the farmer with the loss of his farm.

B. That farm prices be stabilized at cost of production to the working farmer, such stabilization to be made by representatives of organized working farmers and consumers.

C. That the marketing, processing and distribution of farm products be taken over by bona fide cooperatives and other agencies to be created for this purpose.

D. That social insurance be provided against crop failures.

E. The abolition of tenant and corporation farming by the establishment of a use-and-occupancy title for family-sized farms and the convention of plantations and corporation farms into cooperative farms.

8. Civil Liberties

We propose the abolition of all laws that interfere with the right of free speech, free press, free assembly and the activities of labor in its struggle for organization and power; the enforcement of constitutional guarantees of economic, political, and social equality for the Negro and all other oppressed minorities; and the enactment and enforcement of a Federal anti-lynching law.

9. Militarism and War

Not a penny, not a man to the military arms of the government. We reaffirm the historic position of the Socialist Party of the United States of opposition to any war in which the government engages. We propose the elimination of military training from our schools; the abandonment of imperialist adventures of a military or economic nature abroad; the development of internationalism among the peoples of the world; the maintenance of friendly relations with Soviet Russia; the elimination of profits from war and war preparations; and the strengthening of neutrality laws, to the end that we may avert immediate wars while fighting for the attainment of a social order which will eliminate the basic causes of war.

The Socialist party calls upon the workers, farmers and all advocates of social justice to join with it in its struggle to widen the channels through which peaceful, orderly and democratic progress may be made; to resist all trends toward insecurity, fascism and war; to strengthen labor in its battles for better conditions and for increasing power; to refuse to support the parties of capitalism, or any of their candidates, and to unite in the historic struggle toward a cooperative world.[1]

[1] Headquarters Socialist Party, U. S. A., 549 W. Randolph Street, Chicago, Illinois.

Proceed Resolutely: Twelfth Friday

82. THE NAILS

So, you're stretched on the planks, you schemer,
Earth disturber, heaven blasphemer.

You've been a wonder for getting in wrong.
Somebody fetch the nails along!

What's the first one? Envy, is't?
Spread out his fingers, clamp the wrist

To steady his palm for the ragged point.
No, don't set it too near the joint!

There, that's better. Keep it firm.—
Funny he doesn't begin to squirm.—

Hate is the hammer to pound it through.
Strike!... Aha! how's that for you?

He don't wince now much, but he will
Perhaps when his numb flesh feels the chill

Of the bitter metal's tearing bite.
At least his left hand will no more spite

His betters by feigning it can hold
More than rank or power or gold.

Next his right hand. What's the nail?
Scorn. I see his lips go pale.

Well he knows that its iron tooth
Is worse than Envy's barb uncouth.

Strike! Do you flinch to hear him groan?...
Hark! how it crunched the brittle bone.

Silly hand, it's well you're fast, or
You might again be cheating your master,

Giving away what most he needs,
Egging his wits into spendthrift deeds.

Now for the nails to stop his feet
From gathering dust on the common street.

Here is Malice, an ugly spike,
Long with a good broad head to strike?

Send it in straight! . . . No more of your tumbling,
Vagrant foot, so apt at stumbling

In shady places—you know what I mean,—
That pretty street walker, the Magdalene.

As for the other foot, fetch out Fear.
Ho! you have dogged us many a year,

Foot, with your plodding patience, have you?
And all the while no head to save you.

Drive the nail deep there! . . . Good! that's done.
Now, feet, I think you will hardly run

About so freely to stir the rabble
And wake dull mouths to a senseless babble.

Often you used to trouble our peace
With a strange soft tread that never would cease

Night or day. We heard it pursuing
Like a shepherd that drove us to our undoing,

Turned us out of our pleasant ways
To lonely pastures of dangerous days,

Urged us on till we lost our breath
Toward sorrow and toil and shame and death.

But, thank our stars; we've escaped at last,
Pursued you in turn and nailed you fast.

Brothers, to-night we may all sleep fair
And each be proud to have done his share.

Look how we have him, helpless, dumb;
And the worst of his torment is still to come.

Lift him up. Let the show begin.—
Which was the nail, friend, that you drove in?
                                        CHARLES WHARTON STORK.

ONWARD AND UPWARD

I pass the vale. I breast the steep
  I bear the cross: the cross bears me.
Light leads me on to light. I weep
  For joy at what I hope to see
When, scaled at last the arduous height,
  For every painful step I trod,
I traverse worlds on worlds of light,
  And pierce some deeper depth of God.
                                        JOHN CHARLES EARLE.

ONLY LOVE DOES NOT FAIL

Sometimes from our mad world, where men so trust in force,
I come into this church alone and look at the cross above the
altar. It seems to say to me: I am a symbol of apparent failure;
I represent the crucifixion of love by men of violence; but long
ago they passed away, and the empires which by violence they
founded passed away, and I still am here waiting; there is no way
out of human misery but by love; whoever believes in violence
trusts in a god who cannot create or organize anything permanent;
in the long run it is only love that does not fail.
              HARRY EMERSON FOSDICK, *Successful Christian Living.*
                    Published by Harper & Brothers, New York.

WHEN I SURVEY THE WONDROUS CROSS

When I survey the wondrous cross
  On which the Prince of glory died,
My richest gain I count but loss,
  Aud pour contempt on all my pride.

Forbid it, Lord, that I should boast,
  Save in the death of Christ my God:
All the vain things that charm me most,
  I sacrifice them to His blood.

See, from His head, His hands, His feet,
  Sorrow and love flow mingled down:
Did e'er such love and sorrow meet,
  Or thorns compose so rich a crown?

His dying crimson like a robe,
  Spreads o'er His body on the tree:
Then am I dead to all the globe,
  And all the globe is dead to me.

Were the whole realm of nature mine,
  That were a present far too small;
Love so amazing, so divine,
  Demands my soul, my life, my all.

ISAAC WATTS, 1707.

A PRAYER

Almighty God, give us grace to contend always for what is true and right, and to be ready if need be to suffer for it. Give us not over to any death of the soul, but rather lift us into newness of life, and let us glorify and enjoy thee for ever; through Jesus Christ our Lord. *Amen.*

Seek Comradeship: Twelfth Saturday

83. A VAST RELEASE OF ENERGY

The more one examines into the various factors which seem to account for the extraordinary victory of Christianity the more one is driven to search for a cause which underlies them. It is clear that at the very beginning of Christianity there must have occurred a vast release of energy, unequalled in the history of the race. Without it the future course of the faith is inexplicable. That burst of energy was ascribed by the early disciples to the founder of their faith. Something happened to the men who associated with Jesus. In his contact with them, in his crucifixion and in their assurance of his resurrection and of the continued living presence with his disciples of his spirit, is to be found the major cause of the success of Christianity. That experience and that assurance were transmitted to succeeding generations. . . .

It is the uniqueness of Jesus which seems the one tenable explanation of the fact that Christianity is the only one of the many Jewish sects to break off from the parent stem and outstrip it in size and influence. In the impulse which came from Jesus is the primary reason for that growth and that strength which attracted Constantine, for that vitality which enabled Christianity, in the keen competition among religions, to emerge the victor, and for the vision of a fellowship of disciples which led to its organization. Here, too, is the main source of Christianity's inclusiveness. Members of both sexes and of all races, the learned and the ignorant, so Christians held, might share in the salvation made possible by Christ. This new life might express itself in many different cultural forms: hence the flexibility of Christianity. On certain matters of morals and of worship and belief, however, Christians were convinced they must not compromise: hence the intransigence of the Church.

KENNETH SCOTT LATOURETTE, *The First Five Centuries.*
Published by Harper & Brothers, New York.

GREAT AFFIRMATIONS

Reduced to irreducible proportions the Christian faith is expressed in two great affirmations: that love is the ultimate principle of human relationships; and that the high worth of human personality which justifies the principle of love is in turn justified and supported by the character of reality itself. The Christian believes, in other words, that human character, whatever its lowly beginnings and obvious limitations, is potentially capable of moral integrity and on the whole will achieve its highest development by the inspiration of a faith and trust which has its eyes on the potentialities rather than the imperfect realities. The Christian believes, moreover, that this faith in personality is justified by the character of the universe itself, which, whatever its indifference to personal values in the immediate instant, is animated by a concern for the values it has created in human history. . . .

Religion in its most irreducible form is the discovery and the appreciation of the harmonies of life and the universe. The Christian religion goes beyond this, however. It assumes and affirms that a loving personal will is the source of the world's harmonies. This is a tremendous assumption which never can be completely justified in purely scientific terms. . . .

The Christian religion is founded upon a kind of heroic logic. Its affirmations are really logical but they project hypotheses which are not easily maintained; and which cannot be verified if they are not held in heroic defiance of some immediate evidence to the contrary. That is why theistic faith is the world view of either traditionalists or moral adventurers. The traditionalists maintain their faith because they are not sufficiently active intellectually to recognize its difficulties; the moral adventurers maintain it in spite of recognized difficulties because they have discovered a logic in life which negates any premature conclusions of purely analytic intellignce.

When life is vital and morally robust it inevitably universalizes its values, in spite of every philosophical and scientific difficulty which such a process faces. The rational justification of faith is therefore secondary. It is necessary when life is both vital and rational; it is unnecessary when life is vital but not too reflective; and it is futile when an age has reached a stage of sophistication in which the spirit of rationality has enervated moral vitality. Religion, in the final analysis, is justified by life, by morally potent and poetically vital life. Reason may support but it can never create the forces which express themselves in true religion.

REINHOLD NIEBUHR, in *Ventures in Belief,* edited by Henry P. Van Dusen. Published by Charles Scribner's Sons, New York.

ACTIONS NOT PROFESSIONS

There is a sharp distinction between believing in God and believing in the idea of God.

Belief in God is properly an attitude to life which expresses itself in our ways of behaving. If we wish to know what it means to believe in God, we must ask ourselves what this practical attitude is and how it expresses itself. In his parable of the sheep and the goats Jesus was concerned to express this in a striking way. He represented the scene of a final Judgment in which men were divided into two classes, those who were accepted by God and those who were rejected. He represented both classes as being astonished at what happened to them. The reason of their astonishment lay in the fact that the judgment was based not upon their religious professions, but simply upon the way in which they had behaved towards their fellowmen. We must bear this in mind as we try to mark down some of the elements which go to constitute a belief in God. We are concerned with actions, not with professions, and we have repeated warning from the teaching of Jesus that the Divine judgment pays little attention to professions and is likely to have surprising results.

For the Hebrews religion remained the great organizing principle of social life, capable of unifying every aspect of individual and social activity. It never became a particular aspect of human life, relating men to a human existence transcending the earthly life.

Jesus began his public ministry by asserting his continuity with the religious life of his people through the baptism of John. He identified himself with those who remained faithful to the religious development of the Hebrew people, and who looked for the fulfilment of the promises. Then he went out himself, preaching as John did, and saying, "Repent, for the Kingdom of Heaven is at hand." It is a demand for a revolution in mental outlook, in view of the fulfilment of a process of social development.

The repudiation of physical force as a means to the establishment of the Kingdom of Heaven is revealed with great clearness in the story of the temptation in the wilderness. That story represents the spiritual struggle in the mind of Jesus over the question of the means for the establishment of the Kingdom of Heaven on earth. Jesus is represented as being tempted to use power as a means to achieving control over men. He refuses to use miraculous power for the supply of his own bodily needs. He refuses to use the divine power for spectacular purposes which would impress the imagination of men. Lastly, he refuses to accept the power and the glory of the kingdoms of this world on the condition of recognizing the ultimate lordship of the Tempter.

Jesus offered himself to his people from the first as the Messiah of the Old Testament prophecies. But he recognized in doing so that the first task was one of spiritual reform. The fulfilment of the prophecies was conditional upon the acceptance by the Jews of the demand for repentance. The theme of his early preaching was the theme of the preaching of the Baptist: "Repent, for the Kingdom of Heaven is at hand."

In these circumstances the immediate situation was one of inevitable misunderstanding. He was bound to be considered as the leader of a new revolt against the Roman Empire in the cause of Jewish nationalism. It is this that gives historical point to the story of the temptation in the wilderness. It represents an early facing of this situation and a definite choice of programme. The emphasis fell upon the necessity of creating first the inner conditions in the Jewish people which must precede the coming of the Kingdom. The Kingdom of Heaven could not be established by armed force.

JOHN MACMURRAY, *Creative Society.*
Published by Association Press, New York City.

A PRAYER

O Thou who art the light of the minds that know thee, the life of the souls that love thee, and the strength of the hearts that serve thee; help us so to know thee that we may truly love thee; so to love thee that we may fully serve thee, whom to serve is perfect freedom; through Jesus Christ our Lord. *Amen.*

GELASIAN SACRAMENTARY.

Worship God: Twelfth Sunday

84. LONGINGS, VAGUE, INTENABLE.

The sun went down in beauty
While I stood musing alone,
Stood watching the rushing river
And heard its restless moan;

Longings, vague, intenable.
So far from speech apart,
Like the endless rush of the river,
Went surging through my heart.

GEORGE MARION McCLELLAND.

THE IMAGE OF GOD

There is that in the Spirit of God which unfolds itself in the Spirit of the historic Christ, and that in the Spirit of the historic Christ which illuminates the Spirit of God. . . .

When the leper came to Jesus, it is told that Jesus was moved with compassion, and touched him and said, "I will; be thou made clean." That touch, or rather *grasp,* is typical of grace which is wont to do the utmost for the lowest. And in the stooping of the Servant here, was the stooping of the Divine to the life of man, the deepest thing in God appealing to the darkest thing in man.

Wherefore the Christ was but another name for the grace of God, and it was he who brought, as he brings from age to age, the good tidings of the Christlike God. Christ proclaims grace, and grace proclaims Christ. If we speak of the secret of grace, it was revealed in him. If we speak of the mystery of Christ it came to light in grace. In grace it flashed into light, and in grace it was hidden again, and remains mysterious. For the riches of Christ are said to be unsearchable, and great is the mystery of godliness, or of the person or spirit of Christ. Be it understood that the riches of Christ were not merely his teaching, but himself; not merely his words of power, but all that which wrought in his personality in life and in death; his abounding pity and compassion, his seeking after men to bring them to repentance and eternal life, his humbling himself to be their servant, his strong crying and tears of intercession, his confidence in God continuing to the end, and flowing into matchless music in the last hours of the cross—all this and more, by reason of his creative and communicating spirit, is what is meant by the riches of Christ which were the wealth and working of the grace of God. No one can imagine a Being more full of grace than the Christ, nor can one survey a spectacle so perfectly a spectacle of grace as his glorious cross. Let him who emptied himself in perfect fulness and fire of grace, and took the form of a servant, so approach us that we may feel the throb of his heart's appeal; let him but stoop from the cross to touch our soiled and more than half-unfinished lives, and there will come upon us the breath of the brooding Spirit of God, the strange renewing power of His Grace. For what is the Grace of God but the Christ of God bending low to men in the sin-subduing, self-redeeming Passion of his cross, the cross of the God-like servant, the image and glory of the Christlike God? . . .

One can scarcely hope to express the grace, the Christlikeness of God, in nearer terms than those of the Christ who emptied himself, and took upon himself the form of a servant, and as servant proclaimed the fulness of Him that gave him. . . .

If the vague idea still labors to be heard that Christ by virtue of the Cross somehow produced a change in God, reconciling God to man and man to God, it must be understood that it is nearer the truth to say that God was *in Christ* reconciling the world unto himself; in other words, that God is the eternal Christlikeness, and Christ is the grace and truth of God in fashion and in fulness as a man.

JAMES ROBERTSON CAMERON, *God the Christlike*.
Published by the Cokesbury Press.

ZESTFUL JOY

The Divinely intended End of our Life is Joy overflowing and infinite, a Joy closely connected with a noble asceticism.

There is a wholesome, a strengthening zest attached to all action which is right and appropriate for the agent; and there is an unhealthy weakening excitement, which accompanies or follows all activity that is wrong or inappropriate. Hence one great end, and one sure test of right living and right dispositions, is the degree to which such living and dispositions make zest to prevail in our lives and make excitement to disappear from them. Now there is no zest comparable to the zest, the expansion, the joy brought to the soul by God and the soul's close union with Him. . . .

And this love of God, where uninhibited and full, brings Joy— it seeks God, Joy; and it finds Joy, God. I used to wonder, in my intercourse with John Henry Newman, how one so good, and who had made so many sacrifices to God, could be so depressing. And again, twenty years later, I used to marvel contrariwise, in my intercourse with the Abbé Huvelin, how one more melancholy in natural temperament than even Newman himself, and one physically ill in ways and degrees in which Newman never was, could so radiate spiritual joy and expansion as, in very truth, the Abbé did. I came to feel that Newman had never succeeded in surmounting his deeply predestinarian, Puritan, training; whilst Huvelin had nourished his soul, from boyhood upwards, on the Catholic spirituality as it flowered in St. Francis. Under the fine rule by which the Roman Church tribunals require, for Canonisation as distinct from Beatification, that the Servant of God concerned should be proved to have possessed and to have transmitted a deep spiritual joy, Newman, I felt and feel, could indeed be beatified, but only Huvelin could be canonised.

FRIEDRICH VON HÜGEL, *Essays and Addresses, Second Series.*
Published by E. P. Dutton & Co., New York City.

O GOD, OUR HELP IN AGES PAST

O God, our help in ages past,
Our hope in years to come,
Our shelter from the stormy blast,
And our eternal home—

Under the shadow of thy throne
Thy saints have dwelt secure;
Sufficient is thine arm alone,
And our defense is sure.

Before the hills in order stood,
Or earth received her frame,
From everlasting thou art God,
To endless years the same.

A thousand ages in thy sight
    Are like an evening gone;
Shorts as the watch that ends the night
    Before the rising sun.

Time, like an ever-rolling stream
    Bears all its sons away;
They fly, forgotten, as a dream
    Dies at the opening day.

Our God, our help in ages past,
    Our hope in years to come,
Be thou our guard while troubles last,
    And our eternal home.

ISAAC WATTS, 1719.

THE MORE WE LONG TO TASTE

For all the torrents of the grace of God are poured forth, and the more we taste of them, the more we long to taste; and the more we long to taste, the more deeply we press into contact with Him; and the more deeply we press into contact with God, the more the flood of His sweetness flows through us and over us; and the more we are thus drenched and flooded, the better we feel and know that the sweetness of God is incomprehensible and unfathomable.

RUYSBROECK.

A PRAYER

O God, the Help of those that flee unto Thee, the Hope of those who cry unto Thee, cleanse us from our sins and from every thought displeasing to Thy goodness, that with a pure heart and a clear soul, with calm trust and perfect love, we may worship Thee as we seek at this time through these sacred symbols to remember and realize Thy love in Jesus Christ our Lord.

ALBERT W. PALMER.

Concentrate Upon the Ideal: Thirteenth Monday

85. BEAUTY

Bathe me in beauty; beauty of the skies,
  Dawns that surpass all words for loveliness;
  Sunsets not even silence can express,
Though the stilled tongue waits on adoring eyes.
Woods, fields, and hills, whatever Nature's guise,
  All verdure wanting, or in wild excess
  Beauty be mine, and joyance none the less,
Each scene unfolding for me fresh surprise.
Beauty of purpose and unsullied will,
  Humor and courage, and a flash of wrath
  Cleansed and illumined as the lightning's path;
    Such answering of the within to the without
    That all my moods, even despair and doubt
May quicken to the sense of beauty still.

ROBERT WHITAKER, in *Social Song and Other Verse.*
Published by the Banner Press, Emory University, Atlanta, Ga.

MUSIC

Let me go where'er I will
I hear a sky-born music still:
It sounds from all things old,
It sounds from all things young,
From all that's fair, from all that's foul,
Peals out a cheerful song.

It is not only in the rose,
It is not only in the bird,
Not only where the rainbow glows,
Nor in the song of woman heard,
But in the darkest, meanest things
There alway, alway something sings.

'Tis not in the high stars alone,
Nor in the cup of budding flowers,
Nor in the red-breast's mellow tone,
Nor in the bow that smiles in showers,
But in the mud and scum of things
There alway, alway something sings.

RALPH WALDO EMERSON.

SÂDHU SUNDAR SINGH

A strange guest is standing before the door of an English house: a tall, upright figure in a long, saffron-colored robe, with a large turban wound round his head. His olive complexion and his black beard proclaim his Indian birth; his dark eyes, with their gentle expression, reveal a heart at rest, and they shine with an infinite kindness. The stranger gives his name to the girl who opens the door: Sâdhu Sundar Singh. The girl gazes at him for a moment in astonishment, then she hastens to call her mistress: "There is someone at the door who wishes to see you, ma'am; I can't pronounce his name, but he looks like Jesus Christ!" . . . Many men and women, both in Asia and in Europe, who had the good fortune to see him felt as though he were a reincarnation of one of the great men of God from Bible days. . . .

In many ways, however, Sundar Singh is still more like our Lord as He was upon earth. Like Jesus of Nazareth, he wandered homeless from village to village, from town to town; like the Master, often "he had not where to lay his head." Like Him, he withdraws constantly into the solitude of the hills, where, far from his brethren, he spends hours in deep communion with the Eternal Father. Like Him, he proclaims the Gospel in simple language, which can be understood by all; like Him, too, he is a master in the art of teaching through parables which help dull minds to catch something of the meaning of the heavenly mysteries. Like Him, he is full of love for children, and always "suffers the little ones" to come to him. He has left all to follow his Master—home, family, and possessions; in order to serve Him completely he took quite literally the command: "Get you no gold nor silver in your purses; no wallet for your journey, neither two coats, nor shoes, nor staff." And as the instructions of Jesus were literally obeyed by him, so also the prophecy of Jesus has been literally fulfilled in his life: "Before governors and kings shall you be brought for My sake for a testimony to them and to the Gentiles."

So in the life of Sundar Singh we see part of the Bible history begin lived out before our eyes; that life of the Saviour and of His apostle which to so many of our contemporaries seems either an incredible legend or an unattainable ideal has become once more concrete and actual in the life of this man of God. . . .

As we read the Sâdhu's life we realize that we are in the presence of sober, historic fact: we are confronted by a man of our own day who lives entirely in the Eternal, and who is in the closest communion with his Saviour; a man, too, who experiences "miracles" in this life of communion, and who is able to work "miracles" in its power. . . .

The Sâdhu's face is a living sermon about the peace which he carries in his heart. Söderblom says: "He radiates peace and joy. One who went about with him a good deal describes him as the embodiment of peace, gentleness, and loving-kindness." Mrs. Parker says: "That which is so surprising about the Sâdhu is the quite extraordinary joy which one can see upon his face—no picture can give an idea of the beauty of his smile." . . .

The most wonderful experience the Sâdhu has ever had of this peace was on that occasion when he was thrown into a well which was full of dead bodies. "The physical suffering was great, but in spirit I was happy. I began to pray to God, and His joy flowed into my heart to such an extent that I forgot the gruesome place I was in. A wonderful peace filled my heart, so lovely that I cannot describe it." "Never have I experienced greater blessedness in the peace of Jesus, received through prayer, than during those very days. Christ's peace turned that deep well into the Gate of Heaven." "How was it possible to have the peace of God in the pitch-dark night, in the midst of corpses and dead men's bones? Joy like this, peace like this, comes from nothing in this world. God alone can give it. While I was sitting there in the well I reflected that I never felt this kind of happiness while I lived in the house of my parents in comfort and luxury. Whence, then, came this overflowing joy in that terrible den? I saw then, more clearly than ever, that Jesus is alive, and that it was He who was filling my heart with peace and joy." . . .

The West has not lacked holy men who by life and word have called Christendom back to the Living Christ, whose message has been a perpetual summons to repentance. But the present day is not rich in such saints who can show Christians the way back to communion with Christ. There are indeed many learned and able theologians, astute Churchmen and social reformers, but there are very few men of God to whom "Christ is all in all," who therefore can be all in all to their brethren. In the Christian Sâdhu, Western Christianity sees such a man of God. That

which so many Western Christians regard as belonging to the
region of mediæval legend now appears before their eyes as a
living reality. In Sundar Singh the West beholds a man who
lives entirely in the supernatural world, one who brings a message from that world, a man whose heart is fixed in Eternity, and
whose word and life are a sermon of the Living Christ. He stands
before Western Christianity like a loud *Sursum corda!* as one
who summons and leads it to that higher world whose reality is
becoming fainter and fainter and which threatens to fade into
oblivion.

FRIEDRICH HEILER, *The Gospel of Sâdhu Sundar Singh.*
Published by Oxford University Press, New York.

WHAT IS GOOD

Wherewith shall I come before the Lord, and bow myself
before the high God?

He hath shewed thee, O man, what is good; and what doth
the Lord require of thee, but to do justly, and to love mercy,
and to walk humbly with thy God?

MICAH 6:8.

A PRAYER

O Thou Eternal Spirit, who hath set our noisy years in the
heart of the eternal silence, lift us, we pray Thee, out of the control of our empty fears and our vain regrets and our undisciplined
desires that we may see all things in Thy light and again take
courage for great tasks. Amen.

RAYMOND C. BROOKS.

A PRAYER

Love's kingdom is an everlasting kingdom; his dominion endureth throughout all ages. Come then, O lover of our race, and
reign among us, in love and joy and peace; extend thy empire over
human hearts; let the burning vision of thy beauty shine out clear
before the eyes of the world; hasten the consummation of thy
kingdom in which love shall be the only king; that the love wherewith the Father hath loved thee may be in us, and we be made one
in thee. Amen.

Understand the Actual: Thirteenth Tuesday

86. THE DESPISED BECOMES RESPECTABLE

No one would have dreamed in the Middge Ages that the despised creed of the trader and the money lender—a creed of selfishness and worship of the then lowest material values—should rise to be a compendium of everything most respectable in temporal affairs.

THURMAN ARNOLD.

THINGS

A century and a half since, men came to want more things. Men became enthusiastic over things. Men preached a new creed— the faith in things. Men set to work to make and to get things; men devoted the best of human energies to things, men pinned their progress, their civilization to things. To-day the force of things which they developed, the industrial force, may indeed be regarded as having the dominion over men. To-day men may be regarded as cogs in the great machine. But this machine they themselves chose to build.

SAMUEL STRAUSS, in *The Atlanttc Monthly.*

CIVILIZED BARBARISM

The atrophy of European culture was not brought about by the war, but only made swifter and more striking. Not war alone flung up the huge wave of unreasoning barbarism and the primitive, county-fair crudity of mass democracy. Modern man is at once the product and the prey of wild, distracting impressions which assault him, intoxicate his senses, and stimulate his nerves. The amazing development of technology, with its triumphs and disasters, the noisy sensationalism of sports records, the fantastic adulation and overpayment of popular stars, the boxing bouts before hordes of people for million-dollar stakes—these things and more like them make up the picture of our time, together with the decline and obsolescence of civilizing, disciplinary conceptions such as culture, mind, art, ideals.

For those are conceptions from the bourgeois age, idealistic trumpery out of the nineteenth century. And in fact the nineteenth century was above all an idealistic epoch—only today, and with some emotion, does one realize how idealistic it was. It believed not only in the blessings of a liberal democracy, but also in socialism—that is, in a kind of socialism which would raise and instruct the masses and bring them science, art, education, the good things of culture. Today we have convinced ourselves that it is both easier and more important to dominat? the masses, developing to greater and greater perfection the clumsy art of playing on their emotions—in other words, of substituting propaganda for education.

And the masses, it seems, are not inwardly averse; they feel themselves at bottom more intimately drawn to a smart propaganda technique than to any educational ideas. They are easily organized, and it seems that they are grateful for every form of organization, no matter in what spirit, be it even the spirit of violence. Violence is an extraordinarily simplifying principle; no wonder that it is understood by the masses.

If they were simply primitive, these modern masses, if they were only blithe barbarians, then one could do something, one could hope for something from them. But they are two-sided—they are sentimental, and they are given to philosophizing. And that is a catastrophe. The mass mind, extravagantly up-to-date though it is, yet speaks the jargon of romanticism: talks about the "folk," about "blood and soil," and all the old and sacred things; it rails at the industrial age—with which it is one. The result is a false and lying muddle of soulfulness and humbuggery, submerged in raw sensibility. Truly a triumphant combination; it conditions and determines our world today.

It is heartbreaking to see the weakness of the older cultural group in face of this barbarism; its bewildered, confused retreat. Dazed and abashed, with an embarrassed smile it abandons one position after another, seeming to concede that in very truth it "no longer understands the world." It stoops to the foe's moral and mental level, adopts his idiotic terminology, adjusts itself to his pathetic categories, his stupid, spiteful, and capricious propaganda—and does not even see what it is doing. Perhaps it is already lost. It certainly is unless it can take thought and wrench itself free from the creeping hypnosis.

THOMAS MANN, in *The Atlantic Monthly*.

IS CIVILIZATION IN ITS DEATH THROES?

Now that we have built the material instruments and wellnigh perfected the mechanical techniques of a great civilization, what are we going to do with them? Shall we use them for a new and more gigantic barbarism? Or shall we attempt with them to build up here a richer, finer, deeper-reaching, humaner culture in widest commonalty spread? . . .

I do not know what sort of civilization is coming into being. I do not know what will be the fate of western and so-called "Christian" culture. I often fear that we are in for a new Dark Ages, on a vaster scale than the former one. Of one thing only am I certain—the social-economic and political order that emerged from the middle ages and that is called "individualist capitalism," is in its death throes. Let us hope that we are near the birth pangs of a more humane civilization.

I do not wish to be a Cassandra, but I do wish to remind you emphatically; *first,* that the Roman Empire was the greatest, the most prosperous, the most peaceful, and orderly international social system that had ever existed, and that it went to pieces completely. Of course, the barbarians were thundering at the gates, but the barbarians would never have gotten in, if the home defenses had not gone to pieces. Second, that we stand today in the midst of one of the major secular crises of civilization, and our barbarians are not without, but within, the gates of Western civilization. We are not threatened by the onslaughts from without of inferior cultures; the terrible decline of German culture has taken place by actions and inactions at home. The loss of civil and spiritual liberties in Italy and in other parts of Europe have been by actions and inactions at home. We too, like the other free nations, are threatened with these losses unless we address ourselves in the spirit of social intelligence, fair play, and cooperation to a solution of the economic, social, and political problems which confront our increasingly complex mechanized civilization. We shall get, with a dictatorship, the sweeping away of all civil and spiritual liberties and the reign of a brutal tyranny, or we shall have chaos; probably first dictatorship and then chaos, and the ruin of Western civilization. Make no mistake about it. We are fortunately situated in that there are no serious threats to us on our borders. Our barbarians are within our home gates. . . .

What is the root cause of our difficulty? It is, as William James said, worship of that bitch-goddess, Commercial Success, the reign of greed for money and fame and the subordination of every other consideration to profits for the individual or the little group of family or friends. . . . I do not need to recount to you that economic individualism has led to a tremendous contrast, with 42% of our people not having enough to live on decently in the peak year of our prosperity while the total income of one-tenth of one per cent of our population equalled the total income of the aforesaid forty-two per cent; to the gigantic chicanery and fraud in the manipulation of public utilities, holding companies, and other great corporations; to the corruption of officers of the law; to the crookedness in politics; to large scale racketeering and crime; to ten million substandard houses in this prosperous land, etc. The fact is that economic individualism as a social philosophy has been a ghastly failure, and moreover has been strangled by its own most successful practitioners.

JOSEPH A. LEIGHTON, in *The Churchman*.

ENDS AND MEANS

Our dilemma today is due to the fact that though we wish to preserve values, humanity, civilization, we cannot see how we can preserve them without the use or at least the threat of means which if employed destroy that which such means were employed to protect. We repeat, and it is experience which has taught us the lesson, the end does not justify the means. We have learnt it is the method we use not the aim we propose which decides the value of our action and how far its resultant is of worth to humanity.

GERALD HEARD, *The Source of Civilization.*
Published by Harper & Brothers, New York.

A PRAYER

Creative Spirit, who hast through the ages been bringing harmony out of chaos and confusion, make us ready we pray, for the great adventure of living in a growing, changing world. Preserve us from accepting the low goals and cheap compromises of life. We ask not for immunity from risks, but for the courage to meet them with imagination and intelligence; and grant unto us such modesty of spirit that we may constantly feel the need of renewing our purposes in the light of Thy vision. So shall we become co-workers with Thee.

BISHOP PAUL JONES.

Be Concerned: Thirteenth Wednesday

87. THE NEW TESTAMENT SPEAKS

THE ROOTS OF WAR

"Whence come wars and whence come fightings among you? Come they not hence, even of your pleasures that war in your members? Ye lust, and have not: ye kill, and covet, and cannot obtain: ye fight and war; ye have not because ye ask not." (James iv. 1 f.)

"The works of the flesh are manifest, which are these . . . enmities, strife, jealousies, wraths, factions, divisions . . . of the which I forewarn you, . . . that they which practise such things shall not inherit the kingdom of God. But the fruit of the Spirit is . . . peace. . . . Against such there is no law." (Gal. v. 19-23.)

"Ye cannot serve God and mammon." (Matt. vi. 24.)

THE COMMANDMENT OF LOVE

"Thou shalt love the Lord thy God with all thy heart, and with all thy soul, and with all thy mind. This is the great and first commandment. And a second like unto it is this, Thou shalt love they neighbour as thyself. On these two commandments the whole law hangeth." (Matt. xxii. 37-40.)

"The whole law is fulfilled in one word, even in this; Thou shalt love thy neighbour as thyself." (Gal. v. 14.)

"Love worketh no ill to his neighbour: love therefore is the fulfilment of the law. . . . Owe no man anything, save to love one another." (Rom. xiii. 10, 8.)

"Love your enemies, and pray for them that persecute you; that ye may be sons of your Father which is in heaven." (Matt. v. 44 f.)

"A new commandment I give unto you, that ye love one another; even as I have loved you, that ye also love one another. By this shall all men know that ye are my disciples." (John xiii. 34 f.)

"If a man say, I love God, and hateth his brother, he is a liar: for he that loveth not his brother whom he hath seen, cannot love God whom he hath not seen." (1 John iv. 20.)

"Love suffereth long, and is kind; love . . . seeketh not its own, is not provoked, taketh not account of evil; . . . beareth all things, believeth all things, hopeth all things, endureth all things. Love never faileth." (I Cor. xiii. 4 ff.)

"The Lord make you to increase and abound in love toward one another, and toward all men." (I Thess. iii. 12.)

"Seeing ye have purified your souls in your obedience to the truth unto unfeigned love of the brethren, love one another from the heart fervently." (I Pet. i. 22.)

"Above all things be fervent in your love among yourselves; for love covereth a multitude of sins." (I Pet. iv. 8.)

The Duty of Forgiveness

"Jesus said, Father forgive them; for they know not what they do." (Luke xxiii. 34.)

"Whensoever ye stand praying, forgive, if ye have aught against any one; that your Father also which is in heaven may forgive you your trespasses." (Mark xi. 25.)

"If thy brother sin, rebuke him; and if he repent, forgive him. And if he sin against thee seven times in the day, and seven times turn again to thee saying, I repent; thou shalt forgive him." (Luke xvii. 3 f.)

"Put on therefore . . . a heart of compassion . . . forbearing one another, and forgiving each other, if any man hath a complaint against any; even as the Lord forgive you, so also do ye." (Col. iii. 12 f.)

"Let all bitterness, and wrath, and anger, and clamour, and railing, be put away from you, with all malice: and be ye kind one to another, tenderhearted, forgiving each other, even as God also in Christ forgave you." (Eph. iv. 31 f.)

Christ's Way of Meeting Evil

"Christ also suffered for you, leaving you an example, that ye should follow his steps: who did no sin, neither was guile found in his mouth: who, when he was reviled, reviled not again; when he suffered threatened not; but committed himself to him that judgeth righteously." (I Pet. ii. 21 ff.)

"I came not to judge the world, but to save the world." (John xii. 47.)

"When his disciples saw this, they said, Lord, wilt thou that we bid fire to come down from heaven, and consume them? But he turned and rebuked them." (Luke ix. 54 f.)

"Being reviled, we bless; being persecuted, we endure; being defamed, we intreat." (1 Cor. iv. 12.)

"One only is the lawgiver and judge, even he who is able to save and to destroy: but who art thou that judgest thy neighbour?" (Jas. iv. 12.)

"All things therefore whatsoever ye would that men should do unto you, even so do ye also unto them." (Matt. vii. 12.)

"Love your enemies, do good to them that hate you, bless them that curse you, pray for them that despitefully use you." (Luke vi. 27 f.)

"Resist not him that is evil: but whosoever smiteth thee on thy right cheek, turn to him the other also." (Matt. v. 39.)

"Why not rather take wrong? Why not rather be defrauded?" (1 Cor. vi. 7.)

"The Lord's servant must not strive, but be gentle towards all . . . forbearing in meekness, correcting them that oppose themselves." (2 Tim. ii. 24.)

"Bless them that persecute you; bless, and curse not. . . . Render to no man evil for evil. . . . If it be possible, as much as in you lieth, be at peace with all men. Avenge not yourselves, beloved, but give place unto wrath: for it is written, Vengeance belongeth unto me; I will recompense, saith the Lord. But if thine enemy hunger, feed him; if he thirst, give him to drink: for in so doing thou shalt heap coals of fire upon his head. Be not overcome of evil, but overcome evil with good." (Rom. xii. 14 ff.)

"See that none render unto any one evil for evil; but alway follow after that which is good, one toward another, and toward all." (1 Thess. v. 15.)

"Finally, be ye all likeminded, compassionate, loving as brethren, tenderhearted, humbleminded: not rendering evil for evil, or reviling for reviling; but contrariwise blessing; for hereunto were ye called, that ye should inherit a blessing." (1 Pet. iii. 8 f.)

THE WAY OF THE CROSS

"God commendeth his own love towards us, in that, while we were yet sinners, Christ died for us." (Rom. v. 8.)

"Jesus the author and perfecter of our faith, who for the joy that was set before him endured the cross, despising shame." (Heb. xii. 2.)

"Forasmuch then as Christ suffered in the flesh, arm ye yourselves also with the same mind." (1 Pet. iv. 1.)

"We are pressed on every side, yet not straitened; perplexed, yet not unto despair; pursued, yet not forsaken; smitten down, yet not destroyed; always bearing about in the body the dying of Jesus, that the life also of Jesus may be manifested in our body." (2 Cor. iv. 8-10.)

"If any man would come after me, let him deny himself, and take up his cross, and follow me." (Matt. xvi. 24.)

"Wherefore Jesus also, that he might sanctify the people through his own blood, suffered without the gate. Let us therefore go forth unto him without the camp, bearing his reproach." (Heb. xiii. 12 f.)

Passages assembled by G. H. C. MacGregor,
The New Testament Basis of Pacifism.
Published by James Clarke & Co., London.

A PRAYER

Lord, make me an instrument of Thy peace,
Where hate rules, let me bring love,
Where malice, forgiveness,
Where disputes, reconciliation,
Where error, truth
Where doubt, belief,
Where despair, hope,
Where darkness, Thy light,
Where sorrow, joy!
O Master, let me strive more to comfort others than to be comforted,
To understand others than to be understood,
To love others, more than to be loved!
For he who gives, receives,
He who forgets himself, finds,
He who forgives, receives forgiveness,
And dying, we rise again to eternal life.

Attributed to St. Francis.

Endeavor to Transform: Thirteenth Thursday

88. UNLESS TODAY WE CHANGE

Through wars to mockeries and pestilence
All History repeats its cyclic round;
Brute sired by brute to brute bequeaths his breed.
Forever we are what we are today
Unless today we change to be what we
Shall be tomorrow.

EDWARDS DAVIS, *Lovers of Life*.
Published by Baker & Taylor Company, New York.

THE MEANS DETERMINE THE END

Many Americans do not understand that what the communist party in Russia started out to get was not an autocratic, dictatorial state, but democracy. The most widely-based industrial and political democracy in the world was communism's aim. Only, temporarily, they would use ruthless repression as a means, employ violence in the killing or the exile of minorities, and the suppression of liberty of speech and press! Temporarily, as a means, they would take a short-cut through undemocratic methods to reach a democratic goal. And, in consequence, look at Russia. Violence grows by what it feeds upon. The more you suppress liberty, the more you have to suppress liberty. The more you use tyranny as a method, the more you get tyranny as a result. So Mr. Chamberlain, twelve years a resident of Russia, thoroughly convinced at first that communism alone could save civilization, now sums up the matter: "I think the overwhelming weight of historical evidence is to the effect that the means determine the end, and that an idealistic goal, pursued by brutal methods, has a tendency to disappear from view."

We Americans need to learn that lesson by heart. We never can get peace by unpeaceful methods or democracy by undemocratic methods or liberty by illiberal methods. Always the means we use must partake of the quality of the goal we seek. It is a towering falsehood that the end justifies the means. The profound truth is that always and everywhere the means determine the end. . . .

We Americans want two things supremely, democracy and peace. Those are desirable aims. Few things more worth serving invite man's public devotion than a just and effective democracy and a secure and honorable peace. Who among us does not want them? Well, then, if peace and democracy are so supremely desirable, is there anything we would not do for their sake? So we travel the old path worn smooth by the emotions of centuries until we say we care so much for democracy and peace that we will fight for them. Now, if by "fight" you mean wage war, I beg of you walk around that formula for a long time before you let it fool you, as it has fooled millions of our predecessors. Is war an effective method for gaining or defending either democracy or peace?

Twenty years ago we went into a war to make the world safe for democracy. Let no man impugn our motives. No nation ever had a higher aim in view. We, the people, by millions, were willing to make any sacrifice for that high aim. We were out to save democracy and we finished in a world enjoying less democracy than there had been for generations. The reason is not difficult to see. War is not a democratic method. Modern wars must be fought under dictatorship. The day war is declared in any country, conscription starts, totalitarianism begins, liberty of speech and press is limited, and regimentation takes possession of the field. That is inevitable in any modern war. A nation that gets on the military train, crying, All aboard for the San Francisco of democracy, ends necessarily in the Spuyten Duyvil of dictatorship. The means determine the end. Were I to paraphrase Daniel Webster's speech, I should pray that when for the last time my eyes behold the sun in heaven, they may not behold it shining on the tragic spectacle of a great democratic nation that took the warpath to save democracy and ended by itself being no longer a democracy.

Do not suppose that I think the problem easy or that, because I am a Christian pacifist, I think any neat pacifist formula by itself alone covers the case. May heaven have mercy on all prime ministers and secretaries of state in democratic countries today, trying to handle wisely this desperate situation! But let us, the people, keep steadily in mind the law as deeply imbedded in the moral world as the law of gravitation is in the physical: the means we use must partake of the quality of the ends we seek. We cannot get peace by unpeaceful means, justice by unjust means, democracy by undemocratic means. The means determine the end.

HARRY EMERSON FOSDICK, in *The Church Monthly.*

MEANS USED IN SOVIET RUSSIA

Let us now consider examples of planning by political leaders who accept the ideal postulates, whose intentions are good. The first thing to notice is that none of these men accepts the ideal postulates whole-heartedly. All believe that desirable ends can be achieved by undesirable means. Aiming to reach goals diametrically opposed to those of Fascism, they yet persist in taking the same roads as are taken by the Duces and Fuehrers. They are pacifists, but pacifists who act on the theory that peace can be achieved by means of war; they are reformers and revolutionaries, but reformers who imagine that unfair and arbitrary acts can produce social justice, revolutionaries who persuade themselves that the centralization of power and the enslavement of the masses can result in liberty for all. Revolutionary Russia has the largest army in the world; a secret police, that for ruthless efficiency rivals the German or the Italian; a rigid press censorship; a system of education that, since Stalin "reformed" it, is as authoritarian as Hitler's; an all-embracing system of military training that is applied to women and children as well as men; a dictator as slavishly adored as the man-gods of Rome and Berlin; a bureaucracy, solidly entrenched as the new ruling class and employing the powers of the state to preserve its privileges and protect its vested interests; an oligarchical party which dominates the entire country and within which there is no freedom even for faithful members. (Most ruling castes are democracies so far as their own members are concerned. Not so the Russian Communist Party, in which the Central Executive Committee acting through the Political Department, can override or altogether liquidate any district organization whatsoever.) No opposition is permitted in Russia. But where opposition is made illegal, it automatically goes underground and becomes conspiracy. Hence the treason trials and purges of 1936 and 1937. Large-scale manipulations of the social structure are pushed through against the wishes of the people concerned and with the utmost ruthlessness. (Several million peasants were deliberately starved to death in 1933 by the Soviet planners.) Ruthlessness begets resentment; resentment must be kept down by force. As usual the chief result of violence is the necessity to use more violence. Such then is

Soviet planning—well-intentioned, but making use of evil means that are producing results unlike those which the original makers of the revolution intended to produce.

ALDOUS HUXLEY, *Ends and Means.*
Published by Harper & Brothers.

HAIL THE GLORIOUS GOLDEN CITY

Hail the glorious golden city,
    Pictured by the seers of old:
Everlasting light shines o'er it,
    Wondrous things of it are told.
Only righteous men and women
    Dwell within its gleaming wall;
Wrong is banished from its borders,
    Justice reigns supreme o'er all.

We are builders of that city.
    All our joys and all our groans
Help to rear its shining ramparts;
    All our lives are building stones.
Whether humble or exalted,
    All are called to task divine;
All must aid alike to carry
    Forward one sublime design.

FELIX ADLER, 1878.

A PRAYER

Almighty God, our heavenly Father, without whose help labour is useless, without whose light search is vain, invigorate my studies, and direct my inquiries, that I may, by due diligence and right discernment, establish myself and others in thy holy faith. Take not, O Lord, thy Holy Spirit from me; let not evil thoughts have dominion in my mind. Let me not linger in ignorance, but enlighten and support me, for the sake of Jesus Christ our Lord. Amen.

SAMUEL JOHNSON.

Proceed Resolutely: Thirteenth Friday

89. POWER

(In 1930, *The English Poetry Review* offered an international prize for a poem on Power. Five hundred poems were submitted; this sonnet was the winner.)

All worlds lie folded in the arms of Power:
   The live seed lifts its earth-load and is free:
   The filmy moon lifts the eternal sea.
Armed with this might, the insect builds its tower
And lives its little epoch of an hour.
   Man's giant thought, in ever-daring flight,
   Explores the universe, the Ancient Night,
And finds infinity even in a flower.

But there is something that is greater still,
The strength that slumbers in Heroic Will.
   Yes, there is something greater than them all:
It is the high translunar strength that streams
   Downward on man at some imperious call,
And gives him power to perish for his dreams.

                    EDWIN MARKHAM, *New Poems.*
Published by Doubleday, Doran & Company, Inc., New York.

A RADICAL CHALLENGE TO CHRISTIANS

To be thorough, to get at the bottom or root of things, to strive after fundamental understanding and order one's attitude thereby—this, justified by the etymology of the term, is the method of radicalism. Radicalism is not violence or iconoclasm; it is simply the habit of delving down to reality and building one's judgments upon it. That the method of radicalism is the one proper to Christians, no one will be likely to deny. Whatever his problem or task may be, the Christian should touch not the fringe of the issues that face him, but he should lay bare their realities and by their guidance persevere steadily toward his goal. Christianity's way with evil should be to root up, not to apply palliatives. No candid student of the Gospels can fail to acknowledge that Jesus exhibits precisely those qualities of penetration and courageousness of purpose that we have designated above as the marks of radical-mindedness. In his great grasp of seminal principles and in the singleness of his self-devotion, he is excelled by none.

The radical outlook of Jesus can be appreciated if we note the influence upon him of apocalyptic doctrines. A chief element of this belief was the expectation that the present world-age was soon to be ended, and God would at once establish a new order in its place. Just how far Jesus shared in this conception it is not easy to decide, but there is plainly visible in his thoughts its principle of tension, the strain as of one who is astride two worlds, the one already marked for dissolution, the other in the throes of being born. It is in this birth of the new divine order that man's hope lies, so that Jesus is led to portray man's destiny as a fundamental renewal. The tension or conflict of worlds can be resolved only as men repent, become other-minded, and as human relationships are essentially remolded to conform to the pattern of the world that is about to be. Apocalyptic expectations in the time of Jesus helped men to feel that when evil and injustice are inwrought in the texture of things, their removal requires no trifling applications but rebuilding on fresh foundations. Thus it had part in creating the radical spirit. It underlay the crisis ideology in the mind of Jesus himself, by which he envisaged the new righteous order, not as one which would evolve out of the old, but one to be realized through the rejection of the old.

To Christian men and women this conception in itself constitutes a radical challenge. For if a new ordering of life, a complete transposition of human conditions, was what Jesus felt to be needed to achieve righteousness, then we too, if we are to be his followers, must espouse like projects and urge like demands, unless it can be shown that the world is now so different that the achieving of justice is no longer a basal undertaking. This means in the social and economic field, that unless we are satisfied that its major processes, while capable of minor correction here and there, yet are on the whole serving the general welfare and are establishing just and harmonious human relations—unless we are assured of this, we can be loyal to Jesus only if we strive to transform the economic order so that its processes will be given this character.

There are two of these elements in the teachings of Jesus that bear particularly on modern social and economic problems. If it can be shown that their application in economic affairs would entail drastic revision of our business ethics, of our ways of carrying on our economic activity, then Christians are by virtue of their recognition of the truth of Christ's teachings committed to this revision. The two principles are these: the sacredness and supreme worth of human life, and the unworthiness and moral dangers of the desire for material things. Jesus stressed the first by making the test of institutions, even those divinely ordained like the Sabbath, their contribution to human well-being. It is the human quality in men that matters, not the position or rank to which some only may attain; the "little ones" and the "least of these" count equally with the exalted and great. Jesus enforces the second principle by warning against the seductiveness of riches, and by forbidding not only covetousness but even anxiety over material wants.

In what measure, now, are our present industrial order and our social habits in agreement or disagreement with these principles? Only a superman or a man resigned to starvation could have a place in the present-day competitive world without, not merely feeling anxious about his material fortunes, but giving major attention to them. The very nature of competition entails this; for it is psychologically inevitable that competing for a thing should whet the appetite for it, if only for the sake of satisfying the will to power. Hence, in order to live or win his spurs before his fellows, a man in business sets his eye without more ado on that from which Jesus bade him turn away. Our economic individualism, in other words, has the tendency to evoke a reaction upon conditions of life that is radically unchristian. It reverses the values enjoined by Jesus, causing material success to appear, not something the seeker after the Kingdom finds "added" to him, but the precondition of further opportunity, and making the non-rich envious of those for whom Jesus felt commiseration.

Under the capitalistic system the worker's right to work, to maintain himself and his self-respect by honorable exertion, is subject to the interest of those who own the industrial equipment. Thus, not what he may need to fulfil his life, but his economic utility to someone else, determines whether a man shall be employed or not. Such a condition is incompatible with what Jesus taught about human welfare and dignity; for his teaching would at least entail each man's right to the opportunity to provide himself through his own effort with the essentials of life. Nothing could be more unchristian than the denial of this right—a denial that inheres in our present-day industrialism; and which makes the worker's connection with his occupation so factitious as to bar from his mind any interest in it for its own sake or appreciation of its social value. Treated as an instrument in another's scheme for gain, he reciprocates by valuing his own work in turn solely by the wage it brings. . . .

It is, then, on these three grounds that we urge upon Christians a radical purpose and a radical *faith:* the pioneering spirit of Jesus; the demand for bold leadership in the present bewilderment if hope is to be reawakened in men; and the need of a re-affiliation with the *real* fundamentals of its calling, which the Church must seek if it is to overcome uncertainty and futility and regain its potent place in the life of the world.

JOHN LINE, in *The World Tomorrow.*

A PRAYER

Invocation : O God, Our Heavenly Father, we thank Thee for this beautiful world which Thou hast given us, with everything in it which is needful for our welfare. And yet we acknowledge that in a world where there is amply sufficient for all, poverty and suffering are to be found in the midst of plenty. We confess that although all men are children of the same Father, the world is full of hatred and oppression, of war and strife.

Pardon our many sins of greed and hatred, O God; show us the right path and strengthen our minds and our hearts to walk in it, until all mankind shall live together as brothers in a loving family, in a world of peace and plenty.

We ask this, inspired by the memory of Thy Son, Jesus Christ, Who by His teaching and example showed men how they should live.

KENNETH W. PORTER.

Seek Comradeship: Thirteenth Saturday

90. BOUND ORDERLY AND LUMINOUS

By sweet
Submission to the courses of the stars,
Each star serenely fixed in proud content
To shed whatever light may come of it,
Hold to that course your constellation takes
Of gravity, or force centripetal.
So even a lone comet paves a curve
Surrounding Beauty, and obedient
To laws in aggregate, bound orderly
And luminous, prodigiously it moves
Not as a stellar heretic—a force
Unloosed and uncontrolled—but as a Saint
Transcendentally it curves to guiding Power
Supremely surer than itself.

EDWARDS DAVIS, *Lovers of Life.*
Published by Baker & Taylor Company, New York.

NINE AFFIRMATIONS

Not many months ago I had occasion to participate in a ten-day discussion of the Christian message for our times in which these two types of thought, along with other theological points of view, were continually seeking reconciliation. I enjoyed the opportunity not only to observe their capacity for mutual adjustment, but to search out in my own thinking the areas of thought which could be harmonized with other formulations of the Christian faith. The personnel of the group was of such a character as to give the gathering the semblance of an international round table. The leader was a graduate student from Wanganui, New Zealand; the *rapporteur,* a young Indian woman from the faculty of the Isabelle Thoburn College in Lucknow; and the counselor was a theological professor from a midwestern school bordering upon the eastern frontier. The remaining members were Christian leaders from Japan, China, Australia, Germany, Holland, Switzerland, England and from all parts of the United States. Our purpose was to determine, if possible, whether or not Christians representing such diverse cultural backgrounds and theological points of view could discover a common basis of devotion sufficiently genuine to give the feeling of a world Christian community.

There was this qualification: assent did not carry with it complete agreement. The differences theologically were just as pronounced at the close of the discussions as before. The Anglo-catholics remained loyal to the Apostles' Creed. The Barthians persisted in their language of dialectic. And the empiricists, sobered and dazed by the downpour of dogmatics which they had encountered for days, stood firm for the faith of their fathers— that is, their American fathers. There was no concern to wrestle with theological differences; they were to be noted and frankly acknowledged. And when the statement of common faith was set forth members of each group were encouraged to note the points on which they would place greater or less emphasis in presenting it to their constituencies. At the conclusion of ten days of deliberation we found ourselves giving common assent to nine affirmations:

(1) That God, as revealed through Jesus Christ, lives and works among us.

(2) That man and society are dependent upon God for their fulfillment.

(3) That men and women of our generation in great numbers are unmindful of this imperative relationship or indifferent to its demands.

(4) That this blindness and indifference are at the root of our individual and social frustration.

(5) That the hope of personal and social salvation lies in men's return to God as the center of life and in their readiness to yield to him in humility in order to be cleansed of the arrogant self-sufficient attitude that shuts them out from his divine working.

(6) That the way to return to God is to commit ourselves to Christ, who is the revelation of God in human history and the one who did yield utterly to the will of God. In him, therefore, we envisage God and the way that brings life, and we receive the power to give ourselves to God.

(7) That the men and women who have thus turned to God through Christ, in spite of their differences in thought and expression, constitute a world-wide community through which flows

a unifying life strengthening the several members in their common loyalty and inspiring them for Christian living.

(8) These truths have certain direct implication for human living and social organization and therefore lay upon us certain demands in the form of Christian ethics, the exact character of which is to be determined through faithful effort to recognize God at the center of every situation as it arises.

(9) As an aid to Christian living, then, an ardent study of the Bible is imperative, for there we are confronted with a clear portrayal of life lived in relation to God.

BERNARD EUGENE MELAND, in *Christendom*.

TOWARD THE INDEPENDENCE OF THE CHURCH

The relation of the church to civilization is necessarily a varying one since each of these entities is continually changing and each is subject to corruption and to conversion. The history of the relationship is marked by periods of conflict, of alliance, and of identification. A converted church in a corrupt civilization withdraws to its upper rooms, into monasteries and conventicles; it issues forth from these in the aggressive evangelism of apostles, monks and friars, circuit riders and missionaries; it relaxes its rigorism as it discerns signs of repentance and faith; it enters into inevitable alliance with converted emperors and governors, philosophers and artists, merchants and entrepreneurs, and begins to live at peace in the culture they produce under the stimulus of their faith; when faith loses its force, as generation follows generation, discipline is relaxed, repentance grows formal, corruption enters with idolatry, and the church, tied to the culture which it sponsored, suffers corruption with it. Only a new withdrawal followed by a new aggression can then save the church and restore to it the salt with which to savor society. This general pattern has been repeated three times in the past: in the ancient world, in the medieval, and in the modern. It may be repeated many times in the future. Yet the interest of any generation of Christians lies less in the pattern as a whole than in its own particular relation to the prevailing civilization. The character of that relation is defined not only by the peculiar character of the contemporary church and the contemporary culture but even more by the demand which the abiding gospel makes upon Christianity. The task of the present generation appears to lie in the liberation of the church from its bondage to a corrupt civilization. . . .

The captive church is the church which has become entangled with this system or these systems of worldliness. It is a church which seeks to prove its usefulness to civilization, in terms of civilization's own demands. It is a church which has lost the distinctive note and the earnestness of a Christian discipline of life and has become what every religious institution tends to become—the teacher of the prevailing code of morals and the pantheon of the social gods. It is a church, moreover, which has become entangled with the world in its desire for the increase of its power and prestige and which shares the worldly fear of insecurity. . . .

The church's declaration of independence can begin only with the self-evident truth that it and all life are dependent upon God, that loyalty to him is the condition of life and that to him belong the kingdom and the power and the glory. Otherwise the emancipation of the church from the world is impossible; there is no motive for it nor any meaning in it. There is no flight out of the captivity of the church save into the captivity of God. . . . The crisis of modern mankind is like the crisis of the prophets, the crisis of the Roman Empire in the days of Augustine, and that of the medieval world in the days of the Reformation. The last appeal beyond all finite principalities and powers must soon be made. It cannot be an appeal to the rights of men, of nations or religions but only an appeal to the right of God.

The appeal to the right of God means for the church an appeal to the right of Jesus Christ.

H. RICHARD NIEBUHR, *The Church Against the World.*
Published by Willett, Clark & Company, Chicago.

A PRAYER

God, our Father, give to the nations of the world a new heart of comradeship; the old man of ignorance and cruelty being done away, and the new man put on, renewed in knowledge, to strengthen and to serve the brethren; that every people may bring its tribute of excellence to the common treasury, without fear, and without the lust of domination; and that all the world may go forward in the new and living way which he hath consecrated for us; who now liveth and reigneth, with thee and the Spirit of truth, one God, world without end. Amen.

Worship God: Thirteenth Sunday

91. BEYOND PHYSICAL SCIENCE

Physical science set out to study a world of matter and radiation, and finds that it cannot describe or picture the nature of either, even to itself. Photons, electrons and protons have become about as meaningless to the physicist as x, y, z are to a child on its first day of learning algebra. The most we hope for at the moment is to discover ways of manipulating x, y, z without knowing what they are, with the result that the advance of knowledge is at present reduced to what Einstein has described as extracting one incomprehensible from another incomprehensible.

SIR JAMES JEANS, *New Background of Science.*
Published by The Macmillan Company, New York.

WHAT A PICTURE!

We must rid ourselves of any picture of matter as gross or inert. How much matter is invisible like the air! How much is transparent like the water. . . . How much is ever passing from phase to phase like an elusive genie! Those who are inclined to think meanly of matter should look again at its magnificence in the starry heavens, and at its exquisiteness in the miniature architecture of snow-crystals. We must also bear in mind how finely it lends itself to life's purposes—the fashioning of a feather, the sculpturing of a shell, the casting within the bud of those bluebells which ring every day by the wayside.

But when we pass from ordinary sight to scientific vision, how subtle and ethereal matter becomes! What pictures modern physics gives us of a restless activity suggestive of life. . . . The weight of a single molecule of hydrogen is about three million-million-million-millionth of a gram, and its velocity at 0° C. is rather more than a mile a second.

J. A. THOMPSON, *System of Animate Nature.*

WHAT IS REALITY?

"The red brick," says Science, "is a mere convention. In reality that bit, like all other bits of the universe, consists, so far as I know at present, of innumerable atoms whirling and dancing one about the other. It is no more solid than a snowstorm. Were you to eat of Alice-in-Wonderland's mushroom and shrink to the dimensions of the infra-world, each atom with its electrons might seem to you a solar system and the red brick itself a universe. Moreover, these atoms themselves elude me as I try to grasp them. They are only manifestations of something else. Could I track matter to its lair, I might conceivably discover that it has no extension, and become an idealist in spite of myself. As for redness, as you call it, that is a question of the relation between your optic nerve and the light waves which it is unable to absorb. This evening, when the sun slopes, your brick will probably be purple; a very little deviation from normal vision on your part would make it green. Even the sense that the object of perception is outside yourself may be fancy; since you as easily attribute this external quality to images seen in dreams, and to waking hallucinations, as you do to those objects which, as you absurdly say, are *really there.*"

EVELYN UNDERHILL, *Mysticism.*
Published by E. P. Dutton & Company, New York.

MORE AWE-INSPIRING

The progress of modern science has only driven the mystery of physical nature farther back. For the naive wonder of the unscientific man in face of the gross phenomena of experience it has substituted the marvels, multiplied a hundred times, which the scientist discovers through his microscope, in his test tube, or at the end of a telescope. The universe described by Eddington and Jeans is far more mysterious and awe-inspiring than the cozy little playhouse of Greek mythology or Hebrew cosmology. . . .

No matter how educated a man is, he stands baffled before the mystery of the cosmos. Although he knows more about it than has any man in all the history of the human race, yet it remains for him as inscrutable a mystery as it was for any individual who lived in a prescientific age. Where did it come from? What is it coming to? How is it controlled? He has no answers for these questions. Furthermore, he cannot accept the relatively easy answers which less critical generations made. But there it is before him, and in its presence he is inarticulate and bows down with wonder and awe. . . . No amount of scientific sophistication can take away from the twentieth century man the elevation of spirit which he finds in the beauty of his world. The distant mystery of the night sky, the chaste serenity of the moon seen through scudding clouds, the calm majesty of distant mountain peaks—all these stir the consciousness of every sensitive individual and cause him to say that they are good. It is as if there were a homing instinct within man which draws him back to love the beauty of the earth-mother who has brought him forth. Her beauty enters into him and sustains him.

EDWARD H. REISNER, *Faith in an Age of Fact.*
Published by Farrar and Rinehart, Inc., New York.

REDWOODS

I

Long have I felt all gracious trees to wear
    The looks of comrades; but I never knew
Even the flowering almond calmly fair
    As these whose pillars climb the templed blue.

Colossus-footed, with green heads aloof
    As tapering hills that mock at humankind,
They rear a feathery-leafed, tremendous roof
    As though to keep our noblest dreams enshrined.

I think that could the weary world but know
    Communion with these spirits breathing peace,
Strangely a veil would lift, a light would grow,
    And the dark tumult of our lives would cease.

II

Close-massed as brothers in some mystic rite,
    With prayerful heads that search the blue unseen,
They loom in guardian silence on a height
    Where the wind-thunders shake their pointed green.

And while the delicate-fingered leaflets toss
    On brown limbs drooping through the scented air,
Their towers, over banks of fern and moss,
    Seem alien to this earth of dust and care;

Seem like calm spirits from the nebulous skies,
That sour indifferent to our race and age;
Thrown here by chance; and waiting, gravely wise,
For some divine, undreamt-of heritage!
STANTON A. COBLENTZ, *Songs of the Redwoods.*
Published by Overland-Outwest Publications, Los Angeles.

WORSHIPFUL ACTIVITY

Worshipful response manifests itself not simply in moods of relaxation, receptivity, and peace; it also appears as a higher excitement and an intense activity. When "the hand of the Lord" was upon Elijah he outstripped the chariot of Ahab on the road to Jezreel. The word of the Lord is to Jeremiah as a burning fire shut up in his bones, which he cannot contain and which compels him to defy king and nation. George Fox, regardless of consequences to himself, rebukes the judges who have put him in jail because of their injustice to the poor and weak. From the beginning of the Christian era till now men and women have endured hardships similar to those that Paul underwent because they were constrained by the Love of Christ. . . .

The religious function may take the form either of the receptive attitudes of humility, peace, joyful adoration, or of the active experiences of lofty excitement and sustained enthusiasm in which the human rises to superhuman achievement; but in either case man attains in the religious function more unity in himself, discovers more coherence and meaning in his world, and establishes more harmonious interaction between himself and his world in its meaningful character than the ethical function of effortful work is adapted to yield. For ethics in its functioning is by nature selective. . . . Religion can restore the spirit of man, in his very quest of value, to kinship with reality wider than human, and can thereby dissolve tension, refresh the heart, and bring the whole self into play. Religion says, "Be not anxious," "Behold the birds of the heaven," "Consider the lilies of the field." "Seek ye first the kingdom of God and his righteousness."

Thus in the end religion can carry men, even while they stand in the midst of the stress of life and the affairs of human history, beyond the level of effortful work to that of joyous freedom in creative living.
EUGENE WILLIAM LYMAN, *The Meaning and Truth of Religion.*
Published by Charles Scribner's Sons.

Concentrate Upon the Ideal: Fourteenth Monday

92. GOD'S BEAUTY EVERYWHERE

A perfect poem is a shaft of Light,
And there are many rays in it, when soul
Or argent poet, vision-blest, reveals
Elysium. By new experience
Behold, this vibrant eon-echoed Truth,
That not of fading stuffs, carved stones, nor spires,
Idols, gold pavements, pearly gates to towers;
Not of such substance as these are that fade,
Or tarnish, or corrode, for which blind thieves
Break through to steal—reward is where Mind moves
Created and creating to behold
God's beauty everywhere where beauty is.

EDWARDS DAVIS, *Lovers of Life.*
Published by Baker & Taylor Company, New York.

A REVOLUTIONARY ETHIC

Whenever we read the Gospels with fresh and open mind, we cannot help being stuck by the fact that they announce a new way of life. The Sermon on the Mount, the Parable of the Good Samaritan, the story of the Rich Young Ruler, the sayings about the Strait Gate and Narrow Way, about finding one's life through losing it, about the first who are last and the great who serve—there is something stubborn about these things; they resist all attempts to tame them down and explain them away. They mock our conventional morality. Our ethical systems seem drab and unimaginative beside them. They leave us with a breathless sense of reality—the kind of reality whose sign is to expose, condemn and command. They shatter judgments whose weary familiarity had seemed to render them unshakeable. They initiate us into another world which we recognize at once as the real one, and from which nothing separates us any longer except our lethargy and cowardice. . . .

Jesus stands in a tradition whose chief concern was for the common people. The lot of the poor, the needy, the widow, the orphan forms the dominant theme of prophetic morality. . . .

Jesus accepts this prophetic heritage and carries it forward in three ways: First, he identifies himself completely with the hungry, the thirsty, the stranger, the naked, the sick, the prisoner. "Inasmuch as ye have done it unto one of the least of these, my brethren, ye have done it unto me."

Second, he states clearly the moral law of true egalitarianism and true distinction in the coming Kingdom. "Many that are first shall be last, and the last first." This is not a question of spiritual levelling. Neither is it a simple turning of the tables, giving the places of the rich to the poor. It is rather a matter of defining carefully a new principle of greatness, which cuts across established valuations and is open to all alike, rich and poor. It is the greatness of the servant, radically different from the exclusiveness of gentile over-lordship.

Third, Jesus gives a new principle which creates a new man and a new fellowship, whose results are so far-reaching as to be likened to a second birth. It is the principle of finding life through losing it. To find life is not an individualistic matter. It is to be fit for the Kingdom. And that fitness is the only thing that matters. Everything else sinks into insignificance beside it. To gain the whole world and forfeit that is profitless. Pluck out your right eye, cut off your right hand, sell all that you have and give it away—do anything rather than risk the loss of that one thing needful. Where life hangs in the balance any sacrifice is cheap. And what is the way to find life? It is to love, to discover the fact of mutuality and dedicate yourself completely to its service. That dedication will expose the barriers which now divide rich from poor, Pharisee from Amhaarets (the people of the land), priest and Levite from the wounded man, the Jew from the Samaritan. . . .

What is disturbing and revolutionary about the command to love is its challenge to a new way of living which begins immediately, destroys all class divisions, creates a new fellowship, and is ready for the Kingdom of God. Its greatest enemies are those who deny and oppose this new way—also in the name of love. They are the scribes and Pharisees who teach the fatherhood of God and the brotherhood of man, and makes this an apology for the established inequalities of class. Religion, which is life and creates life, becomes a skeleton of ceremonial. The tombs of the prophets are garnished and the voice of prophecy is silenced. This is hypocrisy : the appearance of love serving the reality of division. It is conservatism with a religious sanction. Between that and revolutionary love there can be no peace. Jesus accepted the challenge and paid for it with the cross. . . .

Such an irreconcilable conflict is the meaning of revolution. It begins in religion because religion is the realm of absolute loyalty, of irrevocable choice. The necessity for choice arises when it becomes plain that a human order of value—a particular order of ideas, intuitions and sentiments, as well as of practices and institutions—is beginning to cut across the divine order of value. A product of history is cutting across the grain of historic creativity. A creature of God, estranged from the creator and from its own true nature, sets itself against the creator's will, and whispers to itself : I shall be God. There can be no doubt about the result. It will be destroyed. It cannot be redeemed, unless its old nature be broken. It cannot live, unless its rebellious isolation be ended, unless it be buried deep again in the soil of divine creativity. Revolution is God-made, not man-made. It is the relentless pressure of a structured order that cannot tolerate an incompatible fragment. Man cannot make it, but man can choose it. He can remain in stubborn blindness with the old, prolong its death pangs, and add one or more victims to its fall. Or he can read the signs of the times and cast his lot with the upsurge of the new creative forces.

The final note of the Christian ethic of love in its relevance for our times must be the old reminder : Except the Lord build the house, they labor in vain that build it. The ethic of love is not a matter for further exhortation, for frantic appeals for men to exert themselves and change either their own nature or the nature of the world in which they live. It is a quiet reminder that God is love; that man is made for love and cannot live without it; that the process of human development is necessarily a progressive discipline of interdependence and co-operation; that the present crisis is the tension between a lingering divisive society of economic classes and new possibilities of co-operative community in a classless society; that the issue of that crisis may be retarded by politicians, financiers, industrialists and would-be prophets of social justice, but cannot ultimately rest in their hands; that it can be decided only by the silent, irresistible judgments of the God of Wrath who is also the God of Love. The Christian ethic of love does not counsel a revolution. It announces it. The Kingdom of God is at hand. Repent ye, and believe the gospel.

GREGORY VLASTOS, *Towards the Christian Revolution.*
Published by Willett, Clark and Company, Chicago.

THE LIVING GOSPEL

Christ's Spirit taketh breath again
Within the lives of holy men.

Each changing age beholds afresh
Its word of God in human flesh,

Amid the meek of earth, whose ear
Pure wisdom maketh quick to hear,

Who know the founts of good and ill,
And live in the eternal will,

Sharing themselves and all their good
In universal brotherhood;

In whose sweet lives we still may see
The One who walked in Galilee,

And preaching through the human page
Christ's living gospel to our age.

W. C. BRAITHWAITE.

A PRAYER

Almighty God, breathe into us the spirit of Thy Son that we may love the things which he loves and choose the things which he desires us to have. May the words which we speak and the deeds which we do be spoken and done in his name.   Amen.

CHARLES E. JEFFERSON.

Understand the Actual: Fourteenth Tuesday

93. A POINT OF VIEW

He looks at life from a basement into which no sunbeams can penetrate and from which he sees only feet of men passing by rubbish pails that stand near his windows.

GORKI.

THROUGH THE EYES OF SKEPTICISM

Living is merely a physiological process with only a physiological meaning and that it is most satisfactorily conducted by creatures who never feel the need to attempt to give it any other. . . . The world may be rejuvenated in one way or another, but we will not. Skepticism has entered too deeply into our souls ever to be replaced by faith, and we can never forget the things which the new barbarians will never need to have known. . . . Leaving the future to those who have faith in it, we may survey our world and, if we bear in mind the facts just stated, we may permit ourselves to exclaim, a little rhetorically perhaps,

Hail, horrors, hail,
Infernal world! and thou profoundest hell,
Receive thy new possessor. . . .

Ours is a lost cause and there is no place for us in the natural universe, but we are not, for all that, sorry to be human. We should rather die as men than live as animals.

JOSEPH WOOD KRUTCH, *The Modern Temper.*
Published by Harcourt, Brace and Company, New York.

CITY ROOFS

Roof-tops, roof-tops, what do you cover?
Sad folks, bad folks, and many a glowing lover;
Wise people, simple people, children of despair—
Roof-tops, roof-tops, hiding pain and care.

Roof-tops, roof-tops, O what sin you're knowing,
While above you in the sky the white clouds are blowing;
While beneath you, agony and dolor and grim strife
Fight the olden battle, the old war of Life.

Roof-tops, roof-tops, cover up their shame—
Wretched souls, prisoned souls too piteous to name;
Man himself hath built you all to hide away the stars—
Roof-tops, roof-tops, you hide ten million scars.

Roof-tops, roof-tops, well I know you cover
Many solemn tragedies and many a lonely lover;
But ah, you hide the good that lives in the throbbing city—
Patient wives, and tenderness, forgiven, faith, and pity.

Roof-tops, roof-tops, this is what I wonder:
You are thick as poisonous plants, thick the people under;
Yet roofless, and homeless, and shelterless they roam,
The driftwood of the town who have no roof-top and no home!

CHARLES HANSON TOWNE.

IMPOVERISHED FARM TENANTS

Today, almost half of America's farm families are tenants, tilling land they do not own. For the last half-century the number of tenants has been rising steadily, and it still is growing at the rate of about 40,000 families a year. The problem is not limited to any one section of the country. It is most acute in the Southern cotton belt, but even in Iowa, Illinois, and Nebraska nearly half of all farmers are tenants.

That kind of farming is impoverishing the tenant, the land-lord, and the land itself. It is one of the chief reasons why 1,700,000 American farm families are trying to exist on an average income of only $450 a year, one-third of which is food raised on the farm. Everything else these families get, including the rent they pay for the farm, comes out of the remaining $300. That kind of farming is largely responsible for the erosion which has completely destroyed an area larger than New York and New Jersey combined, and is still sweeping away $400,000,000 worth of top-soil every year—top-soil that nature can build back only over a period of centuries. Ruined land means ruined families. The nation obviously cannot afford to let this process of ruin go unchecked.

WILL W. ALEXANDER, in *Bulletin of America's Town Meeting of the Air.*

ATLAS WEARY OF WORK

Atlas, weary of work, goes home.
Not Atlas, cosmic porter,
Who shouldered all the world himself,
When all the world was young;
But Atlas multifold, a million-brained and million handed Atlas,
An Atlas wrought of many parts, each one bearing earth burdens
    on itself.
He toils in pigeon holes whose many windows gleam from towered
    heights;
He delves beneath the soil with axe and pick;
He stands all day in mammoth stores;
He plies the needle, clicks the keys,
    balances books and presses buttons,
    handles levers, answers bells, arranges files;
He works in many metals, many woods
And leashes all the forces of the world
To heed his pigmy touch and monster will,
This Atlas of the million arms and billion ganglia.

When whistles shriek the call for home
He feels a need for rest.
It croons to him within kaleidoscopic selves;
Maybe in some dim thought each manikin
Dreams once again the dream of his great ancestor
Who shouldered all the world himself
And even dozed with all that burden on his back
Atlas, weary of work, goes home.
They plunge him down in crates from dizzy heights;
They push him out of doors and grates; they turn out lights;
They slam him, cram him, jam him into cars . . .
The wheels of iron cars that clatter overhead,
The wheels of iron cars that thunder underground,
Go round and round and chant a song of home.
He sways upon a strap and marks the beat
On shuffling feet.

His home . . . familiar kitchen smells . . .
He fondles little Atlas wriggling in his crib;
He scolds the other Atlases for making too much noise;
He grumbles at his wife, an ancient privilege,
And then enjoys the meal she sets before him.
This done, he tunes in on the world that never sleeps,
A world of heads gone light on feather toes
And dozes off. . . .
The headlines of the tabloid on his lap
Bawl out their tales of sugar-daddies, vamps, soiled loves,
But wake him not.

He topples into bed;
A man must get the strength to prop up earth again
Tomorrow and tomorrow and tomorrow.

ELIAS LIEBERMAN, in *The World Tomorrow*.

A PRAYER

"Tell me, I pray thee, where is the house of the seer?"

O God of Light and Truth, in a strangely tangled time, when confused cries echo through the world, we pray for the leadership of faith. Hear our prayer for the prophet-vision and the light of the moral mind, lest we lose our way and wander in the dark. Thou Mighty Seer, send us men endowed with the grace of insight, the gift of interpretation, and the accent of command. Speak to Thy people, O Lord, for without vision they become a mob and perish.

God of the Prophets, give us men who share Thy vision of eternal values, and are not afraid of the loneliness of following the highest they know. Show us the shame of the second-best, the bitterness of a joy bought at the cost of a mean timidity. O God, let Thy living word have saving power among us, rebuking our sin, working in us the miracle of love, and leading us out of the night into a new day of the Lord Jesus. In His name, Amen.

JOSEPH FORT NEWTON, *Altar Stairs*.
Published by The Macmillan Company, New York.

Be Concerned: Fourteenth Wednesday

94. CHRISTMAS

We murmur, "Peace on earth—Good will to all!"
And down the grayness of two thousand years
That cry re-echoes; while the moans and tears
Of suffering ages call and vainly call.
The fiery-curtained armies charge and fall;
The nations bleed on their own hurtled spears;
And still the strong, in python-sly careers,
Crush their weak fellows, writhing, to the wall.

"Good will and peace!" we urge; and, far away,
In the rose-vistas of a coming dawn,
We catch that plea, like a white radiance, borne
To stir all men that labor, love and pray.
Then shall the sword and rapier be withdrawn,
And Christmas moods be moods of every day!

STANTON A. COBLENTZ, in *The World Tomorrow.*

BEYOND ARGUMENT

Much as men may argue about the Messiah, the Son of Man, his miracles, his relationship to the figures of the Old Testament, and to various types of thought more or less familiar to his own time, they cease to argue and begin to adore when they touch the threshold of his Spirit. Here is something beyond argument like the radiance of the light, or the haunting loveliness of a melody "that's sweetly play'd in tune." It is felt that this is the supreme thing, the thing that makes the Christ what he was yesterday, and is to-day, and forever. It brings him nearer and makes him more real than creeds, the catechisms, the confessions, by which men have striven to define it. It is that which has attracted and unbound the most enduring of the poets, and the painters, and the builders, and the musicians, whose language is beyond words. More than any Greek god or all the gods of Greece it is that which has drawn, as it has evoked and evolved, the Arts of the modern world, and if we are ever to appreciate the fulness of the Spirit of Christ we must go and learn from the Arts, as well as from the theologies,

and steep ourselves in their visions, and the strange and delicate
vestures wherein the visions are embodied, till at length we gain,
in part, a sense of the Spirit real as that of Christ himself. . . .

"His barque goes singing," said Dante, in its voyage through
the worlds. Singing, because the Spirit of Christ was full of song
and imparted the singing quality to all great Art. The nearer we
draw to the Christ on earth, the more we hear the singing strain of
his Spirit. This is a vital point, as it reveals the beauty and the
breadth of his teaching and manner of life, and the appeal by
which he won the Masters of the Arts. . . .

Truly it is the most joyous spectacle in history to behold him
passing through the haunts of moral failure and despair, unclouded
in his majesty of trust, undimmed in his sense of the beauty of
holiness, unchanged in his strength and depth of sympathy, an
invincible Believer, an utter Saviour. . . .

And is this not the most amazing scene of all?—the lonely,
bruised, rejected Christ standing there amid his judges, and uttering that majestic "I am," soaring serenely in the sky-blue spaces of
the love of God, assured, as St John relates, that they would have
no power against him except it were given them from above.
Radiant as his faith before, it was surely never so radiant as when
he knew that the power committed for a time to Pilate and the
priests was power Divine, but self-abased, which he was himself
in unity. . . .

Only a spirit joyful and melodious could ever have voiced
"the good tidings of great joy," and given them such form in
words, and such finish in deeds "more strong than all poetic
thought." It has been said that "for nineteen centuries Christendom has gazed into his shining face and felt that all things work
together for good." But, too often, his face has been portrayed
as stricken with grief, exciting the pity and pain of men. Undoubtedly that is a half truth, if it is as much, and comes far short
of the whole. To imagine that the face of Jesus was marked, or
"marred," by only one kind of emotion, and that the tone of his
Spirit was but a monotone of grief! The fact is that his Spirit was
many-sided, an unrivalled harmony, or balance of qualities, each
having its part in the consummate unity. No doubt, he may be
truly represented at times as "the man of Sorrows," but he was
habitually and at heart the man of joys, soaring into lofty heights
unknown before. Both in the depth of his sorrow, and the height

of his joy, there was an air of the Infinite breathing without stint
or stay. Yet, if any one word verges to the reality it is joyfulness
rather than sadness, radiance rather than resignation.

JAMES ROBERTSON CAMERON, *God the Christlike*.
Published by the Cokesbury Press.

HE LET ETERNITY BREAK THROUGH

Jesus lived life in its wholeness. He essayed the heights, He
did not shrink from the depths. Three years they say He lived
before men, yet in that time He managed to let eternity break
through, and lifted man's horizon to infinity. He took all that
came to Him, and turned it to the purpose of His mission; circumstance, failure, disappointment, and death. They gave Him a
manger for a cradle, a bench for a pulpit, thorns for a crown, and
a cross for a throne; but He took them and made them the very
glory of His career. He turned sorrow into joy, He found strength
in labour, peace in the storm, rest on the cross, and life in the
grave.

W. E. ORCHARD.

NOT BY HUMAN POWER   UNAIDED

Boccaccio tells the story of a Jew whose Christian friend was
trying to convert him. The Jew was on the point of agreeing, but
before committing himself definitely he decided to go to Rome and
see for himself in what manner the Pope and his cardinals lived,
since they were the men at the head of the Church. This frightened
the Christian, who thought that all his efforts would go for nothing
and his friend certainly refuse baptism when he had seen the
scandals of Rome. The Jew duly went there and observed the
hypocrisy, depravity, corruption, and greed which were rife among
the Roman clergy and in the papal court at that time, and on his
return his Christian friend asked anxiously what impression had
been made on him. The reply was as deeply understanding as it
was unexpected: "Since all the wickedness and abominations that
I have seen in Rome have been unable to overturn the Christian
religion, since in spite of them all it continues to grow stronger,
it must be the true faith."

Christians themselves are the greatest objection to their
religion; they are a scandal to those who are favourably disposed

towards it. . . Our age is too preoccupied with man and what is human, so that Christianity is not seen behind its mask of bad Christians; notice is taken of their wrongdoing and their deformations of the faith rather than of the religion itself; their excesses are more easily seen than the great Christian truth. . . .

Two greats tests were given to Christian mankind, persecution and victory. The first was surmounted, and by its martyrs and confessors under the Romans Christianity triumphed in its beginnings as it does under communist persecution in Russia to-day. But the test of victory is harder, and when the Emperor Constantine bowed down before the Cross and Christianity became the official religion of the Empire there began a very long test of that kind. And it was surmounted less successfully than the other. Christians often changed from persecuted into persecutors, they let themselves succumb to the temptations of the kingdoms of this world and their power; it was then that there crept into Christianity those perversions of its truth that have been made the source of accusations against it. . . .

The Christian renaissance will be above all an appeal to Christ and to his truth freed from all human perversion and adaptation. Man's renewed consciousness of the permanent fact of original sin need not weaken consciousness of his responsibility towards the work of our Lord in the world or nullify endeavours for the forwarding of that work. To make the truth and commands of Christ real sometimes seems a desperate, impossible undertaking, and Christianity itself tells us that it is a task that cannot be achieved by our unaided human powers. But what is impossible for man is possible for God. He who believes in Christ knows that he is not alone: he knows that he is called to realize the truth of Christ in company with Christ himself, his saviour.

NICHOLAS BERDYAEV, *The Bourgeois Mind*.
Published by Sheed & Ward, New York.

Attempt to Transform: Fourteenth Thursday

95. CONSCIENTIOUS OBJECTOR

Die for my country?
Yes, of course I would!
But not the easy way—
Bands playing,
Flags waving,
And the cheers of war-mad thousands in my ears!
And not the useless way—
My body splattered over foreign fields
Or hung in shreds on barbed-wire barriers,
That rabble-rousing slogans be proved false
And millionaires make profits from my blood!
God give me strength
To die the hardest way—
To die for peace,
Conviction,
And a dream of brotherhood—
My only crime that I refuse to kill!
The Pioneer of Peace died on a Cross—
That was before the day of firing squads!

RAY M. JOHNSON, in *The Christian Century.*

A STATESMANSHIP OF PEACE

I am to speak to you this morning on the most difficult question that can be asked of any one who believes in peace and is opposed to war. It is the question as to what we can do when every effort to keep peace has failed, and our enemy, who may be hostile to everything that is precious in human life—all progress, all enlightenment, all freedom—is bent on going to war. If we ourselves are not to take up arms in such a circumstance and fight in defense of what is dearest to mankind, then what are we to do? . . .

There must be a statesmanship of peace to take the place of the statesmanship of war. But if this challenge is valid, it is also, I believe, unfair, at least as offered suddenly in the hour of great crisis, when, as Kipling put it in 1914,

"The Hun is at the gate."

For a statesmanship of peace can be no mere measure of emergency. It cannot be improvised, all of a sudden, to meet some violent contingency. Like a regimen of health, it must be a long-sustained and patient program of procedure achieving step by step what one can never hope to achieve by one dramatic gesture. Imagine preparing for war for years, doing everything in every case to foster war and the things that make for war, and then, when the war comes, asking the pacifist to produce a statesmanship' right out of hand, to keep the peace!

Take the nations of the modern world, for example, which have been following in arrogance and without shame those militaristic policies which every pacifist has known must sooner or later lead to catastrophe! These nations have been piling up armaments, and fortifying boundaries, and grabbing territories, and extending empires. They have been ceaselessly contriving the diplomatic snares with which to entrap their rivals, and in the end resorting to the force and violence which they have accepted as their ultimate reliance for security. Every appeal to reason they have denied; every program of goodwill they have rejected; every endeavor after peace they have either denounced as dangerous or scoffed at as quixotic. Then suddenly and terribly comes war— and instantly those responsible for the disaster turn to the pacifists, who have all along been warning against this very thing, and say, "Well, what is your policy? Haven't we got to fight? Is there anything else in honor and safety that we can do?" Which is like a man of violent and dissipated life, who finds himself stricken with a mortal disease, and frantically, at the last moment, calls upon the physician to save him from death! Is it any reproach to the physician if he throws up his hands, and says, "It's too late. There's nothing I can do. You've got to die"? If the physician had only been listened to, if he had only been summoned in time and asked to take charge of the sick-bed, he could have laid down a program of recovery which would have restored the man to health and kept him well. In the same way, if the pacifist were called early enough into international affairs, he could present a statesmanship which would banish war forever. . . .

But, I hear somebody say in conclusion, this is all very good, but you have not yet faced the real issue. That issue comes not when you have a chance to talk about peace, but when every hope of peace is gone. . . The European Fascists tomorrow will not join the democratic nations for the adoption of any policies of international accord. These barbarians fight. What will you do when they refuse your terms, decline to sit down in your conferences, precipitate a war, and thus destroy every last vestige of your statesmanship of peace?

This is our last question—the pacifist driven into the last ditch! In answer it can only be said that, while this contingency is far less possible than is imagined, it is not impossible. The Fascists may force a war upon Europe, as the Rebels forced a war upon Spain. They have this power in their hands, as any maniac has it in his hands to assassinate the President, or blow up Washington, or set fire to New York. Mussolini or Hitler may choose to wreck our world.

But this does not mean that we must choose to join them in this work of wreckage. A maniac may choose to destroy a city or bomb a crowd, but this places no obligation upon us to aid and abet his lunacy. And that is what we do when we take up arms in answer to the challenge of a madman. All I can see in Spain today is a nation ravaged by the joint efforts of two contending forces. I see Madrid shattered, the country side burned and looted, a million innocent people slaughtered in cold blood, and no end in sight until one of the loveliest lands in Europe is turned into a desert—and all done not by Rebels alone, but by Rebels and Loyalists together. If they were working in concert and not in conflict, they could not do much worse. And this is what we are asked to extend to all of Europe if the Fascists decide to go upon the warpath. We must fight, so we are told, until a continent is laid in ruins from Warsaw to Paris, and from Berlin to Rome.

I cannot see it! I will not do it! I am too much reminded of the Roman historian, Tacitus, who wrote about the conqueror who made a desert and called it peace. So in this age we are asked to make a desert and call it liberty. Let me be frank with you! I had rather see Europe in the hands of the Fascist dictators, and her people alive, her cities still whole, her fields still fair and fertile, than to see Europe free of the Fascists, and her people slaughtered, her cities ashheaps, and her landscapes the dread haunts of wolves and brigands. In the latter case, civilization would be dead, and the last hope gone; in the former case, civilization, though in chains, would be alive—and while there's life, there's hope! . . .

The pacifist has reliance in certain higher qualities of mind and soul which he believes to be distinctive of himself as a man, and is convinced that he can use these weapons to achieve his ends. For are there not in the universe forces of the spirit to match his own? As the stars in their courses yesterday fought against Sisera, so are they not fighting today against Mussolini and Hitler and Franco? Why be so impatient as to believe the stars will fail, or so petty as to imagine that everything depends forever upon a sword, a machine-gun, or a bombing-plane. There are other and mightier forces, and fool or not, the pacifist will trust them to the end.

JOHN HAYNES HOLMES, *A Statesmanship of Peace.*
Published by the War Resisters' League, 171 West 12th Street, New York City.

GETHSEMANE

There is a way which man hath trod
    For, lo, these thronging, countless years;
It is the way of life, of God;
    It is the way of night, of tears;
Its winding we may not foresee;
    It is the way—Gethsemane.

It is the way whereby we know
    Life's larger meanings and its claims,
The fellowship of human woe,
    Our partnership with others' pains.
It is the way which seems to be
    Life's only way—Gethsemane.

CHARLES RUSSELL WAKELEY.

A PRAYER

O God, by whom the meek are guided in judgment, and light riseth up in darkness for the godly; grant us, in our doubts and uncertainties, the grace to ask what thou wouldst have us to do; that the Spirit of wisdom may save us from false choices, and that in thy light we may see light, and in thy straight path may not stumble; through Jesus Christ our Lord. Amen.

BRIGHT.

Proceed Resolutely: Fourteenth Friday

96. MADE LUMINOUS BY SUFFERING

All cosmic knowledge comes of wisdom stored
In minds made luminous by suffering;
Remote or recent orbs of thought flashing
Aflame the bolts of their discoveries
Across the universal architrave
For all men to behold, are repossessed
And utilized by minds ubiquitous,
That, daring to explore the outer zones
Of consciousness, foresee the final fall
Of Chaos.   EDWARDS DAVIS, *Lovers of Life.*
              Published by Baker & Taylor Company, New York.

AS THE CHURCH CONFRONTS THE THREAT OF WAR

What specifically is the duty of the church as it contemplates the imminent possibility of the downfall of civilization in another war? The tragedy of Christianity in 1914-1918 was due to the fact that the church had made no preparation for such a catastrophe. The Christian religion was caught unaware. It had not rehearsed its role. It therefore followed the line of least resistance. It blessed the war and blessed the nations in prosecuting it.

Are we willing that the church shall come up to the next war in such a state of unpreparedness? The greatest business before us now is to envisage the situation in which the church will find itself when the next war comes, and lay down in advance the broad lines which it intends, under God, to follow. What, then, must the church do to make itself ready for the crisis? My answer can be at best only the beginning of an answer.

The first thing, as I see it, which the church must do to prepare itself for war is to establish in its own thought the fact of its complete independence in human society. This includes as its first and major emphasis the independence of the church from the state.

Envisaging now the probability of a new war, it is primary to every other consideration that the church shall establish in its own thought and make it clear to society as a whole, and especially to the state, that it is not here because the state graciously allows it to be here, but that it has an independence of its own. The church is here because God put it here.

In the second place, if the church is to prepare itself for the next war it must excommunicate war from its altars. The fact is that historically the Christian church, in this matter of peace and war, has been on the side of war. The cloak of sanctity which the church threw over war, eased the consciences of German and French and English and American Christians who went forth to kill one another. True, they might have gone anyhow, without this sanction, but they would have done so under profound moral constraint. It is the church's essential business to generate just this constraint in the souls of men. For this the church exists: to create a tension in men's hearts, a tension between the way of the world and the will of God. But the church can generate this tension only if it maintains its character as the institutional expression of the will of God. And God does not will war.

This brings us to the third act in the preparation of the church for the next war. I will state it thus: The church should begin now to prepare itself against internal division over the pacifist issue. As I look forward to another war, I dread its consequences in the internal life of the Christian community. . . .

Room must be made in the church of Christ for both the Christian pacifist and the Christian soldier until God shows his church some solution which is still withheld from its understanding.

In the fourth place, if the church is to prepare itself for the next war, it should begin now to envisage the situation in which it will stand after that war, and determine its present character and activity accordingly. War is the world's greatest destroyer of faith in the living God. We are not left to idle guessing as to the spiritual condition in which the next war will leave mankind. The uprooting and blighting of fundamental Christian convictions as the result of the late war is the most conspicuous fact of the past two decades. And where faith has survived, or where it has been restored, it is a shallow faith, a timid faith, a short-ranged faith. Another war will play havoc with such faith. Its inevitable effect will be to make the world and history look like an affair of chaos and stark confusion, having no meaning, no purpose, no guidance, no goal. . . .

Therefore the church, viewing itself and its world in a wide and long perspective, and envisaging the possibility, nay the probability, of war, must prepare now to deal with the chaos that will ensue. If civilization goes down, every Christian must be anxious that the church shall not go down with it. But it can come through the crisis and minister to a distraught humanity only if it comes through with clean hands. Mankind will turn on its heel in scorn of a church which does once more what the churches did in 1914-1918. And what is meant by clean hands? I have already indicated three things the church must do to make its hands clean. One is the clear affirmation of its own independence. Another is the excommunication of war from its altars. The third is the guarding of its own unity against further division over the pacifist or any other issue. To these I am now adding a fourth. The church must effectively disengage itself from the decadent structure of a civilization whose fate in history is about to be sealed. The church has allowed itself to be flattered and patronized by the secular order. It holds a privileged position in the status quo. It is a chief beneficiary of the very evils which cause the disintegration of the existing order. Obviously, the church cannot expect to minister prophetically to a new order unless its hands are clean of complicity with the money-mad, idolatrous, militaristic and humanistic forces which have produced Western civilization. If the church appears to the world to be bound up with these forces and to be an integral part of the falling structure, it too will fall. Such a church will be hated, as the Russian church is hated for its weak and soft compliance with the will of the old regime.

The hour has come for the church to begin to disentangle its organized life from its dependence upon the secular support and favor which it has sought and enjoyed in the past, and to take a position from which it is able to look at Western civilization with a prophet's eyes. The Christian church should today be uttering her warning and pronouncing God's judgment as Jonah condemned and warned Ninevah. By such a course, the church may at least save herself. And by such a course she may save our modern Ninevah. But in any event, such a church, surviving the next war, will be able to offer the way of salvation to the new civilization whose slow rebuilding will follow upon the destruction of this. The specific steps we are to take will become clear to us when once we see where we ought to go, that is, where God wills that we should go. One thing the church must believe about itself, namely, that it was thrust by a creative act of God into the world to be the bearer of a revelation from him which alone can save the world. Whatever happens to a particular civilization, mankind cannot itself be lost so long as the church survives and proclaims its gospel of redemption unsullied with the privileges, the seductions and the philosophies of this world.

CHARLES CLAYTON MORRISON, in Christendom.

THE PRESENT CRISIS

Count me o'er earth's chosen heroes,—they were souls that stood
    alone,
While the men they agonized for hurled the contumelious stone,
Stood serene, and down the future saw the golden beam incline
To the side of perfect justice, mastered by their faith divine,
By one man's plain truth to manhood and to God's supreme
    design.

By the light of burning heretics Christ's bleeding feet I track,
Toiling up new Calvaries ever with the cross that turns not back,
And these mounts of anguish number how each generation learned
One new word of that grand *Credo* which in prophet-hearts hath
    burned
Since the first man stood God-conquered with his face to Heaven
    upturned.

For Humanity sweeps onward: where to-day the martyr stands,
On the morrow crouches Judas with the silver in his hands;
Far in front the cross stands ready and the crackling fagots burn,
While the hooting mob of yesterday in the silent awe return
To glean up the scattered ashes into history's golden urn.

JAMES RUSSELL LOWELL.

A PRAYER

O merciful Lord, who of thy own free goodness hast given us happy days and an abundance of good things, do not let us be corrupted with so great prosperity lest we forget the Giver in the gifts, but rather increase our love and humility; so shall we offer thee the sacrifice of thanksgiving through Jesus Christ our Lord. Amen.

J. LESLIE JOHNSTON.

Seek Comradeship:

97. HYMN OF THE CITY

Not in the solitude
Alone may man commune with heaven, or see,
 Only in savage wood
And sunny vale, the present Deity;
 Or only hear his voice
Where the winds whisper and the waves rejoice.

Even here do I behold
Thy steps, Almighty!—here, amidst the crowd,
 Through the great city rolled,
With everlasting murmur deep and loud—
 Choking the ways that wind
'Mongst the proud piles, the work of human kind.

Thy golden sunshine comes
From the round heaven, and on their dwellings lies
 And lights their inner homes;
For them thou fill'st with air the unbounded skies,
 And givest them the stores
Of ocean, and the harvest of its shores.

Thy spirit is around,
Quickening the restless mass that sweeps along;
 And this eternal sound—
Voices and footfalls of the numberless throng—
 Like the resounding sea,
Or like the rainy tempest, speaks of Thee.

And when the hour of rest
Comes, like a clam upon the mid-sea brine,
 Hushing its billowy breast—
The quiet of that moment too is thine;
 It breathes of Him who keeps
The vast and helpless city while it sleeps.

WILLIAM CULLEN BRYANT (1794-1878).

THE INNER LIGHT

In the meeting for worship the group waits in silence in the Divine Presence which is manifest in every human heart. The Quaker writers have never given explicit instructions as to what the worshipper should do in the silence. That depends on individual capacity and need. Reverent and devout reflections on events in the worshipper's life, the significance of other proceedings in present or past history, the meaning of Biblical passages or episodes in the life of Jesus, the teachings of certain great human lives and personalities, petitions to God for help and strength, all such and many others which involve a worshipful activity have an important place. But they are not the final rungs on the ladder of spiritual ascent. The time comes when thought is only a door to something higher. The spirit becomes fully awake and alert in an attitude of waiting expectancy. Sensitivity is increased and the worshipper becomes more keenly aware of the needs and feelings of those immediately around him, and of the great world beyond with its myriad voices calling for help and guidance. As sensitivity further increases the world of eternity appears beyond and supporting the world of time. The worshipper is filed with awe and reverence and with a sense of his own utter unworthiness. Self fades away and he becomes vitalized with Divine Life from above which permeates his being with Light and Love. Then he may become aware that God is calling him to do something or to say something. Life acquires new meaning and a new sense of direction because he has been lifted above life to a height from which he can see it in relation to some greater whole of existence. . . .

The meeting for worship should tend toward such results as insight, unity, and power. Religious experience affords the worshipper a wider perspective; he may even glimpse some vista with the eyes of God if he permits God's Spirit to work wholly through him without restraint. Unity results from worship because religious experience is the most powerful solvent for self-centeredness that has ever been discovered. The self is literally dissolved by the flooding in of a greater Life. This is particularly true in silent waiting which is the least self-assertive type of worship. Not only does a wider insight result than that attained from the point of view of narrow selfish interests, but also an attitude of detachment as of one who is in the world, but not of it. Strife ceases and unity comes when a sense of detachment arises which no longer views certain methods or objectives as supremely important. . . .

A silent, expectant worship is not only a source of unity but a source of power. The meeting not only discovers the truth but obtains energy and courage to go forward and act upon it. This doctrine is almost incomprehensible to our modern era in which the whole emphasis is on action. Yet the social worker, the reformer, the person of action in general, must learn that the stream of time flows out of a source which is timeless and that the stream of activity will run dry unless it is fed by an eternal spring. . . .

The doctrine of the Inner Light, as held by the Society of Friends, is associated with unity and power because it is thought of in social rather than in individual terms.

HOWARD H. BRINTON, *Divine-Human Society.*
Published by The Book Committee of The Religious Society of Friends,
302 Arch Street, Philadelphia.

A DIVERSITY OF GIFTS

The Christian sees distinctions of race as part of God's purpose to enrich mankind with a diversity of gifts. Against racial pride or race antagonism the church must set its face implacably as rebellion against God. Especially in its own life and worship there can be no place for barriers because of race or color. Similarly the Christian accepts national communities as part of God's purpose to enrich and diversify human life. Every man is called of God to serve his fellows in the community to which he belongs. But national egotism tending to the suppression of other nationalities or of minorities is, no less than individual egotism, a sin against the Creator of all peoples and races. The deification of nation, race or class, or of political or cultural ideals, is idolatry, and can lead only to increasing division and disaster.

On every side we see men seeking for a life of fellowship in which they experience their dependence on one another. But because community is sought on a wrong basis, the intensity of the search for it issues in conflict and disintegration. In such a world the church is called to be in its own life that fellowship which binds men together in their common dependence on God and overleaps all barriers of social status, race or nationality.

In consonance with its nature as true community, the church will call the nations to order their lives as members of the one family of God. The universal church, surveying the nations of the world, in every one of which it is now planted and rooted, must pronounce a condemnation of war unqualified and unrestricted. War can occur only as a fruit and manifestation of sin. . . . The Christian can acknowledge no ultimate authority but God; his loyalty to the state is part of his loyalty to God and must never usurp the place of that primary and only absolute loyalty. . . .

The responsibility of the church is to insist on the true relationship of spiritual and economic goods. Man cannot live without bread, and man cannot live by bread alone. Our human wealth consists in fellowship with God and in him with our brethren. To this fellowship the whole economic order must be made subservient.

"A Message from the Oxford Conference to the Christian Churches."

The Oxford Conference: Official Report.
Published by Willett, Clark & Company, Chicago.

A PRAYER

Lord Jesus, we beseech thee, by the loneliness of thy suffering on the Cross, be nigh unto all them that are desolate and in pain or sorrow to-day; and let thy presence transform their loneliness into comfort, consolation, and holy fellowship with thee, thou pitiful Saviour. Amen.

SURSUM CORDA.

Worship God: Fourteenth Sunday

98. BURNING BUSHES

I watched the sun slant past a tenement
And splash its gold against a dingy wall,
As though God stooped to give love's sacrament
To that one home. I saw the last light fall
Upon the lacework of a lofty tree,
Consuming it with fiery lavender.
I doffed my hat before this mystery
Revealed to me by God's gay messenger.
One burning bush by Sinai's rugged way
Arrested Moses like a brigand chief,
But this gold glory I have seen to-day
Transcends my grandest dreams of majesty,
Surmounts the limitations of belief
And changes this dirt earth to heaven for me.

HARRY ELMORE HURD, *Christ in the Breadline.*
Published by The Driftwood Press, North Montpelier, Vt.

FROM A HILL RETREAT

There is a harmony that dwells in silence,
    Diviner than the harmonies of sound.—
Here, on a leaf-strewn aisle among the redwoods,
    The mystic arms of quiet fold me round.

Only the peaceful lapping of slow waters,
    A wood-bird's rustle, and a bluejay's call,
Challenge the speechless lull of ridge and canyon,
    Which yet have speech . . . in notes not heard at all.

The stillness of the peaked and gaunt sequoia,
    And the awed hush of sun-barred lanes below;
The sweet, immaculate blue of tree-rimmed heavens,
    And far, brown hills the fog-seas overflow,—

These have a music that the ear of beauty
    May catch when thunder-tones would pass her by,
As though there were a faint, perpetual chorus
    Tuned to the harp-strings of the woods and sky;

As though the gods here lingered lyric-throated,
  And he whose spirit heard that tranquil throng
Would be at one with grove and stream and mountain
  And never wish a more melodious song.
                    STANTON A. COBLENTZ, *Songs of the Redwoods.*
          Published by Overland-Outwest Publications, Los Angeles.

AWARENESS OF GOD

It is needful to revive in this confused generation an awareness of God. Science has made us aware of our material environment and explained many hitherto mysterious forces of nature, but it has also filled our horizon with new and startling artificial material objects. Thus life for most of us tends to superficiality and artificiality to such a degree that many find it easy to lose sight of the realities of nature itself. "Little we see in nature that is ours," complained a poet at an early stage of modern industrialism, and this is true for more people now than then. Still more does our absorption in material interests tend to make us oblivious of God; and this is the commonest kind of atheism today. Neither denying nor affirming his being, men forget God. Not labored argument or scholastic definition but only the confident voice and consistent life of men for whom God is a reality of experience can overcome this devitalizing forgetfulness. We shall not be able to win through to worthful social attainment without first coming to know God with such vivid awareness that we are set free from fear, discouragement and base ambition.

Revolutionary leaven is at work the world over. The future will be perhaps more unlike the past with respect to the external forms of life than we imagine. But external changes mean little if they are not the expression of inward and spiritual change. Invention may be desirable, but no accumulation of gadgets will bring wealth of soul. A redistribution of income and of power may appear to be requisite; but if it has to be advocated with fierce anger, brought about by violence and maintained by terrorism, it loses its attractiveness to the Christian mind. The only external transformations that mark real progress are those which come because the evangel of good will has found lodgment in the hearts of men. The pride and inconsiderateness of our primitive natures must yield to the spirit of "him that serveth"; our greed and self-seeking must vanish, as these native passions have often vanished before that cross "on which the Prince of Glory died." This is the basic price of any "Christian revolution." Social intelligence cannot, important as it is, of itself create a new society. It must be joined with the perhaps even rarer element of social consecration.

JOHN T. McNEILL, *Christian Hope for World Society.*
Published by Willett, Clark & Company, Chicago.

THE TEMPLE OF GOD

Man is made to be the Temple of the Divine Presence; but how is the building marred and broken; how often has it been the haunt, not of the pure spirit of love, but of base thoughts of pride, of lust, of selfishness? Yet let us be thankful that, though the sanctuary has been defiled, though it may be buried beneath earthen masses which the years have only made greater, in the depths of every human heart there is a temple still.

Every man born into the world, be he who he may, has that within him by which he may come into personal communion with the Spirit of God. He can never be at peace until this relation becomes a reality to him. . . .

The food which our souls need is that life, spent for man in unselfish love, poured out for man in the passion of the Cross, triumphing for man in the Resurrection. He is at once the Revealer and the Redeemer, the supreme regenerator of human souls, the unveiler of the reality within us.

RELIGIOUS SOCIETY OF FRIENDS, 1907.

"LISTEN IN!"

Listen in to what the universe is saying,
    Listen in, listen in!
For the trumpets of Eternity are playing
    To the Springtime's violin.
If you'll cease to give your hearing or devotion
    To the little daily tumult that appears,
You will hear a new and wonderful commotion,
    The music of the singing spheres!

Listen in, listen in!
  Only hark to what the radio will tell.
For the viols of the world
Are a melody unfurled
  To summon you and say that all is well.
Though without you are surrounded with disaster,
  And sorrow is the chord you seem to hear,
You shall find the self that triumphs and is master,
  If you listen with the inner ear.

Listen in, listen in,
  While the golden organ peals,
For the music of the soul
Shall rejoice and make you whole,
  If you hark to what the radio reveals.
Though the din of life may fill you with confusion,
  And the roar of cities haunt you with dismay,
You may free yourself from terror and delusion,
  If you'll listen to Eternity to-day!

Angela Morgan's Recitals, Penn Publishing Co., Philadelphia.

A PRAYER

For the gift of wonder and the joy of discovery; for the ever-
    lasting freshness of experience; for the newness of life each
    day as we grow older;
For children and the joy of innocency, for all the sanctities of
    family life and for all that our friendships bring to us;
For the gift of humour and gaiety of heart, and for all pure
    comedy and laughter;
For singers and musicians; for poets and craftsmen, for all who
    work in form and colour to increase the joy and beauty of
    life;
For the gifts of science and invention, and for the recreation
    brought to our homes by books and pictures, and by wireless;
For the image of Christ in ordinary people, their forbearance and
    generosity, their good temper, their courage and kindness;
                        We thank Thee, O our Father.
                                            Acts of Devotion.

PART III

DISCUSSION OUTLINES FOR FOURTEEN SESSIONS OF CLASSES

Discussion Groups and Young People's Meetings

SUGGESTIONS FOR THE LEADER

If at all possible have available a minimum of three copies of this volume: one for your own use, and two copies from which excerpts may be cut out and pasted on loose leaves for assignment to various members of the group.

Maximum value will be derived from the class periods if previously the different members have read the chapter covering the theme under discussion, and the daily readings on this subject. If the various members desire to follow this procedure, it may be preferable for them to read in this order, for illustration: The Ideal, pages 1-34, and readings Nos. 1, 8, 15, 22, 29, 36, 43; and the following week, 50, 57, 64, 71, 78, 85, 92; then The Actual pages 35-56, and readings Nos. 2, 9, 16, 23, 30, 37, 44, etc. Consult the Index for topical readings.

The session may well be closed with a period of corporate worship.

In those instances, where it is not practicable to hold as many as fourteen sessions, portions of these suggested outlines may be combined for seven sessions or whatever number of periods may be available.

THE IDEAL FOR THE INDIVIDUAL AND FOR SOCIETY

1. Human nature being what it is, what would be a normal response from an individual in the following situations:

   (a) When walking along a river bank and hearing the cries of a distressed person in the water who is about to drown?

   (b) When observing a building on fire and hearing the cries of an infant who is rapidly being suffocated by smoke?

   (c) When on duty as a trained nurse during an epidemic of a highly contagious and deadly disease?

2. To what degree is self-sacrifice latent within an average person? Does the report of the Carnegie Hero Fund Commission, as quoted on pages 6 and 7, appear exaggerated to you?

3. Comment on the validity of the oft-repeated statement: "Self-preservation is the first law of life."

4. In the light of your own experience and observation, to what extent are the appreciation of beauty and harmony and capacity to worship latent and prevalent among average people?

5. Comment upon the statement: Human nature is potential; what it becomes is determined by stimuli, the relative impact of various external sensations and internal pressures from ideas, ideals and emotions.

6. Summarize briefly Jesus' estimate of human nature. Cite evidence of his awareness of latent greed, lust and cruelty within man. Do you think he was justified in his high expectations of what his disciples would become and what they would accomplish? Why?

7. Write on the blackboard or read aloud the following summary of Jesus' deepest convictions:

1. God is creator and sustainer of the universe.

2. Personality is the most precious of all values.

3. Kinship with every other human being is the normal relationship.

4. Concern about values and relationships is the most dynamic motivation.

5. Justice is required in all relationships.

6. Fellowship travels far beyond justice.

7. Evil can be overcome only with goodness.

8. Risks must be run and consequences endured.

9. God can be and must be trusted and obeyed.

At what points does this summary appear inaccurate or incomplete? To what extent, if any, did Jesus make exceptions to these general principles? For example, all human beings are my kinsmen—except?

8. Discuss the extent to which the spirit and teaching of Jesus constitute a valid and adequate ideal for personal living and social action in our time under prevailing conditions.

9. Comment on this statement: Stricken humanity in this hour of world crisis needs nothing so desperately as the reproduction and extension of the spirit of Jesus in personal living and social action.

SECOND SESSION

THE IDEAL FOR THE INDIVIDUAL AND FOR SOCIETY (*Continued*)

1. When you pray, "Thy Kingdom come, Thy Will be done on earth as it is in heaven," what ideas about the good society are in your mind? What will be the chief characteristics of the Kingdom of God on earth, if the Lord's prayer is fully answered?

2. Write on the blackboard or read aloud the following interpretation of the economic characteristics of the Kingdom of God on earth:

   (a) Mutual concern and love will provide adequate motivation for efficient economic behavior.

   (b) The method of production will be cooperative endeavor mutually to provide plenty for everybody.

   (c) The method of distributing necessities and comforts will be sharing in accordance with comparative needs, with consideration of relative requirements in the light of responsibilities assumed.

   Discuss the validity and adequacy of this interpretation. In the ideal society, how important will be the role of economic self-interest? How much competition for private gain will there then be? Will society then be divided into classes of rich and poor?

3. Discuss the practicability of this way of life in America today. Evaluate the validity of the following statement:

   Plenty for everybody, work for everybody, and leisure for everybody in the United States could now be provided through mutual concern, cooperative endeavor, and sharing of necessities and privileges. The required resources are available: fertile soil, favorable climate, natural resources, mechanical power, technical skill, administrative genius, labor power, democratic heritage and process, and freedom of religion. The urgent need of the hour is more mutual concern, more cooperative endeavor, more equality of sharing.

4. If the Lord's prayer should be fully answered, what relationships would then prevail among peoples of various races, languages, and classes? In the Kingdom of God on earth, how much significance will be attached to color and dialect?

5. Summarize the practice followed by many missionary societies in providing remuneration for missionaries in foreign lands:

   (a) Basic salary for all unmarried individuals.

   (b) Supplementary salary for wife and children.

   (c) Supplementary salary if located in a city where cost of living is excessively high.

   (d) Supplementary funds to provide special facilities required for specialized responsibilities as a writer, editor, research, etc.

   Comment upon this policy in the light of Christian principles. Would it be more satisfactory to pay missionaries according to their respective abilities? Should the present missionary policy outlined above be extended to other fields of human endeavor?

6. Read aloud Bernard Shaw's statement concerning Jesus' way of life, as printed on pages 378 and 379, and comment upon its validity.

7. Summarize the chief points in the statement by Gregory Vlastos, as printed on pages 516-519, and express a judgment as to their accuracy and importance.

THIRD SESSION

DEEPEN UNDERSTANDING OF THE ACTUAL

1. Summarize the essential facts concerning the extent of idle machinery, idle money and idle men in the United States during recent months and years. (See page 220 for data.) Supplement with information derived from the experience of members of the group.

2. Discuss the point of view outlined on pages 42, 43, that excessive concentration of income, with the consequent lack of adequate purchasing power on the part of millions of families, is a primary cause of idle machinery, idle money, and idle men. (Such a question may easily be assigned in advance for special study by a member.)

3. What are the primary reasons for the prevailing degree of concentration of economic privilege in the United States? Are the larger incomes derived chiefly from wages and salaries, or do they come mainly from ownership of property?

4. Summarize the data presented on pages 41, 42, 192 ff., concerning the concentration of control of giant corporations in this country. Discuss the relationship of this consolidation of control to the prevailing extent of idle machinery, idle money, and idle men.

5. Why is there such an extreme degree of concentration of economic power in the United States? Discuss the significance of these popular and widespread ideas:

   (a) Self-interest must be the driving incentive to efficient economic behavior.

   (b) A man is entitled to all the money that he can get honestly and will use generously.

   (c) Competition is the necessary and wholesome method of achieving economic efficiency.

   (d) Government should keep its hands off business, except for necessary regulation to prevent unlawful and unfair practices.

6. What are the primary causes of industrial warfare in this country? Summarize the situation described on pages 45-48. Discuss the chief reasons for the prevalence of this type of violence.

7. Discuss the significance of idle machinery, idle money, and idle men, together with virulent industrial warfare, as factors which may be forerunners of a patriotic brand of American fascism.

8. To what extent and in what ways is secularism responsible for the diseased condition of American economic and political life? How does loss of vital faith in a righteous and loving God exaggerate and accelerate the destructive tendencies in the social order?

9. Comment upon this statement: "The plain truth is that as a civilization we are less sure of where we are going, where we want to go, how and for what we wish to live, than at any intelligent period of which we have full record."

FOURTH SESSION

DEEPEN UNDERSTANDING OF THE ACTUAL
(*Continued*)

1. What are the chief causes of the militancy and aggressiveness of Germany's present foreign policy? Write on the blackboard or read aloud the following summary:

   (a) Heritage of ideas concerning Teutonic supremacy and the omnipotence of military prowess.

   (b) Violent revulsion against the Treaty of Versailles and other aspects of Allied policy of reducing Germany to the rank of a minor power.

   (c) Economic distress due in part to Germany's handicapped position in controlling essential raw materials and in maintaining access to rich markets.

   (d) Observation of the practices of other imperialist nations in conquering foreign territories and ruling vast empires.

   (e) Determination of Germany to achieve parity of armaments and the refusal of the Allies to make substantial reductions in their own armaments.

   (f) Policy of all great nations in claiming national sovereignty and consequent refusal to establish effective agencies of international justice.

2. In which of these practices is the United States involved, and to what degree? Be specific in your answer.

3. In what ways and to what extent do economic forces cause war? Discuss the statement by V. A. Demant as printed on pages 386, 387. Comment especially upon this sentence: "The key to the tragic situation of a period marked by great peace activities and glaring preparation for war must lie in the aggressive nature of a human activity which is mistakenly regarded as pacific."

4. If the democracies decide that it is necessary to wage war against the fascist powers:

   (a) Where will the fighting occur if the democracies have power to decide?

   (b) In that event, what weapons will be used, and what will be the consequences for the peoples of the invaded lands?

   (c) What will happen to democracy itself while the war continues?

   (d) Is there basis for confidence that wartime dictatorship would be ended at the armistice?

   (e) What would be the effects of such a defensive war upon moral standards and ethical practices?

   (f) In what ways would religion be affected by a war against fascism?

5. Does the description of war as printed on pages 214, 215, appear exaggerated to you? Give reasons for your answers.

6. Summarize the statement by Brigadier General Crozier as printed on pages 380, 381. Discuss the significance and validity of his point of view.

7. Express a rigorous judgment concerning the following statement contained in the official report of the Oxford Conference, composed of delegates from many religious bodies from various parts of the earth:

   War involves compulsory enmity, diabolical outrage against human personality, and a wanton distortion of the truth. War is a particular demonstration of the power of sin in the world and a defiance of the righteousness of God as revealed in Jesus Christ and him crucified.

FIFTH SESSION

BE CONCERNED BECAUSE OF THE GULF BETWEEN THE ACTUAL AND THE IDEAL

1. Copy on a blackboard or summarize the table printed on page 43. Discuss the consequences of this distribution of national income in the light of the ideal:

    (a) the Fatherhood of God,

    (b) the brotherhood of man,

    (c) the supreme worth of personality, and

    (d) the duty of the strong to bear the burdens of the weak.

2. Summarize the estimates of national income for 1935-1936, as printed on page 42, and discuss the meaning of these figures in the light of the ideal. Continue this discussion in relation to the condition of agricultural workers, as described on pages 408-411, 436-439. Comment especially upon this statement:

    "No gifts of clairvoyance are required to foretell that the future of the American farmer is the characteristic one of all peasants for whom, in our present system of society, there is no hope."

3. If concentration of economic power is unavoidable in a complex industrialized society, what safeguards are necessary if progress toward the ideal is to be realized? Discuss the adequacy and validity of these tests:

    (a) Power should be allocated by the community, rather than inherited or wielded because of wealth possessed.

    (b) Power should be administered in a responsible way for the good of the community in terms of the allocation of this power, rather than used arbitrarily for the gain of a privileged few.

    (c) Power should be held temporarily, for a specified period, rather than indefinitely or permanently.

    (d) These differences in the social significance of extreme concentration of power are illustrated respectively by a President of the United States and by a Czar of the old Russia.

4. In the light of these considerations, discuss the meaning of the figures relating to cencentration of control of American corporations, as summarized on pages 41, 42, 292 ff.

5. Discuss the accuracy and validity of the following statement by Professor Slichter of Harvard University:

> "Had we deliberately planned an industrial system which would create intense conflict between capital and labor, we could scarcely have devised one which would have achieved this result more completely than does the existing economic order."

6. Summarize the data concerning industrial warfare, as found on pages 45-48, and discuss its significance in the light of the ideal: the sacredness of personality, and the overcoming of evil with goodness.

7. Discuss the extent to which secularism is prevalent in American economic and political life. Compare or contrast the actual situation with the ideal community in which all life would be characterized by love toward God and love toward neighbor. Discuss the validity of the statements made by W. G. Peck, as printed on pages 356-359.

8. Discuss the significance of penitence in the life of a truly religious person. Illustrate the need for social penitence and point out ways of expressing this contrition.

9. The session may profitably be concluded with a period of quietness, followed by reading of some of the passages printed on pages 57, 58, 61, 62, and ending with prayer.

SIXTH SESSION

BE CONCERNED BECAUSE OF THE GULF BETWEEN THE ACTUAL AND THE IDEAL (*Continued*)

1. Read or summarize the statement by Andre Maurois, as printed on pages 50, 51, and discuss its validity and fairness.

2. List the various wars waged in different parts of the earth since 1919 (see page 213). Discuss the reasons why there has been such an appalling amount of destruction and slaughter.

3. Write on the blackboard the following:

   (a) "Be not deceived, God is not mocked, whatsoever a man sows, that shall he reap."

   (b) "Be sure your sins will find you out."

   (c) "The sins of the fathers will be visited upon the children until the third and fourth generations."

   Discuss the present world crisis in the light of these truths. Is it true that the Allies sowed the Treaty of Versailles and reaped Hitler? Is it fair to say that the sins of the imperialist powers, including Great Britain, France, and the United States, are being visited on the Czechs, the Chinese, the Spaniards, and the Ethiopians? Give reasons for your answers.

4. In the light of the truth that sowing determines reaping, what consequences may be predicted from the prevailing race of armaments and widespread determination to wage war, as a last resort, to preserve national interests? Upon which nations must be placed primary responsibility for the race of armaments? Give reasons for your answers.

5. Summarize the argument of Canon Raven, as printed on pages 161-163. To what extent do you agree and do you differ with his point of view?

6. Is Visser t'Hooft justified in saying that Jesus scandalizes us and that we are afraid of his way of life? (See pages 328, 329.) Comment especially upon this section: "The scandal consists in

his turning upside down all our values. . . . The Christian is a man who has faced this choice, and who has come to the conclusion that Jesus is right and that he himself was and is wrong."

7. Read the statement by Bernard Shaw on pages 378 and 379. Discuss this opinion : "The moneyed, respectable, capable world has been steadily anti-Christian and Barrabasque since the crucifixion."

8. Conclude with a period of corporate penitence because of the gulf between the actual and the ideal. (See pages 61, 62.)

SEVENTH SESSION

ENDEAVOR TO TRANSFORM THE ACTUAL INTO THE IDEAL

1. Discuss the accuracy and adequacy of these three statements:

   (a) We should concentrate on the endeavor to convert individuals to the Christian life, with the assurance that genuinely converted individuals can make satisfactory use of the present social system in the United States.

   (b) We should concentrate on the task of changing the present system into a cooperative commonwealth, with the assurance that a satisfactory social system will produce the desired kind of individuals.

   (c) We should endeavor simultaneously to convert individuals and to change the social system.

2. Summarize the statement about property for use and property for power, on pages 68, 69. Discuss the validity of this distinction.

3. Discuss the accuracy and fairness of the following statement:

   "A genuinely cooperative society cannot be built upon the foundations of private ownership of the chief instruments of production."

   Give reasons for agreeing or disagreeing with this statement.

4. Discuss the validity and relevance of the following statement:

   "There will never be enough private property in users' and consumers' goods for the people of the United States until there is a drastic reduction in the amount of private property in banks, mines, electric power, railways, telephones, and other primary means of production and distribution."

   Give reasons for agreeing or disagreeing with this point of view.

5. Compare or contrast various attitudes toward the present property system:

   (a) The Republican Party

(b) The New Deal

(c) Farmer-Labor Groups

(d) The Socialist Party

(e) The Communist Party

(f) Fascist Leaders

6. If the primary means of production were socialized progressively by rapid stages, are there adequate economic incentives which could be relied upon for efficiency? Is the summary on pages 73, 74, realistic and dependable? Give reasons for agreeing or disagreeing with this point of view.

7. What are the values of the consumers' cooperative movement? Be specific.

8. Discuss the questions: Why labor unions? What kind: company, craft, industrial? Would it be wise or unwise for American industrialists generally to follow the British example of recognizing the unions and seeking to improve the processes of collective bargaining, rather than fighting the unions as they seek to organize the workers?

ENDEAVOR TO TRANSFORM THE ACTUAL INTO THE IDEAL (*Continued*)

1. List the following courses of action open to the democratic powers as they face the menace of aggression by totalitarian nations:

    (a) Wage war against the dictators.

    (b) Rely upon threats of armed action, with the expectation that the fascist governments will yield.

    (c) Rely upon economic and financial pressure that does not go as far as war.

    (d) Seek to remove the basic causes of fascist aggression.

    (e) Suggest other courses of action.

2. Discuss the practicability and efficacy of the method of waging war against the dictators. If the democratic powers proved to be victorious, what would the probable consequences be:

    (a) for the vanquished, and

    (b) for the victors?

3. If the policy of threats of armed action is relied upon, are the democratic or the fascist countries more likely to succeed? Give reasons for your answer.

4. Discuss the types of economic and financial pressure required if by this means the aggression of Germany, Italy and Japan is to be stopped. Would mild or severe measures be required? Why?

5. List the following measures as means of reducing the belligerency and aggressiveness of the fascist nations:

    (a) Help solve their economic problems by providing them with more favorable access to the markets and raw materials of the more favored regions through the lowering of tariff walls.

(b) Help solve the empire problem by reducing the imperialism of the older empires through:

> (1) freedom for India and other parts of empires;

> (2) dominion status or self-government within a commonwealth of equals;

> (3) extension of the mandate system of the League of Nations to include mandates for British and French colonies as well as Germany's former colonies.

(c) Help solve the armaments problem by proceeding to reduce armaments, in spite of the risks incurred.

(d) Help solve the anarchy problem by joining and strengthening international agencies of justice, including a modified League of Nations and the World Court.

Give reasons for agreeing with or disagreeing with these various proposals.

6. Discuss the validity and relevance of the following statement:

> "It is better to proceed down the right road even if progress is slow and the dangers serious than to proceed rapidly down the wrong road to complete catastrophe."

NINTH SESSION

PROCEED RESOLUTELY WHEN CONFRONTED WITH THE CONSEQUENT OPPOSITION AND SUFFERING

1. If you were now living as a youth of twenty in the following countries, what would probably be your point of view concerning economic and international questions:

    (a) Nazi Germany?
    (b) Soviet Russia?
    (c) Imperial Japan?
    (d) Democratic Denmark?

2. If you had lived as a white person in a privileged home in Louisiana in 1850, what probably would have been your attitude toward slavery? Why?

3. Summarize the data concerning slavery as printed on pages 88-92, and comment upon its significance for present-day Americans as they face economic and political problems.

4. What lessons may we learn from the history of feudalism and the divine right of kings? (See data on pages 92-95.)

5. Summarize the statements by Lord Shaftesbury and Harold Begbie as printed on pages 96 and 97, and comment upon their significance.

6. Summarize comprehensively and fairly the arguments used against:

    (a) Universal suffrage.
    (b) Woman suffrage.
    (c) Free public schools.
    (d) Limitation of hours of labor.
    (e) The Interstate Commerce Commission.
    (f) The Federal Reserve Banking System.
    (g) Postal Savings Banks.
    (h) Parcels Post.
    (i) Income Tax.

(j) Unemployment Insurance.

(k) Labor Unions.

7. Discuss the validity and significance of the following statement:

This generation of radicals is especially subject to attack because in times of social convulsion fears are deeper and passions are hotter. Severe tremors are shaking the very foundations of the present economic order, with the result that even the most powerful beneficiaries of the existing system are overwhelmed with a feeling of insecurity and are terribly apprehensive about the future. International lawlessness and aggression are so widespread that peoples everywhere are afraid to reduce armaments, and certain types of patriots feel obliged to combat what they regard as the subversive and treasonable activities of pacifists.

Members of this generation who are endeavoring to bring about vital changes in the structure of society cannot hope to escape the charge that they are public enemies. An effective device used in every period is found in the calling of names, the pinning of labels, the hurling of epithets. The tendency is to pick out the most feared type and then lump together under this designation all individuals who refuse to acquiesce in the status quo. The word "communist" has been worked overtime as a bludgeon with which to beat down non-conformity to existing practices. During the past century this epithet has been hurled at almost every reformer. The individuals who propose freedom for the slaves "are atheists, socialists, communists, red republicans, jacobins." They are "advocates of 'free love,' the 'Socialists,' the Infidels, the 'Red Republicans.' " An editor described the saintly Susan B. Anthony as "a revolutionist, aiming at nothing less than the breaking up of the very foundations of society. . . . The whole plan is coarse, sensual and agrarian, the worst phase of French infidelity and communism." The proposed child labor amendment to the Constitution of the United States was described by one Senator as "a communistic, Bolshevistic scheme," while another Senator described it as "socialistic, bolshevistic, and I would almost say, anarchistic. . . . It assassinates democracy, and upon its grave establishes a hybrid monstrosity."

PROCEED RESOLUTELY WHEN CONFRONTED WITH THE CONSEQUENT OPPOSITION AND SUFFERING
(*Continued*)

1. If you had then been living in a privileged home of a Sadducee, what probably would have been your attitude toward Jesus? Why? (See the poem on page 328.)

2. What were the primary reasons for the hostility toward Jesus manifested by Jewish leaders and Roman authorities? (See pages 106-108.)

3. Express a judgment concerning the probable consequences if Jesus had yielded to pressure and had become a successful leader of armed revolt against Rome. Remember the victorious rebellion under the Maccabees, as summarized by Professor Case:

> "The slumbering discontent of the Jews burst into a new flame of national zeal in the second quarter of the second century B.C., when the Syrian rulers had carried oppression to the point of endeavoring to wipe out the Jewish religion. That heroic struggle, known as the Maccabean revolution, continuing for approximately twenty-five years, finally issued in temporary political independence. Henceforth this was a period of history to be enshrined in memory along with the now idealized national triumph under David. It must have seemed to many Jews that they were now on the verge of realizing a happy theocracy, a veritable kingdom of God on earth. At no previous time since the Babylonian exile had the prospects for Jewish autonomy been so bright. Under the leadership of a John Hyrcanus (135-104 B.C.) the national fortunes of the Jews rapidly approached their zenith. . . . The hope for permanent political autonomy under the Maccabean rulers was soon dispelled. Internal dissensions again rendered the Jews an easy prey for the conqueror, who this time was the Roman general Pompey. In 63 B.C. Palestine became a possession of the Romans."

4. Did Jesus establish a double standard of ethical conduct, one for himself and another for his followers? What degree of loyalty did he expect from his disciples? Discuss the evidence presented on pages 108-112.

5. To what extent and in what ways do the teaching and example of Jesus provide guidance for present-day Christians in their economic and political behavior? Discuss the point of view presented on pages 112-115.

6. If a Christian agrees with the pronouncements of many religious bodies that "war is sin" (see pages 115-118), should he ever approve of war or engage in armed hostilities? Give reasons for your answers.

7. In what sense is a true Christian obliged to be a "radical"? Discuss the point of view presented on pages 504-507. Give reasons for agreeing or disagreeing.

8. Read selections from the verses printed on pages 121-124 and discuss their relevancy and practicability in terms of America's economic and political problems.

SEEK COMRADESHIP IN THOUGHT AND PRAYER AND ACTION

1. Summarize the statement by E. Stanley Jones as printed on pages 126 and 127, and discuss its significance.

2. Comment upon the possibilities open to "inner circles" within churches, as described on pages 425-427.

3. Let some member of the group who is familiar with a Quaker meeting summarize and interpret the statement by Hornell Hart printed on pages 127 and 128.

4. Give reasons for agreeing with or disagreeing with the principles of the Fellowship of Reconciliation. (See pages 128, 129.)

5. Evaluate critically and sympathetically the principles of the Fellowship of Socialist Christians. (See pages 420-423.)

6. In what ways may biography be a means of comradeship? Illustrate.

7. Read the following summary of John Wesley's record:

> He traveled 250,000 miles, chiefly on horseback, averaging 20 miles per day for 40 years, in the days before Fords and streamliners hurled passengers furiously through space.
>
> He preached more than 40,000 sermons.
>
> He produced more than 400 books, as author, editor, and translator, while his own distinctive writings fill upwards of 25 massive volumes. And all in his own handwriting!
>
> He knew ten languages and made good use of them: Arabic, Hebrew, Greek, Latin, French, Italian, Spanish, German, Dutch, English.
>
> He planted, watered and nourished innumerable religious groups, which ultimately became the mighty worldwide Methodist Church.

At the age of 83 he was annoyed by the discovery that he could not write for more than 15 hours a day without hurting his eyes, and at the age of 86 he was ashamed to admit that he could not easily preach more than twice a day! We notice in his diary an increasing tendency to lie in bed in the morning, sometimes as late as 5:30 A.M. In his 86th year he preached in almost every shire in England and Wales, and often rode from 30 to 50 miles per day.

What were the chief sources of his power?

8. Review briefly the autobiography of Miss Vida Scudder. (See pages 130-132.)

9. Let various members of the class testify concerning the stimulus received from reading biographies.

10. The session may well be ended by reading the following poem by Thomas S. Jones, Jr.:

SANCTUARY

How many one hold these days of wonderment
    And bind them into stillness with a thong,
    Ere as a fleeting dream they pass along
Into the waste of lovely things forspent;
How may one keep what the Great Powers have sent,
    The prayers fulfilled more beautiful and strong
    Than any thought could fashion into song
Of all the rarest harmonies inblent?

There is an Altar where they may be laid
    And sealed in Faith within Its sacred care,—
    Here they are safe into the very end;
For these are of the things that never fade,
    Brought from the City that is built four-square,
    The gifts of Him who is the Perfect Friend.

THOS. S. JONES, JR., in *Shadow of the Perfect Rose.*
Published by Farrar and Rinehart, New York.

TWELFTH SESSION

SEEK COMRADESHIP IN THOUGHT AND PRAYER AND ACTION (*Continued*)

1. As an introduction to an interpretation of Charles F. Andrews as a radiant example of comradeship in action, read aloud the tribute from Mahatma Gandhi. (See pages 133-134.)

2. Interpret Mr. Andrews' conception of fellowship as revealed in the statement on pages 340 and 341.

3. Discuss the significance of the attitude toward the other races revealed in the statement by Mr. Andrews on pages 135, 136.

4. Read the following statement by Mr. Andrews and discuss its relevance to American life:

> "What is needed today is a revival of the spirit of martyrdom. That great word 'martyrdom' has a fine background and a noble meaning. It signifies witness in action. It is only those who have carried their faith to the test of action, those who have lived for their faith with the joyful consciousness that at any moment they might be called upon to die for it—it is only such men and women who are able to hold their own position without wavering when the crucial test comes. It is only these who can wrest victory out of defeat. There must be no compromise, no betrayal, no looking back. The test is crucial, for it is always, in some way or other, the test of the Cross. We can not, we must not, we dare not swerve one hair's breadth from the great charter of human solidarity and human redemption, which Christ himself has given us: In Him there can be neither Jew nor Greek, barbarian, Scythian, bond nor free, for all are one Man in Christ Jesus."

5. Summarize the statement on pages 400-402, and discuss the sources of Mr. Andrews' power.

6. Comment upon the statement on pages 172 and 173.

7. Discuss the importance of systematic contacts for discussion and prayer with other seekers after life. Interpret the significance of such groups as described on pages 126, 314 and 315.

8. Summarize the conception of a universal community presented by John MacMurray on pages 173-175.

9. Read the poem by Archibald MacLeish on pages 137 and 138, and discuss its relevance to the Christian task.

10. Discuss the meaning and significance of the following statement concerning fellowship:

> The recovery of Christendom will come, not by the formation of a new party, but by the miracle of fellowship. This we believe; and, believing it, we each desire to learn from others and to be helped by others; we each find that those who seem most to differ from us have often the most to teach us, and that often the very men whom we had been taught to oppose have the highest claim upon our admiration. Because we have been caught in the spirit of fellowship, we find ourselves less and less inclined to deny and ever more ready to respect and to affirm; in this we see the prospect of becoming ourselves more sane and reasonable, since men are apt to deny that which they do not understand, and to affirm those things in which they have found value. If the full presentment of Christ is not given by the Churches or the Church today, it is none the less to be found: it exists, scattered in the hearts of men, who when they come together in Christ's name find Him indeed in the midst of them, and seeing glimpses of His fullness, are made ashamed of their own fragmentariness—their obscurity.

THIRTEENTH SESSION

WORSHIP GOD IN SILENCE AND BEAUTY AND HARMONY

1. Read aloud, and subject to rigorous examination the following statement:

    The longer I meditate the more certain I am that the most thrilling idea that ever entered the mind of man is this: we live continuously in the presence of a wise and powerful and affectionate God, holy and righteous altogether, who eagerly desires to enter into intimate comradeship with human beings created in His own image, and who challenges His children to become co-workers in the glorious adventure of creating a harmonious community of kinsmen.

2. In what ways and to what degree is human nature adapted to worship? Discuss the point of view expressed by Rufus Jones on page 140.

3. Summarize the experience of Charles F. Andrews with silence, as recorded on pages 143 and 144.

4. Concerning the need for regularity and frequency in worship, read the statement by Harry Emerson Fosdick on page 143.

5. In what ways is appreciation of beauty a gateway to worship? Read the following statement by Studdert Kennedy:

    "Nature seems to speak of God. Go, stand out on a summer night and look upwards to the sky where the million stars go sailing through that great wide sea of blue, like silent ships that pass in the night. Go, walk in the woods on a day in April and watch the beauty of nature repeating the eternal resurrection, and rising from the grave of winter to the splendour of spring. Go, stand and watch the daylight die, and all the west grow wonderful with a thousand colours past the power of human artists to express. Look at a mountain towering up to kiss the sun, pluck the tiniest flower that grows upon its side; and if you are a healthy man or a healthy woman there will be something that will call you— call you to the worship of the Maker and Creator of it all, and to the love of the great Artist in whose mind the ever-changing picture that the world presents was born."

6. Let several members testify concerning the relationship in their experience between music and worship. For illustrations see pages 146-148, and consult index for references listed under "Music."

7. The session may well be ended with the reading of this poem by Carl Sandburg:

A SENSE OF WHERE TO GO

On the shores of Lake Michigan
high on a wooden pole, in a box,
two purple martins had a home
and taken away down to Martinique
and let loose, they flew home,
thousands of miles to be home again.
    And this has lights of wonder
    echo and pace and echo again.
The birds let out began flying
north north-by-west north
till they were back home.
How their instruments told them
of ceiling, temperature, air pressure,
how their control-boards gave them
reports of fuel, ignition, speeds,
is out of the record, out.
    Across spaces of sun and cloud,
    in rain and fog, through air pockets,
wind with them, wind against them,
stopping for subsistence rations,
whirling in gust and spiral,
these people of the air,
these children of the wind,
had a sense of where to go and how,
how to go north north-by-west north,
till they came to one wooden pole,
till they were home again.
    And this has lights of wonder
    echo and pace and echo again
for other children, other people, yes.

CARL SANDBURG, *The People, Yes.*
Harcourt Brace & Co., Publishers, New York, Reprinted by permission.

FOURTEENTH SESSION

WORSHIP GOD IN SILENCE AND BEAUTY AND HARMONY (*Continued*)

1. Consider the approaches to God made accessible through corporate worship in a church under favorable circumstances:

    (a) Silence
    (b) Beauty
    (c) Harmony
    (d) Fellowship
    (e) Memory
    (f) Sacrament
    (g) Preaching

    To what extent are these approaches open in the churches with which members of the group are familiar? Discuss rigorously ways and means of opening more widely these doors of worship.

2. Interpret the significance of a Quaker meeting, as described on pages 396-398, and 537 and 538.

3. Consider the meaning of Holy Communion, as interpreted by J. S. Whale in the following statement:

    "We meet together at this Table that Christ may do for us here what He has done for uncounted generations of Christian men. What Christ does for us here is unsearchable, rich in meaning. Plainly enough, this central fact of the Church's life has many aspects, yet three aspects have been determinative from the beginning. There is, first, the historical or memorial aspect; we remember here what was said and done in time of Jesus; this feast is a memorial feast, commemorating the mightiest of God's mighty acts of grace in the cross and the resurrection. There is, second, the timeless or eternal aspect. Here we are lifted out of time and have communion with the very life of God. The feast mediates God's presence and His very Self to us: here our fellowship with God, and in God has all the actuality and wholeness of life. Thirdly, when by an act of faith we partake together of Bread and Wine in this Sacrament, these two aspects become one. At this Table there is a unique fusion or synthesis of what is historical and what is beyond history; of what is in time and is remembered, and what is timeless and is experienced. . . . It is a vitally significant fact that not a single Sunday morning has passed since the first Holy Week without men and women meeting at the Holy Table."

4. Comment upon the statement by Evelyn Underhill on pages 289 and 290 that worship is creative and redemptive.

5. Is it reasonable to think of God as a person? Discuss the interpretations presented on pages 178, 179, 290, 291, 316 and 317.

6. How does God speak to man? Interpret the two statements on pages 373-375.

7. In what sense and to what degree must we trust God for the ultimate outcome of the struggle against evil? Interpret and evaluate the point of view presented by Reinhold Niebuhr on pages 344-346.

8. Read the following statement and express a judgment concerning its validity:

   Human nature being what it is, how does an individual act when he is normal and natural? He may climb or he may plunge. Man's capacity for sordidness and greed and cruelty should never be minimized. But it is equally possible for him to respond to the appeal of beauty and truth and goodness. Truly man does not live by bread alone, but by ecstatic beauty, rapturous harmony, sublime thought, noble deed, and fervent adoration of the Eternal God.

9. This session especially may well be concluded with a period of corporate worship including:
   (a) Adoration
   (b) Thanksgiving
   (c) Confession
   (d) Commitment
   (e) Trust

PART IV

Worship Services for Special Occasions

This section has been prepared for use by leaders of devotional services of various types. Prior to regular meetings of numerous kinds, fifteen or twenty minutes are reserved for a worship service, and it is for such purposes that this material has been assembled. It is hoped that these services will be widely used by leaders of young peoples' meetings, classes, forums, women's meetings, missionary societies, men's clubs, student association cabinets, etc.

Highly desirable is the practice of observing periods of silence between the successive sections of the service. Various tunes of the different hymns are listed in the hope that at least one tune may be found by looking at the index of the hymn book available.

Dozens of similar worship services may be assembled from the material contained in this volume.

Public prayers are a common heritage and are derived from countless sources ancient and modern. The volumes upon which I have drawn most heavily are the following: Morgan Phelps Noyes, *Prayers for Services,* published by Charles Scribners' Sons and Company, New York; *Book of Common Worship,* published by E. P. Dutton and Company, New York; *The Kingdom, the Power and the Glory,* published by the Oxford University Press, New York; Mary Wilder Tileston, *Prayers: Ancient and Modern,* published by Little, Brown and Company, Boston.

574

First Service of Worship

O come, let us sing unto the Lord; let us heartily rejoice in the strength of our salvation.

O come, let us worship and fall down, and kneel before the Lord our Maker.

For he is the Lord our God; and we are the people of his pasture, and the sheep of his hand.

O worship the Lord in the beauty of holiness; let the whole earth stand in awe of him.

For he cometh, for he cometh to judge the earth; and with righteousness to judge the world, and the peoples with his truth.

II

O Lord, Whose eyes are as a flame of fire, and Who searchest the intents of every heart; look mercifully upon us who come in penitence before Thee. Search us, we beseech Thee, and know our hearts; try us and know our thoughts; and see if there be any wicked way in us, and lead us in the way everlasting. Amen.

III

Future historians will write of the epoch through which we are passing as characterized by the most amazing convulsions in human thought. They will write of it as marked by moral as well as economic collapse. They will write of it as dominated by the resurgence of prejudices that were supposed to have been outmoded; by racial and religious persecutions; by the substitution of dictatorial for democratic forms of government; by class consciousness and group pressure; by intolerance and bigotry. They will write of it as evolving to the tune of violated treaties, repudiated debts and undeclared wars. They will write of it as peculiarly astounding because it grew out of a conflict in which ten million men died believing that their sacrifice would end just such things. They will write of it as doubly confusing because of the high hopes and fine ideals which it so suddenly and ruthlessly swept aside.

An atmosphere of tenseness and alarm pervades the world in general. There is a feeling that strife may break out anywhere at any moment, and that it may engulf all humanity. "Best minds" discuss the possibility of Western civilization collapsing as though it were of no great consequence and as though men could and should do little to prevent it. The nonchalance with which approaching disaster is contemplated and fantastic experiments are being undertaken; the complacent disregard of human experience and the vital principles it has disclosed; the lack of firmness in preserving what has been demonstrated as reliable and worthwhile, represent what is perhaps the worst aspect of present-day psychology.

During the last two decades, we have seen millions of people deprived of their right to worship and more millions deprived of their right to earn a living because of the race to which they belong. We have seen the right of free speech and free conscience suppressed throughout two-thirds of Europe. We have seen blood purges and persecutions that smack of the fourteenth century. We have seen armaments increased at an amazing rate though they had to be bought and paid for with the blood and sweat of hungry multitudes. All of it is so different from what was expected twenty years ago, so foreign to the visions and ideals that were then thought to guide the destiny of men, that we find ourselves virtually paralyzed with astonishment. It is against such a background that we must consider and interpret history in the making, with its jungle-like raids, its blasé repudiation of debts, its impulsive, emotional adventuring.[1]

IV

If we say we have no sin, we deceive ourselves, and the truth is not in us.

If we confess our sins, he is faithful and just to forgive us our sins, and to cleanse us from all unrighteousness.

V

O Lord, we acknowledge with shame that we are without excuse. Thou didst send Thy Son to show us the path of life, yet we have erred from Thy way continually. Thou hast magnifested his kingly right, and we have seen His glory; yet, while offering Him the homage of our lips, we have not given Him the loyalty of our lives. We have followed our own pleasures: we have sought our own ends: we have lived in selfishness: we have refused the way of the Cross. Have mercy upon us; rebuke our waywardness and folly, and grant us true repentance, that our sins may be forgiven; through Jesus Christ our Lord. Amen.

VI

Jesus was a Jewish citizen living at a time when his nation was held in political bondage by imperial Rome. Many of the most vital problems of his day emerged from this all-important fact. About six decades before the birth of Jesus, the reign of Rome over Palestine was ushered in by military victory and by a terrible massacre of priests at the altar. Twelve years later 30,000 Jews were sold into slavery.

Political bondage with the accompaniment of economic misery have always produced hatred, conspiracy and rebellion. And so Jewish patriots seethed with venom and implacable hostility toward their conquerors. Four times at least during the days of Jesus, they broke out in armed rebellion against Rome. The most disastrous of these insurrections took place in Sepphoris, the second largest city in the land. The rebellion was quelled with terrible loss of life. The city was burned to the ground and its remaining inhabitants sold into slavery. Outside Jerusalem 2,000 *Jewish patriots were crucified on trees.* In this blazing furnace of enmity and bloodshed, Jesus breathed his every breath.

We may be sure that Jesus gave serious and prolonged consideration to the various proposals being offered by his contemporaries. Yet he rejected them one by one: the armed rebellion of the Zealots, the escape to the desert of the Essenes, the compromising adjustments of the Sadducees, the legalism of the Pharisees, and the reliance by the Apocalyptists upon miraculous military and political intervention of Jehovah. With unequalled insight he saw that the Kingdom of God can be created only by methods which are consistent with the end sought. He, therefore, concluded that the only way to build God's Home on earth is by living every day as a son should conduct himself in the house of his Father. And it was this unswerving resolution which quickly led to crucifixion, a means of execution reserved for "rebels, renegade slaves and the lowest types of criminals."

Nothing more sublime has ever been witnessed than the sight of Jesus, deserted by the populace, denied by his closest friends, suffering the death pangs of the cruelest of executions, yet holding resolutely to his central faith, as voiced in his dying words, "Father, I trust my spirit to thy hands."

The example of Jesus not only furnishes a vivid ideal of personal life, but in his teaching we find also a dynamic ideal of society as it may be constructed. A nobler concept cannot be imagined than the idea of having all men living together as sons in the Father's Home. More attractive even than the ideal of a classless society in which exploitation has been abolished is Jesus' portrait of the Kingdom (or Home) of God on earth, wherein men recognize their sonship and their brotherhood and live every day as good members of the Divine Family. How desperately this ideal is needed becomes evident from even a superficial examination of the countless cleavages which now divide the human race into hostile and warring groups, classes, races, and nations.

If men in their treatment of each other reflected the true spirit of the family, hunger and want could quickly be banished. The resources required in order to provide plenty for everybody are now available—fertile soil, raw materials, manpower, mechanical energy, technological skill. Thus it is apparent that in every realm of life, men are enduring unnecessary suffering and privation because the religious ideal is not being pursued with sufficient vigor and perseverance. The very foundations of orderly society are rapidly being undermined by modes of thought and courses of action which constitute an absolute repudiation of the principles and procedures of the Family of God on earth. Rather than being impracticable, the ideals of Jesus constitute the only means of building a just and enduring society. The law of the harvest is inexorable. "Do not be deceived. God is not to be sneered at. A man will reap just what he sows." Likewise, a civilization reaps precisely what it sows. "And everyone who listens to these words of mine and does not act upon them will be like a stupid man who built his house on sand. The rain came down, the floods rose, the winds blew and beat upon that house, and down it fell—with a mighty crash." [2]

VII

O Merciful Father, as we watch Him steadfastly set His face to go to Jerusalem, ready to meet all the counsels of Thy will, we pray Thee to take from us the faithless mind that shrinks from the hardness of the duty to which Thou callest us. As we see Him refuse the easy way, and tread the lonely path to rejection and the suffering of death, that He might do all Thy will, we pray Thee to fill us with like self-forgetfulness and devotion. Strengthen us by Thy Spirit, that we also may glorify whatsoever cross we may be called to bear. Help us to follow Christ till the sacrifice of ourselves be perfected, and the work finished which Thou hast given us to do; through Jesus Christ our Lord.   Amen.

VIII

That Cause Can Neither Be Lost Nor Stayed

Christian Ostergaard
Tr. by J. A. Aaberg

Danish Folk Tune

1. That cause can neither be lost nor stayed Which takes the course of what God has made;
2. Each no-ble service that men have wrought Was first conceived as a fruitful thought;
3. There-by it-self like a tree it shows: That high it reach-es, as deep it grows;
4. Be then no more by a storm dismayed, For by it the full-grown seeds are laid;

And is not trusting in walls and towers, But slow-ly growing from seeds to flowers.
Each worthy cause with a future glorious By qui-et growing becomes vic-to-rious.
And when the storms are its branches shaking, It deep-er root in the soil is tak-ing.
And though the tree by its might it shatters, What then, if thousands of seeds it scatters!

IX

Now unto him who is able to do exceeding abundantly above all that we ask or think, according to the power that worketh in us; unto him be glory in the church by Christ Jesus, throughout all ages, world without end.   Amen.

1 *Current History Magazine.*

2 *Living Triumphantly,* by Kirby Page.

Second Service of Worship

Lord God eternal; holy, just, and merciful; we adore thee for the wonders of the heavens and the earth; for thy saving love revealed in Jesus Christ, and thy living presence made known by the Holy Spirit. By day and night, with voice and heart, praise and adoration shall be given unto thee, O Lord, from generation unto generation, for ever and ever.

Almighty God, all-seeing and all-holy, Whose eyes behold the children of men and discern the thoughts and intents of the hearts; we are ashamed to lift our eyes to the majesty of Thy glory. We have sinned against Thee through wilfulness and unbelief. We have not sought light through Thy Spirit of wisdom, but, following the counsel of our own will, have erred from Thy way continually. We have not sought strength through Thy Spirit of power; wherefore the good that we would, we have been unable to do, and the evil that we would not, we have done. We have grieved Thy Holy Spirit, and are no more worthy to be called Thy children.

O holy Father, Who didst send Thy Spirit to convince of sin and lead to righteousness; we beseech Thee to bring us to repentance, who confess our faults before Thee. Absolve us from our sins: restore to us the peace of the forgiven: and vouchsafe to us Thy Holy Spirit, that we may learn and do Thy perfect will; through Jesus Christ our Lord.   Amen.

II

I slept, and in my sleep I dreamed.

In my dream I saw the world possessed by demons.

Their name was Legion.

Many of the mighty captains of the realm of Darkness and Death
were among them.

Greed and Selfishness and Tyranny, I saw, and Fear too, with
Suspicion, Lies, Hate, and many others. . . .

Then I saw in my dreams three men arise out of the North.

And they came saying: "Let us do even as the voice bade us. Let
us, as many as will, come together humbly before God. Many
other ways have been tried, but all in vain—the madness has
continued to waste all the earth these several years. Let us
enter now upon the way of prayer." . . .

So they were all with one accord in one place.
No one was leader among them.
All were silent before God and awaited the coming of his Spirit.
Thus they remained for many days.
None spoke to his neighbor.
Sometimes a hand would touch another hand tenderly.
And I saw that the eyes of many were filled with tears of pity.
And there were no angry looks. . . .

And then suddenly it seemed to me in my dream that there came
    from heaven a sound as of a mighty wind and it filled all the
    room where they were sitting.
And they were all filled with the Holy Spirit, and began to speak.

They told first each of his own sins; for having laid their hearts
    open before God, they felt no need to conceal anything from
    one another.
They told how lust of selfish ease and comfort had possessed them,
    body ruling over soul; how indolent they had been in pursuit
    of truth; what pride and self-righteousness had strutted in
    their souls; how cravenly they had feared to obey the heavenly
    vision, to walk God's way to the end; how false and super-
    ficial they had been in the presence of the world's unspeakable
    agony.
And presently all confessed together of how they had been en-
    grossed in struggling after the things of earth instead of
    seeking God's kingdom first, and how they had suffered to
    exist principalities and powers that inflicted ceaseless torture
    upon the people, loading the burdens of the strong and the
    rich upon the weak and poor, and slaughtering the innocents.
And I beheld holy tears of penitence and forgiveness wash away
    all the pain and suffering from their faces, and I saw that
    the stains also were removed from their hearts.
Joy and peace filled them all so that in many tongues they pro-
    claimed the love of God and the great day of Deliverance.
And they were made one in love.

And now in this new power of the Spirit they began to consider
    the grievous state of the world and the multitude of evils
    therein.

Many things were natural and possible to them now which had seemed impossible so long as fear and hate and mistrust ruled their hearts.

They planned for a world in which righteousness should reign supreme.

They saw that the way of love was the sure and only way to bring good to pass on earth, and that ever the Son of Man if lifted up would draw all to himself. . . .

And for one fleeting, ecstatic moment ere I awoke I had a glimpse of a face marred more than any man's but yet radiant with joy, and he said, "Let men hear what the Spirit saith to the churches. This kind cometh not out save by prayer and fasting."

Then all was still.[1]

III

O God, dwelling in light that no man may come unto, whose ways are not as our ways or thoughts as our thoughts, who art able to do for us exceeding abundantly above all that we ask or think; so draw up our affection to Thee, so win us by the vision of the perfect Kingdom of Thy Christ, so kindle our imagination and quicken our ideals, so revive our faith and renew our hope, that we may live wholly unto Thee, neither heeding the fear nor seeking the praise of men. Let our hearts be so surely set toward Thee, that in all our entanglements we lose not Him who is the Way, the Truth, and the Life.

Grant unto us, Almighty God, that we, communing with one another and with Thee, may feel our hearts burn within us, until all pure, and just, and holy, and noble things of God and man may be to us lovely, and we may find nothing to fear but that which is hateful in Thine eyes, and nothing worth seeking but that which is lovely and fair therein. Let the divine brightness and peace possess our souls, so that, fearing neither life nor death, we may look to Thy lovingkindness and tender mercy to lift us above that which is low and mean within us, and at last to give the spirit within us the victory, and bring us safe through death into the life everlasting. Hear us of Thy mercy, through Jesus Christ our Lord — Amen.[2]

IV

Tune—Duke Street or Truro or Mendon. L.M.

1 These things shall be,—a loftier race
Than e'er the world hath known shall rise
With flame of freedom in their souls
And light of knowledge in their eyes.

2 They shall be gentle, brave, and strong
To spill no drop of blood, but dare
All that may plant man's lordship firm
On earth, and fire, and sea, and air.

3 Nation with nation, land with land,
Unarmed shall live as comrades free;
In every heart and brain shall throb
The pulse of one fraternity.

4 New arts shall bloom of loftier mould,
And mightier music thrill the skies,
And every life shall be a song
When all the earth is paradise.

5 There shall be no more sin, nor shame,
Though pain and passion may not die,
For man shall be at one with God
In bonds of firm necessity.

JOHN ADDINGTON SYMONDS, 1890.

V

The peace of God which passeth all understanding, keep your hearts and minds in the knowledge and love of God, and of His Son, Jesus Christ our Lord; and the blessing of God Almighty, the Father, the Son, and the Holy Spirit, be amongst you and remain with you always. Amen.

[1] A. J. Muste, in *The World Tomorrow.*
[2] George Dawson.

Third Service of Worship

I saw the new Jerusalem tonight.
The portals of the sky were opened wide;
The clouds were radiant with celestial light;
My lake gave back its answer, glorified.
Behold, there was a throne set high and clear;
An emerald rainbow circled it, all fair;
And four and twenty thrones, I think, were near,
For jasper, sardius, gold were everywhere.
Before the throne a sea of crystal glass,
And round about were creatures in the sky;
Across the sea a path of burnished brass,
And there, it seemed, angelic hosts drew nigh.
I thought I heard them singing as they trod,
Holy, holy, holy is Almighty God.[1]

II

O magic of a song! here loveliness
May sleep unhindered of life's mortal toll,
And noble things stand towering o'er the tide;
Here mid the years, untouched by time or stress,
Shall sweep on every wind that stirs the soul
The music of a voice that never died![1]

III

If a spiritual interpretation of the universe is to be validated and if personality and society are to be transformed, it is imperative that time be taken for worship. There are many elements in worship: adoration, awe, thanksgiving, confession, penitence, petition, intercession, communion, surrender; and there are many forms of worship: through beauty, harmony, silence, fellowship, the sacraments, human service.

The heights of worship are reached only by a vigorous act of the will through frequent and sometimes prolonged periods of intensive search for God. True enough, spontaneous acts of worship are common experiences and true enough, God is more eager for communion than His children can be. But life under modern conditions is surrounded with countless high barriers that must be surmounted before the rarest of fellowship with God can be experienced with continuity. The pressure consequent upon the performance of daily functions tends to crush spiritual aspiration and expression. Countless temptations to ignoble living are confronted daily. The wider commercialization of sex has magnified manyfold the baser appeal of the flesh, and the crumbling of old standards of morality has plunged many members of this generation into a sea of obscenity. In a society whose economic processes function primarily through the dynamic of self-interest and greed, the acceptance of low ideals and unworthy practices often appears to be the price of mere survival. In a community which operates according to the law of the jungle, every man for himself and the devil take the hindmost, incitations to enmity and hostility are terrific. Exploitation and cruelty are engendering bitter cynicism concerning spiritual values. Frustration and defeat are creating doubt in the minds of millions of victims as to whether life itself is worth the effort required to avoid suffocation. The titanic dimensions of modern industrial society and the appalling impersonality of relentless economic processes are robbing countless individuals of self-respect and self-confidence. Never did men need more desperately a vivid sense of the presence of a loving Father God.

Few men ever drift into a vital religious experience. Vigorous and continuous struggle is essential to a full discovery of God. Time is required and sustained attention must be given to meditation, contemplation, and rigorous thought concerning the nature of the universe and the purpose of life. Emotion must be released and harnessed to determination. Leisure for spiritual devotion is a necessary condition of growth in spiritual insight and power. In a real sense we are what we have taken time to become.

Conscious search for beauty and harmony frequently leads directly to worship. The quality of any man's life may be improved appreciably by increasing the amount of time spent in the enjoyment of the glories of physical nature, and in the appreciation of music and art. Intensified vitality can be gained by spending fewer hours around the bridge-table or on the dance-floor and by spending more time under the stars in adoration of God as one marvels at the beauty and majesty of the firmament. An evening at a symphony or an afternoon before masterpieces of art may become an act of worship. Personally I have discovered that the radio may be used as a means of creating the mood of worship.

By choosing suitable selections by a superb orchestra or by a great violinist as a background and accompaniment of conscious prayer, I have often found myself lifted to heights of spiritual aspiration.[2]

IV

Glory of sunrise and sunset,
Glory of night and the dawn,
Glorious flood of the moonlight
Washing with silver the lawn,
These have bound me and chained me,
Held my heart in the hills
These will envelop, surround me,
Hold my heart when it stills.

Wonder of birches at twilight,
Wonder of lights that enmesh,
Wondrous coolth of the waters
Caressing the swimmer's flesh,
These have conquered me, won me,
Held my heart all the years,
To these I will go on departure
Burying bodily fears.

Beauty of light on the waters,
Beauty of hills in their strength,
Beauty of wind on the corn-fields
Rippling length on length,
These are the things I cleave to,
These will endure to the end;
Beauty, the quest of the ages,
Waits where the lost roads wend.[1]

V

Lovely is daytime when the joyful sun goes singing,
Lovely is night with stars and round or sickled moon,
Lovely are trees, forever lovely, whether in winter
Or musical midsummer or when they bud and tassel
Or crown themselves with stormy splendors in the fall.
But lovelier than day or night or trees in blossom
Is there no secret infinite loveliness behind?

Beautiful is water, running on rocks in mountains,
Or bosoming sunsets where the valley rivers ponder;
Beautiful is ocean with its myriad colors,
In southern blues and purples, its arctic gray and silver,
Blown into green frost-fretted or wine-dark in the evening.
But still more beautiful than waters calm or cloven,
Than ocean thunder-maned or floored for delicate springtime,
Is there no beauty visible save to our eyes? . . .

Who lifteth in the eastern sky the dark, gold moon?
Who painteth green and purple on the blackbird's throat?
What hand of rapture scattereth sunshine through the rain
And flingeth round the barren boughs of spring returned
Dim fire? Who stenciled with caught breath the moth's wide wing
And lit the ruby in his eyes? Whose ecstasy
Set silver ripples on the racing thunder-cloud
And flared the walls of storm with terrible dead green?
What dreamer fretted dew upon the flat-leafed corn
And twined in innocence of useless perfect art
The morning-glory with its bubble blue, soon gone?
Was there no hand that braided autumn branches in
Their solemn brede and stained them with a sombre rust?
Was there no love conceived the one-starred rivered evening,
And dipped in crocus fire the gray horns of the moon?

They say there never was a god men loved but died—
Dead is Astarte, Astoreth is dead, and Baal;
Zeus and Jehovah share a single grave and deep;
Olympus hears no laughter, Sinai no voice;
Spring comes but Freia comes not nor Persephone:
On temple plinth and porch the random grasses run;
Of all their priests alone the white-stoled stars are faithful.
Dead are the gods, forever dead! And yet—and yet—
Who lifted in the eastern sky the dark, gold moon? . . .
There is a loveliness outlasts the temporal gods,
A beauty that, when all we know as beautiful
Is gone, will fashion in delight the forms it loves,
In that wide room where all our stars are but a drift
Of glimmering petals down an air from far away.[1]

VI

Tunes: Oberlin. 11s. 10s. Also Felix.

Still, still with Thee, when purple morning breaketh,
    When the bird waketh, and the shadows flee;
Fairer than morning, lovelier than daylight,
    Dawns the sweet consciousness, I am with thee.

Alone with thee, amid the mystic shadows,
    The solemn hush of nature newly born;
Alone with thee in breathless adoration,
    In the calm dew and freshness of the morn.

As in the dawning o'er the waveless ocean,
    The image of the morning-star doth rest,
So in the stillness, thou beholdest only
    Thine image in the waters of my breast.

Still, still to thee! as to each newborn morning,
    A fresh and solemn splendor still is given,
So does this blessed consciousness awaking.
    Breathe each day nearness unto thee and heaven.

When sinks the soul, subdued by toil, to slumber,
    Its closing eyes look up to thee in prayer;
Sweet the repose beneath thy wings o'ershading,
    But sweeter still, to wake and find thee there.
So shall it be at last, in that bright morning,
    When the soul waketh, and life's shadows flee;
O in that hour, fairer than daylight dawning,
    Shall rise the glorious thought—I am with thee.

HARRIET B. STOWE.

VII

Maker and Lover of beauty, we adore Thee for the splendor of the universe. Help us to use its wonders and its loveliness as an open door through which we shall enter into the imperishable beauty of Thy Kingdom; through Him in whose face the full beauty of Thy being shone, Jesus Christ our Saviour—Amen.

[1] See pages 9, 12.
[2] *Living Triumphantly.*

Fourth Service of Worship

Thou, from whom our life has come, to whom it returns; Thou, Father of our spirit, accept our thanks this day for all we have come to know about Thee. Earth and sea and sky have been vocal with thy messages of power and of beauty; human beings around us have taught us much of thy tenderness; in the face of thy Son we have seen shining the love of thy perfect fatherhood. Our minds worship; our hearts adore. Life is filled with a new glory: help us to live it radiantly, until everything we touch shall be transfigured; until the ordinary and commonplace shall glow with sacred meaning, and the whole of life become a sacrament. Give us, O our Father, the vision of thy Presence through every hour of our days. Give us strength to bear, courage to stand, patience to wait. Help us to make the mind of Christ the standard of our actions, the cross of Christ the measure of our love, until through fellowship with him our life reflects Thee truly.—Amen.[1]

II

After years of contact with human suffering and long vigils of brooding over human agony, Jesus came out of obscurity with a flaming new message and program: the purpose of life is to help create the Family of God, where all men will dwell in filial relations with the Father and with brotherly affection for each other; the method by which the desired end is to be reached is to live constantly as a good member of God's home, live day by day as if the ideal society has already been achieved; run the risks, accept the penalties, and rely upon this manner of life for victory. Here is the most radical program that has ever been offered to mankind. Within a few years its advocates were to be spoken of as "those who turn the world upside down." Well may Jean Paul Richter exclaim: "Christ who, being the holiest among the mighty, and the mightiest among the holy, lifted with His pierced hands empires off their hinges and turned the stream of centuries out of its channel, and still governs the ages." [2]

III

Down through the spheres that chant the Name of One
   Who is the Law of Beauty and of Light
   He came, and as He came the waiting Night
Shook with the gladness of a Day begun;

And as He came, He said: Thy Will be done
  On Earth; and all His vibrant Words were white
  And glistering with silver, and their might
Was of the glory of a rising sun.
Unto the stars sang out His living Words
  White and with silver, and their rhythmic sound
    Was as a mighty symphony unfurled;
And back from out the stars like homing birds
  They fell in love upon the sleeping ground
  And were forever in a wakened world.[3]

IV

The smugness and complacency of this generation need to be shattered by contrition and fruits of repentance. The person who has no higher aim than eating, drinking, lusting and being merry in the midst of hunger, pain, sorrow and strife ought to be filled with shame. "Sinning by syndicate" describes the modern practice. As civilization becomes more urban and complex, relationships become more impersonal. Groups grow larger and larger and affect each other in the mass. We sin against persons we have never seen and who may dwell in distant corners of the earth, and in turn are sinned against by them. Much of our sinning today is done in our capacities as investors, bankers, manufacturers, directors, employers, trade unionists, consumers, citizens, officials, imperialists, militarists, patriots, politicians, lobbyists, journalists, clubmen, Nordics, trustees, educators, deacons, vestrymen and clergymen.

An up-to-date list of notorious sinners would include: investors who live in luxury from unearned income derived from the cruel exploitation of women and children; malefactors of wealth who maintain their privileges and power by corrupting public officials, suppressing collective action on the part of their employees, and poisoning public opinion through a subsidized press; trade unionists who betray their comrades by accepting graft, and those who seek a privileged position for their own craft at the expense of other workers; consumers who purchase in the lowest market, oblivious or indifferent to the fact that these commodities are often covered with the blood of sweated laborers; women who fritter away their time and energies in a meaningless round of social activities; citizens who regard with indifference, indulgence or cynicism the dangerous policies and corrupt practices of public officials; office holders who take petty bribes or wholesale graft in the form of tariff manipulation for their chief supporters; militarists and patrioteers who endanger international peace by generating fear and releasing chauvinistic passions; journalists who debase public morals by pandering to lust and sensationalism, and who create social crises by distortion and jingoism; racial bigots who use the plea of "racial purity" as a smoke screen to hide discrimination, exploitation and barbarity; trustees of educational institutions who victimize professors because they present unpopular truths; educators of craven spirit who hypocritically teach what they do not believe, and hide their real convictions because they fear consequences; church officials who seek to silence the prophetic voice when it menaces vested interests; clergymen who permit their vision to grow dim, their zeal to flag, their courage to ooze away, and their willingness to make sacrifices to become paralyzed—all these are notorious sinners. "If we say, 'We are not guilty,' we are deceiving ourselves and the truth is not in us." If we are to climb the heights of spiritual creativity, we must confess our sins and bring forth fruits worthy of repentance. The pure in heart and steadfast in purpose alone find God.[2]

V

Lord, I Want to Be a Christian

Negro Spiritual

VI

O God, our Heavenly Father, we have sinned against thee and are not worthy to be called thy children. We have not loved thee with our whole heart. We have not loved our neighbor as ourselves. We have not had in us the mind of Christ. We have grieved thy Holy Spirit. We have been conformed to this world which passeth away. We have not endured as seeing him who is invisible. We have not been of the same mind one toward another. We have broken the unity of thy Church. We have not fought in the good fight of faith. We have not rejoiced in hope. Our love has grown cold. These things we remember before thee with sorrow of heart, that thou mayest remember them no more. Unto thee we cry, Lord, have mercy upon us. Forgive us, O most merciful Father. In thy love and pity renew us; through Jesus Christ our Lord. Amen.

---

1 Charlotte Adams.

2 *Living Triumphantly.*

3 Thos. S. Jones, Jr., *Shadow of The Perfect Rose.* Published by Farrar and Rinehart, New York.

INDEX